DESIGN
THE WHOLE STORY

General Editor
Elizabeth Wilhide

Foreword by
Jonathan Glancey

DESIGN

THE WHOLE STORY

PRESTEL

Munich • London • New York

◄ Calico printing at the Morris and
Co workshop in Merton Abbey Mills,
London, in 1931.

Prestel Verlag, Munich · London · New York 2016
A member of Verlagsgruppe Random House GmbH
Neumarkter Strasse 28 · 81673 Munich

Prestel Publishing Ltd.
14-17 Wells Street
London W1T 3PD

Prestel Publishing
900 Broadway, Suite 603
New York, NY 10003

www.prestel.com

© 2016 Quintessence Editions Ltd.

This book was designed and produced by
Quintessence Editions Ltd., London

Senior Editor	Elspeth Beidas
Editors	Rebecca Gee, Carol King, Frank Ritter
Senior Designer	Isabel Eeles
Design Assistance	Tom Howey, Thomas Keenes
Picture Researcher	Sarah Bell
Production Manager	Anna Pauletti
Editorial Director	Ruth Patrick
Publisher	Philip Cooper

ISBN 978-3-7913-8189-3

Library of Congress Control Number: 2016941556

A CIP catalogue record for this book is available from the British Library.

Printed in China

CONTENTS

FOREWORD

William Morris, designer, craftsman, and garrulous socialist, told a Birmingham audience in 1880: "If you want a golden rule that will fit everybody, this is it: Have nothing in your houses that you do not know to be useful or believe to be beautiful." Addressing a gathering in London the following year, he declared: "Simplicity of life, even the barest, is not a misery, but the very foundation of refinement."

Taken together, these two hallowed maxims underpin pretty much the entire history of design. That, at least, is the view of those—the Bauhaus, national design councils, and historians who have wanted a tidy story to tell—who believe that design has proceeded smoothly on Morris's rails ever since he laid them. Morris's own work was flamboyant and, as far as twentieth-century functionalists were concerned, his heart was in the right place. And certainly morality and good design have marched righteously together to create much of the work shown in core sections of this wide-ranging book.

For many decades—ever since, in fact, the Bauhaus, its disciples, and other high-minded moralists spread their mantra of "fitness for purpose"—the history of design has been taken to be a more or less seamless tale of steady progress, with beauty, truth, and refinement emerging as logical by-products of rational functionalism. The inessential decorations beloved in the nineteenth century were stripped away, like barnacles from the hull of a boat, as the design of everything, from teaspoons to trains, became ever more rational.

And yet, as later sections of *Design: The Whole Story* demonstrate, a popular desire for decoration, and also playfulness, texture, and color, has caused design to move almost full circle, back around to lively forms like the expressions of Art Nouveau and Art Deco, for example, that once annoyed Bauhaus professors, iconoclastic historians, and puritanical critics alike.

How have Post-modern and digital-era designers turned what seemed to be a logical story on its head? Turning the pages of this book, the answer becomes increasingly clear. Functionalist design reached its zenith when it was in the service of the public sector, or controlled by civic-minded individuals, businesses, and corporations. In recent decades, with the triumph of neoliberal economics and private enterprise, the wishes of individual consumers have been highly influential, and design has been primarily in their dedicated service. Just look at how, as evidenced in the later sections of this book, "personal" products, such as cellphones, miniature computers, automobiles, wallpaper, and decorative objects, have taken pride of place.

This makes sense. Design, like architecture, is influenced and guided by artistic, academic, moral, and even philosophical ideas, but what perhaps shapes objects most is the political economy. In the communist societies that emerged after the Russian Revolution, for example, consumer design was considered largely unimportant. For society in the early twenty-first century, whether it is directed by the state, as in China, or by corporations and professional lobbyists, as in the United States, consumer design leads the way. And, because consumer desires are thought to be both catholic and insatiable, design has adopted a multitude of forms. Discipline, it might be said, has given way to decadence, and design, freed of moral strictures, has been liberated. Perhaps, though, this is a natural state of affairs. After all, design in nature— from the forms of plankton to planets, seahorses to stars, cactuses to constellations—exhibits infinite forms. And as design mutates and flowers in this natural way, so the certainties of strictly functionalist thinking have given way to a new relativism. Can anyone today say with absolute certainty what good design is? "Ask a toad what is beauty," teased Voltaire in his *Dictionnaire philosophique* of 1764, and "He will answer that it is a female with two great round eyes coming out of her little head, a large flat mouth, a yellow belly and a brown back."

And yet, in a time of ungoverned, haphazard relativism, it is easy to think fondly of eras in which highly purposed design was not only associated with public service but also taken intensely seriously, with enviable results. Think of the intelligent work that has been devoted, over decades, to design in the service of mail offices and state-owned railroads worldwide, of mail stamps and banknotes, of river ferries and electricity pylons, of school furniture and public information graphics.

That, though, is the subject of a different book. *Design: The Whole Story* shows you, boldly and well, how our modern notion of design came about, and what, in terms of the objects we have in our houses, design has become a quarter of a millennium after the Industrial Revolution.

JONATHAN GLANCEY
JOURNALIST, AUTHOR, AND BROADCASTER

INTRODUCTION

Design is hard to define. Most familiarly, as many of the key examples in this book demonstrate, it results in products that can be bought and sold—and eventually, if hallowed by critical approval, placed in museum collections. Yet design may also lead to something as amorphous as the Internet, which shapes every aspect of modern life and communication while remaining intangible. While design often involves problem-solving, it can also anticipate needs that have never been articulated before: in this sense, it is profoundly imaginative. Aesthetic judgement naturally comes into it, yet it is distinct from both art and craft. Similarly, while design can be primarily concerned with function and performance, it cannot be reduced to engineering or technical specification.

If by design we mean intent, then everything that has ever been made by human hands has been designed. In such terms, a pot shaped thousands of years ago and baked in the Mesopotamian sun is a product of design, every bit as much as a concept automobile or an iPhone. But design as a specialist process, or a practice that is distinct from making, has a much shorter history, and dates back only to the beginnings of the Industrial Revolution (see p.20).

Humans have always been toolmakers, but with the dawn of the Industrial Revolution the degree to which human technology could alter the world increased exponentially. The textile industry, which was the first to be mechanized, began the shift that would see the economies of the West transform from largely agricultural ones to those based on manufacturing.

In the late eighteenth century the drive for profit saw manufacturing rationalized into separate elements or processes; similarly, increased volumes theoretically meant lower unit costs and an opening of the market to a broader range of consumers. It was the concomitant need for planning and standardization over the production cycle that led to the emergence of design as a distinct discipline. This constituted a massive shift both in the way work was conceived and the manner in which goods were bought and sold.

Before long, however, the products of the new industrial age, with their often meretricious applied decoration and confused styling, ushered in a crisis of taste. Previously, there had been a broad consensus on what might loosely be termed "style." For much of the eighteenth century, classicism (see p.24), derived from the ancient Greek and Roman orders, informed the design of everyday objects as well as buildings. This underlying point of reference gave a remarkable unity to architecture, interiors, and what they contained.

By the second half of the nineteenth century, consensus was nowhere in evidence. Already, there was nostalgia in certain quarters for a preindustrial way of working and the period was marked by a series of revivals as critics and designers sought to determine an appropriate visual language for the age, a debate that was often couched in moral terms.

"Shoddy is king," was the estimation of William Morris (1834–96; see p.52) of the quality of goods pouring out of Britain's factories. The stylistic confusion on display at the Great Exhibition (1851; see p.38) led directly to calls for reform. That Augustus Pugin (1812–52) championed the Gothic as a morally appropriate style had a strong influence on Henry Cole (1808–82), founder of the South Kensington Museum (later the Victoria & Albert Museum). Cole's mission to educate the public in what constituted good and bad taste included a "chamber of horrors" where the worst stylistic offenders from the Great

▼ A high chest of drawers (c. 1700–20) made in North America from maple, walnut veneer, maple burl veneer, and pine. It personifies the high level of craftsmanship that William Morris regarded as under threat in the late nineteenth century.

◄ William Morris created the "Pimpernel" wallpaper design in 1876 and later chose it to decorate his dining room at Kelmscott House in Hammersmith, London. Its botanical motifs, complex structure, and swirling rhythms are typical of his style.

Exhibition were displayed, including a decorative stoat holding an umbrella. Other occupants of the high ground included John Ruskin (1819–1900), who exerted a powerful influence on Morris and his immediate circle.

The Arts and Crafts movement (see p.74), whose practitioners were hugely influenced by Ruskin and by the work of Morris, promoted an idealized notion of rural simplicity and honesty of construction, harking back to the Middle Ages and early craft guilds. At a time when Victorian clutter was at its greatest, the emphasis on unadorned craftwork sponsored a lightening of the interior, if only among an intellectual elite. Although the Arts and Crafts movement was not without its inherent contradictions, it was to have a significant influence on early twentieth-century design movements in Europe and North America.

During the same period, mass consumption really began to take hold and it was in the United States that mechanical and electrical goods were first produced for use in the home and the office. Advances in printing technology, such as lithography and the new hot-metal process, aided and abetted the advertisement and marketing of new products, in which design played an important role. The electric light bulb, invented by Thomas Edison (1847–1941), stimulated a demand for the supply of domestic electricity and, by extension,

► Joost Schmidt (1893–1948), a teacher at the Bauhaus, designed this poster to advertise a Bauhaus exhibition in the city of Weimar, Germany, in 1923.

appliances such as vacuum cleaners and washing machines that were powered by it. While branding has much earlier antecedents, it was also at this time that it began to emerge as a means of fostering consumer loyalty.

By the beginning of the new century, a rift was opening up between those who believed that there was room for individual artistic expression in design and those who argued that function should be the defining element. The latter part of the nineteenth century had been marked by two chief influences: Japonaiserie (see p.82) and Art Nouveau (see p.92). Both were highly decorative and pervasive in graphics and applied ornament. The short-lived Aesthetic Movement (see p.88) had a similarly febrile *fin de siècle* quality.

By 1913, when Henry Ford (1863–1947) devised his moving production line, functionalism had all but triumphed. Mass manufacture, a design process in itself, demanded standardization. While this had been true ever since the beginnings of industrialization, what had changed was the emphasis on "type-objects," products that proudly proclaimed their manufactured origins.

The machine aesthetic (see p.134), in the hands of masters of modernism such as Mies van der Rohe (1886–1969), Marcel Breuer (1902–81), Le Corbusier (1887–1965), and Charlotte Perriand (1903–99), took inspiration from both modern machines such as bicycles and ocean liners and new materials such as tubular steel. Eschewing ornament of any kind, the emphasis was on pure form derived from function. Few early products of modernism were commercially successful in their time, but their legacy of influence has proved immense. Equally lasting were the revolutionary experiments that emerged from a seminal design school, the Bauhaus (see p.126), and from artists and designers furthering the ideals of the Russian Revolution (see p.120). Along with photography, these conceptual departures founded radical approaches in the way information was communicated and design was practiced.

In the United States, on the other hand, there was a growing appreciation of design's potential to maximize profits. The streamlined aesthetic, applied to domestic products such as meat slicers as much as automobiles, was an early example of design as "styling." This period also saw the emergence of new design disciplines—graphic design, industrial design, and interior design, for example—along with a rise in designers' visibility; Raymond Loewy (1893–1986), one of the first showmen of design, and Russel Wright (1904–76) are cases in point. So, too, was automobile designer Harley J. Earl (1893–1969), head of General Motors' Styling Division, who ushered in the "Annual Model Change," where consumers were persuaded to trade in their old models due to changes in appearance alone. They made no secret of their motivation; nothing, said Loewy, was as beautiful as "an upwardly rising sales curve."

But it wasn't always about profit. Serving the greater good has long been an aim of many designers. In the immediate prewar years, design gained

▼ An armchair (c. 1934) in the streamlined style, made from chromium-plated steel, wood, and leather by the German furniture and industrial designer, architect, art director, and teacher Kem Weber (1889–1963). It is one of his iconic designs.

prominence in the public realm (see p.200) through exercises in corporate identity, such as London Transport's ambitious program in the early 1930s to integrate signage, station design, and route maps, or *The Book of PTT*, created by Piet Zwart (1885–1977) for the Dutch telegraph and telephone service. This was the era, too, of mass-market "people's cars," such as the Volkswagen Beetle.

World War II (see p.212) saw design pressed into a very different kind of public service—armaments, fighter aircraft, and tanks also require design input. Like the American Civil War, generally considered to be the first "modern" conflict, World War II provided a fast track to innovation across a broad range of disciplines, including materials technology. Developments such as radar and the jet engine came to fruition in the war's aftermath.

For shattered postwar economies, especially those on the losing side, design was to prove a means of both revitalizing production and establishing distinct national identities in a new world order. From this period dates Japan's emergence as a major exporter of goods manufactured under the stringent application of "quality control." In Italy, where design was seen as an indivisible part of *la dolce vita*, aesthetics combined with technical innovation created products desirable the world over. Germany's economic miracle rested on

▶ Rationalist principles clearly inform the look of this Braun television set (1957), designed in association with the Academy of Design at Ulm, Germany. Its form is dictated by its function, and no part of it is extraneous to that consideration.

a strictly rationalist foundation, promoted by the Hochschule für Gestaltung (see p.266) in Ulm, which served as a second Bauhaus. Closely allied was a purist, virtuously neutral Swiss approach to design, best characterized by the twentieth century's most successful typeface, Helvetica (see p.276).

On the domestic front, Scandinavian design was a surprise international hit in the postwar period: ceramics, glassware, furniture, lighting, and textiles produced in Denmark, Sweden, and Finland displayed a marriage of a modernist sensibility with natural materials and organic forms. Similarly, mid-century modern US designers such as Charles Eames (1907–1978) and his wife Ray (1912–1988), George Nelson (1908–86), Isamu Noguchi (1904–88), and Eero Saarinen (1910–61), promoted by progressive manufacturers such as Knoll and Hermann Miller, shared a forward-looking aesthetic, reflecting an optimistic faith in the power of science and technology to deliver lasting material progress. During this period, new materials, such as plastic, introduced a new disposability to the marketplace. At the same time, planned obsolescence became a commercial strategy to maintain production volumes.

As the twentieth century progressed, design became ever more mainstream, not merely for an enlightened trendsetting few, but deeply embedded in the contemporary lifestyle. Design became increasingly responsive to, and reflective of, changes in fashion and popular culture, from pop (see p.364) and psychedelia (see p.380) to punk (see p.410) and

▲ US designer George Nelson conceived the Comprehensive Storage System with Desk in 1958, and the Herman Miller Furniture Company manufactured it in 1960 from rosewood, plastic, metal, and glass. By the mid twentieth century, flexibility of use was established as an important design criterion.

▶ "This Mortal Coil" (1993) is an innovative bookcase consisting of a single strip of mild steel formed into a spiral by British artist Ron Arad (b.1951). The steel dividers are hinged at both ends so that the coil may be partly collapsed and reduced in size for transportation.

postmodernism (see p.416). Parallel to the counter-culture movements of the late 1960s, radical "anti-design" groups sprang up, such as Archizoom, challenging the notions of "good taste"; also, the oil crisis of the early 1970s raised the price of plastics, provoking a reevaluation of the throwaway society.

To a greater extent than ever before, design took up permanent residence on the high street. Pioneering retailers, such as Terence Conran (b.1931), founder of Habitat, and Ingvar Kamprad (b.1926), founder of IKEA, brought good design to the ordinary consumer. Design was implicit not only in products created by named designers, but also in time-honored classics, such as bright enameled homewares or flatweave Indian rugs: "designs without designers."

Design was also increasingly a form of celebrity branding. From the "designer decades" of the 1980s and 1990s, when profiles of designers soared into the stratosphere, design became the means to create objects of desire, status symbols for knowledgeable consumers well versed in the language of things. Minimalist, maximalist, high tech, and retro: styles came and went as design was drawn into the fashion cycle. In today's uncertain world of fragile economies and threatened resources, the scope and role of design has continued to evolve. Concerns such as fair trade, inclusivity, and sustainability add new ethical dimensions to design practice. Designers today have to consider not only how their products will be sold and used, but also how their manufacture and eventual disposal will affect the planet and its future.

Yet nothing has had such a profound impact on design's reach across the globe, and the speed with which it connects with its audience, than the arrival of the digital age. This momentous technological revolution, which has given us apps, desktop publishing, computer-aided design, 3D printing, and rapid prototyping, among countless other innovations, has both transformed design practice and given rise to new typologies. For a generation arriving at adulthood today, life before the Internet is virtually unthinkable. Design has always been hard to define, and no more so than today when artificial intelligence is poised to reshape the way we live, work, and play.

Design: The Whole Story takes a close look at the key developments, movements, and practitioners of design around the world, from the beginnings of industrial manufacturing to the present day. Organized chronologically, the book locates design within its technological, cultural, economic, aesthetic, and theoretical contexts. From the high-minded moralists of the nineteenth century to the radical thinkers of modernism—and from showmen such as Loewy in the 1930s to today's superstars such as Philippe Starck (b.1949)— the book provides in-depth coverage of a subject that touches all our lives.

Iconic works that mark significant steps forward or that characterize a particular era or approach are analyzed in detail—such as Breuer's Wassily chair (1925; see p.136); corporate identity work by Eliot Noyes (1910—77) for IBM (1950s; see p. 400); and the Verdana typeface (see p. 478), designed to be read on screen, by Matthew Carter (b.1937).

Throughout the history of design, a fundamental tension between stylistic expressiveness and reductionism, between function and form, has been played out time and time again. But design is not simply a vehicle that records shifts in taste. As a way of imagining, it both defines and anticipates our needs, and as such is expressive both of commerce and culture. Intimately bound up with technology, it provides aesthetic solutions in material form. We are all consumers of design, from the automobiles we drive and the products we buy to the graphics that surround us. *Design: The Whole Story* provides all the information we need to decode the material world.

▼ Industrial designer Samuel N. Bernier used computer-aided design and 3D printing to create customized lids that clip onto empty cans, jars, and bottles to give them new uses. Among the upcycled objects below are a citrus juicer, a rain catcher, a paintbrush cleaner, a piggy bank, a lamp, a bird feeder, a long pasta container, an hourglass, a mug, and a dumbbell. The work is an aspect of Project RE_, which examines how communities might take on their own manufacturing.

1 | The Emergence of Design
1700–1905

INDUSTRIAL REVOLUTION

1 Isambard Kingdom Brunel revolutionized engineering with structures like his Clifton Suspension Bridge (1864) in Bristol, England.

2 Richard Trevithick's passenger-carrying steam carriage made its first journey in 1801 in Cornwall, England.

3 Harrison's Improved Power Loom (1851) was exhibited at the Great Exhibition in London and helped lay the foundation for modern textile mills.

The Enlightenment, or Age of Reason, effected a general shift in social ideals, which was followed by even greater social, political, and economic changes that arose from developments in technology, science, and culture. The period is now collectively termed the Industrial Revolution. Scientific advances and technological innovations improved agricultural and industrial production, eliciting economic expansion and changes in many people's living conditions and working lives. Beginning in England, these developments assisted the growth of national wealth and prosperity for some, while a population surge generated increasing demand.

The Industrial Revolution is usually described as occurring between approximately 1760 and 1840, although there was no sudden transformation. Improved agriculture, industry, and shipping led to an increase in the production of almost everything required by consumers, and the resulting dynamism of the economy transferred from agriculture to industry and trade. Industrialization marked a shift from individual, handmade production to powered, special-purpose machinery, factories, and mass production. The cumulative effect of a number of consequential inventions and designs made this possible. One of several crucial entrepreneurs was the manufacturer Richard Arkwright (1732–92), who created the first water-powered cotton mill, combining skills, machinery, and materials into what became the factory system. He also developed horse power and then water power, which made

KEY EVENTS

1709	1712	1733	1740	1751	1759
Abraham Darby (1678–1717) uses coke to smelt iron ore, replacing wood and charcoal as fuel initiating the mass production of cast iron.	Thomas Newcomen builds the first commercially successful steam engine to pump water out of mines.	John Kay (1704–c. 79) invents the flying shuttle that changes the weaving industry and revolutionizes textile production.	Crucible steel making is discovered by English clockmaker Benjamin Huntsman (1704–76).	English landscape gardener Lancelot "Capability" Brown (1716–83) sets up as an 'improver of grounds."	The first Canal Act is passed by the British Parliament, leading to the construction of a network of waterways for transport and industrial supplies.

cotton manufacture a mechanized industry. Further significant inventions included the power loom (see image 3), developed in the 1780s by Edmund Cartwright (1743–1823), that mechanized the process of weaving cloth.

Momentous achievements also occurred in the field of engineering. The use of fossil fuel was increasingly exploited and mining became more important, but as mines became deeper, many flooded and hand pumps were inefficient. In 1769 James Watt (1736–1819; see p.20) made improvements to an engine designed by Thomas Newcomen (1664–1729) that was intended to pump water out of mines by enabling the replacement of water power by steam. In the early 19th century, engineer Richard Trevithick (1771–1833; see image 2) constructed the first steam train. Iron and steel became essential materials, used to make everything from tools and machines to ships and building infrastructure. One of the most inventive engineers of the 19th century, Isambard Kingdom Brunel (1806–59), designed dockyards, railways, steamships, tunnels, and bridges. He implemented major improvements to docks, and became chief engineer to the Great Western Railway, introducing the broad-gauge railway track that made trains safer and faster because of increased stability. In 1864, five years after his death, Brunel's iron Clifton Suspension Bridge (see image 1) opened. It spanned a gorge in Bristol, south-west England, and was a feat of mankind, only possible through his ingenuity and technological advancements.

Industrial expansion continued to proliferate into the late 19th century, as the work of the early pioneers was followed by new inventions, discoveries, and ideas. As industrialization spread across Europe and the United States, people increasingly addressed questions of industrial design. **SH**

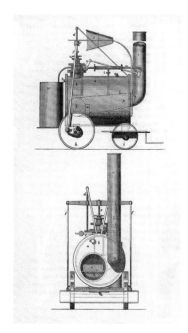

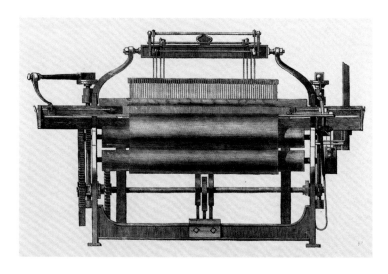

1764	1769	1779	1793	1802	1856
English weaver James Hargreaves (c. 1720–78) invents the spinning jenny that enables workers to produce multiple spools of thread simultaneously.	James Watt patents his improved steam engine as an industrial power source.	The spinning mule, which makes it possible to produce fine yarns by machine, is developed by English inventor Samuel Crompton (1753–1827).	US inventor Eli Whitney (1765–1825; see p.22) invents the cotton gin, solving the problem of supplying cotton speedily for the textile industry.	English chemist William Cruickshank (d.1810/11) designs the first electric battery capable of mass production.	Englishman Henry Bessemer (1813–98) patents the first inexpensive industrial process for mass producing steel.

Single-action Steam Engine 1763–75
JAMES WATT 1736–1819

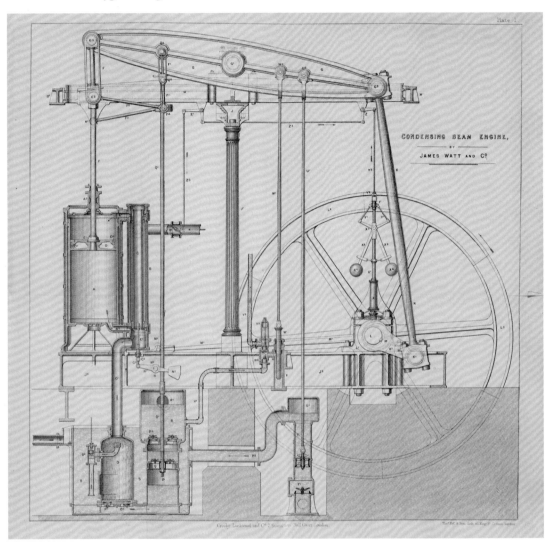

CONDENSING STEAM ENGINE,
BY
JAMES WATT AND C?

Plate from *Stationary engine driving: a practical manual* (1881) by Michael Reynolds

⬡ NAVIGATOR

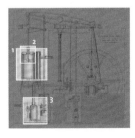

In 1698 the first commercially used steam-powered engine was built by English engineer Thomas Savery (*c.* 1650–1715). Designed to pump water out of coal mines, Savery's invention, consisting of a simple boiler and a pipe, had several problems. In 1712 his partner, Thomas Newcomen, improved Savery's steam pump with his atmospheric engine, which also deployed steam power. Also intended to pump water out of mines, Newcomen engines were fairly complex and were never cost effective. In 1763, while repairing a Newcomen engine, Scottish instrument maker James Watt decided to improve the design. Watt solved the problems of the Newcomen engine by creating a separate condenser outside the cylinder. Watt still had obstacles to surmount in constructing a full-scale engine, including a lack of capital and insufficient technology to make the parts. He formed a partnership with the manufacturer Matthew Boulton (1728–1809). Through Boulton, Watt had access to some of the best ironworkers in the world and gained the means to mass-produce his engines. As a direct result of the invention, the Industrial Revolution was irrevocably activated. **SH**

👁 FOCAL POINTS

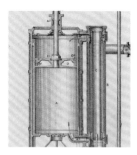

1 CYLINDER
Watt's steam cylinder was constantly hot; there was no enforced cooling required. The shell around the main cylinder helps to keep it hot. The steam cylinder operates on the downward stroke of the steam piston. The weight of the pump side tips the beam so that the steam piston rises.

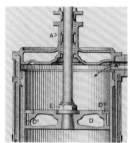

2 PISTON
The engine operated on the principle of a pressure difference created by a vacuum on one side of the piston, which pushed it down. The top of the steam cylinder is sealed. During the upward and downward strokes at atmospheric pressure, steam exists above the piston.

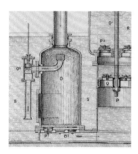

3 CONDENSER
Watt's innovations included a separate condenser. Valves enabled the steam to flow into a separate condenser. When the condenser is under a vacuum, the steam from below the piston then rushes into it. The steam then condenses, and so the vacuum is maintained.

EFFICIENCY AND ECONOMY

The separate condenser was Watt's most significant invention with regards to his steam engine. On each stroke of a Newcomen atmospheric engine, the cylinder was heated by steam and subsequently cooled by cold water so that the steam condensed to water, which created a vacuum, forcing the atmosphere to push the piston down. By making the condensing process occur in a separate vessel, Watt ensured that the cylinder remained hot, which greatly increased the engine's efficiency and so improved economy. It took eleven years from his initial design for his first successful steam engine to be constructed, because the main problem had been the lack of technology to create a piston large enough to preserve a moderate amount of vacuum. Eventually, when technology caught up and Watt had secured financial support, he made his engine available to all. It was immediately used in transport, manufacturing, mining, and more. Watt's faster, more fuel-efficient engine was hugely successful and changed the world.

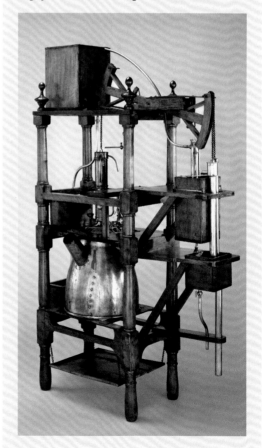

🕐 DESIGNER PROFILE

1736–73
James Watt was born in Greenock, Scotland. He trained as an instrument maker in Glasgow and London. From 1756, he worked as an instrument maker at the University of Glasgow. In 1763 a professor from the university gave Watt a Newcomen engine to repair. Within two years, Watt analysed how to improve it. A patent for his steam engine was granted in 1769.

1774–87
Watt moved to Birmingham. From 1776 to 1781 he spent time in Cornwall, installing engines in copper and tin mines. Next, he adapted his engines to be used to power machines in factories. Watt created a rotary motion in his machines, and in 1782 he invented the double-action steam engine. In 1784, he invented the parallel motion.

1788–1819
Watt invented the centrifugal governor to regulate steam engine speed and in 1790 the pressure gauge. He retired in 1800 and devoted his remaining years to research.

Cotton Gin 1793

ELI WHITNEY 1765–1825

Lithograph from 1793 of the original cotton gin.

O ne of the first great inventions of the Industrial Revolution in the United States was the cotton gin (short for cotton engine), invented by Eli Whitney. This simple machine revolutionized the production of cotton by accelerating the process of removing seeds from cotton fiber.

Inferior versions of the cotton gin had existed since the 1st century AD, but Whitney's invention was the first practical machine. Before Whitney's cotton gin, separating cotton fibers from its seeds was a labor-intensive and unprofitable task undertaken manually— an average cotton picker could remove the seeds from approximately 1 pound (450 g) of short-staple cotton in a day. The cotton gin removed cotton fiber from its seeds. Cotton was run through a wooden drum embedded with a series of hooks that catch the fibers and pull them through a mesh. Although the mesh is too fine for the seeds to pass through, the hooks pull the fine cotton fibers through with ease.

Through the reduction of processing time, cotton became the United States' leading export by the mid 19th century. Whitney's cotton gin revolutionized the cotton industry, saving labor, enabling huge expansion, and reducing the prices of cotton simultaneously. Yet despite the cotton gin's success, it made little money for Whitney due to technicalities in patent laws. It was difficult for him to protect his rights, and even though the laws were changed a few years later, his patent expired before he realized much profit. Another negative factor was that cotton farmers increasingly called on slave labor to work the machines, even though elsewhere increasing numbers supported its abolition. **SH**

 NAVIGATOR

👁 FOCAL POINTS

1 HAND CRANK
With Whitney's hand-cranked cotton gin, one worker could remove the seeds from 50 pounds (22.5 kg) of short-staple cotton in a day, some fifty times more than the average cotton picker could do by hand. Larger cotton gins could be powered by horses and, later, by steam engines.

2 CYLINDER
The cotton gin was a relatively simple machine. Raw cotton was fed into a revolving cylinder via a hopper, short wire hooks pulled the cotton fiber through mesh and dropped it into a pile, while the seeds were deposited separately, ready to be planted next season.

◀ Whitney's cotton gin caused the cotton industry to expand vastly and greatly transformed the US economy. Because of the invention, the yield of raw cotton doubled every decade after 1800. The cotton gin boosted the textile industry, but an accompanying increase in the use of slave labor contributed to the outbreak of the American Civil War (1861–65). By the mid 19th century, the United States was growing 75 per cent of the world's entire cotton supply.

PROFIT-REDUCING PIRACY

Whitney made and repaired machines to support himself through Yale University. On graduating in 1792, he planned to teach while studying law. He travelled to Savannah, Georgia, where he met plantation owner Catherine Greene (1755–1814). Whitney accepted an invitation to stay at her plantation, Mulberry Grove, in Georgia. She and her plantation manager, Phineas Miller (1764–1803), showed Whitney the difficulties cotton farmers experienced in separating seeds from fibers to make cotton usable and gave him the use of a workshop where he created the cotton gin. Whitney received a patent for his invention in 1794 and formed a company with Miller. They planned to build and install cotton gins on plantations throughout the southern states of the United States, being paid a percentage of the cotton produced on each plantation. However, although farmers welcomed the new machine, they had no intention of sharing their expanding profits, and most pirated Whitney's design.

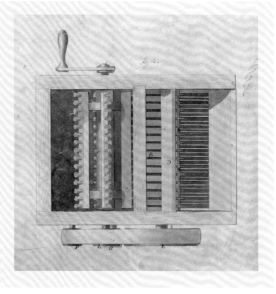

CLASSICAL REVIVAL

1 Made from mahogany and oak with marquetry in satinwood and rosewood, the Kimbolton Cabinet (1771–76) was designed by Robert Adam for Kimbolton Castle in Cambridgeshire, England.

2 Thomas Chippendale completed this gilded beechwood and walnut armchair in 1765 for Robert Adam to satisfy a commission for a grand salon in a great London house.

3 Classical inspiration is evident in this amphora-shaped jasperware Wedgwood vase made c. 1790 at the Etruria pottery in Staffordshire, England. Round the middle are figures of Apollo and the nine Muses.

In the second half of the 18th century, the Industrial Revolution initiated an important period in the history of design. Mass production and mass consumption became possible through the development of new technologies, the introduction of large factories, and changes in urban living, resulting in a consumer revolution in which a new and diverse assortment of goods were available to a more disparate section of the population. The surge of important inventions stimulated a feeling of confidence, sense of progress, and interest in design. Machine-made objects had to be consciously planned; too many were produced to be able to rely on chance or for discrepancies to be practical. So the role of the designer changed. Conceptual work became an essential aspect of machine-made designs.

The custom for young, affluent Europeans and North Americans to go on a Grand Tour of Europe had developed over many years, and by the late 18th century it had become hugely influential on design and taste. The Grand Tour helped to define Rome as the cultural center of the Western world and

KEY EVENTS

1755	1757	1762	1764	1768	1769
German scholar Johann Winckelmann (1717–68) publishes *Thoughts on the Imitation of Greek Works in Painting and the Art of Sculpture*.	Robert Adam returns to Britain after three years in Rome, and amalgamates classical themes with his own ideas to form his Neoclassical style.	In Britain, Josiah Wedgwood is appointed royal supplier of dinnerware.	English weaver and carpenter James Hargreaves invents the spinning jenny, enabling weavers to work eight or more spools at once.	The Royal Academy is established in London, with Joshua Reynolds (1723–92) as its first president.	Scottish inventor and mechanical engineer James Watt (1736–1819) patents his steam engine with separate condenser.

expanded the appeal of classicism. Central figures of the classical revival that occurred at that time were three Scottish architects, the Adam brothers: John (1721–92), Robert (1728–92), and James (1732–94). After spending 1755 to 1757 in Rome during his Grand Tour, Robert designed exteriors and interiors, based on the classical styles he had studied, and established what became known as the "Adam Style." The Adam brothers believed in total design of their interiors, from windows to furniture, paintwork to fireplaces. Combining Neoclassical ornament with impeccable craftsmanship in furniture (see image 2) and grand pieces such as the Kimbolton cabinet (see image 1), Robert in particular led the classical revival in Britain, which then spread across Europe and North America.

Also inspired by Neoclassicism was the cabinetmaker and furniture designer Thomas Chippendale (1718–79). Additionally influenced by Chinese, Gothic, and French Rococo styles, he worked these diverse stylistic elements into harmonious and unified designs, capitalizing on the expansion of the middle classes who were demanding luxury goods. In 1754 Chippendale became the first cabinetmaker to publish a book of his designs: *The Gentleman and Cabinet-Maker's Director* (see p.26), which had an immediate and lasting international impact. Chippendale, Thomas Sheraton (1751–1806), and George Hepplewhite (1727–86) are often classed as the three most important English furniture makers of the 18th century. Sheraton's furniture is characterized by a feminine refinement of late Georgian styles, and Hepplewhite's furniture is light and elegant.

This atmosphere of expansion, intellectual and trade experimentation, and industrial progress was particularly prominent in Britain, and encouraged designers, industrialists, and inventors such as James Hargreaves (*c.* 1720–78), Matthew Boulton (1728–1809), Josiah Wedgwood (1730–95; see p.32), and Richard Arkwright (1732–92) to pursue new ideas and processes. In 1769 Wedgwood founded his Etruria pottery factory, where he produced ceramics inspired by ancient Greek and Roman pottery (see image 3). Aiming to serve the middle classes as well as the aristocracy, Wedgwood became a pioneer of the mass market; he was one of the first manufacturers to advertise in newspapers and to develop retail display. Continually experimenting with his designs and his manufacturing methods, he divided production into separate activities, which contrasted with handmade methods. Each of his factory workers specialized in a single activity, which increased overall output. It was the beginning of a production process that led to the car assembly lines of the early 20th century. The Etruria factory produced two categories of ceramics: "ornamental" and "useful." Both were made of earthenware, but the designs and finishes were different. To complete the ornamental designs, Wedgwood engaged some of the best artists of the day, including John Flaxman (1755–1826), George Stubbs (1724–1806), and Joseph Wright of Derby (1734–97). **SH**

1771	1774	1775	1790	1795	1802
English entrepreneur Richard Arkwright founds the first water-powered cotton-spinning mill in Cromford, England.	The first Shaker community sets up in the United States. The community becomes known for its furniture design and craftsmanship.	Scottish watchmaker Alexander Cumming (1731/2–1814) is awarded the first patent for the flushing toilet (or valve closet).	In the United States, Congress establishes a patent office to protect inventors and give them an incentive to develop new machines and methods.	The first standardized graphite pencils are introduced—they are central to mechanical drawings used in the transition to an industrial culture.	By passing a current through a thin strip of platinum, English chemist Humphry Davy (1778–1829) creates the first incandescent light.

The Gentleman and Cabinet-Maker's Director 1754
THOMAS CHIPPENDALE 1718–79

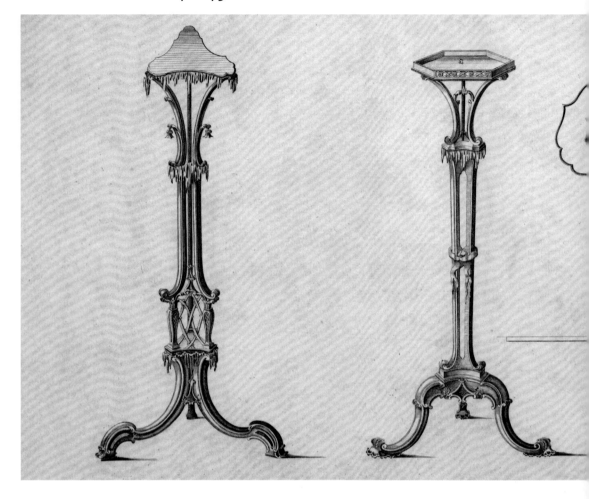

Plate showing tables from *The Gentleman and Cabinet-Maker's Director.*

In 1753 Thomas Chippendale opened a furniture showroom in London's most fashionable shopping street of the time, St Martin's Lane. Profiting from the burgeoning, aspirational middle classes, Chippendale offered a wide range of high-quality furniture.

In 1754 he published an innovative catalog: *The Gentleman and Cabinet-Maker's Director*—a pattern book featuring 160 engravings of his designs. Although other furniture makers had produced catalogs before, none were as comprehensive or on such a large scale. The *Director* claimed to be "a large collection of the most elegant and useful designs of household furniture in the Gothic, Chinese and modern taste."

Published by subscription, Chippendale's *Director* was reissued in 1755 and again in 1762, when it included additional plates of his latest furniture in the new Neoclassical style. It was exceptionally successful. Subscribers included the rich and famous, including the actor David Garrick (1717–79), Catherine the Great (1729–96), and Louis XVI (1754–93), as well as the general public and other cabinetmakers.

Clients often used the *Director* as a guide and ordered simpler pieces for their homes, made with fewer elements or cheaper materials. They also combined elements they saw to create bespoke commissions. By publishing his designs in text and illustrations, Chippendale spread his influence far beyond the reaches of his London workshop. **SH**

✦ NAVIGATOR

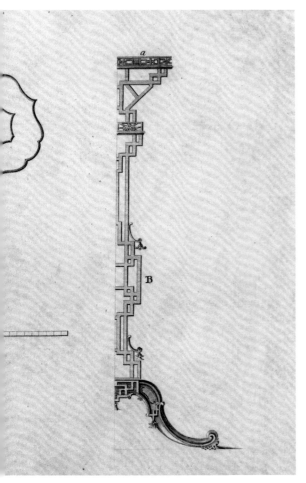

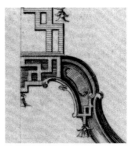

1 ENGRAVED ILLUSTRATIONS
Based on Chippendale's drawings, his friend, the publisher, draftsman and printmaker Matthew Darly (c. 1720–81), engraved most of the illustrations in the *Director*. The 160 plates show the variety of furniture and decorative objects that Chippendale's workshop could produce.

2 VARIETY
The 1754 and 1755 editions of the *Director* displayed furniture in four styles: English; French Rococo; Chinese, which emphasized the effects of chinoiserie, latticework, and lacquer; and Gothic, with pointed arches, quatrefoils, and fretwork. The 1762 edition included Neoclassical lines.

🕐 DESIGNER PROFILE

1718–61
Thomas Chippendale was born in Yorkshire, England. He served an apprenticeship as a carpenter. He moved to London, where he had a showroom and workshop. In 1754 he published *The Gentleman and Cabinet-Maker's Director*. A second edition of the *Director* was published the following year.

1762–79
Chippendale created designs for a new *Director*, which was published in 1762. In 1776 he retired when his son, also Thomas (1749–1822), took over the firm.

MARKETING TOOL

By enlisting subscribers—buyers who prepaid for their copies of his finished book—Chippendale self-published the *Director*. It was a good marketing tool. Chippendale's business soared and he was soon employing approximately fifty skilled craftsmen to keep up with demand. Even though all the plates are signed by him, some of the designs were by other designers who worked for him. Many of the designs include instructions for less experienced cabinetmakers and options for making pieces more or less elaborate, to suit different skill levels or budgets. The patterns were influential across Europe and proved particularly popular in North America, where they were adapted to local materials and tastes.

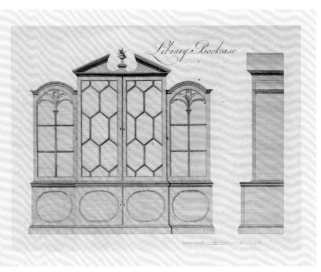

THE CONCEPT OF TASTE

By the mid 18th century, the notion of taste had become an obsession. The idea of being able to discern between vulgarity and decorum—or to have good taste—became a measure of a person's worth, and the period saw an explosion in industries where good taste was essential, such as in Chippendale furniture (see p.26), Wedgwood pottery (see p.32), and Sèvres porcelain (see image 1). Designers sought to bring elegant lines and a lighter touch into people's lives. The focus on taste was linked to the prospering middle classes, who were enjoying the accoutrements of wealth, and it gauged old money against new. While many aristocrats disagreed, most realized a person could have taste even if he or she did not have breeding. Good taste became synonymous with etiquette, sophistication, and refinement.

Trade expansion and the Industrial Revolution generated the increase in consumption, which in turn prompted a rise in the number of designers producing goods, and inspired the extensive debates about taste. The flamboyant, dramatic Baroque style became replaced by two distinct design approaches. Rococo was whimsical and light hearted, inspired by the French court, while Neoclassicism rejected the asymmetrical frivolity of Rococo, and

KEY EVENTS

1704	1709	1710	1711	1718	1749
English physicist Isaac Newton (1643–1727) publishes his discoveries and theories on light and color in *Opticks*.	After years of research, German scientists discover how to manufacture Chinese-style hard-paste porcelain.	The Saxon royal factory at Meissen, Germany, opens. It is the first to produce porcelain in Europe in large quantities and the recipe is kept secret.	Anthony Ashley Cooper, 3rd Earl of Shaftesbury (1671–1713), equates bad taste with vice in his essays *Characteristics of Men, Manners, Opinions, Times.*	English merchant Thomas Lombe (1685–1739) patents a silk thread throwing machine powered by a waterwheel.	English furniture maker Thomas Chippendale (1718–79) opens his first workshop in London.

instead looked to the formality and symmetry of ancient Greece and Rome. On his Grand Tour, amateur architect Richard Boyle, 3rd Earl of Burlington and 4th Earl of Cork (1694–1753), became inspired by the Italian architect Andrea Palladio (1508–80), whose buildings were influenced by the mathematical precision of ancient Classical architecture. Burlington took many ideas he had seen in Palladio's architecture back to Britain and inspired a generation of architects. Palladio was heavily influenced by the writings of the Roman architect, Vitruvius (c. 80–70–c. 15 BC) who, in *The Ten Books of Architecture* (c. 15 BC), wrote that a building should meet "obligations of commodity, firmness, and delight." Commodity addresses how a building serves its function. Firmness means its ability to stand up to natural forces over time, and delight implies that it should look beautiful.

This provoked further discourse on art, beauty, and discernment, and in Germany, the philosopher Alexander Gottlieb Baumgarten (1714–62) gave the term "esthetics" a modern application, using it to mean good taste or a sense of beauty. He defined taste as the ability to judge intuitively rather than through intellectual consideration. Baumgarten's ideas were influenced by ideals of the Enlightenment, a European movement that lasted from the mid 17th century to the late 18th century, when new ideas about the use of reason were considered, a notion that had first been explored by philosophers of ancient Greece. It was during the Enlightenment that several public museums first opened in Europe, including the British Museum in 1759, the Uffizi in 1765, and the Louvre in 1793, which all added to collective sensibilities about taste, connoisseurship, and culture.

In 1757 the British statesman Edmund Burke (1729–97) published his influential philosophical treatise, *A Philosophical Enquiry into the Origin of Our Ideas on the Sublime and the Beautiful*, which concludes that esthetic abilities are improved through experience and knowledge. He argued for the uniformity of taste on the basis of sensibility rather than on judgement, explaining that taste is innate and not logical.

As well as being inspired by Palladianism, Neoclassicism was influenced by the excavations of Herculaneum and Pompeii. In 1738 and 1748 respectively, these two ancient Roman towns had been discovered intact, preserved beneath the ash of Mount Vesuvius, which had erupted in AD 79. The new interest in Classical ideas pervaded all areas of the decorative arts, emphasizing straight lines and geometric motifs, establishing the general belief that the Classical world was the epitome of elegance. While national interpretations varied, from the French Empire style to the Regency style in Britain, from the German Biedermeier style (see image 2) to the Gustavian style in Scandinavia, and the Federal style in the newly formed United States, the Neoclassical style generally engendered the consensus that good taste is discerned by an appreciation of restraint, quality, and harmony. **SH**

1 The exuberant shapes in this Sèvres porcelain coffee and tea service, completed in 1861, evoke the Near East and China, reflecting the contemporary French taste for exoticism.

2 This elegant side chair was made in 1820 by the firm of Viennese furniture maker Josef Ulrich Danhauser (1780–1829). Its simple forms and clean lines are characteristic of the Biedermeier style.

1757	1760	1769	1782	c. 1785	1796
Scottish philosopher David Hume (1711–76) publishes *Four Dissertations*. The essay collection considers taste and esthetics.	The first exhibition of contemporary art in England is held by the Royal Society of Arts in London.	English potter Josiah Wedgwood (1730–95) founds his pottery works at Etruria in Staffordshire, England.	Wedgwood develops a pyrometer for measuring extreme heat in ovens, kilns, and furnaces.	Italian printer and typographer Giambattista Bodoni (1740–1813; see p.30) designs the modern typeface, Bodoni.	German actor and playwright Alois Senefelder (1771–1834) invents the printing technique of lithography.

Bodoni *c.* 1785
GIAMBATTISTA BODONI 1740–1813

S ince movable type was invented in *c.* 1439 by German printer Johannes Gutenberg (*c.* 1398–1468), countless typefaces have been designed, but only a few have endured to become classics that retain popularity for centuries. Bodoni is such an exemplary font. Designed by Italian publisher and typographer Giambattista Bodoni in *c.* 1785, it was inspired by the type designs of English printer John Baskerville (1706–75), and French printers Pierre-Simon Fournier (1712–68) and Firmin Didot (1764–1836).

At the time, book publishing focused attention on illustration, and typography's significance had diminished. Printers were using undistinguished typefaces and substandard printing inks. Printed type lacked clarity and definition, while technical limitations meant that inferior books were the norm. Determined to change this, Bodoni began by copying Fournier and Didot's typefaces. Fournier had first proposed a comprehensive point system in 1737, later adding refinements, and his ideas were perfected by Didot. Bodoni established his own foundry, and began designing a typeface that departed from the French designs and moved towards the Baskerville font he had admired for so long. Resolving to create a classic design, he designed the typeface that became synonymous with his name, characterized by simplicity and emphasizing straight, clean Neoclassical lines with bold, contrasting strokes and an overall geometric construction, reminiscent of ancient Roman inscriptions. **SH**

Roman and italic capitals in the Bodoni typeface designed by Giambattista Bodoni from his *Manual of Typography* (1818).

◉ FOCAL POINTS

1 HAIRLINE STROKES
Picking up on the contemporary preference for classical styles, the Bodoni typeface features clear, simple lines and structure, with thin, hairline strokes. It was one of the first modern typefaces to exhibit extreme contrasts of light and dark in its thick and thin strokes.

2 VERTICAL STROKES
Bodoni is known as a "modern" typeface. Modern typefaces are distinguishable by their vertical emphasis and strong contrasts of vertical and horizontal strokes. Modern serifs and horizontals are extremely thin, almost hairlines. Bodoni's font is the most influential modern typeface.

3 UNBRACKETED SERIFS
The unbracketed serifs and balanced lines made Bodoni's font timeless and classical. From the end of the 18th century, when he first designed it, the Bodoni typeface inspired a number of other type designers to create new versions of it, particularly in the early 20th century.

MANUALE

TIPOGRAFICO

DEL CAVALIERE

GIAMBATTISTA BODONI

VOLUME PRIMO.

PARMA

PRESSO LA VEDOVA

MDCCCXVIII.

▲ Bodoni evolved original typefaces, redefining letters by giving them a more mathematical, geometric, and mechanical appearance. His *Manuale tipografico* (*Manual of Typography*, 1818) discusses more than 300 typefaces, and shows how he used ideas from ancient Greek and Roman lettering and blended them with his concepts, resulting in the elegantly balanced font.

First Edition Copy of the Portland Vase *c.* 1790

JOSIAH WEDGWOOD 1730–95   JOHN FLAXMAN JR 1755–1826

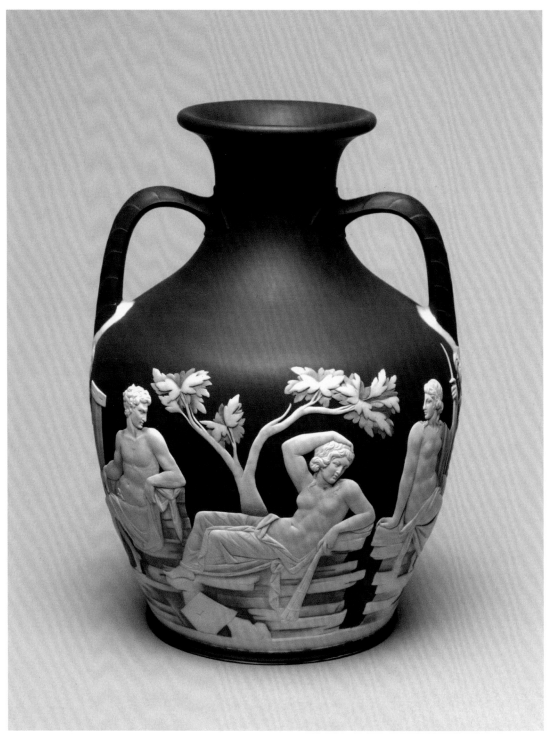

Jasperware, with black dip and white reliefs
Diameter 9⅞ in./25 cm

Made of violet-blue layered glass with a white cameo relief, the Portland Vase dates from between AD *c.* 5 and AD 25. Found in a tomb near Rome in 1582, it was bought by Cardinal Francesco Barberini in 1627 and remained in his family until 1780. After being sold, it reached England and was bought by the Dowager Duchess of Portland in 1784. Two years later her son, the third Duke of Portland, acquired it and lent it to Josiah Wedgwood for a year. Josiah became obsessed with replicating the vase in his own delicate jasperware, a smooth, matt, fine-grained ceramic that he developed in the 1770s. Josiah, his second son, Josiah II, and John Flaxman Junior, a Neoclassical sculptor and designer, toiled to imitate the ancient vase for nearly four years.

In October 1789, Josiah sent the first successful copy of the vase to his friend Erasmus Darwin. The following May, he gave another copy to Queen Charlotte, and then organized a private viewing at the house of the president of the Royal Society, Joseph Banks. By May 1790, Josiah had received twenty subscriptions for the vase. These favorable reactions encouraged him to exhibit the vase abroad, and Josiah II took it around Europe for six months, which reinforced the Wedgwood company's reputation. **SH**

👁 FOCAL POINTS

1 WHITE CAMEO
Although Josiah Wedgwood's modelers produced precise molds of the relief figures on the original vase, replicating the translucent white cameo proved difficult. He wrote to a friend: "My present difficulty is to give those beautiful shades to the thin and distant parts of the figures."

2 FIGURE
A leading figure in European Neoclassicism, John Flaxman Junior was employed by Wedgwood as a modeler. Wedgwood's trademark ancient Greek- and Roman-inspired designs were created mostly by him, and the creative challenges of the Portland Vase owe much to his skills.

EXPERIMENTATION

The Portland Vase (see right) copies are among the greatest of Josiah Wedgwood's achievements, but they took him nearly four years to perfect. After much experimentation, he used a black colored jasperware that he called "basalt ware." The first difficulties he experienced with the jasper body included cracking and blistering, and then lifting of the reliefs during firing. On the original vase, some layers of the cameo are cut thinly in places so that the white is tinted by the dark glass shining through. Initially, Wedgwood worried that his reliefs could never be applied thinly enough to replicate that delicacy, and on some first-edition vases, he achieved the effect by coloring the reliefs lightly with gray and brown shadows. In all, the vases were difficult to make and only about thirty were made between 1790 and his death in 1795, each offered for sale at thirty guineas each, plus £2 10 shillings for the box. After his death, no more Portland vases were manufactured by the Wedgwood company until 1839, when the copied ancient Roman figures were remodeled in consideration of Victorian prudery.

DESIGN REFORM

In 1835 and 1836 in Britain, a report by the Parliamentary Select Committee on Art and Manufactures expressed concern that greater encouragement was being given in France, Germany, and "other manufacturing countries" to "the art of design" and "correct principles of taste." In consequence, British-manufactured goods were lacking in style and risked losing the "export race." Over the rest of the century, the argument for better design rose to prominence among artists and manufacturers.

In 1837 the Government School of Design (later the Royal College of Art) was founded in London to improve the education of designers, but it faced a difficult task as industry continued to respond to the overly ornate styles favored by the public. The Industrial Revolution had created a burgeoning middle class who sought to furnish their new homes lavishly, and many manufacturers were churning out goods to capitalize on this. Most of these manufacturers viewed design as simply a part of production, not a separate consideration requiring specialist thought and planning.

Henry Cole (1808–82) was one of the first critics of this. He decided that if respected fine artists designed everyday objects, public taste would be improved. In 1845 the Society for the Encouragement of Arts, Manufactures and

KEY EVENTS

1810	1826	1829	1830	1832	1836
German printer and inventor Friedrich Koenig (1774–1833) patents a steam-driven printing press.	Scottish civil engineer, architect, and stonemason Thomas Telford (1757–1834) completes two suspension bridges in Wales.	English civil and mechanical engineer George Stephenson (1781–1848) builds his Rocket steam locomotive to compete in railway trials.	The Altes Museum in Berlin, designed by German architect Karl Friedrich Schinkel (1781–1841), is completed after seven years of construction.	English mathematician and inventor Charles Babbage (1791–1871) creates the first calculator, which he calls a "difference engine."	Augustus Pugin publishes his architectural manifesto, Contrasts, which argues for a revival of medieval Gothic architecture.

34   THE EMERGENCE OF DESIGN 1700–1905

Commerce (later the Royal Society of Arts, or RSA) offered a prize for designs for a tea service. Using the pseudonym Felix Summerly, Cole produced a design executed by Minton (see image 1) that won a silver medal. He went on to establish Summerly's Art Manufacturers and commissioned several accomplished artists to design items to be industrially produced. Although short lived, his venture inspired further similar enterprises, which helped his objective of reforming design. Between 1847 and 1849, Cole also organized annual exhibitions for the RSA to promote a greater focus on good design, and in 1849 he founded *The Journal of Design and Manufactures*, edited by Richard Redgrave (1804–88), artist and principal of the Government School of Design. Cole noted that a large problem was that many manufacturers perceived design as an addition, to be added to an object at the end of manufacture, rather than an integral part of it from its conception. Ornamentation was frequently used to disguise inferior materials or poor-quality workmanship.

The poor standards of British design became apparent at the Great Exhibition (see p.38) in London in 1851. Cole, who had instigated the exhibition in the hope of elevating public taste, was particularly concerned. In 1852 he became General Superintendent of the new Department of Practical Art, which was set up to reform training in schools and colleges across the country. He, Redgrave, and the Crystal Palace's interior designer, architect Owen Jones (1809–74), developed guidelines for the study of design at the Government School of Design. Jones had traveled abroad and his attempts to create a modern style were inspired by the Islamic world (see image 2). The men aimed to raise standards, to avoid superfluous ornamentation, and to educate public taste away from the garish designs that dominated the market.

Despite featuring so many meretricious designs, the Great Exhibition was a success and generated a considerable profit. Part of this was used to acquire some of the displays to form a collection in a new Museum of Ornamental Art (later the Victoria and Albert Museum). One room in the museum displayed poorly designed objects, intended to shame the manufacturers who produced such monstrosities, and to educate the public about design. The room was labeled "Decorations on False Principles," but it became known as the "Chamber of Horrors." The museum's purchasing committee included Cole, Redgrave, and the architect, designer and critic Augustus Pugin (1812–52; see p.36). Pugin favored the medieval Gothic style, perceiving it as morally appropriate, and almost single-handedly established Gothic Revivalism as a dominant design style of 19th-century Britain, particularly in architecture.

Aligned with Pugin's medievalism, as well as Cole's and Redgrave's design concerns, the Arts and Crafts movement (see p.74) rejected modernity and industry. Founded by the textile designer, artist, and socialist William Morris (1834–96), the Arts and Crafts movement also followed the teachings of the highly respected art critic and theorist, John Ruskin (1819–1900). **SH**

1 Henry Cole's prize-winning earthenware and porcelain tea service was in production from 1846 to 1871.

2 Inspired by trips to Spain and Egypt, Owen Jones attempted to influence taste with his designs for tiles in Islamic style (*c.* 1840–50).

1837	1840	1849	1853	1854	1856
English schoolmaster Rowland Hill (1795–1879) proposes the idea of the first adhesive prepaid postage stamp.	Construction begins on the Palace of Westminster in London, designed by English architects Pugin and Charles Barry (1795–1860).	The bowler hat is created by London hatters Lock and Co, for a customer who requires protective headwear for his gamekeepers.	Inspired by the Great Exhibition held in London in 1851, the first US World's Fair opens in New York City at the Crystal Palace.	In *Hard Times*, Charles Dickens (1812–70) caricatures Henry Cole as a government inspector who explains the principles of good taste to schoolchildren.	Owen Jones publishes *The Grammar of Ornament*, illustrating patterns and designs from various decorative traditions.

Wallpaper for the House of Lords 1848
AUGUSTUS PUGIN 1812–52

👁 FOCAL POINTS

1 LEAVES
Flat patterns appeared on Pugin's wallpapers, replacing the excessively embellished designs that were popular. The colors are adaptations of medieval pigments. This design is composed of simple repeating forms that articulate the flatness of the wall rather than misrepresenting it.

2 PORTCULLIS
This wallpaper design incorporates the symbol of the Palace of Westminster, the crowned portcullis, and the Tudor rose, a royal emblem. The letters "V" and "R" stand for Victoria Regina, the reigning monarch, so the design symbolizes the authority of the crown and parliament.

D eclaring in his 1836 manifesto, *Contrasts*, that design should move away from "the present decay of taste," Augustus Pugin focused on purity and clarity, initiating the idea of "honesty" and "propriety" in ornament and design. He insisted that only flat patterns should adorn flat surfaces, emphasizing rather than disguising them, and that false illusions of depth, texture, and three dimensions were dishonest and contrived. This became an essential principle of the design reform movement.

Aiming to reform and improve society by idealizing the medieval system, Pugin argued that good design had moral integrity, while bad design was insincere and deceitful. The Gothic Revival that he promoted was to him both ingenuous and Christian. Though he was brought up by his mother in the strict Scottish Presbyterian Church, he converted to Roman Catholicism, believing fervently that architecture with tall spires pointing heavenward, and candidly designed wallpapers, carpets, and furnishings followed the Catholic doctrine and would have a positive effect on society. In 1847 he visited Italy and subsequently incorporated some of the grandest Italian designs into his own. At the Great Exhibition of 1851 (see p.38), he designed a complete range of Gothic-style furnishings, many available to order at relatively modest prices. In their medieval setting, his simply styled tables and colorful dinner plates were new and fresh to contemporary eyes, and appealing to visitors at the Crystal Palace. **SH**

◈ NAVIGATOR

Body colors on red paper
23 x 21 in.
58.5 x 53.5 cm

⏱ DESIGNER PROFILE

1812–26
Augustus Welby Northmore Pugin was born in London, the son of an architect. He attended Christ's Hospital school in London and his father taught him architectural drawing.

1827–35
Pugin was employed to design furniture for George IV at Windsor Castle. He began an antique furniture business and worked as a set designer at King's Theatre in London. He was briefly held in a debtors' prison when his furniture business collapsed. In 1835, he converted to Catholicism.

1836–43
He published *Contrasts*, his first architectural manifesto, and designed churches, cathedrals, houses, and a monastery. He became Barry's assistant on the new Palace of Westminster.

1844–52
His third book, *The Glossary of Ecclesiastical Ornament and Costume*, was published. He designed the interior decorations for the House of Lords, the Medieval Court for the Great Exhibition, and the clock tower at the Palace of Westminster. Suffering from exhaustion, he was committed to Bedlam and died soon after.

THE PALACE OF WESTMINSTER

After the huge fire of 1834, a competition was organized to find an architect to rebuild the Palace of Westminster in London. Pugin acted as draftsman for two of the ninety-seven entrants: Charles Barry (1795–1860) and James Gillespie Graham (1776–1855). As he was so instrumental in Barry's success, Barry asked Pugin to work with him. Construction of the Palace of Westminster began in 1840 and lasted for thirty years. Pugin's contribution can be seen in the distinctive Gothic details, including vanes and spires. He designed almost all the Gothic-style interiors, including more than one hundred wallpapers, carvings, stained glass, floor tiles, metalwork, furniture—and the clock tower that houses Big Ben. Pugin's ideas had a powerful effect on the design reform movement. His belief that even "the smallest detail should have a meaning or serve a purpose," and his principles of historical authenticity in design and reduced ornamentation, had a dramatic effect on designers and the public.

THE GREAT EXHIBITION

The first in a series of world fairs, the Great Exhibition was devised by Henry Cole (1808–82), an English civil servant. Through his membership of the Society for the Encouragement of Arts, Manufactures and Commerce, Cole campaigned to improve standards in industrial design. Prince Albert (1819–61), Queen Victoria's husband and the society's president, supported his ideas, and in 1847 a royal charter was granted to the organization. In 1849 Cole visited the Exposition Nationale des Produits de l'Industrie Agricole et Manufacturière (Exposition of the Second Republic) in Paris and noticed there was no opportunity for international exhibitors. On his return to England, he secured a Royal Commission for an international exhibition to be held in London.

Led by Prince Albert, the society planned the Great Exhibition of the Industry of all Nations. Held from 1 May to 15 October 1851 in London's Hyde Park, the exhibition attracted more than six million visitors and featured over 100,000 exhibits by more than 15,000 contributors. The range of displays was vast, from the overly ornate to the purely functional, from household goods to industrial machines, from quality merchandise to poorly made products. It was the first time that the nations of the world had come together in one place in peace, and it was a showcase for the manufacturers of Britain and the world,

KEY EVENTS

1815	1822	1825	1831	1834	1839
English chemist Humphry Davy (1778–1829) invents the miner's safety lamp, which shields the naked flame to prevent explosions in mines.	French Egyptologist Jean-François Champollion (1790–1832) deciphers ancient Egyptian hieroglyphs using the Rosetta Stone.	Biedermeier furniture, inspired by French Empire style but in light woods that avoid metal ornamentation, becomes popular in Europe.	American farmer Cyrus McCormick (1809–84) invents the mechanical reaper-harvester that frees farm laborers to work in factories.	In London a fire destroys most of the Palace of Westminster and both Houses of Parliament.	Photography is commercially introduced, perfected by William Henry Fox Talbot (1800–77).

a pivotal moment for the development of design in the 19th century. More than forty different countries were represented, but as the host nation, British displays (see image 1) took up half the exhibiting space. Exhibits varied from a hydraulic press invented by civil engineer Robert Stevenson (1772–1850) to a fountain made of four tons of pink glass and a steam hammer that could, with equal accuracy, forge the main bearing of a steamship or gently crack an egg, as well as carpets, cups, chairs, printing presses, and agricultural machines (see image 2). Although the fundamental purpose of the exhibition was the promotion of world peace, the repeating firearms of Samuel Colt (1814–62; see p.48) featured prominently. There were examples of every kind of machine, including a sewing machine by Isaac Merritt Singer (1811–75; see p.40). There was a huge variety of ornamentation, patterns, and historical style references, and the chaotic lack of accord was criticized from all sides.

The exhibition was not only a venue for international competition, but also became an arena that demonstrated national differences. Diversities in attitudes to design across Europe and the United States became immediately apparent. Overall, despite the Industrial Revolution, most Europeans still appreciated the virtues of hand craftsmanship—of embellishment over function. Americans, however, preferred mass production as a means to achieve better-made, simply designed objects in greater numbers. For critics of the day, the contrast between overly ornate household products and those displaying either an unembellished functional esthetic, or those revealing an instinctive connection between hand and eye, established the urgent need for design reform, education, and accord. **SH**

1 A lithograph commissioned by Queen Victoria and Prince Albert depicting the British nave at the Great Exhibition, published by Dickinson Brothers in *Dickinson's Comprehensive Pictures of the Great Exhibition of 1851* (1854).

2 A photograph of various agricultural implements, including a steam traction engine and two types of seed drill, manufactured by Garrett and Sons and shown at the Great Exhibition in 1851.

1848	1849	1854	1855	1856	1869
The Pre-Raphaelite Brotherhood is founded by a group of British artists. It aims to promote art about serious subjects treated with realism.	French gardener Joseph Monier (1823–1906) invents reinforced concrete to use for horticultural tubs and containers.	At the New York World's Fair, Elisha Otis (1811–61) demonstrates his safety elevator, or lift, by cutting the rope holding the platform on which he is standing.	The Christmas edition of the *Illustrated London News* features chromolithographs, becoming the first colored newspaper.	English chemist William Henry Perkin (1838–1907) accidentally produces the first synthetic dye—aniline purple or mauveine.	The Suez Canal is opened in front of thousands of spectators in Egypt. It connects the Mediterranean Sea with the Red Sea.

Sewing Machine 1851

ISAAC MERRITT SINGER 1811–75

👁 FOCAL POINTS

1 TREADLE
Singer's needle moves up and down rather than side to side, and is powered by a foot treadle (not shown), which allowed an unprecedented speed of 900 stitches per minute. The features of his basic machine are evident in the design of later machines by other manufacturers.

2 NEEDLE
Singer's sewing machine was the first to incorporate features that allowed continuous and curved stitching on any part of an item being made. It has a suspended arm holding a straight needle in a horizontal bar. The design helped to reduce thread breakage.

The US inventor and entrepreneur Isaac Merritt Singer did not invent the sewing machine, but in 1851 he patented the first practical and efficient one. Semi-literate Singer had been taking acting jobs when possible, with odd jobs in between, when he began working in a machine-repair shop in Boston. In 1850 he was given a sewing machine to repair and eleven days later he had made a better one, which he patented the following year—after exhibiting it at the Great Exhibition in London. The same year he set up I. M. Singer and Company, later renamed the Singer Manufacturing Company. However, the eye-pointed needle and lockstitch that Singer incorporated had already been developed and patented by Elias Howe (1819–67), and in 1854, Howe won a patent-infringement suit against him, but Singer carried on making his machines.

Until then, sewing machines had been industrial machines, but from 1856 Singer began marketing smaller machines for home use. Singer used the latest mass-production techniques to produce large numbers of machines at economically viable prices. By 1855 his company had become the largest producer of sewing machines in the world, and by 1863 the Singer Manufacturing Company had secured twenty-two further patents for improvements to his machine. In 1867 the company opened its first factory outside of the United States, in Glasgow, Scotland. **SH**

◈ NAVIGATOR

Metal overall, iron mechanisms
16 x 17 x 12 in.
40.5 x 43 x 30.5 cm

① DESIGNER PROFILE

1811–48

Isaac Merritt Singer was born in Pittstown, New York, the eighth child of German immigrants. At eleven, he ran away to join a traveling stage act. In 1839 Singer obtained a patent for a rock-drilling machine. He formed a theàtrical troupe, The Merritt Players, but after five years took a job in Ohio at a sawmill, where he designed a carving machine.

1849–50

Singer moved to Boston and worked at a machine shop where Lerow and Blodgett sewing machines were being built and repaired. He designed a better sewing machine.

1851–55

Singer exhibited his sewing machine at the Great Exhibition in London and obtained a patent for it. He partnered with lawyer Edward Clark (1811–82), who helped him with patent litigation against his sewing-machine design as well as marketing.

1856–75

Several sewing-machine manufacturers formed the Sewing Machine Combination—the first patent pool in US history. That same year, Singer's company manufactured thousands of sewing machines for home use. In 1862 he sailed for Europe where he settled, building a house in Devon, England.

INNOVATIVE MERCHANDISING

Although he yearned to be an actor, acting jobs were not plentiful, so Singer found work as a mechanic and cabinetmaker. He was practical and inventive, and his first invention was a machine for drilling rock, which earned him $2,000 in patent rights. Next, he patented a type-casting machine for printing books. Singer's sewing machines went into production with the backing of Phelps and printer George Zieber. With an astute business brain, Singer initiated several merchandising practices, including mass marketing, using women to demonstrate the machines in venues where they attracted potential buyers, and providing an after-sales service. His business partner, Clark, pioneered the hire-purchase system of buying on credit in easy instalments, which helped assure the company's success. The Singer Manufacturing Company achieved international renown with the opening of factories in Glasgow, Paris, and Rio de Janeiro, and by 1890 it had 80 per cent of the worldwide market share.

BENTWOOD AND MASS PRODUCTION

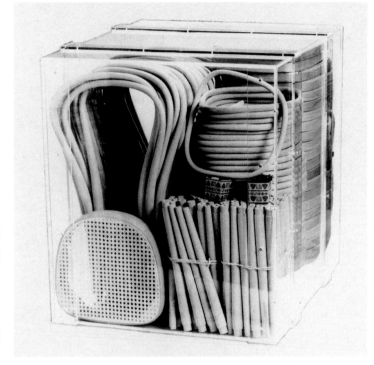

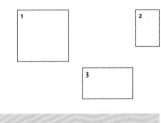

1 When disassembled, thirty-six Model No. 14 chairs could be packed in a transport box of 35⅜ cubic feet (1 cubic meter) to ship around the world.

2 The demonstration chair made from two long, twisted bentwood rods helped the Thonet display win a gold medal at the Exposition Universelle in 1867 in Paris.

3 The Model No. 4 chair designed by Michael Thonet in c. 1850 became popular for use in Viennese coffee houses, such as the Café Griensteidl on Michaelerplatz, depicted here in 1896.

By the middle of the 19th century, the general concepts of machine-assisted manufacture and division of labor were well established in large factories operating across Europe and the United States. Expensive and time-consuming handcrafting was replaced by production systems that used unskilled labor to make standardized components and then assemble them with the aid of specialized machinery. This rationalization of the production process made it possible to produce high volumes of goods at affordable prices, and was instrumental in the success of items such as the Singer sewing machine (see p.40) and .36 Colt Navy Revolver (see p.48). The huge new factories often required raw materials from abroad, while saturation of national markets led to a search for more customers overseas. The growth of manufacturing was accelerated by rapid improvements to transportation methods, which made it easier to reach customers worldwide, so more efficient methods of packaging, marketing, and distribution were also needed.

Most machine-made furniture was imitations of handmade counterparts. However, in the 1830s German cabinetmaker Michael Thonet (1796–1871)

(see p.40) ... (see p.48)

KEY EVENTS

1836	1837	1849	1851	1852	1853
After experimenting with bending laminated veneers, Michael Thonet makes his first successful layer-wood chair.	Thonet gains independence by acquiring the Michelsmühle factory in Boppard, Germany, that makes the glue he uses in his process.	After securing financial backing, Thonet and his five sons found their own workshop in the suburbs of Vienna.	Thonet wins a bronze medal at the Great Exhibition in London (see p.38) for his Vienna bentwood chairs.	Thonet opens a sales office in Vienna and applies for a patent for his bentwood process in the name of his five sons.	Thonet transfers his business to his sons under the name "Gebrüder Thonet."

began experimenting with different ideas. He embraced the notion of mass production, but wanted to create elegant, lightweight furniture with graceful curves. He sought ways of bending wood, aiming to replicate techniques he had seen developed by barrel makers and boat builders. Initially, he tried glueing veneers together, but eventually invented a process where solid lengths of beechwood were bent beyond their natural flexibility through the use of metal clamps and steam. The chairs he produced using this method were innovative in design and suited to factory production because they were made in sections. At first he was refused patents in France, Britain, and Belgium, but he later acquired copyrights, which guaranteed his monopoly on his invention and enabled his global success. He and his five sons founded the Gebrüder Thonet workshop in Vienna, where he proceeded to make furniture for the imperial court of Vienna and for the mass market (see image 3).

Thonet's process eliminated the need for hand-carved joints or fussy ornamentation, and created durable chairs and tables that could be manufactured and sold at low cost. With his astute business sense, Thonet also pioneered "kit furniture," creating his furniture in parts that could be flat-packed and shipped efficiently over long distances (see image 1). On reaching its destination, the furniture was easily assembled with a few screws. This ingenious reduction of elements, flat-packing, and ease of construction made Gebrüder Thonet bentwood furniture suited to high-volume production and export, while the elimination of superfluous embellishment made them appealing to a market saturated with heavy, ornate furniture. Thonet and his sons had contracts with royalty and a worldwide network of retail outlets. Their bentwood furniture was exhibited at international fairs, won awards (see image 2), and established a global reputation, making it an exemplar of early mass production. **SH**

1855	1856	1859	1859	1871	1889
Gebrüder Thonet receives a silver medal at the Exposition Universelle in Paris and receives many overseas orders.	Foundation of the first Gebrüder Thonet furniture factory in Moravia. In the coming years, five more Eastern European production sites open.	Gebrüder Thonet first publishes multilingual catalogs illustrating every item of furniture it manufactures, each individually numbered to facilitate orders.	The innovative bending technique of Thonet's Model No. 14 chair (see p.44) allows for the industrial production of a chair.	Thonet dies, leaving his thriving legacy to his sons.	The seventh and last Gebrüder Thonet factory is established in the town of Frankenberg, Germany.

Model No. 14 Bentwood Chair 1859

MICHAEL THONET 1796–1871

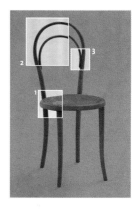
C ombining lightness, restraint, and smooth curves, Michael Thonet's Konsumstuhl Nr. 14 chair, better known as Model No. 14, or the Café or Bistro chair, is one of the most purchased items of furniture ever made. Generally believed to be the first mass-produced chair and one of the most successful products in the history of industrial mass production, it was initially produced in 1859 from Thonet's new factory in the beech woods of Moravia, Czech Republic. Using his revolutionary process of bending solid beechwood with clamps, metal strips, and heat from steam—a process that did not need skilled workers—the chair had instant appeal for its modest, organic design and keen price, and was bought in large numbers, particularly for cafés and bistros across Europe.

Early versions were glued together, but during the 1860s, each chair was made from just six components, ten screws, and two washers. Additionally, Thonet's innovative flat-packing system aided its success as it could be easily and cost-effectively transported to distant locations. Strong yet lightweight, the stylish chair was unique at a time when other furniture designers could only produce such curves through carving. At the Exposition Universelle in Paris in 1867, it won a gold medal and attracted the admiration of eminent architects and designers, including Le Corbusier (1887–1965), which helped to establish Thonet's international reputation. By 1930, more than fifty million No. 14 chairs had been produced and sold around the world. **SH**

Beechwood and cane
36⅝ x 16⅞ x 18¾ in.
93 x 43 x 47.5 cm

FOCAL POINTS

1 SEAT
Woven cane or palm has often been used for the seat section of Thonet's No. 14 chair, because it is light and practical—any spillages pour through the chair. Cane and palm complement the wood esthetically, and the springiness of the weaving enhance the chair's comfort.

2 CHAIR BACK
The unbroken curve of the chair back is made from a single piece of wood that continues down to create the two back legs, which gives it stability and reduces the number of chair parts. A smaller curve reinforces the backrest. The design's clean lines contrasted with contemporary ornate furniture.

3 SCREW
The chair was designed to be fixed together using only ten screws and two washers. Its components could be packed flat and shipped all around the world, where it could be assembled very easily upon arrival. The reduced shipping volume made the design very cost effective to distribute.

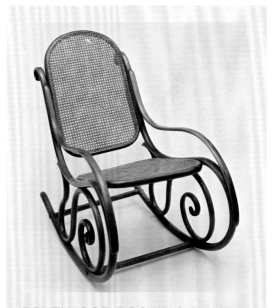

BENTWOOD ROCKING CHAIR

Thonet's bentwood technique lent itself to the creation of rocking chairs, because the rockers were made from long, strong sections of beech wood. He produced several kinds, most featuring fortifying braces that doubled as decorative curves. The bentwood method was liberating for this type of chair, as previously rocking chairs had to have carved rockers. This method was quick and did not need skilled workers. Created in 1860, with elaborate curves and a handwoven cane seat and back, the rocking chair No. 1 is an iconic Thonet design.

MILITARY INNOVATIONS

1 Men of the British Indian Army with revolving chamber Gatling guns, a type of early machine gun.

2 General Ulysses S. Grant (1822–85) in full uniform. He commanded the Union army in the US Civil War from 1864.

3 Joseph Glidden's patent drawing for barbed wire in 1874 shows how it can be used in wire fences.

During the 19th century, the increasing economic might of the United States signalled the start of a new world order, as much as shifting borders and allegiances in Europe. Although the Industrial Revolution had its origins in Britain, it was in the United States that it took hold with the greatest speed. One of the reasons was manpower. The new country was under-populated and machine production was the right answer at the right time. Yet the demands imposed by the US Civil War provided the greatest spur to development. By the outbreak of the war in 1861, the United States was at a point of transition between an economy based on agriculture and the leading industrial nation it would become by the end of the century. The conflict highlighted a division in the economy, with industrialization concentrated in the northern states—the Union or the North—and the Confederacy—or the South—dependent on the sale of its crops, produced by slave labor.

War demands mobilization of resources—armies must be clothed, equipped, fed, and moved where they are needed. At the war's outset, the North had more factories, greater manpower (thanks to more immigrants), and a wider network of railways than the South; it was also more mechanized. The progress of the hostilities heightened these advantages. In the North, production increased—not only of weapons, such as the recently designed .36 Colt Navy Revolver (1851; see p.48) and repeating rifles. Factories processed

(1851; see p.48)

KEY EVENTS

1848	1854	1861	1861	1862	1862
The British Army introduces drab, or khaki, uniforms in India. After the Indian Mutiny of 1857, khaki becomes more widely worn.	Gail Borden invents condensed milk. His tinned food products are later supplied to US Civil War soldiers.	The US Civil War begins. After the first Battle of Bull Run, the Union War Department standardizes the Union uniform.	To raise cash for the US Civil War, President Abraham Lincoln (1809–65) imposes the first federal income tax by signing the Revenue Act.	The Homestead Act grants new settlers outside the founding thirteen states a small acreage of land.	Union soldiers wear the same uniforms and carry the same equipment. They wear early mass-produced leather shoes made for the right and left foot.

food, churned out farm machinery, and equipped the fast-expanding railway network, which meant that the North could rely on a greater number of troops, who were better supplied and equipped, and could move them by train or steamship to the enemy's door. Modern armies need equipment, the funding to see new ideas realized, and they require products in large numbers. This serves as a fast track for innovation, and more than 5,000 patents were issued in 1864. Innovation occurs in peacetime, too: the Swiss Army's need for a multi-tool pocket knife led to the iconic Swiss Army Knife (1890; see p.50).

In addition to developments in small arms design and manufacture, the US Civil War saw the deployment of the first ironclad gunships, which changed naval warfare. It also marked a step toward the first fully automatic weapon, with the patenting of the Gatling gun (see image 1) in 1862, which was capable of continuous firing. Ironically, inventor Richard Gatling (1818–1903) intended to reduce deaths in combat by reducing the need for large armies, since one man could do as much in battle as a hundred with his invention. His gun saw a limited use by Union forces and was not adopted by the US Army until 1866. Later, it was widely used by colonial powers to put down local uprisings.

Wartime innovation can bring wider benefits, some of which might be unforeseen at the time. In 1854 Gail Borden (1801–63) invented condensed milk, which, along with his tinned biscuits and condensed coffee, became staple supplies for Union soldiers during the US Civil War and later for ordinary householders. Standard sizing for clothing and, crucially, boots and shoes was introduced for the first time (see image 2) as the Federal government took over the duty of supplying uniforms, arms, food, and equipment—a development that would directly impact on the emergent mass-market clothing industry. The development of interchangeable parts led to the first affordable pocket watches, which were carried by many soldiers and improved military efficiency, while 15,000 miles (24,140 km) of extra telegraph cable was laid to maintain essential lines of communication for the military.

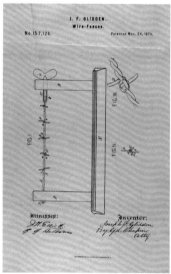

Much of this progress was hastened by legislation, passed by a Republican Congress no longer hampered by Southern Democratic opposition. Crucially, the first income tax was introduced with the Revenue Act in 1861 and paper money became legal tender for the first time. The Pacific Railway Act of 1862 set in motion the construction of an east-to-west transcontinental route, which created jobs, and opened up settlement and commerce along the line. The Homestead Act of the same year gave a small acreage of land away free to settlers. The peace saw ranchers settle on the plains. Farmers needed to protect their land from being trampled by cattle and livestock had to be kept off the railway track. The solution was barbed wire (image 3), patented by farmer Joseph Glidden (1813–1906) in 1873, using a coffee mill to create the barbs. As well as benefiting the North's war aims, the seeds were being sown for expansion in finance, commerce, and manufacturing. **EW**

1862	1862	1862	1862–65	1864	1865
Richard Gatling patents the Gatling gun, which is capable of continuous firing.	The Battle of Hampton Roads sees the first battle between ironclad gunships in the US Civil War.	The Pacific Railway Act specifies an east–west continental route, launching an expansion of the US rail network.	The US government issues more than $450 million in paper money not backed by gold (greenbacks) to help finance the Union cause in the Civil War.	Union soldier John Kinloch (d.1896) patents his Guard Razor aimed at maimed or wounded soldiers and those shaving in dangerous situations.	The US Civil War ends. Northern victory preserves the United States as one nation and ends the institution of slavery.

.36 Colt Navy Revolver 1851

SAMUEL COLT 1814–62

Steel, brass, wood
Length of barrel 7½ in./19 cm

At the age of eighteen, Samuel Colt styled himself "Dr Coult," and began touring the United States as a chemistry lecturer. Three years later he used his lecturing profits to invest in his invention. With its revolving mechanism, his handgun could be fired multiple times without reloading.

As a young seaman, Colt had been fascinated with the way the ship's wheel could either spin or lock in a fixed position through the use of a clutch. He carved a wooden model of a gun based on similar principles and a few years later, in 1836, he developed his idea into a working design. It was a revolutionary repeating gun, replacing the usual single-shot cartridge chamber with a cartridge cylinder that revolved when a hammer was cocked, and so could fire multiple rounds in quick succession. It was also the first handgun to successfully use a percussion action, replacing the flintlock mechanism of established guns. In 1835 and 1836, Colt secured patents for his design in England and the United States respectively, and his revolver was put into production by the Patent Arms Manufacturing Company in New Jersey. In 1842 he ceased production through insufficient orders, but in 1847 the US government ordered 1,000 revolvers for use in the Mexican War. Orders increased even more after the revolver was displayed at the Great Exhibition in London in 1851. Four years later, Colt opened a factory in Hartford, Connecticut, subcontracting Eli Whitney Junior (1820–95), the son of Eli Whitney (1765–1825), because his father had pioneered the mass production of guns. With factories in Hartford and London, Colt developed a production-line system using standardized, interchangeable components, 80 per cent of which were machine made. He was producing 150 guns a day by 1856. During the US Civil War, Colt sold his guns to both sides. By the outbreak of the war in 1861, the reputation of his firearms as accurate, reliable, and of the finest workmanship and design had spread throughout the world.

✦ NAVIGATOR

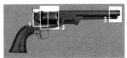

Colt's success owed as much to his guns' practicality as to his original methods of standardized parts, and to his understanding of the potential of effective marketing. He used promotion, publicity, and press advertising as powerful marketing tools. **SH**

👁 FOCAL POINTS

1 CAP CUTOUT
Colt's invention of the percussion cap made ignition faster, safer, and more reliable than the older flintlock design. He allegedly declared: "There is nothing that cannot be produced by machinery." He epitomized the love the Americans had for mass production and simplicity of design, while the Europeans still liked ornate embellishment and handcrafting.

2 REVOLVING CYLINDER
Colt was not the first to invent the revolving mechanism—one had already been patented by US inventor Elisha Collier (1788–1856)—but Colt eliminated the flintlock mechanism with his percussion action, which Collier did not do. Despite its name, the Colt 1851 Navy, or the .36 Navy Revolver, was used primarily by military land forces and civilians.

3 BARREL
The long 7½ in. (19 cm) barrel made seeing the fixed-bead front sight easy and helped the .36 Navy Revolver gain its reputation for accuracy. The 1851 Colt revolvers had octagonal barrels, while later models had round ones. The .36 Navy Revolver was far lighter than Colt's previous designs, which made it suitable for carrying in a belt holster and a popular handgun.

🕐 DESIGNER PROFILE

1814–28
Samuel Colt was born in Connecticut, one of eight children. His father was a farmer turned businessman. He remained at school until he was fourteen.

1829–31
Colt worked in his father's textile plant in Massachusetts while inventing things, then he was sent to sea to study navigation. Inspired by the wheel of the ship he was aboard, he made a wooden model of a gun with a revolving mechanism.

1832–41
Returning to the United States, Colt resumed work with his father, but then toured, lecturing as "The Celebrated Dr Coult of New-York, London, and Calcutta." Using savings and a loan, he built a prototype revolver. In 1835 and 1836 he secured patents in England and the United States.

1842–50
He perfected an underwater mine for use in harbor defense. His remote-ignition submarine battery required a waterproof cable to transmit electricity under water. He adapted an earlier design by telegraph inventor Samuel Morse (1791–1872). In 1847 Colt was commissioned to produce 1,000 revolvers.

1851–62
Colt exhibited his firearms at the Great Exhibition in London. By 1855, his was the largest private arms factory in the world. He pioneered the use of standardized interchangeable parts and an organized production line.

A GROWING INDUSTRY

In 1849 Colt went on a sales tour of Europe, and by 1856 his Hartford factory was the largest privately owned munitions plant in the world. That same year, he was awarded the honorary title of Colonel by the governor of the State of Connecticut. Colt subsequently designed three types of revolver – pocket, belt, and holster – and two rifles. In the 1880s, the Colt Peacemaker became legendary in the Wild West, while the Colt .45 semi-automatic pistol became standard issue to the US Armed Forces during World War I and World War II.

Swiss Army Knife 1890

VARIOUS

Successful incarnations of the multitool pocket knife have proved popular because of their everyday utility.

⬡ NAVIGATOR

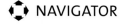

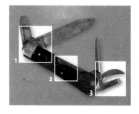

The Swiss military had a problem in the 1880s. The standard service rifle, the Schmidt-Rubin, required a screwdriver for assembly. But a screwdriver was not something that soldiers tended to carry with them. So they ordered a large number of pocket knives to use as a maintenance tool and can opener for ration tins.

The Swiss government would have preferred to manufacture what was designated the Soldier Knife Model 1890 in Switzerland, but there were no domestic suppliers with enough production capacity. So the first order for 15,000 knives went to master cutlers Wester and Co, of Solingen in Germany. That changed when local cutler and surgical-equipment manufacturer Karl Elsener formed the Association of Swiss Master Cutlers, and was able to take over the contract in 1891. Elsener made modifications to the knife, adding tools on both sides of the handle. In 1897 he introduced the Swiss Officer's and Sports Knife. It was not part of a military contract but appealed to officers, who had to buy their own equipment. The knife was sold in grocery stores and sales meant it found its place at all levels of Swiss society. The knife was known mainly in Switzerland until the end of World War II, when US soldiers stationed in Europe began to buy it in large quantities as a souvenir, which is when it became dubbed the "Swiss Army Knife."

As time has passed, more tools have been added to the knife, ranging from tweezers to nail files, and scissors to toothpicks. Some models feature even more functions, like the $1,000 Wenger Giant (2006) collector's knife, which has eighty-seven tools and 141 functions, including a cigar cutter, tire-tread gauge, and magnifying glass. **DG**

FOCAL POINTS

1 FOLDING BLADES
The folding-blade design has a history that dates back to the Iron Age. Folding-blade knives have been found on the Iberian peninsula from pre-Roman times. Contemporary Swiss Army Knives are made from a stainless-steel alloy optimized for toughness and corrosion resistance.

2 GRIP
The first edition of the pocket knife came with a dark wood grip that was later replaced by ebony wood. The most common modern design is the classic red cellulose acetate butyrate scaled knife, although models often have non-slip rubber inlays incorporated for wet conditions.

3 TOOLS
The first pocket knife featured a blade, reamer, can opener, and screwdriver. These were designed to open canned food and aid with disassembling a rifle. The later additions— for the consumer-targeted Officer's and Sports Knife of 1897—consisted of a small cutting blade and a corkscrew.

DESIGNER PROFILE

1860–90
Karl Elsener was born in Zug, Switzerland. He completed an apprenticeship as a cutler and then worked in Tuttlingen, Germany, as a journeyman. In 1884 Elsener founded his factory in the town of Ibach in Switzerland, manufacturing knives and surgical instruments, to help provide local employment.

1891–1911
The decision of the Swiss government to move manufacturing of the Model 1890 army knife to Elsener's company in 1891 was crucial for the business. It produced its first Officer's Knife in 1897. After the death of Elsener's mother, Victoria, in 1909, the company changed its name to Victoria.

1912–18
Elsener was a conservative member of parliament in the Grand Council of Switzerland from 1912 to 1918, and a local councilor until his death. The company was renamed Victorinox in 1921, when the blade was changed to stainless steel—*inoxydable* means "stainless" in French. At the time of Elsener's death, Victorinox had 100 employees.

KNIFE OF PEACE

The Swiss Army knife has never been used in war, despite (or perhaps because of) the fact that Switzerland has one of the world's most heavily armed populations. In the revised Swiss constitution of 1874, every able-bodied male citizen is a member of the federal army. The army has been completely mobilized three times (in response to the Franco-Prussian War, and World Wars I and II) but has never endured wartime combat. Switzerland has a long tradition of neutrality, although it does participate in international peacekeeping missions. Since 1995 the Swiss Army has been progressively shrunk and stands at 220,000 men, with 130,000 on active duty, including an air force. There is also a maritime force, which, as the country is landlocked, is understandably small. Every member of the forces is still issued with a pocket knife manufactured by Victorinox.

▲ Elsener changed the design of the Swiss Army Knife in 1896 to accommodate more blades and tools on the other side of the handle. An innovative spring mechanism allowed him to use the same spring to hold them in place.

MORRIS AND CO

William Morris (1834–96) was a designer, writer, translator, painter, typographer, printer, craftsman, manufacturer, and social activist, who first achieved fame for his poetry, but who later became better known for his designs, his leading role in the Arts and Crafts movement (see p.74), and his contiguous aims to improve both design and the lives of the working poor. His vision in linking art to industry by applying the values of fine art to the production of commercial design became an essential aspect of the evolution of design.

A generous, highly intelligent, sensitive, and energetic man, Morris mastered numerous crafts to ensure that quality in his manufacturing company was always upheld. He passionately opposed industrial mass production, perceiving the profusion of cheap, mass-produced goods as the reason for the undesirable decline in traditional crafts and local industry. Morris believed that esthetic and social issues were intrinsically linked, and that many of the problems of mid-Victorian society could be solved by a return to the working methods of the pre-industrial, medieval period, when the countryside was respected and artisans were valued, and when workers produced goods from start to finish, consequently combining art with production.

KEY EVENTS

1851	1851	1856	1859	1861	1875
William Morris accompanies his family to the Great Exhibition in London (see p.38). He is horrified by what he sees and refuses to tour the exhibits.	The first volume of John Ruskin's *The Stones of Venice*, a three-volume treatise on Venetian art and architecture, is published.	While attending Exeter College at the University of Oxford, Morris and Edward Burne-Jones launch the *Oxford and Cambridge Magazine*.	Morris commissions Philip Webb to design the Red House at Bexleyheath in Kent (now south-east London) as his family home.	Morris, Marshall, Faulkner and Co is established in London. It revives traditional arts swept away by industrialization.	Morris, Marshall, Faulkner and Co becomes Morris and Co. Morris, Burne-Jones, and Webb continue in their roles.

While studying theology at the University of Oxford, Morris became friends with Edward Burne-Jones (1833–98), who shared his interest in medieval art and architecture. They were also influenced by ideas propounded by the Pre-Raphaelite Brotherhood and the writings of the eminent art critic, John Ruskin (1819–1900). In 1861, after training as an architect, Morris started his own firm of interior decorators and manufacturers: Morris, Marshall, Faulkner and Co, which became Morris and Co in 1875. Morris and his associates— among them the painters Burne-Jones and Ford Madox Brown (1821–93), and the architect Philip Webb (1831–1915)—produced handcrafted metalwork, jewellery, wallpaper, textiles, furniture, ceramics, and books. Rather than follow the new factory method of division of labor, the "Firm," as the company became called, emulated the medieval workshop tradition with a community of creators who took control of their own work, complying with Morris's aim to restore "joy in labor." The company was run as an artists' collective, shunning mass production and aiming to create beautifully designed, affordable, handcrafted goods that reflected workers' creativity and individuality. Using bold forms and strong colors based on medieval pigments, Morris's merchandise was devoid of superfluous or excessive decoration, which helped to change the predominant fashions of the day. In 1876 he opened a shop in the most fashionable shopping area of London; by the 1880s he had become internationally known and commercially successful. New guilds and societies formed following his ideas.

His almost perpetual energy and activeness of mind led him to constantly explore new challenges, from poetry and novel writing, to designing typefaces and furniture (see p.54), creating wallpaper (see p.56) and textile designs, translating books and managing his businesses. Morris himself revived the craft of block printing and vegetable dyeing, and even set up looms for tapestry weaving in his home. He produced block printed cotton and velveteen furnishing fabrics like his Wey pattern (see image 2) designed to be printed by indigo discharge to produce a characteristic blue colour.

Morris also adopted the principle of 'truth to materials', focusing on the inherent value and beauty of every material used, as Augustus Pugin (1812–52; see p.36) had advocated with the Gothic Revival. In seeking naturalistic patterns for his designs, Morris researched exhaustively, studying artefacts as diverse as Elizabethan plasterwork and Islamic tiles, and producing interpretations of them. Morris and his colleagues were in demand for projects such as Standen, a country house in Sussex designed by Webb with interiors by Morris and Co, including textiles, wallpapers, furniture and ceramics (see image 1). However, this handcrafting of wares using only quality materials inflated manufacturing costs, and most of the Firm's products were too expensive for any but the rich to afford, which opposed Morris's socialist ideals. Yet his philosophies influenced subsequent designers and design movements immeasurably. **SH**

1 The drawing room in Standen House (1894) in East Grinstead, England, designed by Philip Webb to uphold the highest levels of craftsmanship.

2 Morris and Co produced textiles commercially for sale in two London shops, including this Wey furnishing fabric (c. 1883).

1877	1882	1888	1891	1892	1892
Morris, Webb, and others form the Society for the Protection of Ancient Buildings, to repair old buildings and preserve their cultural heritage.	The Art Worker's Guild is founded in London, a cross-disciplinary forum for its diverse membership that includes craftsmen, artists, and architects.	The Guild and School of Handicraft is founded in London.	Morris sets up Kelmscott Press to produce quality limited-edition books.	Kelmscott Press publishes a chapter from Ruskin's The Stones of Venice outlining key elements of the Gothic style, "The Nature of Gothic."	Webb begins work on the home he has designed for the Beale family, Standen House, in East Grinstead, England.

Sussex Chair *c.* 1860
MORRIS, MARSHALL, FAULKNER AND CO 1861–75

Ebonized beech with
rush seat
33½ x 20½ x 17⅜ in.
85 x 52 x 44 cm

👁 FOCAL POINTS

1 WOOD
Despite his belief in the ethos
of truth to materials, Morris
allowed Sussex chairs to be
made of ebonized beech, which
was fashionable. Staining
wooden furniture to resemble
ebony was a trend inspired in
Europe by travelers returning
from the Orient, where ebony
was used to dramatic effect.

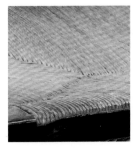

2 SEAT
Woven by hand—usually by
female workers—using
freshwater rushes, the rush
seat enhanced the natural,
unadorned image of the chair,
keeping it light and simple. The
first Sussex chairs had square
seats, but later designs in the
range also had round or
rectangular seats.

Unlike the fussy and often overly ornate furniture that was so popular during the Victorian period, William Morris's furniture was simple, purposeful, and handmade. He aimed to make the handmade furniture his company Morris, Marshall, Faulkner and Co (later Morris and Co) produced available to all. This chair was simply made and competitively priced, embodying Morris's vision for the improvement of design for everyday use.

The chair is thought to have been designed by Philip Webb, who was inspired by a late Georgian country armchair found in Sussex with a rush seat and turned frame. It is a demonstration of vernacular design that relies on traditional artisan skills. Morris used the chairs in his country home, Red House in Kent, and later in his London home, Kelmscott House. Selling it from *c.* 1869 as the "Sussex chair," it was immediately popular and bought in huge numbers. The chair was copied by other furniture manufacturers, including the London stores Heal's and Liberty. Morris and Co went on to produce a range of Sussex furniture, and the Sussex chair remained in production until the 1920s. **SH**

◀ Inspired by British 13th-century architecture, Morris aimed for the Red House to be "medieval in spirit." Plain and well proportioned, the building had no extraneous decoration, except on some functional areas, such as the arches over the windows. Unusually, the windows were positioned to suit the design of the rooms rather than to create an external symmetry.

RED HOUSE

In 1859, Morris commissioned Webb to help him design a house for him and his new wife Jane (1839–1914). It was to be in a rural area not far from London, and he found a plot of land in a village in Kent, ten miles from the city. It was Webb's first independent architectural project. A contractor built the house in a year, costing Morris approximately £4,000. With an L-shaped plan, two storeys, and a high-pitched roof of red tile, the Red House comprises a large hall, dining room, library, morning room, and kitchen on the ground floor, with the main living rooms, drawing room, studio, and bedrooms on the first floor. Reflecting Morris and Webb's socialist beliefs, the servants' quarters were larger than in most contemporary homes. Morris designed most of the interior, including furniture, tiles, and stained glass. Many items of furniture were designed by Webb and the Pre-Raphaelite artists Edward Burne-Jones and Dante Gabriel Rossetti (1828–82). The result was an embodiment of the Arts and Crafts movement—a collaboration between artists using quality materials, with designs inspired by the medieval period.

Willow Bough Wallpaper 1887
WILLIAM MORRIS 1834–96

NAVIGATOR

Block printed in distemper
colors on paper
27⅛ x 20⅞ in.
69 x 53 cm

Many of William Morris's wallpaper designs were based on plant forms that he studied from close observation. Some of his patterns, such as Willow Bough, were inspired by flowers and trees he saw on country walks. The willow was one of his favorite motifs and he used it in several of his designs. In 1874 he designed Willow, a stylized representation of willow branches. Willow Bough is a naturalistic version of the earlier pattern. As one of the freshest of his wallpapers, this is a delicate, flat design, with fine, intertwining stems and soft, curving leaves. The subtle interplay of rhythms suggests Japanese art that was popular among many at the time, while the soft colors express the natural curves and waves of willow trees in the English countryside.

To 21st-century eyes, the design may seem busy and crowded, yet in contrast with heavy, ornate Victorian designs, it seemed fresh, bold, light, and new to Morris's contemporaries. Morris's aim to create goods affordable by all was achieved with such objects as the Sussex chair (c. 1860), but his wallpapers, because of the complexity of the block-printing process they required, were always more expensive than most. **SH**

👁 FOCAL POINTS

1 NATURAL FORMS
The flatness of walls was a pleasure to Morris. He remained particularly fond of his Willow Bough design because it simply yet effectively emphasized smooth surfaces and avoided false illusions of depth, yet managed to remain pliable looking and naturalistic.

2 PATTERN
Many of Morris's early wallpaper designs were based on simple grids, but by the time he designed Willow Bough, he used a complex overlaying of nets or branches, inspired by historic textiles, such as Indian and Italian. The repeats are not as obvious, and the pattern is less predictable.

3 FINE LINES
Morris used a block-printing method for his wallpapers, and he sent this design to Barretts of East London, which hand-cut his pattern on pear-wood blocks. The design was chiseled into the block, while fine lines and detailing were created with metal strips pressed into the wood.

▲ William Morris and Co still sells Morris's Willow Bough design as wallpaper. It is also available as a textile print reproduced in shades of green, red, and blue. The company's papers and fabrics are all produced in British workshops.

TRELLIS WALLPAPER

Some of Morris's wallpaper patterns were drawn from plants in his own gardens. When Morris moved into the Red House in Bexleyheath, Kent, he could not find any wallpapers he liked, so he set about designing some. He designed Trellis in 1862—with the birds drawn by Philip Webb—inspired by the rose trellis in his own garden, and first sold it in 1864. Handprinted from traditional wooden blocks rather than the easier machine-printed method that was used for most other wallpapers, it was expensive to produce. Morris was inspired by nature, and his patterns recall English hedgerows and country gardens. In 1881 he gave a lecture, "Some Hints on Pattern Designing," in which he argued that the ideal pattern should have "unmistakable suggestions of gardens and fields." He was also inspired by the woodcut illustrations in 16th-century herbals—books describing plants and their uses in medicine and cookery.

DESIGNER AS INVENTOR

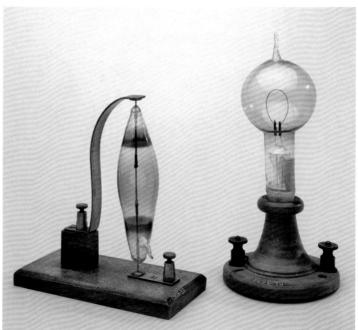

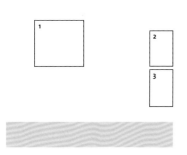

1 Joseph Swan's pioneering electric light bulb (left), made in 1878, and Thomas Edison's lamp (right), made in 1879, were developed independently.

2 Alexander Graham Bell making the first telephone call from New York to Chicago in 1892, sixteen years after he invented the telephone.

3 A poster advertising a film show in France in the 1890s, presented by the first filmmakers, the Lumière Brothers.

During the late 19th century, accelerating industrialization, scientific discovery, and technological developments fostered increasingly inventive design solutions, as manufacturers sought ways of becoming self-sufficient and more productive. The period became a golden age of the designer as inventor, with ingenuity and resourcefulness changing the ways in which ordinary people lived. Self-belief and the desire for improvement propelled the United States to the forefront of industrialization, resulting in the invention of consumer items from textiles to sewing machines (see p.40). The passing of the Patent Act of 1836 created the first US Patent Office and made it easier to protect inventions from infringements, which stimulated even more design research and development. In 1853 New York's Exhibition of the Industry of All Nations showcased the latest global industrial achievements and demonstrated the country's ingenuity, including a safety elevator designed by US mechanic and inventor Elisha Graves Otis (1811–61). Three years later, he installed the first passenger safety elevator in a New York shop.

After the US Civil War ended, a period known as the "Gilded Age" ensued. The nation rapidly expanded its economy into new areas, particularly industry and railways, creating a land of opportunity. The United States' east and west

KEY EVENTS

1865	1869	1869	1877	1878	1881
The US Civil War ends. The reconstruction period to transform society begins and lasts until 1877.	The US First Transcontinental Railroad is completed, and helps set the country on the path to economic abundance.	US inventor George Westinghouse (1846–1914) patents his air brake for railroads. By 1893, air brakes are compulsory on US trains.	Thomas Edison invents the phonograph for the mechanical recording and reproduction of sound.	Edison establishes the Edison Electric Light Company in New York to devise an incandescent light bulb and a public electrical lighting system.	Joseph Swan founds the Swan Electric Light Company in Benwell, Newcastle-upon-Tyne, England, to manufacture light bulbs commercially.

coasts were connected by the First Transcontinental Railroad, shortening the journey between New York and San Francisco from months to less than a week. In the search for cheaper ways to create greater numbers of products, the United States became a world leader in applied technology, and industrial mass production developed there more consistently than anywhere else. In 1874 E. Remington and Sons successfully mass produced the first commercial typewriter (see p.60).

The bright ideas emerged in every aspect of life. In 1876, Scottish-born inventor Alexander Graham Bell (1847–1922) gained the first US patent for the telephone (see image 2). When it was first proposed, the idea that a person's voice could travel through a wire was considered nonsensical. Two years later, the first telephone exchange was built in New Haven, Connecticut, and Bell's harmonic telegraph would change the world.

One of the most prolific US inventors was Thomas Edison (1847–1931), who held 1,093 US patents for inventions such as the phonograph and microphone, plus further patents in Europe. The impact of his inventions and his use of mass-production techniques helped spawn new industries. In 1879, he perfected the electric light bulb (see image 1) independently of English physicist Joseph Swan (1828–1914), who had also developed the light bulb the previous year. The invention revolutionized the world by stimulating a demand for the supply of domestic electricity.

In Europe there was a similar burst of inventiveness. In 1860 Belgian-born engineer Etienne Lenoir (1822–1900) patented the first practical internal combustion engine. Four years later, German-Austrian inventor Siegfried Marcus (1831–98) used a petrol-powered engine to mobilize a car. The combustion engine's main advantage over the steam engine was its weight-to-power ratio, which allowed engines to be used to drive motor vehicles and aircraft. The period from the end of the Franco-Prussian War in 1871 to the outbreak of World War I in 1914 was later labeled "*La Belle Epoque*" (Beautiful Era). Along with technological and scientific innovations, it was a period of optimism, peace, and economic prosperity. Design and invention flourished with the introduction of products as diverse as the Rover Safety Bicycle in 1885 (see p.62) and the vacuum flask in 1892 (see p.64). Influenced by Edison's kinetoscope, in 1895 French brothers Auguste (1862–1954) and Louis (1864–1948) Lumière created the cinematograph—the first moving-picture camera—and made their first film (see image 3). In 1901 Italian physicist Guglielmo Marconi (1874–1937) made the first transatlantic radio transmission, sending a signal across the Atlantic Ocean from Poldhu in Cornwall, England, to St John's, Newfoundland. Two years later, the first engine-powered aircraft was designed and flown by two US aviators, the Wright brothers Wilbur (1867–1912) and Orville (1871–1948). Such advances in communication and transport were to grow markets and give rise to new industries. **SH**

QWERTY Keyboard 1874

CHRISTOPHER LATHAM SHOLES 1819–90

👁 FOCAL POINTS

1 CYLINDER
Each of the letters on the typewriter was mounted on a type bar. The machine also had a cylinder with line spacing, carriage return, and an escapement mechanism. As users tapped the keys, the ink ribbon and type bars jumped up, pressing ink onto the paper held on the cylinder.

2 KEYS
The original QWERTY layout is slightly different to the modern version. It did not contain the numerals "1" and "0," because they could be created using other keys. The letter "M" is on the third row, to the right of the letter "L" rather than on the fourth row, and the letters "C" and "X" are reversed.

I n 1868 a patent was granted to US newspaper editor Christopher Latham Sholes, lawyer and inventor Carlos Glidden (1834–77), and printer Samuel W. Soulé (1830–75) for a "Type-Writer." With the aid of US arms and sewing machine manufacturer E. Remington and Sons, it eventually developed into the first device to feature a QWERTY keyboard that enabled users to type substantially faster than they could write by hand.

Sholes's original machine placed the keys in alphabetical order in two rows, but this arrangement meant that commonly used combinations of letters, such as "ST," were positioned close together. When the keys were hit in quick succession, the adjacent metal arms, or "type bars," in the type basket tended to jam. Glidden and Soulé lost interest in the project but together with newspaper associate and investor James Densmore (1820–89), Sholes developed the machine using infrequent letter pairs to solve the problem. In 1873 they sold the patent for the machine to Remington. Sholes continued to make adjustments to what became his QWERTY keyboard. Remington launched the Sholes and Glidden typewriter, later branded as the Remington No. 1, in 1874. As the typewriter gained in popularity, people became interested in the unusual arrangement of keys and started memorizing it, learning how to type efficiently using all their fingers. Although other typewriter manufacturers tried to enter the market using a different arrangement of keys, most people decided to stay with the QWERTY keyboard. **SH**

The Sholes and Glidden typewriter was manufactured by the Remington Company and launched in 1874.

▲ The Remington No. 1 printed only capital letters, but in 1878 the Remington No. 2, the first typewriter to include both upper- and lower-case letters, was launched. By pressing the shift key, the typewriter carriage shifted position to the front to type a capital letter, which was on the same type bar as the corresponding lower-case one. It boosted the popularity of the QWERTY layout. By 1888, Remington claimed that 40,000 machines had been sold.

XPMCHR FORMAT

Despite the popularity of the QWERTY keyboard, Sholes was not convinced that it was the best system. He continued to invent alternative keyboard layouts for greater efficiency, such as his XPMCHR format that he filed for patent in 1889, a year before he died. However, its chance of success proved short lived, as in 1893 the five largest typewriter manufacturers—Remington, Caligraph, Smith-Premier, Densmore, and Yost—merged to form the Union Typewriter Company and adopted the QWERTY keyboard configuration as standard.

Rover Safety Bicycle 1885

JOHN KEMP STARLEY 1855–1901

The Rover Safety Bicycle changed the face of transport by making cycling safe for all.

⚙ NAVIGATOR

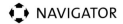

Until the early 1880s, the only commercially available bicycle was the high-wheel or ordinary, disparagingly known as the "penny-farthing" because of its large front wheel and a smaller rear wheel. They were fast but unstable, and really only suitable for use by tall, athletic young men with disposable incomes. In 1877 John Kemp Starley started a business in Coventry, England, with a local cycling enthusiast, William Sutton (b.1843). They began manufacturing tricycles, which were easier to ride and safer than penny-farthings. In February 1885, at the Stanley Cycle Show, Britain's main annual bicycle exhibition in London, Starley showed his Rover Safety Bicycle – a rear-wheel drive, chain-driven cycle, with two similar-sized wheels, it was more accessible and stable than the penny-farthing. Starley said he wanted to "place the rider at the proper distance from the ground . . . to place the seat in the right position in relation to the pedals . . . to place the handles in such a position in relation to the seat that the rider could exert the greatest force upon the pedals with the least amount of fatigue."

Heavier and more expensive than penny-farthings, the bicycle was initially sneered at by penny-farthing riders, but in September 1885 several Rover Safety Bicycles beat the world record on a 100-mile (161-km) promotional race on the Great North Road, which immediately changed perceptions. With the center of gravity low and between the wheels rather than high and over the front hub as with the penny-farthing, the safety bicycle greatly diminished the problem of dangerous falls over the handlebars. Braking was also more effective, and these factors made the bicycle appealing, especially among women. Starley's bicycle was initially equipped with solid tires, but when pneumatic tires were invented by John Boyd Dunlop (1840–1921) and eventually fitted to the bike in 1888, its ride became much smoother and more comfortable. **SH**

1 WHEEL

At first, the two small solid wheels made the ride bumpy and hard, but once Dunlop's inflatable pneumatic tires replaced them, this drawback was eliminated. The Rover Safety Bicycle became popular and was exported worldwide, helping the bicycle become a universal form of transport.

3 SEAT

The Rover Safety Bicycle had an adjustable seat. This meant that it could be enjoyed by all without compromising speed or safety. Because the bicycle was accessible to less athletic men, women, and children, cycling became a common form of transport rather than a specialist hobby.

2 HANDLEBARS

The innovative elements of the Rover Safety Bicycle included a triangular-shaped frame, pedals below the saddle that powered the back wheel through a chain and gears, and handlebars to the front wheel that could be used for steering. These elements are all still part of contemporary bicycles.

4 CHAIN DRIVE

The chain drive joined a large front sprocket to a small rear sprocket that multiplied the revolutions of the pedals, allowing for smaller wheels, and replaced the need for the oversized front wheel that had to be directly pedaled on the penny-farthing.

▲ One of Starley's employees called the safety bicycle the "Rover" because it enabled people to rove freely. In 1896 Starley renamed his firm the Rover Cycle Co. After his death, the company began building motorcycles and then cars.

PENNY-FARTHING

Starley learned about cycle design from his uncle, James (1831–81). Among James's many inventions was the penny-farthing, which he designed in 1871 in response to the desire for a pedal-powered machine that covered the greatest distance in the fastest possible time. Before the advent of gears, the only way to gain speed was to increase the size of the front wheel, which added to the risk of the rider.

Vacuum Flask 1892

JAMES DEWAR 1842–1923

👁 FOCAL POINTS

1 NARROW NECK
In 1872 Dewar created a vacuum jacketed goblet. Twenty years later, he made his experimental flask based on similar principles. He realized that heat was being communicated to the interior of the inner vessel at the neck, so he created a narrow neck to minimize heat loss.

2 WALLS
Dewar's experimental flask contains a partial vacuum between the walls to reduce conduction. Because a perfect vacuum contains no matter, it does not conduct heat. Dewar's flask is closed to maintain the vacuum and stop convection (the transfer of heat by air circulation).

The vacuum flask, also known as a Dewar flask, Dewar bottle, or Thermos, keeps its (usually liquid) contents hot or cold for several hours, irrespective of surrounding temperatures. Invented in 1892 by British chemist and physicist James Dewar, especially to store liquefied gases at extremely low temperatures for his scientific experiments, the vacuum flask consists of two glass vessels, one within the other, joined at the neck, with the air between them pumped out to create a near-vacuum. The vacuum greatly reduces the transfer of heat, providing insulation and preventing a temperature change. Dewar made the walls of his flask in glass, because it is a poor conductor of heat, and he silvered them with mercury to reduce further transfer of heat by radiation. Dewar's aim was to produce a vessel to aid his experiments in keeping liquids cold, so he did not patent his silvered vacuum flask.

However, in 1904 a German glass technician, Reinhold Burger (1866–1954), realized that Dewar's flask could also be used to keep drinks hot and saw it had commercial potential. He recreated it and patented his design, selling flasks under the Thermos name for domestic use. Dewar was furious and tried to sue Burger, but was unsuccessful. Early Thermos flasks were made of handblown glass, which made them expensive and only the wealthy could afford them. They proved essential on expeditions, including Ernest Shackleton's (1874–1922) to the South Pole in 1907. As production became mechanized, the price of the flasks dropped. **SH**

A reproduction of one of James Dewar's experimental flasks that has been cross-sectioned to reveal the inside.

▲ Initially Dewar built insulated boxes to keep liquids cold, but they were inadequate. Cryogenic experiments involving cooling gases to the point where they liquefy were extremely expensive, so it was imperative to him to keep them in that state for as long as possible for his research, which led him to invent his flask.

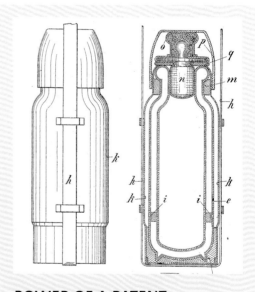

POWER OF A PATENT

Burger stabilized the cavity in Dewar's flask by putting spacers between the two flasks, and patented the design. In partnership with another German glass blower, he held a contest to rename the vacuum flask. The winning entry was "thermos," derived from the Greek word for "heat." They formed the Thermos company in Germany, but sold the trademark rights to three independent companies: the American Thermos Bottle Company, Thermos Limited in England, and the Canadian Thermos Bottle Company Limited.

Gillette Safety Razor 1901

KING CAMP GILLETTE 1855–1932

A Gillette safety razor from 1931. By 1904, Gillette had produced more than 90,000 safety razors and more than twelve million blades.

M an has used many tools for shaving over the centuries—clamshells, shark's teeth, or flint knives in prehistoric times. But shaving has always been dangerous if badly handled. While straight razors need to be kept sharp to shave closely, dull razors are more likely to cut skin.

The earliest safety razor was designed by French barber Jean-Jacques Perret (1730–84) in 1769. It was rather primitive and it was the prolific British inventor William S. Henson (1812–88) who patented the first modern safety razor in 1847. This had the cutting edge at a right angle to the handle, "resembles somewhat the form of a common hoe," with a comb tooth guard to prevent cutting.

The Kampfe Brothers of Brooklyn—German-born inventors Frederick (c. 1851–1915) and Otto (1855–1932)—took this further in 1880, patenting the Star classic safety razor, which held the blade in place with no danger of cutting the skin. However, their blade was still a single piece of forged metal, which required regular sharpening. Then US businessman King Camp Gillette saw a gap in the market, and in 1901 applied to patent a disposable double-edged razor stamped from sheet steel. He soon followed the current trend of charging very little for the razor itself, and a great deal for the replacement blade. It was this razor that was supplied to US soldiers when the United States entered World War I in 1917. With more than 3.5 million razors and thirty-two million blades used by military hands during the conflict, it became the model for every modern razor. **DG**

 **NAVIGATOR**

1 HANDLE

By clamping a smaller version of a straight-edged razor onto a handle, the blade became easier to control. This resulted in fewer nicks and cuts to the skin of the user. A toothed comb guard, or protector, protects the skin from the blade, an innovation pioneered by Henson.

2 BLADE

Keeping a razor blade sharp was fiddly and many outsourced it to barbers to sharpen. Stropping—using a piece of leather to realign the metal's edge—kept the metal sharp for longer, but it needed to be honed once a month. Gillette's blade was replaceable when it became dull.

3 CAP

The razor has a cap with a threaded stem that engages the inner handle. Studs align with holes in the flexible blade. Rotating the handle clamps together the guard, blade, and cap. Twisting the handle exposes the blade edge as the cap squeezes the blade against the guard.

▲ Gillette recognized the value of disposable products, especially ones as difficult to sharpen and maintain as razor blades. Based on the Kampfe Brothers' safety-razor design, his razor featured a stamped steel blade. Gillette began production in 1903.

1855–1900

King Camp Gillette was born in Fond du Lac, Wisconsin, and raised in Chicago, Illinois. In the 1890s he worked as a salesman for the Crown Cork and Seal Company, where he realized the value of a business based on throwaway items when he saw bottle caps, with the cork seal he sold, discarded after the bottle was opened.

1901–16

Gillette founded the American Safety Razor Company, later Gillette Safety Razor Company, to sell his safety razor. He used clever advertising and marketing methods to establish the brand.

1917–32

When the United States entered World War I, Gillette supplied every US soldier with a field razor set. Corporate infighting meant he lost control of the company in the 1920s.

SAVVY MARKETING TECHNIQUE

Gillette succeeded not just because of his razor's technology, but also because he employed packaging, advertising, and publicity techniques superbly. He marketed the numerous perceived benefits of his Safety Razor in advertisements. In 1905 he even used humor in an advert depicting a baby with a face covered in shaving cream (above). Gillette's publicity explained that it was possible for men who used the Safety Razor to shave themselves in the morning in three to five minutes for a tiny cost.

BIRTH OF BRANDS

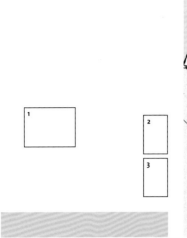

Troupe de
Mᴸᴸᴱ ÉGLANTINE
Eglantine   Cléopatre
Jane Avril   Gazelle

1 Henri de Toulouse-Lautrec created this poster to advertise the "Troupe de Mlle Eglantine" when they performed at the Palace Theatre in London in 1896.

2 Thomas J. Barratt used the work of Royal Academicians in publicity campaigns for Pears Soap, including the *Bubbles* (1886) poster, because it enhanced the brand.

3 The simple color scheme for the Beggarstaffs' poster for Kassama corn flour (c. 1894) made it less expensive to print than if it was polychrome.

The mass manufacturing of the Industrial Revolution led to an increased need for marketing and branding. Advances in printing technology, including bigger and faster steam-powered presses, lithography, the hot-metal printing process, and other color-reproduction techniques made volume printing cost effective and assisted the advertising and marketing of new products. The lithographic rotary printing press sped up the design process from slower flatbed printing, while new methods of papermaking and developments in photography also occurred.

To stimulate customer demand and make a profit, manufacturers spent a great deal on advertising. Products were bestowed with unique identities, individualizing them and assuring potential customers of their quality and price competitiveness. Aiming at the rich and newly burgeoning middle classes, advertisers created press advertisements, leaflets and bills, trade cards, and posters. Slogans and trademarks were printed on umbrellas, banners, flyers, placards, and beer mats. Advertising agencies opened and became specialists in communication, making sure that products and services were seen by and appealed to the relevant people.

Before the 1870s, many goods were sold by weight out of barrels and open containers, while merchandise such as soap and cheese were cut from large slabs, and shoppers were not aware of manufacturers' names, but by the 1880s increasing numbers of manufacturers had begun packaging their goods and creating their own distinctive branding. Patent medicine manufacturers and

KEY EVENTS

1786	1842	1843	1878	1880	1887
The first advertising agency, William Taylor, opens in London. It acts as an advertising sales representative for printers.	Realtor and businessman Volney B. Palmer (1799–1864) sets up the first US advertising agency in Philadelphia.	US inventor Richard March Hoe (1812–86) designs the first lithographic rotary printing press. It speeds up the printing process considerably.	Pioneering English photographer Eadweard Muybridge (1830–1904) photographs horses in motion.	In the United States, the first halftone photographic illustrations are printed in newspapers.	*The Atlanta Journal* runs the first newspaper advertisements featuring the red-and-white Coca-Cola logo (see p.70).

tobacco companies were the first to create proprietary names and decorative labels, closely followed by soap, detergent, and breakfast cereal producers. Early packaging consisted of tin cans, glass bottles, and cardboard boxes, while clothing, now available ready made, had individual labels. Cans had been available for some time and were used to preserve an expanding range of products such as tea, snuff, confectionery, and cookies. Many featured complex and detailed printed designs and were increasingly made in fancy shapes to be kept long after the product inside was used up. In 1879 the printer Robert Gair (1839–1927) invented the prefabricated folding cardboard box, which made previously expensive cardboard boxes affordable for the first time. Also printed with arresting images and strong branding, from the start, cardboard boxes became used extensively by biscuit and breakfast cereal manufacturers. Branding and advertising highlighted unique selling propositions, which were promoted by advertising agencies as something that other manufacturers of similar wares did not have or were not announcing. Through this, consumers began to associate certain brands with characteristics such as reliability, freshness, or value, and less tangible attributes such as glamor or aspiration.

As the need for brand loyalty became apparent, much early marketing offered short-term incentives to buyers: from 1887, British cigarette manufacturer W. D. and H. O. Wills offered collectable illustrated cards. Thomas J. Barratt (1842–1914), chairman of British soap manufacturer A. and F. Pears, pioneered brand marketing by adapting a Pre-Raphelite painting by John Everett Millais (1829–96) of his grandson, *A Child's World* (1886); by adding a bar of soap, Barratt turned it into the Bubbles poster (see image 2), advertising Pear's soap as an endearing product.

With the development of color lithography in the 1880s, Europe took the lead in the production of artistic posters and advertisements. Posters that had previously featured only type included colored illustrations, too. French painter Jules Chéret (1836–1932) pioneered art posters, creating more than 1,000 designs, and inspired French artist Henri de Toulouse-Lautrec (1864–1901; see image 1) and Czech artist Alphonse Mucha (1860–1939). Two British painters, James Pryde (1866–1941) and William Nicholson (1872–1949) who called themselves the "Beggarstaffs," produced pared-down illustrated posters (see image 3), while similarly, German designers Lucian Bernhard (1883–1972), Hans Rudi Erdt (1883–1918), and Ludwig Hohlwein (1874–1949) created understated flat designs with bold colors and simple lettering. During the 1890s, the halftone was perfected, a form of printing that enabled photographs to be converted into small dots and printed on ordinary paper, which had a huge effect on press and poster advertising and packaging. The combination of rising literary interest and falling printing costs expanded the market for and availability of books and newspapers, and the emergence of magazines, which all created new opportunities for advertisers. **SH**

PEARS' SOAP

Beautifies the complexion, keeps the hands white and imparts a constant bloom of freshness to the skin.

1888	1895	1896	1898	1899	1908
US inventor George Eastman (1854–1932) registers the trademark Kodak, and receives a patent for his camera, which uses roll film.	Jules Chéret launches the *Maîtres de l'Affiche* (*Masters of the Poster*) art publication, featuring the best US and European posters of the Belle Epoque.	The National Biscuit Company (later Nabisco) orders two million cardboard boxes from Robert Gair; it is the birth of consumer packaging.	The red-and-white Campbell's soup label first appears (see p.72).	Based on his clinical experiences, Austrian neurologist Sigmund Freud (1856–1939) publishes *The Interpretation of Dreams*.	Swiss chemist Jacques E. Brandenberger (1872–1952) invents cellophane, presaging the era of plastic packaging.

Coca-Cola Logo 1886

FRANK MASON ROBINSON 1845–1923

I n 1882 John Pemberton (1831–88), a pharmacist in Atlanta, created an alcoholic drink. Pemberton made it with extracts from the coca plant, the kola nut, and wine. He sold the drink as Pemberton's French Wine Coca, advertising it as beneficial "for fatigue of mind and body." When Atlanta outlawed the sale and consumption of alcoholic beverages four years later, Pemberton's partner and bookkeeper, Frank Mason Robinson, encouraged him to replace the wine in the drink with sugar syrup and to mix the ingredients with fizzy water. The drink was sold for five cents a glass at soda fountains.

Robinson invented the name Coca-Cola for Pemberton's new drink, as he thought "the two Cs would look well in advertising." He also designed its trademark to be instantly recognizable and valued by fellow Americans. Working closely with a local engraver, Frank Ridge, he experimented with versions of the Spencerian script, a flowing style of writing. The cursive logo was immediately adopted, and the first newspaper advertisements featuring it appeared in 1897. Further publicity schemes followed, accompanied by Robinson's slogans that marketed the drink for all, generating a strong brand awareness. During the 1890s, the Coca-Cola logo underwent some critical changes. Following the fashionable ideas of Art Nouveau (see p.92), from 1890 to 1891 swirls and curls were added. However, Robinson was quick to see that the makeover was a mistake and returned to the original design that has endured. **SH**

An advertisement for Coca-Cola from 1904.

👁 FOCAL POINTS

1 TAIL
The Coca-Cola Spencerian script trademark was registered with the US Patent office in 1893. The trademark was then added to the tail of the first letter "C" of the logo. In 1941 the "Trademark Registered" wording was moved out of the tail to below the logo, instead of inside it.

2 HANDWRITING
The logo uses the Spencerian script, which was a style of handwriting used widely in the United States from approximately 1850 to 1925. The style was taught in schools and used mainly for formal letters and business correspondence before the typewriter became widespread.

ORIGINS OF BRANDING

The ancient Egyptians and Chinese branded certain objects with symbols to establish who owned, or who made, certain products, and this system continued throughout history. Blacksmiths making swords in the Roman Empire are thought to be the first users of trademarks. During the medieval period, European trade guilds used marks to indicate creators of specific products, and soon makers of almost every saleable item marked their goods with individual symbols. The first trademark legislation was passed by the English Parliament in 1266, requiring all bakers to use a distinctive mark for the bread they sold. The first case of trademark infringement also occurred in England, between two cloth manufacturers in 1618. The first comprehensive trademark laws were established in France in 1857. Commercial logo designs developed in the 19th century, with advances in photography, printing methods, and typography. By the 1880s, logos were an important part of business, as manufacturers vied with each other to create awareness and loyalty in a crowded marketplace.

Campbell's Condensed Soup Label 1898

VARIOUS

The layout of the Campbell's soup can label is familiar in the 21st century and has changed little since its initial design.

In 1869, fruit merchant Joseph A. Campbell (1817–1900) teamed up with Abraham Anderson (1829–1915) of the Anderson Preserving Company to form the Joseph A. Campbell Preserve Company, canning tomatoes, vegetables, soups, jellies, condiments, soups, and minced meats. After Anderson left, Campbell took on new partners, renaming the firm the Joseph Campbell Preserve Company. In 1897 one of the partners, Arthur Dorrance, hired his nephew John T. Dorrance (1873–1930), who invented a process for condensing soup, eliminating much of the water without compromising on flavor. This reduced transport costs and made distribution easier. Within five years, more than fifteen million cans of Campbell's condensed soups were selling annually.

Although the original label for Campbell's condensed soup is believed to have been created collaboratively between employees in the company, the first printer to produce the labels, Sinnickson Chew and Sons, is also credited with assisting in the design. The first labels were designed in 1897 in orange and blue. From 1898 the orange and blue were replaced by red and white, after employee Herberton L. Williams, who subsequently became the company's treasurer and general manager, saw a University of Pennsylvania versus Cornell University football game. The cursive script of the logo is generally believed to based on the founder's own signature, intended to create an intimate impression that would appeal to housewives. In 1900 the soup won a Gold Medallion for excellence at the Exposition Universelle in Paris, and from then, an illustration modeled on the medal became an additional feature on the labels. The engraver employed to design this was commissioned to replicate the actual medal as closely as possible. It is the only element of the label that represents something of the real world. **SH**

 NAVIGATOR

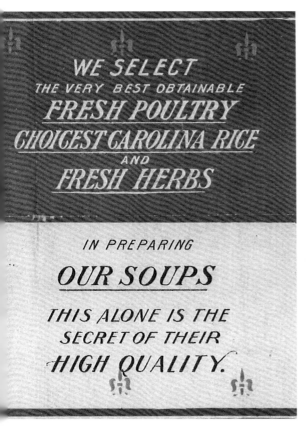

1 RED AND WHITE
Inspired by the red-and-white uniforms of a football team, Williams suggested the soup labels should be changed for similar impact. In keeping with the company attitude of teamwork and collusion, the red-and-white color scheme was adopted.

2 HANDWRITING
The cursive script creates a less formal impression than a more rigid typeface. The product was to be bought predominantly by US housewives, so it needed to impart a homely impression. The script also suggested a handwritten recipe.

3 MEDALLION
The central medallion on the Campbell's label appeared in 1898, two years before the company won a gold medal at the Exposition Universelle. After that it was replaced by the emblem of the French gold seal, as an enduring symbol of excellence.

◀ The Bass Brewery was founded in 1777 by William Bass (1717–87) in Burton-upon-Trent, England. The company's distinctive red triangle became the UK's first registered trademark in 1876. The triangle became well known, symbolizing energy, prosperity, vitality, and enthusiasm. By 1877 the brewery was the largest in the world. In 1882 French artist Edouard Manet (1832–83) featured it prominently in his painting *A Bar at the Folies Bergère*.

ARTS AND CRAFTS

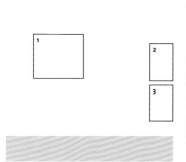

D eveloping in England in the mid 19th century, the Arts and Crafts movement was a protest against the poorly designed and inferior goods being produced in factories, and the inequalities caused by industrialization. Hugely influenced by Augustus Pugin (1812–52), John Ruskin (1819–1900), and William Morris (1834–96; see p.52), it lasted from approximately 1860 to 1910, and evolved into an international movement, although there is no single, recognizable style attached to it. The artists, architects, designers, artisans. and writers of the Arts and Crafts movement believed that industrialization was destroying the environment, suppressing traditional skills and crafts, and eradicating quality in manufactured goods. They were convinced that the decline of artistic standards provoked by industrialization was linked to a social and moral deterioration.

Exponents of the Arts and Crafts movement were against factory environments, and sought to restore self-respect among workers and encourage collaboration throughout the design process. Following Morris's philosophies, they valued human endeavor, and aimed to eliminate artifice, excessive ornamentation, and shoddy workmanship. In 1882 the architect and designer Arthur Heygate Mackmurdo (1851–1942) set up the Century Guild of Artists, with clergyman, designer and poet Selwyn Image (1849–1930),

KEY EVENTS

1884	1884	1887	1888	1893	1893
John Ruskin and William Morris found the Art Workers' Guild, which aims to raise the status of the decorative arts and the individual craftsman.	The Century Guild of Artists begins publishing a quarterly journal, *Hobby Horse*, to promote its aims and ideals.	The Arts and Crafts Exhibition Society is formed in London to promote the exhibition of decorative arts alongside fine arts.	Charles Robert Ashbee sets up the Guild and School of Handicraft cooperative in London to encourage craftsmen's creative potential.	The first issue of *The Studio* illustrated arts magazine is published in London. It disseminates Arts and Crafts ideas internationally.	English designer Ernest Gimson (1864–1919; see p.80) moves out of London to practice architecture and crafts within a traditional rural community.

championing the idea that there is no difference between the fine and decorative arts. The Art Workers' Guild was established in 1884 when two informal groups united: The Fifteen, composed of designers, including artist and illustrator Walter Crane (1845–1915; see image 2), and the St George's Art Society, which was made up of six architects. As well as Arts and Crafts principles, the Art Workers' Guild reflected an additional desire to create social contact between members of different artistic professions. In founding the Guild and School of Handicraft in 1888, designer Charles Robert Ashbee (1863–1942) aimed to destroy the commercial system, and restore workers' dignity and satisfaction in labor. Ashbee's own designs for domestic silverware (see image 1) while at the guild would prove influential on contemporary silverware design in Europe and the United States, as well as in Britain.

By the end of the 19th century, the ideals of the Arts and Crafts movement were inspiring many in North America. The US Arts and Crafts movement, or the Craftsman style, shared the British movement's reform philosophy, focusing on originality, simplicity of form, use of local, natural materials, and handcrafting, but unlike British Arts and Crafts socialist leanings, it aimed to serve a rapidly expanding middle class. These ideals were disseminated throughout the United States through lecture tours given by British Arts and Crafts designers and by publications. Alongside Morris, Charles Francis Annesley Voysey (1857–1941) and Ashbee were also influential. Several Arts and Crafts societies formed, including the Society of Arts and Crafts in Boston, Massachusetts, and the Arts and Crafts Society in Chicago.

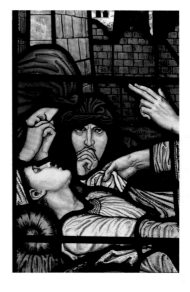

While their values were consistent, creative interpretations diversified. Silversmith Arthur J. Stone (1847–1938) was born in Britain, and trained in Sheffield and Edinburgh. He emigrated to the United States where he became a member of the Boston Society of Arts and Crafts. He set up his own workshop and trained apprentices to produce hand-wrought silver, producing understated domestic silverware. Charles Rohlfs (1853–1936) in Buffalo, New York, created individual pieces of furniture inspired by Moorish, Chinese, and Scandinavian design (see image 3). Gustav Stickley (1858–1942), furniture designer, founder of furniture maker United Crafts, and chief proponent of the Craftsman style, emulated Morris's aims of attempting to improve taste through honest construction, simple lines, and quality materials in pieces like his Morris chair (1901; see p.76).

Despite its high ideals, the Arts and Crafts movement was essentially flawed. Its opposition to modern methods of production meant that it failed in its socialist ideal of producing affordable, quality handcrafted design for the masses, because the production costs of such designs were so high that only the wealthy could afford them. The greatest legacies of the movement were its recognition of the relationship between design and quality of life, and its elevation of the status of design. **SH**

1895	1896	1897	1899	1901	1902
US designer Gustav Stickley visits Europe for the first time and is inspired by William Morris and the Arts and Crafts movement.	The London Central School of Arts and Crafts is founded. It introduces craft workshops to promote Arts and Crafts principles.	Boston becomes the first US city to establish a Society of Arts and Crafts.	English designer Ambrose Heal (1872–1959; see p.78) shows his furniture at the sixth exhibition of the Arts and Crafts Exhibition Society.	Stickley dedicates the first issue of *The Craftsman* magazine to Morris. It promotes Arts and Crafts principles for the next fifteen years.	Members of the Guild of Handicraft move to the Cotswolds. The Cotswold School becomes a center for the British Arts and Crafts movement.

Morris Chair 1901

GUSTAV STICKLEY 1858–1942

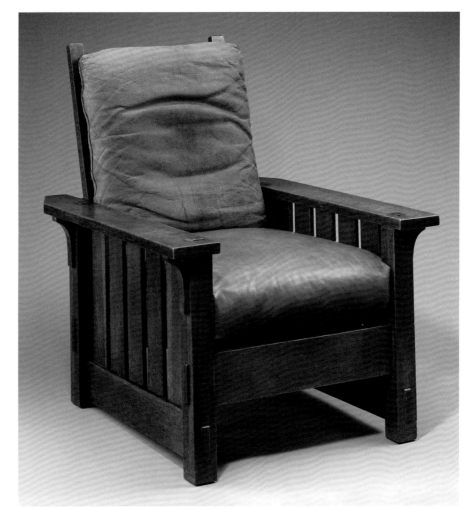

Oak, leather
39 x 31½ x 38¾ in.
99 x 80 x 98.5 cm

❖ NAVIGATOR

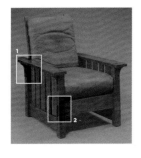

Best known for his wooden furniture featuring simple lines and limited decoration, Gustav Stickley was the greatest influence on the US Craftsman style, an extension of the British Arts and Crafts movement. He worked in his uncle's chair company and, after managing it, opened a furniture manufacturing company with two of his brothers in Susquehanna, Pennsylvania, in 1883. Within five years, Gustav started his own business, in Syracuse, New York. On visits to Europe in the 1890s, he was profoundly inspired by the father of the Arts and Crafts movement, William Morris, and convinced that his company should produce household furniture in the Arts and Crafts style.

Stickley's designs were both nostalgic through being handmade, and modern, in their lack of adornment. This chair was based on designs he had seen in Europe, produced by Morris's English Arts and Crafts design company, although designed by Philip Webb (1831–1915). Simple, solidly built, and functional, Stickley's oak chair with generous brown leather cushions became widely copied. Stickley never called it the Morris chair, but preferred adjustable-back or reclining chair. It was also sometimes described as the Craftsman chair or the Mission Morris chair, although Stickley disliked the terms, but the name Morris chair stuck. **SH**

FOCAL POINTS

1 SIDE SPLATS
The chair is sturdy and of straightforward construction, with vertical side splats, mortise and tenon joints, flat arms at the front supported by short corbels, a drop-in spring seat, and a hinged, reclining back. These features express US Craftsman style rather than English Arts and Crafts.

2 DEEP PATINA
The intense, dark patina of Stickley's chair was achieved by fuming the wood with ammonia. This finishing process consisted of exposing the wood to fumes from a strong aqueous solution of ammonium hydroxide, which reacts with the tannins in the wood, turning it darker.

▲ An image from a page in Stickley's *The Craftsman* magazine in 1909, showing a Morris chair. The magazine influenced the development of Craftsman domestic architecture and interiors.

DESIGNER PROFILE

1858–82
Gustav Stickley was born in Wisconsin. He trained as a stonemason, but in c. 1875, moved with his mother and siblings to Brant, Pennsylvania, where he worked in his uncle's chair factory.

1883–87
Stickley established the Stickley Brothers Company with two of his brothers. In 1888 Stickley partnered with furniture salesman Elgin A. Simonds.

1895–1900
In 1895 and 1896, Stickley visited Europe and was inspired by the Arts and Crafts movement. In 1898 he bought Simonds's share of the company and started to manufactured furniture in the Craftsman style.

1901–14
Stickley launched *The Craftsman*. In 1903 he set up the Craftsman Home Builders Club to spread his ideas on architecture. In 1907 he acquired property in Morris Plains, New Jersey, to create a boarding school, Craftsman Farms.

1915–42
Public taste changed with the advent of modernism, halting the popularity of Stickley's furniture. He filed for bankruptcy and closed *The Craftsman*.

LEOPOLD AND JOHN GEORGE STICKLEY

In 1904 two of Gustav Stickley's brothers, Leopold (1869–1957) and John George (1871–1921), set up their breakaway furniture business, Onondaga Shops. in New York. Two years later, the brothers renamed the company Handcraft. More financially successful than Gustav, they produced cheaper machine-made versions of Gustav's handcrafted designs, taking advantage of his carefree attitude to issues of copyright. They also developed a line reflecting the Prairie esthetic of US architect and designer Frank Lloyd Wright (1867–1959) with pieces like their Prairie settles (1912–13). The brothers acquired Gustav's Craftsman Workshops in 1918, joining the two furniture lines. The company has survived into the 21st century.

Oak Letchworth Dresser 1904–05

AMBROSE HEAL 1872–1959

Oak, chestnut, pine, and brass
53¾ x 18 x 66½ in.
136.5 x 45.5 x 169 cm

⚙ **NAVIGATOR**

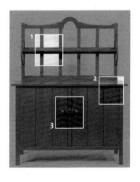

Established in 1810, Heal and Son of London was originally a supplier of beds and bedding, but opened a department for sitting-room furniture in the 1880s. From 1896 the great-grandson of the shop's founder, Ambrose Heal, began designing simple furniture in plain oak that contrasted dramatically with the shop's standard ornate, historical reproductions. Two years later, he published a catalog of his own designs, entitled *Plain Oak Furniture*. In following the Arts and Crafts tradition, Ambrose's furniture design gave the store a new direction. Additionally, his simple, well-made pieces were competitively priced, which made them accessible to a wide section of the public. This oak dresser with chestnut shelves, a pine back, and brass cup hooks and hinges was designed by Ambrose and made by Heal and Son. The dresser was part of a range of homely Country Cottage furniture that was shown at the Cheap Cottages Exhibition at Letchworth Garden City, England, in 1905. It then cost £6 15s. Although influenced by the ideas of John Ruskin and William Morris, Ambrose also embraced the use of machinery where appropriate, which kept costs down. The success of his furniture enabled Heal and Son to open an electrically powered furniture workshop attached to the store. **SH**

 FOCAL POINTS

1 HOOKS

Ambrose commissioned and sold designs that conformed with the Arts and Crafts ideal of simplicity and sobriety, and rejected applied ornament. The oak dresser is typical of his simplified cottage furniture. The dresser has little hardware other than its brass cup hooks and hinges.

2 JOINTS

Heal's original factory was equipped with just a circular saw and a planer, which meant everything was handmade. Timber was cut to rough size and planed square by machine before being passed to the cabinetmakers, who only used traditional methods – as can be seen in the fine joints.

3 DOORS

Ambrose's sober, robust, and well-proportioned furniture intentionally exposed some structural elements, emphasizing the natural qualities and colors of the wood. The two sturdy oak doors open to reveal a single chestnut storage shelf on either side.

⏱ DESIGNER PROFILE

1872–92

Born in London, the great-grandson of the founder of furniture store Heal and Son, Ambrose Heal was the eldest of five children. Educated at Marlborough College, he undertook a two-year apprenticeship to cabinetmakers James Plucknett in Warwick, followed by six months working for Graham and Biddle, furnishers of London.

1893–1924

Ambrose joined the family firm, working in the bedding department. In 1896 he began designing and making his furniture. After his father died in 1913, Ambrose became chairman of Heal's. In 1915 he co-founded the Design and Industries Association. In 1917 he set up the Mansard Gallery at the shop, which later showed work by Picasso (1881–1973).

1925–32

Ambrose exhibited at the Exposition Internationale des Arts Décoratifs et Industriels Modernes (International Exposition of Modern Industrial and Decorative Arts) in Paris, which heralded the Art Deco movement. He expanded Heal's range of products to include china, glass, and textiles. Artists designed Heal's posters and art critics wrote its catalogs.

1933–38

He was knighted for his services in improving design standards. A year later, Ambrose exhibited at the Contemporary Industrial Design exhibition in London. In 1935, he exhibited at the British Art in Industry exhibition, and in 1937, at the Paris International Exhibition.

1939–59

Ambrose was elected to the Faculty of Royal Designers for Industry. In 1953 he resigned as chairman of Heal's. In 1954 the Royal Society of Arts awarded him the Albert Gold Medal for services to design.

AFFORDABLE FURNITURE

In 1905 Heal and Son furnished two cottages in the Cheap Cottages Exhibition at Letchworth Garden City, England, which aimed to help solve the growing housing shortage. Builders and architects built examples of affordable cottages for agricultural workers for the show, which marked a critical juncture for Ambrose and his business. From then on, the concept of affordable furniture became closely associated with his company's image—and Ambrose came close to realizing Morris's dream of "good citizen's furniture." While Ambrose's early furniture was made of oak, during the 20th century he began using other English woods, including walnut, elm, cherry, and chestnut, and produced a range of cheaper, machine-made furnishings.

Oak Settee 1906

ERNEST GIMSON 1864–1919

Oak, rush seat, and woven-
wool upholstery
Height 34⅞ in./88.5 cm
Width 66 in./167.5 cm
Depth 23⅝ in./60 cm
Seat height 16½ in./42 cm

Ernest Gimson was an English furniture designer and architect who helped to establish what became known as the Cotswolds School of Arts and Crafts. As a young man, Gimson had met and become inspired by William Morris after hearing him talk on art and socialism. After training as architects and experimenting with the London cabinetmaking enterprise Kenton and Company, in 1893 he and the Barnsley brothers, Sidney (1865–1926) and Ernest (1863–1926), moved to the Cotswolds to make furniture as a community of craftsmen, learning from each other and following local traditions in a workshop environment as Morris had advocated. Using locally available woods, such as ash, deal, and oak, and creating their furniture and buildings using traditional crafts, they attracted more like-minded designers and became known as the Cotswolds School. Many of their pieces were based on rural forms, such as ladder-back chairs and oak dressers or wardrobes, while others drew on 18th-century techniques such as inlays or marquetry. Like Morris, Gimson sought first-hand experience of the materials and practical processes relating to his work, and mastered many disappearing craft techniques. For instance, in 1890 he learned the techniques of chair bodging—a traditional wood-turning craft—from influential chairmaker Philip Clissett (1817–1913).

From 1900 Gimson set up further workshops, and he continued exploring and learning traditional craft techniques, creating Arts and Crafts furniture that emphasized textures and surfaces with naturalistic patterns and motifs drawn from life. Completely avoiding imitations of past furniture styles and creating his own unembellished pieces, he demonstrated his commitment to the honesty that John Ruskin and Morris advocated. This settee, with its shaped, chamfered three-section lattice back, shaped arms, and upholstered seat on a rectangular box frame, is a typical example of his unadorned, truth-to-materials approach that closely adhered to Arts and Crafts objectives. **SH**

✦ NAVIGATOR

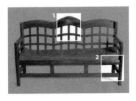

1 CHAIR BACK
Inspired by medieval and Tudor design, Gimson's work has an organic quality, as can be seen in this curving chair back, which adds a lightness to an otherwise plain and boxy design. This settee demonstrates Gimson's preoccupation with simplicity and quality of workmanship.

2 WOOD
Celebrating the beauty of solid wood, Gimson focused on precise details and proportions, using locally sourced woods where possible. His style was fundamental and pared down, and he remained concerned with honesty of structure and truth to materials throughout his career.

DESIGNER PROFILE

1864–85
Ernest Gimson was born in Leicester, England. After attending Leicester School of Art, he was articled to local Arts and Crafts architect, Isaac Barradale (1845–92).

1886–88
Inspired by meeting William Morris, Gimson moved to London. Architect John Dando Sedding (1838–91) employed Gimson on Morris's recommendation, where he met Ernest Barnsley.

1889–92
Gimson joined Morris's Society for the Protection of Ancient Buildings and in 1890 co-founded the furniture firm Kenton and Company with Sidney Barnsley and others.

1893–1910
Gimson moved to the Cotswolds in England with the Barnsley brothers. In 1900 he married and set up another furniture workshop. Striving to create a utopian craft village, he continued to design handmade furniture.

1911–19
Gimson designed Lupton Hall at Bedales School in England, intended to be the first of a quadrangle of buildings. World War I broke out and only a memorial library was built in 1921.

▲ One of the most prominent Arts and Crafts societies was the Guild and School of Handicraft, started by Charles Robert Ashbee in London. When the lease on its workshop ran out in 1902, members moved to the Cotswolds where Gimson already had his enterprise.

LADDER-BACK CHAIR REVIVAL

Ladder-back chairs like this ash version were first made during the medieval period, but became particularly fashionable among furniture makers between 1700 and 1900. Clissett taught Gimson how to make these chairs, including the complicated rush weaving of the seating. Gimson made the chairs from 1892, but gave up in 1904, after which his designs were made by his assistant, Edward Gardiner (1880–1958), at Gimson's workshop at Daneway in Gloucestershire, England.

THE JAPANESE INFLUENCE

1 An ebonized mahogany sideboard designed by Edward William Godwin in 1867.

2 A late 19th-century example of Japanese earthenware from the Satsuma region.

3 A Limoges porcelain plate, Setting Sun, designed in 1876 by Félix Bracquemond.

Japan had been a closed society for over 200 years when it responded to pressure from the United States and Britain to open up to the rest of the world in 1854. Once trade was established, the export of Japanese art, artefacts, ideas, and culture had a profound impact on the West. At the 1867 Exposition Universelle in Paris, Japanese had its own pavilion, which attracted acclaim. The following year, a revolution in Japan saw the restoration of the power of the Meiji emperor. Aiming to create an accord with the West, the new government initiated changes and the country subsequently participated in all international exhibitions.

As Europe and the United States became obsessed with Japan, artists and designers began to express clear Japanese influences. They drew inspiration from Japanese prints with their calligraphic lines, simplification of shapes and decorative patterns. Such elements featured in Impressionist paintings, as well as designs attributed to the Aesthetic Movement (see p.88) and Art Nouveau (see p.92). In France, the craze became called *japonisme* and *japonaiserie*; in Britain, it was known as the Anglo-Japanese style. Among those incorporating Japanese artistic principles into their work was architect and designer Edward

KEY EVENTS

1854	1862	1862	1872	1875	1876–77
The US Navy succeeds in forcing Japan to open its ports to traders from the West.	La Porte Chinoise, a shop specializing in Japanese goodsn opens in Paris on the Rue de Rivoli.	Japanese objects are displayed in large numbers at the International Exhibition in London.	French critic Philippe Burty (1830–90) coins the term *japonisme* to describe the craze for Japanese art in Europe.	Arthur Lasenby Liberty (1843–1917) opens his store Liberty and Company. It specializes in selling goods imported from Asia.	On his trip to Japan, Christopher Dresser amasses selected objects for import by Tiffany of New York City and Londos of London.

William Godwin (1833–86), who created a range of furniture in the Anglo-Japanese style that included a sideboard designed in 1867 (see image 1). Its simple geometric form, use of ebonized wood, and Japanese embossed leather paper epitomize Japanese influence on decorative arts at the time.

The minimal lines, asymmetrical compositions, elongated formats, organic motifs, and blocks of flat color in many Japanese *ukiyo-e* (pictures of the floating world) prints, ceramics, textiles, bronzes, cloisonné enamels, furniture, fans, lacquers, and porcelains (see image 2) became fashionable and emerged in almost every aspect of Western design. *Ukiyo-e* was a style of woodblock printing and painting depicting everyday scenes, kabuki actors, sumo wrestlers, landscapes, and beautiful women. One of the leaders of the use of Japanese imagery was French printer and industrial designer Félix Bracquemond (1833–1914), who perpetuated Japanese style with his designs for furniture, jewelry, bookbindings, tapestries, ceramics, and enamels. He is often credited with discovering the work of one of the best-known *ukiyo-e* artists, Katsushika Hokusai (1760–1849), whose prints inspired many artists and designers. Bracquemond's Service Parisien dinner set (1876; see image 3) draws inspiration from the Japanese artist's series *Hokusai Manga* (*Hokusai Sketches*, 1814–75).

British designer and writer Christopher Dresser (1834–1904) also played a prominent role in disseminating Japanese art in the West. The first European designer to go to Japan as a guest of the Japanese nation in 1876, he wrote and lectured about his experiences there on his return to England. As a dealer, he also imported Japanese art and objects, and endorsed the styles in his own designs from silver teapots (see p.84) to pottery and furniture.

Siegfried "Samuel: Bing (1838–1905), a German art dealer working in Paris, also contributed to the spread of *japonisme*. From 1888 to 1891, he edited a monthly journal, *Le Japon Artistique*, which generated more enthusiasm about Oriental art and design. Then in 1895, he opened La Maison de l'Art Nouveau, a gallery where he displayed imported Japanese prints, contemporary fine art, and various designs in styles inspired by Japanese ideas. He arranged every room in the gallery as a living area, complete with furnishings, textiles, and ornaments, and became a pivotal figure in the development of Art Nouveau.

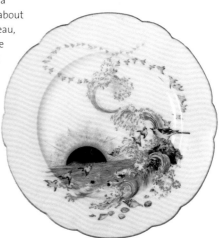

The reach of *japonisme* was seen in the United States in the work of designers such as brothers Charles (1868–1957) and Henry Greene (1870–1954), who incorporated Japanese joinery techniques into pieces like their sideboard for the David B. Gamble House in Pasadena, California (see p.86). The influences worked both ways. After the Meiji Restoration, Japanese trade flourished and art dealer Tadamasa Hayashi (1853–1906) and critic Iijima Hanjuro (1841–1901) were just two people who moved to Paris from Japan and established successful careers there. **SH**

1878	1878	c. 1880	1882	1882	1893
Tadamasa Hayashi arrives in Paris to work as an interpreter at the Exposition Universelle.	Dresser establishes the company Dresser and Holme to import Japanese art.	Liberty fosters the craze for Japan. He commissions works from British designers, particularly those influenced by Japanese art.	Hayashi opens a shop selling *japonaiserie*, which attracts a large clientele from both artistic and business circles.	Dresser publishes *Japan: Its Architecture, Art and Art Manufactures*, which became influential in both the UK and the United States.	Charles and Henry Greene are inspired after a visit to the Japanese section at the World's Columbian Exposition in Chicago.

Silver Teapot 1879

CHRISTOPHER DRESSER 1834–1904

Electroplated nickel silver with
ebony handle
Height 5⅛ in./13 cm
Width handle to spout
9 in./23 cm

NAVIGATOR

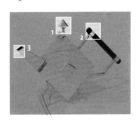

Christopher Dresser was one of the most talented British designers of the 19th century. Often considered to be the first industrial designer, he understood the properties of many materials and production processes, which enabled him to design for production in ways few of his contemporaries could. During his career, he worked for a number of manufacturers and created designs in silver plate, cast iron, ceramics, and glass, as well as furniture, textiles, carpets, and wallpapers. This teapot epitomizes his approach, amalgamating the influence of Japanese design with his ideas.

Dresser began creating a number of silver-plated tea sets for James Dixon and Sons of Sheffield in 1879. Most contemporary tableware was rounded and ornately decorated. In contrast, this is pure and unadorned. The striking, diamond-shaped body is pierced by a smaller diamond-shaped aperture in the centre. The straight legs, handle, and spout are attached to the body at ninety- and forty-five-degree angles. The lid is an integral part of the stringently geometric body, with a dramatically angled finial, and the ebony handle is both a design feature and a practical consideration, because wood remains relatively cool when the teapot is filled with boiling water. Partly derived from his enthusiasm for natural forms, and partly from his admiration of Japanese design, this innovative design meets Dresser's criteria of maximum effect with minimum means. Although he considered keeping production costs down, the teapot was not mass produced and remained an expensive item that only the wealthy could afford. **SH**

1 FINIAL
The oversized pyramid-shaped finial, with its angles and curves that contrast with most rounded finials of the day, is practical because it makes the lid easy to lift. Esthetically, the straight lines and diagonal contours echo the angled contours of the lid and the body of the object.

2 HANDLE
Aligned with the body of the teapot, the ebony handle is held in place by two silver-plated tubes and brackets. They had a practical purpose because they were used in other designs, and indicate Dresser's awareness of industrial requirements and how to reduce production costs.

3 SPOUT
Straight and solid looking, the spout offsets the delicate, angled handle on the opposite side of the teapot. The plain, rectangular pouring hole at the top of the spout does not have a distinct lip, yet is designed not to dribble. The spout base matches the angle and width of the aperture in the center.

▲ After Dresser returned from Japan, he started to design silver and electroplate for Hukin and Heath of Birmingham, including this silver-and-glass decanter with ebonized wood handle (1881).

TUREEN AND LADLE

Made in c. 1880, this tureen and ladle show the influence of the objects Dresser admired during his four-month trip to Japan from December 1876 to 1877. It demonstrates his blending of Japanese, ancient Egyptian, and Asian styles, and fits his ideas regarding truthful expression: there is no attempt to conceal any joints or other structural elements. Adhering to his belief in the importance of form over ornament, the gently curving soup tureen and ladle reveal his admiration for Japanese metalwork and the reduced shapes of Eastern design. He produced versions in sterling silver and electroplate, with ebony or ivory handles. The tureen's angular, oblique feet emphasize its clean contours and assist its practicality—when full of hot soup, the bowl is raised above any surface upon which it has been placed.

Sideboard c.1908

CHARLES GREENE 1868–1957   HENRY GREENE 1870–1954

👁 FOCAL POINTS

1 EBONY PEGS
In addition to being decorative, the Greene brothers' signature ebony pegs were sometimes used to reinforce joints or to hide screws. These shallow pegs of exotic wood were arranged in precise, sparse patterns, as here, to contrast directly with the lighter wood of the cupboard itself.

2 JOINERY
Traditional Japanese joinery techniques were used to fasten together pieces of wood. Where possible, the Greene brothers used the Japanese method of cutting the wood precisely and then slowly hammering a small piece of wood—a plug—between the pieces, forcing an exact fit.

🕐 DESIGNER PROFILE

1868–92
Charles and Henry Greene were born in Cincinnati, Ohio, fifteen months apart. In 1884 Charles entered Calvin Woodward's Manual Training School, and Henry joined him the following year. In 1888 they both studied architecture and in 1891, they began apprenticeships in Boston.

1893–1901
The brothers visited the Columbian Exposition (1893) in Chicago. In 1894 they opened their architectural practice, Greene and Greene, in Pasadena, California.

1902–21
Magazines such as *The Craftsman* featured articles on Greene and Greene. From 1903 they offered integrated design services, including bespoke furniture and fittings. From 1905 they began collaborating with Peter and John Hall, who produced many of their furniture designs. Their distinctive bungalows became archetypes of the Craftsman style.

1922–57
Greene and Greene dissolved. In 1952 the brothers were recognized by the American Institute of Architects for fostering new ways of considering buildings and furnishings.

This stained-glass sideboard by Greene and Greene is from the dining room of the David B. Gamble House in Pasadena, California.

The design esthetic of brothers Charles Sumner Greene and Henry Mather Greene developed mainly as a fusion of the English Arts and Crafts and Japanese styles. In particular, they were inspired by the designs in the Japanese section of the World's Columbian Exposition in Chicago and later by the work of artist Will H. Bradley (1868–1962) and architect Frank Lloyd Wright (1867–1959), which featured in the *Ladies Home Journal*, as well as by Arts and Crafts ideals promoted in *The Craftsman* magazine. After meeting master craftsmen Peter (1867–1939) and John Hall (1864–1940), the Greene brothers embarked on what was to become a very successful collaboration. Using their expert skills and an almost obsessive attention to detail, the Halls produced many of the Greene brothers' furniture designs. The use of ebony pegs to provide simple decoration and a contrast of color, and to disguise joinery, became a hallmark. In this sideboard, the pegs punctuate the rounded corners, while the slightly elongated handles reinforce horizontal aspects of the design. The curved edge of the door balances against the angled solidity of the overall structure, combining the strong appearance with a smooth patina.

Although they were inspired by many different sources, the Greene brothers explored unique ideas. They ensured that their mortise and tenon joints, for example, became part of the visual design, supplanting the need for traditional ornamentation. Always employing quality materials and complex manufacturing methods, they favored the joinery techniques seen in Japanese design. However, the restrained style of US furniture maker Gustav Stickley (1858–1942) was another influence, and the refined rendering of this sideboard is an example of the brothers' distinctive integration of all these notions, which strongly affected the evolving US Craftsman style. **SH**

GREENE AND GREENE CHAIR

Chairs are among the most difficult items of furniture to make. Yet the Greene brothers designed and produced many different varieties, even for one room. The workshop of Peter and John Hall was forever challenged by their designs; sometimes legs were dramatically trapezoid or parallelogram, frequently back crest rails had complex carved shapes and in contrast with the usual plain Arts and Crafts-style arm rests, Greene and Greene chairs were often sinuous and curving. They also included variously sized back splats: a common design was a wide central back splat flanked by narrower splats on either side, exemplified by the living room armchair for the Robert R. Blacker House in Pasadena, California (1907; right). The rear legs often featured ebony splines to complement the decorative ebony pegs. This ebony detailing, as well as restrained inlays and elegantly pierced splats, was commonly the only form of decoration. The Greene brothers skilfully managed to combine multiple design elements in all their chairs, yet retained a sense of simplicity, quality, and restraint.

AESTHETICISM AND DECADENCE

1 James McNeill Whistler's Peacock Room (1876–77) was once the dining room in a grand house in London.

2 This furnishing fabric (1887) was sold through Liberty's shop in London. The tail feathers of peacocks were popular motifs for Aesthete designers.

3 Frederic, Lord Leighton, created the Arab Hall Extension (1877–81) for Leighton House, his home in London.

Aestheticism was a British development of design reform that emerged in the late 19th century as a reaction to the Industrial Revolution. Deriving from the Gothic Revival, the Arts and Crafts movement (see p.74), and the Pre-Raphaelite Brotherhood, it was a rejection of Victorian morality and promoted the notion of "art for art's sake." The idea was popularized by French poet and arts critic Théophile Gautier (1811–72), but it was adopted by Aesthetes after one of the movement's leading proponents, English writer and critic Walter Pater (1839–94), used the phrase in a review in 1868 of poetry by William Morris (1834–96; see p.52). Aestheticism emphasized the sensual and visual qualities of art and design, embracing the importance of the object itself separate from social, political, and moral considerations. The informal movement became part of a wider debate among artists, designers, and manufacturers regarding the value of craftsmanship.

Exponents of Aestheticism were particularly inspired by exhibits at the International Exhibition held in London in 1862, which displayed early work by Morris, Marshall, Faulkner and Company as well as a range of Japanese artefacts — a novel design culture to most of them. The Japanese exhibits at the Paris Exposition Universelle in 1878 similarly aroused interest among artists and designers, and the ideas gleaned became a strong feature of Aestheticism. The movement's ideals manifested in art in the paintings of Anglophile US

KEY EVENTS

1862	1864	1868	1873	1875	1876–77
The International Exhibition is held in London. China and Japan show porcelain, lacquerware, ivory carvings, cotton tapestries, and more.	Frederic, Lord Leighton, starts to build Leighton House in London, a groundbreaking example of Aesthetic architecture.	University of Oxford professor Walter Pater reviews William Morris's poetry in the *Westminster Review* and extols "the love of art for art's sake."	A modified form of Pater's review appears in his *Studies in the History of the Renaissance*. It becomes a key text for Aesthetes.	Arthur Lasenby Liberty opens a shop in London. He aims to change the look of homeware and fashion with his vision of an Eastern bazaar.	James McNeill Whistler designs the Peacock Room in London. Its green-blue walls, copper and gold leaf, and Orientalism are defiantly Aesthetic.

artist James McNeill Whistler (1834–1903), and artists Frederic, Lord Leighton (1830–96), and Albert Moore (1841–93). In the applied arts, it emerged in the work of architect and designer Edward William Godwin (1833–86), illustrator Aubrey Beardsley (1872–98), and ceramicist William De Morgan (1839–1917), among others. Many leading manufacturers of furniture, wallpapers, ceramics, and textiles employed professionals such as illustrator Walter Crane (1845–1915) and designer Christopher Dresser (1834–1904) to create objects in the Aesthetic style. In 1875 Arthur Lasenby Liberty (1843–1917) opened a London shop, Liberty and Company, creating an outlet for items from the Far East, fabrics, *objets d'art*, and decorative furnishings, which proliferated the Aesthetic style (see image 2).

From its beginnings, the movement was especially fashionable among a certain circle in west London, who even adopted styles of Aesthetic dress of Japonaise gowns and velvet jackets that contrasted with prevailing fashions. In 1864 Leighton acquired a plot of land there and collaborated with fellow Aesthetes, including De Morgan and Crane, to build an opulent Aesthetic home and studio, decorated with Turkish, Persian, Sicilian, and Syrian elements, channeling Arabic influences (see image 3). The interest in the decoration of entire rooms with all decorative elements complementing each other is one of the features of Aestheticism. Whistler completed Harmony in Blue and Gold: the Peacock Room (see image 1) in 1877 for the London home of shipping magnate Frederick Leyland (1832–92). Resembling the inside of a Japanese lacquer box, the walls were sumptuously adorned with stylized peacocks in gold on rich turquoise. Its lavish style epitomizes Aestheticism, and contributed to the development of Art Nouveau (see p.92) and the Vienna Secession. The interest in interior decoration grew after US author and critic Clarence Cook (1828–1900) published his book *The House Beautiful: Essays on Beds and Tables, Stools, and Candlesticks* in 1878 and was championed by Aesthete writer Oscar Wilde (1854–1900).

Yet the ethos of Aestheticism perplexed the general public. In 1879 French-British cartoonist and author George du Maurier (1834–96) published a series of cartoons, "Nincompoopiana," in the satirical magazine *Punch* ridiculing its ideals. From 1887 to 1889, Wilde was the editor of *The Woman's World* periodical aimed at educated, middle-class female readers. Unperturbed, he continued to advocate the ideas of *The House Beautiful* in it, suggesting that everyone should aim to create their own beautiful environment. Along with his friend and fellow Aesthete, Beardsley, Wilde shocked the public with his decadence, and Beardsley's illustrations, such as those for *The Yellow Book* (see p.90), and the English edition of Wilde's controversial play *Salome* in 1894 celebrated lasciviousness. Nonetheless, ultimately, Aestheticism helped to reinforce the importance of design and the need for refinement in the creation of mass-produced goods. **SH**

1877	1878	1878	1881	1885	1895
The Grosvenor Gallery opens in London. It displays work by Aesthete artists shunned by the Royal Academy.	The third World's Fair, the Exposition Universelle, is held in Paris. It features a Japanese pavilion.	Clarence Cook proposes what is desirable in interior design in his book on home furnishings, *The House Beautiful*.	*Patience*, an opera by W. S. Gilbert (1836–1911) and Arthur Sullivan (1842–1900), mocks the Aesthetes and has characters like Whistler and Oscar Wilde.	Whistler delivers his "Ten O'Clock" lecture in the Prince's Hall, London, explaining his Aesthetic creed.	Wilde is found guilty of gross indecency and sentenced to two years' hard labor. His death five years later marks the end of Aestheticism.

The Yellow Book 1894–97
AUBREY BEARDSLEY 1872–98

Cover of *The Yellow Book: An Illustrated Quarterly*, Volume 1, April 1894.

👁 FOCAL POINTS

1 YELLOW
Beardsley's choice of name and color was provocative. In imitation of illicit French novels, he created covers with black illustrations on lurid yellow cloth boards, and called it *The Yellow Book*. Its layout differed dramatically from contemporary periodicals with an almost square format.

2 FIGURES
Flattening perspectives and stylizing forms with curving, asymmetrical, sinuous lines, Beardsley introduced a new illustrative style. The influence of elegant Japanese prints is apparent. Although his use of subjects such as masked carnival goers was sensational, the journal was successful.

In April 1894, a new quarterly journal of the arts was published in Britain that became associated with Aestheticism and Decadence. Intending to be avant-garde, it contained both literary and artistic elements, giving equal weight to each, and did not include serial fiction or advertisements. Devised by English illustrator Aubrey Beardsley and his friend Henry Harland (1861–1905), a US writer living in London, it was published by John Lane (1854–1925) and Charles Elkin Mathews (1851–1921) through their firm the Bodley Head. Harland was literary editor and Beardsley art editor. The magazine was progressive in commissioning up-and-coming writers and artists, too. Commissioned artists included John Singer Sargent (1856–1925), Philip Wilson Steer (1862–1942), Walter Crane, and Frederic, Lord Leighton. The contributing authors were similarly exemplary and included Max Beerbohm (1872–1956), Henry James (1843–1916), H. G. Wells (1866–1946), and William Butler Yeats (1865–1939). Yet it was Beardsley's artistic contributions that gave the journal its distinctive character and established its decadent reputation. Despite Lane's remonstrations, Beardsley repeatedly shocked readers by including erotic details in his imagery. Other critics berated his sensual illustrations, and the satirical magazine *Punch* parodied several of them. In its three years of production, thirteen volumes of *The Yellow Book* were published. **SH**

⏱ DESIGNER PROFILE

1872–91
Aubrey Beardsley was born in Brighton, England. From six years old, his education was disrupted by frequent attacks of tuberculosis. In 1889 he began working in London as an insurance clerk, but dreamed of being an artist. Encouraged after meeting painters Edward Burne-Jones (1833–98) and Pierre Puvis de Chavannes (1824–98), he enrolled at London's Westminster School of Art in 1892. That year he traveled to Paris and became inspired by the posters of Henri de Toulouse-Lautrec (1864–1901) and fashionable Japanese prints.

1893–94
The publishing house J. M. Dent commissioned Beardsley to illustrate *Le Morte d'Arthur* (c. 1470). He also illustrated *Bon-Mots of Sydney Smith and R. Brinsley Sheridan. The Studio* arts magazine launched with a feature on him, accompanied by several of his characteristic black-and-white drawings. His fame increased with his erotic illustrations for Oscar Wilde's play *Salome*. He co-founded *The Yellow Book*.

1895–96
After Wilde was arrested on a criminal charge of committing indecent acts, Beardsley was dismissed from *The Yellow Book* because of his association. Beardsley continued working profusely as an illustrator, caricaturist, and writer. In 1896 he co-founded *The Savoy*, another magazine of literature, art, and criticism, but only eight issues were published. He also produced Rococo-style illustrations for an edition of Alexander Pope's *The Rape of the Lock* (1712).

1897–98
Beardsley converted to Roman Catholicism, and subsequently begged his publisher Leonard Smithers (1861–1907) to destroy all his erotic illustrations. Smithers ignored him, and continued selling reproductions and forgeries of his work. Beardsley moved to France, but died a year later of the tuberculosis he had contracted as a child.

IMMORALITY

After Beardsley read the original text in French of Oscar Wilde's play *Salome*, he drew Salome embracing the head of John the Baptist with stylized arcs of blood spurting forth. Wilde saw the drawing and asked Beardsley to illustrate the English edition. Beardsley then experienced notoriety when the combination of the grotesque and the graceful in his illustrations led to allegations of immorality.

ART NOUVEAU

A rt Nouveau was more an international movement than a particular style. It manifested in all forms of art and design, and its exponents aimed to produce original designs that reached a broad public, transcending class boundaries and reconciling mass production with craftsmanship. Its inspiration was found in natural forms, and sinuous, organic shapes predominated. Art Nouveau evolved from the Arts and Crafts movement (see p.74) and Aestheticism (see p.88), which both reacted against the predominance of historicism, ornate styles, and poorly made mass-produced objects. They rejected the traditional hierarchy of the arts established by the academic system that had dominated art education since the 17th century, which maintained that fine art, such as painting and sculpture, was superior to craft-based decorative art. In attempting to raise the status of craft and the decorative arts, Art Nouveau was applied to all types of art and design, with practitioners endeavoring to produce total works of art in which every aspect coordinated. Art Nouveau emerged almost simultaneously across Europe and the United States, and lasted from 1890 to 1914. It was a conscious

KEY EVENTS

1883	1888	1894	1894	1895	1900
Wren's City Churches is published. Arthur Heygate Mackmurdo's title-page design depicts swirling, rhythmic abstract forms based on plants.	The London-based Arts and Crafts Exhibition Society show of decorative arts includes Art Nouveau works of art and design.	Victor Horta completes the first Art Nouveau structure, the Hôtel Tassel in Brussels. Its attention to detail and curvilinear ironwork attract attention.	Alphonse Mucha introduces his distinctive style to Paris with a poster for the play *Gismonda*, starring Sarah Bernhardt (1844–1923).	Siegfried Bing opens Maison de l'Art Nouveau in Paris; the shop and gallery become a meeting place for Art Nouveau designers and artists.	The first Art Nouveau entrance designed by Hector Guimard for Paris Métro stations opens. Made from glass and cast iron, the last is built in 1912.

attempt to create a unique and modern form of expression that evoked the spirit of the age, that did not imitate the past, that embraced modern technology, and that was truly international.

The first Art Nouveau designs are believed to have been made by English architect and designer Arthur Heygate Mackmurdo (1851–1942) in the 1880s. His designs for a fretwork-backed chair and the title page for the book *Wren's City Churches* (1883) are reminiscent of Japanese *ukiyo-e* (pictures of the floating world) compositions. The undulating, asymmetrical, and abstracted plant-like designs convey an impression of dynamism. They generated many reinterpretations, and became some of Art Nouveau's key characteristics. Japan as a source of artistic inspiration had developed with the re-establishment of its trade with the West after more than 200 years in 1854. Western artists and designers were inspired by the flattened perspectives, minimal lines, asymmetrical compositions, elongated formats, organic and decorative motifs, and blocks of flat color (see p.82).

In France, the Art Nouveau style was seen originally in the paintings, posters, and interiors of Alphonse Mucha (1860–1939), who had moved to Paris from Czechoslovakia in 1887 to study art. By then hoardings of lithographed posters were common, serving as a street gallery that popularized the artistic style as well as the items advertised. Mucha found work creating posters that reflect life in fin-de-siècle Paris, for stage productions (see image 1), as well as consumer items from bicycles and beer to champagne and chocolate. His commercial work often featured women in flowing robes surrounded by decorative floral motifs. Also in Paris, German art dealer Siegfried "Samuel" Bing (1838–1905) opened his Maison de l'Art Nouveau in 1895, displaying imported Japanese prints, contemporary fine art, and many designs in the new styles. Bing encouraged Art Nouveau styling in the decorative arts, and it became evident in the glassware of Emile Gallé (1846–1904), the furniture of Louis Majorelle (1859–1926), and the glassware and jewelry of René Lalique (1860–1945). Lalique was innovative in his designs, creating fantastical jewelry (see image 2) influenced by the organic shapes of nature, and employing the latest techniques and novel materials—including translucent enamels and semi-precious stones—to add color.

In Belgium, Art Nouveau appeared first in the architectural schemes of Paul Hankar (1859–1901), Victor Horta (1861–1947), and Henry van de Velde (1863–1957). Horta's Hôtel Tassel in Brussels is credited as the first example of the Art Nouveau style in architecture, and it influenced French architect Hector Guimard (1867–1942; see p.96) when he created entrances for the Paris Métro from 1900.

In Britain, during the 1880s, the London shop Liberty and Company sold various ornaments, fabrics, and furnishings from the Orient. The shop also commissioned objects from several progressive English designers of the period.

1 A poster designed by Alphonse Mucha for *Amants*, a comedy at the Théâtre de la Renaissance, Paris, in 1895.

2 René Lalique used novel materials, such as enamel, to add color to jewelry like this pearl-and-gold ring of c. 1900.

1900	1901	1902	1904	1909	1914
At the Exposition Universelle in Paris, René Lalique causes a sensation with jewelry and *objets d'art* made from glass, ivory, and bronze.	Charles Rennie Mackintosh designs four pavilions for commercial organizations at the Glasgow International Exhibition in Scotland.	The 'Prima Esposizione Internazionale d'Arte Decorativa Moderna' (First International Exposition of Modern Decorative Arts) opens in Turin, Italy.	European luminaries of Art Nouveau exhibit at the St. Louis World's Fair in Missouri, helping to disseminate the esthetic.	Mackintosh finishes his building for the Glasgow School of Art. It is the first example of British Art Nouveau architecture.	World War I breaks out. Art Nouveau is regarded as being overly elaborate.

The most notable was Archibald Knox (1864–1933), who often incorporated Celtic ornamentation into his pieces (see image 3). His work in silver, pewter, and jewelry came to epitomize the English variant of Art Nouveau. Consequently, Liberty became identified with the Art Nouveau movement.

Along with those shops selling Art Nouveau goods, improvements in printing and distribution resulted in the publication and wide circulation of numerous periodicals, including *The Studio* in Britain, *Pan* in Germany, and the magazine of the Vienna Secession, *Ver Sacrum*. Many such periodicals reached an international audience and spread the concepts of Art Nouveau.

The style proliferated in Germany, Austria, and Scotland, with the architecture, furniture, and household goods of Josef Hoffmann (1870–1956), the paintings of fellow Vienna Secessionist Gustav Klimt (1862–1918), and the elegant, rectilinear architecture, furniture, and interior designs of Charles Rennie Mackintosh (1868–1928; see p.100). In Spain, Antoni Gaudí (1852–1926) created highly individual and expressive architecture. Innovative, undulating buildings such as Casa Batlló (1906; see image 5) in Barcelona reflect Gaudí's vision of Art Nouveau. In the United States, Louis Comfort Tiffany (1848–1933; see p.98) produced multicolored and iridescent glass that came to exemplify the US interpretation of the movement that became known as 'Tiffany Style' in recognition of his distinctive designs.

In different countries, different names were used to describe the style and its localized variants. For instance, Jugendstil (Youth Style) arose in German-speaking countries after the magazine *Jugend: Münchner illustrierte Wochenschrift für Kunst und Leben* (*Youth: the Illustrated Weekly Magazine of the Art and Lifestyle of Munich*), first published in 1896. In Austria, it was known as Sezessionstil after the Vienna Secessionists, a group of painters, sculptors and architects who opposed the conservatism of the Association of Austrian Artists, and were inspired by the linear style of Mackintosh. In France names included the Style Moderne, Style Jules Verne, and Style Métro. It was known as Modernisme in Catalonia, Arte Joven in Spain, Arte Nova in Portugal, and Nieuwe Kunst in the Netherlands. In Italy it was called Arte Nuova and Stile Liberty after the London shop.

In Scotland it was mainly known as the Glasgow Style, in recognition of the group of designers known as The Four:

Mackintosh, Herbert MacNair (1868–1955) and their wives, the sisters Margaret (1864–1933) and Frances MacDonald (1873–1921). The phrase that stuck, Art Nouveau, originated from Bing's Parisian gallery, especially after he exhibited works at the Exposition Universelle in Paris in 1900. From then, the name became synonymous with the style.

In 1900, the Paris Exposition Universelle was a showcase of Art Nouveau. It captured the public imagination, and Art Nouveau became the first international decorative style of the modern age. Also intended to celebrate the start of the 20th century, the Exposition Universelle flaunted new technologies and ideas. It featured the elaborate dome-shaped Porte Monumentale entrance designed by René Binet (1866–1911); the Palais d'Electricité (Palace of Electricity), fitted with thousands of colored and white lamps; the Pavillon Bleu (Blue Pavilion), a grand restaurant at the foot of the Eiffel Tower designed by Gustave Serrurier-Bovy (1858–1910); and Bing's acclaimed pavilion Art Nouveau Bing , which featured six domestic interiors displaying graphics, fine art, and other objects produced by notable artists and designers, including Eugène Gaillard (1862–1933), Edouard Colonna (1862–1948), Georges de Feure (1868–1958), Henri de Toulouse-Lautrec (1864–1901), Mucha, Tiffany, and Lalique. Pieces such as Gaillard's carved walnut chair (see image 4), with its sinuous patterning and organic sculptural form resonant of the twisting branches of a tree in nature, would have seemed novel to visitors. The pavilion of the Union Centrale des Arts Décoratifs (Central Union of Decorative Arts)—an official body committed to the reinvigoration of crafts in France—offered a further display of Art Nouveau objects. In the international pavilions, national differences in the interpretations and expressions of Art Nouveau became apparent. The Exposition Universelle was followed by three further world fairs at which many of the luminaries of Art Nouveau exhibited.

Then in 1914, abruptly and brutally, it all ended with the outbreak of World War I. Art Nouveau was seen as a luxurious and expensive style, making way for the more streamlined look of modernism. **SH**

3 This cigarette box (1903–04) was part of the range of designs Archibald Knox created for Liberty's Cymric range of silverware and jewelry.

4 Art dealer Siegfried Bing showed this walnut and leather dining chair by Eugène Gaillard at the Exposition Universelle in Paris in 1900.

5 The organic forms of Art Nouveau led to a new approach to architecture evident, in the billowing shapes of Antoni Gaudí's Casa Batlló (1906) in Barcelona.

Porte Dauphine Métro Entrance 1900

HECTOR GUIMARD 1867–1942

The Porte Dauphine Paris Métro entrance is made from painted cast iron, glazed lava, and glass.

 NAVIGATOR

Chiefly made of cast iron and glass, Hector Guimard's Paris Métro entrances were designed to enhance the underground train system that was being built beneath Paris to meet the needs of an expanding city, and to coincide with the Exposition Universelle world fair in 1900. The Exposition was intended to display progress in art, industry, and science, particularly French achievements, and the new Métro was to serve visitors and demonstrate developments in transport. In 1899 the Compagnie du Chemin de Fer Métropolitain de Paris (Paris Metropolitan Railway Company) held a competition for designers to submit ideas for the station entrances, but the company directors were unhappy with the submissions. Guimard was invited to submit proposals and then commissioned to design the entrances. Over twelve years, he created 141 Métro entrances in two different styles: simple balustrades without roofs, and kiosks with large or small canopies, known as *édicules*, as in Porte Dauphine. Produced in standard parts, all the entrances were relatively cheap to produce and easy to assemble.

Porte Dauphine was inaugurated on 13 December 1900, a month after the Exposition Universelle had closed and before that section of the Métro was complete. Two iron pillars shaped like flower stalks flank the molded, cast-iron green frame of the inverted, glass, fan-shaped awning. However, the organically styled Art Nouveau design was unfamiliar to contemporary eyes and generated controversy. Guimard's designs for the Métro became a lasting embodiment of Art Nouveau, with Style Métro becoming one of the terms used to describe the entire style. **SH**

1 SIGN

The sign is made of glazed lava, allowing for bright colors and a smooth texture. The green on yellow lettering is in an organic-style typeface. The curvilinear, flowing lettering was hand-drawn by Guimard. The lettering varied on station signs until Guimard arrived at a consistent style in 1902.

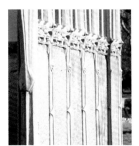

2 SUPPORT

The cast-iron supports that hold up the sign look like flower stalks. The curvilinear lines were inspired by flowers. Parisians nicknamed the entrances in this style *libellules* (dragonflies). The entrance is protected by a small canopy that flares in an upward curve to drain off the rain.

3 METAL

The cast-iron elements were painted green to resemble bronze that had acquired the patina of age. Guimard's concept of luxurious design demonstrates the idealist aspirations of Art Nouveau, in creating something for everyone—beautiful design was not only for the rich.

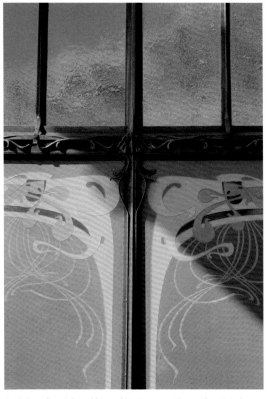

▲ Guimard envisioned his architecture as a *Gesamtkunstwerk* (total work of art). The sensuous curves and elaborate flourishes decorating the glazed lava panels lining the walls of the interior space correspond to the flowing forms of the exterior structure.

CASTEL BERANGER

At first, Guimard's Paris Métro entrances appeared bizarre and extraordinary to most Parisians, but the term "Style Guimard" became one of the ways the new exotic ideas were described. For visitors to the Exposition Universelle, the Métro entrances with their giant, stylized, unfurling supports must have seemed the height of modernity. Yet Guimard had already become known as the first Art Nouveau architect of Paris with his Castel Béranger on Rue Jean de la Fontaine, built from 1895 to 1898. Started when Guimard was unknown, the block of thirty-six apartments is an example of the development of his style after meeting with his Belgian colleague, Victor Horta, in 1895 in Brussels. Guimard created both the exterior structure and the interior decoration, including woodwork, metalwork, stained glass and glazing, wallpaper, and furniture. As with his Métro entrances, Guimard used inexpensive, easily obtainable building materials, including prefabricated wrought-iron parts for the balcony railings.

Tiffany Wisteria Table Lamp *c.* 1902

LOUIS COMFORT TIFFANY 1848–1933

Patinated bronze and leaded glass
18¼ x 26½ in./46.5 x 67.5 cm

Comprising nearly 2,000 pieces of glass, this lamp was created in the workshop of Louis Comfort Tiffany in New York. Although he was responsible for the design's inception, Clara Driscoll (1861–1944), the head of his glassworking team, created it. In jewel-toned shades of blue, purple, green, and yellow, tiny glass pieces are shaped to resemble a wisteria in bloom. The delicate glass shade contrasts with the lamp's solid bronze stand. Tiffany and Driscoll were inspired by a love of nature, developments in Art Nouveau, the Aesthetic movement (see p.88). and Japanese design (see p.82). Having set up his glassmaking company in 1885 to produce stained-glass windows, Tiffany patented his iridescent Favrile glass in 1894 and expanded into producing colored-glass lampshades a year later. His first lamps were lit with kerosene, then he took advantage of the new electric light bulbs that his friend Thomas Edison (1847–1931) made commercially viable in 1880. Made by hand, small petal shapes were traced onto the glass using a template, cut out with pliers, and then fused together with thin strips of copper foil that became integral to the design. Favrile glass is variegated, and selecting pieces of glass required an artistic eye because variations in colors and tones enhanced the lamps' richness and individuality. Tiffany believed that women had a superior sense of color, so he mostly employed female technicians to make the lamps. This was one of his most popular lamps and it has become an international icon of Art Nouveau. **SH**

👁 FOCAL POINTS

1 COPPER FOIL
Tiffany started with color sketches of the design on paper and then made brass templates for each piece of glass to be cut. Workers cut out each small shape and assembled them by hand. They were soldered in place by thin copper foil that had been coated in beeswax on one side.

2 GLASS
In this lamp, Tiffany used his mottled Favrile glass in rich colors to create a soft, glowing light. When light bulbs were first produced, their light was harsh and sharp, but from his interior-design projects, Tiffany had an extensive knowledge of how to soften, diffuse and deflect light.

3 BASE
The bronze lamp stand was created to draw attention to the colorful shade. Sinuous and sculptural, the stand mirrors the natural motifs on the shade and suggests the actual stem of a wisteria plant. Like each lampshade, all Tiffany's lamp bases were slightly different.

▲ The Peony (c.1905) table lamp has a profusion of dynamic-looking peony buds and blossoms in shades of red and pink with yellow centers that contrast with a mottled amber and green background. The smoothly curving canopied shape appears delicate and natural, and when the light is turned on it emits a warm glow. The curving bronze and iridescent base is decorated with red glass mosaics, known as "turtleback" for their shape.

Hill House Ladder-back Chair 1903

CHARLES RENNIE MACKINTOSH 1868–1928

Ebonized ashwood, seagrass
fabric, horsehair
Height 55½ in./141 cm

⊕ NAVIGATOR

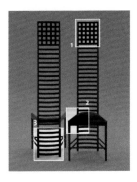

ill House in Helensburgh, Scotland, is one of Charles Rennie Mackintosh's most
famous works, designed and built for the publisher Walter Blackie (1816–1906)
and his family between 1902 and 1904. As well as the house itself, Mackintosh
designed most of the interiors, furniture, and fittings, and despite his formal training and
proficiency as an architect, he became known for his interior design schemes and
furniture. Striking for its straight lines and minimal decoration, he designed furniture to
augment his interior spaces, rather than stand alone, and at a time when popular tastes
favored curving lines, his style was a combination of gentle curves and stark vertical lines,
fusing traditional Celtic craftsmanship and design with the purity of Japanese esthetics.
Mackintosh made two chairs for the main bedroom at Hill House. The stark linear
geometry of his design deliberately contrasted with the delicate white, pink, and silver
decorative scheme of the room. The high back and rows of horizontal bars topped with a
grid illustrate his articulation of space. The elongated elements are characteristic of his
Japanese-inspired style, as is the disguise of the ashwood with black lacquer. **SH**

1 HEADREST
Characterized by an economy of line, with the headrest grid echoed around the white walls of the room for which it was made, this chair's distinct geometric lines demonstrate Mackintosh's modernist inclinations and contrast definitively with many other Art Nouveau interpretations.

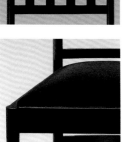

2 SEAT
The fan-shaped seat is small and decorative, but not very functional. The chair was likely intended to have clothes placed on it rather than to be sat upon. The small seat emphasizes the chair's fragility, but the structure is strong with lengths of wood intersecting at right angles to create a sturdy frame.

3 SLATS
From the floor to the top, the horizontal back slats are identically spaced and counterbalance the vertical sides. Straight lines echo elements of Japanese linear ideals of beauty and the Vienna Secessionists. Although the chair appears straight, the back rungs are curved for comfort.

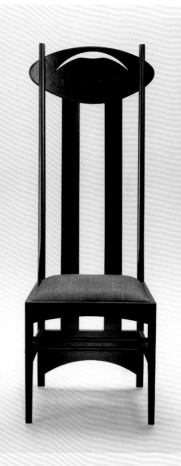

▲ Mackintosh designed much of his furniture for specific spaces. In the Hill House bedroom, the chair's horizontal back slats and long vertical uprights suggest a trellis that complements the rose patterns that were originally stenciled onto the walls.

HIGH-BACKED CHAIR

In 1896 Mackintosh met Kate Cranston (1849–1934), an entrepreneurial businesswoman who opened four tearooms in Glasgow. Between 1896 and 1917, Mackintosh designed all four of Cranston's tearoom interiors. This chair, created when he worked on the Argyle Street tearooms between 1898 and 1899, was intended for their luncheon rooms. It was the first of many high-backed chairs that he produced, allowing him to manipulate the space, so when people were grouped around tables, they could not be seen and the high backs created the illusion of a private space. The crescent cut-out shape within the oval headrest echoed a motif of a bird in flight that featured around the room, while the two hroad, widely spaced back splats, the narrow, tapering uprights, and the slender legs echoed the verticality throughout the interior. Although the chair appears simple, the back legs are complex, changing from circular to oval to square, and the tapering front legs are both robust and delicate.

WIENER WERKSTÄTTE

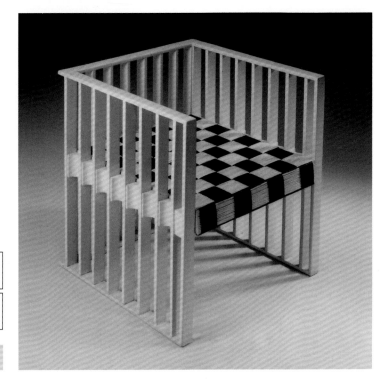

1 The cube shape of Koloman Moser's armchair, created in 1903 and used at the Purkersdorf Sanatorium, is typical of the many simple geometric forms adopted by the Wiener Werkstätte designers.

2 Josef Hoffmann's lithograph of 1907 depicts the Wiener Werkstätte design for the Bar Room at the Cabaret Fledermaus, which included the interior decor, furnishings, and tableware.

3 The patterning of the goblets on these wineglasses (c. 1907) by Otto Prutscher, harmonizing with the elegant, elongated stems, is a striking feature of Wiener Werkstätte glassware design.

The Wiener Werkstätte (Vienna Workshops) was an innovative multidisciplinary design collective established in 1903. An offshoot of the Vienna Secession, it sought to reinvigorate the decorative arts by providing a creative outlet for artists, designers, and craftspeople. Cross-fertilization between the fine and applied arts was key. Active for three decades, the Wiener Werkstätte electrified every branch of the applied arts.

The prime movers initially were the architect Josef Hoffmann (1870–1956; see p.106) and the painter and graphic artist Koloman Moser (1868–1918). Over time, the Wiener Werkstätte became increasingly eclectic, reflecting the diverse input of designers from different spheres. Continuity was provided by Hoffmann, who remained as artistic director until 1931. The gifted Dagobert Peche (1887–1923), who joined in 1915, also made a significant contribution. His balletic patterns added a new dimension to the Workshops' collections.

Two major architectural projects that established the reputation of the group were the Purkersdorf Sanatorium (1904–05) near Vienna and the Palais Stoclet (1905–11) in Brussels, both designed by Hoffmann. The Cabaret

KEY EVENTS

1897	1901	1903	1907	1908	1910
Austrian artist Gustav Klimt (1862–1918) leads a rebellion against the Viennese art establishment and establishes the Vienna Secession.	Koloman Moser's pupil Jutta Sika (1877–1964; see p.104) co-founds the Wiener Kunst im Hause (Viennese Art in the Home) group.	The Wiener Werkstätte headquarters opens in October at 32–34 Neustiftgasse in the city.	The Wiener Werkstätte showroom opens at 15 Graben in the city. Koloman Moser resigns, leaving Josef Hoffmann in charge.	The 'Kunstschau' exhibition in Vienna features a room of posters designed by members of the Wiener Werkstätte.	The Wiener Werkstätte establishes a textile and fashion department; it is headed by Eduard Josef Wimmer-Wisgrill until 1922.

Fledermaus (1907; see image 2), a nightclub and restaurant in Vienna, provided a lively creative platform. The Wiener Werkstätte created arresting, coordinated furnishing schemes for these interiors, conceived as *Gesamtkunstwerke* (total works of art) in which every detail was harmonized. Pronounced geometric and angular forms with strong outlines and checkerboard patterns characterized their approach (see image 1). Black and white featured prominently, contrasting with injections of bright, singing colors.

As an artist-led enterprise, the Wiener Werkstätte was able to be more adventurous and experimental than conventional firms. The fact that it controlled the means of production meant that it could take more risks while maintaining high standards. Many products were handcrafted in its own workshops, which included facilities for metalwork, bookbinding, leatherwork, and lacquerwork. External manufacturers were carefully vetted, and the Wiener Werkstätte supplied the designs and dictated how they were produced.

Glass was made on its behalf by various Bohemian glassworks via the agency of the Viennese distributors E. Bakalowits and Söhne and J. and L. Lobmeyr. Particularly striking were the tall wineglasses designed by Otto Prutscher (1880–1949), with their elaborately cut geometricized stems (see image 3). Ceramics were manufactured by Wiener Keramik, established in 1906 by two Wiener Werkstätte members, Michael Powolny (1871–1954) and Bertold Löffler (1874–1960), who created striking vessels and figurines.

Textiles were another important aspect of the Wiener Werkstätte, initially Jacquard-woven furnishing fabrics manufactured by Johann Backhausen and Söhne. Following the establishment of an in-house textile and fashion department in 1910, block-printed dress fabrics became a significant area of activity. These vibrant, abstract and floral patterns, created by numerous contributors in styles ranging from folk art to Fauvism, contrasted sharply with the pared-down simplicity of the loose-fitting dresses in which the Wiener Werkstätte specialized. Under the direction of designer Eduard Josef Wimmer-Wisgrill (1882–1961), the fashion department became extremely successful, influencing leading international designers such as Paul Poiret (1879–1944).

Although Wiener Werkstätte products were made in only relatively small quantities, they gained a high profile internationally. Stylistically, the Wiener Werkstätte can be seen as a bridge between fin-de-siècle Art Nouveau (or Jugendstil, as it was known in Germany and Austria; see p.92) and interwar Art Deco (see p.156). Fearlessly modern in outlook, the Wiener Werkstätte showed what could be achieved when designers seized the artistic reins. Proto-modernism is an apt description of the Wiener Werkstätte: it inspired emergent modernist architects such as Le Corbusier (1887–1965) and paved the way for the Bauhaus (see p.126). However, the Wiener Werkstätte was more pluralistic and less didactic than the Bauhaus. Free spirited and exuberant, its products celebrated of the visual potency of decorative art. **LJ**

1913	1914	1916–17	1922	1924	1931
The Wiener Werkstätte registers its trademark, featuring its logo of two letters, "WW."	The Austrian pavilion at the Werkbund (Work Federation) Exhibition in Cologne, Germany, features a room dedicated to the Wiener Werkstätte.	The Wiener Werkstätte opens showrooms in Vienna, one of them specializing in textiles, and a Swiss branch is established in Zürich.	Austrian-born stage designer Josef Urban (1872–1933) opens a US branch of the Wiener Werkstätte on Fifth Avenue, New York City.	The New York City branch of the Wiener Werkstätte folds. An attempt to revive it in 1929 fails.	Because of financial difficulties following the Stock Market Crash of 1929, the Wiener Werkstätte ceases to operate and is liquidated a year later.

Coffee Service *c.* 1901–02

JUTTA SIKA 1877–1964

👁 FOCAL POINTS

1 HANDLES
What makes this design so striking is its handles. Instead of conventional curved handles and circular knobs, it has flat "fins" pierced by holes. Although eye-catching, these features proved rather impractical, as they were problematic to manufacture and difficult to use.

2 SPOUT
The vessel shapes are quirky, particularly the spout on the lidded coffee pot, resembling the beak of a puffin. The service has an animated, jaunty quality with anthropomorphic overtones. The recesses for the cups were originally positioned off center on the saucers, but this feature was later modified.

3 PORCELAIN BODY
Made of hard-paste porcelain, a high-fired vitreous ceramic material traditionally used in the European ceramics industry, the service was produced by the Viennese firm of Josef Böck. The vessels were likely manufactured on their behalf by a Bohemian factory, then decorated in house.

4 PATTERN
The pattern of overlapping circles and dots has been stenciled in overglaze enamel. Its flattened abstract motifs and asymmetrical composition were unconventional at the time. It is one of several alternative patterns created for the service by Sika and students at the School of Applied Arts.

Porcelain and enamel
Height of coffee pot
7½ in./19.3 cm

This coffee service, with its unusual handles, looks so modern that it is hard to believe that it dates from the early 20th century. The shape was created by a young Austrian designer called Jutta Sika, who was still a student at the time. Sika was studying at the Kunstgewerbeschule (School of Applied Arts) in Vienna, where one of her tutors was the graphic artist Koloman Moser. The stenciled decoration on this piece was created by Moser's students as part of an academic exercise.

Moser was one of the most influential figures in the Viennese art world at this date. A founder member of the Vienna Secession in 1897, he established the Wiener Werkstätte (Vienna Workshops) with Josef Hoffmann in 1903. One of its precursors was a group called Wiener Kunst im Hause (Viennese Art in the Home), established in 1901. Sika co-founded this alliance, along with nine fellow students at the School of Applied Arts. Like the Wiener Werkstätte, Viennese Art in the Home promoted the concept of the *Gesamtkunstwerk* (total work of art), the idea that the different components within an interior should be visually integrated. As well as ceramics, members of the group designed textiles with patterns derived from Austrian folk art.

Made from porcelain, this coffee service was initially produced in plain white. Its unusual shape clearly made a dramatic impact, as it was exhibited at the Austrian Museum of Applied Arts in Vienna at the time. It was later featured in an exhibition called 'Der Gedeckte Tisch' (The Laid Table), originally held at the Moravian Museum in Brno (now Czech Republic), in 1905 and subsequently at the Wiener Werkstätte showrooms in Vienna the following year. So, although Sika did not design for Wiener Werkstätte, she shared similar ideals and was an integral part of the same artistic milieu. **LJ**

⏲ DESIGNER PROFILE

1877–96
Jutta Sika was born in the Austrian city of Linz. In 1895 she enrolled at the Graphic Education and Research Institute in Vienna.

1897–1904
From 1897 to 1902, Sika studied at the School of Applied Arts, where one of her tutors was Koloman Moser. In 1901 she co-founded the Viennese Art in the Home alliance.

1905–12
Sika designed accessories for the Flöge Sisters haute couture salon and embroidery for the Wiener Stickerei (Viennese Embroidery) group, as well as practicing as a graphic designer.

1913–64
Sika returned to the School of Applied Arts for two years to study costume design under Alfred Roller (1864–1935). From the 1920s, Sika devoted her energies to painting, specializing in floral subjects, and teaching.

◄ This figurine typifies the decorative ceramics associated with the Wiener Werkstätte. It was designed c. 1907 by Michael Powolny, who teamed up with Bertold Löffler (1874–1960) to create a company called Wiener Keramik in 1906. The cherub figure is classical in origin but his floral cascade, symbolizing spring, is unmistakably contemporary. Some versions were decorated in black and white; others were painted in bright colors that gave a very different character to the piece.

Fruit Bowl *c.* 1904

JOSEF HOFFMANN 1870–1956

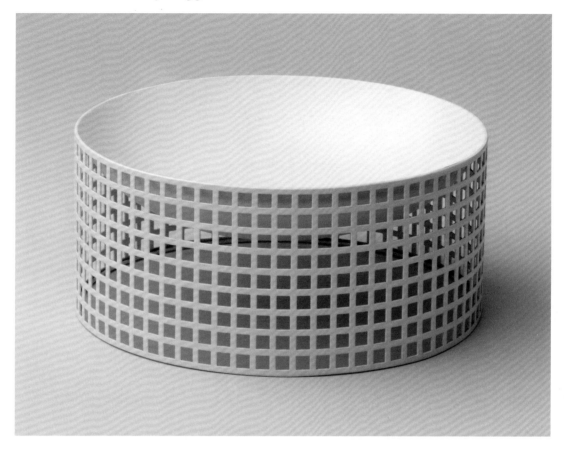

Painted metal
Height 3¾ in./9.5 cm
Diameter 8½ in./21.5 cm

 **NAVIGATOR**

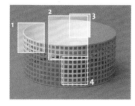

Josef Hoffmann is an intriguing designer because his work is highly restrained, yet overtly decorative. An admirer of the Glasgow architect and designer Charles Rennie Mackintosh (1868–1928), whose work was shown in the Vienna Secession in 1900, Hoffmann developed a similar penchant for grid patterns and geometric forms as an alternative to the prevailing organic forms of Art Nouveau (see p.92). Although opposed to historicism, he frequently drew on classical shapes, stripped back to their purest elements. His three-dimensional designs are elegant and beautifully proportioned, but he also had a flair for dynamic surface patterns. Both aspects of his design character—the plain and the decorative—are encapsulated in this design.

Created as part of a range of basket-like vessels in various geometric forms, this fruit bowl was one of Hoffmann's earliest creations for the Wiener Werkstätte (Vienna Workshops). Made of sheet metal, perforated on the exterior like a cage, it represents Hoffmann at his most austere and radically simple. With its clean lines, pristine white finish, and industrial esthetic, it is clear why designs such as these have been regarded as precursors of Modernism. Fabricated in various metals, including enameled iron or zinc and nickel-plated brass, some pieces were produced in silver, giving a richer and more luxurious impression.

Although Hoffmann regarded himself first and foremost as an architect, he was more prolific as a designer. His shapes have an architectural rigor and he brought the same precision to the design of a bowl as he did to a building. Because his objects display a complementary esthetic to his interiors, the two could be seamlessly combined, a key motivation being to create a *Gesamtkunstwerk*, a complete work of art. **LJ**

FOCAL POINTS

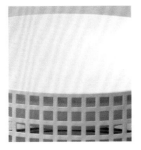

1 GEOMETRIC FORMS
The shape and pattern in the bowl are perfectly geometrical. The rim is circular, the vessel sides are straight. and the latticework perforations are square. It is rare for a vessel to be as uncompromisingly pure as this in its shape and decoration. The bowl must have seemed stark at the time.

2 SUSPENDED BOWL
At first glance the vessel appears cylindrical, but the base is open and the shallow curved bowl is suspended from the top rim. The pierced sides give it a light. airy quality and create interesting shadow effects. The bowl has a sculptural presence, making it visually satisfying when empty.

3 WHITE PAINT
White is often used by designers to evoke purity and cleanliness. Many of Hoffmann's designs exploit the visual contrast between black and white. Although this piece is monochrome, the square perforations create infinite differentiations between light and shade.

4 PERFORATED METAL
The use of grille-like perforated sheet metal for the structure of a vessel was daring. Because the metal is quite thin, the rim has been folded over and strengthened with wire. The pieces in this range were made in base metals, such as iron, zinc, and nickel-plated brass, and precious metals such as silver.

DESIGNER PROFILE

1870–99
Born in Moravia, Czech Republic, Josef Hoffmann studied architecture at the Akademie der Bildenden Künste (Academy of Fine Arts) in Vienna, then joined the office of architect and urban planner Otto Wagner (1841–1918). A founder member of the Vienna Secession in 1897, Hoffmann set up in practice independently in 1898 and was appointed professor at the Kunstgewerbeschule (School of Applied Arts) in Vienna in 1899.

1900–11
He visited Britain where he met Charles Rennie Mackintosh. After co-founding the Wiener Werkstätte in 1903, it became the main avenue for Hoffmann's designs. Two of his major buildings, the Purkersdorf Sanatorium (1904–05) near Vienna and the Palais Stoclet (1905–11) in Brussels, provided a showcase for his early furniture and textiles.

1912–36
Hoffmann continued as artistic director of the Wiener Werkstätte until its closure in 1931, creating numerous designs in many different media, including glass, silver, metalwork, furniture, and textiles. He also remained closely involved with the School of Applied Arts, where he taught until 1936.

1937–56
Hoffmann carried on practicing as an architect, later focusing on housing projects for Vienna.

JOSEF HOFFMANN TEXTILES

It is rare for a designer to be equally adept at three-dimensional form and surface decoration, but Hoffmann was a highly original pattern designer as well as an accomplished architect and product designer. His earliest textiles were Jacquard-woven furnishing fabrics for curtains and upholstery. Later, from 1910 onward, he turned his hand to block-printed dress fabrics for the Wiener Werkstätte's fashion collections. Grid patterns feature prominently in his patterns, sometimes juxtaposed with triangles or chevrons, but his decorative vocabulary also encompassed stylized plants, as in Pilz (1902; above). While operating within strict self-imposed parameters, Hoffmann created dynamic designs. One of the most striking features of his textiles is the preponderance of black and white.

2 | The Age of the Machine 1905–45

THE PRODUCTION LINE

1 Workers trying out the new Ford moving assembly line in Detroit, Michigan, in 1913—the first for the mass production of an entire automobile.

2 Women operating machinery in a British munitions factory during World War I. The women worked at individual stations assembling gun components.

3 A Buick motor car is driven off a flatbed using a ramp in 1924. As demand for automobiles grew in the 1920s, General Motors set the pace of production.

One of the most important technological influences upon modern design was the development of mass production in factories. Factory production eliminated the elements of chance, and the reliance on tacit knowledge, iteration, and improvization, that had characterized making by hand. Above all, it made possible the mechanized manufacture of standardized products from interchangeable parts, which could be sold at lower prices as a result of the economy of scale that was achieved.

With manufacturing carried out by teams of skilled and semi-skilled workers, operating as part of a divided labor system, design became a highly planned activity, with products fully envisaged before the production process commenced. There was no room for improvization or variation. Furthermore, the machines used in the factories exerted an influence upon the final appearance of products, and prototypes had to be designed with the constraints of available production machinery in mind.

The mechanization of production was a relatively slow process in Britain, but it was introduced much more speedily in the United States, where a shortage of manpower meant that it was a necessity. Starting with its arms industry, for which the interchangeability of parts was essential for the quick repair of weapons used in war, the United States developed a highly rationalized mass-production system that was implemented in the design and

KEY EVENTS

1908	1910	1913	1914	1915	1918
Albert Kahn Associates designs the Highland Park factory for Ford Motors in Detroit, Michigan. The design is of reinforced concrete with large windows.	Henry Ford opens the Highland Park Ford factory in Detroit, Michigan. It is the largest manufacturing facility in the world.	Ford introduces his moving assembly line into his factory. Although he did not invent the concept, he applies it at a larger scale than before.	World War I breaks out. French industrialist André-Gustave Citroën persuades the French government that it needs to mass produce munitions.	Citroën builds a munitions plant; its production of shells reaches 55,000 per day.	World War I ends. Citroën decides to convert his original arms factory into a plant to mass-produce a small, inexpensive automobile.

manufacture of many other (mostly metal) products, including locks, clocks, and bicycles. By the early 20th century, the so-called "US system of manufacture" was nearly complete.

However, one element of the fully fledged system was still absent, namely the moving assembly line. That was put in place by Henry Ford (1863–1947), who took his inspiration from the meat-packing industry, which used moving belts to speed up the process of disassembling carcasses. It changed the nature of mass production: rather than the factory workers having to work on static objects, moving around them as they added components, they could remain in one place while the products moved past them. It significantly increased the speed of manufacture and therefore of profitability. In 1913 Ford introduced a fully fledged model of mass production in his Highland Park plant in Michigan (see image 1). It combined divided labor, product standardization, interchangeable parts, and mechanization with a moving assembly line.

The benefits of the assembly line were immediate and dramatic. Over the course of a single year, 1913 to 1914, the hours required to assemble a Model T (see p.112) dropped from 12.5 to 1.5. There was a concomitant decrease in price for an entry-level model, from $1,200 in 1909 to $690 in 1914. However, workers did not find the new conditions congenial, and to encourage staff to stay, Ford introduced his policy of paying $5 per day. Cannily, this also had the effect of providing his workforce with the means to buy his products.

In retrospect, the timing of such developments could not have been more opportune. The year after the moving assembly line was introduced, World War I broke out. The production line entered a new and deadlier phase, pressed into service to create vehicles and armaments (see image 2) for the war effort. Ambulances, trucks, aircraft, and army transport of all kinds, along with shells and weaponry, were churned out in factories on both sides of the conflict, firmly wedding mass production to mass global warfare. André-Gustave Citroën (1878–1935), the first mass producer of automobiles outside the United States, started as a manufacturer of munitions in Paris during the war, operating an assembly line.

After the war ended, the pure model of mass production underwent a shift. By 1927 more people were buying a second car than were buying their first, and what they increasingly demanded was greater choice and a better specification. By the late 1920s, Ford's chief competitor, General Motors (see image 3), with its strategy of "a car for every purse and purpose," was ahead of the game. To give its customers the variety they wanted, and to build a brand portfolio that enabled the buyer of a basic Chevrolet to aspire to owning a luxury Cadillac one day, General Motors employed a more flexible model of mass production called "batch production." This market-oriented approach sacrificed a degree of production efficiency in the interests of increased sales. It also had the effect of placing styling—and designers—at the heart of the motor industry. **PS**

1919	1923	1927	1927	1928	1930
The first Citroën car, the Type A, comes off the assembly line in May.	Alfred P. Sloan (1875–1966) becomes head of General Motors and instigates a market-oriented approach that makes it financially successful.	Ford launches his new Model A automobile in response to competition from General Motors. It is more stylish than the Model T.	Sloan introduces an Art and Color (later Styling) Section into General Motors and invites Harley J. Earl (1893–1969) to lead it.	Ford's River Rouge Complex in Dearborn, Michigan, begins its operations. It has its own electricity plant and an integrated steel mill.	Sloan introduces the concept of the model year, which markets cars on annual cosmetic changes, setting a new direction for the motor industry.

Ford Model T 1908

HENRY FORD 1863–1947

The tensile strength of the vanadium steel alloy used in the Model T helped the car withstand being driven on bumpy roads with potholes.

The Ford Model T, also known as the "Tin Lizzie," is a basic car. First produced in 1908, the automobile is a product of its materials and the efficiencies of the Ford Motor Company factory's production process, which enabled company founder Henry Ford to sell his cars at cheaper price than his competitors could. It consists of a separate chassis and a body that came together at the point of the assembly. The impression that it was little more than an assemblage of its component parts—which characterizes the Model T and distinguishes it from later models—is reinforced by the gap visible between the chassis and the body, the sense that its headlights have been added to its body, and the semi-separateness of the running board. Yet the Model T's appeal lay in its price and its efficiency—all had 2.9-liter engines and two-speed gearboxes. The fact that it was the first car purchased by members of a rural population that had hitherto only used horses and carts for transportation meant that ownership alone was a status symbol.

Ford worked at improving and rationalizing its means of production, which allowed him to reduce costs and drop the sales price. The Model T was the company's first automobile mass produced on moving assembly lines with completely interchangeable parts. Production of the Model T ceased in 1927, but it is one of the best selling cars of all time. Sales of 16.5 million in nineteen years were aided by design revisions over its lifetime and its availability as a roadster, coupe, saloon, wagon, or pickup. The Model T was the first mass-produced, affordable car and brought car ownership to middle-class US families. It was also the first global car: by 1921 it accounted for almost 57 per cent of the world's automobile production and was being assembled in several countries. **PS**

◆ NAVIGATOR

◉ FOCAL POINTS

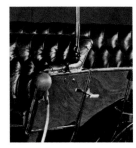

1 BODY PANELS
The Model T made no attempt to present a curved, unified form to the world. Instead the planes of its body panels, its upright, flat windshield, and the straight lines of its radiator cover suggest a car that did not make speed one of its selling points, unlike aerodynamically shaped cars that came after it.

2 STEERING WHEEL
The Model T's simple, open cast-iron steering wheel attached to a column contributes to the lack of integration of the design. However its position on the left of the car helped standardize the practice when the Model T became popular and other manufacturers followed suit.

3 SEATING
The only aspect of luxury and comfort to be found in the Model T is its upholstered leather seating. The lack of luxury is because Ford intended the automobile to be an affordable mode of transport for the mass market rather than a novelty item that only the wealthy could afford.

4 WHEEL SPOKES
The link between the Model T and the rural cart on which it was based is epitomized by its exposed wheel spokes. There were few paved roads in the United States when the Model T was launched; the car's wheels and transverse springs suited muddy conditions and gravel roads.

◷ DESIGNER PROFILE

1863–1912
Henry Ford was born on a farm in Greenfield, Michigan. He went to Detroit to become a machinist's apprentice. He later became an engineer at the Edison Illuminating Company. He built his first car in 1896. He established the Ford Motor Company in 1903; five years later, it produced the Model T.

1913–47
Ford introduced the moving assembly line at Ford Motors' plant in Highland Park, Michigan. He launched the Model A in 1927, and opened the River Rouge Plant in Dearborn, Michigan, in 1928, by which time sales of the Model T were in decline.

▲ The production line at Ford's Highland Park factory in Detroit, Michigan, in *c.* 1914. The innovation reduced the time it took to build a car from 12 hours and 30 minutes to 1 hour and 30 minutes.

SO LONG AS IT'S BLACK

The famous statement made by Henry Ford that people could buy his Model T in any color, "so long as it is black," is only a half truth. It was only after 1914 that black became the dominant color of the cars that came off the Highland Park production line because of its quicker drying time. From 1908 to 1913, the Model T was chiefly available in gray, but red, green, and blue models were also produced. Red was only used for touring cars and gray only for town cars. Even when black became the main color employed, a variety of black paints were utilized depending on the application and drying methods used for the different components of the automobile. When the Model A was launched in 1927, black no longer dominated and the car was available in four colors.

PIONEERS OF MODERNISM

1 Gerrit Rietveld designed Red Blue Chair in 1918. Initial versions were simply stained wood; painted versions were produced from 1923.

2 The German Werkbund invited pioneering designer Peter Behrens to create this poster advertising an exhibition in Cologne, Germany, in 1914.

Although the fully fledged modern movement in design and architecture did not emerge until the 1920s, there were many signs that, prior to that decade, designers and architects were beginning to think along those lines. Indeed what has been called "Proto-modernism" revealed itself in the late 19th century in response to the rampant stylistic eclecticism of those years, and also to concepts relating to the design of the new domestic machines that were beginning to appear in the marketplace. This was combined with a growing dissatisfaction with conspicuous consumption on the part of an international group of progressive architects and designers, and their belief that the rationalism of engineering provided a better basis on which to move forward than the commercial pragmatism of the capitalist marketplace. The group began to search for a new language of design, many of them rejecting the idea of decoration.

KEY EVENTS

1904	1907	1907	1907	1914	1917
Hermann Muthesius publishes *The English House*, a study of British Arts and Crafts architecture, which has an enormous impact in Germany.	The Deutscher Werkbund (German Word Federation) forms in Munich. The group comprises designers, architects, and industrialists.	German electrical equipment maker AEG hires Peter Behrens as a consultant to rebrand the company from its buildings to its products (see p.118).	Mariano Fortuny designs his Fortuny lamp (see p.116), based on a new indirect lighting system for the stage.	The Werkbund mounts its first exhibition in Cologne celebrating German industry, design, and art.	The De Stijl group forms in the Netherlands. It aims to align art, design, and architecture through the creation of a new abstract language.

The roots of modernist thinking lay within the reformist ideas that were expressed in the writings of architect and designer Augustus Pugin (1812–52) and critic John Ruskin (1819–1900), and which re-emerged in the thoughts of designer William Morris (1834–96; see p.52) and others allied to the British Arts and Crafts movement (see p.74). Central to their ideas was a sense of unease with what they felt to be the over-embellished, inauthentic products of the factory. Their influence soon spread across Europe, impacting the work of designers, including Spanish designer Mariano Fortuny (1871–1949). His pleated silk Delphos gown (1907), which hugged the contours of the body and was intended to be worn without undergarments, was a natural development of the movement's drive for dress reform.

These concepts took particular root in Germany, where architect and author Hermann Muthesius (1861–1927) helped establish the Deutscher Werkbund (German Work Federation). The federation was an association of artists, architects, designers, and industrialists, and their aim was to link designers with industry and thereby improve the quality of German goods. Key figures involve in the group included the architects and designers Theodor Fischer (1862–1938), Peter Behrens (1868–1940), Richard Riemerschmid (1868–1957), and Bruno Paul (1874–1968). The group organized an influential exhibition in Cologne in 1914, for which Behrens designed a poster depicting a man holding a torch (see image 2), which is thought to indicate that the group was lighting the way ahead for German product design. Although World War I was to create a hiatus in the development of those ideas, they surfaced again in the 1920s in Germany and elsewhere in Europe.

The work of modernist architects, artists, and designers active in the Netherlands in the years around World War I, and associated with the De Stijl (The Style) movement, were hugely influential. De Stijl was both a group of artists and architects and the name of a journal published by group member Theo van Doesburg (1883–1931). Key members of the group included painters Piet Mondrian (1872–1944) and Bart van der Leck (1876–1958), and architects Gerrit Rietveld (1888–1964) and Robert van't Hoff (1887–1979). The De Stijl designers proposed that function should drive everything, and that the language of art—form, surface, and color—should be used to communicate that. A number of radical designs emerged as a result, especially from Rietveld, including his starkly geometric Red Blue Chair (see image 1). Rietveld started out with the idea of creating a sitting object made up of a series of planes and their intersections. He let the planes overlap with each other to emphasize their intersections, and he used colors—red, blue, yellow, black, and white—to identify the planes. Van Doesburg went on to join the German Bauhaus (see p.126) school in Weimar, taking with him Dutch ideas, which, together with influences from the Russian Contructivist group (see p.120), were seminal to the formulation of modernist architecture and design thinking. **PS**

1918	1920	1922	1924	1927	1934
Gerrit Rietveld designs his Red Blue Chair. It is among the first items of furniture to be designed according to a set of abstract formal principles.	Lilly Reich (1885–194/) becomes the first female director of the Werkbund. Later she works with Ludwig Mies van der Rohe (1886–1969).	Theo van Doesburg joins the Bauhaus. The De Stijl principles of Neo-Plasticism are an important input into the Bauhaus's design esthetic.	The Werkbund stages an exhibition in Berlin. It plays an important role in the spread of modernist design ideas.	The Werkbund creates the Weissenhof Estate in Stuttgart for an exhibition. Leading modernist architects create buildings for the housing estate.	The Werkbund is taken over by new leaders affiliated to the Nazi regime.

Fortuny Lamp 1907
MARIO FORTUNY 1871–1949

⊙ NAVIGATOR

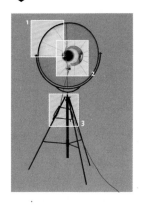

Powder-coated steel frame, cotton shade
Height 75–94½ in./190.5–240 cm
Width 37 in./94 cm
Diameter 32½ in./82.5 cm

Mariano Fortuny was a couturier, architect, inventor, set designer, and lighting technician. Fortuny's versatility as a designer made him one of the most interesting creative minds of his era. His 1907 floor light is based on the principle of his patented cyclorama dome, which made it possible to change stage lighting instantly from bright sky to faint dusk. The original version of the lamp is a black steel frame with a rotating diffuser shade that is black on the outside and white inside. The light is indirect and diffused, and the lamp has a 360-degree swivel-and-tilt capability. The lamp performs effectively, illuminating an area with an emphasis on the quality rather than the quantity of the light created. It is a simple yet strikingly functional artefact that appears timeless, and is an iconic design of the early 20th century. **PS**

⊙ FOCAL POINTS

1 SHADE
Fortuny decided to turn the typical shade of the time upside down when he created his sizable, rotating shade. The absence of color in the original version and the simple circular form of the cotton shade add to the uncompromising focus that is given to its functionality.

2 TILTING MECHANISM
Fortuny gave the shade a tilting mechanism that adds to the light's flexibility. A dimmer switch on a cord was introduced to enhance the variety of lighting effects. The lamp makes its greatest impact in large spaces, where the subtlety of the light it generates is most effective.

3 LEGS
The simple black frame of Fortuny's light takes its visual cue from a camera tripod. In so doing, it aligned itself with a contemporary, high-technology object that had captured the public's imagination. The central leg is adjustable so that the height and position can be changed as needed.

▲ The lamp's design was influenced by experiments being undertaken in the field of indirect lighting for the stage, which made it possible to change the mood of a set very quickly and thereby increase the dramatic effect. This simple, yet hugely flexible, reflector lamp works in the same way.

INTERDISCIPLINARY DESIGNER

Fortuny was one of the first interdisciplinary designers. He trained as a painter and then applied his artistic skills to a range of media, from fashion to architecture, interiors, set design, and lighting. Fortuny was ahead of his time in understanding the way in which design moves across material and spatial boundaries. His work on lighting and set design influenced his work in interiors and architecture, because he was interested in the way in which spaces support the human interactions that occur within them. Dress—whether in the form of stage costume or everyday wear—was a key component of this. Fortuny's Delphos gown (1907), a finely pleated silk dress that adjusts to the body, served as informal tea gown as well as evening wear.

AEG Electric Kettle 1909

PETER BEHRENS 1868–1900

Brass and cane
Height 9¼ in./23.5 cm
Width 8⅛ in./20.5 cm
Depth 6⅛ in./15.5 cm

✿ NAVIGATOR

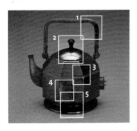

From 1907 to 1914, Peter Behrens worked as a consultant for AEG, designing its corporate identity. The commission came from the company's director, Emil Rathenau (1838–1915), who had been implementing a progressive commercial policy at AEG since the company's formation in 1887. The Behrens project was one of the first instances of a modern company seeking to brand itself in this way. Behrens designed its electrical products, including fans, kettles, lights, and clocks; the cutlery in the staff canteen; and a range of graphic and publicity materials. In so doing, he largely abandoned his previous affiliation with the decorative Jugendstil style and developed a highly functional esthetic that was considered appropriate for the project, and which was being promoted by the German Werkbund to which Behrens was connected. This was a fresh approach to design that deliberately transformed the look of the factory and its contents into a self-conscious esthetic that represented functionality.

Behrens's designs for electrical products combined a level of decoration in those goods destined for a domestic setting (the kettles) with utilitarian simplicity for those intended for an industrial environment (lights, fans, and clocks). Behrens' work for AEG marked him out as a pioneer industrial designer, creating a model that many were to emulate. **PS**

1 HANDLE

All the models had wicker-covered handles, which gave these modern items a traditional appearance. Wicker was chosen to protect the user's hand, but it also gave the kettles a Japanese feel and aligned them with Japoniste objects that became popular in the late 19th century.

2 FINIAL

A black finial of painted wood sits at the top of the domed lid, reinforcing the link between this modern artefact and older, more familiar objects. In the domestic setting, this was a means of ensuring that people felt comfortable using what might otherwise have been a daunting new technology.

3 BEADING

Although they were designed for a progressive manufacturer of domestic goods, the electric kettles were intended for the domestic setting and exhibit decorative features such as the beading around the top of the main body and the detailing where the body meets the two ends of the handle.

4 SURFACE

This is one of a range of electric kettles Behrens designed for AEG, which were available in various models. They were made of nickel-plated and copper-plated brass, and some had hammered surfaces. Although technologically progressive, they recall conventional kettles.

5 STAND

Because the electric kettle does not sit on a hob, it has a stand integrated into the main body that contains the electric element. The electric socket at the kettle's rear, which connects to the plug and the electricity supply, is carefully positioned to avoid a sense of visual imbalance.

▲ The kettle was designed in three styles—octagonal, oval, and round—with different materials and finishes, and with a choice of handle shape to fit in with living rooms and kitchens. The interchangeability helped promote consumer choice.

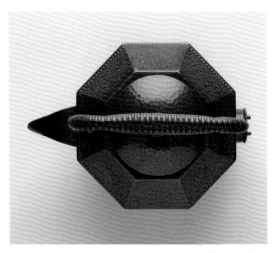

CORPORATE IDENTITY

When Behrens designed the AEG logo, he created a simple, geometric design analogous to a beehive—a hexagon with three smaller hexagons within it, each of which contained one of the letters of the company's name—which was appropriate for the rational image of a powerful industrial manufacturer. He introduced the concept of corporate identity, and even designed AEG's Turbine Factory near Berlin, which made unprecedented use of concrete, glass, and steel, setting the tone for the many other functional modern factories built in the 20th century.

REVOLUTIONARY GRAPHICS

1 Alexander Rodchenko's poster of 1924 has become one of the most memorable and imitated images in Soviet art.

2 The cover of the second edition of the Vorticist literary magazine *Blast* features a woodcut by Wyndham Lewis.

3 Varvara Stepanova's dramatic typographic book cover for *Gornye dorogi* (*Mountain Roads*, 1925).

Following the upheaval of the Russian Revolution in 1917 and the devastation of World War I, reverberations were felt across a wide range of disciplines, design included. Movements such as Constructivism were attempts not so much to formulate responses to these cataclysms, but to help forge a new world order in the wake of them.

The seeds for change were planted before the first shots were fired in either conflict. Conceived as an alternative to Cubism and Futurism, Vorticism caused a brief stir in British artistic and literary circles just as World War I broke out. One of its leading lights was painter and writer Wyndham Lewis (1882–1957); those who signed the movement's manifesto included French artist and sculptor Henri Gaudier-Brzeska (1891–1915) and US poet Ezra Pound (1885–1972), who coined the term "Vorticist." Like Cubism and, to a greater degree, Futurism, Vorticism rejected traditional artistic subject matter—portraits, nudes, landscapes, still life, and so on—in favor of more abstract representations that sought to capture the driving pulse of the emerging machine age. Lewis edited the Vorticist arts magazine *Blast* (see image 2), which appeared in only two numbers between 1914 and 1915 and featured a sans serif typeface and daring departures in typographic style, which proved to be the movement's greatest influence.

KEY EVENTS

1914	1915	1915	1916	1917	1917–22
The first issue of the Vorticist magazine *Blast* is published in July. World War I breaks out in August.	Kazimir Malevich paints *Black Square* and *Black Circle*, expressing the precepts of Suprematism.	The Second Battle of Ypres sees poison gas used for the first time in warfare. The second and last issue of *Blast* is published.	Romanian author and performer Tristan Tzara (1896–1963) founds the Dada art movement. It develops Cubism's collage techniques.	The February and October revolutions lead to the creation of the Soviet Union. The new order adopts Suprematism as its artistic voice.	The Russian Civil War breaks out, erupting immediately after the Russian revolutions. It ends five years later with the Communists in control.

Similarly, in Russia new directions in art and graphics were signalled before the revolution took place. Kazimir Malevich's (1879–1935) *Black Square* (1915)—a black square painted on a white ground—represents a dramatic rupture from previous notions of what art could or should be. Malevich was instrumental in the formation of Suprematism, a movement that exalted pure abstract forms—the supremacy was of geometry over representational imagery. Circles, squares, a limited range of solid colors—elements that readily lent themselves to graphic work. Among the most influential of those who took up these ideas was designer and typographer El Lissitzky (1890–1941), whose experimental and dynamic compositions had a lasting impact on later modernist movements such as the Bauhaus (see p.126). In turn, Suprematism had an abiding influence on the defining artistic movement that emerged after the revolution: Constructivism.

Where Constructivism departed from Suprematism was in its insistence on the roles that art, architecture, and design should play as agents of social change. Such disciplines were no longer to be indulged for their own sake or on behalf of an elite of taste makers, but harnessed to the greater good. In the new Communist era, the Constructivist movement had a profound influence on every sphere of design, from propaganda posters and packaging to book covers, textiles, and theatrical sets. Among the most prolific practitioners of the revolutionary new style was painter and graphic designer Alexander Rodchenko (1891–1956), who later moved into the fields of photomontage and photography. He became associated, along with his wife Varvara Stepanova (1894–1958), with Productivism, which promoted the infiltration of art into the life of the masses via everyday graphic means. Stepanova was dedicated to the use of art to change society; her work encompassed textile design, posters, and book covers (see image 3).

It is difficult to underestimate the impact avant-garde Russian artists and designers such as Lissitzky and Rodchenko have had on successive generations of graphic designers. While initially such ideas spread to modernist circles such as the Bauhaus, with time their impact became more pervasive, part of a contemporary visual language. A case in point is the poster that Rodchenko created for publisher Gosizdat in 1924 (see image 1). The principal image is a photograph of Lilya Brik (1891–1978), who was a muse for the Russian avant-garde. In 1915 Brik openly became the lover of poet Vladimir Mayakovsky (1893–1930) at a time when she was still married to literary critic and publisher Osip Brik (1888–1945); even in the ferment of revolutionary times, their *ménage à trois* was shocking. Brik's beauty and forceful personality inspired many of Rodchenko's works, although it is the Gosizdat poster that has become iconic. From Brik's open mouth issues a diagonal wedge that proclaims: "BOOKS." In 2005 the same graphic style was employed by Franz Ferdinand on the cover of the band's album, *You Could Have It So Much Better*. **EW**

1918	1918	1919	1923	1924	1924
Constructivism starts to elbow aside Suprematism as its supporters work in art establishments and advocate a utilitarian artistic culture.	World War I ends in November with the signing of the Armistice. The Spanish flu pandemic sweeps the world.	El Lissitzky creates his *Beat the Whites with the Red Wedge* poster (see p.122).	Influenced by Lissitzky, German graphic designer Karl Schwitters (1887–1948) publishes the first issue of *Merz* magazine (see p.124).	Alexander Rodchenko creates his iconic poster, featuring a photograph of Lilya Brik, for Gosizdat.	Vladimir Lenin (1870–1914) dies. The rise of Stalinism sees the decline of the Russian avant-garde and Socialist Realism imposed.

Beat the Whites with the Red Wedge 1919

EL LISSITZKY 1890–1941

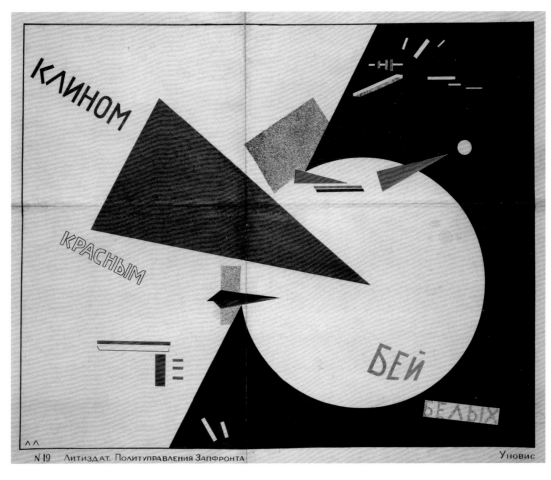

N 19 Литиздат. Политуправления Запфронта   Уновис

Lithograph
18¼ x 21⅞ in.
46 x 55.5 cm

⚙ **NAVIGATOR**

This Soviet propaganda poster was created during the Russian Civil War (1917–22) following the Russian Revolution, and is one of the most influential graphic designs of the 20th century. Its creator, El Lissitzky, was a Russian Jew born in 1890 who became a key figure in the avant-garde and a titan of graphic and exhibition design. The lithograph is one of Lissitzky's early works, produced for the Red Army while he was head of graphics and architecture at the People's Art School in Vitebsk. There, Lissitzky met artist Kazimir Malevich, leading force of Suprematism, which was a movement using a daring visual alphabet of geometric forms and oppositional color to agitate the viewer into political awareness. Lissitzky was influenced by Malevich, but developed his own forms. He was interested in communicating beyond the Soviet horizon to lives that were touched by industrial processes that might affect social change. *Beat the Whites with the Red Wedge* became influential in the West when Lissitzky moved to Berlin to become Russian cultural ambassador to Germany in 1921. He influenced Hungarian painter and photographer László Moholy-Nagy (1895–1946), who led the typography course at the Bauhaus, German typographer Jan Tschichold (1902–74), the Dutch De Stijl group of artists and architects (see p.114), and many others across Europe. The poster is considered the central image of the Russian Civil War in Western publications, although for decades it was almost unknown in Russia. It continues to inspire graphics and political movements internationally. **JW**

👁 FOCAL POINTS

1 STYLIZED OBJECTS

Objects are distilled into an idealized geometric form, alluding to similar shapes on military maps. A red wedge pierces the white circle—a symbol of the Bolsheviks breaching the anti-Communist White Army. A broad base of red support tapers into an efficient tool of war.

2 COLOR

Color is a key tool in Lissitzky's attempt at a new visual paradigm. Here it is reduced to a palette of primary red, black, and white, distilling their psychological effects and placing them in opposition to form. The bold color planes maximize visual focus and accelerate the dynamic effect.

3 WEDGE

The red wedge piercing the white orb references the Jewish proverbial symbol of the mote in the eye, an interesting counterpoint lending additional energy to the image. The title *Beat the Whites with the Red Wedge* is thought to be a play on the anti-Semitic slur. "Beat the Jews!"

4 RED TRIANGLE

There have been various interpretations of the shapes. The small red triangles to either side of the red wedge may represent groups of Red Army soldiers and allies. The circle may be a Suprematist symbol for the unchanging, or conservative. The red dashes may be symbols of change.

5 TEXT

The text on the left side, *klinom krasnim*, means "with [the] red wedge;" the text to the right, *bey belych*, means "beat [the] whites." The paucity of text and use of a well-known color scheme helped to make the poster effective propaganda, universally appealing to a literate and illiterate audience.

▲ From 1919 to 1927, Lissitzky produced a body of work including prints, paintings, drawings, collages, and assemblages that he categorized under the title *Proun*, a Russian acronym for his "Project for the Affirmation of the New." The works concern a new evaluation of spatial dimensions. They go beyond purely pictorial representation to act like technical designs, and their interlocking, simple geometric forms represent three-dimensional space.

🕐 DESIGNER PROFILE

1890–1911

Lazar Markovich Lissitzky was born in a small Jewish community near Smolensk in Russia. Lissitzky renamed himself in a homage to the painter El Greco (1541–1614). He was refused entrance to study art at an academy in St Petersburg because he was Jewish. He left for Darmstadt in Germany to study architectural engineering.

1912–16

He toured Italy and then traveled to France, associating with Russian Jews in Paris. When World War I broke out in 1914 he returned to Russia, where he worked in architectural firms and as an illustrator for Yiddish children's books.

1917–20

The head of the People's Art School in Vitebsk, Jewish artist Marc Chagall (1887–85), invited Lissitzky to teach at the school. With Malevich, he became involved in Suprematism.

1921–24

As cultural ambassador in Germany, Lissitzky promoted Russian-German relations and the avant-garde. In 1923 he wrote his essay, "Topography of Typography" for *Merz* magazine (see p.124) on the relationship of type and content.

1925–41

Returning to the Soviet Union, Lissitzky worked on exhibition design, including for the Soviet contribution to the "Pressa" press industry exhibition in Cologne, Germany, in 1928.

Merz Magazine 1923 – 32
KURT SCHWITTERS 1887–1948

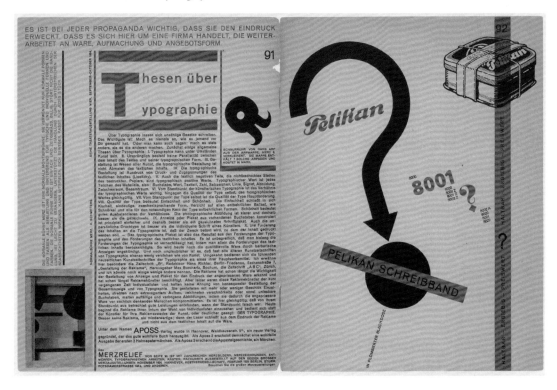

Merz 11 (1924)
Printed paper, wire stitching
11½ x 8⅞ in.
29 x 22.5 cm

Kurt Schwitters created *Merz* magazine from 1923 to 1932 in Hanover, Germany. He had trained in traditional art and architectural drawing, but soon became involved in the anti-rational Expressionist and Dada art movements, and in poetry. The twenty-five issues of *Merz* magazine he designed include three double issues; numbers 10, 22, and 23 were never published. Schwitters produced *Merz* magazine to disseminate his ideas, and its influence continues today in art, typography, and architecture.

In 1918 Galerie Der Sturm, the leading avant-garde gallery in Berlin, included two Schwitters paintings in the summer show. Shortly after, Schwitters began making collage pieces that grew into a lifework, reassembling fragments of timber, wire, and magazine advertisements, old tram tickets, and detritus, including off-cuts from the Molling commercial printworks in Hanover. Schwitters called his process-driven method "Merz": the title comes from the very first collage to which he fixed a paper strip upon which was written *Kommerz und Privatbank*. He observed how the essence of things changes as soon as they are placed out of context and put to different use, and he called this process the "detoxification of material."

In 1919, as the Treaty of Versailles was signed, Der Sturm devoted a solo show to Schwitters' Merz pictures, and published the artist's statement: "In the war, things were in terrible turmoil. . . Everything had broken down and new things had to be made out of the fragments; and this is Merz. It was like a revolution within me. . . ."

Schwitters met the Russian Constructivist typographer El Lissitzky, who became a fundamental influence as he embarked on the publication of *Merz* magazine. Each issue focuses on a central theme, and is a text-based work printed predominantly in black, white, and red, with some covers in Prussian blue. Schwitters compared typography to architecture—and considered them parallel applications of abstract art. *Merz* magazine traveled far beyond Germany to the United States and elsewhere. **JW**

 **NAVIGATOR**

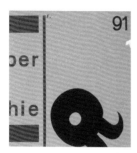

1 BLANK SPACE

Schwitters used printmaking to express concerns central to his artistic project in collage, assemblage. and poetry. He constructed experimental layouts according to Dadaist and Futurist theories. Blank spaces in the page are positive typographical values with dynamic interrelationships.

2 PELIKAN WORDING

Through *Merz* magazine, Schwitters became so expert at typography that the city of Hanover employed him to design municipal print. He also handled advertising for Pelikan inks and Bahlsen biscuits. Sometimes these designs, test prints, and proof sheets appeared in his layouts.

1887–1922

Born in Hanover, Germany, Kurt Schwitters studied art in Hanover and Dresden until 1914. Deeply impressed by Expressionism and Cubism, in 1918 he created the first Dada collages and assemblages, called "Merz," using found printed materials and bits of detritus. In 1919 he published *Anna Blume: Dichtungen* (*Anna Flower: Poetry*), a collection of poems and prose whose influence was felt internationally, and had his first solo show at Galerie Der Sturm in Berlin.

1923–39

Schwitters began to publish *Merz* magazine and to construct large sculptural Merz spaces, or "Merzbau," in his family home in Hanover. He transformed the rooms of his home into works of art, and his assemblages anticipated the emergence of installation art. The Nazis declared his work degenerate; he fled to Oslo in 1937 and embarked on a second Merzbau.

1940–48

Schwitters fled to Britain. After months in an internment camp, he was released following pressure from the Rhode Island School of Design. In 1945 he began a last Merz construction in an old barn in the Lake District, funded by New York's Museum of Modern Art. He died at Kendal in England.

▲ *Merz* magazine was a forum for exchanges between Dadaists, and between Dada and Russian Constructivism. *Merz 8–9* (1924) was a collaboration between Schwitters and El Lissitzky, who typeset it. The magazine also highlighted Russian Constructivists' innovations in architecture and painting, including a photograph of El Lissitzky's *Proun (City)* and the drawing *Monument to the Third International* (1920) by Vladimir Tatlin (1885–1953).

MULTIMEDIA EXPERIMENTATION

Merz magazine disseminated the seeds of change and bridged a gap between the end of Surrealism and the explosion of mid-century US art movements. Schwitters also used *Merz* magazine to promote his abstract sound poetry. In 1932 he published his most famous sound poem, the *Ursonate*, as a twenty-nine page special and final issue of *Merz* magazine.

BAUHAUS

1 Walter Gropius designed the Bauhaus School (1925–26) in Dessau, Germany, with a huge curtain window facade.

2 Benita Koch-Otte and Ernst Gebhardt created the Haus am Horn kitchen (1923) for a show in Weimar, Germany.

3 The cover of the Bauhaus school manifesto features *Cathedral* (1919), a woodcut by Lyonel Feininger, the head of the printmaking workshop.

The Bauhaus was a design school set up in 1919 by the architect Walter Gropius (1833–1969) in Weimar, Germany. It was created through a merger of the Grand Ducal School of Arts and Crafts and the Weimar Academy of Fine Arts. Gropius's vision was to create a school led by architecture that crossed all the art and design disciplines.

The first phase of the Bauhaus was influenced by the artistic movement German Expressionism, which rejected traditional stylistic conventions and subjects in favor of boldly simplified forms and exaggerated colors. The cover for the school's manifesto featured a line woodcut of a cathedral (see image 3), created by artist Lyonel Feininger (1871–1956), and had a strongly Expressionist flavor. Along with Feininger, artists Gerhard Marcks (1889–1981) and Johannes Itten (1888–1967) were among the first staff members to be recruited by Gropius. Artists Oskar Schlemmer (1888–1943), Paul Klee (1879–1940), and Wassily Kandinsky (1866–1944) followed soon after. In 1922 Theo van Doesburg (1883–1931) arrived from the Netherlands, bringing with him experience of the Dutch De Stijl artistic movement (see p.114), which fed into the thinking at the Bauhaus, alongside the ideas of the Russian Constructivists, brought to German soil by graphic designer El Lissitzky (1890–1941; see p.122).

The Bauhaus was an experiment in design education that encouraged its students to work with abstract form applied to a range of materials—wood,

KEY EVENTS

1919	1922	1923	1923	1924	1925
Walter Gropius founds the Bauhaus in Weimar, Germany. It brings together two existing schools in the area.	Theo van Doesburg organizes a course on the Dutch De Stijl movement that inspires and influences Bauhaus students.	Johannes Itten, who led the preliminary course, leaves the Bauhaus because his pedagogical approach is questioned.	The exhibition "Art and Technology – A New Unity" proclaims the Bauhaus philosophy to a general audience.	Local conservative parties call for the Bauhaus in Weimar to be closed down and slash its funding.	The Bauhaus moves from Weimar to Dessau in Germany. Work begins on a new building designed for the school by Gropius.

ceramics, metal, and textiles—to create functional products, from chairs to teapots to lamps to rugs. The preliminary course was, perhaps, the most radical of all the Bauhaus's pedagogical innovations. It had several longer-term influences, including feeding into 20th-century art and design education in the form of foundation courses during which students can work across a range of disciplines. At the outset, the Bauhaus preliminary course had a strongly Expressionist approach. It was led by Itten, who also brought to it ideas deriving from a cult called "Mazdaznan" to which he was affiliated. Students were encouraged to engage with a certain style of dress and adopt a particular diet. This extreme approach soon fell from grace and Itten left in 1922. He was replaced by painter and photographer László Moholy-Nagy (1895–1946), who focused instead on esthetic ideas and theories of form influenced by Constructivism. Students followed a very open curriculum on the preliminary course, engaging with the broad, underlying principles of art and design. Klee and Kandinsky focused on teaching about color and composition.

The first years of the Bauhaus were difficult ones financially, and the local government was not totally supportive of it. An exhibition, themed "Kunst und Technik—eine neue Einheit" (Art and Technology—A New Unity), was held in 1923 to show the local region what was being achieved at the school. Bauhaus students and staff created the Haus am Horn as part of the exhibition. It embraced a number of novel features, including the use of color to denote different interior spaces and built-in furniture. The kitchen (see image 2), designed by Benita Koch-Otte (1892–1976) and Ernst Gebhardt, was especially interesting. It contained a workbench and a stool on which a housewife could perch while she performed her tasks, and eye-level cupboards with doors to prevent any contamination of their contents by dust. One of the kitchen's most memorable features was the inclusion of a set of standardized, labeled ceramic containers, designed by Theodor Bogler (1897–1968), a design solution that still features in many contemporary kitchens.

At the time, Gropius declared his intention to ensure that the skills acquired by students at the Bauhaus could be applied to the world of industry. However, in 1925 the Weimar school closed because of political pressures. The institution relocated to Dessau, to a purpose-built building (see image 1) designed by Gropius, which had impressive workshops and a residential block for the students, with each room featuring a balcony.

After their time on the preliminary course, Bauhaus students went to work in one of the materials workshops, where they were taught craft skills by specialists, and they also continued to learn about form and integrated that knowledge into their materials-focused work. The objects created in the Bauhaus workshops were conceived as prototypes for factory production, although few tentative links with industry were forged. Its most memorable objects went into production after the school was closed by the Nazis in 1933.

1925	1928	1928	1930	1933	1937
Marcel Breuer takes over the running of the carpentry, or furniture, workshop. A Bauhaus graduate himself, Breuer stays there for three years.	Gropius resigns as the director of the Bauhaus. He is replaced by Hannes Meyer. Herbert Bayer, László Moholy-Nagy, and Breuer also leave.	Artist Josef Albers (1888–1976) takes over the leadership of the preliminary course and injects new ideas and energy into it.	Ludwig Mies van der Rohe replaces Meyer as the director of the Bauhaus and two years later the school relocates to Berlin.	The Nazis shut down the Bauhaus. Many of the teachers leave Germany for other European countries and the United States.	Moholy-Nagy establishes the New Bauhaus in Chicago, which revives and develops the teaching approach of the German design school.

The metal workshop was among the most productive of all, and resulted in some of the best-known Bauhaus objects. Lasting iconic pieces include the glass table lamp by Wilhelm Wagenfeld (1900–90; see p.130) and the metal tea infuser by Marianne Brandt (1893–1983; see p.132). These radical reformulations of existing objects were made possible by their designers' deep questioning of the ways in which these objects performed their functions and exploited their materials. They succeeded in creating a radically new esthetic for the modern home and its contents. Importantly, their ultimate aim was not esthetically focused. Rather, they set out to rethink the question of form from scratch, to change behaviors, and to realize a vision of modern living.

Ceramics also played an important role at the Bauhaus. Key teachers included Bogler and Otto Lindig (1895–1966). Lindig's training in sculpture is evident in the simple, clear form of his coffee (see image 6) and tea services, which continue to be popular. The wood workshop had a furniture focus, and Marcel Breuer (1902–81; see p.136) was among the star pupils to emerge from it. Like several of his peers, he went on to become a member of staff at the Bauhaus and to have a huge influence throughout the 20th century. Breuer extended the De Stijl principles, promoted by Gerrit Rietveld (1888–1964), of seeing furniture items as a set of geometric elements that need to be joined in a visibly obvious way. Above all, a new vision of the home was developed at the Bauhaus, which focused on space rather than mass and required domestic objects to blend seamlessly with the architecture that contained them.

There was a strong male bias at the Bauhaus, with the exception of the textiles workshop, which was largely peopled by women, both staff and students. Anni Albers (1899–1994) and Gunta Stölzl (1897–1983; see p.152) were influential figures in that context. Albers's experiments at the Bauhaus, producing wall hangings devoid of representation with straight lines and solid colors (see image 5), reveal the influence of De Stijl. Her use of geometric patterns also highlights the materials, in keeping with Bauhaus principles.

The Bauhaus also influenced modern graphic design and typography. When Moholy-Nagy was appointed in 1923, he introduced to the Bauhaus the principles of what came to be called the "New Typography," an approach to graphic design that had been developed by others, including Lissitzky in Russia. It focused on clarity of communication and prioritized the use of sans serifs and asymmetry. Herbert Bayer (1900–85) led the Bauhaus typography workshop, working there with his Universal typeface. Later, after he set up home in the United States, Bayer became one of the 20th century's most influential graphic designers.

Although students worked hard at the Bauhaus, they also played hard and undertook a great deal of extra-curricular work. The theatrical performances with which they engaged, led by Schlemmer, brought the pedagogical and esthetic ideas together, demonstrating that the Bauhaus was advocating a new way of life. Schlemmer saw the body as an artistic medium and pioneered abstract dance. His *Triadic Ballet* (see image 4) premiered in 1922 and explored the relationship of the body to its surroundings.

Although Gropius had seen architecture as the ultimate medium, it was not taught at the Bauhaus until 1927 when it was introduced by Hannes Meyer (1889–1954), a radical functionalist who rejected the role of esthetics in design and advocated instead an approach entirely based on rational principles. This marked a pendulum swing at the Bauhaus away from the more subjective work of Itten and others, and the primarily esthetically oriented work of the fine artists.

When Gropius resigned in 1928, Meyer took over as head of the school and took it in quite a different direction. He only lasted a couple of years and was replaced by architect Ludwig Mies van der Rohe (1886–1969). In 1932, the Bauhaus came under attack by the National Socialist Party and Mies moved it to Berlin. It lasted there for ten months before it was closed by the Nazis.

Although it only had a life of fourteen years, the Bauhaus completely radicalized art and design education, and it also consolidated a modern design esthetic that was to remain in place for many decades. The idea of combining the principles of abstract art with crafts skills led to a radically new approach toward the material environment.

After 1933, the Bauhaus's legacy continued as its leading protagonists took their ideas elsewhere. Gropius, Breuer, and Moholy-Nagy all settled for a while in Britain in the 1930s, but it was in the United States, to which they, as well as Mies, all subsequently traveled, where their greatest influence was felt, both in design education and in the world of modern architecture. **PS**

4 Bauhaus principles were applied to performance, too. Oskar Schlemmer's costumes for *The Triadic Ballet* (1922) explore the body and movement.

5 Anni Albers's cotton and silk wall hanging (1927) avoids representation and concentrates on elemental forms to exploit the nature of the material.

6 The slightly flared body, rounded shoulder. and base of this earthenware coffee pot (c. 1923) by Otto Lindig hint at his experience as a sculptor.

WG24 Lamp 1923–24
WILHELM WAGENFELD 1900–90   KARL J. JUCKER 1902–97

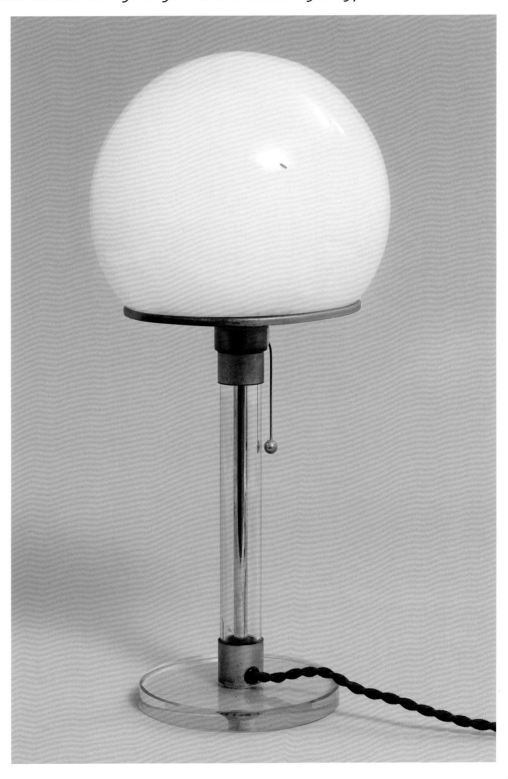

W ilhelm Wagenfeld's elegant little lamp, intended for a side table, is one of the most lasting icons from the Bauhaus. Wagenfeld was a student in the Bauhaus's metal workshop, where he worked under László Moholy-Nagy. The light was created with the help of Karl J. Jucker, because Wagenfeld did not have a formal training in electrics.

The WG24 comprises a small number of components—a glass cupola, a post, a base, and the electrical components—which perform an essential functional role. The lamp's impact derives from the strong visual contrast between the pole and the cupola, and the glass and the metal. True to the Bauhaus principle of reducing objects to their elements and using them to create an abstract form, the lamp is nothing more than the sum of its parts, and its visual simplicity and rationality are part of its appeal. Such are the choice of the materials used—opaque and clear glass and metal—and of the proportions and scale of the object, that it is harmonious esthetically. Following Bauhaus principles, it is the nature of the illumination provided—the object's function—that is most important. The light cast by the lamp is diffused and soft. During the Bauhaus years only fifty of these lamps were produced, as it was such a radical design. However, it has been mass produced since the 1980s and is a familiar sight in contemporary living and working spaces. **PS**

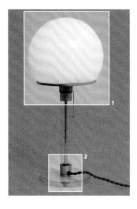

Chromed metal and glass
Diameter 18 x 8 in./
45.5 x 20.5 cm
Diameter at base 5½ in./14 cm

👁 FOCAL POINTS

1 CUPOLA
The cupola is the most striking form in the lamp. Its simple curve suggests a globe although, because of the need to direct light downward, it is not a complete one. The point at which the globe is cut gives the object its balanced appearance and maximizes the illumination.

2 BASE
Consisting entirely of geometric forms, this design is a classic Bauhaus object. The designer has transformed it into a functional artefact that has no extraneous components. The combination of curved surfaces with straight lines lies at the heart of this design.

◀ The little glass teapot that Wagenfeld designed for the Jena glassworks in 1931 is another 20th-century classic design. Like the Bauhaus lamp, it utilizes industrial materials—in this case, glass alone—and has no elements that do not contribute to its primary function of making and serving tea. Attention has been given to the visual harmony of the object and its effective pouring capacity.

Tea Infuser 1924

MARIANNE BRANDT 1893–1983

I n 1924 Marianne Brandt was the first women to join the Bauhaus metal workshop, where she was taught by the Constructivist artist, László Moholy-Nagy. She designed this little tea infuser, Model No. MT 49, as a student the same year. A remarkably mature piece of work, it has become a modern icon, admired for its simplicity and elegance. Her teacher's rigorous approach to form is apparent in the object, which consists of a number of geometrical elements, inspired by the machine esthetic (see p.134), carefully combined into a satisfying whole. Brandt has combined a hemisphere, a circle, and a cylinder to create a form that is highly sculptural and that reflects the design thinking at the Bauhaus. The aim was to create a harmonious form while not forgetting the function of the artefact, which was to infuse and pour tea. There are several elements of the design that reinforce its function, among them its neat built-in strainer, its non-drip spout, the off-center positioning of the lid, and the fact that heat-resistant ebony was selected for the handle. The push-on lid is away from the spout so it does not drip, unlike metal hinged lids. Thus while this jewel-like object is strikingly beautiful it can still produce a good cup of tea. Brandt made several versions—in Tombac brass alloy, silver, nickel silver, and ebony—and each one is slightly different. The materials from which this design was made render it an exclusive object. At the same time, although the tea infuser was handmade in the first instance, and was seen as a prototype, its relationship with the esthetics of machinery is reflected in its form. Brandt succeeded in combining luxury with democracy and esthetics with practicality. She went on to apply her ideas to a number of designs intended for mass production. **PS**

✪ NAVIGATOR

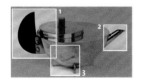

👁 FOCAL POINTS

1 HANDLE
The exclusive materials—brass and ebony—from which the tea infuser is made suggest it is a decorative object to be valued highly. However, its form suggests otherwise: that this is a machine-age design, created for mass production and destined for a wide range of environments.

2 SPOUT
In spite of the dominating sculptural form of this object, its purpose is not neglected. Thought has been given to all its functioning parts, from the non-drip spout to the fact that the ebony handle will not burn its user. Although it is not visible, the built-in strainer also performs its task effectively.

3 BASE
The elements create a harmonious whole. Seen from the side, it sits well on its four-pronged base, while the spout and handle offset each other on each side of the body of the object. The position of the lid and its handle to one side complete the balanced asymmetry of the composition.

Tombac brass alloy, ebony handle, silver-plated interior, with silver strainer
Height 3⅛ in./8 cm
Width 6 in./15 cm
Diameter 4 in./10 cm

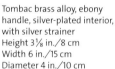

▲ Brandt designed this brass and nickel-plated ashtray with cigarette holder in 1924. As with her tea infuser, she used basic geometric shapes. The ash container is spherical and the cigarette holder is cylindrical. The lid has an off-center opening and the bowl sits on two bars that form the cross-shaped base.

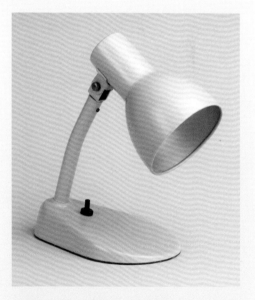

BEDSIDE TABLE LAMP

The little Kandem task light was designed by Brandt in collaboration with fellow Bauhaus student Hin Bredendieck (1904–95) in 1928. First handcrafted in the Bauhaus metal workshop, it went on to be mass produced and became a widely accessible object through the 20th century. Made of lacquered steel, it allows the user to create a spot of light where desired and ably fulfils the Bauhaus dictum of "form follows function."

THE MACHINE ESTHETIC

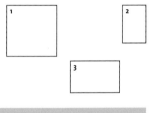

1 The clean lines of Wells Coates's Isokon round table (1933) are typical of the modernist style he advocated.

2 MR10 chairs in the Villa Tugendhat (1929–30), Brno, Czechoslovakia, designed by Ludwig Mies van der Rohe.

3 Oliver Percy Bernard's SP4 (1931) for PEL was upholstered in synthetic plastic with a tubular steel frame.

The sense of rationality that pervaded modernist architecture extended to the way in which the interior was conceived. Decoration and domesticity were rejected; the emphasis was upon space and the rational way of life that went on in it. The separation between inside and outside was minimized, and the idea of open planning, made possible by steel and concrete construction, was encouraged.

In response to the requirements of the modern home, which took the metaphor of the machine, or rather the logic of mechanized production, as its starting point, architects took various approaches to furniture. These included seeing furniture as an extension of the architectural frame. This meant cantilevering tables from walls and depending upon fitted furniture, whether wardrobes or shelving systems. Another approach was to acquire functional, off-the-peg furniture. Modernist architects also designed their own furniture. The favored material was tubular steel, because it was a strong, industrial material that had no domestic connotations and because it could be made into skeletal furniture pieces that did not block the spatial flow.

KEY EVENTS

1923	1925	1925	1925	1927	1927
Le Corbusier publishes *Vers une Architecture*, (*Towards a New Architecture*), the leading polemic of modernist architecture.	In his book *L'Art Décoratif d'aujourd'hui* (*The Decorative Art of Today*), Le Corbusier defines three different furniture types.	Mart Stam begins experimenting with gas pipes. He develops the principle of cantilevering chairs.	Marcel Breuer takes over leadership of the Bauhaus furniture workshop and starts conducting his experiments with bent tubular steel.	The German Werkbund creates the Weissenhof Estate in Stuttgart, Germany, for which most modernist architects create a building.	Ludwig Mies van der Rohe designs his cantilevered tubular steel MR10 chair with the help of German interior designer Lilly Reich (1885–1947).

The most famous items of tubular steel furniture from the 1920s were designed by Dutchman Mart Stam (1899–1986), Le Corbusier (1887–1965), Bauhaus graduate Marcel Breuer (1902–81), and Bauhaus director Ludwig Mies van der Rohe (1886–1969). They created chairs in metal, including Le Corbusier's LC4 chaise longue (1928; see p.140) and Breuer's Wassily chair (1925; see p.136), all of which depended upon the same technique of bending tubular steel. Mies created the most dramatic, the cantilevered MR10 (1927; see image 2), based on ideas developed by Stam. Mies bent the tubular steel while it was cold to retain its elasticity. Irish architect Eileen Gray (1878–1976) designed the furnishings for her house at Roquebrune-Cap-Martin in France, completed in 1929, including the E-1027 (1927; see p.138) tubular steel side table.

By the late 1920s, the idea that a home should feature industrial materials and have an emphasis upon open forms that did not disrupt the possibility of open planning, a sense of space, and visual continuity between inside and outside had become widespread among avant-garde architects in mainland Europe. It had even spread to the United States, especially the West Coast, where the weather permitted outdoor living. Britain was more resistant to the idea of the home emulating the machine. However, there were some exceptions. Architect Wells Coates (1895–1958) adopted the European approach and created furniture for apartment blocks he designed, such as the wood-and-steel Isokon round table (1933; see image 1) for the Isokon building (1934) in London. British company Practical Equipment Limited (PEL) began producing cheap bent tubular steel chairs, including the SP4 (1931; see image 3), designed by architect Oliver Percy Bernard (1931–33), which were destined for the public rather than the private sphere. **PS**

1927	1929	1929	1931	1932	1934
Stam designs his cantilevered tubular steel chair.	Mies designs his Barcelona Pavilion, representing Germany, at the International Exposition in Barcelona, Spain.	Le Corbusier completes the Villa Savoye modernist villa in Poissy, France, which puts his idea of the "house is a machine for living in" into practice.	British company PEL begins producing tubular steel chairs designed by Oliver Percy Bernard.	"The Modern Architecture International Exhibition" opens at the Museum of Modern Art in New York City.	The "Machine Art" exhibition at New York City's Museum of Modern Art shows the close alliance between machines and modernist design.

Wassily Chair 1925

MARCEL BREUER 1902–81

Chrome-plated tubular steel
with leather slings
28⅛ x 30¼ x 27¾ in.
71.5 x 77 x 70.5 cm

⊕ NAVIGATOR

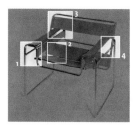

When it was designed in the 1920s, Marcel Breuer's "Wassily" chair was known as the Model B3, but it was later named after his friend and fellow Bauhaus instructor, the Russian painter Wassily Kandinsky (1866–1944). Made of bent tubular steel, it is one of the Bauhaus's most lasting icons. It was made while Breuer was leading the cabinetmaking workshop, and grew out of experiments he undertook there.

In essence, it was a reworking of the traditional leather club armchair. Breuer is said to have been inspired to use bent tubular steel by the curves of his bicycle frame. German steel manufacturer Mannesmann had also developed a process to make seam-free tubular steel, which made production possible. The steel enabled Breuer to develop a skeletal version of a chair without sacrificing any of its comfort. Dependent on steel's inherent strength, the design reduced the traditional chair to its essential lines and planes. Emphasizing structure rather than volume, and using at first canvas and later leather strips as supports for the body, Breuer's radical vision was of a comfortable and visually pleasing object that had significant presence without disturbing the architectural space it occupied. It epitomizes the idea of the machine esthetic, and repudiates the concept of Victorian domesticity. **PS**

◉ FOCAL POINTS

1 METAL
The way in which functionality was defined at the Bauhaus related less to the use of an object than to how the appearance of an object reflected its materials and its manufacturing process. The chair's esthetic is determined by the bent metal and leather or fabric from which it is made.

2 SINGLE COLOR
Many Bauhaus designs relied on neutral colors, particularly black, white, and gray. This emphasized the industrial materials used and the importance of forms and their relationship with space. However, the chromed surface of the tubular steel adds some sensoriality to the chair.

3 CHAIR BACK
In spite of its minimal materiality, such are the strength and the flexibility of the materials used that the chair is comfortable. It holds the body in a relaxed position. This is reinforced by the gentle slopes of the back and seat, and the armrests provide support where needed.

4 FRAME
The Wassily chair is defined by its transparency, which allows the viewer to see right through it. The Wassily chair does not block out any other features of the surrounding space, unlike conventional bulky upholstered chairs and sofas that render the surrounding architectural frame invisible.

▲ Breuer first turned to his bicycle manufacturer, Adler, for help in creating his B3 chair, but the company was uninterested in making furniture. Breuer then went to Mannesmann. He paid a plumber to help him build the first prototypes and then founded a company, Standard-Möbel, to manufacture his tubular steel furniture.

BENT TUBULAR STEEL
Breuer created a number of items from bent tubular steel, including a cantilevered side chair (the B32; 1928), which had a bentwood and cane seat and back. But he was not alone in developing the cantilevered form in tubular steel. Breuer lost the battle for the patent and was unable to claim the design as his own. He ceased designing in tubular steel as a result. However, by the early 1960s the B32 design was once again produced under Breuer's name.

E-1027 Adjustable Table 1927

EILEEN GRAY 1878–1976

Chrome-plated tubular steel,
sheet steel, and glass
Minimum height 21¼ in./54 cm
Maximum height 36½ in./93 cm
Diameter 20 in./51 cm

✦ NAVIGATOR

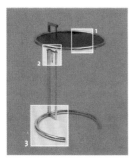

Eileen Gray designed this asymmetrical, height-adjustable, tubular steel side table as part of the bedroom furnishings for her house at Roquebrune-Cap-Martin in France. The house, known as E-1027 (1926–29), was designed for herself and her partner, Romanian architect Jean Badovici (1893–1956). Its coded name commemorates their association: E stands for Eileen and the numbers refer to letters of the alphabet: 10 for J, 2 for B (hence Jean Badovici), and 7 for G (Gray).

Like Le Corbusier in France and Marcel Breuer in Germany, Gray chose tubular steel for her table, although she had fewer ideological reasons for working with it. Inspired by Breuer's work in tubular steel at the Bauhaus, Gray is said to have created the table for one of her sisters so she could eat breakfast in bed. It was also positioned next to chairs in the interior and on the terrace at her house, acting as an occasional side table. Visually striking, it rejected the symmetry of other tubular steel designs. Gray did not use tubular steel often, although steel in other forms features as the structural element in some of her chairs and tables. The close association between form and function that defines the table makes it a supremely modern object. She developed the table for production with British furniture designer Zeev Aram (b.1931) in the 1970s, and they decided to produce the chrome-plated version first. The table is made under license by Aram Designs. **PS**

FOCAL POINTS

1 TABLETOP
Gray experimented with versions of the design of the E-1027 table throughout the 1920s. The frame was made of tubular steel with either a black powder coating or a chrome-plated surface. The tabletop was of clear crystal glass, gray smoked glass, or black lacquered metal.

2 CHAIN
The table was intended as a bedside table, either for people who were ill or bedridden, or simply for someone who wanted to eat or drink while in bed. A mechanism on the table enables its height to be adjusted, to cater for different heights of bed and thicknesses of bed coverings.

3 BASE
The most striking formal feature of the table is its asymmetry. This is also functional, because it enables the table to be positioned right alongside a bed so that the occupant can reach it. The incomplete circle at the base of the table means that it can surround a bed leg.

BONAPARTE CHAIR

In 1935 Gray used tubular steel again, this time for a side chair with black leather or fabric upholstery. Although the chair was in the tradition of Marcel Breuer's famous tubular steel design produced while he was at the Bauhaus, and Le Corbusier's and Ludwig Mies van der Rohe's chairs constructed of the same materials, it is more heavily upholstered than those examples and, as a result, more comfortable. Gray also includes a reference to the work of Breuer and Mies by leaving a gap between the seat and the back, thereby creating a cantilevered structure.

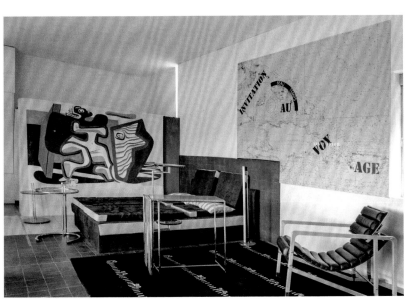

◀ The main living area at E-1027, Gray's house in the south of France. She designed most of the furniture and furnishings at the house in a modern style. Although she was aware of the modernist work of Le Corbusier and others, she chose a slightly softer version of that idiom, introducing texture and embracing the sensuousness of modern materials. She also included abstract patterns on her rugs (see p.154). Her chairs often featured upholstery, with an emphasis on comfort—like the Transat chair (1925–27), with its plump rolls of soft leather suspended from a wooden frame.

LC4 Chaise Longue 1928

LE CORBUSIER 1887–1965

Chrome-plated steel, fabric, and leather
26⅜ x 23 x 62⅜ in.
67 x 58.5 x 158.5 cm

T he LC4 chaise longue was designed by Swiss-French modernist architect, Le Corbusier. He was helped by his cousin, Pierre Jeanneret (1896–1967), and his assistant, French designer Charlotte Perriand (1903–99), who worked with him on the development of most of his furniture designs. Originally, the chaise longue was conceived as a piece of seating for the Villa La Roche, a house built in Paris in 1925. Le Corbusier was particularly inspired by publicity for a contemporary chair, the Surrepos, which was invented for therapeutic purposes by Parisian doctor Jean Pascaud (1903–96). Le Corbusier's dependence upon non-domestic models reinforced his concerns regarding 19th-century bourgeois domesticity, and underpinned his commitment to bring a sense of modernity into his environments. Designed for mass production, the chaise longue went through several evolutionary stages until it reached its final form. A version of it was shown at the "Salon d'Automne" (Autumn Salon) in Paris in 1929 on the designers' stand "Equipement Intérieur d'une Habitation" (Interior Equipment for the Home)—an installation of an apartment with modular furniture.

 NAVIGATOR

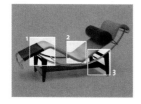

Austrian furniture maker Thonet acquired rights to the design and produced it in limited numbers from 1930. By 1934 licenses were granted to firms in Switzerland and what was Czechoslovakia. In 1959 the production rights were transferred to Swiss gallery owner Heidi Weber, and in 1965 to Italian furniture maker Cassina.

The predominance of industrial materials used in the LC4 chaise longue contribute to the machine esthetic to which Le Corbusier and his collaborators aspired. Its visual, material, and spatial characteristics combine to communicate the core messages of modernism, and it remains one of the iconic objects from the 1920s. **PS**

FOCAL POINTS

1 SILHOUETTE
The chair's silhouette mirrors that of a reclining human body. Perriand undertook studies of figures and, when describing the chair's creation said she thought of "a simple soldier, who, when he is tired lies down on his back, puts his feet up against a tree, with his knapsack under his head."

2 MATTRESS
The LC4 was inspired by the elegant curves of 18th-century daybeds as a machine for relaxing. The designers' contemporary sources included reclining invalid chairs such as those used in tuberculosis sanitoria. It has a self-supporting mattress that is attached directly to the frame.

3 FRAME
Black-painted steel was used for the base and chrome-plated tubular steel for the support frame. Rubber, springs, and screws were used to link the canvas of the first model to the frame, while the footrest and headrest were made of leather. In later versions, the canvas was replaced by black leather.

DESIGNER PROFILE

1887–1916
Le Corbusier was born Charles-Edouard Jeanneret in the Swiss town of La Chaux de Fonds. He was educated at the local art school, where he studied to become an engraver of watch cases but he became interested in architecture. From 1907 to 1911, he traveled extensively in Europe, and from 1910 to 1911 worked in the office of German architect and designer Peter Behrens (1868–1940) near Berlin. In 1912 he set up his own architectural practice in Switzerland.

1917–22
Settling in Paris, he created a new persona as Le Corbusier and took up painting. He also worked as an architect, creating concrete structures for government contracts. In 1920 he helped found the influential journal *L'Esprit Nouveau* (*The New Spirit*), which advocated functionalism. In 1922 he opened an architectural partnership with his cousin, Pierre.

1923–34
Le Corbusier published a collection of essays, *Vers une architecture* (*Towards a New Architecture*, 1927). His writing inspired Perriand to seek work in his studio and they collaborated on interiors, producing tubular steel chairs and the LC4 chaise longue. He designed several residences.

1935–50
He turned from designing modernist villas to urban master plans and in 1935 he published *La Ville Radieuse* (*The Radiant City*). Between 1947 and 1952, he worked on the Unité d'Habitation (Housing Unit) apartment block in Marseille, reinventing his style with *béton brut* (raw concrete).

1951–65
Le Corbusier worked on designing government buildings at Chandigarh, the new capital of the Punjab, India, with British architects Maxwell Fry and Jane Drew (1911–96).

◄ Perriand posed for the publicity shots of the LC4 chaise longue. She is shown with crossed legs wearing a short skirt and a necklace made from industrial ball bearings. She demonstrated how the LC4's inclination can be adjusted incrementally, reaching full recline with the hip and knees bent. The reclining surface is independent of the base and fixed on a pair of bows, so it can be lifted off the base, to suit the user.

LESS IS MORE

The concept of "less is more" is firmly associated with Ludwig Mies van der Rohe (1886–1969), although he did not actually coin the phrase. German architect Peter Behrens (1868–1940) had used it when he employed the young Mies to work with him on the AEG turbine factory in Berlin from 1907 to 1910. Later, Mies recalled hearing the expression: "I heard it in Behrens's office for the first time. I had to make a drawing for a facade for a factory . . . I showed him a bunch of drawings of what could be done and then he said, 'Less is more.' but he meant it in another way than I use it." Mies effectively made the phrase his own as he reduced and distilled his buildings, their components, and furniture designs into simple, integrated forms. Throughout his career, he demonstrated his view that less decoration, properly deployed, makes more impact than an abundance of it. In addition to Behrens, he was inspired by Prussian architect Karl Friedrich Schinkel (1781–1841) and the ideas of Russian Constructivism and Dutch De Stijl. Schinkel focused on clean lines, Constructivists aimed to use architecture to benefit society, and the De Stijl philosophy advocated simplicity, a sentiment that cohered with Mies's use of "less is more." Like several others around him, he sought to create a new design style to exemplify modern times. His focus on minimal components and

KEY EVENTS

1910	1915	1925	1925	1930	1930
Gabrielle "Coco" Chanel (1883–1971) opens her first shop—Chanel Modes—in Paris.	US industrial designer Earl R. Dean (1890–1972) designs the Coca-Cola contour glass bottle.	The "Exposition Internationale des Arts Décoratifs et Industriels Modernes" in Paris inspires a craze for a new design style: Art Deco (see p.156).	Scottish inventor John Logie Baird (1888–1946) transmits the first television image.	Mies van der Rohe becomes the last director of the Bauhaus school, overseeing its move from Dessau to Berlin.	Mies designs furnishings including his Barcelona glass and steel coffee table (see p.148) for the Villa Tugendhat in Brno, Czechoslovakia.

the reduction—or abandonment—of ornament underpinned his design philosophy and led to furniture made of glass, steel, chrome, brick, concrete, and leather with unique structural interpretations.

After the austere war reparations agreed at the Treaty of Versailles in 1919, Germany suffered economically. The Deutscher Werkbund, which had been founded in Munich in 1907, was an organization of artists, designers, and architects that aimed to inspire good design and craftsmanship in architecture and mass-produced goods. It reasserted itself with greater strength after the war with an exhibition in Stuttgart in 1927, organized by Mies, the Werkbund's director. Primarily, it addressed social housing, aiming to minimize waste in both construction and upkeep. The resulting Weissenhof project of twenty-one buildings, constructed by leading architects such as Walter Gropius (1883–1969) and Le Corbusier (1887–1965), were typified by plain, unadorned facades, flat roofs, open-plan interiors, prefabricated elements, and a strong geometric formalism. In the same year, Mies and interior designer Lilly Reich (1885–1947) designed a tubular steel cantilevered chair—the MR 10—which, like the earlier S33 model (see image 2) designed by Mart Stam (1899–1986), eliminated superfluous details. In 1928 they were commissioned as artistic directors of the German section of the Barcelona International Exposition. In addition to the design of several exhibition areas, Mies was also responsible for an official reception building: the German, or Barcelona, Pavilion (see image 1). He devoted as much time to designing the furnishings as to the building itself. With Reich, he designed the Barcelona chair and ottoman (1929). Intended as thrones for the Spanish king and queen during the exhibition's opening ceremony, the chairs are based on the ancient *sella curulis*, a Roman magnate's stool. With smooth, angular forms and clean lines, the classical X-frame is made of chrome-plated, tubular steel, which contrasts with the deep, rectangular, leather-covered cushions forming the seat and backrest.

The simplified, streamlined, stripped-back and functional aspects of Mies's "less is more" approach emerged in the work of other architects and designers, and found expression in all forms of design, including packaging (see p.144), graphic design, and typography (see p.146). Combining purity with the avoidance of fussiness and nostalgia, the concept of "less is more" became a precursor to minimalism (see p.444) and a recurring theme throughout the 20th century. It was echoed in various quarters, for example by US architect, theorist, author, designer, and inventor Richard Buckminster Fuller (1895–1983), who was an early environmental activist and keenly aware of the finite resources of Earth. In 1927 he promoted his principle that we must all find ways of "doing more with less" in order that everyone can share in the planet's resources. Half a century later, in the 1970s, the highly influential industrial designer Dieter Rams (b.1932) explained that his unobtrusive approach followed his belief in "less but better"– or the use of as little design as possible. **SH**

1 The Barcelona Pavilion (1928–29) was designed by Mies to house the industrial exhibits commissioned by the German government.

2 The S33 cantilever chair (1927) by Mart Stam was the result of the designer's experiments with gas pipes in 1925.

1931	1933	1933	1933	1935	1938
The Empire State Building is completed in New York City; it remains the world's tallest building for many years.	The Bauhaus is forced to close by the Nazi Party and Mies emigrates to the United States.	US inventor George Blaisdell (1895–1978) designs the Zippo lighter, inspired by an Austrian cigarette lighter.	Italian designer Alfonso Bialetti (1888–1970) creates the stovetop Moka Express coffee maker.	US architect Frank Lloyd Wright (1867–1959) designs Fallingwater in Pennsylvania. It has a cantilevered structure.	Volkswagen launches the simple, economical, two-door Beetle (see p.210) onto the market.

Chanel No. 5 Perfume Bottle 1921

GABRIELLE "COCO" CHANEL 1883–1971

Chanel's friend Misia Sert described the Chanel No. 5 bottle design as "solemn, ultra-simple, quasi-pharmaceutical."

NAVIGATOR

The No. 5 perfume was French fashion house Chanel's first, and its bottle is a classic of modernist design that has retained its market appeal and relevance. As with much surrounding fashion designer Gabrielle "Coco" Chanel, a supreme self-publicist and brand builder, the facts of the bottle's origins remain elusive. Some authors claim that illustrator Georges Goursat (1863–1934), known as "Sem," who had drawn Coco in Deauville, France, with her lover Arthur "Boy" Capel (1881–1919) in 1913, designed the iconic bottle and packaging. However, it is more likely that Coco chose the elements of the design. The bottle was conceived in tune with the avant-garde of the Jazz Age. Coco worked with perfumer Ernest Beaux (1881–1961), who combined more than eighty synthetic ingredients into an olfactory abstraction in his laboratory. In 1921 he sent Coco samples and she chose the fifth sample, which she launched alongside her collection on 5 May that year. Proudly machine made and mass produced in Normandy by Verrerie Brosse, the bottles are thought to have been inspired by the rectangular beveled flacons of Charvet toilet water that Capel carried in his traveling case. The white packaging was edged with a black stripe reminiscent of funeral stationery, which may reference Capel, who died in 1919. The branding has remained consistent to the 21st century. **JW**

👁 FOCAL POINTS

1 SQUARE BEVELED GLASS
Originally the shoulders were slightly round. Chanel designer Jean Helleu (1938–2007) altered the bottle in 1924, adding a sharp bevel cut to facilitate export to the United States. The bevel cut was inspired by an 18th-century mirror in Coco's apartment.

2 STOPPER
The stopper was originally a flattened square glass plug, small in size and marked with Coco's initial. It was altered by Helleu in 1924, who replaced the plug with an octagonal stopper. He adapted the design slightly every fifteen years to reflect contemporary tastes.

3 SEAL
The Canson paper label looks like fine stationery and over the years has been enlarged in size. The only other adornment is the black seal around the neck. The unpretentious title No. 5 was a bold contrast to fanciful names of competing perfumes in 1921.

4 LABEL
Sans serif fonts were not a widespread fashion in Europe when No. 5 launched. The font was custom made. The plain white label and upper-case black lettering underline the modernist look. The Chanel logo and font were registered at the US patent office in 1924.

▲ French caricaturist Sem paid tribute to Chanel No. 5 in a sketch of 1921 that is known as the first advertisement for the perfume, although it was not a paid promotion. It features Coco Chanel, in a slim-hipped flapper dress with pearls, androgynous and modernist, gazing up adoringly at a bottle of Chanel No. 5.

CHANEL PERFUMES

In 1924 the Société des Parfums Chanel was founded, with Ernest Beaux as director of production and chief perfumer. He created many other perfumes for Chanel, including No. 22 (1922), Gardénia (1925), Bois des Iles (1926), and Cuir de Russie (1927). In 1970, shortly before her death, Coco Chanel launched No. 19, named after the day of her birth. During her lifetime, subsequent Chanel perfume bottles echoed the design of No. 5 with plain white labels, except for Coco, which has a black label framed in gold.

Futura 1927

PAUL RENNER 1878–1956

A map of Berlin, issued by the German tourist board for use at the Olympic Games in 1936, featured the Futura font.

 NAVIGATOR

Futura is one of the most successful typefaces of the 20th century. A geometric sans serif font typeface, it was created by German typographer Paul Renner. Its clean, geometric shapes are synonymous with the principles of Bauhaus design, although Renner was not a Bauhaus member. He first drew the font by hand some time between 1924 and 1926. Subsequently Futura was commissioned and released, promoted as "the type of our time" by the Bauer type foundry in Frankfurt in 1927.

The mid 1920s saw exceptional innovation in German arts, design, and engineering, and the Weimar Republic had more magazines and newspapers than any country in the world. The debate concerning the importance of nostalgic Gothic letterforms versus roman type became a heated political issue. Avant-garde thinkers and artists began using typography as a significant medium within their compositions, and typography took on a new aspect through their work. The leader of the New Typography movement was Jan Tschichold (1902–74). Renner was a friend of Tschichold, an author and a contributor to the debate. He was a member of the Deutscher Werkbund (German Work Federation; see p.114), and became principal of several important schools. Futura remains popular, and Volkswagen and Ikea use Futura exclusively in their advertisements. **JW**

1 CAPITAL LETTERS

Futura was created entirely from geometric forms (almost perfect triangles, circles, and squares). The width of the capital letters changes markedly from character to character. While "O" and "G" are almost perfectly round, letters such as "E," "F,"and"L" are only half a square wide.

2 LOWER-CASE LETTERS

Later, the geometric structure of the upper case was applied to the lower-case letters as well; however, they were not drawn with triangle and compass. Only some early letterforms were truly constructed, for example a, g, m, n, and r, but they were gradually left out of the font.

3 LARGE POINT SIZE

Futura had width strokes of near-even weight and contrast. It was refined by Bauer to work in small point sizes as well as large, and above all to achieve clarity. Several optical corrections had to be applied to Renner's drawings in order to safeguard the impression of mono-linearity.

4 SANS SERIF

Futura appears clean, legible, efficient, and unmannered. In keeping with the philosophical stance of the Bauhaus, Futura was functional, universal, and focused on mass production for a new period in history. The Bauhaus dream was to reunite art and craft to design high-end functional products.

🕐 **DESIGNER PROFILE**

1878–1906

Paul Renner was born in Wernigerode, Germany. He studied architecture and painting in Berlin, Munich, and Karlsruhe, and worked as a painter in Munich.

1907–24

In Munich, Renner became production assistant and designer for Georg Müller (1877–1917), a forward-thinking publisher of plays, fairy tales, and adventure novels. In 1911 Renner co-founded a private school for illustration in Munich.

1925–31

Renner became head of the commercial art and typography department at the Frankfurt Art School. In 1926 he returned to Munich and became director of the Grafische Berufsschulen school for the printing trades. In 1927 he became head of the Meisterschule für Deutschlands Buchdrucker (Master School for German Book Printers) in Munich, inviting Tschichold to join the faculty. Renner created several typefaces, including Futura (1927), Plak (1928) and Futura Black (1929).

1932–56

In 1932 Renner published a booklet *Kulturbolschewismus?* (*Cultural Bolshevism?*), which criticized the Nazi's cultural policy. As the power of the Nazis grew in the same year, Renner was arrested and he was pronounced subversive. Only after Rudolf Hess (1894–1987) pleaded directly with Adolf Hitler (1889–1945) was Renner released. Renner was design director of the German section at the Milan Triennale 1933 and was awarded the Grand Prix. Soon after, he was dismissed as director of the Master School for German Book Printers. To avoid the Nazis taking over the school, Renner struck a deal allowing his friend George Trump (1896–1985) to take his place. Renner devoted the rest of his life to painting.

FUTURA IN SPACE

Renner's aim that Futura be a new and modern typeface was borne out when US film director Stanley Kubrick (1928–1999) used Futura for the titles and credits of his movie *2001: A Space Odyssey* (1968). Futura even became the first typeface on the moon. The commemorative plaque left on the moon by the Apollo 11 astronauts in 1969 is inscribed in Futura, using upper-case letters set in Futura Medium.

Barcelona Table 1930

LUDWIG MIES VAN DER ROHE 1886–1969

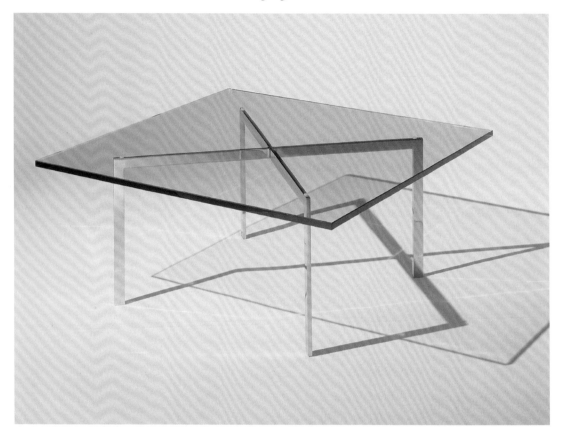

👁 FOCAL POINTS

1 STEEL
The evenness and shiny surfaces of the polished chrome frame and the glass mean the table plays on reflections of light, mirroring and melting into its surroundings. By helping to dematerialize the architectural surface, the table is consistent with the contemporary modernist trend.

2 TABLETOP
The table is one of Mies's most minimal designs. He uses simple contours and modern materials. The tabletop is made of polished, thick, clear glass with a beveled edge. Like the glass, the chrome-plated steel bars used for the table's structural support are overtly industrial in origin.

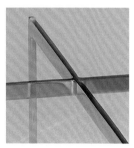

3 X SHAPE
Made from a glass square and an X-shaped steel support, the table's appeal derives from the juxtaposition of its two elements. The visibility of the X-shaped support and the L-shapes of the four chromed bars provides interest in an object that has no surface decoration or ornamentation.

4 GLASS
The transparent nature of the table is in keeping with the design of the open-plan floor of the Villa Tugendhat. There the table sat alongside a large expanse of plate-glass windows, panels of which opened via an electric rolling mechanism, helping the space to merge with the landscape.

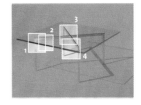
A long with a leather-upholstered daybed, Ludwig Mies van der Rohe's glass and steel coffee table is marketed by US furniture company Knoll as one of a number of pieces of furniture that he designed for the Barcelona Pavilion he created as the German national pavilion for the International Exposition in Barcelona in 1929, where he presented his concept of flowing or unrestricted space. However, the only designs by Mies to feature at the show were a leather-upholstered chair, later known as the "Barcelona chair," and an ottoman.

A number of items of furniture were designed in Mies's Berlin office in the late 1920s, two for the Barcelona Pavilion and the rest for the Villa Tugendhat in Brno, in what is now the Czech Republic, a commission from the Tugendhat family. Mies's assistant, Lilly Reich, played an important design role in them all. The Barcelona chair was used in the villa, as were some other pieces, subsequently known as the "Tugendhat" designs. The coffee table featured in the open-plan sitting area of the villa—along with a range of Barcelona and Tugendhat chairs, and an ottoman—so it is also known as the "Tugendhat coffee table" or "X table." The square table comes with a frame of polished stainless steel or polished chrome, and is so minimal in its design as to be almost self-effacing: restrained and transparent, it is practically invisible. **PS**

Stainless steel and plate glass
18 x 40 x 40 in.
45.5 x 101.5 x 101.5 cm

◄ The second storey of the Villa Tugendhat houses the main living area that contained the original Barcelona table. This was an innovative space when it was designed, inviting its inhabitants to live a modern lifestyle in unrestricted space. The positioning of the furniture suggested different ways of using the space and moving around within it.

OPEN-PLAN LIVING

The Villa Tugendhat (1929–30) in Brno, Czechoslovakia, was among the first modernist buildings to include an open-plan floor. The three-storey building is situated on a hillside. The top floor at street level is laid out as separate bedrooms. However, the middle floor is open plan with a half-circular wall of ebony wood and a free-standing wall of onyx; a garden is visible through large plate-glass windows. Industrial materials including steel and glass were heavily utilized in the villa's construction, as well as luxurious materials, such as Italian white travertine marble. Velvet, Shantung silk, and other fabrics were employed to screen the windows and partition space.

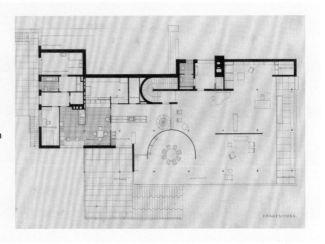

MODERNIST TEXTILES

The emergence of modernism during the 1920s triggered an exciting period of cross-fertilization between art and design. Modernist designers embraced abstraction and experimented with revolutionary new artistic idioms, such as Cubism, Futurism, and Expressionism. Painters, designers, and craftspeople all enthusiastically engaged with textiles, which became one of the most dynamic and progressive areas of the applied arts.

In Britain the Omega Workshops, an artist-led collective spearheaded by painter Roger Fry (1866–1934) from 1913 to 1919, paved the way for future initiatives. In addition to furniture and ceramics, the Bloomsbury-based group designed furnishing fabrics with colorful, energetic, painterly patterns, which were block printed in France. Eschewing conventions, the raw-edged designs appeared deliberately unfinished. Patterns such as Maud (see image 2) by painter Vanessa Bell (1879–1961), with its overlapping squares and triangles, echo the explosive forms of Fauvism. Another modernist pioneer was Sonia Delaunay (1885–1979), a Ukrainian-born painter based in Paris. Delaunay's textile designs, derived from her vibrant paintings, encapsulated the vitality of modern life (see image 1). She began experimenting with block printing in 1923, creating bold, brightly colored dress fabrics with geometric patterns. Showcased to dramatic effect in the custom-designed garments in her

(see p.102)

KEY EVENTS

1910	1911	1913	1919	1923	1923
Wiener Werkstätte (Vienna Workshops; see p.102) sets up a textile and fashion department, creating block-printed fabrics in proto-modernist idioms.	Paul Poiret (1879–1944) opens Atelier Martine in Paris, employing untrained young women to create authentically Primitive textile designs.	Omega Workshops in London produces a collection of artist-designed block-printed fabrics in modern styles.	The Bauhaus is founded at Weimar in Germany, where Gunta Stölzl and Anni Albers produce groundbreaking handwoven textiles.	Sonia Delaunay develops her *tissus simultanés*, abstract-patterned printed textiles fusing art and fashion.	Liubov Popova (1889–1924) and Varvara Stepanova (1894–1958) design abstract-patterned printed fabrics for workers' clothing.

Boutique Simultané, Delaunay's textiles were a highlight of the "Exposition des Arts Décoratifs et Industriels Modernes" (International Exposition of Modern Industrial and Decorative Arts) in Paris in 1925. Also based in Paris was Irish furniture and textile designer Eileen Gray (1878–1976). Initially working in an Art Deco (see p.156) style, Gray produced lacquerwork notable for its figurative imagery and Cubist-inspired geometric designs, as well as rugs (see p.154) and furniture. After she embraced the modern movement, Gray collaborated with her partner, Romanian architect Jean Badovici (1893–1956), on their house E-1027 (1926–29) at Roquebrune in the south of France, for which she created modernist furnishings (see p.138).

In Britain there was a surge of interest in block-printed textiles during the 1920s, and the medium was well suited to small-scale, artist-led workshop production. Phyllis Barron (1890–1964) and Dorothy Larcher (1884–1952), leading lights of the movement, had trained as painters but joined forces to run a block-printing workshop in 1923 after becoming enthralled by textiles. Experimenting with the mellow tones of vegetable dyes, they created simple, energetic designs with the rhythmic spontaneity of ethnographic textiles. However, modernist textiles took a different course in Germany following the establishment of the Bauhaus (see p.126) art school in 1919. There the emphasis was on weaving, rather than printing. The textile hangings of Gunta Stölzl (1897–1983; see p.152) and Anni Albers (1899–1994), the two most influential weavers at the Bauhaus, explored the technique to the full.

The advent of screen printing, which was enthusiastically adopted in the British textile industry from 1930, fostered the dissemination of modernism. Because it was so much more flexible than roller printing, it encouraged manufacturers to produce short runs of more adventurous designs. The positive creative climate in Britain at this time, which encouraged artists to cross over freely into textiles, was another reason why modernist textiles flourished there. US-born Marion Dorn (1896–1964), who was based in London during the 1930s, was the most high-profile freelance designer of the decade. Equally adept at printed and woven fabrics, she collaborated with many leading textile firms. Originally trained as a painter, Dorn was celebrated as "the architect of floors," creating bespoke carpets with subtle textures and calligraphic motifs for modernist ocean liners and luxury hotels. One of her most sympathetic clients was Edinburgh Weavers. Under the inspiring leadership of Alastair Morton (1910–63), Edinburgh Weavers commissioned influential artists such as Ben Nicholson (1894–1982) and Barbara Hepworth (1903–75) to create a groundbreaking collection of Constructivist fabrics that were at the cutting edge of the modern movement. Produced in the form of large-scale jacquard weaves and hand screen-printed furnishing fabrics, these ambitious designs translated the esthetics of Constructivist painting and sculpture into textiles with pure, abstract patterns in subtle colors. **LJ**

1 The silk *tissu simultané* No. 46 (1924) by Sonia Delaunay features a bold geometric print but retains a hand-drawn painterly aspect.

2 A printed linen furnishing fabric, the Maud pattern was designed by Vanessa Bell in 1913 and was available in four colorways.

1923	1923	1925	1931	1934	1937
Munich-based Deutsche Werkstätten establishes a textile division producing geometricized florals by Josef Hillerbrand (1892–1981).	Phyllis Barron and Dorothy Larcher establish a workshop producing hand block-printed textiles, first in London and later in Gloucestershire.	The "Exposition Internationale des Arts Décoratifs et Industriels Modernes" in Paris features Art Deco and modernist textiles.	English artist Allan Walton (1892–1948) sets up Allan Walton Textiles, making artist-designed, screen-printed furnishing fabrics.	Marion Dorn founds her own firm, Marion Dorn Limited, in London. She designs rugs and carpets for prestigious hotels and ocean liners.	Edinburgh Weavers launches Constructivist Fabrics, featuring artist-designed furnishing fabrics by Ben Nicholson and Barbara Hepworth.

Wall Hanging 1926 – 27
GUNTA STÖLZL 1897–1983

👁 FOCAL POINTS

1 RED STRIPE
This textile is woven from three colors of yarn: red, yellow, and blue. The warp is red but the weft changes color at intervals, creating horizontal bands. The red stripe near the center indicates a section where the warp and weft are the same color, producing a band of solid monochrome.

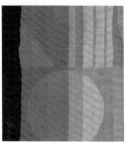

2 CIRCLES
Influenced by the theories of her Bauhaus tutor Johannes Itten, Stölzl created this design from a limited vocabulary of pure geometric shapes. In addition to circles, squares, and rectangles, the pattern includes triangles, stripes, and hemispheres arranged in a lively composition.

3 BANDS OF PATTERN
Made from a combination of silk and cotton yarns, Stölzl handwove this colorful hanging on a small-scale, jacquard loom. Without such a loom, only simple repeats can be produced, whereas this abstract design is complex and each band of pattern is very different.

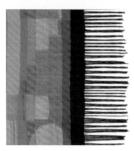

4 FRINGE
The red warp threads running lengthwise through the cloth are tied off at either end to form a fringe that highlights the verticality of the design and counterbalances the bands of horizontal pattern. The fringe reinforces the fact that the object is not a painting, but a piece of woven cloth.

Jacquard-woven silk and cotton
51⅛ x 28⅛ in.
130 x 73.5 cm

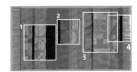

The key principles behind the textiles created at the Bauhaus were that woven patterns should be abstract rather than figurative, and that they should reinforce the structure of the weave. This is why the woven hangings and rugs created by German textile artist Gunta Stölzl and her associates, such as Anni Albers, in the weaving workshop at the Bauhaus are so emphatically geometrical: they consciously highlight the interplay of vertical warp threads and horizontal wefts underlying the construction of the cloth.

One of the Bauhaus's aims was to foster creative exchange between fine and applied arts. Stölzl was influenced by Swiss Expressionist painter Johannes Itten (1888–1967), who taught art theory to students in the weaving workshop up to 1921. Swiss artist Paul Klee (1879–1940), who joined the Bauhaus that year and taught there until 1931, also exerted a potent influence on textile students. Itten's theories about primary colors and elementary forms are encapsulated in this hanging, with its geometric vocabulary of circles, checkerboards, and stripes. By the time Stölzl created this piece, however, the Bauhaus had begun to change direction. After the school moved from Weimar to Dessau in 1925, the emphasis shifted from individualistic craft production to design for industrial mass production. Although color remained a key feature of the upholstery fabrics later developed at the Bauhaus, texture and weave structure assumed greater significance than pattern. Stölzl always remained committed to handweaving, yet it is her more expressive early textiles, such as this wall hanging, that have proved the most enduringly popular and influential. **LJ**

ANNI ALBERS

Alongside Stölzl, the other major figure to emerge from the Bauhaus's weaving workshop was Anni Albers, who enrolled in 1922. She continued her studies after her marriage to artist and fellow Bauhaus member Josef Albers (1888–1976), and completed her diploma in 1929. In addition to her husband, the artist who had the greatest impact on her development was Paul Klee. Anni took his class for weaving students, where she learned the importance of rhythm and movement, and the interaction between colors. Klee drew parallels between weaving and music, a concept graphically illustrated by Anni's woven hangings and rugs. Often she began her weaving projects with sketches, such as this *Design for Smyrna Rug* (1925; right). In spite of confining herself largely to patterns composed of stripes, she achieved variety and dynamism through strategic shifts in color and depth. By mastering complex techniques, such as triple weave, she was able to create textiles that were multilayered. With their visual ingenuity and architectural rigor, Anni's designs epitomize the ideals of the modern movement in its purest form.

Blue Marine Rug 1926–29

EILEEN GRAY 1878–1976

👁 FOCAL POINTS

1 ABSTRACTION
Gray trained as a painter, and this carpet design displays an artist's eye for color and pattern. Here, she exploits the classic modernist vocabulary of abstract forms, using circles, ovals, and stripes, contrasting flat planes of color with dynamic linear motifs.

2 BLUE
During the 1920s and 1930s, Gray spent time in the south of France, where she designed and furnished two houses. Her design contains marine colors. The vivid blue evokes the intense hue of the Mediterranean Sea, contrasting with black, white, and pale blue elsewhere.

3 ASYMMETRY
Traditionally carpets had been symmetrical, but Gray abandons convention in favor of abstract motifs. Although the composition is asymmetrical, she creates a sense of balance through the contrast between light and dark tones and the interplay between shapes.

4 WAVY LINES
Nautical themes are suggested by several motifs. Undulating lines recall lapping waves, while the large black circle conjures up the steering wheel of a boat. This playful imagery injects a hint of jauntiness into an otherwise serious abstract design.

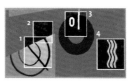

Hand-knotted pure new wool
43 x 85 in.
110 × 215 cm

Eileen Gray became interested in carpets after a trip to Morocco, where she and her friend Evelyn Wyld (1882–1973) learned the basics of dyeing and weaving wool. Wyld later became an accomplished weaver, and oversaw the production of Gray's carpets in their Paris workshop, established in 1910. Gray was very particular about her how designs were translated and wrote detailed annotations on her artwork, which was usually painted in gouache, sometimes with collaged elements in cut paper, cardboard, or fabric. Wyld continued to produce some of Gray's designs after their partnership ceased, although not the Blue Marine rug, which was created after they went their separate ways. Also known as Marine d'Abord, this carpet was one of several created for E-1027 (see p.138), the modernist house designed by Gray and her partner, Jean Badovici, at Roquebrune-Cap-Martin in the south of France in the late 1920s. By then Gray had been practicing successfully for many years as an interior decorator, creating luxurious Art Deco interiors furnished with her own lacquered furniture and carpets. E-1027 was significant because it was the first time she had ventured into full-blown architecture. The code E-1027 was imbued with personal symbolism: E stands for Eileen and the numbers refer to letters of the alphabet: 10 for J, 2 for B (hence Jean Badovici), and 7 for G (Gray). The number 10 is subtly incorporated into the design of this carpet, which was created specifically for the terrace of E-1027.

This carpet reveals Gray at the height of her powers, making a conscious shift from deluxe modernistic Art Deco to more rigorous, minimalist modernist design. Her palette echoes that of Henri Matisse (1869–1964), another artist mesmerized by the south of France. With its striking abstract composition and vivid coloring, Blue Marine is as potent as a painting, a work of art for the floor that equally could be hung on the wall. **LJ**

⏱ DESIGNER PROFILE

1878–1906
Born in Ireland, Eileen Gray studied at the Slade School of Art, London. In 1900 she visited the Exposition Universelle in Paris.

1907–25
Gray settled in Paris. She studied lacquerwork with Japanese craftsman Seizo Sugawara (d.1937), and in 1910 established a workshop producing carpets, furniture, and lacquerware. She exhibited at the Société des Artiste Décorateurs (Society of Decorative Artists) from 1913. In 1922 she opened the Galerie Jean Désert shop to sell her rugs, furniture and lighting.

1926–39
After working with Badovici on E-1027, Gray designed her own house at Castellar (1932–34). She developed innovative modern furniture to complement the interiors. Her work featured at the Paris International Exposition of 1937.

1940–76
Having lost all her possessions during World War II, Gray led a reclusive existence in Paris and her work was largely forgotten. Her achievements were recognized posthumously.

▲ Gray also incorporates the number 10 in this rug design, alluding to the letter J for her partner. Other numbers appear also, along with short parallel lines that evoke the markings on a ruler.

ART DECO

1 This pair of Ducharne armchairs (1926)
by Emile-Jacques Ruhlmann epitomizes
the glamor of the Art Deco style.

2 This poster advertising the Holland
America cruise line (c. 1932) echoes
the visual language of Cubism.

3 The Chrysler building in New York City,
designed by architect William Van
Alen, was the tallest building in the
world when it was completed in 1930.

The first use of the term "Art Deco" is sometimes attributed to architect Le Corbusier (1887–1965), who wrote a series of articles in his journal *L'Esprit nouveau* under the headline "1925 Expo: Arts Déco." He was referring to the Exposition Internationale des Arts Décoratifs et Industriels Modernes (International Exposition of Modern Decorative and Industrial Arts) held in Paris. However, the term did not come into general use until 1966, when an exhibition titled "Les Années '25' Art Déco/Bauhaus/Stijl/Esprit Nouveau" was mounted in France. It compared the French decorative arts of the 1920s with other similar contemporary styles, such as Bauhaus (see p.126) and De Stijl (see p.114). Two years later, British design historian Bevis Hillier (b.1940) published *Art Deco of the 20s and 30s*, which defined Art Deco as "an assertively modern style, developing in the 1920s and reaching its high point in the 1930s . . . a classical style that . . . ran to symmetry rather than asymmetry, and to the rectilinear rather than the curvilinear."

Art Deco flourished between the two world wars and throughout the Roaring Twenties and subsequent Great Depression, affecting all forms of design, from the fine and decorative arts to fashion, photography, product design, and architecture. Exuding glamor (see image 1), the style contrasted with the depressed economic conditions and sense of anxiety that arose as another war became inevitable. Whereas the simultaneous modernist movement celebrated functionalism and pared-down design, Art Deco focused

KEY EVENTS

1917	1919	1920	1923	1923	1924
De Stijl is first formed as a magazine by a group of artists, including Theo van Doesburg (1883–1931) and Piet Mondrian (1872–1944).	Combining fine art and design, the innovative Bauhaus school opens in Weimar, Germany. It is the brainchild of Walter Gropius (1883–1969).	The Harlem Renaissance begins; it is a cultural, social, and artistic movement based in New York City.	László Moholy-Nagy (1895–1946) takes over the metal workshops at the Bauhaus and encourages students to design using a simple, austere focus.	Industrial designer Willem Wagenfeld (1900–90) designs his chrome and glass hemispherical MT 8 table lamp.	Ceramic artist Clarice Cliff (1899–1972) begins work on her Art Deco-inspired Fantasque range of ceramics (see p.160).

on the exuberance and excitement of the flapper era, Hollywood glamor, and the optimism of the Harlem Renaissance that exploded after World War I.

At the end of World War I, there had been a general determination that the world should never go to war again, along with a belief that it was possible to construct a new and improved environment through design. Despite the many negative political and economical undercurrents, the period was also a time of optimism: women received the vote in many countries; mass production made a number of domestic appliances affordable, such as telephones and electric irons; wealthier members of the population were buying cars and taking holidays on cruise ships; and trains, ships, and skyscrapers across the world exemplified the widespread sense of progress. In response Art Deco emerged as an eclectic style, drawing on both tradition and the mechanized modern world. Like Art Nouveau (see p.92), it embraced both handcraft and machine production, and the ideas spread quickly.

Although Art Deco had become an international phenomenon by the 1930s, its place of origin was Paris. There, in the 1910s and 1920s, architects and designers worked with specialist makers to create opulent designs for furniture, glassware, metalwork, lighting, textiles, and wallpapers. From 1910 to 1913, architect Auguste Perret (1874–1954) designed the Théâtre des Champs-Élysées in Paris. With its straight lines, geometric forms, and bas-reliefs, the facade is one of the earliest examples of Art Deco. However, the movement did not reach a mass audience until 1925 and the Exposition Internationale des Arts Décoratifs et Industriels Modernes in Paris, which was attended by more than sixteen million visitors. There, Art Deco interiors were displayed in juxtaposition with more avant-garde modernist schemes, and the two most influential displays were the interiors for the Pavillon du Collectionneur. designed by Emile-Jacques Ruhlmann (1879–1933) and built by Pierre Patout (1879–1965), and the Pavillon de l'Esprit Nouveau, designed by Le Corbusier.

Before the Wall Street Crash of 1929, many people around the world could afford to buy luxurious and costly items for their homes, and Art Deco became popular for its diverse range of historic sources, from African tribal art to the arts of pre-Columbian Meso-America and those of ancient Egypt. The style was also influenced by contemporary artistic developments such as Cubism (see image 2) and Futurism, the rich colors and exotic themes of the Ballets Russes, and the shiny, streamlined components of machines. The spread of Art Deco ideas was rapid and far reaching. Its influence emerged in designs of transport, public and private buildings, interiors, household goods, typography, jewelry and fashion. In the United States, the smoothly contoured forms were perceived as less extravagant than more recent styles, and many mass-production processes were relatively inexpensive, which complemented attitudes during the Depression. The style was particularly prominent in newly constructed buildings across New York City (see image 3). **SH**

Skyscraper Furniture 1926
PAUL T. FRANKL 1886–1958

FOCAL POINTS

1 SHELF
With their boxy lower parts and tall upper sections, Frankl's Skyscraper furniture displays the strength of his architectural skills. He counterbalanced elongated vertical lines with stabilizing, horizontal planes, as well as delineating surfaces and edges with contrasting colors.

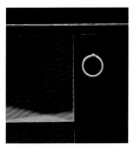

2 HANDLE
As it became more popular, Frankl's Skyscraper furniture became more refined looking and elegant, as with this bookcase from c. 1928. He added decorative additions, such as silver leaf detailing and polished handles, that created an antithesis to the chunky forms of the furniture itself.

After training as an architect in Berlin, Austrian-born Paul T. Frankl moved to the United States in the 1920s. Enchanted by the optimism he experienced in New York City, he settled there and soon after built himself a bookcase based on the staggered Manhattan skyline he could see outside his window. When his neighbors admired the bookcase, he designed similar items of furniture for them, following the shapes and forms of the city skyscrapers. His ideas conveyed the sense of freedom felt by many during the period between the two world wars and before the Great Depression. By the 1920s the skyscraper had become a symbol of US modernity, independence, and power; nowhere else in the world had furniture that mirrored the urban landscape. Calling it simply "Skyscraper furniture," he sold it in Frankl Galleries, his newly opened interior design showroom on East 48th Street. His Art Deco and modernist-inspired designs reflected the common feelings of wanting to discard the past, of confidence in the present and hope for the future. Frankl's range of stacked structures, including bookcases, desks, cupboards, closets, and other pieces, were immediately popular with the public, even though a little costly for most pockets.

In dispensing with retrospective design styles in this playful, stylish way, Frankl helped to make Art Deco and modernism accepted—and even mainstream—in many parts of the United States. Yet his success did not last long. Although the clean, pure lines of his Skyscraper furniture became fashionable, they were easy to copy. By 1927 several other furniture manufacturers were emulating his designs, and some even managed to mass produce them, making them more affordable. **SH**

Lacquered wood
Height 95 in./242 cm
Width 43 in./109 cm
Depth 13 in./33 cm

⏱ DESIGNER PROFILE

1886–1911

Paul Theodore Frankl was born in Vienna. He studied architecture at the Vienna Technische Hochschule (Institute of Technology) and then the Berlin Institute of Technology.

1912–25

Before settling in New York City, Frankl traveled around the United States and Japan. During World War I, Frankl returned to Europe. In 1920 he returned to the United States.

1926–58

Frankl's Skyscraper furniture had instant appeal, and was featured in many newspapers and magazines. Frankl opened a shop in Beverly Hills, California, that was patronized by Hollywood celebrities. He introduced biomorphic shapes into his furniture, and employed rattan as a material for furniture. Frankl wrote several books and articles about the modern style, and after he moved to Los Angeles in 1934, he also taught at universities.

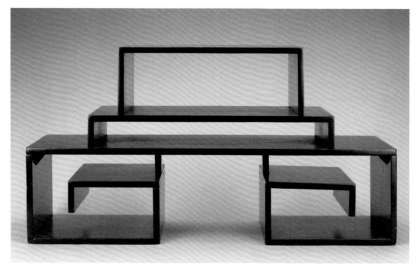

◀ In his lecture "The Skyscraper in Decoration" at the 1927 Art in Trade exhibition at Macy's department store in New York City to promote modern design, Frankl explained his theories, especially his belief that geometry is the key to good design. Frankl asserted that straight lines and sharp angles were modern, while curves could be used to create highlights. His modern esthetic is evident in pieces like this pine and lacquer coffee table of 1929. He also wrote about it in his books, including *New Dimensions: the Decorative Arts of Today in Words and Pictures* of 1928, and *Form and Reform: A Practical Handbook of Modern Interiors* of 1930.

Fantasque Ceramics 1928–34

CLARICE CLIFF 1899–1972

👁 FOCAL POINTS

1 CUP
This tea set is handpainted in the Gibraltar pattern. It depicts a seascape of the Rock of Gibraltar in pastel colors, with yachts on a blue sea and sailing boats. Banding in blue, lilac, pink, and yellow frames the pattern. It embodies Cliff's bold design and semi-abstraction.

2 TEAPOT
This Stamford teaware shape, with flat-sided teapot and solid-handled cups, is characteristic of Cliff. Its curves and angles capture the Art Deco style, and the teapot's flat sides provide an ideal surface for painting and displaying the range of Cliff patterns.

🕐 DESIGNER PROFILE

1899–1926
Clarice Cliff was born in Tunstall, Staffordshire, England. At thirteen, she became an apprentice enameler. At seventeen, she joined A.J. Wilkinson's Royal Staffordshire Pottery at Burslem in Stoke-on-Trent. From 1924 to 1925 she attended classes at Burslem School of Art and her talents attracted the attention of her boss, Arthur "Colley" Shorter (1882–1964).

1927–28
Shorter sent Cliff to the Royal College of Art in London for two brief periods of study. She returned to Wilkinson's where she was given a studio in the Newport Pottery. There she decorated traditional white-ware in freehand designs, using bright enamel colors. She called this her "Bizarre" range.

1929–72
Between 1929 and 1935, Cliff issued numerous shape ranges, including Conical and Trieste. In 1930 she was made art director of Newport Pottery. By 1932, her popular Appliqué range had fourteen patterns, and despite the economic recession, sold well. In 1940, after Shorter was widowed, Cliff and he married. After his death, she sold the factory to Midwinter Pottery and retired.

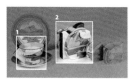

Painted polychrome majolica Gibraltar pattern tea set from the Bizarre Fantasque service (1932) made by Wilkinson, Newport Pottery.

From early in her career, Clarice Cliff created bold, distinctive ceramics in an original, vibrant style. Working at Newport Pottery in Staffordshire, England, a branch of Wilkinson's Pottery, she used brilliant enamel colous on plain white ceramic bisque—or pottery that has been fired once but not glazed—often called "biscuit" or "blanks." Her designs were brighter than most, and she became recognized for her palette of reds, oranges, yellows, blues. and greens. In 1927 she named her first range Bizarre, painting the designs on the available traditionally shaped ceramics produced at the pottery. However, once this stock was depleted, she began designing shapes for her wares that harmonized with her Art Deco-inspired patterns, such as square or hexagonal plates, conical coffee pots and sugar shakers, and cups and teapots with triangular handles. She painted her patterns by hand, and from 1929, supervised a team of mainly young women to keep up with demand. She followed Bizarre with further exotic-sounding ranges, such as Black Luxor, Fantasque, and Ravel, and every style was immediately successful. She developed her Fantasque range between 1928 and 1934, primarily for tax purposes because Bizarre had made such huge profits, so it was sold as Wilkinson rather than Newport Pottery. Fantasque originally included eight patterns, including Umbrellas and Rain, Broth, and Fruit. As it evolved, it featured abstracts, landscapes of cottages and trees. and Art Deco-inspired patterns. The first Fantasque landscape was Trees and House, which sold well, but the slightly later, more sophisticated Autumn pattern, issued near the end of 1930, became the most popular. Originally in coral red, green, and black, it soon appeared in other color combinations and continued to sell well for years. Throughout the Great Depression, along with the other ranges, Fantasque continued to sell in volume around the world at what were high prices for the time. **SH**

CROCUS PATTERN

Cliff taught her painters to follow her designs with straightforward steps. One of her most popular patterns was Crocus (1928–64), which was created with three or four converging strokes that made up the flower, then turned upside down and painted with thin green lines for leaves. Cliff originally painted Crocus in vibrant orange, blue, and purple, with a band of yellow above representing the sun, and brown for the earth below. She later produced several other color variations, including Purple, Blue, Sungleam, and Spring. Initially, the design only needed one painter, but as orders poured in, teams of girls were trained, with two or three painting the petals, a leafer, and a bander. For a large part of the 1930s, for five and a half days every week, twenty young women painted only Crocus patterns. Crocus was produced as tableware, tea and coffee sets, and gift ware.

LABOR-SAVING DESIGN

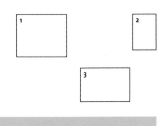

1 In the 1930s, electricity was cheap enough in Britain to allow heating appliances, such as Christian Barman's chrome-plated electric fan heater designed in *c.* 1934, to find a market.

2 A woman smiles while she vacuums a living-room carpet in an advertisement for Hoover from the 1940s. Labor-saving devices were marketed as bringing happiness by saving time.

3 J. J. P. Oud's kitchen design for the exhibition by the Deutscher Werkbund in Stuttgart, Germany, in 1927 aimed to provide logical and efficient workspace for the housewife while she prepared food.

By the 1920s. designers began to examine how to reduce the levels of work in the home and make the housewife's life easier. These primarily focused on changes to the design and layout of the kitchen. One of the most influential figures in the rational household movement was US home economist Christine Frederick (1883–1970), who applied the principle of step saving to the domestic sphere. Frederick produced diagrams illustrating interior planning. She positioned the kitchen at the rear of the house, creating a small, efficient, domestic laboratory where the housewife was seated on a high stool from which she could reach everything she needed. Translations of Frederick's book were read by European modernist architects, among them Austrian architect Margarete Schütte-Lihotzky (1897–2000), who developed one of the most famous examples of rational kitchen planning, the Frankfurt fitted kitchen (1926; see p.164), for a public housing scheme in Frankfurt.

In 1927 the Deutscher Werkbund (German Work Federation; see p.114) created the Weissenhof Estate in Stuttgart for an exhibition exploring modes of contemporary living. Leading modernist architects, including Ludwig Mies van der Rohe (1886–1969) and Le Corbusier (1887–1965), created buildings for the housing estate, and the influence of Germany's answer to Frederick could be seen. She was economist Erna Meyer (1890–1975),author of the popular *Der neue Haushalt: ein Wegweiser zu wirtschaftlicher Hausfuhrung* (*The New*

KEY EVENTS

1913	1922	1923	1924	1926	1926
Christine Frederick's *The New Housekeeping: Efficiency Studies in Home Management* is published and it applies motion studies to household tasks.	A translation of Frederick's *The New Housekeeping* is published in Germany as *Die rationelle Haushaltsführung.*	The Bauhaus holds its "Art and Technology: A New Unity" exhibition in Weimar. The Haus am Horn with its rational kitchen is a key exhibit.	The Electrical Association for Women is formed in Britain. It aims to modernize the home and educate women in the use of labor-saving devices.	Erna Meyer's *The New Household* is published in Germany. It quickly becomes an important text for modernist architects.	Margarete Schütte-Lihotzky designs the Frankfurt fitted kitchen. It is produced for new apartment blocks in Frankfurt.

Household: A Guide to Economical Housekeeping). Meyer acted as a consultant, creating a kitchen for the show with Dutch architect, J. J. P. Oud (1890–1963) that featured open shelving, a housewife's stool, and workbench (see image 3).

The downside of this new design, which was not immediately apparent, was that it tended to isolate the housewife from the family and eventually women reacted against it. Another disadvantage was that Frederick still advocated the use of simple kitchen utensils. She did not embrace the innovative, electric, labor-saving devices that were coming out of US factories and being consumed in large numbers. In esthetic terms, the ideas about reducing labor in the home that were developed in the 1920s reinforced visual minimalism and served as another influence on the development of modernist design that eventually affected the appearance of the furnishing and equipment of the whole house.

When the economic depression arrived in the 1930s, domestic appliance manufacturers stimulated the market with modern designs in curvilinear, streamlined forms that suggested efficiency and rendered older yet functional goods stylistically obsolete. They employed industrial designers to apply their skills to electrical labor-saving devices. For example, in Britain, HMV Household Appliances commissioned Christian Barman (1898–1980) to design various appliances, including his convector heater (see image 1). In the United States, the Hoover Company commissioned Henry Dreyfuss (1904–72) to streamline the Model 150 vacuum cleaner (1936; see image 2), and the Hobart Manufacturing Company hired Egmont Arens (1889–1966) to create the KitchenAid Model K Food Mixer (1937; see p.166). **PS**

1927	1933	1934	1934	1936	1936
The exhibition by the Deutscher Werkbund in Stuttgart, Germany, promotes labor-saving kitchens.	Christian Barman begins designing electrical appliances for HMV Household Appliances in Britain.	General Electric's Flattop refrigerator appears on the US market; it is one of the first to be designed in a modern style with a hidden compressor.	US designer Raymond Loewy (1893–1986) creates the Coldspot refrigerator for Sears Roebuck. It borrows features from automotive design.	Henry Dreyfuss designs the Hoover Model 150 vacuum cleaner with a streamlined design that suggests speed and efficiency.	Barman designs a streamlined, thermostatically controlled electric iron for HMV Household Appliances.

Frankfurt Fitted Kitchen 1926

MARGARETE SCHÜTTE-LIHOTZKY 1897–2000

Based on examples from outside the home—ship's galley, dining-car kitchen, and lunch wagon, in particular—Margarete Schütte-Lihotzky created a kitchen layout that emphasized the importance of step-saving and efficient storage. Like Christine Frederick before her, she devised a small, laboratory-style kitchen in which the housewife could reign supreme and where she could work like a scientist, seated on a stool at a worktop. Also like Frederick, she developed a work station where all the implements were within easy reach of the operator's hand. Furthermore, she added a continuous work surface, which gave the kitchen a more unified modern appearance, and fitted a wooden plate holder below the glazed wall cupboards. She also provided doors for her cupboards and shelves. This visual integration meant that Schütte-Lihotzky's kitchen greatly appealed to contemporary architects. Even the color choice was designed to promote efficiency. Although the original blue was supposedly effective in repelling flies, it also added considerably to the kitchen's visual impact. The materials—linoleum, glass, and steel, among them—enhanced the rooms' sophisticated, modern look.

Schütte-Lihotzky created this kitchen for Frankfurt's new public housing scheme, designed by German architect Ernst May. It went straight into mass production and set a precedent for many new housing developments of the late 1920s and early 1930s. However, housewives began to turn against the idea of the laboratory kitchen from the late 1930s. **PS**

Wood, glass, metal, linoleum
paint, and enamel
11 ft 3 in. x 6 ft
344 x 187 cm

👁 FOCAL POINTS

1 STOOL
As in Frederick's kitchen, the housewife in the Frankfurt kitchen was expected to do her work sitting down. To this end, a high stool was included that could be tucked away in a space under the worktop. The stool was situated in the food preparation area, where most kitchen work took place.

2 CLOSED DOORS
The kitchen cupboards and shelves were fitted with sliding and hinged doors, which meant that their contents were better protected against dirt and dust. Although time was lost in opening and shutting the doors, they gave the room a more streamlined, modern appearance.

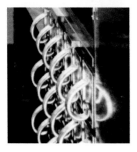

3 ORGANIZATION
The kitchen was organized so that the housewife had everything close to hand. The tasks were isolated; food preparation and cooking were separated from washing up. Small storage cupboards housed individual canisters designed to store single items, such as flour, sugar, and salt.

🕐 DESIGNER PROFILE

1897–1937
Margarete Schütte-Lihotsky was born in Vienna and was the first female to study at the University of Applied Arts Vienna. In 1926 architect Ernst May asked her to join him in Frankfurt to work on his public housing scheme. There, she designed the Frankfurt kitchen. She spent a large part of the 1930s in Moscow, helping to realize Stalin's five-year plan.

1938–2000
Schütte-Lihotsky left Russia and eventually settled in Istanbul, Turkey, in 1938 where she worked as an architect and teacher. She returned to Vienna but was imprisoned for treason until 1945. She spent most of the remainder of her life in Vienna.

▲ The fitted Frankfurt kitchen could be installed in three different sizes, depending on the dimensions of the apartment. The lack of moldings and ornament meant that it was easy to clean.

KitchenAid Model K Food Mixer 1937

EGMONT ARENS 1889–1966

Stainless steel and aluminum
14 x 14¼ x 8¾ in.
35.4 x 35.9 x 22.2 cm

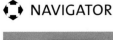 NAVIGATOR

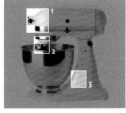

The Hobart Manufacturing Company, founded in Troy, Ohio, which owned the KitchenAid brand, began developing commercial food mixers from 1914. It released its first consumer version in 1920, but despite the fact that the model was sold in hardware stores and, later, by a female door-to-door sales force, it did not sell well. In the mid 1930s, the company asked Egmont Arens to design a food mixer. Launched in 1937, Arens's low-cost Model K proved to be a design classic. Its elegant, streamlined form, light weight, and fully interchangeable attachments appealed to consumers, and it was a commercial success for the company.

Arens had earned himself a reputation in a number of fields, including publishing and product design. In 1932 he co-authored an influential book entitled *Consumer Engineering*, which introduced the idea of planned obsolescence. The book suggested that objects needed to be well designed, continually redesigned, and aggressively sold. After its publication, numerous manufacturers asked him to work on their products for them. Arens's reputation as an industrial designer was quickly established, and he worked on a number of products, although few proved as long lasting as the sleek food mixer. KitchenAid components are still compatible with the 1937 model and the design has changed little since then. **PS**

1 BODY SHELL

In the United States during the 1930s, the visual motif of streamlining was transferred from cars to static consumer goods. Arens's KitchenAid mixer has a streamlined body shell. Not only did that render it stylish, it helped persuade consumers that electrical goods were safe to use.

2 HEAD

The bullet-shaped mixer head tilts backward, making it easy to change attachments. The mixer comes with a range of fully interchangeable attachments, so it can be used for a variety of tasks from shredding vegetables to chopping meat, and shelling peas to opening cans.

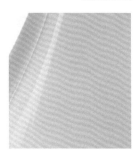

3 WHITE

Initially, the KitchenAid mixer came only in white. Color options were added in the mid 1950s: Petal Pink, Sunny Yellow, Island Green, Antique Copper, and Satin Chrome. The black and silver of the interwar years was replaced in the kitchen by a range of colors from pastels to bright hues.

MODERNIZATION OF THE HOME

The introduction of labor-saving devices into domestic kitchens was a marker of the modernization of the US home in the interwar years. In spite of the economic recession, domestic consumption increased as people sought to embrace these features of modernity.

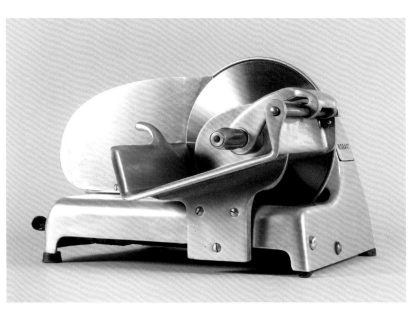

◄ Four years after his design for the KitchenAid mixer, Arens worked on another industrial design for Hobart. This time it was a meat slicer, the Streamliner, for which he developed a striking aerodynamic form. Completely made of steel, with its rivets exposed, the slicer combines streamlining with a utilitarian appearance. It includes a two-stone sharpener, a StaySharp stainless-steel blade driven by a Bakelite gear, and a proprietary motor. Like the mixer, the design received widespread press attention. The Streamliner is considered one of the most successful US designs of the period, and almost 100,000 were made between 1944 and 1985.

FORM FOLLOWS FUNCTION

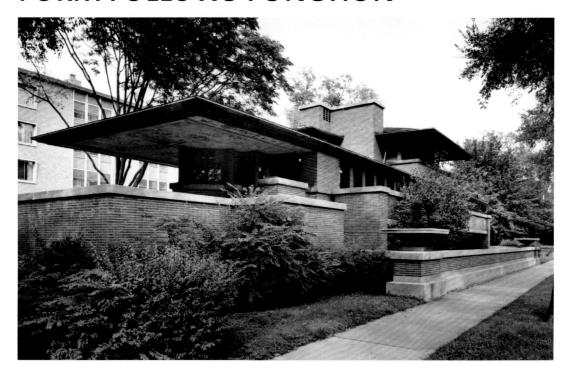

I n the early 20th century, the esthetic shift that took place from the use
of surface decoration to a commitment to pure, unelaborated form is one of
the most important stylistic transformations in the story of modern design.
However, mechanized production did not lead directly to machine-styled
products. Instead, a couple of generations of forward-looking designers took
their cue from contemporary architects and fine artists who had been quicker
to respond to the cultural imperatives of the machine age. and applied them to
the factory-made products that had inspired the architects and artists.

The idea that pure form derives from function, and that products should
not display surface decoration, does not mean that the use of an object
determines its appearance. Rather, the concept is based on the notion that
inner structure should influence outer form. "Form follows function" was a
phrase coined by US architect Louis Sullivan (1856–1924), who believed that,
just as a flower grows out of the root and stem of a plant, so the outer
appearance of a building should be determined by its inner structure. As
Sullivan advocated the use of a steel frame structure for a modern building,
he suggested its outer form should reflect that simple underlying geometry.

KEY EVENTS

1900	1901–02	1907	1908–10	1908	1910
Adolf Loos publishes *Spoken into the Void*, attacking the decorative work of the Vienna Secessionists.	Louis Sullivan's *Kindergarten Chats*, in which he elaborates many of his ideas about architectural form, are serialized.	The Deutscher Werkbund (German Work Federation; see p.114) adopts the principle of "form follows function" for product design.	Frank Lloyd Wright constructs Robie House in Chicago. He also designs the interiors, including the lighting, furniture, rugs, and textiles.	Loos argues that mankind has become more civilized by rejecting ornament in his essay *Ornament and Crime*.	Loos presents *Ornament and Crime* as a lecture in Vienna. His ideas prove influential and help define modernism in Europe.

Although he did not always practice what he preached—several of his buildings had decorative details on their exteriors, especially at their entrances—his idea was influential on early modernist architects and designers. Sullivan's ideas were picked up by US architect Frank Lloyd Wright (1867–1959), who became a key influence on later modernist thinking. Wright employed the principle of "form follows function" in early projects, such as Robie House (1908–10; see image 1) in Chicago; the client wanted to see neighbors without being seen, and Wright used horizontal planes cleverly to achieve his goal.

In the development of the functionalist philosophy of modern design, these architecturally focused principles were supplemented by others that drew on ideas coming out of the mass production of goods. Early European modernist writings expressed a sense of awe at the simple products of US mass production. Clocks, keys, bicycles, farm machinery. and standardized bookcases were widely revered as functional, visually unselfconscious products of the machine. The modernists' shared nostalgic longing for that age of innocence was a response to their anxieties about the commercial context of design.

As the 20th century progressed, architects and designers sought an objective formula that took the ideas of Sullivan and Austrian architect Adolf Loos (1870–1933) as a starting point. A dilemma for the supporters of design modernism was whether it represented an attempt to develop a modern esthetic using the idea of the machine as a key metaphor, or an attempt to design for machine production and thus facilitate the widespread availability of modern goods for the mass market. The goals merged in tubular steel furniture such as that of Bauhaus (see p.126) teacher Marcel Breuer (1902–81). The evenly distributed compartments of his Model No. B22 shelf unit (1928; see image 2) serve their purpose; the polished metal frame encasing the stark horizontal planes of stained blockboard allows whatever objects they house prominence because of their lack of decoration.

By the 1930s, the idea that "form follows function" had become widespread. The fact that simplicity and geometric form had become the esthetic for the modern age can be seen in designs such as Giò Ponti's (1891–1979) 0024 Suspension lamp (1931; see p.170). The purity of its shape, created out of concentric circles, the use of unadorned modern industrial materials, such as steel and glass, and the reduction of a hanging light to its bare essentials is a clear expression of the rationalism adopted by prewar Italian designers.

A rather different interpretation of the "form follows function" concept is demonstrated by another iconic lamp, the Anglepoise task light (1932–35; see p.172), whose mechanical form spells out the functionalism of the object. A maneuvrable task light, designed to target light exactly where it was needed, the Anglepoise is the product of engineering thought, and shows it. The mechanics of the design are not hidden away: they are the design. The form thus directly arises out of the job the lamp has to do. **PS**

1 Frank Lloyd Wright used structural steel framing to support the cantilevered roof of Robie House (1908–10), and designed the interior using a modular grid system.

2 The lean appearance and simple lines of Marcel Breuer's chromium plated tubular steel shelving (1928) is typical of the 'form follows function' ethos.

1910–12	1914	1924	1925	1928	1933
Loos builds the Loos House in Vienna, in which he puts many of his ideas into action. Its lack of decoration causes controversy.	European architects Henry Van de Velde (1863–1957) and Hermann Muthesius (1861–1927) debate how craftsmanship and industry relate.	Sullivan publishes his memoirs, *The Autobiography of an Idea*, where he mentions the idea of "form follows function."	Marcel Breuer creates the Wassily chair, the Model B3, made of bent tubular steel while he is at the Bauhaus.	Giò Ponti starts the magazine *Domus* to raise awareness about design issues and ideas of the time.	Ponti is instrumental in organizing the first Milan Triennale art and design exhibition.

0024 Suspension Lamp 1931

GIÒ PONTI 1891–1979

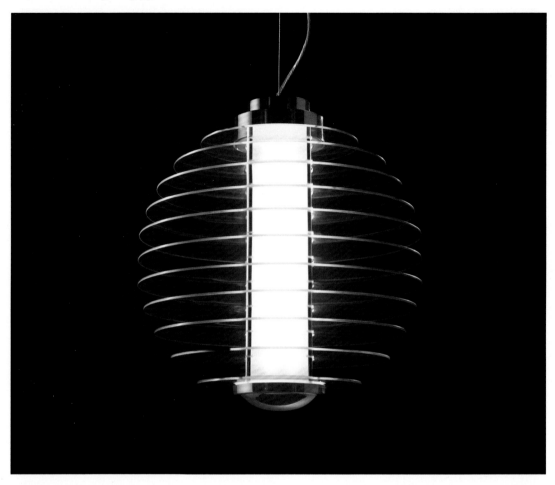

👁 FOCAL POINTS

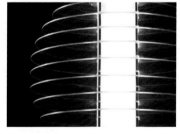

1 GLASS AND METAL

The 0024 comprises eleven transparent, tempered glass discs, stacked horizontally and fixed to a chrome-plated brass frame. A central diffuser is made of sandblasted glass. Ponti used glass because of its modern esthetic appeal and for the way in which it distributes the light.

2 GEOMETRY

Essentially a sphere, created from the varied sizes of the glass discs positioned in parallel with each other, the 0024 is a piece of abstract geometry. Ponti contrasted the horizontal discs with the verticality of the cylindrical central diffuser to create an arresting sculpture.

3 ILLUMINATION

In addition to its appeal as a hanging artwork, the 0024 is innovative in the way in which the illumination that emanates from the light source at its center is diffused. The use of satin glass has a very particular effect. The lamp can also be dimmed to enable low energy consumption.

By the late 1920s Italy had introduced its own version of modernist architecture and design. A group of Italian architects developed a movement called Rationalism, which was influenced by the work of Le Corbusier (1887–1965) and Walter Gropius (1883–1969), and from which a number of modernist furniture and product designs emerged. Alongside this architectural approach, several Italian designers who had worked in the decorative arts also embraced the modern style. Architect Giò Ponti was one of them.

The 0024 suspension lamp epitomized the designer's innovative way of working with glass in combination with metal. Hanging from the ceiling, it was a piece of sculpture that also emitted light. Although its form was essentially abstract, Ponti's choice of materials and shapes resulted in a highly decorative modern object that also functioned effectively. The esthetic that Ponti achieved in his 0024 lamp was influenced by the French Art Deco movement, which sought to establish a decorative modern style to accompany the more minimal forms of architectural modernism. Known as the "moderne," it became the more luxurious, commercial branch of modernism and was widespread in the traditional decorative arts. In 1932 Ponti formed FontanaArte, a branch of leading glass manufacturer Luigi Fontana, for whom he created these modern, decorative designs in traditional materials. **PS**

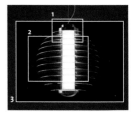

Transparent tempered glass discs, tubular sandblasted glass diffuser, chrome-plated brass frame
Diameter 20 in./50 cm

○ DESIGNER PROFILE

1891–1932

Born in Milan, Giò Ponti studied architecture at Politecnico di Milano but interrupted his studies temporarily during World War I to serve in the army. In 1923 he entered into architectural practice, and from 1927 he worked with Emilio Lancia (1890–1973), designing in the Novecento style. In 1928 Ponti established *Domus* architecture and design magazine. Throughout the 1920s he also worked in industrial design and was appointed art director for porcelain manufacturer Richard-Ginori.

1933–79

Ponti began working with engineers Eugenio Soncini and Antonio Fornaroli in 1933. Together they were involved in the creation of Fiat's offices, as well as the headquarters for Montecatini, an Italian chemicals company. In 1956 construction began on the Pirelli tower in Milan, designed by Ponti. From this point onward, the architect was involved in the design of many other important Italian landmarks, and he continued to work in the decorative arts, collaborating, for example, with Piero Fornasetti.

SUPERLEGGERA CHAIR

More than two decades after his design for the 0024 suspension lamp, Ponti created an iconic "super lightweight" chair, the Superleggera (1957; right), manufactured by Milanese furniture company Cassina. It weighed a mere 3¾ pounds (1.7 kg). By this time, the style was less Art Deco and more "contemporary." Once again bringing tradition and modernity in touch with one another, Ponti modeled the stable little side chair—made of varnished wood and finely woven cane—on the vernacular fisherman's Chiavari chair (1807). However, he subtly altered the traditional design to give his version a more up-to-date appearance. More minimal than the 0024 hanging light, the chair demonstrated how Ponti had moved on to help create the highly original Italian design esthetic of the post-war years. It combined artistic minimalism with elegance, practicality, and comfort.

Anglepoise Task Light 1932–35

GEORGE CARWARDINE 1887–947

Steel, cast iron base with steel cover
Height (maximum reach): 24 in./60 cm

The Anglepoise task light epitomizes "form follows function;" it contains no parts that do not contribute to its purpose and its appearance is determined by its functional components. It has become a design classic. The light was the brainchild of George Carwardine, a British car designer who was an expert in suspension systems. In 1932, while he was working in that field, he discovered a mechanism that he thought could be utilized in other engineering contexts. In essence, he created a spring that could be moved in a number of directions but that remain rigid. He went on to develop a joint that, through the addition of a set of springs (three or four), could be moved into many positions and remained where it was placed without extra support. Carwardine realized that the best use of his mechanism was in a task light, as it would allow the beam to be focused on multiple points. He also decided that he needed to collaborate with a specialist manufacturer to take his idea into production. He joined forces with the Terry Spring Company (later Herbert Terry & Sons) and produced the 1227 Anglepoise in 1935. **PS**

◈ NAVIGATOR

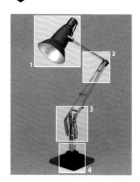

◉ FOCAL POINTS

1 SHADE
The shade was added to prevent glare. It has a mechanism within it that allows it to be pivoted, which means that the beam can be directed wherever the user wants it to go. This contributes to the advanced functionality of the Anglepoise.

2 ARM
There is a strong resemblance between the Anglepoise's three-part metal column and a human arm. Carwardine was aware of this when he was designing his task light and thought of its joints working in a similar way to those in the human body.

3 MECHANISM
The Anglepoise mechanism consists of a metal column with two joints linked by springs. The articulated column is completely stable once it is moved into position, a function made possible by the special springs that Carwardine developed.

4 BASE
The lamp requires a heavy base to ensure that it does not fall over. This one is made up of two metal squares, one on top of the other. The base was the only element of the original design that had any styling; its ziggurat-like appearance had an Art Deco feel to it.

COPIES AND REDESIGNS

By the end of the 20th century, the Anglepoise light had become a British design classic. It had been copied widely and inferior versions could be bought across the globe. In 2003 Herbert Terry and Sons commissioned British product designer Kenneth Grange to redesign the original 1227 model. He had enjoyed a successful design career since the 1950s—Ronson shavers, Kenwood food mixers—but leapt to the challenge, producing three new models. The first was the Anglepoise Type 3, which had a double skin shade that could withstand a 100-watt bulb; the second was the Type 75, which resembled the original very closely; and the third was the Type 1228 (right), which had a colored shade and was the most styled of the three.

PLYWOOD AND LAMINATED WOOD

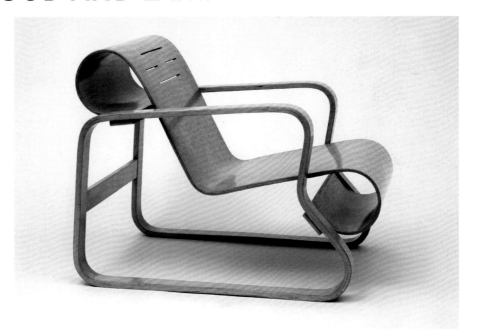

lywood and laminated wood are closely associated with 1930s modernist furniture, but they were by no means new materials at that time. German-born cabinetmaker Michael Thonet (1796–1871) had experimented with bent laminated wood as early as 1830, boiling strips of timber in glue and shaping them in molds, and his innovations in wood technology paved the way for later technical breakthroughs. The first US patent for plywood was registered in 1865. Initially known as veneered wood, it was fabricated from multiple layers of thinly sliced timber veneers glued together with the grain in alternating directions. Because early plywood was of fairly poor quality, it was used mainly as a substitute for solid wood on cabinet backs and drawer bottoms, for example. However, plywood has many advantages over solid wood, because it is more stable and less likely to warp or crack. The fact that it can be manufactured in large sheets is also beneficial, but its greatest asset is its strength. Laminated wood is similar to plywood but it is made from thicker slices of timber, with the grain running in the same direction layer upon layer. Laminated wood is stronger than both plywood and solid bentwood.

When modernist architects turned their attention to furniture in the 1920s, they focused initially on metal. However, Finnish architect Alvar Aalto (1898–1976) found tubular steel rather harsh and was drawn instinctively toward wood. The

KEY EVENTS

1927–29	1931	1931–32	1932–33	1933	1934
Alvar Aalto begins to experiment with bent laminated wood and molded plywood in conjunction with Otto Korhonen.	Makers of Simple Furniture is established in London by Gerald Summers. The company specializes in plywood furniture.	Aalto designs Armchair 41 and Armchair 31, using bent laminated wood for the frame and molded plywood for the seat.	Aalto designs the Stacking Stool 60 (see p.176), made from solid and laminated birch, with a flat, circular seat and three bentwood legs.	Aalto's furniture is exhibited at the London shop Fortnum and Mason.	Finmar is founded to import Aalto's furniture from Finland into the United Kingdom.

challenge was how to overcome its physical limitations, and laminated wood and plywood provided the solution: they were elastic and malleable, but incredibly strong and could be manipulated into interesting organic shapes. Aalto combined the two materials in his groundbreaking Armchair 41 (see image 1) for the Paimio Sanatorium, using laminated wood for the looped frames and mouded plywood for the curvilinear seats. He went on to develop a whole range of furniture, including the Stacking Stool 60 (1932–33; see p.176).

When Bauhaus architect Marcel Breuer (1902–81) came to London in 1935, he adopted the same techniques and materials as Aalto. The two-part cantilevered frame of his Long Chair (1935–36) was made of bent laminated wood, while the undulating reclining seat was molded plywood. Writing in 1937, he stressed the innovative nature of this design solution: "Here the plywood is not used merely as a panel or as a plane surface borne by separate structural members; it performs two functions at one and the same time—it bears weight and forms its own planes." He designed numerous other pieces of furniture for Isokon Furniture Company, including a trio of nesting tables (see image 2) cut from a sheet of thick birch plywood. However, Breuer was not the first designer to create a piece of furniture from a single sheet of plywood. Two years earlier, Gerald Summers (1899–1967) had designed a plywood armchair for Makers of Simple Furniture, in London. A fluid, curvilinear form, bent in various directions to create the integral arm rests and legs, it was cut from a sheet of plywood composed of thirteen layers. Although this was Summers's best-known design, it was not a one-off. He created a pioneering collection of plywood furniture, including a stylish trolley with an S-shaped frame in 1934 and the innovative Z table, a plywood spiral with a circular top and shelf, in 1936. **LJ**

1 Armchair 41 (1931–32) by Alvar Aalto was manufactured using bent plywood, bent laminated birch, and solid birch.

2 The nesting tables (1936) by Marcel Breuer were notable for the fact that each table was cut in one piece, then molded into shape.

1934	1935	1935	1936	1936	1939
The Eva chair is designed by Bruno Mathsson (1907–88) for Swedish firm Karl Mathsson, with a bent laminated beech frame and jute webbing seat.	Artek is set up by Alvar and Aino Aalto, art critic Nils-Gustav Hahl (1904–41), and patron Maire Gullichsen (1907–70) to market Aalto's furniture.	Isokon Furniture Co. is established in London by Jack Pritchard (1899–1992) as an offshoot of modernist building development company Isokon.	The Long Chair by Marcel Breuer is produced by Isokon Furniture Company. Its shape derives from Breuer's earlier aluminum furniture.	Breuer designs a range of laminated wood and plywood chairs and tables for Isokon Furniture Company, then emigrates to the United States in 1937.	The Penguin Donkey (see p.178), designed by Egon Riss (1901–64), is launched by Isokon Furniture Company, but the firm closes the following year.

Stacking Stool 60 1932–33
ALVAR AALTO 1898–1976

Birch and birch veneer
Height 17¼ in./44 cm
Diameter 13¾ in./35 cm

 NAVIGATOR

Many of the most notable pieces of furniture over the past two centuries have been designed by architects, and the Stacking Stool 60 by Alvar Aalto provides a good example. Aalto pioneered a new style, typified by the Paimio Sanatorium (1929–33) in Finland and its light, airy, clean-lined interiors. Sympathetic furnishings were vital to this project, and this impelled the architect to engage with furniture design. He recognized the potential of wood as an engineering material and teamed up with Otto Korhonen to establish a joint workshop. Together the two men developed techniques for producing structures from laminated wood, bent into organic shapes with the aid of jigs.

With its circular seat and three L-shaped legs, Stacking Stool 60 was a radically simple piece of furniture. Aalto was so proud of the leg structure, which is laminated at the top and bent into shape, that he patented this element of the design. Although a four-legged version was produced later in the 1930s, the original three-legged model made the stool light in weight and economical to manufacture because of the reduced materials and labor costs. Stacking Stool 60 has remained in continuous production up to the present day, marketed from 1935 onward by Aalto's furniture company, Artek. **LJ**

FOCAL POINTS

1 THREE-LEGGED STRUCTURE
The stool's three-legged structure has practical benefits because it facilitates stacking. The way in which the legs are offset when several stools are stacked together creates an ascending spiral, which adds to the overall esthetic appeal of the design.

2 BIRCH WOOD
Birch has been widely used for furniture in Finland because the material is readily available. With its pale coloring and fine grain, birch wood is visually appealing and lends itself well to veneers. Structurally, it is ideal for laminated wood, the key to this stool design.

3 CIRCULAR SEAT
In addition to being pleasant to sit on, the circular seat is satisfying from an architectural point of view, complementing the curved legs. The seat was either veneered in birch or padded and upholstered; either way, the same depth and proportions were retained.

4 BENTWOOD LEGS
The legs are made from bentwood and screwed to the seat's underside. The lower part of the leg is solid wood; the upper section is laminated. Gluing slices of wood together greatly strengthens the timber. It also makes it flexible enough to bend without fracturing.

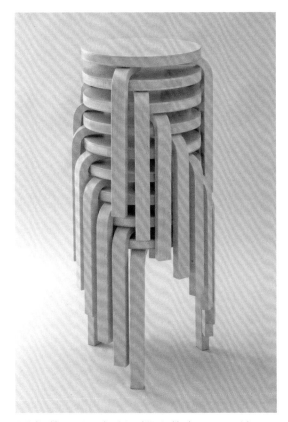

▲ Aalto, like most modernist architects, liked pure geometric forms but he also used more organic shapes in his furniture design. When they are stacked, the stools form a pattern that clearly relates to natural phenomena, including plant forms.

ORGANIC DESIGN

Although organic design is often associated with the 1940s and 1950s, it originated during the 1930s and Aalto was a pivotal figure in its genesis and evolution. Like other Finnish designers, such as Tapio Wirkkala (1915–85), he created forms rooted in the natural world, but he was also interested in abstraction and admired artists such as Constantin Brancusi (1876–1957) and Hans Arp (1886–1966). In this way, Aalto pioneered a more human esthetic that was clean lined yet fluid. It is this melding of the organic and the abstract that makes his furniture and glassware designs, such as the Savoy vase (1937; above), so timeless and pure.

Penguin Donkey 1939

EGON RISS 1901–64

Birch plywood and
laminated wood
17 x 23½ x 16½ in.
43 x 60 x 42 cm

NAVIGATOR

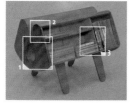

The Isokon Furniture Company, which produced this quirky hybrid—part bookcase, part magazine rack—was established by Jack Pritchard, an idealistic maverick who developed a keen interest in modern architecture and design. Since the 1920s, veneered plywood panels had been used increasingly as a substitute for solid wood in wardrobes and chests of drawers, but Pritchard realized that plywood had wider potential applications in the furniture industry. Lighter, stronger and more malleable than solid wood, it could be used as a material in its own right to create new furniture forms that were radically different to those in the past.

Houses built in the 1930s tended to be more modestly proportioned than their Victorian and Edwardian predecessors and increasing numbers of middle-class Londoners opted to live in serviced apartments. Because space was at a premium, this prompted a vogue for dual-purpose furniture. In 1937 Pritchard commissioned several designs from Egon Riss, a Viennese émigré architect, and the unusually named Penguin Donkey is one of four very practical items that the latter created for Isokon. The others were a bookstand called Gull, and two devices for storing and carrying bottles and glasses: the Bottleship and Pocket Bottleship. More playful than previous designs, the Penguin Donkey bookcase is technically ingenious, witty, and visually dynamic, as well as multipurpose: the recess between the bookshelves serves as a rack for newspapers and magazines. The whole design is extremely organic, too, complementing the forms of contemporary sculptors such as Barbara Hepworth (1903–75) and Henry Moore (1898–1986). **LJ**

⊙ FOCAL POINTS

1 DONKEY
The name "Donkey" derives from the pannier-like shape of the main bookcase, which is designed and built to carry the maximum amount of weight. The horseshoe-shaped end panels and round peg-like feet enhance the exuberant character of this perky little design.

2 MOLDED PLYWOOD
The bookcase is made from a combination of thin molded plywood and thicker laminated wood. The plywood folds back on itself to create a narrow-necked pocket in the center for magazines. The flat end panels, shelf dividers, and legs are cut from a single sheet of laminated wood.

3 PENGUIN
The "Penguin" component of the name arises not from the shape of the bookcase, but from the fact that the design was created specifically to accommodate Penguin paperbacks, with their distinctive orange spines. The shelves are designed to fit the books' proportions.

POCKET BOTTLESHIP

Designed by Riss and produced by Isokon Furniture Company, the Pocket Bottleship (1939; above) was a charming domestic accessory, designed for carrying up to two wine bottles and six wine glasses, with a recess in the center for rolled-up magazines. Small enough to be placed on a table, it could also be hooked onto the wall. With its fluid lines and aerodynamic form, it was exciting to look at and demonstrated the sculptural potential of mouded plywood.

◄ In the 1970s Pritchard relaxes in an Isokon Long chair (1935–36) designed by Marcel Breuer, alongside an Isokon Penguin Donkey Mark 2 (1963) designed by Ernest Race (1913–64). Pritchard asked Race to redesign the original Riss design with a flat top to allow it to be used as a side table.

TAKING PICTURES

1 Gerda Taro used the medium-format 2¼ x 2¼-in. (6 x 6 cm) Rolleiflex Old Standard Model (left).

2 The cover of the first issue of *Life* magazine in 1936 features a photograph by Margaret Bourke-White.

While the introduction of the daguerreotype process in 1839 was the beginning of practical photography, taking pictures remained the preserve of studio-based professionals and leisured amateurs until the 1880s, when US entrepreneur George Eastman (1854–1932) released the first Eastman Kodak camera, modified the following year to take roll film.

The democratization of photography was prompted by sound business sense. Eastman wanted to sell film. Eastman understood the potential market for film rested on persuading non-professionals that great pictures could be taken by everyone. To do this, he not only produced an affordable camera that was easy for amateurs to operate, he also separated what was arguably straightforward—picture taking—from what was more apparently complicated—processing photographs.

Eastman's advertising slogan "You Press the Button, We Do the Rest" spelled out this message in the catchiest terms. All his customers had to do was point the camera and take the pictures. They then sent the camera to the factory, fully loaded, for the film to be processed, receiving in return not only the camera but prints, negatives, and a new roll of film. In 1930 Eastman brought

KEY EVENTS

1900	1908	1917	1925	1930	1933
Eastman Kodak introduces the Brownie, which uses roll film. The age of mass photography arrives.	Kodak produces the first commercially practical safety film using a cellulose acetate base instead of the highly flammable cellulose nitrate base.	Three leading Japanese optical manufacturers merge to form Nippon Kogaku Tokyo, which will eventually become the firm Nikon.	The world's first high-quality 35mm camera, the Leica, is made available commercially.	Kodak launches the Beau Brownie, a box camera specifically designed to appeal to women.	Hungarian photographer Brassaï (1899–1984) publishes *Paris de nuit* (*Paris by Night*), his collection of photographs of Parisian nightlife.

out the Beau Brownie No. 2 (see p.184), styled like an accessory and specifically targeted at women. A new dimension was added with the launch of Kodachrome, the first modern color film, in 1935.

As picture taking became part of family life, recording every birthday, vacation, and momentous occasion, photography reached a mass audience through the medium of magazine publishing. The US periodical *Life* started out as a humorous general-interest weekly in 1883. In 1936 Henry Luce (1898–1967) the publisher of *Time*, bought the title and transformed it into a vehicle for photojournalism. The first issue (see image 2) of the refocused magazine featured a photograph taken by Margaret Bourke-White (1904–71). *Life* helped the careers of numerous significant 20th-century photographers. Bourke-White was one of the magazine's first four staff photographers, and she went on to become the first female documentary photographer to work with the US armed forces. *Picture Post*, the British equivalent of *Life*, first came out in 1938. The same year saw the launch of the French photographic news magazine *Match*, which closed in 1940 and reappeared in 1949 as *Paris Match*.

If easy-to-use cameras such as those produced by Kodak helped to create a market of amateur photographers and a multimillion-dollar industry, 35mm cameras such as the Leica (1925; see p.182) transformed reportage. Readily transported into the field, the Leica rapidly became the favored camera of photojournalists such as Robert Capa (1913–54), who covered the Spanish Civil War (1936–39). Together with his companion and partner Gerda Taro (1910–1937), who used a medium-format Rolleiflex camera (see image 1), and who is regarded as the first female photojournalist on the front line, Capa helped to establish the genre of war photography. His *Death of a Loyalist Militiaman* (1937) became one of the defining images of that conflict.

On the eve of another war, the Minox (see p.186) was launched. Designed by Latvian designer Walter Zapp (1905–2003), this miniature camera, first produced in 1938, rapidly came to the attention of those engaged in clandestine operations on behalf of both Axis and Allied powers; it was later used as a spy camera during the Cold War. Yet its real commercial success came about in the 1960s, when it became a desirable status object.

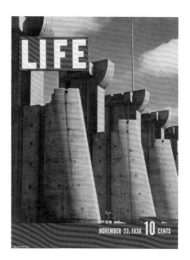

Photography's influence on design, particularly graphics, was immense. Capable of capturing "the decisive moment," to use Henri Cartier-Bresson's (1908–2004) famous phrase, it was in tune with the rapid pace of early modern life; both photographs and photocollages were readily adopted by avant-garde artists and designers. As a form of visual communication, the photograph was upheld as an objective truth teller, despite the fact that images have been manipulated since the earliest days of picture-taking. Advertisers found it a boon, and product and packaging shots became an important selling tool. Along with moving pictures in the cinema and later on television, the advent of mass photography played a key role in a shift toward a visual culture. **EW**

1935	1936	1936	1937	1938	1940
Latvian designer Walter Zapp designs the innovatory Minox subminiature camera. It goes into production in 1938.	Kodak releases Kodachrome as slide film in 35mm format. It is the first commercially successful amateur color film.	Henry Luce buys *Life* and relaunches it as a photojournalistic magazine. Within four months, its circulation exceeds one million copies per week.	*Popular Photography* magazine launches in the United States.	The "American Photographs" exhibition at the Museum of Modern Art in New York City raises the profile of straight photography.	The Museum of Modern Art in New York City develops a department of photography.

Leica 35mm 1925
OSKAR BARNACK 1879–1936

👁 FOCAL POINTS

1 CINEMA FILM
The Leica was the first 35mm stills camera to use standard cinema film rather than glass plates. The Leica feeds the film horizontally, unlike the cine camera, which fed the stock vertically. In order to improve the quality of the still, Barnack doubled the frame size to 24 × 36 mm (2:3 aspect ratio).

2 ELMAR LENS
The Leica I has a two-speed shutter, an automatic frame counter, and Berek's f3.5 Elmar lens, which collapses into itself when not in use, making the camera even more compact. Utterly functional, the Leica fits comfortably into the hand and could be used in outdoor settings with only daylight.

🕐 DESIGNER PROFILE

1879–1913
Oskar Barnack was a German optical engineer who became known as the father of 35mm photography. In 1911 he was appointed head of microscope research and development at Ernst Leitz in Wetzlar, Germany. He was passionate about landscape photography, but his asthma rendered him incapable of carrying heavy large-format equipment. Consequently, he created the first mass-market camera that could be held in the palm of the hand, and introduced the 24×36 mm film format, which came to be known as 35mm.

1914–20
After Barnack created the Ur-Leica, he used it extensively himself. From 1914 until his death, he took a series of photographs documenting events such as the historic flooding of Wetzlar in 1920.

1921–36
Barnack's cameras went into production in the 1920s. Little is known about the designer's later life, but in 1979 Leica established the Oskar Barnack Award to mark the one hundredth anniversary of his birth. It remains an annual event with an international jury and prize of €5,000. A small museum to his life and work exists in Lynow, Germany.

The first 35mm Leica camera was designed privately by Oskar Barnack in 1913, and its lightweight, small format went on to cause a revolution in the nascent world of photography. Although the prototype was created in 1913, World War I delayed production and it was not until 1923 that Barnack convinced his employer at the Ernst Leitz optical firm to make thirty-one prototype cameras for testing. Responses were mixed, but in 1924 the company ordered production of the Leitz Camera (Lei-Ca) and the Model A, or Leica I, was introduced to the public at the Leipzig Spring Fair of 1925. It was an enormous success and a landmark in the history of photography. Its outstanding quality gave it iconic status almost as soon as it was launched, and it has since been used by the world's leading photographers, as well as by legendary film-makers from Alfred Hitchcock and Stanley Kubrick to Brad Pitt.

Designed to use small rolls of film that could be carried with ease, rather than bulky glass plates, the Leica I featured a cloth focal plane shutter and a built-in optical viewfinder, and had shutter speeds ranging from $\frac{1}{20}$ to $\frac{1}{500}$ of a second. Taking one frame at a time, Barnack could expose a small area of 35mm film to create a negative before enlarging the image in a darkroom. The film was wound manually by a sprocket wheel that connected with holes on the strip. In addition to a Z for Zeit (time) position, the camera had an accessory shoe to which a flash unit or other accessories could be attached. These professional features were complemented by a precision lens that could record images sharp enough to withstand enlargement. This invaluable contribution was made by Max Berek, Barack's colleague in the Ernst Leitz microscope department. **JW**

Leica I (1927)
Aluminum, glass, brass, synthetic leather

▲ The Leica 250, also known as the Reporter, became an invaluable tool for photojournalists such as Henri Cartier-Bresson. It contained 30 feet (9 m) of film, which allowed 250 shots to be taken without reloading.

FREEDOM TRAIN

Ernst Leitz had a good track record of caring for its employees. Pensions, sick leave, and health insurance were instituted early on. The company depended on skilled employees, many of whom were Jewish. When Hitler came to power in 1933, Ernst Leitz II quietly established what Rabbi Frank Dabba Smith called the "Leica freedom train." Until the borders were closed, the company helped Jewish employees and friends leave Germany by sending them to their sales offices in the United Kingdom, Hong Kong, and the United States. Leitz's daughter, Elsie Kühn-Leitz, was imprisoned by the Gestapo when she was caught helping Jewish women to cross into Switzerland.

Kodak Beau Brownie No. 2 1930

WALTER DORWIN TEAGUE 1883–1960

Metal, enamel, glass,
faux leather, cardboard
5 x 3½ x 5 in.
13 x 9 x 13 cm

 NAVIGATOR

The Beau Brownie box camera was part of the popular Brownie range made by Eastman Kodak in Rochester, New Jersey. It was designed as a special edition for women and had an Art Deco (see p.156) front motif and faux leather sides. Produced from 1930 to 1933, it was available in two sizes—for using 120 film and 116 film—had an instantaneous and time-rotary shutter with three stops, and was capable of taking eight exposures. Known in some circles as the camera that democratized photography, the Beau spread the desirability of the camera across the sexes as well as the classes. Its cute appeal was augmented by the fact that it was more compact than many other models, thanks to a doublet lens that allowed the pictures to be projected on a film plate over a shorter distance. In order to appeal to young women of the period, the Beau was also less austere than previous cameras. It was not about optics and technicalities, but was designed as an easy-to-use, desirable object. The two-tone styling of the facade was by Walter Dorwin Teague, and the cardboard packaging was decorated with jazz age geometric shapes and colors, too. Teague pioneered the discipline of industrial design, and one of his specialties was packaging. **JW**

FOCAL POINTS

1 VIEWFINDERS
The Beau was designed with two viewfinders. It takes rectangular pictures, and this format results in two options: images can be taken in portrait (long-side vertical) or landscape (long-side horizontal). To complement each position, Teague designed a viewfinder for each format.

2 COLORWAYS
The front panel was decorated with highly polished nickel inlaid with two-tone enamel. The rose and green colorways were not produced after 1931, and these two models were never available outside the United States. Consequently, they are now the rarest and their packaging is even rarer.

3 DOUBLET LENS
The camera was fitted with a fixed-focus Eastman doublet lens. This type of optic lens is made up of two simple lenses paired together, either cemented or held close with space between, enabling optical aberrations to be corrected. The doublet lens also allowed for a shorter body.

4 ART DECO STYLING
Composed of vertical batons, squares, and oblongs arranged around a central circle, the geometric front plate echoes non-objective paintings by Sonia Delaunay and others in the Art Deco period. Teague designed it on 6 January 1930 and was granted a patent on 26 July the same year.

▲ The Beau Brownie No. 2 was manufactured in five color combinations with matching faux leather casing: black and burgundy, two-tone blue, two-tone rose, brown and tan, and two-tone green.

STRATOCRUISER INTERIOR

Teague designed the interior of the Boeing Stratocruiser 377 (right), which made its first flight in July 1947 and was retired in 1963. His designs for the 6,600 cu ft (187 cu m) of luxury interior space heralded a new beginning in aviation for civilians after World War II, and became a blueprint for the interiors of later Boeing 707s and 747s. In 1988 Teague also designed the interior of President Ronald Reagan's Air Force One, which included two fully equipped kitchens, one hundred telephones, seven bathrooms, sixteen televisions, and thirty-one sleeper suites.

Minox Subminiature Camera 1936

WALTER ZAPP 1905–2003

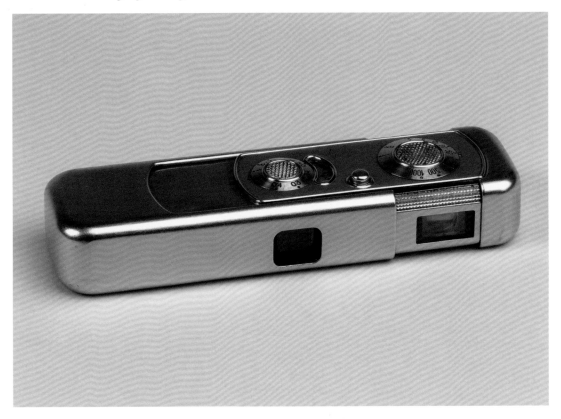

Stainless steel
⅝ x 3⅛ x 1 in.
1.5 x 8 x 2.5 cm

Miniaturization seems such a preoccupation of late 20th-century designers, particularly in the field of electronics, that the early date of this compact camera comes as a surprise. Yet the appearance of the Minox at a time when mass photography was rapidly gaining ground could be seen as a logical development. Manufacturers such as Eastman Kodak had already placed easy-to-use portable cameras in the hands of ordinary people. What Walter Zapp did was to design one small enough to be concealed in a pocket.

At first, the appeal of the Minox was not immediately apparent, and its launch was met with indifference in Latvia, where it was first produced in 1938 by the radio and electrical firm VEF. Nevertheless, in the following two years nearly 20,000 were sold worldwide, many of which found military use—aside from its small size, the camera's macro focusing ability, which meant that it was ideal for photographing documents, recommended it for spy purposes. After World War II, the camera was redesigned and production eventually resumed in Wetzlar, West Germany. Commercial success followed, with the most popular model being the Minox B, launched in 1958 and discontinued in 1972. In the climate of the Cold War, the camera's obvious suitability for covert operations and espionage gave it a particular glamor that made it irresistible as a luxury item: its manufacturing costs meant that it was never cheap enough to become the mass product Zapp had originally intended.

Inventive, curious, and technically adept, Zapp was fortunate in his associates, particularly Richard Jürgens, a German businessman who was a backer and with whom he launched the Minox company after the war. Early on he was encouraged by the photographer Nikolai Nylander (1902–81), who devised its name and mouse logo. **EW**

✦ NAVIGATOR

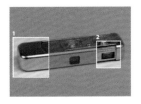

FOCAL POINTS

1 SHELL
The original Minox had a stainless-steel shell over a brass chassis. Later models produced had plastic bodies clad in aluminum, which made them lighter and somewhat cheaper. Special-edition luxury models, plated in gold, platinum, or anodized aluminum, were also issued.

3 CLOSE-FOCUSING LENS
The Minox was never as popular as its 35mm peers, but its Minostigmat 15 mm f/3.5 lens could focus at distances of only 7 ⅞ in. (20 cm). Many models were supplied with a measuring chain, which at the full length of 23 ⅝ in. (60 cm) is perfect for photographing letter-size documents.

DESIGNER PROFILE

1905–29
Walter Zapp was born in Riga, Latvia. He worked as an apprentice to an art photographer in Estonia. In 1925 he patented a design for a paper cutter.

1930–35
Zapp made a prototype miniature camera, which Nikolai Nylander named "Minox." After the German firm Agfa turned it down, Zapp approached VEF at Richard Jürgens's suggestion.

1936–44
Zapp signed a contract with VEF and production began in 1938 in Riga. Advertised in Europe and the United States, the Riga Minox achieved modest success. In 1941 Zapp went to work for AEG in Berlin. Production of the Minox ceased in 1943.

1945–50
Zapp and Jürgens set up a company in Wetzlar, West Germany. In 1948 production of the redesigned Minox II began. Zapp left the company in 1950 after a dispute with one of its backers.

1951–2003
Minox models sold well in the luxury market. From the 1970s, the company introduced electronic versions and branched into other film formats. In 1989 Zapp renewed his association with the firm.

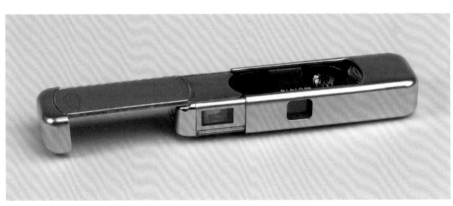

◀ The camera shell telescopes open and closed. This action advances the film and contributes to the camera's compactness. In its closed position, the lens and viewfinder are covered and hence protected from being scratched.

SPY VS SPY

The Minox's compact size, along with its close-focusing lens, ideal for photographing documents surreptitiously, made it attractive for espionage. US, British, and German intelligence agencies were known to have used the camera for spying in World War II. The camera found a similar role during the Cold War. British and US intelligence services supplied Minox cameras (right) to Soviet spy Oleg Penkovsky (1919–63) in the early 1960s.

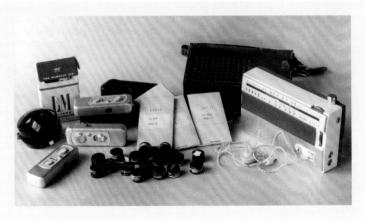

EARLY PLASTICS

1 A hexagonal Bandalasta Ware bowl made by Brookes and Adams of Birmingham in *c.* 1926.

2 An employee of the US National Bureau of Standards measures the length of nylon hose to define a new standard.

3 A Galalith casein plastic lamp (1925–30) manufactured by Italian chemical company Montedison.

The development of plastics was the result of technological advances. It also arose to meet the demand for goods and novelties by a group of middle-class consumers in the industrialized world who had hitherto not been able to indulge in luxuries. The first natural and semi-synthetic manmade materials emerged—celluloid, casein, gutta-percha, vulcanite, and shellac among them. These were all developed as substitutes for a range of luxurious materials that included ivory, jet, amber, tortoiseshell, and horn. Such were the enhanced demands for items such as jewelry and hair decorations made from these expensive natural materials that the supply of them was diminished and substitute materials had to be found.

The result of the development of early plastics was a huge expansion in the production of commodities for the middle classes, and the emergence of large number of manufacturers emerged keen to invest in the new industry. Plastics were not confined to being used for decorative items but came to be used for domestic items, too. For example, casein plastics are made from dairy by-products and hardened with formaldehyde. They could be dyed in bright colors and could withstand washing and ironing, so casein plastics like Galalith became popular for buttons and jewelry, but were also used to make household objects like lamps (see image 3).

KEY EVENTS

1910	1913	1924	1930	1931	1933
Stockings made from viscose, the precursor of nylon, are produced in Germany.	US company Westinghouse Electric patents Formica. First used for electrical parts, by the 1930s it is used for decorative laminate products.	Research chemist Edmund Rossiter (1867–1937) discovers the thiourea-urea-formaldehyde polymer used in Bandalasta.	US company 3M invents a transparent sticky tape, Scotch Cellulose Tape.	German company IG Farben (now BASF) begins manufacturing polystyrene commercially.	British scientists discover polyethylene, or polythene. It becomes widely used after World War II.

The first fully synthetic material was Bakelite, invented in 1907 by Belgian-born US chemist Leo Baekeland (1863–1944). It went on to dominate the story of plastics through the early 20th century. Bakelite was a substitute material that enabled the acquisition of luxury goods to spread through society. It was promoted by popular magazines as a substance with magic properties and was available in dark brown or black.

Plastic products had curved forms, which made it easier to extricate them from the molds, and helped foster the craze for the streamlined style that became synonymous with objects whose forms had little to do with their utilitarian functions. The transformation of the new materials into products was made possible by designers who employed them to fashion the streamlined bodies of objects such as telephones and radio sets. The Ekco AD-65 radio (1934; see p.190) was one of Britain's most modern-looking radio models of the interwar years; its shiny Bakelite body shell disguises the set's complex inner workings and displays the curved forms of objects fabricated in molds. It also brought a taste of the US lifestyle into the lives of British people.

However, Bakelite's dominance was challenged by the new plastics entering the marketplace. These new materials—cellulose acetate, Plexiglas or Perspex, polyethylene, and nylon among them—improved on what had been previously available by offering a range of attractive colors, along with other new features. Among them was Bandalasta Ware, the trade name of a range of lightweight household articles, picnic sets, and tableware (see image 1) made by British company Brookes and Adams from a synthetic resin in the Art Deco (see p.156) style. Like Bakelite, Bandalasta could be molded into a range of shapes, but items came in a range of translucent and marbled pastel shades.

While some new plastics were hard, others were soft. Nylon, or polymer 6.6, was invented by US chemist Wallace Hume Carothers (1896–1937) for the US chemical company DuPont in 1935. It transformed the toothbrush by providing material to replace the natural animal hair bristles used for its tufts. The first nylon bristle toothbrush, Doctor West's Miracle Toothbrush, went on sale in 1938. Made with nylon yarn, it formed the basis for the modern toothbrush. Nylon was capable of being woven, which led to new possibilities in the area of textiles, including nylon stockings (see image 2). The transparent material could make legs appear smooth and shiny, and was marketed as an affordable alternative to silk stockings. Launched at the New York World's Fair in 1939, nylon stockings revolutionized the market. Nylon was also initially used as sewing thread and in parachute fabric. Synthesized from petrochemicals, nylon opened the door to the discovery of new kinds of manufactured fibers.

By 1945, plastics had transformed the everyday environment of the industrialized Western world on an enormous scale. Plastics were being used in a host of ways in variety of products from ballpoint pens (see p.192) to fabrics, automative parts, and domestic interiors. **PS**

1934	1934	1936	1938	1940	1943
British chemical company ICI launches Perspex acrylic in the form of sheets, rods, tubes, and other shaped pieces.	Interiors on the RMS *Queen Mary* luxury ocean liner are fitted out in wood-grain Formica.	Aircraft canopies are made from Perspex see-through plastic. They allow for a combination of protection and visibility.	The first toothbrush to have nylon tufts is manufactured. It proves more effective than those made with natural bristles.	PVC is produced in the United Kingdom for the first time. It is widely used for rain wear.	DuPont discovers the synthetic material known by the brand name "Teflon."

Ekco AD-65 Radio 1934

WELLS COATES 1895–1958

Bakelite, stainless steel, cloth
16 x 15½ x 8¼ in.
40.5 x 39.5 x 21 cm

 NAVIGATOR

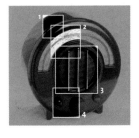

The appearance of radios during the interwar period was transformed by the arrival of plastics. Prior to that time, radios had been contained in wooden cabinets, designed to resemble conventional pieces of furniture. Taking pride of place in a living room, they had shared a similar esthetic to chests of drawers and cocktail cabinets. Once molded plastic body shells were used to encase the workings of radios, they ceased to resemble pieces of furniture and became equipment, more visually aligned with electric kitchen appliances.

Designed in Britain in 1932 and produced a couple of years later, the Ekco AD-65 radio is the work of Canadian architect and designer Wells Coates. Its Bakelite body shell, combined with steel and woven fabric, had no stylistic precedents. Instead, it took its form from the process of plastic molding. Its manufacturer, E K Cole Limited, was based in Southend-on-Sea, England. The firm's founder invited a number of modernist architects to create innovative designs for radios. It represented a step forward in the design of household goods for everyday life. **PS**

◉ FOCAL POINTS

1 CURVED SHELL
The availability of Bakelite meant that the AD-65 radio could take on a modernist look that had no associations with the past. The molding technique used in manufacture allowed the development of the curved profile for the object's body shell, which created its distinctive appearance.

2 SEMI-CIRCULAR DIAL
Once the circular form had been decided upon, the other elements had to be positioned to complement it. A semi-circle was chosen as the appropriate form for the tuning dial, which is functional and attractive. Being circular, the radio required two small plastic feet to stabilize it on a surface.

3 CIRCULAR FORM
The circular form of the radio aligned it with other modernist designs, such as those that emanated from the German Bauhaus, the shapes of which were geometric in nature. Coates knew about modern European design and intended his design to have a similarly progressive profile.

4 CONTROL KNOBS
The three circular control knobs on the lower part of the radio are positioned to create a harmonious composition. They echo the shape of the body shell and complete the pleasing appearance of the face of the radio. The radio was available in black, walnut, ivory, and green.

◷ DESIGNER PROFILE

1895–1927
Wells Coates was born in Tokyo, Japan, the eldest son of Canadian missionaries. The Japanese esthetic he encountered in his youth would influence his work later. Coates served in World War I, first as a gunner and then as a pilot with the Royal Air Force. He studied at the University of British Columbia in Canada. He went to London in 1922, where he trained as an engineer at the East London College, gaining his doctorate two years later. He worked as a journalist and then for a design firm.

1928–33
Coates set up his own firm in England. Among his first design projects was work on shops and the interior of the Cresta Silk Factory (1928) in Welwyn Garden City in Hertfordshire, and studios for the BBC's Broadcasting House (1930) in London. He began his collaboration with E K Cole Limited in 1932. In 1933 he co-founded the Modern Architectural Research Group, the British wing of the Congrès Internationaux d'Architecture Moderne, to further the practice of modern architecture.

1934–39
He designed apartment blocks in England, including the Isokon building on Lawn Road, Hampstead, London (1934), the Embassy Court flats (1935) in Brighton, Sussex, and 10 Palace Gate (1939) in Kensington, London.

1940–58
Coates served in the Royal Air Force during World War II, developing fighter aircraft. Afterward, he continued his architectural career and became involved in yacht design. In 1954 Coates left London. He spent two years teaching at Harvard University's Graduate School of Design and then moved to Vancouver, Canada.

ISOKON FURNITURE

Coates founded the Isokon Furniture Company in 1929 to design and build modernist houses and apartment blocks, as well as the furniture and fittings for them. He is most famous for designing the Isokon building (1935) in Hampstead, London, as an experiment in minimalist living. It became the home of various intellectuals and artists, including Bauhaus émigrés Walter Gropius (1883–1969), Marcel Breuer (1902–81), and László Moholy-Nagy (1895–1946). In 1939, when World War II started, the firm's supply of plywood dried up, and Isokon ceased producing furniture until 1963, when it was revived by British furniture designer Jack Pritchard (1899–1992).

Ballpoint Pen 1938

LÁSZLÓ BÍRÓ 1899–1985

An early Biro ballpoint pen, made by the Miles-Martin Pen Company in *c.* 1945.

The search for a pen that would facilitate writing with ink in a way that was cleaner than the fountain pen began in the late 19th century, with several patents being granted for a variety of solutions. The most promising was the concept of the ballpoint pen, which involved ink flowing over a little ball at the tip. The biggest breakthrough came in 1938 when László Bíró, a Hungarian painter and newspaper editor, working with his brother György, filed a British patent for a ball-socket mechanism. Keen to find an ink writing implement that did not smudge and dried fast, László invented one that combined a ball bearing and quick-drying ink. György was a chemist and helped him develop the ink, which is fed to the ball by capillary action.

Three years later, the brothers left Europe to settle in Argentina, where they set up a company and in 1943 filed a US patent. There they met the English accountant Henry Martin, who observed that—unlike a fountain pen—the ballpoint could be used at high altitudes without leaking. With Martin's backing, László licensed his idea to the Royal Air Force, and its air crews used the pens during World War II to write their logs. The British Miles Aircraft Company produced the pen called a "Biro." By Christmas 1945, the Miles-Martin Pen Company had taken over and Biros were on sale at 55 shillings each.

The postwar story of the Biro involved a number of US companies acquiring the rights to produce a pen with the ballpoint mechanism, including the Eversharp Company and Eberhard-Faber. In 1945 Reynolds Ball Point Pen produced a ballpoint pen and in 1954 Parker Pens created the "Jotter." None of the ventures were successful, and the ballpoint pen fell out of favor with consumers. The French firm BIC, formed in 1945, ultimately took the lead in the international marketplace, mass producing cheap BIC ballpoint pens in enormous numbers from 1950. Plastic had already been used for fountain pens, and the availability and cheapness of plastics at that time made them an obvious material for the body of the ballpoint pen. Indeed, ballpoint pens became one of the ways in which plastics entered the everyday environment. In the second half of the 20th century, the BIC ballpoint pen became a cheap, ubiquitous, throwaway item, so simple and effective that its presence was hardly noticed. In many ways, objects such as these can be thought of as modern vernacular artefacts. **PS**

✦ NAVIGATOR

Picture Post, December 8, 1945

Biro

MARKS A TURNING POINT IN THE HISTORY OF

Writing

"BIRO" is unique: it writes with a ball-bearing point —a point that never goes wrong, never floods, bends or splutters —a point that rolls your writing on to the paper with effortless ease. "BIRO" ink dries as you write; you cannot smudge it; you need no blotter. "BIRO" writes six months or

more without refilling—according to the amount you write. To replenish "BIRO" for a similar period of trouble-free service, a refill unit is inserted while you wait.

The demand for "BIRO" has far exceeded production capacity. Consequently you may have to be patient until your turn comes round.

Retail Price 55/-
including purchase tax.

Biro —for perpetually perfect WRITING

◄ The advantages of the Biro ballpoint pen were heavily promoted in advertisements when it launched to the public. The ballpoint pen was then marketed as an expensive luxury item.

👁 FOCAL POINTS

1 TIP
The ballpoint pen employs a simple mechanism that involves the insertion of a tiny ball bearing at the tip of the pen, over which the ink flows. This allows it to flow smoothly and evenly, avoiding the messiness of working with a fountain pen.

2 CLIP
The early ballpoint pen borrowed the traditional appearance of a fountain pen. It featured a number of already familiar elements, from the bands of metal around the body to the metal clip that fitted to the top jacket pocket of its—assumedly male—user.

BIC CRISTAL

The ballpoint pen's resemblance to a fountain pen came to an end with the appearance of the BIC Cristal pen in 1950, which features a transparent polystyrene body that shows the ink level, a hexagonal barrel that affords a comfortable grip and does not roll on a desk, and a streamlined polypropylene cap in the color of the ink. No effort was made to link the pen to the past. The look and ergonomic design reflected the modernity of the writing tool. Produced in vast quantities, the pen had to be bought by large numbers of people if the investment in its manufacture was to be worthwhile, and it was promoted successfully in several wide-ranging advertising campaigns.

THE CONSULTANT DESIGNER

1 Norman Bel Geddes created the Futurama model city in 1939 for the New York World's Fair. Sponsored by General Motors, Futurama introduced the concept of expressways.

2 The black enamel and chrome clamshell case of Walter Dorwin Teague's Kodak Bantam Special in 1936 is an example of Art Deco streamline styling.

The role of consultant designer to industry came of age in the United States in the years between the two world wars, primarily as a result of the effect of the economic depression in manufacturing, but also of expanding consumer needs. Building on the work of earlier practitioners, such as Peter Behrens (1868–1940) in Germany, consultant designers needed to combine high visual and conceptual skills with the ability to work across a broad range of disciplines. Several of the leading designers—including Norman Bel Geddes (1893–1958), Walter Dorwin Teague (1883–1960), Raymond Loewy (1893–1986), and Henry Dreyfuss (1904–72)—had begun their working lives in stage design, advertising, and retail, all spheres that had been quick to embrace the modern style. Bel Geddes first worked as a stage designer, and his training in theatrical effects led to work creating window displays and products; Teague had designed decorative borders for advertisements for the Calkins and Holden agency; Loewy started out as a window designer for department stores, including Saks Fifth Avenue and Macy's in New York City; and Dreyfuss, first apprenticed as a stage designer to Bel Geddes, had then worked for Macy's.

The arrival of the consultant designer represented the moment when designer culture came into being. Objects, images, or environments gained added value when the names of well-known designers were attached to them.

KEY EVENTS

1924	1926	1927	1928	1929	1932
Norman Bel Geddes and Henry Dreyfuss design the set for *The Miracle*, which played on Broadway in New York City.	US industrial designer Donald Deskey (1894–1989) sets up a consultant design office that specializes in furniture, textiles, and lighting design.	Bel Geddes opens his industrial design studio, one of the first consultancy agencies to work with a range of manufacturers.	Walter Dorwin Teague begins his relationship with Kodak, which leads to a range of innovative designs for the company.	Dreyfuss opens his consultant design office. One of his first clients is Macy's department store in New York City.	Bel Geddes publishes *Horizons*, one of the first of a spate of books written by consultant designers setting out their design philosophies.

Time and *Life* magazines reported on the details of the consultants' daily lives as though they were Hollywood stars. Their celebrity status was important to them as individuals but it was more crucial for the manufacturers who employed them, because it bestowed an instant cachet on their goods. Indeed, the designers' names were used as a form of product endorsement.

Bel Geddes was among the most visionary of them all. In his early career he worked on experimental forms of transport that employed dramatic aerodynamic styling. He used his experience in stage design to create theatrical interiors for the corporate headquarters' of advertising agency J. Walter Thompson in New York in 1927. He also played an important role at the 1939 New York's World Fair, which celebrated the "World of Tomorrow" and was dominated by the futuristic, streamlined vision offered by consultant designers, and his Futurama (see image 1), a model city for General Motors, depicted a world twenty years into the future.

Teague has a number of seminal streamlined designs to his name, including Texaco petrol stations (1934) and cameras such as the Kodak Bantam Special (1936; see image 2), which suggest modernity and progress. Teague was a member of the Board of Design for the 1939 New York's World Fair and designed many of its exhibits, including the Wonder World of Chemistry for DuPont, which included a 105-foot (45-m), test-tube-shaped tower that simulated bubbling chemicals when lit at night.

Loewy launched his career as an industrial designer streamlining the Gestetner Duplicator (1929; see p.196). His Coldspot refrigerator (1934) for mail-order firm Sears Roebuck borrowed details from automotive design, including a recessed door handle. His greatest achievement is the streamlined GG-1 electric locomotive (1936) for the Pennsylvania Railroad Company.

Dreyfuss was commissioned by a wide range of manufacturers—from the Hoover vacuum cleaner company to the Westclox clock company—demonstrating that he could combine the esthetic language of streamlining with concern for what came to be called products' "human factors." His skill for ergonomics combined with the streamlining esthetic is evident in products such as the Bell Model 302 handset telephone (1937; see p.198).

As well as developing a number of spectacular streamlined designs, the consultants were innovative in the area of business practices. Bel Geddes gained his market knowledge via detailed consumer questionnaires. He styled his Highboy, Lowboy, and Lazyboy radio cabinets for Philco Radio in 1931 with the aid of his market-survey results to appeal to different market segments.

Many other industries engaged in producing consumer products benefited from hiring consultant designers from the late 1920s. Soon other countries emulated the model of consultant design that emerged in the United States, as they searched for ways of embedding design into their emerging industries and encouraging consumer interest. **PS**

1933	1934	1934	1936	1939	1940
The "Century of Progress" exhibition is held in Chicago. Art Deco style is prominent but new materials—steel, aluminum, and so on—also feature.	Chrysler's Airflow automobile, one of the first streamlined cars to enter the motor marketplace, is launched. It proves to be ahead of its time.	The "Machine Art" exhibition opens at New York City's Museum of Modern Art, showing how industry influences ideas about art.	Raymond Loewy establishes a relationship with the Pennsylvania Railroad Company, which leads to some of his most striking designs.	The New York World's Fair is held in Queens. It represents the pinnacle of streamlining, which penetrated all walks of life at that time.	Teague publishes *Design This Day*, an overview of his work and an account of the ideas underpinning the streamlined movement in design.

Gestetner Duplicator 1929
RAYMOND LOEWY 1893–1986

Metal, rubber, wood
Mechanism 13 x 15 x 24 in.
34 x 38 x 61 cm

🕐 DESIGNER PROFILE

1893–1919
Loewy was born in Paris, served in the French Army during World War I. and emigrated to New York in 1919.

1920–28
He worked as a fashion illustrator for *Vogue* and *Harper's Bazaar*, among other magazines, and as a window dresser for Macy's and Saks in New York City.

1929–43
In 1929 Loewy received the commission from Sigmund Gestetner to redesign the duplicator. The job led to many more industrial design commissions, and he set up his own office as a consultant designer in 1930. Work during the 1930s included several redesigns of the Hupmobile motor car.

1944–1963
He established his industrial design firm Loewy Associates in 1944. It was incredibly successful and he appeared on the cover of *Time* magazine in 1949. Notable designs included the new Coca-Cola bottle in the 1950s and the Avanti automobile for Studebaker in 1963.

1964–86
During the 1960s and early 1970s, Loewy worked with NASA on habitability systems and interior design for its spacecraft.

In 1929 Sigmund Gestetner approached Raymond Loewy and asked him to improve the visual appeal of his rather outdated office duplicator. The existing machine had a complex, mechanical metal top that did all the work (and looked a little like a sewing machine) and a base that resembled an old-fashioned filing cabinet. Loewy's modernization retained the functional divide between the copying machine and the wooden cabinet, but, importantly, he removed the physical gap between the two, thereby transforming the duplicator into an integrated object that was attractive to both consumers and users. It was a classic piece of redesign.

The most significant addition was the large Bakelite body shell, which encased all the workings and kept the machinery safe and dust free. Its curvaceous profile was in keeping with the new streamlined esthetic of the day, and it transformed the duplicator from a mundane machine into a shining symbol of progress. Indeed, Loewy's design was intended as a progressive addition to the modern office environment that was emerging in the United States in the 1920s. It was part of the move toward enhanced efficiency and production, a result of the time-and-motion studies initiated earlier in the century. The success of the Gestetner Duplicator enhanced Loewy's reputation, and he went on to become one of the most renowned consultant designers of the mid 20th century, working on a wide range of products, from cars and trains to crockery. **PS**

👁 FOCAL POINTS

1 MIXED MATERIALS
In his redesign of the duplicator, Loewy retained the original combination of materials—wood and metal—and added Bakelite. Although the result was complex to produce, the new visual language he employed succeeded in making the materials work together harmoniously.

2 STREAMLINING
Loewy designed a streamlined body shell, realized in molded Bakelite, for the top half of the machine. However, the size of the shell presented technical challenges because plastics molding was still in its infancy. He echoed the curves of the casing by rounding the top edges of the cabinet.

3 NEW LEGS
One of the significant changes that Loewy introduced was to replace the cabriole-style legs with shorter, sturdier, and more modern-looking ones. This enhanced the overall stability of the duplicator and transformed the old-fashioned cabinet into a stylish piece of office equipment.

THE COLDSPOT REFRIGERATOR

In 1934 Loewy redesigned the Coldspot refrigerator for Sears Roebuck. He took much of his inspiration for the design from automobile manufacture. The refrigerator he created was one of the first to boast a fully streamlined body. Its bulbous shape was made possible by the introduction of new techniques in steel manufacturing and bending.

Bell Model 302 1937

HENRY DREYFUSS 1904–72

The Model 302 was the first Bell telephone to include the ringer and network circuitry in the same unit.

The Bell 302, also known as the Model 302 handset telephone, was designed in 1937 by US industrial designer Henry Dreyfuss. It was inspired by principles of functionality, which Dreyfuss described as "the human factor." Manufactured by Western Electric, the Model 302's curving sides swoop upward from a square base to cradle the gentle arc of the handset.

Dreyfuss had trained as apprentice to theater designer Norman Bel Geddes, before setting up his own studio. He was not the only one. A new breed of industrial designers had started out as artists, set designers, and illustrators who, when the Great Depression struck, were forced to find new jobs. A revolutionary notion that companies could boost profits through good design began to spread. Dreyfuss, Raymond Loewy, and others were reinventing the relationship between people and the products they would use. To make a product more user friendly, they would often encase any mechanical parts inside streamlined, sculpted shells.

In 1930 Bell Labs sponsored a competition for a new handset to replace the old candlestick telephone and invited Dreyfuss to enter. He refused, preferring to work directly with engineers. The competition ended and the company called Dreyfuss back. It was the start of a decades-long relationship. The Model 302 had a receiver and transmitter in a combined handset resting on a horizontal cradle. Molded in black phenol resin, it was produced until 1954. Collectors sometimes refer to the Model 302 as "the Lucy phone," because it was often seen in the 1950s' TV comedy show, *I Love Lucy*. **JW**

✪ NAVIGATOR

☁ FOCAL POINTS

1 HANDSET

Dreyfuss conceived the Model 302 holistically, according to how it would relate to the human body. He softened his design, rounding corners and smoothing edges. For example, the triangular handle follows the shape of the palm when holding the phone. When cradled, it rests on the shoulder.

2 HOUSING

Model 302 sets were issued in black. Sets with painted metal housings were available in several colors. Metallic hues, such as dark gold, statuary bronze, old brass, and oxidized silver were available by order. Later, plastic sets were available in ivory, red, gray, green, dark blue, and rose.

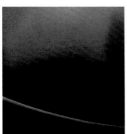

3 DIAL

Built on a rectangular steel base plate, the Model 302's housing was made out of cast zinc alloy and then plastic when metal was scarce in World War II. The dial plates were made of steel covered with white vitreous enamel. The metal finger wheels were replaced with clear plastic.

▲ Dreyfuss's studio, Henry Dreyfuss Associates, also designed the innovative Trimline corded telephone for Bell in 1965. The dial was moved from the telephone's base to the underside of the handset.

⏱ DESIGNER PROFILE

1904–37

Born in Brooklyn, New York City, Henry Dreyfuss was an apprentice stage designer before opening a design office in 1929. His 1933 refrigerator for General Electric radically improved looks and functionality, as did his Toperator washing machine for Sears Roebuck. In 1934 he was featured in *Fortune* Magazine. Soon he was making $25,000 a year for Hoover Co, designing the Model 150 upright vacuum cleaner.

1938–1954

Dreyfuss designed steam engines for the New York to Chicago line. He produced the John Deere Model A tractor, the Big Ben alarm clock, and the futuristic city 2039 at the New York World's Fair in 1939. In 1941 he co-designed wartime strategy rooms for the US Department of Defense Joint Chiefs of Staff.

1955–1972

Dreyfuss wrote *Designing for People* (1955) and *The Measure of Man* (1960). In 1965 he became the first president of the Industrial Design Society of America.

CONSISTENCY AND LONGEVITY

The Model 302 was an immediate success and remained more or less unchanged until the 1960s—an incredibly long shelf life by design standards. Consistency became a Dreyfuss byword, and he even streamlined his own wardrobe by wearing only brown suits. He would only stay at the Plaza Hotel when in New York City, so clients knew where to find him, and it is said he missed only five days of work over the course of twenty-two years.

PUBLIC SERVICE DESIGN

1 Percy Metcalfe's designs for Irish coinage feature a harp as the national symbol and a series of animals important to the country's agricultural economy.

2 Fiat's Littorina railcars displayed the symbol of Benito Mussolini's fascist party on the front, the fasces—bound rods with a projecting axe.

3 Herbert Matter pioneered photomontage in commercial art with posters promoting travel to Switzerland, such as this example from 1936.

N ational flags, emblems, military uniforms, and coinage have been ways of branding a kingdom or state since early times. As national and local government offered citizens a variety of goods, services, and information in the 20th century, the art of public relations became officially linked to government, coinciding with a search for universal and timeless standards of design. Guided by the widespread moral and intellectual rejection of laissez-faire capitalism of the 19th century, the early 20th century saw a blurring between public and private sectors and the creation of intermediate entities such as the London Passenger Transport Board, while publicly owned services conveyed the qualities of efficiency and up-to-dateness associated with enlightened commerce. The public sector had the opportunity to give design a role in branding, connected not primarily to selling (being in many cases monopoly providers), but to building a sense of familiarity and security.

Shattered by World War I, the Germany of the Weimar Republic (1919–33) developed modern design in many fields. In Frankfurt a regular municipal magazine in the late 1920s showed the new tenants of modernist houses what furniture was suitable for their homes, while in 1926 they were also offered the convenient Frankfurt kitchen design (see p.164) with its minimal units.

After the Irish Free State was founded in 1922, one of the ways it symbolized its status was to issue its own coinage. Such was the success of English sculptor Percy Metcalfe's (1895–1970) design of 1928 (see image 1) that it remained in use until Ireland adopted the euro as its currency in 2002.

KEY EVENTS

1907	1909	1915	1923	1926	1930
German electrical equipment maker AEG hires architect Peter Behrens (1868–1940) to redesign the company logo (see p.118) and brand.	Danish architect Knud V. Engelhardt (1882–1931) adopts a proto-modernist layout for the Copenhagen telephone directory.	Industrialists, retailers, and journalists found the Design and Industries Association in London to promote civic design and responsible industry.	Engelhardt designs road signage for Gentofte in eastern Denmark, using white sans serif lettering on black; a red heart is the dot on the letter "j."	Austrian architect Margarete Schütte-Lihotzky (1897–2000) designs the Frankfurt kitchen (see p.164) for workers' housing in the city.	The Sceaux rail line from Paris introduces railcars in green and white with Art Deco-style lighting.

In Britain a lead for public-utility design was given by the London Underground Railway when seeking to unify its image as a public service on a level above capitalism. Commercial manager Frank Pick (1878–1941) commissioned an alphabet that would belong "unmistakably to the times in which we lived." Pioneer of authentic hand-lettering Edward Johnston (1872–1944) designed Johnston, his monoline sans-serif typeface, in 1916. It was the precursor of many such typefaces and remains in use in the 21st century. From an anonymous diamond-shaped original, Johnston also developed the Underground roundel used to carry station names. Charles Holden's (1875–1960) station architecture, derived from Arts and Crafts movement (see p.74) principles but using flat roofs and concrete, beamed out a message of reassurance without complacency or escapism. As the network expanded, navigating it became confusing. Pick sought to resolve the problem by commissioning engineering draftsman Harry Beck (1902–74) to create a diagrammatic map. Beck's radical design of 1933 (see p.202) is still in use.

Not all public service design between the wars was modernist. From 1910 until 1940, classical styles were revived to counter Art Nouveau (see p.92), which was thought too personal, and stripped classical—in lettering as in architecture—remained in use across the political spectrum from Stalinist Russia to the United States, accompanied by mural paintings and heroic sculpture. The Nazis simultaneously promoted the nostalgic rural *Heimatstil* style and Fraktur or blackletter type, but also modern motorways and the *Kraft durch Freude* (Strength through Joy) people's car that became the Volkswagen Beetle (1938; see p.210). Streamlined Art Deco (see p.156) was a feature of Italian design under Fascism, leading to Fiat's streamlined Littorina railway passenger cars (1932; see image 2) for the Ferrovie dello Stato (State Railway) and named for Benito Mussolini's (1883–1945) regime.

The PTT (Postal Telegraph and Telephone) service in Holland was an example of state sponsorship of a spritely modernism in its phone boxes and printed matter, from stamps to public information materials (see p.204). However, the country most thoroughly engaged in modernism before 1930 was Switzerland, where the photomontage posters (see image 3) by graphic designer and photographer Herbert Matter (1907–84) for the Swiss National Tourist Office and Swiss resorts were widely admired.

A series of national and international exhibitions continued a 19th-century tradition of national self-representation in architecture and displays of art and industry. Ludwig Mies van der Rohe's (1886–1969) German Pavilion at the 1929 International Exposition in Barcelona lacked the usual national symbols and spoke volumes by omission. It inspired the head of Britain's Empire Marketing Board and future public relations officer for the British Post Office, Stephen Tallents (1884–1958), who saw the future in terms of intangible assets of culture and language rather than the productions of industry. **AP**

1931	1932	1932	1932	1935	1939–40
Dutch architect Leendert van der Vlugt (1894–1936) designs the PTT telephone box with a flat top, much glass, and lower-case sans serif signage.	Stephen Tallents publishes *The Projection of England*, an essay on promoting a post-industrial nation and selling it to the world with design.	Typographer Stanley Morison (1889–1967) redesigns *The Times* newspaper, using his Times New Roman typeface based on classical principles.	Danish architect Steen Eiler Rasmussen (1898–1990) organizes the "Britisk Brugskunst" (British Applied Art) show in Copenhagen.	English architect Giles Gilbert Scott (1880–1960) designs the K6 Jubilee red telephone box, with a mdomed top and small window panes.	The World's Fair in New York City has sixty pavilions projecting national commerce, as the United States identifies with consumerism.

London Underground Map 1933

HARRY BECK 1902–74

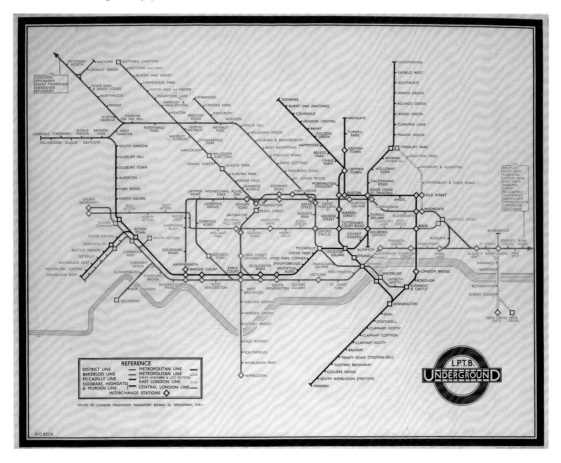

Color lithograph
6⅝ x 9 in.
16.8 x 22.8 cm

By 1931, Edward Johnston's sans serif typeface and Charles Holden's architecture were starting to create a sense of unity and a corporate identity for London Underground. However, the poster maps and the pocket-sized card folders showing the extent of the network and its intersections remained unreformed. As the network was extended into new suburban areas, it became difficult for mapmakers to balance the dense texture of the central area against the distant tails of lines to the newly built suburbs at a consistent scale.

By abandoning realistic scale and aiming for the topological rather than the topographical, Harry Beck made a conceptual leap that the directors of London Transport initially thought was beyond the ability of the ordinary traveler to understand. Beck was an engineering draftsman at the London Underground signals office, who began mapping the network schematically in his spare time. After rejecting his design when he first offered it in 1931, they decided to give it a trial in 1933, and it was immediately popular among customers, showing that their fears were unfounded.

Beck's design synthesized features of earlier maps while making major innovations. The color-coded map allowed travelers to plan their route without redundant information about features above ground, the shapes of the routes were simplified, and easily read symbols were used for interchange stations. These principles were adopted over time by almost every transport system in the world and Beck's diagram still forms the basis for the underground map used in London in the 21st century. **AP**

✦ NAVIGATOR

⊚ FOCAL POINTS

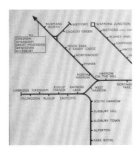

1 TICKS

Beck's first drafts of the diagram used a round blob to denote the non-interchange stations. He then substituted a tick, which lies in the direction chosen for the text, itself determined by the available space in the diagram. It directs the reader's eye toward the relevant name.

2 SQUARES

Beck indicated interchange stations in the 1933 map as open diamond shapes. Some are repeated on each line passing through the station, while others serve a dual purpose. From 1949, he adopted the white-line connector, still in use, which clarifies the nature of the interchange.

3 BOX

The Metropolitan and District lines extended as surface railways into the countryside, bringing new housing in their path. Beck compressed the actual distances involved, and in the 1933 version, he dealt with the eastern arm of the District by putting the offstage station names in a box.

4 RIVER THAMES

Beck's self-imposed rule omitted all surface features apart from the river Thames, although even this was left out of some versions of the map. Here it is submitted to Beck's geometric discipline of 45-degree angles and horizontals. Underneath is a key to the line colors and other information.

🕐 DESIGNER PROFILE

1902–32

Harry Beck was born in London. In 1925 he became an engineering draftsman for London Underground. In 1931 he proposed a design to illustrate the expanding underground system, but it was rejected and he made modifications.

1933–74

A trial pocket version of Beck's design was published. As the system expanded, he continued to modify the map for London Transport until 1960. From 1947 he taught typographics and color design at the London School of Printing.

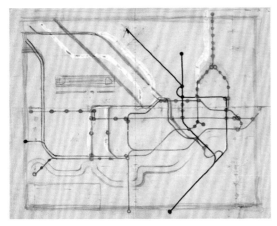

▲ Created in 1931, this is Beck's first rough sketch for the London Underground map. Inspired by electrical-circuit diagrams, Beck used only vertical, horizontal, and diagonal lines.

AMATEURISM AND EFFICIENCY

While the British tended to be conservative and suspicious of foreign professionalism in design and foreign ideas about art, the tradition of amateur engineering and invention continued to win respect, and it is in this context, rather than that of the Bauhaus (see p.126) or De Stijl (see p.114) that Beck's work should be understood. At the turn of the century, British culture became obsessed by the idea of efficiency—often paraphrased as fitness for purpose. Darwinian ideas of evolution encouraged the idea that everything had the potential to achieve ideal form by dropping superfluous or outdated features. New technologies, such as the electric motors that drove the London tube trains, showed this evolutionary pattern in contrast to the steam trains they replaced.

The Book of PTT 1938
PIET ZWART 1885–1977

Zorg, dat de post met

één oogopslag

kan zien naar welke plaats een stuk verzonden moet worden; zet daarom een **streep** onder de plaatsnaam.

Er zijn stukken voor allerlei plaatsen; die stukken moeten eerst worden uitgezocht en gerangschikt. Dit gebeurt in kasten met vakjes voorzien van een plaatsnaam. In elk vakje komen de stukken die voor die plaats bestemd zijn.

Dit gebeurt zeer snel; er is geen tijd te verliezen, de posttrein wacht niet; de post kan alleen maar kijken naar de plaats van bestemming; al het andere komt later wel in orde.

Het is dus van groot belang een streep onder de plaatsnaam te zetten.

Daardoor gaat het rangschikken vlugger en dus ook de verzending.

Zet onder de plaatsnaam een streep

Hengelo (Gld)

8

n 1912 Jean-François van Royen(1878–1942), the legal clerk to the directors of the Dutch PTT (Postal Telegraph and Telephone) service, complained about the ugliness of its existing government-produced design. By 1920 Van Royen was secretary general and given the scope to influence the public face of the organization in a manner unique in Europe at the time. Van Royen was a typographer himself, and a friend of many of the contemporary leading designers. Rather than imposing a unified style on the organization, he allowed designers as varied as Jan Toorop (1858–1928), one of the founders of Art Nouveau (see p.92), and the modernist Paul Schuitema (1897–1973) to work in an individual manner. In addition, a telephone booth was commissioned from architect Leendert van der Vlugt (1894–1936) as part of his aim to improve design.

Into this lively culture, Van Royen brought Piet Zwart to design stamps that were the first to use photographic imagery, plus leaflets and posters. Zwart's most famous work for the company was *Het boek van PTT* (*The Book of PTT*). This was given to children to encourage them to make more use of the company's services. With photomontages of cut-out paper dolls and graphic representations of statistics, it pushed the existing technology of reproduction to its limits and made a dull subject a memorable fantasy, which was quite the contrary of ordinary trade literature. It is an example of how design of public information materials helped to modernize and transform the PTT's image. **AP**

Rotogravure
9⅞ x 7 in./25 x 17.5 cm

FOCAL POINTS

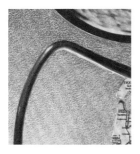

1 BLUE
Full-color printing was expensive and designers often used spot color, creating a page to print in a limited number of specified colors by making separate drawings in black for each of the colours. Zwart used versions of the three primary colors favored by the De Stijl movement.

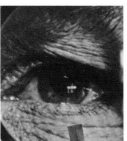

2 EYE
Although the scatter of text and image on the page seems random, there is a structure that uses the convention of reading from top to bottom and left to right, so that the eye travels in a diagonal sequence, apparent where the visual story begins with the eye of the worker in the sorting office.

3 PINK LETTERS
Contemporary ideas advocating that only sans serif typefaces should be used, or employing entirely lower-case letters, can be found in Zwart's book, where he introduces emphasis and variety by using different type sizes and colors in an unconventional and poster-like fashion.

THE INFLUENCE OF CINEMA

Graphic designers of Zwart's generation were the first to experience moving pictures—he designed a poster for an international film festival at The Hague in 1928. Designers learned from the way avant-garde cinema in the early 1920s developed techniques for showing familiar things in unfamiliar ways. These included close-ups that focused attention on part of a larger object or scene, famously in the sequence on the Odessa steps in Sergei Eisenstein's (1898–1948) *Battleship Potemkin* (1925), contrasted with long-distance shots. Scenes might be shot at an angle, and devices were used to frame part of the action like the monocle round the eye in *The Book of PTT*. Silent cinema encouraged storytelling purely through images, and it is possible to imagine how the page of *The Book of PTT* might become a film, moving across the map of the Netherlands to explain the importance of writing the address correctly on the envelope.

THE RISE OF MOTORING

The mass production of the Ford Model T in the United States in the early part of the 20th century kick-started an era of mass car ownership, and from that point onward motoring became part of everyday life. As more people invested in cars, there was an increased need for the vehicles to look good. The financial crisis that led Ford Motor Company to close its River Rouge factory for a year in 1926, in the face of competition from General Motors Company (GM), marked an important turning point in the emerging role of the automobile designer. In response to changing consumer demands, GM rejected product standardization in favor of a more flexible manufacturing system. Its launch in 1927 of a styling section represented the first attempt to introduce an esthetic element into the mass-produced automobile.

During the interwar years, cars remained large and stylish in the United States, but in Europe—where traveling distances were shorter—the concept of the small, low-cost, mass car, or "people's car," took hold. Appearance was subservient to utility, and the engineer rather than the automobile stylist reigned supreme. In the United Kingdom, the cars produced by Herbert Austin (1866–1941) and William Morris (1877–1963) led the way. The most popular of the former's cars was the Austin 7 (see image 2), introduced in 1922. It had four seats, although the two at the rear were only suitable for children. Morris's first Minor was launched six years later and once again prioritized price over style.

1 The Citroën 2CV had a crude, minimally streamlined body and its accessories and fittings were very basic.

2 Known as "Chummy," the Austin 7 was the United Kingdom's response to the Ford Model T.

3 The Fiat 500 C Topolino was a small, two-passenger car with a simple, streamlined body shell.

KEY EVENTS

1913	1919	1922	1928	1931	1932
The Morris Oxford Bullnose is manufactured in the United Kingdom; it is one of the country's first low-cost, mass-produced cars.	The Citroën company is founded in France. It is quick to introduce Fordist production techniques and aims its cars at a mass market.	The little Austin 7 is launched in the United Kingdom; it is the country's first people's car.	The Morris Minor is introduced in the United Kingdom. Designed by Alec Issigonis (1906–88), it becomes very popular after World War II.	Ferdinand Porsche (1875–1951) establishes his automotive company in Stuttgart, Germany, and begins to develop a small car for the masses.	Flaminio Bertoni is employed by Citroën and begins work on the design of the Citroën 2CV three years later.

Germany's version of the people's car was the Volkswagen Beetle (1938; see p.210), which today is recognized as a design classic. In France the Citroën company was influential in bringing Fordist manufacturing techniques across the Atlantic, and in the interwar years began to develop an innovative utility model. This development was crystallized by the appointment of Pierre-Jules Boulanger (1885–1950) to the Paris factory in 1936. In collaboration with Italian sculptor Flaminio Bertoni (1903–64), he began work on what was to become the Citroën 2CV (see image 1), which was launched in 1948. The car was designed specifically with the needs of French farmers in mind. It was able to cope with almost any road surface and was cheap to run. Although Italy did not produce its fully fledged version of the people's car until after World War II—in the form of the Fiat 600, launched in 1956—its designer, Dante Giacosa (1905–96), worked on an earlier version (see image 3) during the interwar years.

The advent of the people's car facilitated mass travel and tourism on a scale never experienced before. In turn, this led to the emergence of a number of subsidiary industries, the sole purpose of which was to support motoring. The need for rubber tires on a mass scale saw the growth of the Michelin and Dunlop tire manufacturers, while the concomitant requirement for a widespread fuel distribution system led to the construction of gas stations across the globe (see p.208). Above all, mass travel necessitated the construction of new roads and road signage systems. Mass motoring transformed leisure, too. Day trips to the countryside, roadside picnics, and sightseeing tours were nothing new, but for the first time they were brought within the reach of ordinary people. This democratization of leisure and lifestyle provided designers and manufacturers with a variety of new challenges. **PS**

1933	1936	1936	1939	1948	1953
Hitler comes to power. One of his aims is to see a people's car developed for Germany, a project in which Porsche becomes involved.	Pierre-Jules Boulanger is hired by the managing director of the Citroën factory in Paris. He initiates the pre-war development of the Citroën 2CV.	Italy's Fiat Topolino is launched. Designed by Dante Giacosa, it is the first of that country's low-cost popular cars.	The prototype of the Citroën 2CV produced in this year becomes the model for the post-war, mass-produced version.	The Citroën 2CV finally appears in its fully fledged form at the Paris Salon de l'Automobile. It is quickly adopted as an urban car.	The Ford Popular is launched as a cheap family car in the United Kingdom and rapidly lives up to its name.

"You Can Be Sure of Shell" Poster 1933

EDWARD MCKNIGHT KAUFFER 1890–1954

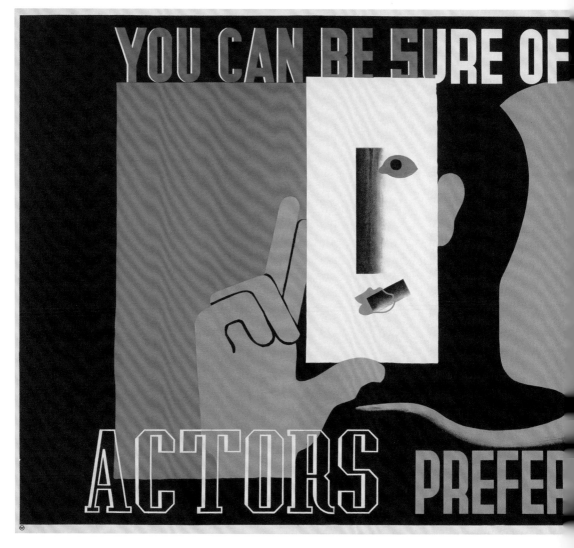

Lithograph
30½ x 44½ in./77 x 113 cm

⬥ NAVIGATOR

To the new motoring public taking to the roads in their people's cars, one supplier of fuel appeared much the same as the next. At the same time, driving for pleasure, rather than as a necessary means of getting from A to B, was a relatively new concept. The first challenge for the ancillary industries who supported mass travel, therefore, was to stimulate and increase demand for their products by promoting the notion of touring: more car journeys meant more fuel sold. The second was to achieve brand differentiation and brand loyalty when their products were less than exciting. One of the ways in which Shell promoted itself was through innovative advertising campaigns, which stressed the reliability of its fuel and the pleasures of the countryside.

The "You Can Be Sure of Shell: Actors Prefer Shell" poster designed by Edward Kauffer was part of a campaign undertaken by the Shell advertising department in the United Kingdom, led by Jack Beddington from 1932. His approach was hugely innovative in that he brought in a number of artists to create posters, among them Paul Nash (1889–1946), John Piper (1903–92), Vanessa Bell (1879–1961), and Graham Sutherland (1903–80). **PS**

FOCAL POINTS

1 COLOR
The artist has employed a basic palette. In so doing he was reflecting modernist thinking manifested by the Dutch De Stijl artists and designers and by the craftsmen and designers at the German Bauhaus. Kauffer was among the first to bring this use of color into the world of advertising.

2 ABSTRACTION
Kauffer's greatest contribution was to bring avant-garde movements, such as Futurism and Cubism, into advertising. This poster owes much to Cubist collage techniques, and those of Picasso in particular. The use of geometry and strong form projects a very effective commercial message.

3 TYPOGRAPHY
Typography is used by Kauffer in a very sophisticated way. In this poster he has combined three typefaces; two of them are sans serif faces, which were associated with the modern movement in graphic design. Although he studied fine art, he was well versed in modernist design and typography.

DESIGNER PROFILE

1890–1912
Kauffer first displayed his artistic skills when he painted stage scenery for a local opera house. He went on to study fine art at the California School of Design, San Francisco, where a tutor offered to sponsor his travel to Paris to continue his studies.

1913–14
In Paris Kauffer spent a couple of years studying art before the outbreak of World War I. It was here that he acquired his knowledge of the avant-garde at first hand, which stood him in good stead for the rest of his career.

1915–39
Kauffer moved to London and immediately began to apply what he had learned in Paris to the world of advertising. In 1915 Frank Pick commissioned him to design a number of posters for London Underground. Shell was Kauffer's biggest client in the 1930s, but he also worked for Fortnum and Mason and Lund Humphries.

1940–54
In 1940 Kauffer returned to the United States, where he continued to work. One of his last projects was a series of posters that he created for American Airlines in the 1950s.

EDWARD KAUFFER AND MARION DORN

Kauffer met US interior and textile designer Marion Dorn (1896–1964) on a trip to Paris in 1923 and promptly left his wife and daughter to set up life with her in London. Together, they undertook a number of projects, such as interior schemes for offices and a range of designs—interiors, a logo, a luggage label, and a brochure—for the Orient Line's flagship modern ocean liner, the *Orion*, which traveled between England and Australia. Kauffer was responsible for the cover of the brochure, which featured his characteristic combined use of geometrical forms and modernist typography. They also created a collection of rugs, and a replica of one of Dorn's abstract designs can be seen in the entrance hall of Eltham Palace, London (right).

Volkswagen Beetle 1938
FERDINAND PORSCHE 1875–1951

A 1953 Volkswagen Export Type 1 Beetle. Adolf Hitler advised that the people's car be streamlined to "look like a beetle." In 1981 the Beetle became the first car to sell twenty million units.

In the early 1930s, what was later to be known as the Volkswagen "Beetle" emerged as the result of a project led by the Czech automotive engineer Ferdinand Porsche, working in Germany and supported by Adolf Hitler. Compared to other Western countries, levels of car ownership were low in Germany. The Führer wanted to develop a low-priced *volkswagen* (people's car)—a German equivalent of Ford's Model T—which the majority of the population could afford to purchase. He decreed the vehicle should be able to travel at 60 mph (100 kph), carry a family of five. and cost thirty weeks' average pay. Porsche had an extensive track record in automobile design and had worked with a number of companies along similar lines. With Hitler's encouragement and influenced by the layout of a Czech car, the Tatra, Porsche developed the "Type 60."

The car was tested extensively and went through several stages. In 1937 Hitler decided that its production should be state funded and his government founded Volkswagen. The next year the design was finalized and the *KdF-Wagen* (Strength through Joy Car) was finally launched, accompanied by a promotional campaign. When World War II broke out in 1939, steel supplies were redirected to war production and the car was shelved. The car would have remained a symbol of a defeated fascist regime had it not been for the British decision to reopen the Volkswagen plant at Wolfsburg immediately after the war in an attempt to stimulate German reconstruction and the recovery of its manufacturing base. The Beetle's subsequent introduction to the US market in 1949 paved the way for its eventual commercial success and status as a design icon. By the late 1960s, the budget two-door saloon had become a cult classic, with a particular appeal to the young, who often customized it with painted images. When production ceased in 2003, some 20.5 million models had been built. **PS**

⊕ NAVIGATOR

⊙ FOCAL POINTS

1 ROUNDED PROFILE
The Beetle has a dramatic profile. With its rounded front hood, slanting windshield, and tapering rear, the shape of the body shell is that of a classic aerodynamic teardrop. To reinforce its visual unity, the headlights are integrated and the bumpers and tail lights flow with the body form.

2 REAR WINDOW
The early prototypes of the Beetle had no rear window. Later, a small rear window was introduced, a split design known as the *brezelfenster* (pretzel-window) model. In 1953 the two-part window was replaced with an oval, one-piece glass window that was 23 per cent larger.

3 LOUVERED VENTS
One of the Beetle's most defining characteristics is its air-cooled engine located at the rear of the vehicle. Another is the horizontal louvered vents, situated just below the rear window to provide ventilation. They also give the car a utilitarian appearance and reinforce its functionality.

▲ The Beetle is a car with a strong visual personality and that is reflected by its star role in Walt Disney's "Herbie" films, beginning with *The Love Bug* (1968), in which an anthropomorphized 1963 Beetle helps a racing-car driver become a champion.

◷ DESIGNER PROFILE

1875–1930
Born in Maffersdorf in Bohemia (later the Czech Republic), Ferdinand Porsche worked as an engineer in automotive companies in Vienna. In 1906 he joined Austro-Daimler as chief designer, then in 1923 he joined Daimler-Motoren-Gesellschaft in Stuttgart, Germany, as technical director.

1931–38
Porsche set up his own company. Three years later, working with his son, Ferry, he became involved with Adolf Hitler's people's car project, producing what would become the Beetle. He became a member of the Nazi Party and the SS.

1939–51
Porsche was involved with designing Tiger tanks and the V-1 flying bomb for Germany during World War II. In 1945 he was arrested as a war criminal and imprisoned for some months. He aided his son in designing the Porsche sports car of 1950.

THINK SMALL

The Beetle's huge commercial success in the United States was in no small part due to a brilliant advertising campaign by the agency Doyle Dane Bernbach, which eschewed the typical bright, brash hard sell of the time in favor of black-and-white photography and wry copy that emphasized the car's quirky charm and reliability. The Think Small campaign of 1959 invited readers to turn the perceived disadvantages of the model—its comparative slowness, small size, and unusual shape—into virtues.

WORLD AT WAR

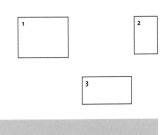

The Willys MB 8 Jeep at work in 1941.
The 4 x 4 truck was suitable for
traversing difficult terrain. Its windshield
tilts forward on top of the bonnet.

1 The Willys MB 8 Jeep at work in 1941. The 4 x 4 truck was suitable for traversing difficult terrain. Its windshield tilts forward on top of the bonnet.

2 The V-2 rocket was developed at the German Rocket Test Centre at Peenemünde and first successfully tested in 1942.

2 Red Army soldiers head into battle on board T-34 tanks during World War II. Easy to mass produce, the tank won the production battle against Germany.

If necessity is the mother of invention, it is not surprising that many significant advances in medical science, materials technology, engineering, and design have had their origins in conflict, when stakes are high and needs acute. World War II was no exception—the radical design of the Supermarine Spitfire (1936; see p.214) was in response to an British Air Ministry specification calling for a high-performance fighter in 1934. In some cases, such advances represented true breakthroughs, innovations spurred by the demands of wartime. Others built upon previous developments, broadening their scope and application. Radar, synthetic rubber, and the jet engine were all inventions that resulted from government investment in research and development, either by Allied or Axis powers.

World War II was a global conflict that was mechanized to a hitherto unprecedented degree. On land, the foremost war machine was the tank. While these armored behemoths made their battlefield debut in 1916, it was during World War II that tank divisions proved their mettle. In terms of sheer menace and fighting efficiency, the Soviet T-34 tank (see image 3), designed by Mikhail Koshkin (1898–1940), was arguably the most successful. Although the design of the T-34 dates to before the war, it first appeared in 1940. Fast and maneuvrable, even in mud and snow, one of its key advantages was the fact that it was simple and economical to manufacture and repair. Some 57,000 T-34s were produced by 1945—more than any other wartime tank.

KEY EVENTS

1936	1939	1940	1940	1940	1941
The prototype Supermarine Spitfire is flown for the first time. It is based on the Type 300 fighter plane designed by Reginald J. Mitchell (1895–1937).	Germany invades Poland, triggering the outbreak of World War II.	The German *blitzkrieg* overruns Denmark, Holland, and Belgium. In June the British Expeditionary Force evacuates from Dunkirk; France falls.	The Spitfire plays a crucial role in the Battle of Britain. The London Blitz begins in September. Luftwaffe attacks on other British cities follow.	The Soviet T-34 tank appears for the first time. It remains in production until 1958.	The Sten sub-machine gun is put into production in January. Adolf Hitler invades the Soviet Union. The United States enters the war in December.

When labor and materials are in short supply, those that make cost-effective use of scarce resources have an edge—as do those that can be repaired easily. The British Sten sub-machine gun (1941; see p.216), which could be manufactured with a minimum of effort and material, was produced in its millions. A gun that could be mastered with relatively little training was often more effective when human casualties were so high. Similarly, simplicity of operation often won out over technical sophistication. The jeep (see image 1) was the most famous vehicle of the conflict. It originated in 1941 because the US War Department needed a cheap yet robust vehicle for basic tasks. Made by various manufacturers, it was used in guises from battlefield ambulance to staff car.

Materials were applied in ways that broadened their possibilities. Plexiglas was pressed into service to make lightweight, shatter-resistant, bulletproof cockpits, windshields, and aeroplane glazing. Plywood found an important role as an economical means of using scarce timber resources—for aircraft fuselages, for example. New molding techniques were devised, notably by Charles (1907–78) and Ray Eames (1912–88), who were commissioned in 1942 by the US Navy to use the material to make lightweight transport leg splints for injured personnel, resulting in a mass-produced, modular, shaped splint that was easy to transport. The results of the Eameses' experiments were seen in the molded plywood furniture (see p.284) that they designed after the war.

Technical innovation is an obvious means by which weaponry can deliver an advantage. Many modern technologies that continue to shape the world, such as computing, navigation systems, and rocket science, emerged during the war. Wernher von Braun (1912–77), the German aerospace engineer who helped to design the German V-2 (see image 2), later went to work for the National Aeronautics and Space Administration on the US space program, developing the Saturn V rocket that eventually put a man on the moon. **EW**

1942	1943	1944	1944	1945	1945
The US Navy commissions Charles and Ray Eames to make shaped splints out of molded plywood for injured airmen.	The Germans surrender at Stalingrad, their first major defeat. The Allies are victorious in North Africa. Italy surrenders.	The first jet-powered fighter plane, the Messerschmitt Me 262 of Germany, is introduced in April.	D-Day: the Allies invade German-occupied France in June. Paris is liberated in August.	Soviet troops liberate Auschwitz. Germany surrenders on 7 May after the Russians reach Berlin, and Hitler commits suicide.	Atomic bombs are dropped on Hiroshima and Nagasaki. Japan announces its surrender in the afternoon of 15 August (local time).

Supermarine Spitfire 1936

REGINALD J. MITCHELL 1895–1937

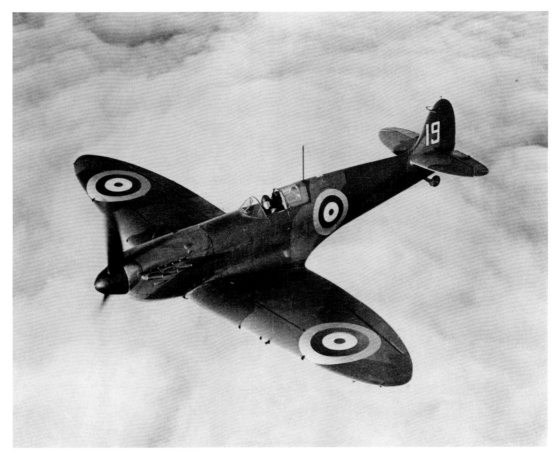

A Spitfire I, equipped with a radio, in flight on 16 February 1939. It belonged to 19 Squadron at Duxford, England, and was one of the first Spitfires to be supplied to the RAF.

⬡ **NAVIGATOR**

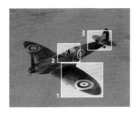

Few wartime designs are held in greater affection than the Spitfire—esteemed not only by the pilots who flew it, but also by those grateful for its key role in winning the Battle of Britain in 1940. While the plane shares certain features with other World War II fighters, it is the small, barely visible choices made by its lead designer, Reginald J. Mitchell, that guaranteed its success as a defender of the skies.

All aircraft design represents form following function at its purest. During the 1930s, when the Spitfire was being developed, aeronautical designers and engineers were sharing information to a surprising degree and working to briefs that differed very little from one another. This accounts for a number of apparent similarities between the Spitfire, the Hawker Hurricane, and the German Messerschmitt Bf 109, or Me 109, all of which have a large cowling up front to house a huge engine, a retractable undercarriage to reduce drag in flight, and a tail wheel. What made the Spitfire such a pre-eminent fighter was largely due to its wing design. The Spitfire had an elliptical wing to minimize wing-tip vortices. The Royal Air Force (RAF) brief had specified wing-mounted guns, which meant that the wing could not be as thin (and hence as fast) as Mitchell would have liked. However, he designed the wing to be exceptionally strong, which meant that it was able to bear the weight of the even more powerful engines and heavier armament that emerged as the war progressed. Just as crucially, in the twists and turns and dives of a dogfight, the plane could be flown at the very limit of its capabilities by a relatively inexperienced pilot. Some 20,334 Spitfires in various versions were made. **EW**

FOCAL POINTS

1 WING
The Spitfire wing, with its distinctive silhouette, was thin enough to achieve high speeds, yet exceptionally strong. Mitchell introduced a curve at the wing root to ensure that during a stall, the ailerons remained responsive for as long as possible, which facilitated recovery.

2 COCKPIT
Mitchell, who gained a pilot's license in 1934, kept safety firmly in mind, insisting, among other things, on a bulletproof cockpit. The cockpit was also relatively roomy, which meant that the control stick had plenty of space for movement, especially fore and aft.

3 SHELL
Mitchell maximized the Spitfire's performance by using an aluminum monocoque shell, which meant that loads were carried by a structural skin rather than an internal framework, leaving the interior of the fuselage unobstructed. The all-metal construction reduced fire risk.

DESIGNER PROFILE

1895–1916
Born in Staffordshire, England, Reginald J. Mitchell was apprenticed at the age of sixteen at an engineering works specializing in locomotives. He subsequently worked for the same firm as a draftsman while studying at night school.

1917–20
Mitchell went to Southampton to work for the Supermarine Aviation Works, which manufactured seaplanes. He was promoted to chief designer in 1919 and then chief engineer in 1920.

1921–31
As chief engineer and—from 1927—technical director, Mitchell was responsible for the design of twenty-four aircraft, including a number of flying boats and racing seaplanes. When Vickers took over Supermarine in 1928, Mitchell was asked to stay on. In 1931 his Supermarine S.6B racing plane won the Schneider Trophy and subsequently broke the world airspeed record.

1932–37
Mitchell designed the Type 224 fighter aircraft to an Air Ministry brief. It was not successful. However, his Type 300 attracted RAF interest and formed the basis of what would become his Spitfire. Mitchell died of cancer the year after the prototype Spitfire flew for the first time in 1936.

THE BATTLE OF BRITAIN

During the Battle of Britain, the Spitfire was most commonly pitted against the German Me 109 (above). Design differences inevitably made an impact in the air. Unlike the Spitfire, the Me 109 had fuselage-mounted guns, which allowed it to have a thinner wing. This, in turn, gave the German plane a narrow speed advantage and a tighter turning radius, vital in close aerial combat. However, the Me 109's closely grouped guns required an expert marksman at the controls, whereas when the Spitfire pilot fired he was effectively spraying a larger area and thus stood a greater chance of hitting a target. The Me 109 also had a cramped cockpit, with the control stick having only about 5 inches (12.5 cm) of fore–aft movement. Spitfire pilots quickly learned to encourage Me 109s to follow them into a vertical dive, knowing that the enemy would not be able to maneuver his stick back far enough to pull up at the last moment.

9 mm Sten Machine Carbine Mark 1 1941

REGINALD SHEPHERD 1892–1950   HAROLD TURPIN d.1977

Mark 1 Sten guns were made at a former Singer sewing machine plant at Clydebank, Scotland. The first guns were delivered in October 1941.

In June 1940 the British Expeditionary Force was evacuated from the beaches of Dunkirk following the Nazi's blitzkrieg advance through Europe. While the human casualties, although grave, were much less catastrophic than anticipated, the retreating army had left much material behind—not only tanks and artillery, but also rifles and pistols. With the real possibility of invasion looming on the horizon, rearmament was a matter of desperate urgency.

It was in response to this crisis that the Sten gun was developed. Commissioned by the Royal Small Arms Factory at Enfield Lock in north London, the Sten took its name from the first initials of its designers—S for Major Reginald V. Shepherd and T for Harold Turpin—plus EN for Enfield. It was conceived as a British-made alternative to the US Thompson sub-machine gun, imports of which could not meet demand.

Designed as a weapon to be used at close quarters, the Sten was robust, cheap to produce, compact, and easy to conceal. It was also very light, weighing just over six pounds (2.7 kg) unloaded. Capable of being fired without lubrication, the Sten was also an asset in desert conditions where a conventional weapon would need oiling that would attract and retain sand. On the downside, it was prone to jamming and not very accurate at distances greater than 110 yards (100 m). However, it soon proved indispensable, not only for providing troops and tank crews with short-range firepower but also for arming partisans and resistance fighters in occupied countries. Huge numbers were dropped by parachute behind enemy lines, along with bullets to fire them, although the gun also shot many types of Axis ammunition obtainable from enemy munition dumps.

The Sten was extremely simple and economical to manufacture. Small workshops could tackle most of the machining, and the parts were then assembled at Enfield. The most basic versions could be produced in hours. Neither the unrefined appearance of the gun nor its occasional malfunctioning went unnoticed by troops on the ground, who nicknamed it "Plumber's Nightmare;" "[Made] by Marks and Spencers out of Woolworth" was another common saying of the time.

The chief advantage of the Sten was the fact that it required a minimum of materials and labor when both were in short supply. More than four million in various versions were produced during the 1940s, almost half of which were the Mark II model. **EW**

NAVIGATOR

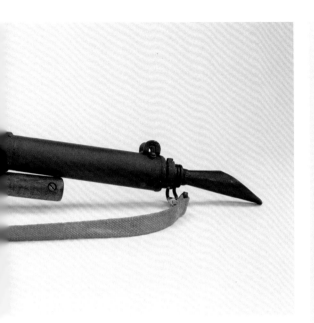

RESISTANCE AND INSURGENCY

The utilitarian design of the Sten gun, along with its low production costs and simple operation, made it an effective weapon for resistance fighters and insurgents. The Sten could be packed in small spaces by removing the butt and the barrel, then rotating the magazine downward. During World War II, large numbers of Sten guns were dropped by parachute in territories occupied by Axis powers to aid local fighters such as the French Resistance (below). Its firepower was especially welcome in close street-to-street fighting in urban areas. The Sten's basic construction meant that it was easy to repair, copy, and reproduce. During the German Occupation of Norway, commandos and resistance fighters were armed with Sten guns made in clandestine workshops on home ground; the same was true in Denmark and Poland. Captured Sten guns were also used by the Germans, who were manufacturing a very similar version by the end of the war. After World War II, the Sten continued to play a key role in conflicts around the world and variations were produced in many different countries. During the 1948 Arab-Israeli War, both sides employed Sten guns; Arab fighters were armed with British-made guns, while paramilitary Jewish groups had been making copies secretly in various locations since 1945. The Korean War (1950–53) saw the last use of the Sten by British forces on foreign soil.

👁 FOCAL POINTS

1 BUTTSTOCK
The Sten was a basic weapon and looked it. The working elements were enclosed in a simple pressed steel tube, with a barrel at one end and a rudimentary skeletal shoulder support at the other. It could also be easily assembled and disassembled for transport.

2 TRIGGER
The open-bolt blowback operation of the Sten was based on that of the German MP 38 sub-machine gun. This made it simple to operate; when the trigger was pressed, the bolt shot forward, stripped the round from the magazine, chambered it, and fired it.

3 MAGAZINE HOUSING
Each detachable box magazine had a 32-round capacity. The Sten was chambered for the 9 x 19 mm Parabellum pistol cartridge and capable of firing at a rate of 500 rounds per minute, compared to 15 rounds for standard bolt-action infantry rifles.

ON THE HOME FRONT

1 "Your Britain, Fight for it Now" (1942) by Abram Games depicts a school destroyed by bombing and a modern replacement in Cambridgeshire, England. The aim was to boost morale.

2 The London Wall design (1941) by Arnold Lever was used for both neck and head scarves. Slogans include "Your courage, your cheerfulness, your resolution" and "Save for victory."

World War II had a major impact on designers and manufacturers in the United Kingdom. Government restrictions, such as controls on the supply of timber, came into force within a few days of the outbreak, and the furniture and furnishings industries were drastically affected by shortages of materials, fuel, and labor, not only for the duration of hostilities, but right through until the early 1950s. Moreover, many small companies, such as the pioneering Isokon Furniture Company, shut down altogether during the war and struggled to re-establish themselves afterward. Those that continued in operation, including Morton Sundour Fabrics, used their equipment and skills to produce vital wartime necessities, such as blackout fabrics and camouflage netting. Furniture Industries (now known as Ercol), a large factory in High Wycombe run by Lucian Ercolani (1888–1976), undertook contracts for military accessories, including wooden snowshoes and tent pegs. Ercol's post-war recovery was closely linked to a significant wartime order for 100,000 Windsor kitchen chairs, because this triggered the idea for the firm's highly successful range of Windsor furniture.

Apart from bulk orders for essential goods, furniture manufacturing was limited to basic domestic items for "bombees" (people who had been bombed out). Initially known as Standard Emergency Furniture, the name Utility Furniture (see p.220) was adopted in 1942 after the government established a

(see p.220)

KEY EVENTS

1939	1940	1941	1941	1941	1942
Following the German invasion of Poland, the United Kingdom and France declare war on Germany on 3 September.	The Royal College of Art relocates to Ambleside in the Lake District, England, and operates there on a limited scale until 1945.	Graphic designer Abram Games is appointed as the official War Office poster artist.	All men under the age of forty are conscripted in the United Kingdom, causing severe labor and skills shortages in many fields of manufacturing.	The Japanese attack on the US naval base at Pearl Harbor prompts the United States to enter World War II.	The UK Advisory Committee on Utility Furniture is established by the Board of Trade. The first collection of Utility Furniture is launched in 1943.

design panel, headed by furniture manufacturer Gordon Russell (1892–1980), to develop a set of simple, plain, economical, standardized designs. Production was limited to a list of approved manufacturers and because the furniture was exempt from purchase tax, it was sold for a reasonable price.

The war disrupted the careers of many designers who were either called up for military service or prevented from practicing by the lack of outlets for their work. The US duo textile designer Marion Dorn (1896–1964) and graphic designer Edward McKnight Kauffer (1899–1954), who had dominated the British design scene during the 1930s, never achieved the same degree of success after returning to the United States in 1940. Emergent designers, such as Robin (1915–2010) and Lucienne Day (1917–2010), had to put their careers on hold because of the lack of opportunities in the furniture and furnishing industries. It was not until the Festival of Britain in 1951 that they were able to get back on track. Although abnormal conditions prevailed during the war, some positive initiatives did emerge. Important technical advances, such as the development of synthetic resin adhesives for molded plywood, were a direct result of wartime research, because strong, lightweight materials were needed for military aeroplanes such as the Mosquito Bomber. Such breakthroughs were of great benefit to the furniture industry after the war, and they were harnessed by designers such as Charles (1907–78) and Ray Eames (1912–88) in the United States.

One design field in which creativity flourished during the war was graphics, because posters were an important tool for disseminating information. Abram Games (1914–96), who was already well established as a commercial artist during the late 1930s, spent the war years designing government advertising campaigns. His first design, "Join the ATS" (1941), encouraging women to join the Auxiliary Territorial Service, proved somewhat controversial because it featured an image of a glamorous female, referred to as the Blonde Bombshell. Games's other wartime posters were more serious. In "Your Talk May Kill Your Comrades" (1942), a sound wave spiraling out of a man's mouth terminates in a bayonet piercing three soldiers; "Grow Your Own Food" (1942) cheerfully chivvied people to dig for victory by growing their own vegetables; whereas "Your Britain, Fight for it Now" (see image 1) sought to raise public spirits with idealistic images of modern architecture superimposed against the rubble of bomb-damaged buildings. Posters were also an important propaganda vehicle in the United States. One of the most iconic images was "We Can Do It!" (1942) by J. Howard Miller (1918–2004), which featured Rosie the Riveter flexing her biceps and encouraging the US public to pitch in and support the war effort.

Scarves were also co-opted for light-hearted propaganda in Britain and the United States. Arnold Lever (1905–77), chief designer at the British firm Jacqmar, often incorporated witty patriotic messages in his designs. London Wall (see image 2) features a brick wall emblazoned with handwritten signs, including "Careless talk costs lives" and "Give us the tools and we will finish the job." **LJ**

1944	1945	1946	1946	1947	1948
The UK Council of Industrial Design (COID), the precursor of the Design Council, is established in December.	The "Design at Home" exhibition at the National Gallery is organized by the newly established Council for the Encouragement of Music and the Arts.	Two new ranges of Utility Furniture called Chiltern and Cotswold are launched at a Board of Trade exhibition in March.	The COID organizes the "Britain Can Make It" exhibition at the Victoria and Albert Museum. It showcases wartime innovations in UK design.	Gordon Russell, formerly chair of the Utility Furniture committee's design panel, is appointed as director of the COID.	Utility Scheme regulations are relaxed to allow "freedom of design," but Utility Furniture and furnishings continue to be produced until 1952.

Utility Furniture: Cotswold Sideboard 1942

EDWIN CLINCH HERBERT CUTLER

👁 FOCAL POINTS

1 FLUSH SURFACES
The sideboard is simple and plain, with no surface decoration, thereby epitomizing the ideals of the modern movement. Not only are the sides of the cabinet flush, but also the drawer fronts and doors. Flat surfaces made the sideboard easier to clean.

2 ECONOMICAL DESIGN
The modest scale of the Cotswold sideboard and the way in which it is constructed reflect the fundamental premise behind the Utility Furniture scheme. It was designed to use the minimum quantity of wood to create the maximum amount of storage.

3 ROBUST CONSTRUCTION
Utility Furniture was neither flimsy nor temporary. The products were remarkably solid and robust so that they would stand up to domestic wear and tear. The joints were mortised or pegged, to make them as strong as possible, rather than being nailed, screwed, or glued.

4 DURABLE MATERIALS
In order to ensure that Utility Furniture was tough and durable, hardwood was a prerequisite. Mahogany and oak were the standard timbers, but light-colored oak was more attractive in color and grain. The panels were made from veneered hardboard.

By 1941 furniture-grade timber had become so scarce that the government introduced a quota system for domestic furniture, with manufacturing concentrated in a nucleus of factories. The Advisory Committee on Utility Furniture controlled the design of all furniture being produced and approved the first prototypes in 1942. An influential figure in the project from the outset was Cotswold-based furniture designer and manufacturer Gordon Russell. Inspired by the simplicity of Arts and Crafts movement design, Russell ensured that Utility Furniture was made to the highest possible standards within the tight constraints. The economical use of materials was the key criteria, followed by practicality and strength. Simplicity of construction was another essential ingredient, because workers in the furniture industry at that date had limited skills and restricted timescales. Most of the initial Utility Furniture designs were created by two experienced designers from the furniture-making town of High Wycombe: Edwin Clinch and Herbert Cutler. Clinch was the in-house designer for Goodearl Brothers, whereas Cutler was a lecturer at High Wycombe Technical Institute. Their designs, including the basic Chiltern and the more expensive Cotswold ranges, remained in production well into the post-war period. **LJ**

✧ NAVIGATOR

Rectangular oak sideboard
33⅞ x 48 x 19½ in.
86 x 122 x 49.5 cm

▲ The first prototypes of the Utility Furniture were shown at a trade fair in London in 1942. The collection included a sideboard with matching dining table and chairs, as well as a range of beds.

🕐 DESIGNER PROFILE

1892–39

Gordon Russell moved to Broadway in Worcestershire, England, at the age of six. He joined the family business in 1908 and began restoring and designing furniture for the historic Lygon Arms hotel. After serving in World War I, Russell devoted more time to furniture design, publishing a booklet titled *Honesty and the Crafts* in 1923. He stopped designing in 1930 to concentrate on running his rapidly expanding business.

1940–80

He left his firm in 1940 and two years later joined the Utility Furniture Advisory Committee, where he was appointed chair of the Utility Furniture design panel in 1943. Closely involved with the "Britain Can Make It!" exhibition in 1946 and the Festival of Britain in 1951, Russell was director of the Council of Industrial Design from 1947 to 1960 and was knighted in 1955. His autobiography, *Designer's Trade*, was published in 1968.

UTILITY TEXTILES

Another main area of domestic design affected by the Utility scheme was furnishing fabrics. When the Utility Furniture design panel was established, one of its members was textile designer Enid Marx (1902–98). In 1945 she teamed up with Carlisle-based manufacturer Morton Sundour Fabrics to develop a range of woven cotton furnishing fabrics, such as Ring (right), for the Utility scheme. As with Utility Furniture, the economical use of materials was paramount, hence the limited number of colors in each design. The pattern repeats were also deliberately small, partly because they were easier to weave but also because there was less wastage when the cloth was cut. Marx's dynamic Utility designs were mostly geometric, but some had stylized organic motifs.

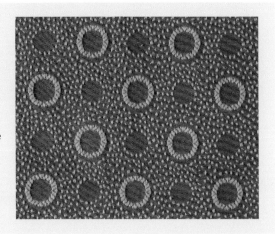

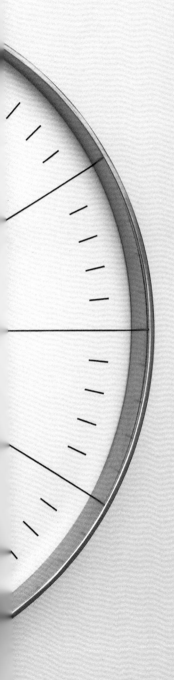

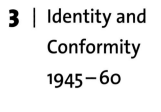

3 | Identity and Conformity 1945–60

DANISH MODERN

Of all the Scandinavian countries, Denmark made the greatest impact on the international design scene in the mid 20th century. By that time, Sweden and Finland had developed their own distinct modern movements, but neither country was so influential, nor did their practitioners embrace such a diverse range of media. The concept of Danish modern, which made a huge impression in Europe and the United States, had its origins in the 1930s. In the craft-based industries of furniture, textiles, metalwork, ceramics, and glass, a new generation of innovative Danish designers came to the fore during this period and developed their own version of modernism. Using traditional materials—wood, metal, clay, and glass—and working with small-scale manufacturers, they offered an alternative to the highly rational objects made from industrial materials that were emerging from Germany at that time. More humanistic and organic than Germany's version of modernism, Denmark's design movement was oriented toward the domestic sphere and directly inspired by nature. Its aim—to offer everyone the opportunity to bring high-quality modern design into their homes—was profoundly democratic.

Furniture design was among the first disciplines to be rethought along these progressive lines. A key figure in this field was Kaare Klint (1888–1954), head of the Royal Danish Academy of Fine Art's School of Architecture in Copenhagen.

KEY EVENTS

1945	1945	1947	1949	1951	1951
Børge Mogensen designs his model no. 1789 sofa. It is conceived to be adaptable for use in a small space.	Finn Juhl sets up his design office. He becomes known for abstract sculptural furniture produced in collaboration with Niels Vodder.	Hans Wegner designs the Peacock chair. Based on traditional Windsor chairs, its form and proportion are altered to give it a modern appearance.	Wegner designs the Round chair, perhaps the ultimate icon of Danish modern design. It is the result of his tireless pursuit of perfection.	Kay Bojesen designs his articulated wooden monkey toy. Brimming with personality, it is still in production today.	Bojesen's Grand Prix flatware wins a prize at the Milan Triennale.

Under Klint's instruction, forms were taken back to basics. As one of the first furniture designers to apply anthropometric principles in his work, he carried out extensive studies measuring the human body in motion and repose in order to ensure that furniture was fit for purpose. Looking back at traditional items of functional furniture, for example pieces used by the military, he evolved designs that were defined more as "equipment" than "furnishings" (see image 1). These were attuned to the decreasing size of the average Danish home and came to represent the modern way of life for many people.

Danish craftsmen working in metal also embraced modern design thinking. Georg Jensen, a leading silverware company that had been established in the early part of the century, set high standards. One of Denmark's leading silver designers of the 1930s, Kay Bojesen (1886–1958), was trained at Jensen's. His Grand Prix flatware (1938), made of polished steel, was simple, elegant, and a pleasure to use thanks to its functional, ergonomic design; this was Danish modern at its best. Bojesen also played an important role in promoting Danish design. The exhibition space Den Permanente, an artists' co-operative that he set up in 1931, showcased the best Danish designs of the era. It remained an arbiter of good design for several decades and was active until 1981.

Denmark had always had a strong ceramics tradition. The best-known manufacturer, then and now, is Royal Copenhagen, founded in the late 18th century. Although the company's designs were chiefly traditional during the interwar years, the strikingly modern stoneware pieces in natural, muted colors (see image 2) by Axel Salto (1889–1961) promoted a completely new image. Another ceramics manufacturer, Bing & Grøndahl, similarly embraced the modern style alongside its more traditional ware. Glassware was another field of design that responded early to the new design thinking, and textiles were transformed by designers such Marie Gudme Leth (1895–1997), who revolutionized screen printing and set up her own studio in 1941.

Lighting manufacturer Louis Poulsen quickly established an international reputation for innovation and excellence. The company's collaboration with architect Poul Henningsen (1894–1967) resulted in designs that were novel both in their appearance and in the quality of their spatial illumination. Henningsen's well-known PH light, produced in 1925, remains a design classic to this day. He also created a number of other innovative light fittings during the mid-century years, including the Artichoke light (1958; see p.232).

The 1930s saw the foundations of Danish modern laid in place, but in the immediate post-war years the movement grew from strength to strength and established its influence worldwide. A new generation of Danish designers came to the fore, keen to establish modernism as the defining style of domestic design. Like their predecessors, the abiding aim of this cohort was to improve the lives of ordinary people through design. Great emphasis was placed on affordability, and to that end craft joined hands with industry. Once

1 The Safari chair (1933) by Kaare Klint is well known for its simple functionality. It can be assembled without the use of tools.

2 Axel Salto designed this heavy stoneware vase in 1956. Manufactured by Royal Copenhagen, its organic form is covered in a rich oxblood glaze.

1952	c. 1954	1958	1958	1959	1960
Arne Jacobsen designs the Ant chair, a molded plywood chair with metal legs. It is produced by Fritz Hansen.	Erik Herlow designs the Obelisk pattern for a set of flatware for Copenhagen Cutlery.	After the success of his PH light in 1925, Poul Henningsen creates another design classic with the Artichoke light.	Poul Kjaerholm receives the Lunning Prize for the PK22 chair. It goes on to win prizes at Milan.	Nanna Ditzel designs the Hanging chair, which represents the beginning of a shift in the Danish modern movement.	Verner Panton designs the S chair, the first injection-molded, all-plastic, cantilevered chair to be made.

3 This silver necklace (1947) designed by Henning Koppel was manufactured by Georg Jensen. The fourteen cast "links" are abstract and amoeba-like in form.

4 The PK 24 chaise longue (1965) by Poul Kjaerholm is one of his signature designs. The curved plane appears to hover in the room, supported by a minimal angular steel frame.

again, furniture played a leading role. At the craft end of the spectrum, Hans Wegner (1914–2007) created a number of very simple designs that quickly became iconic, among them the Chinese chair (1944), Peacock chair (1947), and Round chair (1949; see p.228). Today, Wegner's designs, which are made using traditional joinery techniques, represent the very best of Danish modern. Furniture designer Børge Mogensen (1914–72) is often linked to Wegner. Trained as a cabinetmaker and an architect, he worked briefly for Klint, then formed his own studio in 1959. Many of Mogensen's designs reflected Klint's interest in traditional furniture archetypes. The model no. 1789 sofa, which he designed in 1945, recalls both the classic Windsor chair in its spoke back and the Knole sofa in its drop-down side held in place with leather ties. More overtly sculptural in his approach was furniture designer Finn Juhl (1912–89).

Danish modern took off in the United States, too. There, the initial impetus was largely due to Edgar Kaufmann, Jr., the son and heir of the tycoon for whom Frank Lloyd Wright had built his masterpiece Fallingwater (1936–39) in southwestern Pennsylvania. Kaufmann was involved in the running of the Museum of Modern Art in New York and was seen as a prominent esthete. Consequently, his purchase of Danish furniture for Fallingwater sent a clear message to New York taste-makers. Soon Danish modern was not only featuring in journals and magazines, but it was also stocked by leading US retailers and produced under license by US manufacturers. Juhl's designs were especially popular. Danish modern's relative affordability, human scale, and use of familiar domestic materials found an increasingly enthusiastic reception from the US public. International exhibitions spread its popularity even wider.

Nanna Ditzel (1923–2005) was one of the few female Danish designers whose work became known to a world audience. Her Hanging chair (1959), a wicker egg shape designed to be suspended on a chain from the ceiling, was frequently featured in fashion and interiors magazines, suggesting a new, liberated lifestyle. Ditzel's wide-ranging work included designs for interiors, exhibitions, jewelry, and textiles. Danish modern textiles in general were another success story, notably the work of Lis Ahlmann (1894–1979) and the products made by textile manufacturer Kvadrat. In addition to Jensen designs, the organic forms of silverware (see image 3) by Henning Koppel (1918–81) and Erik Herlow (1913–91), among others, were well received internationally.

Danish modern continued to evolve. The 1950s saw the beginning of a shift away from the craft esthetic, as designers began to incorporate metal and plastic into their pieces. Poul Kjaerholm (1929–80), a craftsman by training, produced some strikingly minimal pieces, among them the PK series (see image 4). Inspired by the work of US designers Charles (1907–78) and Ray Eames (1912–88), architect Arne Jacobsen (1902–71) utilized molded plywood and steel rods in his Ant chair (1952), a design created for the canteen of a Danish pharmaceutical company, and the later 3107 chair (1955; see p.230). Jacobsen went on to design a number of iconic furniture pieces, among them the Swan and Egg chairs (both 1958), whose seat shells were made of molded fiberglass.

In the 1960s, the highly individual work of Verner Panton (1926–98) represented a radical departure from Danish modern as it had been conceived up to that point. Trained as an architect, Panton briefly worked for Jacobsen and came up with a number of proposals for interiors that featured organically shaped plastic forms. In the field of furniture, his best-known design is the S chair (1960)—the first injection-molded, all-plastic chair—which was notoriously beset by production difficulties. Panton's work marked a dramatic shift in Danish design. Gone was the reliance on craft skills and natural materials, as was the emphasis upon domesticity and everyday home life. Instead, a much more industrial ethos was emerging, alongside a strong internationalism.

By the late 1960s, Danish modern had had its day. Its very success had contributed to its eventual fall from favor. Cheap reproductions and knock-off designs that cashed in on the style's popularity tarnished the look by association. Those in search of sleek European modernity now turned their gaze to Italian design. Yet this was not the end of the story. In the early 21st century, as part of an enduring vogue for mid-century style, Danish modern is again being prized for all the qualities that made it so appealing in the first place, not least its concern to maintain a human element in the designs we live with every day. **PS**

Round Chair 1949

HANS WEGNER 1914–2007

Solid ash, leather
30 x 20½ x 24¾ in.
76 x 52 x 63 cm

◆ NAVIGATOR

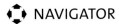

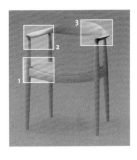

Dubbed "The Round One" by its creator Hans Wegner because of the shape of its back support, this design was the initial result of a collaboration with manufacturer Carl Hansen & Son. It is the epitome of Danish modern, and its form is extremely well proportioned and highly elegant. The use of natural materials, organic form, simplicity, humaneness, modernity, comfort, and modesty all add to a design that could only have come from Denmark in the 1940s. However, simplicity is its defining characteristic. Wegner thought through the minimal requirements of comfortable sitting and produced an object that is pared down to its essentials. As a result, its highly sculptural form suggests the presence of the body even when it is absent. The Round chair was the first Wegner design that did not take an existing model as its inspiration. Unlike the earlier China chair, which was modeled on a Chinese emperor's throne, or the Peacock chair, which was inspired by the traditional Windsor design, the Round chair represents the ultimate refinement of its constituent parts. It remains Wegner's most important chair and it is still highly respected today. Indeed, the Round chair became the benchmark for a number of designs created by Wegner over the years, among them the Wishbone chair and several other variations on the same theme. **PS**

FOCAL POINTS

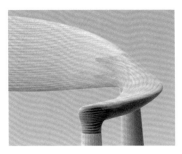

1 NATURAL MATERIALS
The materials used in the chair are all natural. Solid wood (oak, ash, cherry. or walnut) is the principal element. It is supplemented by either woven cane or leather for the seat. In the cane version, additional material is used on the backrest to add to the comfort of the sitter.

2 CRAFTSMANSHIP
Given its simplicity, the chair is dependent on immaculate craftsmanship because the slightest fault would be noticeable. The designer is also very happy for users to see how he has constructed the chair: Wegner does not disguise the joints, where one plane meets another.

3 CURVED LINES
There are no straight lines in the design. Widest at the midpoint to provide support, the chair back is in the form of a semicircle, and the curved armrests sit on four tapered legs. The seat is also curved, and the space between the seat and the back rail is crucial to the composition.

◀ In 1960, the Round chair was chosen as seating for the live televised presidential debates screened on CBS between John F. Kennedy and Richard Nixon. It was Kennedy, a long-time sufferer from intense back pain, who specifically requested the design, as he believed it would be comfortable. The exposure brought the chair instant recognition and it was mentioned in the press coverage after the event.

WISHBONE CHAIR

Hans Wegner's Wishbone chair (right), so called because of the splayed Y-shaped back strut, is a variation on the theme of the Round chair. In this design, the curved top rail becomes unsupported arm rests that are not directly attached to the front legs. Only the back legs are connected to the top rail in this way. A dramatic space is therefore created between the armrests and seat. The handwoven seat is made of paper cord rather than from cane or leather. Both chairs were designed in 1949 and the Wishbone has been in production by Carl Hansen & Son since 1950.

3107 Chair 1955

ARNE JACOBSEN 1902–71

Pressure-molded sliced walnut
veneer, chromed steel
Height 31½ in./80 cm

⊕ **NAVIGATOR**

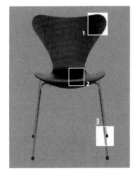

In his furniture designs of the 1950s, manufactured by Fritz Hansen, architect Arne Jacobsen brought together European modernism and Nordic organic form. In so doing, he created a series of furniture items that have remained timeless and much sought after. Following on from the Ant side chair of 1952, which Jacobsen made in molded plywood, he developed the more elegant 3107 chair as part of Series 7. It had a simple and well-proportioned profile, and quickly became a huge success. One of the main reasons for its success is the way in which it can be adapted to different settings and purposes. Unlike early Danish furniture designers, Jacobsen was not preoccupied with domesticity, and his chairs can exist as easily in an office or reception area as they can around a dining table. This erosion of public and private space was a feature that Jacobsen took from modernists Le Corbusier (1887–1965) and Ludwig Mies van der Rohe (1886–1969). Given the small size of many Danish homes in the 1950s, stackability was a great advantage for occasional and dining chairs. Although the 3107 cannot be stacked very high, this feature enhances its practicality. **PS**

1 PROFILE

Unlike the Ant model, which had a round back, the 3107 had two distinctive "ears" or "shoulders." The curves of the chair's back are balanced by the slimness of its "waist" and the curve of the seat. The appealing anthropomorphic shape helps it to relate to the body of its sitter.

2 MOLDED PLYWOOD

In his use of molded plywood, Jacobsen was indebted to the work of US designers Charles and Ray Eames, who had been experimenting with that material during the war years. Before then, it had only been possible to bend laminated plywood along one axis.

3 TUBULAR STEEL LEGS

The elegant appearance of the 3107 chair is partly achieved by the juxtaposition of the curvaceous molded shell and the slim, splayed, chrome-covered tubular legs. The purpose of the tiny ball feet at the end of the steel legs is to prevent the chair from damaging the floor.

FRITZ HANSEN

Furniture maker Fritz Hansen played a key role throughout the 20th century working with leading designers linked to the Danish modern movement, including Kaare Klint (1888–1954), who designed the Church chair (above right) in 1936. The company flourished during the war and established stockpiles of wood to use in the post-war period. It produced the China chair in 1944 by Hans Wegner and the Spokeback sofa of Børge Mogensen a year later. The firm's collaboration with Jacobsen began in 1934, but became important in the 1950s when the architect's classic designs were marketed. Fritz Hansen's work with Jacobsen established its international reputation.

◀ To meet the needs of the variety of environments into which the Series 7 chairs could be placed, a number of modified versions were created. These included an upholstered model and an office chair with five wheels (both at left), and a version with armrests (at right). Also made was a bar stool and a chair with a writing table attached to it.

Artichoke Light 1958

POUL HENNINGSEN 1894–1967

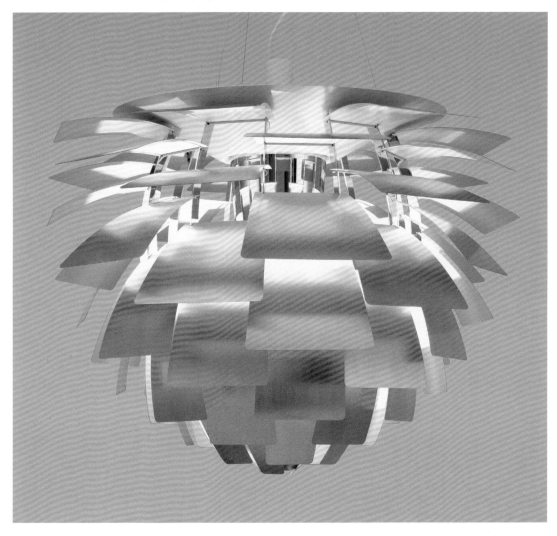

Brushed copper,
paint, chrome, glass
Height 28⅜ in./72 cm
Diameter 33¼ in./84.5 cm

✦ NAVIGATOR

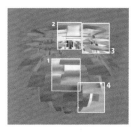

Poul Henningsen spent his childhood living in gaslit interiors. When he grew up, he remembered the softness of that lighting fondly and wanted to recreate the same ambience and to reduce the harsh glare that often came with poorly shaded electric lighting. In 1925 he designed a multishade light, the first in what came to be known as the PH series. This was the initial result of the designer's extensive analysis of the way in which the design of fittings can affect the distribution and diffusion of light. His first lamp, which won a prize at the Paris Exhibition in 1925, was produced by Louis Poulsen, the company with which he was associated for the rest of his career. His best-known designs are the PH5 and the Artichoke lights.

Created more than three decades after Henningsen's first design for Poulsen, the Artichoke quickly became a design classic, not least because of its dramatic presence. Its rows of overlapping blade-like reflectors or shades resemble leaves, and they are painted white on the underside to give a soft reflection. The lamp was based on the same principles as his earlier designs but visually it is more spectacular, especially when hung in commercial spaces or large, open-plan, modern domestic interiors. **PS**

FOCAL POINTS

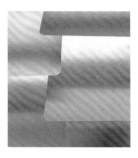

1 DIFFUSION
Henningsen's Artichoke light is all about harmonious light diffusion. Through the use of layers of pliant reflectors, carefully positioned to conceal the light source, illumination is distributed softly and evenly. This means that the lamp does not emit a harsh glare from any angle.

2 MULTI-ELEMENT SHADE
All Henningsen's light fittings are made up of multiple elements to disguise the electrical components and to create a diffused illumination that generates a warm ambience. The effect is also to transform the light fitting into a glowing sculptural object in space.

3 MATERIALS
A large part of the visual effect of the Artichoke light originates from the metal surfaces—either copper or brushed stainless steel—of its leaves. The chrome inner diffuser continues the metallic theme and conceals the light bulb. A white painted version is also available.

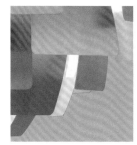

4 INSPIRED BY NATURE
The leaf-like elements of the design recall an artichoke or a pine cone. However, the design is not superficially decorative and is underpinned by stringent functionality. Compared to the rational, geometric products of German design, this humane type of modernism is typically Danish.

DESIGNER PROFILE

1894–1924
Poul Henningsen studied at the Danish College of Technology in Copenhagen and subsequently trained as an architect. In 1920 he set up his own architectural office in Copenhagen, but also worked as a journalist and critic.

1925–67
Henningsen designed the first lamp of his PH series in 1925. He worked for Louis Poulsen for many years and designed more than 500 lights for the company.

▲ The Langelinie Pavilion in Copenhagen commissioned Henningsen to design its restaurant lighting and the Artichoke light was the result. It was inspired by the PH Septima (1927).

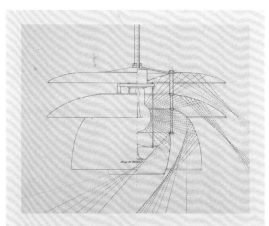

LOUIS POULSEN

Without Henningsen's long-standing collaboration with Louis Poulsen, the PH series would never have existed. His creativity, combined with the firm's marketing and manufacturing skills, lay at the heart of the range's success. Designed by Henningsen to hang down low over tables, the PH5 pendant light (1958; above) is a design classic. Poulsen started out as a wine-importing company. This venture lasted only a few years, and by 1914 the firm was marketing machines and tools. At first it was only involved in marketing Henningsen's lights, but in 1941 the company acquired a manufacturing plant and began producing them, too. Louis Poulsen is now recognized as a leading lighting manufacturer.

SCANDINAVIAN GLASS AND CERAMICS

1 The bowl of the Spectrum Leaf tureen (1947) has a straight rim and low foot, whereas the tip of the domed cover tilts gently to one side.

2 Orrefors continued to produce the Tulip glass (1954) in various colors and proportions until 1981.

3 The delicate and sculptural Apple (1955) was designed for the H55 exhibition in Hälsingborg and remains an icon of the golden age of art glass.

The Nordic countries distinguished themselves in the applied arts during the early post-war period, particularly in glass and ceramics. Significant industries had developed in Sweden, Denmark, and Finland by the late 19th century, and, from the 1920s onward, there was a gradual shift toward modernism, or Functionalism as it was known in this region. After World War II, a surge of creativity in Scandinavia prompted a host of gifted designers to channel their energies into ceramics and glass. Supported by enlightened manufacturers, they pushed the boundaries of these materials, esthetically and technically, creating exquisite artworks and attractive tableware.

The two principal glass companies in Finland were Iittala and Nuutajärvi. Iittala had championed modern glass since the 1930s, when it put the prize-winning designs of architects Alvar (1898–1976) and Aino Aalto (1894–1949) into production. Tapio Wirkkala (1915–85; see p.238) also came to the firm's attention as a result of a design competition in 1946. He was joined four years later by Timo Sarpaneva (1926–2006), and their combined achievements put Finnish glass on the map. Abstract organic shapes characterized the work of both designers. The fluid flared form and finely cut lines on Wirkkala's

KEY EVENTS

1942	1945	1946	1948	1949–50	1950
Finnish ceramicist Rut Bryk (1916–99) joins the art department at Arabia, established in 1932 to enable studio potters to work freely in an industrial context.	Kaj Franck designs tableware for Arabia and is later appointed head of utility ware.	Finnish artist Gunnel Nyman (1909–48) starts designing for Iittala and Nuutajärvi, having previously worked for Riihimäki glassworks.	Swedish ceramics and glass win acclaim at the Milan Triennale; a gold medal is awarded to Stig Lindberg at Gustavsberg.	Timo Sarpaneva starts to work for Iittala, Nanny Still (1926–2009) joins Riihimäki, and Franck is appointed art director at Nuutajärvi.	In Sweden, Marianne Westman joins Rörstrand and Vicke Lindstrand teams up with Kosta.

Kantarelli vase (1946) were inspired by chanterelle mushrooms, whereas Sarpaneva's Orkidea (1953) took its name and inspiration from the orchid flower. While Wirkkala and Sarpaneva won acclaim for their breathtaking art glass, Kaj Franck (1911–89) focused on utilitarian glassware at Nuutajärvi. His ceramic tableware for Arabia was similarly spartan (see p.236): austere vessels pared down to their simplest elements, glazed in monochrome. Stig Lindberg (1916–82), who collaborated with Swedish ceramics factory Gustavsberg, was an altogether more playful and decorative designer. His onion-shaped Spectrum Leaf tureen (see image 1) was hand painted with small leaves in rainbow colors on a white tin-glazed ground. Rörstrand's Picknick range (1956), designed by Marianne Westman (b.1928), was similarly joyful. Culinary imagery such as sliced vegetables and fish was used as decoration.

The Swedish glass industry, centered in Småland, was substantial and wide ranging. As in Finland, two well-established firms—Orrefors and Kosta—stood out. Orrefors had been a pioneer of modern glass since the interwar years, having forged alliances with two outstanding designers: Simon Gate (1883–1945) and Edward Hald (1883–1980). Vicke Lindstrand (1904–83) also began his career at Orrefors but later moved to Kosta in 1950, where he created remarkable vessels, sometimes abstract but often decorated with striking figurative imagery. Orrefors employed a large team of designers during the post-war period, including Nils Landberg (1907–91), whose gravity-defying Tulip glass (see image 2) was characterized by tall, finely blown vessel forms with attenuated necks and stems. Ingeborg Lundin (1921–92), one of the first female designers in the Swedish glass industry, created subtly arresting artworks that exploited the unique qualities of glass. Although some were made from clear crystal, cut or engraved with abstract patterns or quasi-surreal figures, others made daring use of color, notably Apple (see image 3), a giant free-blown spherical vase. Whereas Landberg and Lundin explored the delicacy and translucency of glass, Edvin Ohrström (1906–94) and Sven Palmqvist (1906–84) exploited its malleability and monumentality. Palmqvist's vibrant Ravenna series (1948) was a cross between stained glass and mosaics, while Ohrström's thick-walled Ariel vessels (1940s) contained evocative watery patterns created from pockets of air.

Danish glass designer Per Lütken (1916–98) enjoyed a productive career at Holmegaard. Free blown and organic, his vessels were well suited to mass production, being relatively simple in shape and color. Lütken's Beak vase (1951), with its swollen body and asymmetrical lip, highlighted his skill in harnessing the plasticity of molten glass. Plasticity was also a key feature of ceramics created by Axel Salto (1889–1961) for Royal Copenhagen. With their gourd-like shapes and fluid treacly solfatara glazes, Salto's stoneware vases and bowls were more like studio pottery than industrial ceramics. As these objects demonstrate, Scandinavian post-war ceramics and glass were multifaceted—often restrained and austere, but sometimes exuberant and offbeat. **LJ**

1951	1954	1955	1956	1957	1960
Frederik Lunning establishes the Lunning Prize, awarded to outstanding Scandinavian designers. The first recipient is Wirkkala.	Norwegian glass and ceramics are exhibited at the Milan Triennale, alongside work from Sweden, Denmark, and Finland.	The H55 exhibition (see p.240) is held at Hälsingborg and acts as an international showcase for Scandinavian design.	Sarpaneva wins the Lunning Prize. Finnish designer Oiva Toikka (b.1931) begins to design ceramics for Arabia.	Radical Swedish glass designer Erik Höglund (1932–98) is awarded the Lunning Prize, having joined Boda glassworks in 1953.	Wirkkala wins a gold medal and the Grand Premio at the Milan Triennale.

Kilta Tableware 1948

KAJ FRANCK 1911–89

Earthenware, colored glaze
Height 2¼ in./6 cm

Kaj Franck's primary design interest was in ceramics and glass for everyday use. His vessels were pared down to their essence, with no superfluous embellishment in form or decoration. Although his ethos appears to derive from modernism, Franck's principal source of inspiration was traditional rustic objects created to meet basic needs. Motivated by a strong sense of social purpose, his aim was to harness industrial technology to create useful and affordable objects. This fueled his obsession with simplicity, because the more complex and ornate an object, the more expensive it usually is to produce. Although Franck's ceramics and glass met with considerable success, he disapproved of the cult status accorded to other Scandinavian designers and deliberately sought anonymity. The enforced austerity of World War II had a lasting impact on Franck's mindset, and his designs remained extremely economical throughout his career.

The Kilta tableware for Arabia, designed in 1948 and launched in 1952, represented the culmination of ideas that the designer had been refining since joining the firm in 1945. Initially consisting of ten pieces, Kilta was revolutionary not only for the minimalism of its shapes, but also because it broke with the formal conventions of tableware. Instead of a large, elaborate dinner service, in which each item was designed for a specific application, Kilta was more flexible and informal. Many items were stackable, too. Based on the concept of mix and match, the idea was that consumers could build up their service gradually, according to their means and requirements, while still achieving visual coherence. All the shapes were complementary, as were the monochrome glazes. **LJ**

NAVIGATOR

1 PARED-DOWN FORMS

All the pieces in the original Kilta range were as plain and simple as possible. Angular in profile but without being hard edged, vessels have straight sides tapering to the foot, rather than curved forms. These shapes were easy to manufacture, thereby reducing production costs.

2 MONOCHROME GLAZES

Kilta's white earthenware body provides the perfect foil for the monochrome glazes. Initially produced in five colors—black, white, yellow, green, and brown (later replaced by cobalt blue)—Kilta works equally well as a service in a single color, in two contrasting tones, or in a mix-and-match ensemble.

3 FAIENCE BODY

Made from a tough, high-fired body known as faience, Kilta was more robust than other tableware and could be heated in the oven. Most ceramics are fired in two stages—biscuit and glaze—but Kilta was produced in a single firing, which sped up the manufacturing process and reduced costs.

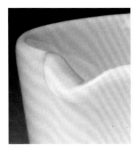

PRACTICAL GLASSWARE

Franck's glassware is remarkably similar to his ceramic tableware. The Kartio hourglass-shaped carafe and conical tumbler (1958; above) are plain and simple, with the emphasis on angular forms and rich dark monochrome colors (violet, blue, red, green, and gray). Because they were turn-mold blown, these pieces have thin walls. Franck later designed some thicker-walled, pressed-glass tableware, which was cheaper to produce.

◄ Kilta initially consisted of only core pieces: a cup and saucer, sugar bowl, cream jug, flat plate, deep plate, vegetable dish, oblong platter and lidded pitcher. Further items were added over the years, including an egg cup, cruet set, flour sifter, casserole dish and hors d'oeuvre dish, all in complementary forms.

Tapio Glassware 1954
TAPIO WIRKKALA 1915–85

Mold-blown glass
Height 5 in./13 cm
Diameter 2½ in./6.5 cm

⬡ NAVIGATOR

Originally trained as a sculptor, Tapio Wirkkala brought an artist's eye for form, texture, and color to the applied arts. His esthetic was rooted in the natural world, particularly the lakes and forests of the Finnish countryside. Glass was therefore a suitably elemental material. As hard as stone and as transparent as ice, it was extremely expressive and could be blown, molded, or cast into a variety of shapes and surface textures. Tapio was one of Wirkkala's first tableware ranges. Made by hand, the vessels were shaped by turn mold-blowing. A blob of molten glass was collected from the furnace on the end of a blowing iron. The glass was blown into a cuplike mold that shaped the profile of the bowl, and the blowing iron was rotated to ensure a smooth, clean surface. More like a chalice or goblet than a conventional wine glass, the flared bowl grows seamlessly from the trunklike stem, counterbalanced by the heavy solid foot. The air bubble in the stem appears to be rising up through the glass, a simple but ingenious device. Although this design has a smooth finish, Wirkkala's later tableware became increasingly textural, with pitted surfaces resembling charred wood and melted ice. **LJ**

👁 FOCAL POINTS

1 ORGANIC LINES
The subtly curved profile is gentle on the hand and eye. Created as an organic whole, esthetically and physically, the vessel has a satisfying unity. The sensuous fluidity of its form is typically Scandinavian, conjuring up the contours of the human body in an understated way.

2 STEM, FOOT AND BOWL
The solid glass base roots the vessel to the ground. Wine glasses traditionally consist of three distinct elements—bowl, stem, and foot—each made separately, then joined together. Here, all three components are created simultaneously as a harmonious whole.

3 AIR BUBBLE
The sole decoration is the air bubble suspended in the stem. Created by pressing a wet wooden stick into the molten glass, causing a release of steam, the bubble appears to be ascending through the glass. It was an appropriately simple decorative feature for this utilitarian drinking glass.

▲ Wirkkala's breakthrough design was Kantarelli (1946), a wide-necked vase with a softly undulating rim, cut with fine lines that evoke mushroom gills. Other early pieces, such as Tree Stump (1948) and Lichen (1950), were also overtly organic and similarly tactile.

ART GLASS

One of the distinctive characteristics of Scandinavian glass factories was that they created limited-edition art glass alongside tableware. The same designers were often responsible for both ranges, but their art glass was more experimental and allowed greater creative scope. Paader's Ice (1960; right) is a classic example of Wirkkala's nature-inspired art glass. Named after a lake in Lapland, this is a work of pure abstract sculpture and it is not intended to be functional. Powerfully tactile, the striated sides contrast with the soft, bubbling rim. The fingerlike wells, created by pushing a rod into the molten glass, evoke icicles or glacial shafts.

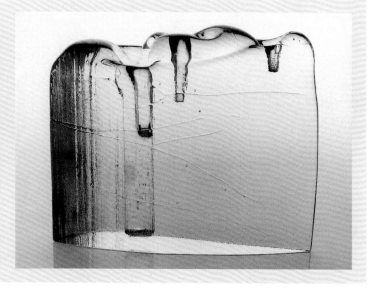

THE HÄLSINGBORG EXHIBITION

1 A selection of items from the Terma kitchenware collection designed by Stig Lindberg.

2 The On Board Pavilion by Carl-Axel Acking helped to attract around 1.2 million visitors to the H55 exhibition.

3 This Fuga bowl (1954) by Sven Palmqvist was made using a technique derived from a hand-operated machine that spun the glass into shape.

In 1955 the Swedish city of Hälsingborg (known today as Helsingborg) hosted an international exhibition of architecture, industrial design, and home furnishings called H55. Organized by the Swedish Society of Crafts and Design, H55 provided an international showcase for Swedish applied arts, which had been flourishing since the 1920s, especially in ceramics, glass, metalwork, and textiles. Finland and Denmark had also flowered during this period—the Danes excelling in furniture making and the Finns in glassware—so it was a good time to celebrate the region's collective achievements. The complementary esthetic of these three design superpowers, along with the emergent Norway, was collectively described as Scandinavian modern.

Unashamedly optimistic, H55 embodied the idealistic post-war zeitgeist, reflecting the positive aspirations of designers and consumers for the brave new world of modern design. In addition to highlighting groundbreaking recent designs, such as the String shelving system (1949; see p.242) by Nils "Nisse" Strinning (1917–2006), H55 provided the launch pad for many new products. These included the sleek, brown-glazed Terma kitchenware (see image 1) designed by Stig Lindberg (1916–82) for Gustavsberg and the Servus stainless-steel cutlery designed by renowned silversmith Sigurd Persson (1914–2003) for KF (Swedish Cooperative Union). Scandinavian design took center stage at H55, presented in two large pavilions and various room settings in furnished apartments. Three of the architects responsible for these interiors—Alvar

KEY EVENTS

1939–45	1948	1949	1951	1951	1954
Sweden remains neutral during World War II; there is less disruption in Swedish applied art industries than in those elsewhere in Europe.	Swedish designers excel at the Milan Triennale: Stig Lindberg and Berndt Friberg (1899–1981) win gold medals for their ceramics.	The exhibition of Swedish design titled "From Town Plan to Cutlery," held in Zürich, is a precursor of the themes later explored in H55.	Swedes, Danes and Finns exhibit at the Milan Triennale, establishing the collective idea of Scandinavian modern design.	The Festival of Britain held on London's South Bank acts as a stimulus and model for the H55 exhibition at Hälsingborg four years later.	Norway exhibits at the Milan Triennale for the first time, alongside Sweden, Denmark, and Finland.

Aalto (1898–1976), Finn Juhl (1912–89), and Børge Mogensen (1914–72)—were also furniture designers, a fact that illustrated the dynamic cross-fertilization between architecture and design in Scandinavia at this time.

Adept at creating exquisite handcrafted luxury items, the Swedes were also committed to affordable, well-designed, functional objects produced on an industrial scale and promoted under the slogan "More beautiful things for everyday use." Sven Palmqvist (1906–84), a leading glass artist at Orrefors, demonstrated this dual approach. Alongside his richly colored, technically complex Ravenna glassware (1948), he developed a range of plain, practical bowls called Fuga (see image 3), produced by the innovative technique of centrifugal casting. Textile designer Astrid Sampe (1909–2002), who was chief designer and art director at Nordiska Kompaniet's textile division, adopted an equally broad-minded approach. In addition to designing geometric-patterned furnishing fabrics in vibrant colors, she commissioned a boldly experimental collection of artist-designed, screen-printed fabrics called Signed Textiles (1954).

The democratic principles nurtured in Sweden were reflected in other aspects of H55. The Swedes believed that the environment in which people lived—both indoors and outdoors—had a huge impact on their quality of life. "The things that surround us at home, outside, and at work all have significance not only in the functions they fulfil but in their esthetic qualities," observed designer Sven Erik Skawonius (1908–81) in *Scandinavian Domestic Design* (1961). H55 provided a tangible illustration of the benefits of intelligent, public-spirited architecture and town planning. Located on the pier overlooking the Øresund strait, the nautical On Board Pavilion (see image 2) designed by Carl-Axel Acking (1910–2001) resembled a ship's bridge perched on stilts crowned by fluttering pennants. The site as a whole, with its juxtaposition of light, airy buildings and attractive open spaces, created a pleasant, welcoming atmosphere. The lucid graphic identity developed by Anders Beckman (1907–67) for H55 complemented the coherent exhibition design.

Whereas exhibitions such as "Design in Scandinavia," which toured North America during the mid 1950s, were targeted at an international audience, H55 had a different atmosphere and a different agenda. It was less about commerce and more of an expression of national and regional identities. Just as the Festival of Britain in 1951 had marked the birth of "contemporary" style, so H55 confirmed Sweden's creative coming of age and boosted the profile of Scandinavian design at home and abroad. Having adopted a position of neutrality during World War II, the Swedes sought to re-engage with their European neighbors and to develop international links. The public and media interest in design generated by H55 was sustained over the coming years by the annual Scandinavian Design Cavalcade, hosted on a rotating basis by each Nordic country in turn. **LJ**

1954	1954	1954	1955	1956	1957
'Design in Scandinavia' begins a four-year tour of North America, disseminating and popularizing the concept of Scandinavian modern design.	Swedish designer Evar Bergström introduces Tebrax, an adjustable aluminum shelving-bracket system.	Astrid Sampe designs the patterns Angles, Soft Sand, and Thermidor for the Signed Textiles project.	The *New York Times* hails Focus de Luxe flatware by Folke Arström (1907–97) as one of the 100 best designed products of modern times.	Stockholm-based technology firm Ericsson launches the one-piece Ericofon (see p.244) on the domestic market.	Bruno Mathsson (1907–88) exhibits his furniture at 'Interbau' in Berlin. It is displayed in an apartment designed by Sampe.

String Shelving System 1949

NILS "NISSE" STRINNING 1917–2006

Oak, plastic-coated wire,
stainless steel
Flexible dimensions

 NAVIGATOR

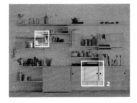

Scandinavian modern appealed to post-war consumers on many fronts. The organic forms, use of natural materials. and concern for comfort that characterized the style represented an approachable version of modernism, and one that was in tune with contemporary post-war lifestyles. The well-proportioned furniture designs were space saving, too, which was an important factor for those setting up home in much smaller surroundings than those enjoyed by their parents' generation.

Among the many new products on display at the Hälsingborg Exhibition of 1955 was the groundbreaking modular storage system String, created by Swedish designer Nils Strinning with his wife, Kajsa. The design came about when he entered and won a competition organized by Sweden's largest publisher, Bonnier, to create a shelving system for books that was affordable and easy to assemble. In conjunction with manufacturer Arne Lydmar, Strinning developed a way of coating wire with plastic, a technique he put to good use in the shelving system. Importantly, String addressed a common problem of home organization, then and now, which was how to store the accessories of daily life in a discreet and logical way. The wall-mounted system, with its minimal ladderlike supports, was visually unobtrusive and supremely functional. It could be extended and configured in many different ways and did away with the need for cumbersome free-standing storage furniture, such as traditional bookcases or cupboards. Although it was conceived principally for storing books, String can be used to organize other types of possessions as well. The focus falls on the items that are shelved, rather than on the shelving itself. From a producer's point of view, the kit of shelving parts was easy and cheap to package and transport. **EW**

1 KIT OF PARTS
The shelving system consists of modular elements that can be packed flat for ease of transport. Assembly is very straightforward and the system is fully adjustable even once it has been fitted. String can be configured in many different ways to suit diverse locations and needs.

2 LADDERLIKE SUPPORTS
A key feature of the light, airy and unobtrusive design are the economical ladderlike supports, which are made of strong, plastic-covered wire. Baskets, trays, and other items made from plastic-coated wire have become ubiquitous elements of behind-the-scenes storage.

🕐 DESIGNER PROFILE

1917–46
Architect and designer Nils Strinning was born in Kramfors, Sweden. During the 1940s, he studied architecture at the Royal Institute of Technology in Stockholm. In 1946, while he was still a student, he designed a simple plastic-coated wire rack used for drying dishes, called Elfa.

1947–51
Strinning further developed his method of coating wire with plastic in the late 1940s. By this time the Elfa dish rack had become very popular, and its success inspired the designer to incorporate the wire technique into a versatile shelving system.

1952–2006
In 1952 Strinning and his wife founded String Design AB. The company still produces the iconic storage system, which today includes many different components such as cabinets with sliding doors. The String system was awarded a gold medal at the Milan Triennale in 1954, it was shown at the "Design in Scandinavia" exhibition in the United States in the same year, and was exhibited at H55 in 1955. Strinning, who went on to design other plastic products, won numerous awards in his native Sweden and internationally.

▲ Nils Strinning in an early publicity shot for his shelving system. String became an iconic Swedish design and its adaptability meant that it provided storage solutions throughout the home: in living rooms, bathrooms, and work spaces, for example.

MODULAR SHELVING

The earliest modular shelving systems date from the 1930s and reflect the "furniture as equipment" esthetic of early modernist designers such as Le Corbusier (1887–1965). More visually refined modular systems were produced during the 1950s and 1960s. These include the Comprehensive Shelving System (1957) by George Nelson (1908–86) for Herman Miller and the self-supporting Ladderax (1964) for British firm Staples. However, perhaps best known today is the 606 Universal Shelving System (above), designed in 1960 by Dieter Rams (b.1932) for Vitsoe.

Ericofon 1956

ERICSSON f. 1876

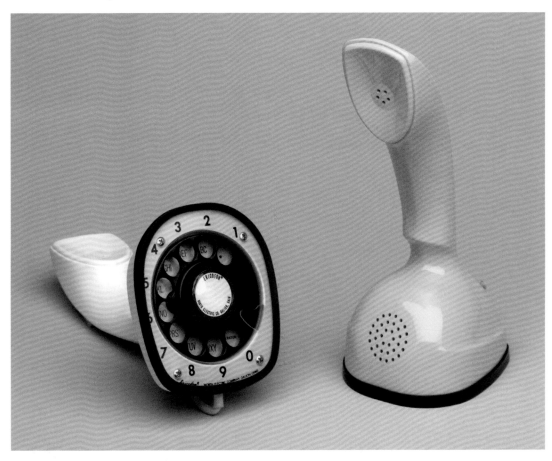

ABS plastic, rubber, and
nylon casing
8 ⅝ x 3⅞ x 4⅜ in.
22 x 10 x 11 cm

✦ NAVIGATOR

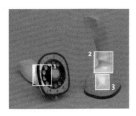

As soon as plastics came on the scene, designers began to look for ways in which to express the sculptural potential of this versatile family of materials. Closely allied was the ambition to create seamless one-piece products. Experimentation focused initially on the eternal design challenge of the chair, but during the 1940s a number of designers began to investigate the possibilities of creating a one-piece telephone. The Ericofon was the first realization of this aim.

Designed by Swedish firm Ericsson, the model went into production in 1954 and it was launched on the domestic market in 1956. Its antecedents were an upright, slightly taller version created by Hugo Blomberg (1897–1994) and Ralph Lysell (1907–87), patented by Ericsson in 1941, and the horizontal Unifon (1944), developed by Hans Kraepelin and styled by Gösta Thames (1916–2006), which was molded in two halves. The revolutionary Ericofon design was the first commercially available telephone to house the dial, receiver, and speaker within a single unit. Nicknamed the "Cobra" because of its resemblance to a coiled rearing snake, it was shaped ergonomically to facilitate a comfortable cradling posture. The rotary dial was positioned out of sight, underneath the mouthpiece in the base of the unit.

More than 2.5 million Ericofons were sold in the decades that it remained in production. Although the design was discontinued in 1972, it was subsequently reissued a number of times in updated and anniversary versions, and the Ericofon telephone now forms part of the collection at New York's Museum of Modern Art. **EW**

👁 FOCAL POINTS

1 SINGLE UNIT
The earliest version of the Ericofon featured a plastic casing that was manufactured in two halves, which were then glued together. However, by 1958 the design was injection-molded in a seamless single piece, thereby underscoring the unity of the original concept.

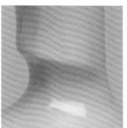

2 ORGANIC FORM
The designers of the Ericofon exploited plastic's sculptural potential and ensured that the one-piece telephone had a gently curved organic form, carefully shaped for comfortable use. Although the product's appearance was snakelike, the broad base gave it stability.

3 COLOR
When the Ericofon was launched on the European and US markets, it was available in eighteen different colors—with the exception of black. Bright red and white were the most popular. The vibrant colors were enhanced by the glossiness of the molded plastic.

🕐 COMPANY PROFILE

1876–13
The Swedish communication technology company Ericsson was founded by Lars Magnus Ericsson in 1876 as a telegraph and telephone repair workshop. It rapidly moved into the manufacture of telephones and by 1900 had 1,000 employees.

1914–39
World War I, the Russian Revolution, and the Depression hit sales and development. In the 1930s a failed takeover bid and corrupt share dealing brought the company to the brink of bankruptcy. It was saved by the Wallenberg family.

1940–96
During World War II, business focused on the domestic market, but in 1950 Ericsson hit the headlines when the world's first international call was made on an Ericsson telephone exchange. A hands-free speaker phone was launched in the 1960s, and by the late 1970s the firm was moving into digital.

1997–PRESENT
In 1997 Ericsson had 40 per cent of the global mobile market, and by 2000 it was the world's leading supplier of 3G mobile systems. In 2009 Ericsson collaborated with Verizon to carry out the first data call on 4G.

TELEPHONE FASHION

In the post-war era, it became increasingly common for middle-class households to own more than one telephone; kitchens and bedrooms were common locations for extensions. Consequently, a number of telephones were launched and marketed on the basis of their chic styling. Henry Dreyfuss Associates designed the Princess telephone (1959; above), a compact model produced in a range of colors and targeted at women, and the Trimline (1965), a sleek, slim design with a lighted dial set on the underside of the handset. In the United Kingdom, the Trimphone (1964), designed by Martyn Rowlands (1923–2004), was equally slim, but perhaps the most revolutionary styling was seen in the Grillo (1965), by Marco Zanuso (1916–2001) and Richard Sapper (b.1932), which was an exceptionally compact clam-shell design.

▲ Early telephones were styled as serious instruments, but by the 1950s familiarity was starting to breed fun. Here, the Ericofon is used by Peter Sellers in the comedy film *The World of Henry Orient* (1964).

LA RICOSTRUZIONE

In the mid 1940s, Italy emerged as a vibrant new force in modern design. This development was a result of a number of converging factors at the end of the war. One was the presence, mostly in Milan, of a generation of modernist-trained architects who found themselves without work after the war. To earn a living, architects such as the Castiglioni brothers—Achille (1918–2002) and Pier Giacomo (1913–68)—Vico Magistretti (1920–2006), Marco Zanuso (1916–2001), and Ettore Sottsass (1917–2007) turned to furniture and product design. They aimed to exploit the opportunities offered by the new industries that were beginning to rise up in the Brianza region and elsewhere. These new firms sought to distance themselves from a fascist past by adopting a different esthetic, and the architect-designers were ready to provide it.

This spirit of renewal underpinned the years of La Ricostruzione. During the war, Italian cities had been devastated by bombing, and their widespread destruction created an urgent need for housing. Most of the homes built immediately after the war were located in apartment blocks on the periphery of cities. The concomitant need for these dwellings to be furnished stimulated production. Firms such as Cassina, Artemide, Arteluce, and Flos rose to the challenge and invested in new machinery. This gave architect-designers an

KEY EVENTS

1946	1946	1946	1946	1947	1951
Domus magazine is re-established after the war. Ernesto Rogers (1909–69) is appointed editor.	In the new political climate of the Italian Republic, design is aligned with progressive modernity and the future.	Enrico Piaggio (1905–65) files a patent for the Vespa design (see p.248), referring to a "model of a practical nature."	Pininfarina designs the Cisitalia car, an Italian design icon that is later included in the collection at New York City's Museum of Modern Art.	The focus of the Milan Triennale is post-war reconstruction and the building and furnishing of new homes.	The theme of the design section of the Milan Triennale is "Form of the Useful." Olivetti typewriters are featured.

opportunity to create new lines of furniture. Giò Ponti (1891–1979), for example, worked with Cassina and produced the Superleggera chair (1957), while Marco Zanuso (1916–2001) joined forces with the firm Arflex, which was using plastic foam to upholster its chairs. The curves of Zanuso's design for the Lady armchair (see image 1) were inspired by the possibilities of this new material. Moreover, product design companies, such as Kartell, employed the new plastics to create striking designs that made a mundane object, such as a bucket, take on the appearance of a work of art. Large technical firms such as Olivetti, known for its typewriters (see p.250), also joined in the search for dynamic new forms.

Another sphere of Italian manufacturing to embrace modern design at this time was the automobile industry, founded largely on traditional coach-building. While Fiat entered the world of Fordist mass production, which led to the 600 and 500 models in the 1950s, a range of more upmarket producers—Alfa Romeo (see p.252), Lancia, Ferrari, Maserati, and Pininfarina (see image 2) among them—produced more stylish vehicles aimed at an international elite.

Modern Italian design was clearly aspirational rather than democratic, and the late 1940s to 1950s was a time of dramatic improvement in the quality of goods for both the domestic and international markets. This was fuelled by economic expansion and the emergence of the concept of *dolce vita* or the "good life." Events such as the Milan Triennales, held in 1947, 1951, and 1954, acted as a stimulating international forum for debate, with exhibition themes including "Form of the Useful" (1951) and "The Production of Art" (1954). The late 1950s marked the high point of what came to be known as the "economic miracle" in Italy. Export figures were high and Italy was seen as the home of stylish modern design. However, by the early 1960s growing industrial unrest indicated that this era of optimistic economic expansion was beginning to slow down. **PS**

1 The Lady armchair (1951) is constructed from four separate elements. It won the Gold Medal at the Milan Triennale in 1951.

2 Inspired by the aerodynamic shape of racing cars, the coachwork of the Pininfarina Cisitalia 202 GT (1946) was conceived as a single shell.

1954	1954	1956	1956	1957	1958
The Golden Compass industrial design award is instigated by La Rinascente department store in Milan.	*Stile Industria* magazine is launched. It adopts a highly artistic approach to industrial design.	The Italian Association of Industrial Designers is formed in Milan; it is a marker of the esteem in which the profession is held.	The Fiat company launches its model 600. A people's car, it is the first example of a minivan.	The Milan Triennale marks the high point of design's role in the Italian "economic miracle."	Ettore Sottsass is employed by the Olivetti company and works on its new computer, the Elea 9003.

Vespa 1946
CORRADINO D'ASCANIO 1891–1981

Vespa GS 150 (1955)
Painted steel and metal frame,
rubber, leather, and plastic
42½ x 28⅜ x 67⅜ in.
108 x 72 x 171 cm

NAVIGATOR

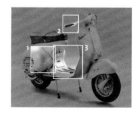

Corradino D'Ascanio designed the Vespa motor scooter for industrialist Enrico Piaggio, and it was named the "Wasp" in reference to its body shape and antenna-like wing mirrors. Like D'Ascanio, Piaggio's background was in aeronautical engineering and the Vespa borrowed many of its features from that industry. The brief from Piaggio to D'Ascanio had been to design a simple and affordable vehicle for the masses, but one that was not a motorcycle. It needed to be easy to ride and able to carry a passenger. The Vespa was introduced at the Milan Fair of 1946 and it quickly became one of the most iconic objects of La Ricostruzione. For many Italians, keen to abandon their bicycles for any kind of motorized transportation, it symbolized a new era of freedom and a carefree modern lifestyle. The way in which all of its mechanical parts were covered made it a particularly desirable object, as did the fact that it could be paid for by instalments. Indeed, so visually and symbolically potent was the Vespa design that the scooter quickly attracted a cult following and appeared in a number of Hollywood films. Most notable among them was *Roman Holiday*, made in 1952, in which Gregory Peck and Audrey Hepburn ride together on a Vespa, the latter in a side-saddle position.

Once the patent had been filed, production expanded rapidly, rising to nearly 20,000 units in 1948. Piaggio marketed the Vespa aggressively, both in Italy and abroad, and introduced the concept of Vespa clubs to help grow its popularity. From 1950 onward, the Vespa was manufactured in Germany, the United Kingdom, and France, among other places, and production began outside Europe in the 1960s. **PS**

FOCAL POINTS

1 BODY SHELL

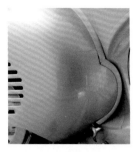

The aerodynamic appearance came from aircraft technology. With its unified, painted, pressed-steel body shell, it also owed something stylistically to American streamlining. It was one of the first vehicles to use monocoque construction, which meant that the body was an integral part of the chassis.

2 NEW TECHNOLOGY

In addition to being visually innovative, the Vespa was technologically radical. Unlike previous motorbikes, it was built on a spar frame with the gear change positioned on the handlebars. The fact that the engine was mounted onto the rear wheel was also new and required much testing.

3 FEMALE DRIVERS

The pass-through leg area was designed with consideration for women wearing skirts, and the absence of a drive frame meant that women were unlikely to get dirty from oil. Although the scooter was designed for men and women to drive, typically women rode on the rear passenger seat.

▲ The Vespa acquired cult status in the United Kingdom. In the early 1960s, it became the preferred mode of transport for "Mods," a predominantly male youth subculture. They decorated their scooters with multiple side mirrors, headlamps, and furry tails on sticks.

LAMBRETTA

The Vespa's main competitor was the Lambretta motor scooter (right), launched in 1947. Manufactured by Innocenti, the name derives from Lambrate, the region where the factory was located. Its design was based on that of a World War II military vehicle, and although the Lambretta looked a little similar to the Vespa, it lacked its innovative technology and body shell design. However, it was similarly suited to the narrow back streets of Italian cities and was easily navigable with a female passenger on the rear seat. Large numbers of Lambrettas were produced, but it never achieved the same cult status as the Vespa.

Olivetti Lettera 22 1950

MARCELLO NIZZOLI 1887–1969

Enameled metal housing,
inked ribbon, rubber
3¼ x 11¾ x 12¾ in.
8 x 30 x 32.5 cm

☼ NAVIGATOR

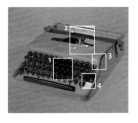

Designed as a portable typewriter that would free its users from being office bound, Marcello Nizzoli's Olivetti Lettera 22 broke new ground. In contrast to his earlier typewriter for the same company, the Lexicon 80, which was more bulky and heavy, the little Lettera was compact and elegant. By today's standards it would be seen as too heavy to carry around, but in 1950 it was perceived as relatively light. It was especially appreciated by journalists who needed to be able to work on the move. Furthermore, the design received much acclaim. It was awarded the Golden Compass in 1954, and in 1959 the Illinois Institute of Technology selected the Lettera 22 as the best product design of the past hundred years.

Nizzoli had first been employed by Olivetti as a graphic designer, an area of expertise that he took up after painting. He had spent the 1930s working in that field, and also engaging in the design of exhibitions. Company chair Adriano Olivetti was quick to recognize his employee's visualizing skills and approached him to create new forms for his firm's typewriters. Olivetti had visited the United States in the 1930s and seen the slick, streamlined machines that were being produced there. He realized that in order to compete with US products, post-war Italy needed to go one stage further and make its industrial objects look more attractive, like pieces of sculpture. Nizzoli brought his eye for composition and visual harmony into this new professional arena. **PS**

1 SENSORIALITY
Great attention was paid to the user interface. It had a sharp, clear action and felt good to use. Nizzoli was aware that the visual, tactile, and aural all had to come together if he was to create a well-designed object. The awards given to the design were a tribute to his rigorous approach.

2 SCULPTURAL FORM
The sculptural quality is clear in the way in which form and space interact. The kidney-shaped space above the keys, for example, is as important compositionally as the object's solid form. Nizzoli was aware of the way in which contemporary sculptors were working and emulated their methods.

3 BODY SHELL
The style of the Lettera 22 is described as restrained streamlining. The steel body shell conceals its mechanism and gives the design visual unity. Its restraint lies in the absence of chrome strips to conceal seam lines and in the decision to counteract straight lines with subtly curved ones.

4 COLOR
Nizzoli's choice of color contributed to the Lettera 22's modesty and functionality, as it did not assert itself in any way. Soft blue was the most common, but light green and gray were also available. Nizzoli could not resist adding a single red key to act as a striking visual highlight.

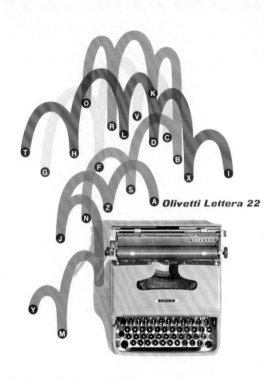

▲ Giovanni Pintori (1912–99) designed this advertisement poster for the Olivetti Lettera 22 typewriter in 1955. The graphic designer is well known for his minimalist designs for the company.

LEXICON 80

The Lexicon 80 (above), designed a year before the Lettera 22, was a very different kind of typewriter. Intended to be used in an office, it was conceived as a solid piece of machinery that gave its users confidence in its performance. The heavy metal shell featured a curvaceous, sculptural form, and one of its most striking features was the curved seam line that joined together the two molded components of the shell. Nizzoli made the decision to leave it exposed and let it contribute to the overall design. This sculptural approach distinguished Italian streamlining from its US roots. Nearly 800,000 Lexicons were produced before the model was replaced by the Diaspron 82 in 1959.

Alfa Romeo Giulietta Sprint 1954

GIUSEPPE "NUCCIO" BERTONE 1914–97

The Giulietta Sprint was manufactured at the Bertone Group's coach-building plant, which was located in Grugliasco near Turin, Italy.

Italy's post-war successes in furniture and product design were extended to include automobile design, an area in which the country had excelled since the early part of the 20th century. Its particular strength lay in its coach-building traditions and the skills that were developed and sustained in that field. Companies such as Bugatti and Alfa Romeo were already internationally renowned, specifically in the production of racing cars, but in the years after World War II, Alfa Romeo decided to move into the mass-produced family car market. The company simply transferred its expertise in high-quality engineering and immaculate styling to a new arena. Nothing was lost in translation.

The Giulietta was an example of its success in this new venture, and the car remained in production from 1954 to 1965. A number of models were developed, including the 2+2 Sprint coupé (1954), the four-door Berlina saloon (1955), and the open-top, two-seater Spider roadster (1955). The Giulietta Sprint was the first off the production line and it was an extremely elegant, streamlined car. Although it was designed in the studio of Giuseppe "Nuccio" Bertone, one of the great names in post-war Italian car styling, the designer who actually worked on the car was Bertone's partner, Franco Scaglione (1916–93), who has been described as the unsung hero of post-war Italian streamlining. He had a background in aeronautical engineering and began to design independently in 1959, working with Porsche among others. Some 40,000 cars were produced before the Giulietta was discontinued. It marked a big turning point for Alfa Romeo and was one of the Bertone Group's most successful designs. **PS**

◆ NAVIGATOR

FOCAL POINTS

1 RADIATOR GRILLE
The Giulietta Sprint features the familiar shield-shaped Alfa Romeo grille. It is flanked by additional, chrome-trimmed grilles on either side to give the car a dramatic appearance at the front. It is from this angle that the Sprint most closely resembles the styling of US automobiles.

2 CHROME DETAILING
Although the streamlining is more subtle than would have been the case in a US automobile, chrome strips are used in several places—around the windshield and radiator grille, and along the bottom of the doors—to create visual highlights and to accentuate the car's sculptural form.

3 PROFILE
The Giulietta Sprint has a classic streamlined profile and a subtle teardrop shape. The hood gently slopes to the slant of the windshield and the same curve extends from the slope of the roof right down to the back bumper. The fact that it has no mudguards leaves its profile undisturbed.

DESIGNER PROFILE

1914–51
Giuseppe "Nuccio" Bertone joined his father in the family business in 1934. After the war, he took over the Bertone Group and developed it into a significant car manufacturing and designing operation. He initiated the move into mass production, making a huge investment in new technology.

1952–97
In 1952 Alfa Romeo commissioned him to design and manufacture the Sprint. He brought in several innovative car designers, including Giorgetto Giugiaro (b.1938). Bertone oversaw the design and manufacture of cars for all the major Italian car companies, including Lamborghini, Lancia, and Fiat. He kept up his interest in the business until his death at the age of eighty-two.

▲ The Spider roadster came hot on the heels of the Sprint in 1955. The convertible bodywork of the Spider was designed by Pininfarina, one of Italy's leading independent car design companies, and it was most distinctive and impressive in Alfa Romeo red.

BRAVE NEW WORLD

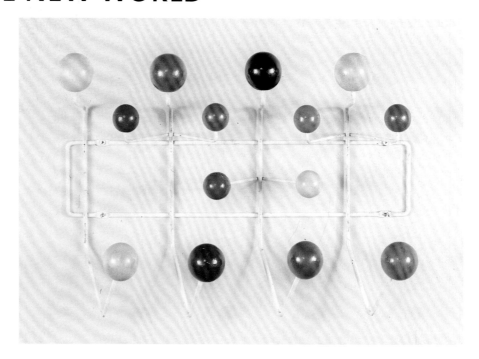

After World War II, there was a collective feeling of optimism in the design profession and the scientific community: both were committed to creating a better world. The early post-war period was a momentous era for scientific research, with significant progress in fields such as X-ray crystallography, molecular biology, nuclear physics, space exploration, and astronomy. Many vital technological and medical breakthroughs were made during the late 1940s and 1950s. There was also a keen interest in popular science among the general public.

After a decade of disruption, manufacturers were able to re-establish their operations and respond to growing consumer demand. Design flourished as a consequence. Self-consciously modern designs enjoyed a wave of popularity during the 1950s. Confidence in the future prompted designers to explore new sources of inspiration for the form and decoration of everyday products that purposely evoked modernity, such as the ball-shaped feet and knobs on furniture and appliances, echoing the ball-and-spoke models of atomic structures, as seen in George Nelson Associates Ball clock (1947; see p.256) and the Hang-It-All coat rack (1953; see image 1), designed by Charles (1907–78) and Ray (1912–88) Eames. Contemporary art proved fertile territory, hence the vogue

KEY EVENTS

1945	1947	1950	1951	1952	1953
British crystallographer Dorothy Hodgkin works out the atomic structure of penicillin by means of X-ray crystallography.	The British Medical Research Council establishes a Unit for the Study of the Molecular Structure of Biological Systems in Cambridge, England.	The Plastic chair by US designers Charles and Ray Eames is manufactured by Herman Miller.	The Festival of Britain highlights scientific innovations in the Dome of Discovery in London.	The United States conducts its first nuclear test of an hydrogen bomb, or H-bomb, at Enewetak Atoll in the Marshall Islands.	The Soviet Union explodes its first H-bomb at the Semipalatinsk test site in Kazakhstan.

254 IDENTITY AND CONFORMITY 1945–60

for Abstract Expressionist textiles inspired by the action paintings of Jackson Pollock (1912–56), and organic vessels in ceramics and glass such as the Lancet Blade dish (1951; see p.258) by Stig Lindberg (1916–82), echoing the sculpture of Henry Moore (1898–1986). The vogue for free-form amoeboid shapes during the 1950s, which affected everything from coffee tables to tableware, can be linked to developments in molecular biology.

One of the most intriguing science-inspired initiatives was the Festival Pattern Group project. Instigated by the Council of Industrial Design as part of the 1951 Festival of Britain, the aim of the scheme was to stimulate a new approach to decoration by encouraging manufacturers to use diagrams of crystal structures as the basis for patterns on textiles, wallpapers, plastics, glass, ceramics, and metalwork. Helen Megaw (1907–2002), a highly respected scientist from Cambridge University, came up with the idea, having recognized the decorative potential of crystal structures (X-ray crystallography diagrams showing the relationship between atoms) or atomic structures, as they were also known: "A crystal structure, like a wallpaper, consists of a unit of pattern which repeats itself indefinitely," explained Megaw.

Having been enlisted by the Council of Industrial Design to act as the scientific consultant for the Festival Pattern Group, Megaw selected a group of X-ray crystallography diagrams illustrating the structures of minerals, such as mica, beryl, and afwillite, and biological materials, such as hemoglobin and insulin. Although the crystallographers who participated in the scheme chose to remain anonymous at the time, they included world-renowned Nobel Prize-winning scientists, such as Dorothy Hodgkin (1910–94) and John Kendrew (1917–97). The diagrams were of two distinct types: ball-and-spoke structures in which atoms were depicted as circles and the bonds between them were drawn as lines; and electron density maps recording the distribution of matter, resembling the curvilinear contour lines on maps. Whereas the former were geometric in outline, the latter were fluid and asymmetrical. Both proved equally stimulating, resulting in some highly unusual and memorable designs.

These drawings were circulated to a select group of companies, including Wedgwood, Warner and Son, ICI, and Chance Brothers, where they were used as the basis for patterns on products as diverse as machine-woven lace, Jacquard-woven and screen-printed fabrics, vinyl leathercloth, ceramic tiles, and window glass. Resulting designs such as the fabric based on a diagram of afwillite (see image 2) were showcased in the Dome of Discovery and the Regatta Restaurant at the Festival of Britain in London and the "Exhibition of Science" at London's Science Museum, alongside scientific drawings and artefacts. The Regatta Restaurant was decked out with carpets, drapes, and plastic laminates featuring these weird and wonderful patterns. Fusing art and science, the Festival Pattern Group represented the ultimate embodiment of the brave new world of post-war design. **LJ**

1 The Hang-It-All coat rack, designed by Charles and Ray Eames and produced by Herman Miller in 1953, evokes the molecular structures revealed by the electron microscope.

2 The design of this screen-printed spun rayon fabric is based on the structure of the afwillite mineral, and was made for British Celanese as part of the Festival Pattern Group in 1951.

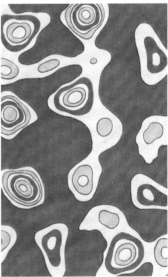

Ball Clock 1947

GEORGE NELSON ASSOCIATES 1947–86

Lacquered wood, steel
Diameter 13 in./33 cm

 NAVIGATOR

Architect George Nelson (1908–86) had an extremely positive influence on US post-war design. As design director at Herman Miller from 1947 onward, Nelson recruited some outstanding artists and designers to work for the company, such as Charles and Ray Eames, Isamu Noguchi (1904–88), and Alexander Girard (1907–93). His own design practice, George Nelson Associates, also provided an umbrella for a group of talented individuals who were responsible for some of the most imaginative designs of the period, including the Coconut chair (1955) and Marshmallow sofa (1956). It was Nelson's colleague Irving Harper (1916–2015)) who took the lead in developing a series of table and wall clocks for the Howard Miller Clock Company from 1947 to 1953.

The Ball clock not only dispensed with the standard clock face and casing, but also with traditional numerals. Witty and playful, it married the language of contemporary art and science to create a visually stimulating object serving a practical purpose. Other designs in the series included the Asterisk clock (1950), featuring a typographic symbol of an asterisk cut from zinc-plated steel, and the Spider Web clock (1954), a skeletal star strung with decorative cord. A perennial favorite, the Ball clock is still in production. **LJ**

👁 FOCAL POINTS

1 BALL AND SPOKE
The ball-and-spoke shape of this design derives from scientific models of atomic structures. Models of this kind, composed of colored balls representing atoms, connected by steel rods denoting the links between them, were commonplace in scientific laboratories at this date.

2 FACE
Challenging the conventions of clock design, the Ball clock has an open structure, rather than a glazed frame, and there are no numerals on the clock face. The hours are represented by twelve balls made of painted birch, attached to narrow steel rods radiating from a circular disc hiding the clock mechanism.

3 HAND
Whereas much modernist design was very serious, the Ball clock is an overtly playful and humorous design. Deliberately eye-catching and thought-provoking, it encapsulates the upbeat mood of the early post-war period and injected a note of color and fun into interior design.

🕐 DESIGNER PROFILE

1908–34
George Nelson was born in Hartford, Connecticut. He studied architecture and fine art at Yale University. From 1932 to 1934, he studied at the American Academy in Rome.

1935–86
Nelson became an associate editor at *Architectural Forum*. From 1936 to 1941 he ran an architectural practice. He began designing furniture for Herman Miller in 1945 and was design director from 1947. He also ran George Nelson Associates from 1947 to 1983. His firm also designed offices, restaurants, and stores.

▲ Following the success of the wall clocks, George Nelson Associates was asked to develop a range of lighting. Produced in an array of shapes and sizes, the Bubble lamps (1952) were created by spraying a layer of thin white plastic over a wire cage, exploiting a manufacturing process developed by the US military.

CALDER SCULPTURES

Drawing on the visual language of contemporary art, George Nelson Associates' Ball clock evokes comparisons with the work of US sculptor Alexander Calder (1898–1976; right), whose newly developed mobiles featured colored geometric and organic elements floating in space suspended on rods and wire. Calder made the colored kinetic and standing sculptures from 1931, using abstract shapes and bold colors to create visual and spatial rhythms. Constellation motifs, as reflected in the radiating structure of the Ball clock, were a recurrent form of imagery in Calder's sculptures. Calder attempted to evoke the dynamism of the cosmos in his work in the 1930s. Constellation motifs also appear in one of his textile designs.

Lancet Blade Dish 1951

STIG LINDBERG 1916–82

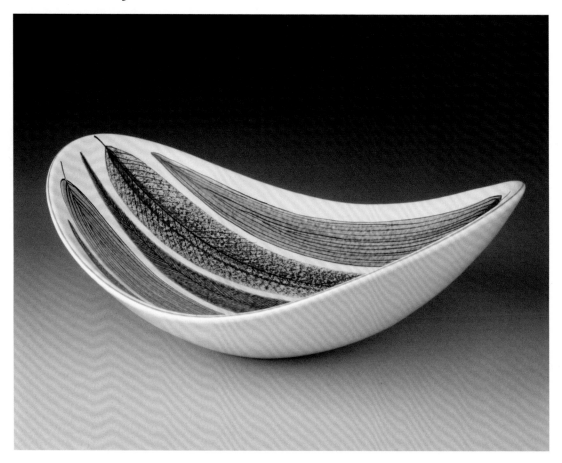

Tin-glazed earthenware
Length 10⅝ in./27 cm

◆ NAVIGATOR

An unashamedly decorative designer, Stig Lindberg introduced a new vocabulary of pattern-making into Swedish post-war design. In his colorful hand-painted faience pottery for Gustavsberg, developed during the early years of World War II and first exhibited in 1942, he married fluid curvaceous forms with stylized organic motifs. Whereas manufacturers elsewhere in Europe were severely disrupted at this date, Swedish firms were able to continue in operation. After the war Sweden rapidly emerged as an international design superpower, with Lindberg as one of its star designers, winning awards at the Milan Triennale between 1948 and 1957. His faience pottery, with its seductive sculptural shapes and brightly colored patterns, is visually arresting and consciously joyful, embodying the positive spirit of post-war Scandinavian modern design.

Pastoralism had been rife in Swedish textiles throughout the 1940s, a conscious reaction against the widespread destruction elsewhere. Swedish printed fabrics were awash with wild flowers during the war years, exemplified by the vibrant floral patterns created by exiled Danish architect Arne Jacobsen (1902–71) and the lush botanical prints designed by Josef Frank (1885–67) for Svenskt Tenn. Lindberg's faience pottery, with its hand-painted leaves and floral sprigs, can be seen as another manifestation of this heightened pastoral trend. The shapes of his ceramics were also exaggeratedly organic. Lindberg's fascination with biomorphic forms and quasi-biological imagery continued throughout the 1950s, affecting not only his tableware and ornamental faience pottery for Gustavsberg but also his printed textiles for Nordiska Kompaniet. **LJ**

👁 FOCAL POINTS

1 LEAF MOTIFS
The long, narrow, pointed leaves on this dish complement the elliptical vessel form. Painted in two shades of earthy green, the leaves are simplified and stylized, with stalks and veins added in fine black lines. There is a biological quality to the patterns, which are as exaggeratedly organic as the shapes.

2 RIM
With its ovoid outline and scooped rim, this dish is fluid and organic. Whereas hard-edged geometric forms and machine imagery prevailed in the 1920s and 1930s, Lindberg pioneered a vocabulary of soft plastic forms in the 1940s and 1950s that were rooted in the natural world.

3 WHITE
The whiteness of this dish arises from a glaze containing tin. Tin-glazed earthenware, known as "delftware" or "faience," had been produced in Europe for centuries. By the early 20th century, this medium had gone out of fashion, but it was given a new lease on life by Lindberg.

FRUKTLÅDA FABRIC

The strongly biological character of Lindberg's early post-war designs is reflected in his screen-printed fabric Fruktlåda (above)—meaning "fruit box." A witty pattern depicting rows of apples in cross section, each piece of fruit is decorated individually, some with core and pips, others with a worm inside. The shape of the fruit and the motifs inside resemble the forms and patterns of Lindberg's pottery for Gustavsberg. The style he developed had a strong impact on designers in neighboring Denmark and Finland.

◄ Because the decoration on Lindberg's faience pottery was painted entirely freehand, each piece was individual. Considerable skill was required to paint these motifs on the soft, unfired tin glaze. The pigment and glaze fused during the firing process, giving a soft-edged quality to the decoration. The white ground provides a foil for the vibrant colors, intensifying the visual impact of the pigments.

THE FESTIVAL OF BRITAIN

1 The twin iconic structures—the Dome of Discovery and the Skylon—sitting side by side at the Festival of Britain site.

2 This wallpaper is by Robert Sevant, a member of the Festival Pattern Group.

3 The side walls of the Lion and Unicorn Pavilion had eye-shaped portholes.

The origins of the Festival of Britain held in 1951 go back to 1943 when the Royal Society of Arts proposed a celebration of the centenary of the Great Exhibition of 1851, which had been mounted in Hyde Park, London. The idea was revived in 1945 under the new Labour government, and the Festival ultimately expressed the spirit and ideals of Labour, especially those of its deputy leader, Herbert Morrison. Although industry was still struggling with shortages and many cities remained war ravaged in 1951, the country was ready to embrace a sense of progress and recovery.

Unlike the "Britain Can Make It" exhibition of 1946, which had presented products in a museum setting, the Festival was conceived as an ambitious program involving the entire country. For example, the HMS *Campania* toured the coast, local exhibits were staged, an exhibition of housing was held at Poplar in East London, and the Festival Pleasure Gardens were built at Battersea. It was concerned with both architecture and design, as well as with the arts more generally. The two key buildings—the Dome of Discovery and the Skylon (see image 1)—were reminiscent of the Perisphere and Trylon that had featured at the New York World's Fair of 1939. They were equally futuristic in nature, thereby expressing the promise of a brave new world governed by advanced technology and science. These landmarks were visual highlights on

KEY EVENTS

1943	1945	1946	1948	1948	1949
The Royal Society of Arts (RSA) proposes an international exhibition to celebrate the centenary of the Great Exhibition of 1851 in London's Hyde Park.	World War II comes to an end and the United Kingdom elects a Labour government. The landslide victory reflects a strong public mood for social change.	The RSA's proposal for an international show is shelved. Instead, a Festival of Britain is planned, featuring art, design, architecture, science, and technology.	The Arts Council of Great Britain, the British Film Institute, and the Council for Industrial Design are involved in planning the Festival.	Manufacturers are asked to submit details of their best designs for inclusion in the exhibition.	Labour Prime Minister Clement Attlee lays the foundation stone of the Royal Festival Hall; it is the only structure that survives after the festival.

the South Bank site near Waterloo station, positioned among other structures containing a range of exhibits and displays. While Gerald Barry (1898–1968) oversaw the event, Hugh Casson (1910–99) had overall responsibility for the architecture. James Gardner (1907–95) was responsible for the Battersea gardens and Ralph Tubbs (1912–96) for the Dome. The main similarity between the events of 1946 and 1951 was that the Council of Industrial Design played a key role in both exhibitions, vetting all the products that were included.

Although the Festival was forward thinking in its approach, focusing on the role of design and architecture in creating a new world, it also embraced tradition, in an acknowledgement of the fact that the United Kingdom was largely defined by its past. Nowhere was this theme more evident than in the Lion and Unicorn Pavilion (see image 3), designed by students at London's Royal College of Art under the leadership of R. D. Russell (1903–81) and Robert Goodden (1909–2002). The displays subtly embraced the past, not only referencing heraldry and other historic images, but also projecting that nostalgic nationalistic vision into a new future. Other main themes of the displays at the Festival included the Land of Britain, Sea and Ships, and Transport. The aim was to provide an overview of the nation's achievements and aspirations. Inevitably design played a significant role, particularly in the House and Gardens Pavilion designed by Bronek Katz (1912–60), which depicted the way in which people would lead their lives in their homes in the not-too-distant future. The room sets were light and bright, and featured new furniture and textiles (see p.264) designed by Robin (1915–2010) and Lucienne Day (1917–2010), among others. However, modern furniture was not restricted to the inside spaces, as the Council of Industrial Design selected some striking pieces for outside, too. The slender, metal Antelope (see p.262) and Springbok chairs by Ernest Race (1913–64) punctuated the exterior landscape of the South Bank, sitting alongside litter bins designed by Jack Howe (1911–2003).

One of the most influential design initiatives arising out of the event in 1951 was the work of the Festival Pattern Group (see image 2). Referencing scientific developments and imagery—for example, molecular structures—the contemporary patterns produced by this group were intended to be applied to a wide range of products, from textiles to kitchen laminates. These striking abstract designs came to epitomize the progressive esthetic of the Festival.

In the summer of 1951, the Festival came to an end. Subsequently, the newly elected Conservative government decided to destroy all the structures, except the Royal Festival Hall, which remains on the site to this day. However, the influence of the Festival lingered throughout the remainder of the 1950s, especially in the new towns that were built during that decade. The architecture of these developments, the design and furnishing of the new homes that comprised them and, above all, the radical approach to urban planning owed a great deal to what had been achieved on the South Bank. **PS**

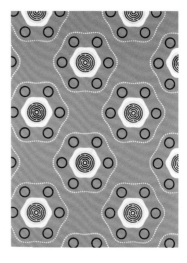

1950	1951	1951	1951	1951	1952
Festival director Gerald Barry visits Rome to observe the city's treatment of fountains and floodlighting.	Crystallographer Helen Megaw (1907–2002) coordinates the Festival Pattern Group, which comprises twenty-eight manufacturers.	On May 3, King George VI declares the Festival open. Later that day, 2,000 camp fires are lit across the nation.	The Festival runs throughout the summer, attracting huge visitor numbers. A smaller group of displays tours the coast on HMS *Campania*.	Labour fails to capitalize on the success of the Festival and loses the October election to the Conservative Party.	Conservative Prime Minister Winston Churchill orders the scrapping of the Skylon, the iconic emblem of the Festival.

Antelope Chair 1951
ERNEST RACE 1913–64

Bent steel, molded plywood
31½ x 19¾ x 20¾ in.
80 x 50 x 53 cm

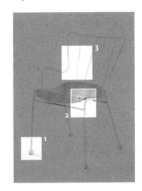

Created by Ernest Race for the Festival of Britain, the Antelope chair has stood the test of time and remains an iconic, mid-century modern British design. Made of bent steel and molded plywood, it owes much to the work of US designers Charles (1907–78) and Ray Eames (1912–88), who were the first to experiment with wartime developments in molded plywood for chair seats and shells. It is nonetheless a highly original design, noted for its lightness and elegance. Produced by Race's own manufacturing company, the Antelope was one of two chairs—the other was the Springbok—commissioned as exterior seating for the areas around the Royal Festival Hall on the South Bank site. Thanks to the large number required, it was profitable to produce.

Both chairs were designed in the Festival spirit, which encouraged a union of science and design. The use of steel rod, which defined the form of the Antelope, was technologically advanced, and the chair had a playful, sculptural appearance that was in keeping with the optimistic mood of the day. After the Festival, Race put the chair into mass production and created a number of different versions, including a two-seater. The Festival chair had had a yellow plywood seat, but new colors were introduced and it remained a popular design throughout the 1950s, visible in a range of environments such as outdoor eating areas, new towns, and swimming baths. It exported the spirit of the Festival to new arenas and helped to sustain the event's forward-looking ethos. **PS**

👁 FOCAL POINTS

1 BALL FEET
The humorous little ball feet primarily exist to give the thin legs a visual finishing point, but they also ensure that the legs do not damage any flooring. The shape of the feet recalls the "atom" theme of the Festival, which inspired a number of other designs that appeared at the same time.

2 STEEL ROD
The strong, resilient, slender steel rods that were used for the main structure—legs, back, and armrests—of the Antelope meant that this very minimal, sculptural design could withstand outdoor weather conditions. The steel was coated with enamel, which was colored white.

3 SPACE
The Antelope's skeletal form and splayed legs were in keeping with the modernist idea that furniture should not visually impede the appreciation of architectural space. In this case, the intention was to highlight the architectural features of the buildings nearby.

SPRINGBOK CHAIR

A less dramatic design than the Antelope, the Springbok (1951; above) was nonetheless a handsome, modern-looking chair. Although it was commissioned for outdoor use, it offered enough comfort to be used inside as required. Comfort was provided by a number of horizontally positioned springs that were covered in PVC. They came in a range of colors, including red, yellow, blue, and gray. The legs were fixed to the outside of the steel rod seat frame in order to make the chair stackable.

Calyx Furnishing Fabric 1951

LUCIENNE DAY 1917–2010

Instead of representational motifs, flowers are suggested by simple, pared-down cup-and-saucer shapes, some in vivid hues, others decorated with textural effects, connected by lines evoking stems that resemble the strings of a kite.

✪ NAVIGATOR

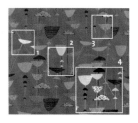

After World War II, there was an explosion of creativity in design. Designers such as Lucienne Day, who had trained during the late 1930s but whose careers had been put on hold during the war, were bursting with ideas. Calyx captures the moment when this pent-up artistic energy was released. In this revolutionary printed furnishing fabric, Day broke with the conventions of floral pattern design and introduced an exciting vocabulary of abstraction. She admired US sculptor Alexander Calder (1898–1976), and the motifs in Calyx are similar to the metal shapes suspended on wires in his mobiles. The dynamism and playfulness of Calyx chimed with the esthetics of modern art, as well as encapsulating the upbeat mood of the early post-war period.

Calyx was created for a room setting designed by Day's husband, Robin (1915–2010), for the Homes and Gardens Pavilion at the Festival of Britain in 1951. Her adventurous furnishing textile complemented his innovative molded-plywood furniture. Initially, Heal's Wholesale and Export (later Heal Fabrics) was reluctant to produce this design, as they thought it was too radical for British taste, but she persuaded them to take a risk. Contrary to expectations, Calyx proved successful, both critically and commercially, remaining in demand for many years and winning a string of awards. Day's groundbreaking approach to pattern design had an electrifying effect on the British market, heralding the arrival of contemporary design. **LJ**

FOCAL POINTS

1 MOTTLED TEXTURE
Co-opting radical modern art idioms, Day applied this esthetic to textiles in an original way. One of the first post-war designers to make this transition, she adopted a collage-like approach, juxtaposing solid planes of color with broken, mottled, and spongelike textures.

2 LINES
A keen gardener, Day used plants as a source of inspiration in many of her textile designs, but in stylized or abstracted forms. Calyx, the title of this design, refers to the sepals of a flower. The cup-shaped forms and spindly lines are loosely derived from stalks and flowers.

3 FLAT COLOR
The hand screen-printing technique was used for Calyx. The large scale of the pattern, much bigger than could be produced by roller printing, was one of the advantages of this flexible process. Screen-printing was ideally suited for reproducing the flat colors and subtle textural effects.

4 BLACK AND WHITE
Calyx was innovative in its use of color. Although it was produced in several colorways, the best-known version had an olive greenish-brown background, contrasting with crisp black and white elements and striking color highlights, which were novel at the time.

DESIGNER PROFILE

1917–40
Dèsirèe Lucienne Conradi was born in Coulsdon, Surrey, England. She studied at Croydon School of Art, then at the Royal College of Art, specializing in printed textiles.

1941–2010
She married furniture designer Robin Day. After the war, she began practicing as a freelance textile designer. She was very successful during the 1950s and 1960s, enjoying a close relationship with Heal Fabrics. She and Robin acted as design consultants to the John Lewis Partnership from 1962 to 1987.

▲ Day found inspiration in the quirky imagery, rhythms, and colors of the abstract paintings of Paul Klee (1879–1940) and Joan Miró (1893–1983). Her designs have esthetic similarities to pieces such as Miró's *The Escape Ladder* (1940; above).

SKELETAL PATTERN DESIGNS

In 1953 James de Holden Stone from the Royal College of Art said of the textiles popularized by Day: "Artists still in revolt against the old-time floral have turned to frost-gripped trees, dry leaves, twigs, grasses, ferns, creepers." He predicted that in the future: "Emphasis will be less on flowers than on the total growth: stalks, thorns, leaves and tendrils will be given disproportionate attention, mostly in line, with color as an afterthought." Day's skeletal designs triggered these developments, typified by Fall (1952; above), a printed furnishing fabric for Edinburgh Weavers.

GERMAN RATIONALISM AND RECOVERY

1 The chrome-plated wall clock model no. 32 (1957) by Max Bill reflects the designer's focus on clarity and precision.

2 This 1960s magazine advertisement for German airline Lufthansa exemplifies Germany's post-war design spirit.

3 Hans Roericht designed the glazed porcelain stacking tableware model no. TC 100 (1959) for Rosenthal. It had been developed initially as part of his degree studies.

In the aftermath of its defeat in World War II, Germany looked for a way to regain its pre-eminence in the field of modern design. The post-Nazi climate encouraged a reappraisal of the work of the Bauhaus (see p.126), which had been closed down by Hitler in 1933. Consequently, the post-war German spirit in design was rooted in a commitment to rationalism and geometric minimalism. Existing firms, including decorative arts companies such as ceramics manufacturer Rosenthal, reinvented themselves to face the challenge of recovery; others, such as Braun, renewed their place in the technology sector.

This new spirit of rationalism manifested itself in a number of ways, including the formation in 1953 of an education establishment: the Hochschüle für Gestaltung at Ulm (Ulm School of Design). The specific aim of the school was to revive and develop the program of the Bauhaus. Its first rector, Swiss designer Max Bill (1908–94), made sure that the school adopted a highly rational approach toward design, both intellectually and formally. The emphasis was upon systems rather than style: design was conceived as a rational process in which the end products reflected a problem-solving approach (see image 1). The curriculum featured graphics and product design at its heart, but the

KEY EVENTS

1948	1949	1950	1951	1953	1954
Porsche launches the 356 (see p.268). It is the company's first mass-produced car.	Wilhelm Wagenfeld (1900–90) becomes the artistic director for metal and glass at tableware manufacturer WMF in Stuttgart.	Braun manufactures its first dry shaver. Electric shavers go on to become key products for the company.	Erwin and Artur Braun take over the company and bring in Dieter Rams to work for them, first as an interior designer and later as a product designer.	The Ulm School of Design is founded by Inge Aicher-Scholl (1917–98), Otl Aicher (1922–91), and Max Bill. Bill models it on the pre-war Bauhaus.	German design is displayed at the Milan Triennale. Its rational approach and geometric forms make a huge impact there.

decorative arts were absent, as was architecture. When Argentinian designer Tomás Maldonado (b.1922) took over in the late 1950s, he introduced the study of semiotics, a direction that was to dominate the Ulm approach to design until the schools's closure in 1968. In essence, Maldonaldo's strategy was to employ linguistic theory as a model for a theory of design practice: in other words, to place the emphasis on the meanings of designed objects rather than their forms.

One of the aims of the school was to have an impact on its surrounding community, and Ulm staff and students collaborated with manufacturers whenever possible. Hans Roericht (b.1932), an Ulm student, designed a very simple set of white crockery (see image 3), which Rosenthal put into production. Joint ventures included a graphic identity for Lufthansa airline (see image 2) and a very successful collaboration with Braun. Ulm teacher Hans Gugelot (1920–65) worked with Braun designer Dieter Rams (b.1932) to create a radical hi-fi system in 1956 (see p.270). He also created a number of other iconic designs, among them a carousel slide projector for Kodak (1963; see p.272). Rams's highly rational forms epitomized Germany's post-war product design. His approach was always to work from an object's function outward and to create strikingly simple, geometric forms with no surface decoration. His most influential designs included audio equipment, a food processor with multiple accessories, electric razors, and, by the 1970s, pocket calculators.

The new spirit in German design was much admired when it was exhibited abroad, for example at the Milan Triennale in 1954. It was further helped by a support system at home, which included the newly reformed Deutscher Werkbund (German Work Federation) and the publication *Form* magazine, which disseminated its ideas. Companies such as AEG and Bosch, producers by this time of white goods, also embraced the rigid geometry and respect for high-quality technology that came to epitomize German design. **PS**

1955	1955	1957	1958	1968	1968
Braun products are displayed at the Dusseldorf Fair. The Braun brothers' new approach to design receives much acclaim.	Hans Gugelot joins the staff at Ulm. He becomes one of the school's most influential teachers through the 1950s.	Braun launches the Multimix food processor by Dieter Rams. Its strict, functional esthetic provides a model for other designs.	The Deutscher Werkbund is responsible for the design and contents of the West German Pavilion at the Brussels Expo.	The Ulm School of Design closes. Like the Bauhaus, it had become the object of mistrust by the local authority that helped fund it.	The Braun Prize is launched, a prestigious design award that is widely respected. Rams is a member of the awards committee.

Porsche 356 1948
ERWIN KOMENDA 1904–66 AND FERDINAND PORSCHE 1909–98

The Porsche 356 (1962) not only looked good, it also handled well and its performance was highly efficient.

The Porsche 356 remains one of the most iconic of the company's automobiles and it helped to create the reputation for stylishness that the firm retains to this day. It also represents the rigor and quality that were associated with German design in the years immediately after World War II. Although the 356 was Porsche's first mass-produced car, it was one of the most elegant and stylish on the market when it was launched, combining lightness and compactness with high speed. A two-door luxury sports car, it was created by Ferdinand "Ferry" Porsche, the son of the company's founder. Ferry's idea was to create a highly powered small car that gave its driver a great deal of pleasure. Although the striking, aerodynamic body of the 356 was a completely new design, created by Porsche staff member Erwin Komenda, many of its mechanical components (apart from the chassis) derived from the earlier Volkswagen Beetle, which had been designed by Ferdinand Porsche Senior in the 1930s. Like the VW Beetle, the 356 was a rear-engined, rear wheel-drive car and everything about its design—in terms of both styling and engineering—was geared toward high performance. The early 356s had a split front windshield, but by the early 1950s this had been replaced by a V-shaped version. Several other subtle changes occurred in later models: for example, a solid chromed-metal hub was added to the wheels in the 1950s.

Only fifty 356s were manufactured in the first two years of production. After that, however, they were made in greater numbers (76,000 in total) and the model remained in production until 1965. Both open- and hard-top versions were available. **PS**

 NAVIGATOR

FOCAL POINTS

1 AERODYNAMICS
The form of the 356 was determined by aerodynamics. The sharp curve of the front gives way to the gentler curve that runs from the roof to the rear bumper. Wind-tunnel testing suggested that the "teardrop" shape was the most resistant to wind and therefore fitting for a high-speed car.

2 MATERIALS
The earliest 356s were hand made in aluminum. Left unpainted, this enhanced the car's functional appearance. When the 356 began to be mass produced, steel replaced aluminum and it was inevitably a little heavier. The bodies were painted in a range of colors, including cream.

3 BODY SHELL
The absence of mudguards serves to give the car a simple, almost utilitarian look that was synonymous with the idea of "form follows function." The sleek body of the 356 has no excrescences that would slow the car down, but chrome trimmings were added to provide visual highlights.

PORSCHE 911

By the late 1950s, it was clear to Porsche that it needed to replace the 356. Ferry Porsche oversaw the new design of a more powerful and larger car, assisted by his son Ferdinand "Butzi" Porsche (1935–2012) and once again by body engineer Komenda. Launched in 1964, the Porsche 911 (right) instantly became an iconic design. Like the 356, it was designed to be both a racer and a road car, which gave it its distinctiveness. Also like the 356, the styling and engineering of the 911 work in tandem, resulting in one of the late 20th century's most memorable cars.

Braun SK4 1956
HANS GUGELOT 1920–65 AND DIETER RAMS b.1932

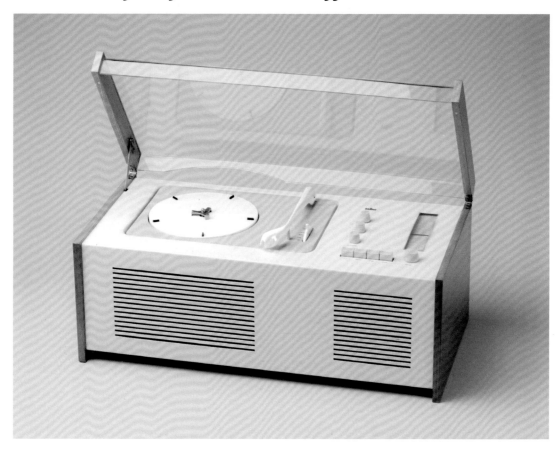

👁 FOCAL POINTS

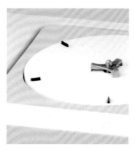

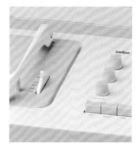

1 RATIONAL FORM
The SK4 was designed to be completely logical. Every element was included because it had a function to fulfil. This sense of logic was reflected in the minimal, geometric form of the product, which consists mostly of straight parallel lines, rectangles, and circles.

2 MINIMAL COLOR
The only colors employed are white, gray, and black. The exception is the brown of the wood that acts as a container for the functioning parts. This is the only natural material. The use of neutral colors emphasizes Braun's commitment to performance.

3 CONTROLS
The simple forms of the round radio knobs and the curved arm of the record player were designed for ease of operation. This sense of accessibility is enhanced by the transparent Plexiglas lid, which earned the design the nickname "Snow White's Coffin."

4 ANTI-DOMESTICITY
The only "domestic" reference is noted in the use of wood for the casing and the frame of the lid. Although the SK4 would most likely have been positioned in the living area of the home, it was not designed as a domestic object, but rather as a functional music player.

B raun's SK4 radio and record player was the result of a collaboration between Dieter Rams and Ulm School of Design teacher Hans Gugelot. It was the company's first piece of radical design in the audio equipment field, and it set a benchmark for many others that followed. Rams and Gugelot decided to put a radio and record player together as one unit to create a new hybrid object that could be understood as a "system" rather than as a single-function artefact. Furthermore, for the first time, a piece of audio equipment did not present itself as an item of furniture, designed to fit into a living room. Instead, the SK4 was unapologetically a piece of equipment, a functional tool. So influential was this departure that it set in motion the future trajectory of Braun audio designs, including the pioneering portable world-band radio, the T1000 (1962).

The SK4 was the first post-war German product of its type to go into mass production. Its design was a reflection of its function: every feature was there for a reason; nothing was superfluous. Furthermore, the designers ensured that all its components were positioned in such a way that the product was not only easy to use, but it also looked as if it were easy to use. All the technological workings of the SK4 are hidden from view inside a box, and the logic behind this decision is that the user does not need to see the working parts of the radio or record player in order to be able to use them. Instead, they need only engage with the controls and the record arm. **PS**

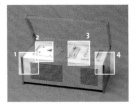

Bent steel, elm, Plexiglas
22¾ x 9½ x 11½ in.
58 x 24 x 29 cm

DESIGNER PROFILE

1932–87

Born in Wiesbaden, Germany, Dieter Rams joined Braun in 1955, initially as an architect and interior designer. However, by 1961 he had become the head of the company's product design and development division. He created many memorable products, from audio equipment to styling products and juicers. He also worked for the furniture manufacturer Vitsoe from 1959 onward.

1988–PRESENT

Rams was asked to join Braun's board of directors in 1988 and seven years later he became the company's executive director of corporate identity. He retired from the firm in 1997. Rams continues to engage with design in a range of different ways. In 2002 he was honored with the Order of Merit of the Federal Republic of Germany for his long-standing contribution to design.

THE BRAUN COMPANY

Established in 1921 in Frankfurt by engineer Max Braun, the Braun company began by making radio components. By the end of the decade, it had a reputation as a leader in that field and in 1932 it became one of the first manufacturers to combine a radio and a phonograph. The firm also ventured into dry razors and household appliances in 1950, and notable among them was the Multimix food processor. Max Braun died the following year and left the firm to his sons, Artur and Erwin. They instigated a period in the company's history in which design came to the fore, especially through the work of Dieter Rams. The brothers also commissioned Wilhelm Wagenfeld (1900–90) to work on their radios, such as the Braun Combi portable radio with record player (1957; right). Rams became the head of Braun's design department in 1961, taking over the role from Fritz Eichler, and the next few decades saw the company's products becoming increasingly respected, especially for their innovative design. In 2005 the Proctor and Gamble group acquired Gillette, which had already taken over Braun.

Kodak Carousel-S 1963

HANS GUGELOT 1920–65

Painted aluminum and plastic
6 x 11¼ x 10½ in.
15 x 28.5 x 27 cm

 **NAVIGATOR**

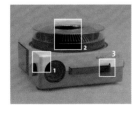

Slide projectors became popular in the 1950s, in tandem with the growth of air travel, as the post-war generation began inviting friends over to view their vacation snaps magnified on a screen. With the early models, each photographic slide had to be inserted manually. New versions were introduced swiftly in which a rectangular tray held a stack of slides in waiting, but these machines were notorious for jamming. In response, Neapolitan inventor Louis Misuraca—based in Glendale, California—came up with a design for a circular tray with an automatic slide feed. He sold it to Kodak for a buy-out fee. Misuraca's carousel was operated by the click of a button and did not jam. Kodak tinkered with the design and introduced a somewhat clunky version in the United States in spring 1962. However, the German branch of the company, based in Stuttgart, thought it could do better and hired Hans Gugelot to work on a version for the German market. His Carousel-S slide projector was launched in 1963, and it was so perfectly fit for purpose that it was sold worldwide and remained in production with almost no modification until 2004.

When Kodak approached Gugelot, he had already established a distinguished name and been producing best-selling products for Braun since 1955. He was also an influential teacher at the Ulm School of Design in Germany. The school's design philosophy, which Gugelot helped to define, involved an uncompromising focus on functionality and ease of use. Gugelot rarely mentioned esthetics and was emphatically unconcerned with beauty, but his designs always involve clean lines, neutral colors, and elegant finishes. **JW**

1 FORM FOLLOWS FUNCTION
Edges were gently curved and detailing was kept minimal. It was reported that Gugelot kept the casing off the workings of the prototype until the last minute; his major focus was the smooth operation of the interior mechanism. The slides were projected with lenses from 60 to 180 mm focal distance.

2 THE WORKINGS
The tray was rotated by a motor contained within the projector body below. As the tray advanced, a reciprocating mechanism pushed the currently loaded slide back out into the tray, and the tray was rotated, dropping the next slide into position between the light source and the lens.

3 UTILITY, BEAUTY, AND NOSTALGIA
Made from painted aluminum and plastic, in gray-on-gray tones grounded with black, the anti-esthetics design solution resulted in an object that was balanced, considered, and sober. And yet the name "Carousel" brings to mind childhood fun on a merry-go-round or a circus ride.

▲ In 1962, most families who owned a slide projector would have had a version that held the slides in a straight tray. The first timer for automatic viewing was introduced around this time.

🕐 DESIGNER PROFILE

1920–54
Hans Gugelot was born in Indonesia and moved with his family to Switzerland in 1934. He studied in Lausanne from 1940 to 1942 and at the EtH architecture school in Zurich until 1946. He then freelanced in Max Bill's architecture practice for eight years and designed the built-in furniture M125 storage system. From 1954 Gugelot taught at Ulm School of Design in Germany, where he developed the principles of his practice. He felt that good design should never be a means to boost sales; design was a much greater, cultural necessity. In 1954 Gugelot also embarked on his association with Braun.

1955–65
Gugelot's products for Braun were modeled on geometric forms and realized in sober colors. Many products, such as his Sixtant 1 shaver (1961), became international best sellers. Its black and silver modeling also became part of the Braun corporate identity. Gugelot designed for the Pfaff Sewing Machine Company and developed the underground rail system in Hamburg with Herbert Lindinger (b.1933) and others. As an architect, he specialized in prefabricated housing.

BRAUN SIXTANT SM 31

Electric razors were invented in the 1920s in the United States, and in 1950 Braun introduced a wire mesh to protect the skin from direct contact with the blades. In 1962 Gugelot collaborated with Gerd A. Müller to create the iconic Braun shaver, the Sixtant SM 31 (above). The foil cover was made by electrotyping in a hexagonal shape, hence the name. It introduced black into the bathroom, became the go-to precision machine for men's grooming, and sold eight million units.

SWISS NEUTRALITY AND VIRTUE

Switzerland, neutral during World War II, was one of the few European countries to emerge largely untouched by conflict in 1945. It had suffered neither mass bombing nor any of the devastation that invasion and foreign occupation had wreaked on infrastructure, and despite trade blockades imposed by both Allied and Axis powers, its manufacturing base—chiefly concentrated in the production of precision instruments, watches, chemicals, and pharmaceuticals—had never been placed on a war footing.

During the post-war period, Switzerland's tradition of neutrality and prudence translated into a design style, predominantly expressed in graphics, that aspired to universal application. Known as the International Typographic style, the Swiss Grid style, and variations on the same theme, the Swiss approach to typography and layout spread far beyond Europe during the 1940s and 1950s, and came to dominate the design of public and corporate communications worldwide. Focusing on simplicity, clarity, and legibility, its antecedents lay in the early modernist experiments of De Stijl (see p.114), Constructivism (see p.120),

KEY EVENTS

1947	1951	1953	1955	1954	1956
Armin Hofmann begins his teaching career at the Basel School of Arts and Crafts.	Josef Müller-Brockmann begins to design posters for Zurich Town Hall, advertising concerts and theatrical entertainments.	Ulm School of Design opens in Germany, co-founded by Inge Aicher-Scholl, Max Bill, and Otl Aicher.	Müller-Brockmann designs his Beethoven poster, which has since been highly imitated.	Adrian Frutiger designs the Univers family of sans serif fonts.	Max Bill designs his simple, elegant wall clock for German manufacturer Junghans. It is one of several minimal timepieces.

and the Bauhaus (see p.126); taking up such a lineage, it embraced abstraction, which had been deemed a feature of "degenerate art" by the Nazi Party.

Swiss designers adhered to the modernist principle "form follows function" (see p.168), to which they added their own concerns to make design socially useful. The movement originated in two schools—the School of Arts and Crafts in Zurich and the Basel School of Design—and Josef Müller-Brockmann (1914–96) at Zurich and Armin Hofmann (b.1920) at Basel were among its leading proponents. The style was noted for its use of unjustified sans serif type, mathematically constructed grids, and asymmetrical layouts that gave equal prominence to white space. Photomontage was preferred to illustration, as it was believed to be more objective. The key elements were unity of composition, clarity of communication, and problem solving based on an underlying scientific approach (see image 2).

Müller-Brockmann was a founder member of the collective that produced *Neue Grafik* (*New Graphic Design*), an influential magazine published between 1958 and 1965, which championed the notion that a designer's chief role was as communicator. He was an advocate of the geometric grid: "The grid is an organizational system that enables you to achieve an orderly result at a minimum cost." The best-known examples of his work are the posters that he created for Zurich Town Hall from 1951 onward; his poster for a Beethoven concert in 1955, featuring black and white concentric curves, has been much imitated. Hofmann is also highly regarded for his poster designs (see image 1), often executed in black and white with strong, clear, sans serif type. "A primary objective of my work with black and white posters is to counteract the trivialization of color as it exists today on billboards and in advertising," he said.

Emblematic of this period of Swiss design are the sans serif typefaces Univers and Helvetica (see p.276), both released in 1957 (Helvetica, as Neue Haas Grotesk). Univers, designed in 1954 by Adrian Frutiger (1928–2015), is notable for its consistency across the type family and for the fact that it is not purely geometric, unlike earlier modernist faces such as Futura (see p.146). Designed by Max Miedinger (1910–80) and Eduard Hoffmann (1892–1980), Helvetica is one of the most specified typefaces of all time, its very ubiquity—some would say corporate blandness—a cause of criticism in some quarters.

The Swiss drive for cleanness, clarity, and legibility led inevitably in the direction of minimalism. Swiss designer Max Bill (1908–94) is well known for the elegant restraint of his timepieces, such as the wall clock (1957) he designed for German manufacturer Junghans. Bill, who had studied at the Bauhaus in its pre-war heyday, co-founded the Hochschule für Gestaltung (Ulm School of Design) in Germany in 1953 with Inge Aicher-Scholl (1917–98) and Otl Aicher (1922–91). The school, which was highly influential during its fifteen-year existence, is where the story of German post-war recovery (see p.266) and Swiss design overlap. **EW**

1 LEFT: The exhibition poster (1955) titled *Theater Bau Von der Antike bis zur Moderne* (Theater Construction in Antiquity and Modernity) by Armin Hofmann is striking for its simple asymmetrical composition.
RIGHT: Hofmann designed this bold black and white poster (1961) for the "Kunsterziehung in USA" (Art Education in the USA) exhibition in Basel, Switzerland.

2 Josef Müller-Brockmann's poster titled *Schützt das Kind!* (Protect the Child!) was designed in 1953. It is an offset lithograph on woven paper.

1957	1958	1965	1965	1967	1968
The sans serif typefaces Neue Haas Grotesk (later renamed Helvetica) and Univers are released.	Müller-Brockmann co-founds the influential graphics periodical *Neue Grafik*, which helps popularize the Swiss style in the United States.	Hofmann publishes his *Graphic Design Manual: Principles and Practice*. It becomes a classic for generations of students.	The last issue of *Neue Grafik* is printed, produced by Müller-Brockmann, Richard Paul Lohse, Hans Neuburg, and Carlo Vivarelli.	Müller-Brockmann is appointed European design consultant by IBM.	The Ulm School of Design closes after a series of internal disagreements.

D. Stempel AG
Frankfurt am Main
Schriftgießerei

helvetica
helvetica

H elvetica is a modernist sans serif typeface developed by Swiss type designer Max Miedinger, with Eduard Hoffmann, president of the Haas Type Foundry in Basel. They set out to create a typeface of clarity that was adaptable to wide usage and not associated with any political stance. Based on the early sans serif Akzidenz-Grotesk of 1898, the realist design was originally named Neue Haas Grotesk. In 1961 it was licensed by Linotype, who renamed it Helvetica to suggest its Swiss origins. The handset type, however, continued to be sold as Neue Haas Grotesk for several years. It was marketed as a symbol of Swiss technology at the Graphic 57 trade show in Lausanne and became one of the most successful typefaces of all time. It is used on street signs in many cities from Vienna to Chicago, for the National Theatre logo in London, and the New York City subway.

Helvetica is associated with the Swiss graphic style of the 1950s and 1960s, and with neutrality and peace. It is relied upon not to impart additional meaning to any given content. It neither appeals to fashion nor changes with it. Since its launch, a wide range of variants has been released and there are now some thirty versions in the font family. In 2004 Christian Schwartz (b.1977) was commissioned to digitize Neue Haas Grotesk. The project was referred to as a restoration and it was completed in 2010 with "as much fidelity to the original shapes and spacing as possible." Schwartz redrew the typeface to match Miedinger's originals and to rekindle a hint of warmth lost over the years. **JW**

This Helvetica type sample was produced by the Stempel Type Foundry in Frankfurt.

◉ FOCAL POINTS

1 LEGIBILITY
The most distinctive features of Helvetica are the large x-height and horizontal—rather than angled—stroke terminals, which make it easy to read even in small point sizes and at distance. These features resulted in the typeface's characteristically dense and dynamic texture.

2 PRACTICALITY
Helvetica suggests plainness and practicality, drawing a peaceful line under history and looking toward the future. As international trade expanded, glyphs that were not associated with any given region became desirable in commercial communications, which further explains Helvetica's popularity.

3 PRECISION
The tremendous precision of the Helvetica typeface conveys a reassuring dependability, but it has also become associated in recent years with a conservative culture, and has garnered criticism in some circles for being too corporate and too much a favorite of US big business.

AfricanAmerican
AsianAmerican
HispanicAmerican
NativeAmerican
AmericanAirlines®

We believe success comes from diversity. At American, we take pride in working with companies who offer quality products and services through our Diversified Supplier Program. If you are a diversified supplier and would like to explore opportunities with us, we'd like to hear from you. Visit our Web site at www.aa.com/supplierdiversity to register your company with American Airlines or e-mail Sherri Macko, manager of our Diversified Supplier Program, at supplierdiversity@aa.com.

We know why you fly
AmericanAirlines
American *Eagle*

Dedicated to the growth of minority/women-owned diverse and small businesses.

▲ American Airlines is one of many companies to have used Helvetica for its corporate logo. The typeface is sober and durable, and is relied upon not to impart additional meaning to any given content. It neither appeals to fashion nor changes with it.

SCULPTURAL FORM

A key feature of mid-century design was the stimulating new vocabulary of sculptural forms. The inspiration for these shapes can be traced directly to contemporary art. The tall, thin bronze figures of Italian-Swiss sculptor Alberto Giacometti (1901–66) fueled the trend for spindly steel rod legs and attenuated vessel forms. One of the most influential artists of the mid-20th century was Romanian-born Constantin Brancusi (1876–1957). His austere minimalist sculptures held great potency for post-war Scandinavian designers, such as Danish silversmith Henning Koppel (1918–81) and Finnish glass artist Timo Sarpaneva (1926–2006). Koppel's elegant canoelike Eel dish for Georg Jensen (1956) and Sarpaneva's blade-shaped Lancet sculpture for Iittala (1952) both display the same pared-down simplicity as Brancusi's works. It was no coincidence that the US sculptor Isamu Noguchi (1904–88), who created some of the most iconic furniture and lighting designs of the post-war era, including the Akari light (1951; see p.280), had spent time working as Brancusi's assistant in Paris in 1927.

The abstract organic sculptures of the German-French artist Hans Arp (1886–1966) also exerted a powerful influence on many mid-century designers from Alvar Aalto (1898–1976) onwards, reaching their apotheosis in the fluid, free-blown vessel forms of glass designers such as Per Lütken (1916–98) at the

KEY EVENTS

1940	1946	1946	1947	1948	1950
The Museum of Modern Art in New York City holds a competition called "Organic Design in Home Furnishings."	Charles and Ray (1912–88) Eames's molded-plywood chairs are manufactured by Evans Products.	Eva Zeisel's Town and Country tableware is produced by Red Wing Pottery.	Frank Lloyd Wright (1867–1959) designs the Guggenheim Museum in New York City with an outward-coiling spiral shape. It is completed in 1959.	Eero Saarinen's Womb chair is launched by Knoll Associates, its seat molded from fiberglass-reinforced polyester resin.	The Eames's Plastic chair and armchair are produced by Herman Miller, with sculptural, colored fiberglass seats.

Danish firm Holmegaard. The pierced forms and bimorphic figures of British sculptors Barbara Hepworth (1903–75) and Henry Moore (1898–1986) also subtly informed the esthetics of contemporary designers. The abstract organic salt and pepper pots created by Hungarian-born US designer Eva Zeisel (1906–2011) for her Town and Country tableware for Red Wing Pottery (1946; see image 2) are closely related to Moore's family groups.

In the applied arts the impulse to create expressive sculptural forms became all pervasive from the mid 1940s. Following Aalto's lead, the Museum of Modern Art in New York City held a competition called "Organic Design in Home Furnishings" in 1940. This proved highly significant, as it brought to the fore two leading exponents of organic design, Charles Eames (1907–78) and Eero Saarinen (1910–61). Their prize-winning organic seating concepts later materialized in a series of groundbreaking production furniture designs.

In Scandinavia the seed planted by Aalto during the 1930s continued to bear fruit for several decades. Recognizing the sculptural potential of furniture, the Danes not only exploited molded plywood, but honed their skills in shaping solid wood into appealing soft-edged forms. Hans Wegner (1914–2007) combined these dual technologies in his Shell chair for Fritz Hansen (c. 1950), with its cupped plywood seat and sculpted wooden frame. The Ant chair (1952) by Arne Jacobsen (1902–71) was also sculptural in two respects, with its dynamic curvilinear outline and bent plywood seat.

Swedish mid-century ceramics and glass designers, such as Wilhelm Kåge (1889–1960), Edvin Ohrström (1906–94), Nils Landberg (1907–91), and Stig Lindberg (1916–82), were masters of sculptural design. Kåge's Soft Forms tableware for Gustavsberg (1938) paved the way for Lindberg's exaggeratedly organic faience bowls and vases painted with quasi-biological patterns. Ohrström's Ariel vessels for Orrefors, also pioneered during the 1930s, were sculptural in both form and decoration with their fluid air-bubble patterns trapped inside chunky glass walls. Landberg's colored underlay vessels were similarly organic, whether thickly cased or thinly blown, as in his Tulip glass (1957). Meanwhile, in Finland, art glass ascended to new heights in the hands of two master sculptor-designers, Tapio Wirkkala (1915–85) and Sarpaneva, who dissolved the barriers between fine and decorative art.

Elsewhere in Europe, sculptural design also flourished in Italy, although it tended to be rather more extravagant. Flamboyant architect Carlo Mollino (1905–73) created some extraordinary organic furniture. His Arabesque table (1949; see image 1), with its dynamic, undulating, bent-plywood structure, was described at the time as "Neo-Liberty" because it conjured up the whiplash forms of fin-de-siècle Art Nouveau (see p.92). Flavio Poli's (1900–84) vividly colored sculptural vessels for Seguso Vetri d'Arte also took full advantage of the intrinsic plasticity of glass, but in a much more uninhibited way than his contemporaries in Scandinavia. **LJ**

1 Carlo Mollino's curving Arabesque table (1949) was inspired by the work of Surrealist artists, such as Hans Arp.

2 Eva Zeisel's glazed salt and pepper shakers (1946) for her Town and Country range nestle into each other like a mother and child.

1951	1952	1955	1956	1956	1958
The Festival of Britain in London features the sculptural Dome of Discovery, the elegant Skylon, and Robin Day's (1915–2010) plywood chairs.	Arne Jacobsen's Ant chair is produced in Denmark by Fritz Hansen, featuring an insectlike design with a curvilinear plywood seat on steel legs.	The sculptural Citroën DS 19 car (see p.282), designed by Italian sculptor-designer Flaminio Bertoni (1903–64), is launched.	Saarinen designs the sculpturally expressive TWA Terminal in New York, which is completed in 1962.	Brazilian architect Oscar Niemeyer (1907–2012), starts designing a group of civic buildings in an overtly organic style for Brasilia.	Jacobsen designs two sculptural upholstered chairs for the Royal Hotel in Copenhagen, the Swan and the Egg, both manufactured by Fritz Hansen.

Akari Light 1951
ISAMU NOGUCHI 1904–88

👁 FOCAL POINTS

1 LEGS

The paper-covered bamboo shade is complemented by patented wire stretchers and thin metal legs that form a tripod structure, allowing the object to be freestanding. The spindly legs give the lamp an insectlike appearance, highlighting the lightness and nimbleness of the design.

2 BAMBOO RIBS

The delicate ribs supporting the paper shade are made from bamboo. An organic and flexible material, bamboo is ideal for lampshades because of its lightness and elasticity. As well as shielding the intense glare emitted by a light bulb, the paper used for the shade is effective at diffusing light.

samu Noguchi was one of the first US sculptors to embrace organic abstraction, an esthetic he subsequently applied to furniture design and lighting. Although born in the United States, he spent much of his childhood in Japan and retained strong cultural ties with Japan for the rest of his life.

Noguchi collaborated with two leading US furniture manufacturers, Herman Miller and Knoll Associates, during the mid 1940s. A few years earlier he had begun experimenting with "Lunars." as he called them: small sculptures incorporating artificial illumination. Noguchi's Akari lamps, developed in 1951 after a trip to Japan, were inspired by traditional Japanese paper lanterns, known as *chochin*. The term "Akari" means "light," in the sense of illumination, but it also suggests physical lightness. Produced by the firm of Ozeki in the historic lantern-making city of Gifu, the lampshades were made of *washi*—fine paper made from the inner bark of the mulberry tree—over a thin, ribbed framework of bamboo. The framework was created by stretching long lengths of finely cut bamboo over molded wooden forms. Strips of paper were then glued to both sides of this framework. Once dried, the internal wooden structure was disassembled and removed. Designed to be collapsible, the paper-covered bamboo structures can be compressed and flat-packed without being damaged.

Noguchi's initial Akari lamp had an ovoid shade perched on a slender steel tripod stand. He went on to create other lampshade designs, some organic, others geometric, including cones and cubes, as well as composite forms. Noguchi's Akari lamps are varied in form, but unified in esthetic. More than just functional lamps, they are illuminated organic sculptures for the home. **LJ**

This Akari floor lamp is made from *washi* paper with bamboo ribbing, supported by a metal frame.

⏱ DESIGNER PROFILE

1904–21
Isamu Noguchi was born in Los Angeles. His mother was American, his father Japanese. He lived in Japan from 1907, returning to the United States in 1918 to complete his schooling.

1922–37
Noguchi moved to New York where he attended classes at the Leonardo da Vinci Art School, then established his own studio in 1924. In 1927 he spent six months as assistant to Romanian sculptor Constantin Brancusi (1876–1957) in Paris. The simplicity of Brancusi's organic forms made a lasting impression on Noguchi, prompting him to embrace abstraction. After traveling in the Far East, he returned to New York in 1931, creating stage sets for dancer Martha Graham (1894–1991).

1938–51
He won a commission to create bas-reliefs for the Rockefeller Center in New York City. The president of the Museum of Modern Art in New York City, Anson Goodyear (1877–1964), commissioned Noguchi to design a table in 1939. Noguchi designed his Akari lamps after visiting Japan in 1951.

1952–88
Noguchi continued producing organic sculpture, working mainly in wood, stone, metal, and clay, moving to Long Island City in New York in 1961. He also designed outdoor sculpture gardens.

NOGUCHI'S FURNITURE

As well as designing lighting, Noguchi applied his artistic talents to furniture. His Rudder table (1949; above) for Herman Miller had one wooden rudder-shaped leg and two hairpin supports made of bent steel rods. Having teamed up with Knoll Associates, Noguchi designed a rocking stool (1953) with a circular wooden base and top connected by crisscrossing steel rods; it later evolved into the Cyclone side table and dining table. Noguchi's last furniture design, the Prismatic table (1957), was commissioned by the aluminum firm Alcoa for an advertising campaign. Hexagonal in form, it was made from overlapping sheets of folded aluminum.

Citroën DS 19 1955

FLAMINIO BERTONI 1903–64   ANDRÉ LEFÈBVRE 1894–1964

👁 FOCAL POINTS

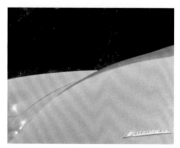

1 BONNET
The sweeping lines of the Citroën DS 19 are appealing from a sculptural point of view. The projecting bonnet has all the sleekness of a modernist sculpture. Designed as an organic whole so that the body, roof, and windows complement and enhance each other, the curvaceous form of the vehicle's exterior is satisfying from any angle.

2 WINDSHIELD
Co-designed by aeronautical engineer Lefèbvre, the Citroën DS 19 is genuinely aerodynamic. With its bullet-shaped bonnet and slanted wraparound windshield, it not only looks good but is shaped to minimize wind resistance, sloping down gradually from the top of the roof to the tip of the trunk.

3 SUSPENSION
With its hydropneumatic suspension, the Citroën DS 19 can adapt to different driving conditions and road surfaces. The body can be raised or lowered to variable heights by means of compressed gas. When the engine is switched on, the car rises up like a hovercraft, and when in motion, it seems to glide above the ground.

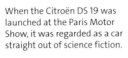

When the Citroën DS 19 was launched at the Paris Motor Show, it was regarded as a car straight out of science fiction.

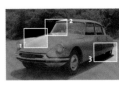

This elegant, streamlined, organic car is like a sculpture on wheels. Styled by an Italian designer, Flaminio Bertoni, who had originally trained as a sculptor, the Citroën DS 19 was beautifully proportioned and subtly curvaceous. Without resorting to exaggerated tail fins or chromium trims, the Citroën DS 19 was extremely stylish, epitomizing the suave sophistication of European car design.

Naturally gifted, Bertoni was talent-spotted by technicians from the French automobile industry as early as 1923 while working as a drafttsman for Italian firm Carrozzeria Macchi in Varese. It took nearly a decade before he decided to move to Paris, teaming up with Citroën in 1932. Following Citroën's takeover by tire manufacturer Michelin, the forward-looking Pierre-Jules Boulanger (1885–1950) was brought in to run the firm. At his instigation, Bertoni began working on a new small car—the 2CV—in 1935, assisted by aeronautical engineer and former Grand Prix racing driver André Lefèbvre. However, although it was completed by 1939, the 2CV was not launched until 1948 because of World War II.

The Citroën DS 19 was a much more sophisticated and glamorous model than the modest low-cost 2CV. Launched in 1955, it was christened "the goddess" (déesse in French, a pun on DS). With its sculptural bonnet and sloping roof, the DS 19 was aerodynamic and futuristic, reflecting the heightened aspirations of French consumers. Because the roof was made of fiberglass, it reduced the weight of the car and lowered its center of gravity. Exuding an air of luxury, it had many remarkable technical features, including state-of-the-art hydropneumatic self-leveling suspension. Immediately heralded as revolutionary, the DS 19 rapidly became an icon and was manufactured for twenty years. Still regarded as one of the most beautiful cars ever produced, it was lovingly shaped by an artist-designer with a sculptor's eye. **LJ**

LOVE FOR SCULPTING

Bertoni was born in Masnago, Varese. After attending technical school, he studied drawing, carving, and sculpture. Initially apprenticed as a joiner at Carrozzeria Macchi in 1918, he became a draftsman in 1922. Although car design was Bertoni's profession, he continued to practice as a sculptor throughout his career. Being an artist gave Bertoni a different perspective, and set him apart from other designers in the automobile industry. The first Citroën car he styled was the Traction Avant (1934; right), a handsome saloon car remarkable for its front-wheel drive. His last design for Citroën was the Ami 6 in 1961.

US MID-CENTURY MODERN

W orld War II resulted in a dramatic shift in momentum within the design world. Germany and France, the dual progenitors of modernism during the interwar period, were no longer the dominant creative hotspots. A new alliance of international design superpowers emerged during the late 1940s led by Sweden, Denmark, Finland, Italy, and the United States, each bringing a fresh perspective and new ideas. The Americans had made a decisive contribution to modern architecture since the late 19th century through the invention of the skyscraper. However, in the field of furniture and furnishings, US design remained somewhat derivative until the 1920s, with the notable exception of Frank Lloyd Wright (1867–1959). With the widespread adoption of Machine Age styling and streamlining during the 1930s, the United States began to assert its own design identity, although on a commercial level, progress was hindered by the Depression.

A key figure in the US design world during the mid 20th century was Russel Wright (1904–76), a product designer who pioneered the concept of American modern. The term "American modern"—denoting a contemporary style that expressed the unique character and culture of the United States—was adopted initially for a range of ceramic tableware designed by Wright for Steubenville Pottery Company in 1939 (see image 1). Expressively organic and sculptural, the

KEY EVENTS

1940	1945	1946	1948	1948	1950
Charles Eames and Eero Saarinen win two first prizes—for domestic seating and storage—in the Organic Design in Home Furnishings competition.	Eames and Saarinen design Case Study Houses #8 and #9 for an experimental programme instigated by *Arts and Architecture* magazine.	The Eameses' Plywood chairs are manufactured by the Molded Plywood Division of Evans Products Company.	Saarinen's Womb chair is produced by Knoll Associates; it is the first mass-produced chair shell made of fiberglass-reinforced polyester resin.	The Eamses design La Chaise (see p.288) for the Low-Cost Furniture Design competition held by the Museum of Modern Art (MoMA) in New York City.	The Eameses' ESU Storage Unit (see p.290) is produced by Herman Miller, along with the designers' Plastic chair and armchair.

designs were characterized by relaxed informality, vivid colors, and malleable shapes. Ahead of its time when it first appeared, American modern remained extremely popular throughout the 1950s, along with Wright's aptly named Casual China (1946) for the Iroquois China Company, an oven-to-tableware range embodying similar esthetic and functional ideas. Complementing the new fitted kitchens, Formica tables, and chrome-trimmed refrigerators that came on the market during the early post-war period, American modern encapsulated the material aspirations of the American dream.

The delayed involvement of the United States in World War II, combined with its remoteness from the main conflict zones, meant that US designers and manufacturers were considerably less disrupted than their European counterparts during the 1940s. On a creative level, the US architecture and design community had benefited greatly from the influx of European émigrés who settled in the United States during the 1930s, including leading figures from the modern movement such as architects Marcel Breuer (1902–81) and Ludwig Mies van der Rohe (1886–1969) and weaver Anni Albers (1899–1994). North America had long been a magnet for immigrants seeking to make a fresh start, attracted by the American Dream. Finnish architect Eliel Saarinen (1873–1950) immigrated in 1923, for example, spurred by the hope of creative opportunities in the United States. He later became director of the Cranbrook Academy of Art in Michigan, a progressive art school modeled on the Bauhaus (see p.126), which acted as a seedbed for US mid-century modern design. It was here that his son, Eero Saarinen (1910–61), met Charles (1907–78) and Ray Eames (1912–88), who emerged as the foremost designers of the post-war era.

The cross-fertilization between furniture and architecture, so crucial to the work of Eero Saarinen and Charles Eames, was central to the development of US mid-century modern design. Like Saarinen, Eames had originally practiced as an architect and continued to regard architecture as his profession even after his focus shifted to furniture: "I think of myself officially as an architect," he said. "I can't help but look at the problems around us as problems of structure—and structure is architecture." The early post-war period was also an exciting time for US art, with the flowering of many different forms of abstraction in both painting and sculpture, including Abstract Expressionism. The active interplay between the fine and applied arts that flourished during the 1940s and 1950s affected not only the shape of objects, but also their color, texture, and materials.

The energetic Eameses encapsulated the spirit of adventure in US mid-century modern design and the free flow of ideas between art, architecture, and design. Charles first came to prominence in 1940, when he and Saarinen collaborated on two prize-winning entries to the Organic Design in Home Furnishings competition (see image 2) organized by the Museum of Modern Art in New York City. Following their marriage, Charles and Ray Eames worked

1 The Casual China dinnerware (1946) by Russel Wright is a classic example of US modernism. It was manufactured by Iroquois China Co.

2 The exhibition "Organic Design in Home Furnishings" was installed at the Museum of Modern Art in New York City between 24 September and 9 November 1941.

1950	1950	1951	1952	1956	1958
Russel Wright and his wife, Mary (1904–52), publish their bestselling book *Guide to Easier Living*.	MoMA begins a series of exhibitions called "Good Design." A touring exhibition titled "Design for Use USA" departs for Europe the next year.	The Eameses' Wire chair is launched by Herman Miller and remains in production until 1967.	Harry Bertoia's Diamond chair enters production at Knoll Associates, following a two-year development period.	Eero Saarinen's Pedestal chair is manufactured by Knoll Associates and quickly becomes known as the Tulip chair.	The Eameses design a range of furniture known as the Aluminum Group. It later becomes particularly popular as office furniture.

closely together, establishing a joint design office in California in 1941. The war and the ensuing period of austerity forced designers to become more resourceful, partly in order to overcome the problem of materials shortages but also to take advantage of the latest war-time technology. In addition to embodying the idealistic, democratic ethos of the early post-war period—the desire to create universal designs that were widely available and affordable—the Eameses' furniture was consciously economical. Not only were their creations physically lean with no unnecessary wastage of resources, but the designers also exploited technological developments in order to ensure that their furniture was manufactured in the most effective and efficient way.

Initially focusing on creative applications for molded plywood, which they harnessed for its sculptural and design potential, the Eameses' first major breakthrough was their Plywood chair (see image 3). Made from five-layer plywood, veneered in ash, birch, or walnut, the chairs were fabricated originally by the Molded Plywood Division of the Evans Products Company and subsequently by Herman Miller, who later manufactured the Eames Storage Units (1950; see p.290). What made this chair so unusual was its fluid profile and the lightness and elasticity of its structure. Designed to complement the contours of the human body, it gave the impression that the sitter was floating.

Having mastered molded plywood, the Eameses became increasingly interested in plastics. Although Bakelite had been used widely in product design since the early 20th century, plastics technology was still in its infancy. As with plywood, the key issue with plastics was how to mold a seat that was tough enough to support the weight of the human body, but at the same time light and thin. Although it was Saarinen who designed the first one-piece plastic seat—his Womb chair for Knoll was launched in 1948—the Eameses were hot on his heels with their groundbreaking Plastic chair (1950). Produced in an armchair and side chair version, the shells were molded from polyester resin strengthened with glass fiber (known as GRP). However, whereas the Womb chair had to be upholstered in order to make it usable, the Plastic chair

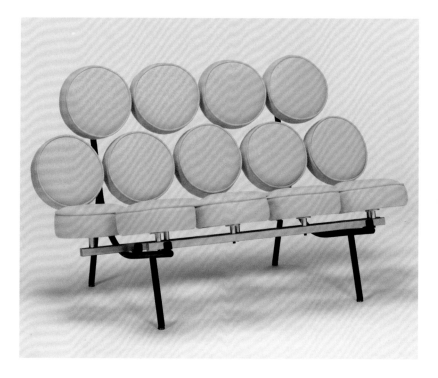

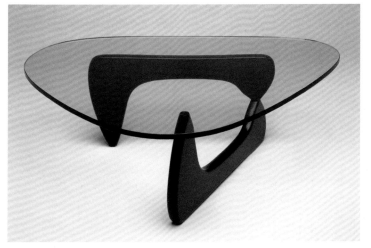

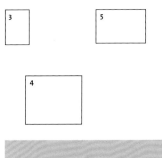

was so refined that it could be utilized "in the raw." Tirelessly inventive, the Eameses also experimented with various metals. Their Wire chair (1951) was made of welded steel wire and steel rod, while their Aluminum Group (1958) consisted of a range of pedestal chairs with cast aluminium frames.

In addition to the Eameses, Herman Miller collaborated with a number of other designers. The company's design director George Nelson (1908–86) made a significant contribution to the firm's output, both directly and indirectly. As well as designing office furniture and ingenious storage wall systems, he and his colleagues at George Nelson Associates created playful domestic seating, such as the Marshmallow sofa (see image 4). Eschewing conventional forms, the Marshmallow consisted of four rows of disc-shaped seat pads mounted on a steel frame. Nelson was also responsible for bringing on board sculptor Isamu Noguchi (1904–88), who created one of the most iconic pieces of US mid-century modern furniture: a glass-topped table of organic form supported on sculptural carved wooden supports resembling giant bones (see image 5).

Herman Miller's principal competitor, Knoll Associates, was similarly committed to innovative modern furniture design. Established in 1943 by Hans (1914–55) and Florence Knoll (b.1917), the company was run single-handedly by the latter after her husband's death. In addition to producing Florence's well-proportioned, understated, upholstered seating, Knoll Associates enjoyed fruitful partnerships with several other designers, notably Saarinen and Harry Bertoia (1915–78). Although furniture was something of a digression from the latter's main activity as a sculptor and graphic artist, Bertoia made a memorable contribution to mid-century modern design through his Diamond chair (1952; see p.292), an expressive sculptural lounge chair made from welded steel wire. Saarinen's interest in furniture dated back to the 1930s, when he had designed furnishings for his father's buildings, but it was his alliance with Charles Eames in 1940 that triggered his interest in organic design. His Womb chair, with its giant fiberglass shell, was a remarkable concept, both sculpturally and technically. The embodiment of organic design, it was intended to "achieve psychological comfort by providing a great big cup-like shell into which you can curl up and pull up your legs." Saarinen's second major design for Knoll, the Tulip chair (1956; see p.294), was memorable not only for its cupped seat, but also for its striking curvilinear stem and pedestal base. Working in parallel and very much in tune, Saarinen and the Eameses revolutionized the language of US mid-century modern furniture. The impact of their work was considerable at the time and continues to resonate in the present day. **LJ**

3 The Plywood chair (1946) by Charles and Ray Eames was manufactured in two sizes, known as the DCW (Dining Chair Wood) and the LCW (Lounge Chair Wood).

4 Although the Marshmallow sofa (1956) is a classic George Nelson Associates product, it was actually designed for the firm by Irving Harper (1916–2015).

5 The glass-topped table (1946) designed by Isamu Noguchi was produced by Herman Miller.

La Chaise 1948

CHARLES EAMES 1907–78   RAY EAMES 1912–88

Fiberglass, iron rods, wood
32½ x 59 x 33½ in.
82.5 x 150 x 85 cm

 NAVIGATOR

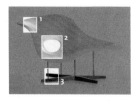

Charles and Ray Eames designed La Chaise as their entry for a competition held by New York City's Museum of Modern Art. The competition, on the theme of "Low-Cost Furniture Design," was intended to encourage designs that would stimulate production and meet the needs of post-war housing. La Chaise was much admired, and appeared in the catalog and show in 1950.

Wartime developments in the low-pressure molding of fiberglass combined with resin had made the organic contoured seat possible. The Eameses had become familiar with the molding process through their wartime work in plywood.

The chair was notable for the fact that it was not upholstered, which gives it an unusual, raw appearance. It is also highly sculptural, which was a strikingly new look for a chair, so it appeared in numerous contemporary magazines and journals. La Chaise was a highly experimental chair and was not destined for mass production, but it has been manufactured in wet painted polyurethane by Vitra since 2006. **PS**

👁 FOCAL POINTS

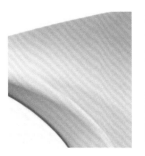

1 FIBERGLASS
The flowing, organic form is made of two very thin fiberglass shells that have been glued together. They are separated by a hard, rubber disc and the cavity between the shells is filled with styrene.

2 HOLE
The hole in the seat was included for its visual effect. Ray was familiar with contemporary artists such as the British sculptor Henry Moore (1898–1986), who had created pierced works.

3 BASE
Five intersecting metal rods have been arranged partly diagonally to create a visual counterpart to the organic form of the seat. They fit into a cross-shaped wooden base that sits well on the floor.

THE DAR

In addition to the experimental La Chaise, the Eameses designed a number of other plastic chairs at around the same time. The DAR armchair (right) was created for the Museum of Modern Art's "Low-Cost Furniture Design" competition. It was produced in different versions in a variety of colors, with various bases including metal rod or wooden cat's-cradle legs. A rocking version was also available. The DAR chair has a molded plastic seat that is organic in form but less dramatic than the sculptural version. The curves of the DAR lend themselves to sitting in a more conventional, upright manner.

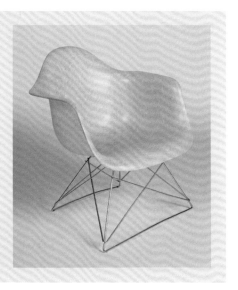

🕐 DESIGNERS' PROFILE

1907–39
Charles Eames was born in St. Louis, Missouri, in 1907. Bernice "Ray" Kaiser was born in Sacramento, California, in 1912. In 1925, Charles started an architecture course but left after two years. In 1938 he went to study architecture at Cranbrook Academy of Art in Michigan. Ray studied Abstract Expressionist painting with German-born artist Hans Hofmann (1880–1966).

1940–41
Charles won the Museum of Modern Art "Organic Design in Home Furnishings'" competition with Eero Saarinen (1910–61). Charles and Ray married and began to work together in 1941.

1942–49
The Eameses moved to Los Angeles. The US Navy placed an order for 5,000 splints the Eameses had made from a mold of Charles's leg. They worked creating molded plywood furniture and designed Eames House (1949) in Pacific Palisades, California.

1950–88
The Eameses designed furniture in fiberglass, plastic, and aluminum. They also produced multimedia presentations, exhibitions, and films. After Charles's death in 1978, Ray continued to work on their unfinished projects. She died of cancer in 1988, ten years to the day after Charles.

Eames Storage Unit – 400 Series 1950

CHARLES EAMES 1907–78   RAY EAMES 1912–88

Steel, plywood, and Masonite
58½ x 47 x 16 in.
148.5 x 119 x 40.5 cm

The Eames Storage Unit, known as ESU, grew out of the designers' earlier Case Goods range, a series of interchangeable wooden storage cabinets in standardized sizes supported on low benches. The impetus to design low-cost storage reflected the concerns of the austerity-conscious early post-war period. By creating modular cabinets, the Eameses sought to maximize the amount of storage in the minimum amount of space. What is striking about the ESU series is the radical simplicity of the concept and the use of inexpensive off-the-peg industrial components, notably the angled steel frame and criss-cross bracing rods. These features bear a striking resemblance to the construction techniques used to build the Eameses' home at Pacific Palisades near Santa Monica in California, completed in 1949: both employ a steel-framed grid structure clad with multicolored panels. Even the palette is similar: the ESU units use black plastic laminate or white glass cloth for the sliding doors, while Masonite panels were enameled in eight colors, including red, yellow, and blue, thus recalling the abstract paintings of Piet Mondrian. Although overtly utilitarian, the varied colors and textures of the interchangeable panels, shelves, and drawers were visually stimulating, reflecting the creativity and playfulness of this imaginative design duo. **LJ**

◈ NAVIGATOR

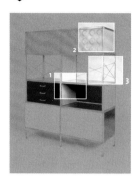

◉ FOCAL POINTS

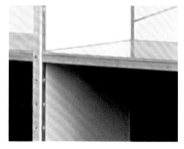

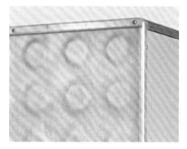

1 PLYWOOD AND MASONITE
The materials used for the shelves and panels were standard industrial products. The plywood shelves were sufficiently strong to provide structural stability and to bear significant weight. The panels were made from Masonite, a form of hardboard with a baked enamel finish.

2 TEXTURE
Apart from the structure, the most striking feature of these units was the visual and tactile variety of the textured surfaces. Perforated metal backs and panels of thin, vacuum-pressed, birch-veneered plywood with relief-patterned circular motifs added a sculptural dimension.

3 STEEL FRAME
Made from chromium-plated, cold-rolled steel, the frame has an overtly industrial esthetic more typical of office or factory storage than domestic cabinets. Resistance-welded steel rods, positioned diagonally, act as braces between the uprights, giving stability to the structure.

◄ Manufactured by Herman Miller, the units were produced in various formations, as single storey cabinets (100 series), two-tier units (200 series; far left), and tall four-level systems (400 series). The range also included the Eames Desk Unit (EDU; left).

Diamond Chair 1952

HARRY BERTOIA 1915–78

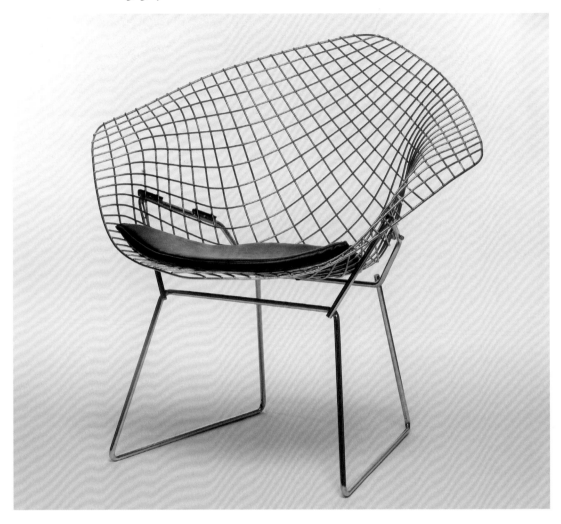

Welded steel rod, vinyl, plastic
30 x 28¼ x 33½ in.
76 x 72 x 85 cm

NAVIGATOR

Harry Bertoia was a metalwork artist who ventured briefly into furniture design during the early 1950s. Although sculpture was his primary field of activity, the Diamond chair typifies the cross-fertilization between the fine and applied arts in US mid-century modern design. After Bertoia was invited by Florence Knoll to collaborate with Knoll Associates in 1950, he spent the next two years refining the design of his Diamond chair. One of the reasons for the delay was that the chair proved difficult to manufacture. In spite of its industrial esthetic, the complex curvature of the seat meant that the chair had to be made by hand, rather than being shaped by machine. Nonetheless, it was a great commercial success.

Bertoia's fascination with welded steel extended into his architectural sculpture. His best-known work was a screen for the Manufacturers Hanover Trust in New York in 1954, made from welded steel fused with brass, copper, and nickel. He also created a shimmering fountainlike sculpture for the chapel at Massachusetts Institute of Technology (1955), designed by Eero Saarinen. The connecting thread between these works is the lightness and airiness of the structures: the gaps between the steel elements are as significant as the metalwork itself. **LJ**

FOCAL POINTS

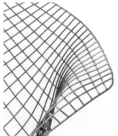

1 WIRE MESH
The curved chair was made from welded steel wire coated with vinyl to create a uniform appearance. Visually, the exposure of the wire mesh is highly effective because the contours of the chair are fluid and sculptural, resembling a draped net.

2 DIAMOND FORM
The squares of the wire mesh have been distorted into diamonds using a complex mathematical calculation. The pattern is echoed in the outer rim of the seat, which is roughly diamond-shaped, too. The front edge is rounded off for comfort.

3 STEEL ROD BASE
Thicker steel rod was used to make the base that cradles the seat. It was produced in two parts, shaped on a jig, and welded together. Instead of conventional legs and feet, the chair has two sledgelike runners, raised slightly above the floor on plastic glides.

4 UPHOLSTERED SEAT
From a sculptural perspective, Bertoia would have preferred the seat to be left uncovered to highlight the intricacy of the metalwork and the airiness of the structure. This would have been uncomfortable, so an upholstered cover was produced to soften the interior.

DESIGNER PROFILE

1915–43
Harry Bertoia was born in the village of San Lorenzo near Venice and moved to the United States in 1930, where he attended Cass Technical High School in Detroit followed by the Art School of the Detroit Society of Arts and Crafts from 1936 to 1937. He then won a scholarship to study painting and drawing at Cranbrook Academy of Art in Michigan, and became part of the gifted circle who flourished there. He taught at the academy until 1943, overseeing the metalwork studio.

1944–52
Bertoia began producing abstract monoprints during the 1940s. His metalwork and jewelry also reflected the influence of contemporary art. He moved to California to work with Charles and Ray Eames, and to pursue experimental designs in molded plywood in particular. Although the alliance was short lived, there were clear crossovers between the trio's work during the early post-war period. Following an invitation from Hans and Florence Knoll to design furniture for Knoll Associates, the designer relocated to eastern Pennsylvania and established a metalwork studio there in 1950. His Diamond and Bird chairs for Knoll were launched in 1952. The Diamond chair was more sculptural than the Eameses' Wires chair that influenced it.

1953–78
Metalwork sculptures and architectural commissions were Bertoia's principal activity from the 1950s onward, and he worked with some of the most prolific architects of the era, including Eero Saarinen, Henry Dreyfuss (1904–72), and I. M. Pei (b.1917). Bertoia received numerous awards throughout his career, including a Gold Medal from the Architectural League of New York (1955–56).

▲ Charles and Ray Eames' Wire chair appeared on the market in 1951, a year before Bertoia's Diamond chair. Although there are obvious similarities between the two designs, there are also clear differences. The Wire chair has a much simpler form, with a regular square mesh running down the center, for example.

Tulip Chair 1956

EERO SAARINEN 1910–61

A pivotal figure in US mid-century modern furniture and architecture, Eero Saarinen had all the right design credentials to guarantee his success: cultural background, family connections, and educational advantages. Like his Finnish compatriot Alvar Aalto (1898–1976), whose work he greatly admired, Saarinen aspired to create fluid, organic furniture that complemented the forms of contemporary sculpture. However, rather than pursuing an interest in molded plywood and laminated wood, he put his faith in plastics—fiberglass in particular—because he believed that this material was better suited to the all-in-one sculptural chair shells he wished to create. His iconic Womb chair, a large lounge chair with a capacious seat made from the recently developed fiberglass-reinforced polyester resin (GRP), was launched by Knoll Associates in 1948.

The same material was used for the shell of Saarinen's Tulip chair, a small armchair supported on a pedestal base. However, by 1956 the technology had been improved so that the plastic had a much smoother finish. Ideally, Saarinen would have liked to make the whole chair from one material, but GRP was not strong enough for the thin stem and wide circular foot. The sculptural pedestal combined with the white plastic gave this design a space-age appearance. A daring alternative to conventional furniture forms, it still looks incredibly modern today. **LJ**

◆ **NAVIGATOR**

Varnished fiberglass-reinforced polyester, varnished cast aluminum, foam rubber, textile
32 x 21¼ x 20 in.
81 x 54 x 51 cm

👁 FOCAL POINTS

1 PEDESTAL BASE
The most radical feature of this design is the pedestal base, as virtually all chairs prior to this were supported on four legs. "I wanted to clear up the slum of legs," declared Saarinen. The base appears to be plastic, but for structural reasons it was made from aluminum with a white plastic coating.

2 FIBERGLASS SHELL
The cupped seat is molded from fiberglass-reinforced polyester resin. With its fluid sculptural form and integral armrests, the Tulip chair is similar to the Eameses' Plastic chair (1950), but the shiny white finish and upholstered lining create a different esthetic.

TWA TERMINAL

The sensuous curves and organic form of the Tulip chair relate closely to contemporary sculpture, particularly the works of Hans Arp, Henry Moore, and Barbara Hepworth. Saarinen was clearly attracted to this esthetic because it also forms the basis for his architecture, notably the fluid, curvaceous, forms of buildings such as his TWA Terminal (1962; right) for Trans World Airlines at John F. Kennedy International Airport in New York. According to the architect: "The shapes were deliberately chosen in order to emphasize an upward-soaring quality of line. We wanted an uplift."

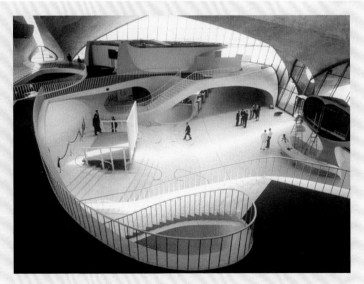

POST-WAR PLASTICS

1 David Harman Powell's two-color melamine cup and saucer design integrates the handle and cup.

2 A British advertisement for Formica decorative laminates from the 1950s. After World War II, Formica entered the European market.

3 Gino Colombini made award-winning everyday household objects like this carpet beater using polyethylene.

The story of plastics in the post-war years was one of experimentation, expansion, and democratization. The replacement of gas by oil in plastic manufacture saw an increase in the number of types available; new forming techniques, such as injection molding, widened the application of this family of synthetic materials. By 1960, the visual and material world was radically transformed. This was as true in the home as it was in industrial, commercial, and retail spheres. In the process, plastics moved from being seen as substitute materials and became valued for their own characteristics.

Many of the new technological possibilities arose from wartime developments. After the war, plastics were ready to be developed for the mass market. Nowhere was this more in evidence than in the United States, where chemical companies such as DuPont were in the forefront of the new materials technology. DuPont's development of polyethylene was especially notable, and the material was a component of a wide range of products, from buckets to bottles to hula hoops.

Plastic was a key factor in the US post-war consumer boom. Color was a significant part of its cheap and cheerful appeal. For the first time, everyday objects began to be available in bright, contemporary shades, and at a price that ordinary families could afford. Manufacturers enlisted the aid of designers to create products that would appeal to those living in the new suburban

KEY EVENTS

1947	1948	1948	1949	1950	1953
Color is introduced into Tupperware containers, which allows users to organize them by color coding.	US recording label Columbia Records introduces the vinyl long-play (LP) 33⅓ rpm microgroove record. It transforms how people listen to music.	Charles (1907–78) and Ray (1912–88) Eames design their Plastic chair, the first significant use of the material in furniture design.	The Italian firm Kartell is founded. It quickly becomes associated with high-quality plastic products.	New York City's Museum of Modern Art holds an international competition on the theme of "Low-Cost Furniture Design."	The Chevrolet Corvette, the first mass-produced car to be built with a fiberglass-reinforced plastic chassis, is launched.

housing developments, leading to items like the fiberglass La Chaise chair (1948; see p.288). Kitchens, in particular, were given radical makeovers by the new materials, heavily marketed as hygienic and easy to keep clean. Plastic washing-up bowls, dustpans and brushes, and lemon squeezers, among many products, became widely available. Tupperware (1946; see p.298) plastic storage containers transformed kitchens as well as providing a new marketing model via Tupperware parties. Kitchen worktops and tables were covered with Formica (a brand name for melamine), a plastic laminate that allowed strongly colored patterns to be printed onto its surface (see image 2). Children's toys were also transformed when plastics came on the mass-market scene.

The United States was not the only country to embrace plastics in the post-war years. Italy also took a proactive role. A key figure was Giulio Natta (1903–79), who was among the first to discover polypropylene and who was awarded the Nobel Prize for Chemistry in 1963. While the United States had set out to democratize plastic products, making them as cheap as possible, Italy took a more upmarket approach and focused on the ways in which the new materials could be used to express a modern esthetic. Nowhere was that more in evidence than in the products of Kartell, which used high-quality plastics in goods such as trays, bowls, and dining chairs. Founded in 1949 by Giulio Castelli (1920–2006), Kartell's highly innovative and desirable products included Gino Colombini's (b.1915) carpet beater (1957; see image 3) and Marco Zanuso's (1916–2001) child's chair. Zanuso also worked with Arflex to created strikingly modern-looking seating formed of a new, plastic-based form of foam rubber. The magazine *Stile Industria* celebrated these new uses of plastic in photographs that made the products look like works of art.

Britain was less enthusiastic about plastic, seeing the material as symbolic of an invasive US popular culture. Nonetheless, some striking British plastic products did emerge in the 1940s and 1950s from designers such as Gaby Schreiber (1916–91) working with Runcolite, Ronald E. Brookes working for Brookes and Adams creating tableware, and David Harman-Powell (b.1931), who created a highly sculptural cup and saucer set (1957–58; see image 1) for Ranton and Co. For the most part, however, the British public associated plastic products with bad taste and did not embrace its esthetic possibilities like the Italians. The Design Council was equivocal about the new materials and tended to reserve its praise for contemporary designs made out of more traditional materials, in particular wood and steel.

By the end of the 1950s, plastic products were ubiquitous in the industrialized world and, as a result, what had first been so eye catching became invisible, part of the everyday landscape. From a design perspective, there were only a few exceptions to that general rule—the work of furniture designers in both the United States and Europe whose quest to create the first all-plastic chair was about to be realized. **PS**

1954	1954	1957	1958	1958	1959
Polypropylene is first made into a polymer by Italian chemist Giulio Natta.	Plastics expert Bill Pugh (1920–94) designs the Jif lemon (see p.300), a squeezy plastic container for lemon juice.	US company Monsanto's "House of the Future," made from plastic structural parts, opens at Disneyland's Tomorrowland in Anaheim, California.	Lego files an application for a patent for its system of interlocking plastic bricks (see p.302).	Anglo-Dutch company Unilever launches Sqezy washing-up liquid contained in a plastic bottle. It is the first squeeze-to-use detergent container.	US toy company Mattel introduces the Barbie doll. It is made mostly of PVC and the doll's swimsuit is made of Lycra.

Tupperware 1946

EARL TUPPER 1907–83

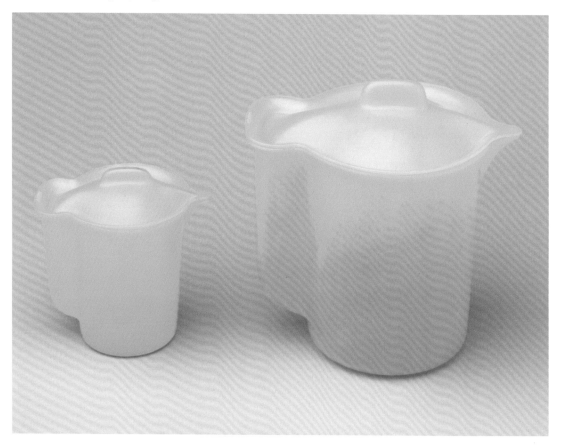

Pitcher
6½ x 6⅝ x 4¾ in.
16.5 x 17 x 12 cm
Creamer
4¼ x 4¼ x 3³⁄₁₆ in.
11 x 11 x 8 cm

⚙ NAVIGATOR

While employed at US chemical company DuPont, Earl Tupper discovered a see-through, colorless plastic that was a waste product of the oil-refining process. In 1938 he used this material, Poly-T, to create a bell-shaped container. In 1946 a version of this early plastic design was launched to consumers as Tupperware, a light, durable, airtight, watertight food storage container for keeping food and leftovers fresh in the refrigerator. The lidded Wonder, or Wonderlier, bowl available in nested trios set a new direction for the company.

Two things distinguished Tupperware's plastic storage containers from those of its competitors. First a noise—the Tupperware burp—was emitted when the lid was taken off. This aural indication of airtightness was a result of a patented seal developed by Tupper—modeled after the metal lid used on paint cans—to create a partial vacuum. Secondly, the company initiated a means of direct marketing through the Tupperware party—a party-plan system of informal get-togethers where women bought items from other women who hosted events to demonstrate the products for neighbors and friends in their own homes. Attending the parties became part of post-war US suburban life.

The success of Tupperware was due to its effectiveness and timeliness. It serves its purpose of keeping food fresh, it does not affect the taste of the food it contains, and it fits easily in refrigerators. Tupperware was also produced and marketed in a post-war, pre-feminist culture when weekly grocery shopping became the norm and women were expected to be domesticated. Buying the product helped women meet that expectation, while hosting parties helped liberate them by giving them an income. **PS**

FOCAL POINTS

1 PLASTIC

The first post-war Tupperware products were made from polyethylene at a time when consumers were used to glass, metal, and earthenware, so Tupperware parties helped explain how to use the product. Over the years the company used other plastic materials, including polypropylene.

2 COLOUR

Tupper introduced color into his containers in 1947, which helps users organize by color coding. The move was in keeping with the trend of the time to move away from the dreariness of the wartime period. The five bright pastels he introduced matched those used for other kitchen items.

DESIGNER PROFILE

1907–41

Earl Tupper was born in Berlin, New Hampshire. In 1937 he went to work for the plastics manufacturing division of DuPont. A year later he started his first business, the Earl S. Tupper Company, producing his Welcome Ware containers made of see-through plastic.

1942–47

He opened his first factory in Farnumsville, Massachusetts. He launched the Tupperware bell tumbler and bowl to the consumer market in 1946. A year later, an article on Tupperware appeared in *House Beautiful*, describing the Wonder bowl as "Fine Art for 39 Cents."

1948–57

Brownie Wise held her first Tupperware party and joined Tupperware in 1949. The same year Tupper patented the Tupper seal. In 1956 the Museum of Modern Art in New York featured Tupperware containers in an exhibition of contemporary design.

1958–83

Tupper fired Wise over a difference of opinion and sold the company for $16 million. He divorced his wife, bought an island in Central America, and moved to Costa Rica.

▲ Tupper's products were never meant to be seen much, but were intended to be stacked in the then newly popular refrigerators. Tupperware's simple appearance has barely changed and does not date.

THE TUPPERWARE PARTY

The Tupperware products were marketed and sold during the Tupperware party (above), a combination social and sales event. Brownie Wise (1913–92), who became vice president of the company in 1951, was responsible for developing the social networks that made the parties possible. Tupper quickly saw the potential and stopped selling his goods through retail outlets. Wise also introduced the idea of incentives for sales staff. Holding parties in a saleswoman's home made customers feel at ease and able to imagine using the containers in theirs. Women earned money by hosting the parties, which challenged the ideal of the unpaid housewife that was the norm in the United States in the 1950s and gave women a sense of independence.

Jif Lemon Packaging 1954

BILL PUGH 1920—94

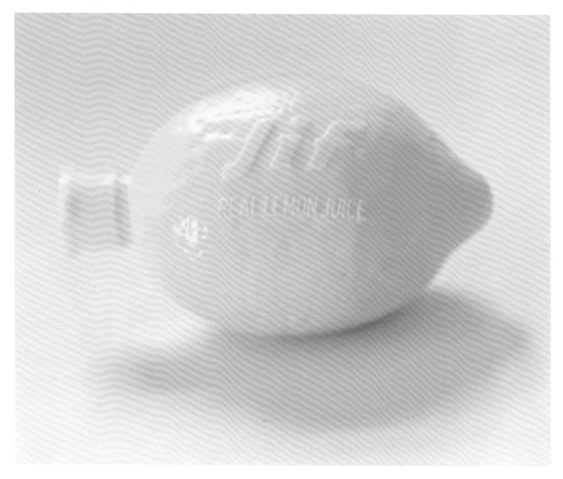

Blow-molded polyethylene
Height 3⅛ in./8 cm
Diameter 2 in./5 cm

The Jif lemon plastic container is a playful piece of packaging that tells consumers at a glance exactly what they are buying. With the growing popularity in the 1950s of both processed foods and self-service supermarkets, it was becoming increasingly important for manufacturers to guide consumers in making their purchases and feeling comfortable with their selection. Whereas most processed foodstuffs relied on cardboard packaging emblazoned with graphics to signal their contents, this product went one step further: the iconic packaging was made to resemble the natural fruit from which the juice was extracted. However, there remains some debate about the original design of the product. Most accounts claim that British designer Bill Pugh, who worked for a Leicester-based plastics company named Cascelloid, created it based on a prototype by Edward Hack, but others credit an ex-RAF pilot named Stanley Wagner. The idea was bought by domestic products company Reckitt & Colman, which launched the Jif lemon in 1956, two years after its design.

The fact that the plastic Jif lemon looks like a real lemon puts it into an esthetic category known as "kitsch," which is characterized by the use of irony and humorous messaging. At the same time, the move was astute commercially because it meant that consumers understood straight away that they were buying lemon juice, without the need for any additional information. The modernist idea of "form follows function" (see p.168) is subverted and replaced by "form follows communication." **PS**

✪ NAVIGATOR

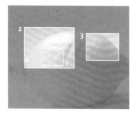

⊚ FOCAL POINTS

1 TEXTURE

The most striking and realistic feature of the plastic Jif lemon bottle is the way in which the surface is textured so that it looks and feels like dimpled lemon peel. This removed the focus from the "plasticness'" of the material and gave the product a hint of tongue-in-cheek authenticity. The container was made using a mold that was covered with real lemon peel in order to recreate the texture.

2 SCREW TOP

The feature that immediately gives away the Jif lemon as a synthetic product is the small screw top. Beneath the cap is a nozzle, which releases the lemon juice when the container is squeezed. In this sense the "lemon" resembles a number of other containers of liquids. When the product was launched in 1956, it was marketed with the tag line "Real lemon juice in a Jif."

PLASTICS

The number of available plastics vastly increased after World War II, and the material quickly found many uses in the consumer goods industry, transformed by designers into a range of wondrous new products that were readily available in the marketplace. Blow-molded polyethylene (also known by the brand name Polythene) was used for the Jif lemon packaging.

▲ This magazine advertisement from 1966 promotes the idea that Jif lemon juice can stay fresh and last much longer than a real lemon, even as long as a month. In many countries, the product has since become inextricably linked with Pancake Day, which falls on Shrove Tuesday.

🕐 COMPANY PROFILE

1814–1938

Based in Norfolk, Jeremiah Colman was a miller of flour and mustard seed and he founded Colman's of Norwich in 1814. In 1823 he was joined by his nephew and the company was renamed J. & J. Colman. Having also started out in the business of milling, Isaac Reckitt bought a starch mill in Hull in 1840 and diversified into household products. Reckitt & Sons was established when his sons were old enough to be involved. In 1913 the two companies began to work together and Reckitt & Colman was formed in 1938.

1939–74

The company continued to trade successfully internationally, supplying mustard and numerous other household products. It began producing the plastic Jif lemon in 1956. In 1964 Reckitt & Colman bought Airwick products, thereby widening its portfolio even further. The firm continued to acquire a number of other companies that specialized in household cleaning products, and later sold off the Colman's food business.

1975–PRESENT

In 1975 a court case began between Reckitt & Colman and Borden Inc., a US company that had been making a product called Realemon since the 1930s, and had been marketing it in the United Kingdom. The latter's plastic lemon had a flat bottom, but otherwise it bore a close resemblance to the Jif product. Reckitt & Colman sued Borden for "passing off" its product as if it were Jif lemon. The situation was made more complex by the fact that Jif was not a registered trademark. The case came to an end in 1990 in the Court of Appeal, in favor of Reckitt & Colman. In 1999 the company merged with Netherlands-based Benckiser to become Reckitt Benckiser Group.

Lego 1958

OLE KIRK KRISTIANSEN 1891–1958   GODTFRED KIRK KRISTIANSEN 1920–95

Lego bricks from 1997. The bricks are injection molded and a single mold produces 2,880 Lego blocks an hour.

◆ NAVIGATOR

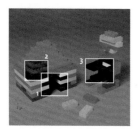

Lego founder Ole Kirk Kristiansen named his company after the Danish phrase for "play well" — *leg godt*. He subsequently discovered that Lego is also Latin for "I join together." Lego began manufacturing interlocking toy bricks in Billund, Denmark, in 1949, but did not file a patent until 1958.

Ole began to make small toys in the new plastic materials in 1947. Inspired by the Kiddicraft Self-Locking Building Bricks created by British designer Hilary Fisher Page (1904–57) in 1939, Lego released its first building bricks. Originally there were few sales. From 1954, Ole's third son, Godtfred, became junior managing director of the firm, with a growing interest in toy systems. In 1955 the Lego Town Plan themed play set was launched, offering a larger imaginative landscape, and the fortunes of the company rose. In 1958 the bricks were improved with hollow tubes in the underside adding support and improved locking. The company patented the new design and several similar designs.

Despite a slow start Lego has grown into the world's largest toy company, with around seven sets sold every second. The last Lego patent expired in 1989, and since then there have been imitators, but the family-run group remains leader of the field. **JW**

FOCAL POINTS

1 COLORS
Lego's bright colors and shiny surface were thought to be appealing to children. Lego toys are seen as more than recreational. Their educational benefits include patterning practice, fine motor development, and thinking in three dimensions. Originally, the bricks were meant for children aged six and more, and in 1969 the larger Duplo was created for children under five.

2 STUDS
Lego's stud-and-tube coupling system and modular design—functional parts of scalable, reusable pieces—means that a project of growing complexity can be fashioned from simple repeated elements connected with ingenuity. The beauty of modular building is that a user can replace or add any component without affecting the rest of the system. Many architects cite Lego among their early influences.

3 PLASTIC
The use of plastic means Lego bricks are light, cheap, and robust. They can be manufactured on a large scale and distributed internationally. The bricks can also be washed in water, making them easy to clean. Lego's cellulose acetate material was replaced in 1963 by an oil-based plastic, acrylonitrile butadiene styrene (ABS). Lego is committed to finding a sustainable alternative to ABS.

DESIGNERS' PROFILE

1891–31
Ole Kirk Kristiansen was born in a village in Jutland, Denmark. He trained to be a carpenter under his older brother, Kristian, and in 1916 bought the Billund Woodworking and Carpentry Shop where he had several successful years. Ole married and had four sons.

1932–46
The Great Depression was biting in Denmark and Ole was a widower, with four young children and no work. He set up a carpentry business making household items, such as ironing boards and stools. The toys he carved from wood proved his most successful products and in 1934 he created the Lego toy brand. In 1935 he introduced the pull-along Lego Duck on wheels that became popular and was produced until 1958.

1947–54
After acquiring one of the first plastic injection-molding machines in Denmark in 1947, Ole introduced his plastic Automatic Binding Bricks in four colors in 1949. A forerunner to Lego Bricks, they used a stud-and-tube coupling system. In 1953 the bricks were renamed "Lego Mursten," or "Lego Bricks." Lego was registered as a trademark in Denmark in 1954.

1955–95
Ole's son, Godtfred, introduced the Lego System of Play with twenty-eight sets and eight vehicles to the range, enlarging Lego's scope and increasing its popularity. In 1958 the bricks were redesigned with a different stud-and-tube coupling system that made more stable models, and the new system was patented. The same year, Ole died and Godtfred took over the company. Godtfred oversaw the introduction of Lego into the United States in 1961.

▲ Lego building blocks were originally marketed as toys for both boys and girls. In 1971 Lego released the Homemaker line, the first of several sets aimed specifically at girls. The Lego Friends range, which launched in 2012, contains mini-dolls and has been one of the biggest successes in Lego history.

DESIGNING FREE TIME

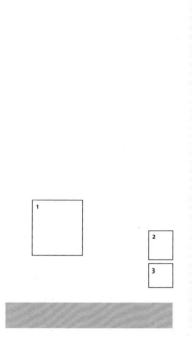

1 The brightly colored leatherette covering of Dansette record players was specifically aimed at the young.

2 The CBS Eye logo helps suggest the US radio and television network is all-seeing.

3 Alex Steinweiss's LP cover designs, like this one from 1952, use playful typography and eye-catching images.

During the 1950s, television began to supplant radio as a form of mass entertainment that could be enjoyed in the privacy of people's homes. By 1954, 55 per cent of US households had television; the next year radio listening had halved. But it was not merely brands of soap powder that competed for airtime on the new medium. Television companies also sought to establish their own identities. The CBS Eye logo (see image 2), which serves as a perfect visual summary of television news reporting, dates from 1951. The brainchild of CBS's creative director Bill Golden (1911–59), aided by graphic artist Kurt Weihs (1918–2004), the logo was inspired by the hex signs painted on the sides of Amish barns in Pennsylvania Dutch Country.

If television was uncharted territory for advertisers, who were accustomed to radio and print media, so too was an new group of consumers. The greatest shift in leisure culture occurred among young people. Despite a reputation for rebelliousness, they proved no less status conscious than their parents.

KEY EVENTS

1939	1948	1951	1951	1952	1954
Alex Steinweiss persuades Columbia Records to try out illustrated record sleeves.	Columbia unveils the new long-playing record, or LP, at a press conference in the Waldorf Astoria in New York City.	The British-designed Dansette portable record player is manufactured for the first time.	The CBS Eye logo debuts. It is advertised as "The sign of good television."	In the United States, the LP represents almost 17 per cent of unit sales and a little more than 26 per cent of dollar sales.	More than half of US households own a television set. Radio listening goes into steep decline.

Previously, adolescents had been viewed as superannuated children or adults in waiting. They emerged as a demographic in their own right and were given a new name: teenagers. The reason was their spending power. A typical US teenager in the 1950s made $10 to $15 weekly in allowance from their parents, supplemented by what they could earn in casual jobs. By 1959 teenage disposable income in the United States amounted to $10 billion; in the United Kingdom a study identified British teens as worth £1.5 billion a year. Unlike previous generations of adolescents, who would have been expected to contribute their earnings to supplement their family's income, the new prosperity meant that teenagers could spend their money on themselves as they pleased. And spend it they did—on records and record players, magazines, cosmetics, movies, clothes, and a host of other products that both defined their identity and were essentially leisure based.

Music was one of the chief ways in which the teen identity was expressed. Rock and roll burst raucously onto the scene during the 1950s, paving the way for the popular-music explosion of the following decade. In the United Kingdom, teenage spending accounted for 44 per cent of record and record-player sales in 1957. Singles, or 45s, rather than LPs, comprised the bulk of record sales. The Dansette record player (see image 1), first manufactured in 1951, was a familiar feature in many British homes (or teenage bedrooms), with its hinged, latched lid, carrying handle, front speakers, and control knobs. One million were sold in the 1950s and 1960s. A key factor in its popularity was that it was portable—teenagers wanted to be able to listen to music anywhere but where their parents were. An important design element was its auto-changer, which allowed singles to be stacked and listened to one after the other.

Adult listening was transformed by the introduction of the LP by Columbia Records in 1948, which held twenty minutes of music on each side. This was the first time that people could enjoy longer pieces of music without having to jump up and change the discs at frequent intervals. Shortly before the introduction of the LP came a new graphic art form that the LP would popularize: the album cover. In 1939 Alex Steinweiss (1917–2011) was art director at Columbia when he suggested replacing the then-standard brown paper record wrappers with an illustrated sleeve. His idea was taken up and within months Columbia's record sales increased by 800 per cent. Over thirty years, Steinweiss created classical, jazz, and popular music record covers (see image 3), featuring characteristic bold typography and original illustration. "I wanted people to look at the artwork and hear the music," he said.

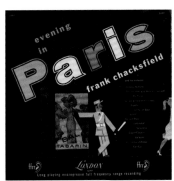

US graphic designer Saul Bass (1920–96), who designed many iconic movie posters throughout his career, had a similar aim: to distil the essence of a film into a single arresting image. Bass's designs for Alfred Hitchcock (1899–1980) in the 1950s, like that for *Vertigo* (1958; see p.306), achieved this memorably and in the process turned the director into a form of brand. **EW**

1955	1955	1956	1957	1958	1959
Saul Bass's stylized poster for the film *The Man with the Golden Arm* uses jagged typography to help communicate the film's key elements.	The film *Blackboard Jungle* plays "Rock Around the Clock" by Bill Haley and His Comets over its title sequence. The rock and roll era begins.	US singer Elvis Presley (1935–77) releases "Heartbreak Hotel." The single sells 300,000 copies in its first three weeks and tops the Billboard chart.	The musical *West Side Story* opens on Broadway in New York City, retelling the story of *Romeo and Juliet* (1597) with rival teenage street gangs.	Bass creates the film poster for Alfred Hitchcock's *Vertigo*. Its spiraling curves and bright color suggest disorientation, mystery, and fear.	The disposable income of US teenagers is $10 billion a year. They are important consumers for novel lifestyle goods and services.

Vertigo Film Poster 1958

SAUL BASS 1920–96

The poster's central geometric pattern
is based on spiraling curves, creating an
sense of disorientation, mystery, and fear.

S aul Bass was an Academy Award-winning film-maker and a graphic designer who created many memorable film posters and title sequences, mostly during the 1950s and 1960s. "Symbolize and summarize" was Bass's motto. His poster design for the romantic thriller *Vertigo* (1958) is based on a simplified two-color process that uses hand-cut lettering against a bright orange-red background. The text and imagery are handled like a symbol of great importance: strong, simple, memorable, and metaphorical.

Bass had been in Hollywood creating film advertisements since the late 1940s. He was soon assigned to posters and title sequences and by 1958, when he made the *Vertigo* poster, he had become a master. Before Bass, film posters were static, often unsophisticated excerpts pulled from the most dramatic scene. Nobody had thought to distil the entire film into one succinct image, and few have achieved that since. Bass saw that both poster and title sequence were integral to a film, and help to engage a powerful mood and expectation. Stripped down and urgent, Bass's style became immediately recognizable and immensely influential. **JW**

FOCAL POINTS

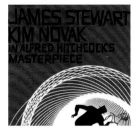

1 CREDITS
Bass creates expectation. The names of the stars are at the top, followed by the bold claim that this is a masterpiece by the director Alfred Hitchcock, then follows the central image and lastly, before the small print, comes the title.

2 RED
The main visual element is the background red—a dramatic color used by Russian and German designers of the 1920s and 1930s, and unmistakably aligned with avant-garde Constructivist philosophies and a modernist world view.

3 FIGURES
At the center, the figures are caught in mid-movement, silhouetted against a blinding light as they tumble into the eye of a swirling storm. Outlined in white mesh, the vortex is a net trapping the couple into its heart.

4 LETTERING
The lettering is in bold upper case printed with streaks as if hastily carved in wood. Bass references German Expressionist film posters of the 1920s, which used hand-drawn lettering with dizzy perspectives and oblique angles.

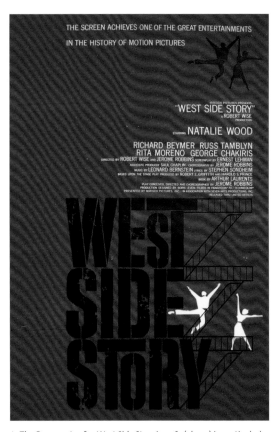

▲ The Bass poster for *West Side Story* in 1961 (above) is particularly memorable. Two, small, silhouetted figures, repeated in white and black on the bold red ground, give a masterful impression of modernist choreography and a romantic storyline. The bold, hand-drawn typeface of the title becomes the central image. Bass deftly extends the horizontals in the letters into an outline of a New York City fire escape, and an urban environment is perfectly conveyed. Bass filmed the prologue, storyboarded the opening dance sequence, and created the ending title sequence, so his visual impact on the film was considerable.

POST-WAR DOMESTIC DESIGN

1 Aerial view of rows of modest houses in the post-war housing development at Levittown, New York. The suburbs were about having the American dream.

2 In 1948 Frigidaire made the first refrigerator with a separate freezer section. Innovations were necessary to attract consumers as fridges became integral to modern kitchens.

3 Post-war optimism is visible in pieces like this Cannes coffee pot of 1954 by Hugh Casson for Midwinter, depicting a street café inspired by the trend for travel.

The years between 1945 and 1960 saw an emphasis fall on the design of the home and its contents. In Britain and mainland Europe, there was a need for reconstruction, notably of housing destroyed by wartime bombing. With the return of soldiers from arenas of conflict, women who had been employed during World War II in essential industries were encouraged to leave the paid workforce to free up employment for homecoming veterans. The arrival of peace saw a return to domestic life.

Stylistically, the war years created a rift with the past. The attitude of new homeowners was forward looking and the style of domestic goods was modern. The term "contemporary" was coined to describe the style, which was less abrasive and uncompromising than its pre-war equivalent. Natural wood, wallpaper, and fabric came back into vogue. Abstract fine art proved a fruitful source of inspiration for many fabric and wallpaper designers, as did more representational motifs drawn from scientific advances.

In the United States, suburban housing burgeoned. Levittown (1951; see image 1) on Long Island in New York was a post-war development that featured sweeping lawns, automobiles in the drive, and giant appliances in the kitchen. In Britain, the new towns of the post-war period were similarly progressive, while in Italy, Germany, and the Scandinavian countries, apartment blocks were created on the peripheries of cities, promising a similar vision of the future.

KEY EVENTS

1945	1946	1947	1950	1951	1951
George Nelson's book *Tomorrow's House* is published in the United States, popularizing the concept of open-plan domestic layouts.	Isamu Noguchi designs his Freeform sofa—an organic shaped piece of furniture like a soft rock—for the contemporary home.	The first post-war Ideal Home Exhibition is held at Olympia in London following its suspension during the war years.	Northgate Mall, in Seattle, opens. It is one of the first post-war, suburban malls in the United States.	The US television show *I Love Lucy* is first broadcast. It depicts an aspirational model of domestic life.	Levittown, the planned New York suburban community founded by William Levitt (1907–94) for returning war veterans and their families, is completed.

In many cases these new homes were less spacious than their pre-war equivalents. Instead, a sense of space, light, and air was promoted by open-plan layouts. No longer were rooms built as individual cells. Rather, the kitchen typically overlooked the dining and living areas, minimally partitioned by open shelving filled with books and plants. The housewife was no longer shut away, but a convivial hostess complete with a patterned apron. The information needed by housewives to cook, clean, and keep house was available in advice books and in the advertisements that filled the glossy magazines and were shown on television.

Furniture and domestic products soon flooded onto the market as manufacturers increased their output during the post-war consumer boom. In the United States shopping malls built on the outskirts of towns and cities, and accessible only by car, replaced more conventional "Main Street" shopping. At the upper end of the market, Herman Miller and Knoll led the way in the United States, working with designers Charles Eames (1907–78), George Nelson (1908–86), Eero Saarinen (1910–61), Isamu Noguchi (1904–88), and others. More downmarket Grand Rapids companies emulated the novel furniture items these designers created. Where kitchen goods were concerned, General Electric, Westinghouse, and others created bulbous refrigerators (see image 2) and stoves in a range of bright colors. In Britain, Hille and Race, working with Robin Day (1915–2010) and Ernest Race (1913–64), provided the radical new furniture items that companies such as G-Plan keenly emulated. Lucienne Day (1917–2010) designed some strikingly modern patterned fabrics for Heal's. In both countries ceramics and glass companies—such as Midwinter and Whitefriars in Britain—rose to the challenge of designing for the new domesticity. The former used abstract patterns created by Jessie Tait (1928–2010) and scenes of Cannes and the French Riviera by Hugh Casson (1910–99) to evoke the romance of aspirational vacations abroad as ways of making their ceramic dining and tea sets attractive to new consumers (see image 3).

Exhibitions played an important role in making consumers aware of what was fashionable and available. In the post-war years, the Ideal Home Exhibition held at London's Olympia became hugely popular, offering visitors a range of displays from entire homes to kitchen gadgets. Visitors to the show in 1956 could see the House of the Future, a visionary home designed by Alison (1928–1993) and Peter Smithson (1923–2003) that utilized many of the new materials that became available after World War II.

However, by the end of the 1950s—the peak of the post-war consumer boom—a new critical awareness was awakening. This was first expressed in concerns around the concept of planned obsolescence and in the powerful growth of advertising that had reached new levels of sophistication. US commentator Vance Packard (1914–96) attacked both strategies in his books *The Hidden Persuaders* (1957) and *The Waste Makers* (1960). **PS**

1951	1954	1955	1957	1960	1960
US industrial designer Russel Wright (1904–76) launches his Highlight dinnerware set and accompanying stainless steel flatware (see p.310).	Hugh Casson's Riviera design for Midwinter launches in Britain. Its seaside scenes appeal to people taking holidays abroad for the first time.	Cumbernauld New Town is designated as an overspill from Glasgow. Similar developments follow.	*The Hidden Persuaders* is released. It warns of the effects of subliminal advertising on unsuspecting consumers.	British company Russell Hobbs launches the K2 fully automatic electric kettle (see p.312). It becomes the bestselling kettle in Britain.	*The Waste Makers* is published. It highlights the effects of companies in the automobile sector planning obsolescence into their products.

Highlight Flatware 1951
RUSSEL WRIGHT 1904–76

👁 FOCAL POINTS

1 SURFACE
The Highlight flatware is one of Wright's few forays into stainless steel. He had worked extensively with spun aluminum before the war. The subtle shine on the surface of the polished metal gave it a modern look. The set comprises twenty pieces and was intended for a family of four.

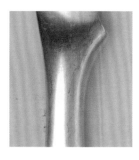

2 HANDLE
Wright nicknamed the set "the pinch" because of the narrowness of the top part of the knife's handle just before it became the blade. The organic shape of the knives, forks, and spoons that make up the Highlight set owe much to contemporary sculpture, furniture, and ceramics.

R ussel Wright was best known for his ceramic dinnerware set, known as American Modern, which was produced in the United States between 1939 and 1959. It was made by the Steubenville Pottery in Ohio, and it came to stand for the aspirations of a generation who wanted to live a modern lifestyle after World War II and who required cheap and available domestic accessories to make that dream possible. Wright believed in the centrality of domestic life and he focused his career on designing for it.

As well as creating his colorful ceramics Wright also designed a range of spun aluminum dining accessories, along with wooden furniture, textiles, and other tableware items. His designs were simple and modern, and they helped many Americans to embrace modernism in their homes.

Wright's stainless-steel flatware of 1951, which was intended to accompany his Highlight dinnerware created in the same year, was modern yet accessible. Stylistically owing much to the organic designs coming out of Scandinavia at that time, it was the first set of modern flatware designed in the United States after the war and was widely copied. Manufactured by the John Hull Cutlers Corporation in New York, it was reasonably priced and appealed to people who already had Wright's ceramic dinnerware and furniture at home. **PS**

⬖ NAVIGATOR

Stainless steel
Salad fork 6¾ in./17 cm
Dinner fork 7 in./18 cm
Dinner knife 8¾ in./22.5 cm
Butter knife 6⅜ in./16 cm
Tablespoon 6⅞ in./17.5 cm
Teaspoon 6¼ in./16 cm

⏱ DESIGNER PROFILE

1904–38
Russel Wright was born in Lebanon, Ohio. He studied art and sculpture at Cincinnati Academy of Art. He then worked in theater design with Norman Bel Geddes (1893–1958). In 1930 he set up a design business with his wife, Mary. In 1934 he began designing furniture.

1939–76
Wright designed the "Food Focal" exhibit at the New York World's Fair of 1939 and, in the same year, launched his American Modern dinnerware. In 1950 he and his wife published the *Guide to Easier Living* on maintaining a home.

Mary + Russel Wright

GUIDE TO

EASIER LIVING

INTRODUCTION BY **MASSIMO VIGNELLI**
FOREWORD BY **ANN WRIGHT**

MARY WRIGHT

In 1927 Russel Wright married Mary Small Einstein (1904–52). She was a designer and a businesswoman who had studied sculpture under Alexander Archipenko (1887–1964). The husband and wife team went into business together. While Russel designed, Mary was responsible for marketing. It is possible she developed the idea of designing for modern domesticity. The book they wrote together, *Guide to Easier Living* (1950), focuses on reducing the amount of work in the home and increasing leisure time.

▲ Wright created glassware like this wine goblet as part of his American Modern dinner service in an effort to create visual unity and a harmony of design for table settings.

Russell Hobbs K2 Kettle 1960

WILLIAM RUSSELL 1920–2006

The original Russell Hobbs K2 kettle was produced in spun copper and polished chrome.

NAVIGATOR

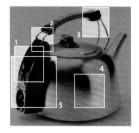

British small domestic appliances company Russell Hobbs was formed by William Russell and Peter Hobbs (1916–2008) in 1952. The same year, Russell Hobbs designed the world's first automatic coffee percolator, the CP1. The company followed it with the world's first automatic kettle, the K1, and in 1959 Russell went on to create its successor, the K2. The latter proved to be the company's winning design and it remained in production for the next thirty years. It was launched in 1960 and earned a place on the Council of Industrial Design's list of well-designed products.

The automatic kettle, which meant that it switched itself off when the water had boiled, replaced its predecessor, which had to be heated on the hob and announced that it was ready with a whistle. While the K1 had done the job it was neither modern looking nor stylish, so the arrival of the sleek, chromed steel K2 made all the difference.

The K2 was not a cheap kettle but it was reliable and long lasting, and it proved to be a classic design, a staple object in the British kitchen through the 1960s and 1970s. In 1982 it was finally replaced by the K3. **PS**

1 RED SWITCH

A particular design detail of the K2 kettle is the inclusion of a small switch at the back made of bright red plastic. This provides a strong color contrast with the silver of the metal and the matt black of the plastic, and aligns the K2 with the esthetic language of design modernism.

2 METAL STIRRUP

The K2 kettle has an elegant, streamlined shape. This is especially obvious in the way in which the handle slopes toward the rear, meeting the switch housing via a metal stirrup to create a smooth, continuous curve. The sleek, curved form of the body of the kettle reinforces its elegance.

3 HANDLE

As well as being functional and attractive, the K2 was designed to be pleasant to use. This was a function of the balance of the object when it was lifted, the ease with which it could be filled with water, and the way in which the handle was formed to fit easily in the hand of its user.

4 CONTAINER

The first K2 kettle had a body of chrome-plated copper. This gave it a shiny, polished look. Plastic was used for the switch housing, the kettle handle, and the smaller handle of the lid. Later the chrome-plated copper was replaced by brushed stainless steel, which gave the kettle an updated appearance.

5 SWITCH HOUSING

The kettle can switch itself off once the water is boiled due to the presence of a bimetallic strip at the rear. Steam is forced through a hole in the lid of the strip. This knocks the switch, which turns the kettle off. For a nation of tea drinkers, automating the boiling of water was a step forward.

1920–46

William Morris Russell was born in Islington, London. He won a scholarship to High Wycombe Technical Institute. He was an apprentice at electrical engineering company Rheostatic in Slough, where he completed an engineering diploma. He served in the British army during World War II.

1947–62

Russell left the army and went to work for domestic appliance maker Morphy Richards, where he contributed to the design of the pop-up toaster, the electric iron, and the hairdryer. While working there he met engineer Peter Hobbs, with whom he formed Russell Hobbs in 1952. The pair set up a factory in Croydon, England, to manufacture the CP1 coffee percolator. The K1 kettle (1955) gave Russell Hobbs a reputation for elegance and innovation, which was furthered by the launch of the K2 kettle in 1959.

1963–2006

In 1963 Russell Hobbs was sold to British engineering company Tube Investments. Russell became technical director of its subsidiary Creda, before moving to run Turnright, a Tube Investments company that made control and regulation devices. He died in 2006.

CP1 ELECTRIC COFFEE MAKER

The Model CP1 (above), made by Russell Hobbs in 1952, was both the first appliance made by the company and the first automatic electric coffee percolator. The CP1 had a green warning light and automatically cut out when the coffee was ready. It came with a built-in coffee strength adjuster, as well as matching sugar basins and cream jugs. In 1967 Russell Hobbs teamed with Wedgwood to make the ceramic bodies.

THE PERSONAL LUXURY CAR

1 A US drive-in theater in 1955. The number of drive-in theaters increased along with car ownership in the post-war era.

2 The four-seater Ford Thunderbird of 1959 was conceived as a compact luxury car with a distinctive style.

3 The parking lot at the Southdale Center shopping mall in Minneapolis in 1956. It had 5,200 parking spaces.

W hile appearance and status were persuasive issues from the beginning of the automobile industry, the emphasis remained largely on engine power and performance. Relatively quickly, however, producers of cars, gasoline, and tires found it useful to promote the concept of touring to stimulate demand for their products. It was in the post-war period that styling as a driver for car sales was taken to its logical conclusion, as seen in the marketing for cars such as the Ford Thunderbird (see image 2), which created a new market segment: the personal luxury car.

Styling was beginning to be a significant feature of the car industry when Alfred P. Sloan (1875–1966), the president of General Motors, put Harley J. Earl (1893–1969) in charge of the newly formed Art and Color Section in 1927 (officially renamed the Styling Section in 1937). Earl was in part responsible for the marketing strategy known as "dynamic obsolescence," and its near-relative "annual model change," whereby car manufacturers deliberately enticed customers to purchase new models on an annual basis, then a new concept in marketing. Unlike planned obsolescence, where the programmed or built-in breakdown of an appliance gave it a short functional lifespan, this approach rested on nothing more substantial than the flamboyant design of a tail fin or the tweaking of a radiator grille, resulting in the Cadillac Coupe de Ville of 1959

KEY EVENTS

1947	1948	1950	1951	1953	1954
William Levitt begins building Levittown, New York, a suburb constructed of mass-produced housing.	Harley J. Earl puts tail fins on the Cadillac, the first appearance of this characteristic feature of 1950s car styling.	Opening of the Northgate Mall, Seattle, generally acknowledged to be the first out-of-town shopping mall.	The first drive-through-focused fast-food chain, Jack in the Box, opens in San Diego, California, taking advantage of the burgeoning car culture.	The Chevrolet Corvette, designed by Earl, is launched. It is the first sports car produced by a US manufacturer.	Ford unveils its first Thunderbird, a two-seat convertible, at the Detroit Auto Show and positions it as an upscale model.

with its exaggerated tail fins and jewel-like grille (see p.316). A car that was designed to break down or stop working would undermine the reputation of a brand. A car that looked obsolete, on the other hand, might be more readily discarded. During the 1950s, the annual practice of trading in last year's model for the latest off the assembly line became a marker of status and affluence for middle-class Americans. It is worth noting, however, that most European manufacturers remained resistant to such strategies, with models of brands such as Citroën and Peugeot changing little in appearance from year to year.

The emphasis on styling, which elevated the latest Buick, Chevy, or Cadillac to ultimate symbols of the American dream, coincided with a widespread shift in culture. During the 1950s, the United States became a much more car-oriented society—and celebratory of the apparent freedoms this promised. The Federal-Aid Highway Act, signed by President Dwight D. Eisenhower (1890–1969) in 1956, saw the construction of 41,000 miles (65,983 km) of freeways, a massive expansion of road network stretching coast to coast. With the accompanying infrastructure of full-service gas stations staffed by attendants ready to fill the tank, wash the windshield, and pump the tires, and roadside motels catering for overnight travelers, distance was now no object.

The same period saw an equivalent shift to suburban living, with new housing springing up all around the United States. Attracting city dwellers and rural populations alike, the suburbs often functioned as bedroom communities, with a consequent reliance on cars for commuting to work in nearby urban areas. The first mass-produced suburb was Levittown, New York, constructed from 1947 to 1951 by William Levitt (1907–94), who applied assembly-line techniques to house construction. The Federal Housing Administration, which made cheap loans possible after the war, stimulated such developments and made affordable houses and gardens available to a wider section of the population than ever before. A similar move toward decentralization saw the emergence of the out-of-town shopping mall, with its concentration of retail outlets and acres of parking. The first such example is generally considered to be the Northgate Mall in Seattle, which opened in 1950; the Southdale Center in Minneapolis opened in 1956 and was the first enclosed mall (see image 3). Other symbols of the new car culture were the drive-in fast food restaurants and drive-in movie theaters (see image 1) that opened in their thousands during the same period.

If the car was emblematic of post-war mobility, it also helped to generate an attitude of restlessness rather than rootedness, particularly among the young. The state of mind was summarized by Jack Kerouac's (1922–69) novel of the beat generation, *On the Road* (1957): "What is that feeling when you're driving away from people and they recede on the plain till you see their specks dispersing?—it's the too-huge world vaulting us, and it's good-bye. But we lean forward to the next crazy venture beneath the skies." **EW**

FORD THUNDERBIRD '59
The car everyone would love to own!

1956	1956	1957	1957	1957	1959
The opening of the Southdale Center, Minneapolis, the first enclosed mall in the United States.	The Federal-Aid Highway Act is signed by President Dwight D. Eisenhower, inaugurating a massive expansion of US road networks.	*Popular Science* magazine notes the phenomenal number of US movie theaters: there are 6,000 catering to a weekly audience of 35 million.	The All-Weather Drive-In movie theater opens in Copiague, New York. Covering more than 28 acres (11 ha), it can park 2,500 vehicles.	*On the Road* by Jack Kerouac is published, the book of the beat generation.	Earl's Cadillac Coupe de Ville is launched, the model with the most exaggerated tail fins of all time.

Cadillac Coupe De Ville 1959

HARLEY J. EARL 1893–1969

The curved windows and large amount of glass in the Cadillac Coupe de Ville of 1959 is reminiscent of a fighter plane.

The pre-eminent US luxury car brand, Cadillac, is also among the oldest in the world. Founded in 1902, the company was acquired by General Motors in 1909, by which time it already had a reputation for producing well-built, reliable automobiles with top-of-the-line features and powerful engines. During the Great Depression the brand suffered, but it recovered lost ground by World War II, thanks in part to the overturning of a policy that had previously discouraged sales of the car to African-Americans.

The Cadillac Coupe de Ville of the post-war years comprised a series of models that combined high specification—power brakes, power steering, power windows, and so on—with the distinctive sharp styling of the period. It owed the latter to the pervading influence of Harley J. Earl, the head of General Motors' Styling Section, one of the world's foremost motor designers. Exaggerated tail fins, chrome plating, and two-tone paint finishes, which characterized many US cars at the time, were all introduced by Earl.

When the motor industry was in its infancy, what a car looked like was low on the list of priorities for manufacturers and customers alike. Henry Ford's (1863–1947) famous statement "any color so long as it is black" reflects Ford's reluctance to engage in style wars. "There is a tendency to keep monkeying with styles and to spoil a good thing by changing it," Ford wrote in his autobiography. Alfred P. Sloan, president of General Motors in the 1920s, had no such reservations when he put Earl in charge of the Art and Color Section in 1927. Earl's focus on appearance and his freeform approach to the design of car bodies resulted in demonstrable commercial success. **EW**

 NAVIGATOR

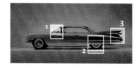

1 WINDSHIELD

The wrap-around windshield, with its curved glass, offers panoramic visibility and is an Earl innovation, as is the use of chromium plating. A decorative grille pattern at the front of the car is heightened by the use of chrome, and it complements the elaborate features at the rear of the car.

2 REAR WHEEL

The form of the Coupe de Ville, with its long, low, sweeping lines, is evocative of high-speed jet planes and rockets. The mudguard skirts covering the rear wheels contribute to the long, low emphasis of the car body. Earl lengthened and lowered the appearance of the US automobile.

3 TAIL FINS AND LIGHTS

The most distinctive features are the car's exaggerated tail fins and dual bullet-shaped tail lights. Tail fins first appeared on the 1948 Cadillac, inspired by the Lockheed P-38 Lightning, a World War II US fighter aircraft. The tail fins of the 1959 Coupe de Ville are the largest and most complex ever of any car.

BUICK Y-JOB

The classy Buick Y-Job (right) was the first concept car. Designed and built by Earl's Styling Section in 1938, it was a two-seater, two-door coupé, almost 20 feet (6 m) long and only 5 feet (1.5 m) high. With its streamlined form, wrap-around bumpers, gunsight hood ornament, power windows, and concealed headlights, it was designed to attract attention and test out public taste. Earl drove one himself.

JAPAN AND QUALITY CONTROL

Compact Luxury at its Best!

1 The Datsun Bluebird (1959) was introduced as a new product for a new generation.

2 A Japanese factory worker at Sony checks the functioning of transistor components in 1962.

3 The Sony 8-301W (1959) was the first all-transistor television set in the world.

It is usually unwise to attribute significant historical trends to the intervention of a single idea. However, after World War II, the quality-control concepts communicated by Jewish-Romanian-US engineer Joseph M. Juran and US statistician W. Edwards Deming revolutionized Japanese manufacturing and led to its dominance of technology markets in the late 1960s and 1970s.

Prior to World War II, Japan had a manufacturing sector. Indeed, compared to its Asian neighbors, it was an economic powerhouse, producing a wide range of goods for domestic consumption. However, most of the goods manufactured by independent companies were state mandated, under the auspices of the country's desire to be a great military power. With the cessation of hostilities, the country's manufacturers had to shift away from a war footing to target export markets, but many of their original products had been banned by the occupying forces: for example, they were not allowed to produce cars again until the late 1940s. Once they had worked out which goods to make and where to sell them, the low quality of Japanese goods became rapidly evident. "Made in Japan" communicated low price, not merit.

Nevertheless, the collaborative Japanese *keiretsu* system meant that manufacturers, suppliers, distributors, and banks cooperated to ensure that the economy kept going, aided by powerful unions and coordinated by the Ministry

KEY EVENTS

1945	1947	1951	1954	1955	1958
After the nuclear bombings of its civilian centers, Japan surrenders to the United States, which proceeds to reshape the country in its image.	W. Edwards Deming visits Japan and introduces the concept of statistical control.	Joseph Juran's *Quality Control Handbook* is widely taken up as a guide to improve Japanese products.	US firm Texas Instruments produces the first transistor radio—the Regency TR-1—although Sony is working on one simultaneously.	The Sony TR-55 is the first Japanese transistor radio. It is followed in 1958 by the TR-610 (see p.320).	Honda launches the Super Cub (see p.322): a small, mass-market motorcycle.

of International Trade and Industry. Furthermore, the US occupying forces were extremely keen to get the country back on its feet as a democracy in order to keep militarism and communism at bay, and so poured huge sums of money into the country for it to rebuild. In 1947 Deming was dispatched to Japan to aid with the country's first post-war census. While there, he met with the leaders of the Japanese Union of Scientists and Engineers (JUSE), who wished to learn about statistical control of processes, in which Deming was a specialist. Juran, on the other hand, had been a quality-control specialist at Western Electric/ AT&T for more than twenty years before embarking on a career as a professor of industrial engineering and moonlighting as a consultant on quality control. In 1951 he published his *Quality Control Handbook*, which soon came to the attention of JUSE. The union invited him to visit Japan and took him around major manufacturing companies and universities.

The quality-control message of Juran and Deming was the opposite of the "pile-it-high, sell-it-cheap" model. They believed that although high-quality goods had higher initial costs, due to standardization and improved control systems, in the long term they were more competitive, easier to sell, and enjoyed higher margins. However, the message was not only about improving the quality of the goods; Juran also advocated improving the quality of the staff through training and the general culture of planning and organization. These ideas were widely seized upon.

Quality control transformed Japanese manufacturing. Its application coincided with a period of innovation when companies such as Sony experimented with commercial applications for new technologies, such as the transistor (see images 2 and 3). The first Sony transistor radio, the T-55 (1955), made miniaturization highly desirable. It was a quality that would increasingly be associated with a Japanese approach to design. Similarly, the Nikon F (1959; see p.324) married superb engineering and design with technical innovation—all made possible through the implementation of Juran's thinking. By the time restrictions were lifted on car production in the late 1940s, companies such as Toyota and Nissan, who had spent the intervening years in research and development, were primed to adopt a new approach. In 1958 Nissan began to export its vehicles to the United States, where the comfortable and stylish Datsun Bluebird (see image 1) became a surprise hit. Nissan opened dealerships across the United States very quickly.

Japan's recovery was in notable contrast to events in the United States, where the lessons learned from wartime quality control were slowly forgotten in the face of huge demand for their products from around the world. It was not until the 1980s, and the unexpected dominance of Japanese manufacturing, that the United States woke up to what it had lost. **DG**

1959	1959	1960	1977	1979	1991
The Nikon F displaces the German Leica as the professional photographer's camera of choice.	The Datsun Bluebird is launched in August. By 1970 Nissan is one of the world's biggest car exporters.	Sony launches the 8-301W. It is the first portable transistor television.	Japan's products are so dominant abroad that the US government forces it to implement export restrictions or face tariffs.	The first low-cost portable stereo, the Sony Walkman (see p.408), goes on sale in Japan for around USD150.00.	Some 46.7 per cent of color televisions and 87.3 per cent of video recorders produced in Japan are exported.

Sony TR-610 Transistor Radio 1958

SONY

Alloy and plastic
5 x 2¾ x ¾ in.
13 x 7 x 2 cm

👁 FOCAL POINTS

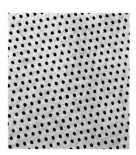

1 SPEAKER GRILL

The design emphasizes the punched metal grill panel, which stands out against the glossy body of the radio. A ring around the grill pins it to the main body using flanges hidden inside the unit, behind the grill itself. This allows the device to appear screwless and to retain a sleek form.

2 DIALS

The tuning and volume dials are both on the right-hand side, thereby allowing a user to operate the radio with one hand. They are small and tucked away, unlike previous versions, such as the TR-63, which had large dials that sat on the front of the box, looking outlandish and ugly.

M any of the Japanese companies that succeeded after World War II were survivors of the pre-war period. However, Sony was co-founded in 1946 by Masaru Ibuka (1908–97) and Akio Morita (1921–99) as the Tokyo Telecommunications Engineering Corp. It consisted solely of a small office in Tokyo, which repaired radios and added innovative devices that turned short-wave radios into all-wave radios. A sales trip to the United States in 1952 introduced Ibuka to the newly invented transistor. Today, the transistor is the key active component in all modern electronics. As a semiconductor, it can act as either a switch or an amplifier, but it has huge advantages over the valves that preceded it because it is much lighter, more reliable, and more robust. Although Ibuka was sceptical, he decided to license the manufacturing rights and work on practical uses for the transistor.

The TR-55 (1955) was the first Japanese transistor radio; it weighed 20 ounces (560 g) and featured a contemporary Americanized appearance. It was followed two years later by the TR-63, which was the world's first pocket-sized radio, made in cream plastic with a speaker grill of punched aluminum. Finally, came the TR-610, which was well known for its design, in which the textured round speaker almost escapes the frame of the radio's casing. This handsome device, with its foldable wire stand, was designed for shirt-pocket storage and sold half a million units. **DG**

COMPANY PROFILE

1908–45

Born in Nikko City, Japan, Masaru Ibuka studied science and engineering at Waseda University. His nickname was "genius inventor." Upon graduation, he invented a modulated-light transmission system that won him a prize at the Paris Exhibition. He then joined Photo-Chemical Laboratory, which specialized in the recording and processing of motion picture film, before moving to the Japan Measuring Instrument Co.

1946–70

Ibuka co-founded Tokyo Telecommunications Engineering Corp, which was later renamed Sony for use in the Western

market. In 1949 the firm developed magnetic recording tape, followed by the first tape recorder in Japan. Subsequent products included the first transistor radios (1955), transistor televisions (1960), calculators, record players, and many more objects. In 1967 Sony created the first Trinitron color television.

1971–97

In 1971 Ibuka published a book titled *Kindergarten is Too Late*, which argued that the most important learning happens before the age of three. After his retirement from Sony in 1976, he continued his work for the company in an advisory role. He also actively worked with the Boy Scouts of Nippon.

◀ The use of transistors in models such as the TR-6 (1956) meant that Sony could massively decrease the size of the radio, compared to the valve radios that existed before. Sony went on to build transistor versions of many devices, which contributed to the Japanese reputation for miniaturizing everything.

Honda Super Cub 1958

HONDA

The Super Cub was not aimed at the typical macho motorcycle rider. Its smooth design was reminiscent of modern kitchen products.

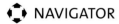
NAVIGATOR

Like Sony, the Honda company is another post-war success. Before the war, mechanic Soichiro Honda (1906–91) worked in a garage, tuning cars and racing them, but he always had a desire to be a manufacturer. After a series of disasters—his first business lost a vital contract after producing subpar goods, one factory was bombed by the Americans, and another was destroyed by earthquakes—he gradually realized his aim. By 1956 Honda was a stable and successful business. Soichiro remained interested in racing but his business partner, Takeo Fujisawa, wanted to make a small, high-performance, mass-market motorcycle. The technology had to be simple, so it could survive in places without spare parts or trained mechanics, and the model had to be quiet, reliable, and easy to use. It also had to be possible to drive the motorcycle with one hand while carrying a tray of noodles: "I don't know how many soba noodle shops there are in Japan, but I bet you that every shop will want one for deliveries," said Fujisawa.

The Super Cub, or Honda 50, hit the market in 1958. It featured a pressed steel frame with an attractive plastic fairing, step-through design, clutchless three-speed gearbox, and a 50cc four-stroke engine, which was later upgraded to 70cc and 90cc. Despite the fact that Fujisawa had been keen to produce the motorcycle on an enormous scale, to benefit from economies of scale, it sold poorly at first, owing to a Japanese recession. However, it is still in production today and is the most produced motor vehicle in history. **DG**

👁 FOCAL POINTS

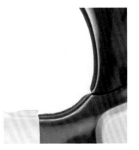

1 MOPED OR MOTORCYCLE?
The design of the Super Cub was a hybrid. The plastic fairing makes it look like a scooter, as does the step-through arch. But the engine sits in the middle of the bike like a true motorcycle, to give it proper balance. It also features 17-inch (43-cm) motorcycle wheels rather than 10-inch (25-cm) scooter models.

2 KICK-START
The four-stroke engine of the Super Cub was a huge improvement on the earlier 50cc models, managing up to nine times the horsepower. It could also consume cheap, low-octane fuel and was easy to kick start, thus removing the need for an expensive and heavy electric starter.

3 ENCLOSURES
The multiple enclosure points on the Super Cub certainly look good, but they have more than an esthetic value. The covering around the chain prevents lubricant being spattered across the rider's clothing, while the leg shield stops wind and road debris hitting the motorcyclist.

🕐 DESIGNER PROFILE

1906–27
Born near Mount Fuji to a blacksmith and a weaver, Soichiro Honda was not formally educated and left home at the age of fifteen to work in a garage in Tokyo.

1928–45
At the age of twenty-two, he returned home to set up an auto-repair business and to build racing cars. In 1937, after an injury in a racing accident, he changed direction and founded

Tōkai Seiki to produce piston rings for Toyota. After attending engineering school, he created a method of mass producing the rings.

1946–91
Soichiro founded Honda in 1946. He started out turning surplus two-stroke radio generators into motorcycle engines, but the business grew rapidly. Its first motorcycle was the two-stroke D-type (1949), but by 1964 Honda was the world's largest manufacturer of motorcycles.

BRANCHING OUT

In 1962 the Japanese parliament planned to pass a law that would restrict the manufacturing of cars and trucks to existing manufacturers. Honda did not want to be locked out forever, so quickly designed a sports car—the S360—which was never put into production, and the T360 (right), a small two-door pick-up truck. The latter was available as a flatbed, folding flatbed, or van. Furthermore, the rear wheels could be replaced with tracks, in case of snowy weather. The law was never passed, but it forced Honda into new markets.

Nikon F Camera 1959

NIKON

Stainless steel, titanium, glass,
chrome, plastic
5¾ x 4 x 3½ in.
14.5 x 10 x 9 cm

 NAVIGATOR

Nikon is one of Japan's older manufacturing companies, founded in 1917. Originally called Japan Optical Industries Co., it specialized in optical lenses for binoculars, microscopes, and cameras. During World War II, it worked for the Japanese government, running more than thirty factories, but after the war the company shrank back to a single factory and adopted the Nikon brand name for its cameras. The creator of the majority of Nikon's early cameras, including the Nikon Model 1 (1948), was Masahiko Fuketa (1913–2001). He worked on all the cameras up to the Nikon F before being appointed a vice president of the company in the 1970s.

The Nikon F was released in 1959 and within a year nearly every US photographer and photojournalist had abandoned their German Leicas (see p.182) and adopted the Nikon. It was the first SLR camera from Nikon, and as such did not need to be advertised very hard: one slogan simply read, "Today, there is almost no other choice." A year after the launch, the shared offices of *Time* and *Life* magazines were full of Nikon Fs. Their camera repairman, Marty Forscher, commented, "It's a hockey puck that takes pictures." He meant that it was indestructible, something that owners still say today. Drop it, hit it, let it sit there for fifty years . . . it keeps taking pictures. The Nikon F was so popular that it was the first camera to be taken to the Moon, and a specially made edition—the digital Nikon NASA F—was used on the space shuttle until 1991. **DG**

FOCAL POINTS

1 LENSES
The Nikon F had a wide range of lenses, ranging from 21mm to 1,000mm focal length, some of which were drawn from Nikon's existing rangefinder models. Nikon also introduced "mirror lenses," thus allowing for long focal length lenses to be much more complex than standard telephotos.

2 ADAPTABILITY AND ACCURACY
In addition to the lenses, the viewfinder, prism, and focusing screens could be changed. It also had a 100 per cent viewfinder as standard, which meant that the image you saw through the viewfinder was exactly what you would get on the film—no cropping and no hidden extra material.

COMPANY PROFILE

1917–38
Nikon was established when three of Japan's leading optical manufacturers merged to form a new company that specialized in microscopes and binoculars. It was based at the Oi Plant from 1918. The Nikkor brand of lenses was introduced in 1932.

1939–45
Nikon's factories were invaluable to the Japanese government during World War II, and they manufactured bombsights, periscopes, and all sorts of lenses. After the war, the company significantly decreased in size.

1946–87
The business continued to focus on cameras and optical instruments, as well as survey instruments, and established a number of new branches around the world. The design for the first Nikon brand camera was completed in 1946 and the Model 1 was released two years later.

1988–PRESENT
The company was renamed the Nikon Corporation, after its cameras, in 1988. Today, it is still based at the Oi Plant, doing exactly the same thing, nearly one hundred years after it was founded.

▲ This silk screen poster advertising Nikon cameras was designed by Yusaku Kamekura (1915–97) in *c.* 1955. He worked hard to elevate the status of design in Japan in the 1950s and Nikon was one of the clients that allowed him to experiment with his abstract style.

NIKON RANGEFINDER

Rangefinder cameras such as the Nikon S (1951; above) work in a slightly different way to SLR cameras. They typically show two images of the subject, one of which moves when a wheel is turned. When the images fuse, the distance can be read off the rangefinder and fed into the camera, for a shot that is in super-sharp focus. The Nikon SP rangefinder (1957) was a professional model favored by photojournalists and it was the most advanced rangefinder of its time, surpassing any cameras manufactured by Leica. It was smooth as butter and super quiet, much more so than modern DSLR cameras.

4 | Design and the Quality of Life 1960–80

BRAND LOYALTY

1. The Apple Records logo created by design firm Wolff Olins is seen here on the A side of the Beatles' *Abbey Road* album (1969). The B side featured the apple cut in half.

2. Raymond Loewy's version of the Shell logo (1971) is still in use today. It is so iconic that it is often used without the word "Shell."

3. This magazine advertisement for Nike was first seen in *Runner's World* in 1976. It was created by John Brown and Partners advertising agency.

B rand loyalty is the manufacturer's holy grail. Having tempted consumers to try a product, companies want them to choose it time and again, and to extend their loyalty across the entire range of goods. From the early days of mass manufacturing, packaging design has been crucial. A package carries the all-important product name, generally in a recognizable livery, and occasionally badges of quality or authenticity. One of the oldest examples of such hallmarks in the United Kingdom is the Royal Warrant. A Royal Warrant implies high quality: the inference is that if the product is good enough for the royal household, it is good enough for anyone. However, quality cannot always be determined. If there is only one soap powder on the market, consumers will buy it as long as they need to wash their clothes. If there is an outstanding soap powder available, they might, within reason, pay more for it. In reality, there are many soap powders on the market and they all broadly do the same job, at the same price point, so branding becomes an important means — sometimes the only means — of distinguishing one product from another.

KEY EVENTS

1960	1961	1961	1962	1962	1964
More than 45.7 million US households and some 16.3 million UK households own a television set.	Romek Marber (b.1925) devises the cover for the Penguin crime series (see p.332), creating an overarching brand that allows for individual author identities.	The Kikkoman soy sauce bottle (see p.330), designed by Kenji Ekuan (1929–2015), expresses a Japanese identity.	Paul Rand (1914–96) designs the lower-case logo for the American Broadcasting Company.	The McDonald's Golden Arches logo (see p.338) makes its first appearance.	The "First Things First" manifesto, signed by Ken Garland (b.1929) and twenty-one other creative professionals, calls for design to serve public service ideals.

The early 1960s saw an explosion of brands. Airlines, soft drinks, cereals, cigarettes, and a host of other goods vied for attention in an increasingly crowded marketplace. The growth of television opened up a new marketing arena on both sides of the Atlantic. Designers were drafted in to create logos and packaging, to work on advertising and corporate identity campaigns, and generally to aid and abet commerce and retail in all its forms. Although design agencies had long been established in the United States, they began to emerge in the United Kingdom, too. Wolff Olins, founded in 1965 by Michael Wolff (b.1933) and Wally Olins (1930–2014), designed the iconic identity for Apple Records in 1968 (see image 1), which featured a bright green Granny Smith apple on the record label. However, successful logos are not always the result of expensive design consultancy. In 1971 Phil Knight, a University of Oregon track athlete, and his coach, Bill Bowerman, were seeking to launch a line of running shoes and were on the lookout for a logo. They approached university student Carolyn Davidson (b.1943), who devised what has since become one of the world's best-known symbols. The brand was Nike (see image 3), and Davidson's "Swoosh"—recognizable today without accompanying brand name or specific color—cost the new company only $35.

The more successful the product, the more reluctant companies are to tamper with their logos. When designs have been updated in line with changing graphic fashion, something of the original DNA has generally been retained. The name Shell dates back to the 19th century, and the pecten or scallop-shell motif was introduced in 1904. Early representations of the logo were realistic and monochrome, with the distinctive red-and-yellow colorway being introduced later. Today's logo, bar a slight color adjustment, dates back to a redesign by Raymond Loewy (1893–1986) in 1971 (see image 2). It is a sharp, simplified version that is distinctive, easy to reproduce, and true to its origins.

Not all creative professionals were happy to develop commercial brands. A growing unease was reflected in 1964 with the publication of the "First Things First" manifesto, which criticized the wasting of design talent in the promotion of such products as "cat food, stomach powders, detergent, hair restorer, and striped toothpaste." It called for a return to public service ideals, in which design would be used to educate, inform, and improve society in the broadest sense: "We hope that our society will tire of gimmick merchants, status salesmen, and hidden persuaders, and that the prior call on our skills will be for worthwhile purposes." The manifesto attracted significant media attention, and anticipated the rejection of mainstream consumer values by the countercultural movements of the late 1960s and 1970s. The reissuing of a reworked "First Things First" manifesto in 2000 demonstrated that such ethical concerns have not gone away. Published in the Canadian magazine *Adbusters*, it was signed by Jonathan Barnbrook (b.1966), Milton Glaser (b.1929), Zuzana Licko (b.1961), and Erik Spiekermann (b.1947), among other design luminaries. **EW**

MADE FAMOUS BY WORD OF FOOT ADVERTISING.

1965	1968	1969	1971	1971	1978
Leading UK design group Wolff Olins is founded by Michael Wolff and Wally Olins.	Wolff Olins designs the iconic logo for Apple Records, record label of the Beatles, which was founded in the same year.	The Olivetti Valentine portable typewriter (see p.334) is designed by Ettore Sottsass (1917–2007). He is heavily involved in the marketing campaign.	Raymond Loewy gives the Shell logo a sharp, modern update, while retaining the essential features of the original.	Carolyn Davidson designs the Nike "Swoosh" logo. Nike is now one of the world's most recognized brands.	Milton Glaser designs the now iconic "I ♥ NY" logo for New York City. The heart symbol is red and the typeface is American Typewriter.

Kikkoman Soy Sauce Bottle 1961

KENJI EKUAN 1929–2015

✪ NAVIGATOR

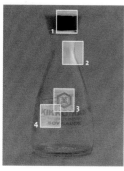

Glass and polystyrene plastic
5¼ x 2½ in.
13.5 x 6.5 cm

In 1957, leading Japanese food and drink manufacturer Kikkoman Corporation had opened a sales and marketing offices in San Francisco, and had its sights on a large export market. Soy sauce was an essential ingredient in Japanese cuisine, but it came in unwieldy, large bottles. The brief from Kikkoman was to develop a small bottle that would be easy to stock and to ship, but also acceptable on the domestic table. It took Japanese designer Kenji Ekuan three years and 100 prototypes to settle on his graceful, sloping-shouldered design. The elegant curves are redolent of a traditional Japanese water carrier in a (red) hat, with the widest part of the bottle occurring, as if on a robed figure, somewhere below knee height. The top has a convex curve, in the manner of a water carrier's hat, or a bow of bamboo carrying a pole weighted with buckets on either side. Two spouts, which jut out either side of the red top, are cut inward on the diagonal, extending the curve of the top. Before Ekuan's iconic bottle appeared in 1961, packaging as a distinct design discipline was unknown in Japan, a state of affairs that rapidly changed. By the time of Ekuan's death in 2015, more than 300 million bottles had been sold. **JW**

FOCAL POINTS

1 RED CAP

The sauce dispenser never leaks. It does not create rings on tables, and the exterior of the bottle is never streaked with drips nor does it clog. Inside the red cap, an inner mechanism channels the sauce slowly through a narrow chute, angled on a climbing gradient, and out through the spouts.

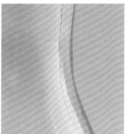

2 CURVE

"The ultimate design is little different from the natural world," said Ekuan, and the beautiful curving silhouette of his Kikkoman bottle evokes organic, natural forms. In terms of three of his watchwords—comfort, convenience, and function—his little sauce bottle is an unqualified success.

3 LOGO

In Japanese folklore, the tortoise lives for 10,000 years and is a symbol of longevity. *Kikko*, means "tortoiseshell" in Japanese, and *man* means "10,000," so together they form the company name. The hexagonal logo shows a tortoise shell with the Chinese character for 10,000 inside.

4 GOLD LETTERING

The plain lettering expresses contemporary style and confidence in the future. But the use of gold refers back to the past. In Japanese tradition, gold is associated with royalty—and Kikkoman had made soy sauce for the Imperial Household since 1917. Gold represented the color of the heavens.

DESIGNER PROFILE

1929–54

Born in Tokyo into a line of priests from Hiroshima, when Kenji Ekuan was one year old, his father moved the family to Hawaii to work in a Buddhist mission, returning to Hiroshima seven years later. Ekuan was deeply influenced by both Buddhism and early US industrial design. He was away at naval college when the atomic bomb struck Hiroshima in 1945, killing one of his sisters. He returned home soon after. His father died of radiation sickness the following year, and Ekuan began training in Kyoto to become a monk. However, the devastation he saw around him led him to change his direction.

1955–69

Ekuan graduated from the Tokyo National University of Fine Arts and Music and, in 1957 founded the design studio that eventually became GK Industrial Design Group.

1970–2015

Ekuan became president of the Japan Industrial Designers' Association and in 1975 was elected president of the International Council of Societies of Industrial Design. His designs include the Narita Express airport train (1991) and Yamaha VMAX (2008) motorbike. In 1998 he became head of Design for the World, an organization using design to solve problems of the poor. Ekuan won the Japanese Good Design Award 2003 for shell-shaped Japan Airlines seats, which allowed more privacy and a flatter sleeping position.

E3 BULLET TRAIN

Personifying the speed and futurism of a brave new world, the bullet train seemed to carry Japan away from a troubled past. Ekuan's E3 bullet trains for the East Japan Railway Company were not designed until 1997, but they are the most beautiful of all Japan's bullet trains. Ekuan pushed the boundaries of the streamlined esthetic even further into the future. Without ever straying into the nostalgic or the saccharine, his E3 train and carriages are wildly futuristic while remaining within the traditional Japanese idiom. Japan began discussing the need for high-speed trains in the 1930s, and when the first Shinkansen (new trunk line) was launched in time for the Tokyo Olympics in 1964, it became an international symbol of just how advanced Japan had become. Characteristically, Ekuan designed the train that passes through some of Japan's most glorious countryside.

Penguin Crime Series 1961–65

ROMEK MARBER b.1925

Published in July
1962, Romek Marber's
Hangman's Holiday
(1933) book jacket was
designed according
to his influential
grid principle.

◆ NAVIGATOR

The distinctive look of Penguin Books' Crime series, which emerged in 1961, was the result of an open brief from art director Germano Facetti (1926–2006) to refresh the design approach, but the job ended up changing the look of the publisher's covers more widely. Prior to this intervention, Penguin had been content with an esthetic that had served the company well for more than twenty-five years. Though updated in 1947, the familiar tri-band colors and Gill Sans typography were in need of modernizing. Romek Marber's solution was to employ striking imagery and an approach to cover design based on a consistent grid system that would prove highly influential. In notes Marber made on his concept for the series, he stated that "the pictorial idea, be it drawing, collage, or photograph, will indicate, if possible, the atmospheric content of the book." He aimed to offer a continuation with the past through "a common denominator"—the "strong horizontal movement, which is emphasized in the current crime cover, and which is repeated in the new cover by the use of horizontal rules and the occasional use of a white horizontal panel." Marber kept the familiar green color coding, brightening its hue a little, and used Standard as the typeface. The result was a range of more than seventy covers that balanced clean design and a fixed identity with evocative, often dark and mysterious graphics. The formula of bringing a range of imagery into a unified identity system was applied to Penguin's orange fiction titles and its blue Pelican range. **MS**

👁 FOCAL POINTS

1 EYE
Marber used a range of techniques across his Crime covers, from distorted type to line drawing, to a host of experimental photography. Marber regularly used himself as a model. Often he opted for dark visual images, suggestive of crime. The dribble of ink here has an ominous, creepy feel.

2 WHITE FIGURE
Marber's covers for Dorothy L. Sayers's titles showed how a confident sub-series could emerge for an individual author within the wider Crime range. On Sayers's covers a white figure—a caricature of the chalked outline of a murder victim—was shown in various settings.

3 GEOMETRIC GRID
The "Marber grid," as it became known, places the colophon, the book's title, and the author's name in a tri-band panel at the top of the cover. It allows for "variations in the length and the placing of titles," while enabling the pictorial element to run across the remaining area.

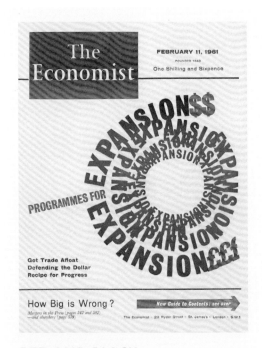

RED AND BLACK

Marber provided designs for magazines *The Economist* and *New Society*. Facetti was impressed by Marber's covers for *The Economist*, particularly the way in which he distilled social and political issues into bold black and red graphics, and invited him to enter a competition to revamp Penguin Crime for the company's Silver Jubilee.

Olivetti Valentine 1969

ETTORE SOTTSASS 1917–2007

ABS plastic and other materials
4⅝ x 13½ x 13⅞ in.
12 x 34.5 x 35 cm

E ttore Sottsass was an architect, product designer, artist, writer. and theoretician, as well as a notable glass maker and ceramicist. Throughout his career he constantly sought to blur the distinctions between art and industrial design, to demonstrate, in his own words, that "design should be sensual and exciting."

In 1958 Sottsass accepted an invitation from Adriano Olivetti (1901–60) to act as a creative consultant alongside his son, Roberto (1928–85), in Olivetti's newly established electronics division. In subsequent years, along with engineer Mario Tchou (1924–61), they were responsible for a number of products that combined Sottsass's flair for aesthetics with technical innovation. Although the Valentine typewriter was not the first portable on the market, it represented the first time a standard piece of office equipment had been reinvented as a desirable consumer product. Sottsass, who called the design an "anti-machine machine" and "a biro among typewriters," was heavily influenced by Pop Art and the beat culture. A co-designer on the project was Perry A. King (b.1938).

Unlike most office machines, which were still largely made of metal, the Valentine flaunts its shiny plastic casing, which contributes both a sassy allure and makes the typewriter lightweight and portable. Sottsass was always interested in new materials. ABS (acrylonitrile butadiene styrene), the thermoplastic resin used here, is a glossy, rigid, and tough material, commonly used to make luggage; Lego bricks (see p.302) are also made of ABS. The Valentine typewriter proved both a critical and a commercial success, winning the prestigious Compasso d'Oro design award in 1970. **EW**

 **NAVIGATOR**

◉ FOCAL POINTS

1 CARRIAGE-RETURN LEVER
Unlike the upright carriages of most typewriters of the era, the carriage on the Valentine is set level with the keys and the carriage-return lever folds back when it is put away—an advantage when fitting it into its case. The slim profile that resulted also underlined its go-anywhere Pop esthetic.

2 RIBBON SPOOL COVER
Although the Valentine was also made in gray, blue, and green, red is its signature shade (according to Sottsass the "color of passion"), which also spells out the name. The orange ribbon spool covers create a jolting contrast. The color choice also recalls the glossy bodywork of US cars.

◷ DESIGNER PROFILE

1917–57
Sottsass was born in Innsbruck, Austria, but grew up in Milan. He studied architecture in Turin and after World War II set up his own practice in Milan. In 1956, a visit to New York City introduced him to modern US art and industrial culture. On his return to Italy, he began designing furniture for Polotronova.

1958–79
As creative consultant to Olivetti, Sottsass was responsible for a number of innovative products, including the Valentine. From 1972 he became involved in avant-garde design groups such as Studio Alchimia and Archizoom.

1980–2007
He founded the Memphis design collective. In 1985 he returned to architecture and industrial design. His firm Sottsass Associati designed the new Milan airport, Malpensa, in 2000.

▲ The integral case of the Valentine visibly promotes its portability. The rear of the typewriter forms the fixed lid of the case. Rather than an appendage, the case is conceived as part of the total design.

MARKETING THE VALENTINE

Unusually for a product designer, Sottsass was highly involved in the marketing of the Valentine typewriter. From the choice of name, appearing in lower-case lettering, to the red plastic casing, the Valentine was as much about concept as it was about technical innovation. Appropriately, the launch of the product was on Valentine's Day, 1969. The advertising campaign for the typewriter, which Sottsass art-directed, featured advertisements and eye-catching posters that made the Pop Art references of the design explicit. In some advertisements the typewriter is shown alongside couples lying on the grass or being held by different people all over the world. The message is clear: here is a lightweight, portable office machine with personality, meant to be used anywhere but the office.

DISPOSABLE DESIGN

For many nations, the immediate post-World War II period was marked by extreme austerity. However, once the desire for basic goods—food, clothes, shelter—had been satisfied, the population discovered it had disposable income and demanded products on which to spend it. In the 1950s and 1960s, manufacturers fought to supply these, repeatedly updating models of cars, white goods, and homewares for the population to buy again and again.

Modern consumerism was shaped and driven, according to the economist J.K. Galbraith (1908–2006), by "the machinery for consumer-demand creation," which included advertising. Galbraith's book *The Affluent Society* (1958) outlined the increasing and self-perpetuating division in the United States between the wealthy private sector and the impoverished public sector. The writer Vance Packard (1914–96) shared Galbraith's concerns about this "consumerism." His book *The Waste Makers* (1960) deplored "the systematic attempt of business to make us wasteful, debt-ridden, permanently discontented individuals." By contrast, Marshall McLuhan (1911–80), in his book *Understanding Media: The Extensions of Man* (1964), was happy to see society shaped by media technologies, believing it empowered mankind. Others sought to present consumerism as a new-found economic freedom that empowered rather than impoverished the population.

Despite the misgivings of some commentators, the US population went on a spending spree that drove the nation's economy to new heights. Spending was

KEY EVENTS

1960	1961	1963	1964	1966	1966
Vance Packard publishes *The Waste Makers*, warning of the dangers of unbridled consumerism to the environment and ourselves.	Ray Kroc buys out McDonald's from the brothers McDonald and sets it on the road toward becoming a global fast-food corporation.	The Anthora paper coffee cup is designed and launched, becoming a symbol of New York City's fast-moving society.	Marshall McLuhan publishes his far-seeing book *Understanding Media*, with its central idea that "the medium is the message."	Barclaycard launches the first non-US credit card, expanding take-up of the radical idea that goods bought today may be paid for tomorrow.	A group of California banks issue Master Charge: The Interbank Card, a credit card that was jointly honored by the participating banks.

aided in the 1950s by the advent of accessible debit and credit cards, such as Diners Club, American Express, and Carte Blanche. By 1970 approximately 100 million credit cards had been sent unsolicited to US citizens. Getting into debt, which previous generations had widely considered the result of failed economic management, was repackaged and marketed as "credit."

Disposable design and planned obsolescence were key components of this new consumerism. Exploiting the new materials that arrived in the post-war era, manufacturers designed devices that lasted only just as long as their warranties, and clothes that quickly wore out or faded in sunlight; foods were doctored to last a day rather than weeks. Disposable items, such as the Anthora coffee cup (see p.340), were presented as stylish and practical—consumers could take their coffee away, and restaurants had no washing up to do. The Post-it note (see p.342), whose technology was first conceived in 1968, was similarly intended to serve a short-term function and be disposable.

Other objects were designed to have obsolescence of desirability. Here, new objects were designed primarily to be more desirable than their predecessors, rather than to be as durable and attractive as possible. For example, Alfred P. Sloan at General Motors established a rigid pricing structure for GM makes, running from Chevrolet (see image 1) to Pontiac, Oldsmobile, Buick, and finally Cadillac, encouraging each buyer to stay within a GM family. Each make would release new designs every year to ensure that there was always a new object of desire, even if the driver couldn't afford to move up to the next make.

Advertising helped here. As early as 1938, the De Beers cartel used advertisements (see image 2) to create the concept that engagement rings had to be diamond; the US public agreed (as they did to the later concepts that size didn't matter—prompted by smaller Soviet diamonds entering the market—and that a second diamond ring bought later in life reaffirmed romance). In Japan in the 1970s, when marriages were arranged and hence devoid of premarital romance, De Beers marketed diamond rings as tokens of modern Western values, a trick the company has recently repeated in China. The expansion of the McDonald's Corporation was assisted by the instantly recognizable "golden arches" of its restaurants (see p.338), and the logo that was based on them.

From the 1950s, design had a vital role in changing consumers' expectations and helping them buy into economic materialism—the ethos of chasing the new, preferring the new-looking over the practical. The ascendancy of design meant that, as long as an object had the look of the new about it, it was perceived as good. And just as a person was defined by their pattern of consumption, conspicuous consumption became a marker of status. Today, both Packard and McLuhan seem to have been right. The pursuit of economic happiness has made Americans richer than ever before, but the United States also seems impoverished in key ways, with health care, job security, and secure property ownership the privilege of the richer classes alone. **DG**

1 In the 1960s, ownership of a car such as this Chevrolet Corvette Sting Ray Sport Coupe (1963) signaled achievement of a glamorous, carefree lifestyle that was light years away from the grim deprivation of the post-war years.

2 A De Beers advertisement of the 1970s helps to create a new market for small Russian diamonds. The message was that, incorporated into "eternity" rings, they signified undying love.

1968	1960s	1970	1976	1979	1980
The adhesive technology of the disposable Post-it note is first invented, although at first its uses are not apparent.	De Beers pioneer the idea of the "eternity ring," with small diamonds set around its outer edge, as a means of marketing small Russian stones.	Mass mailings of unsolicited credit cards (known as "drops") are outlawed in the United States because of the high levels of debt that they cause.	The Visa credit card is launched, with licensees including BankAmericard, Barclaycard, and Carte Bleue.	The Master Charge card of 1966 is renamed MasterCard and expands its credit provision operations worldwide.	The first branded Post-it notes go on sale, and are a runaway success as people realize how useful they can be.

McDonald's Golden Arches 1960s
MCDONALD'S CORPORATION est. 1961

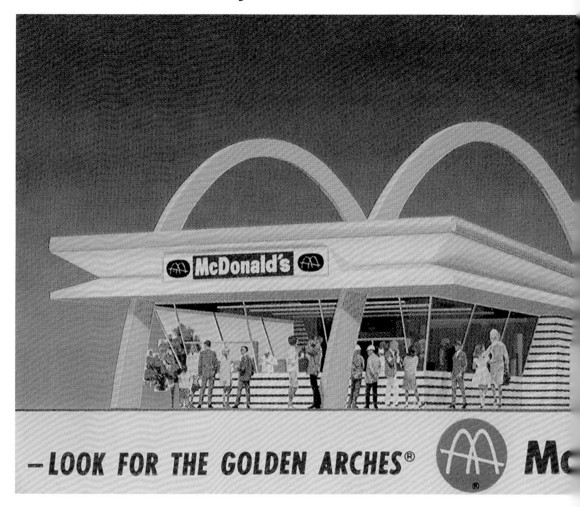

Exhorted to "Look for the Golden Arches," customers were tacitly encouraged to overlook rival establishments in their home areas.

The famous McDonald's "golden arches" logo originated in Googie architecture, a subdivision of Futurism that was popular in southern California from the 1940s to the mid-1960s. Commonly used on low-profile roadside buildings, such as motels, gas stations, and coffee shops, Googie was influenced by car, jet, and spaceship design and features curves, geometric shapes, and unabashed use of glass, steel, and neon. Googie influenced the design of the McDonald brothers' popular restaurant in San Bernadino, California, and in 1952 architect Stanley Meston designed their franchised restaurant, in Phoenix, Arizona. Dick McDonald added the large semicircle on either side of the building to Meston's rendering. The arches didn't act as an entry point and had no structural, cultural, or historic function; they weren't even conceived as looking like an "M" at this point—that did not occur until 1962. The aim was simply to make the restaurant more visible. The arches were later refined by signmaker George Dexter into two wide parabolas, 25 feet (8 m) tall, built from sheet metal trimmed with neon.

When national franchise agent Ray Kroc bought out the McDonald brothers in 1961, McDonald's ventured into advertising. His Minneapolis franchisee had tried radio advertising and seen his sales explode in 1959, so Kroc encouraged all his operators to follow suit. The "Look for the Golden Arches" campaign was a key part of this advertising drive. **DG**

✦ NAVIGATOR

👁 FOCAL POINTS

1 LOGO
When McDonald's was seeking a new logo in 1962, Fred Turner, the vice president of operations, sketched a prototype design. The head of engineering and construction, Jim Schindler, refined it to an "M" that was designed to resemble a McDonald's store viewed from an angle.

2 GOLDEN ARCHES
McDonald's has retained the golden arches theme throughout almost all of its later campaigns, and as a logo they remain central to the business's visual identity. In 2003 McDonald's spent around $600 million on advertising to generate sales of $6 billion.

3 SLOGAN
The slogan "Look for the Golden Arches" refers not to the current logo, but to the restaurants' physical arches. Ironically, the giant golden arches were eventually dropped, and franchisees were obliged to rebuild to a new design. The arches remained on the restaurants' road sign, however.

🕐 COMPANY PROFILE

1937–53
In 1937 two brothers of Scotch-Irish descent, Richard and Maurice McDonald, started a drive-in hot dog stand in Pasadena, California, before opening a barbecue restaurant in San Bernardino in 1940. Their first franchise opened in Phoenix, Arizona, in 1953.

1954–60
In 1954, Ray Kroc, born in Chicago to a Czech family, became the brothers' national franchise agent. He helped to build the business, but realized that the brothers were not interested in realizing its full potential.

1961–PRESENT
Kroc bought out the brothers for $2.7 million in 1961 and established a "Hamburger University" for franchise owners in his home state of Illinois. Today, of McDonald's 1.9 million employees, no fewer than 1.5 million work for franchisees.

THE HAPPY MEAL

McDonald's has always been innovative in its packaging design—from the unique curves of the flat-pack fries packaging of 1970 to the kooky Halloween bags issued in the 1960s. The origins of the Happy Meal go back to the 1960s and early 1970s, when McDonald's owner-operators across the United States began toying with the idea of creating a children's meal. While a few different formats were tested and proved fairly successful, none of the concepts were repeated or rolled out nationally. It was not until 1977, when St. Louis regional advertising manager Dick Brams challenged his advertising agencies to create a children's meal concept, that the Happy Meal was born. The idea was conceived by the Kansas firm Bernestein-Rein, who designed the well-known lunch pail (right) with golden arches serving as a handle.

Anthora Paper Coffee Cup 1963

LESLIE BUCK 1922–2010

For decades, the naive design and cheering message of the Anthora paper cup made it an unlikely icon of New York City.

NAVIGATOR

The Anthora paper coffee cup—blue and white, with a faux ancient Greek design—was designed in 1963 by Leslie Buck of the Sherri Cup Company. Up until the 2000s, it was an iconic symbol of New York City, with 500 million sold in 1994 alone (though almost none outside the city limits). On TV it was to be seen on almost any New York-based entertainment show, with characters holding Anthoras appearing in *NYPD Blue*, *Law & Order*, *Mad Men*, *Men in Black*, and many other productions.

In the early twentieth century, there were hygiene concerns over the shared drinking utensils—glasses or dippers—used at drinking-water sources such as water barrels and public faucets. Shared utensils were widely banned and the first paper cups, known by the brand name of Dixie Cup, were introduced. They had a waterproof coating, usually stiff paper, and the lip was rolled to stiffen it further. Versions used for hot beverages, including the Anthora, also have a second layer to trap an insulating layer of air.

Sadly, the Anthora was heavily copied, and a wide variety of designs and slogans diluted the brand. When modern coffee chains, such as Starbucks and Costa, supplanted the Anthora completely, it faded from public view. By 2005 the Sherri Cup Company, which is now owned by the Solo Cup Company, was selling only 200 million Anthoras a year. By the time of Buck's death in 2010, it was only available as a special request. **DG**

👁 FOCAL POINTS

1 MOTTO

New Yorkers enduring their city's famous cold responded favorably to the design of three gold coffee cups, steaming to indicate the welcome heat within. The cheering motto, "We are happy to serve you," appears in a faux ancient Greek font inspired by ancient Greek inscriptions.

2 ANTHORA

On the side are two Greek amphorae; these, when named in Buck's Czech accent, account for the name "Anthora." Buck's amphorae are unusual in that they have only a single carrying handle, angular rather than curved sides, and a flat base—but then he never claimed to be an artist.

3 GREEK COLORS

Buck designed the cup in the blue and white colors of the Greek flag, using a classic Greek meander for the borders. He wanted to get the cup into New York's diners and restaurants, which were mainly run by Greek Americans, so marketing considerations strongly influenced the design.

▲ In a still from the film *The Wolf of Wall Street*, Leonardo DiCaprio strides thoughtfully along the eponymous thoroughfare. His coffee is contained in the city's emblematic Anthora, naturally.

🕐 DESIGNER PROFILE

1922–45

Leslie Buck was born Laszlo Büch to a Jewish family in Khust, Czechoslovakia. Buck and his family were imprisoned by the Nazis in the Auschwitz and Buchenwald concentration camps, where his parents died.

1945–65

Moving to New York with his brother Eugene after the war, Büch anglicized his name and launched an import–export business. In the late 1950s, the brothers moved into paper cup manufacture, launching Premier Cup.

1965–92

Buck joined the start-up paper cup maker Sherri Cup as its sales manager, before becoming marketing director. He designed the Anthora cup in the early 1960s, and continued to work for the company for the next thirty years.

1992–2010

Retiring from Sherri Cup in 1992, Buck received 10,000 specially made Anthora cups. He died in 2010.

ANCIENT ANTECEDENT

In China, paper cups have been in used since the Tang dynasty (618–907 CE). Tea was served from baskets made of rushes that held cups of tea, known as *chih pei*. They were made in different sizes and colors, and adorned with decorative designs. Only later was tea served in porcelain, as in the tomb painting above.

Post-it Note 1968

ART FRY b.1931　SPENCER SILVER b.1941

In the first large trial of Post-it notes in Boise, Idaho, in 1978, 94 percent of consumers said that they would buy them.

Dr Spencer Silver was tasked by 3M (the Minnesota Mining and Manufacturing Company) with developing a superstrong adhesive. Instead, in 1968 he developed a low-tack adhesive in which tiny acrylic spheres made of acrylate copolymer ensured the glue didn't bond firmly. Obviously, his work was regarded as useless in the context of his task and he was reassigned to other projects, but Silver was convinced that the material was useful. The low-tack material ensured that this glue, however weak, could be reused over and over. He thought it could be used as a spray or a surface for bulletin boards, so that temporary notices could be easily posted and removed. His problem was that he couldn't convince anyone else.

For five years, he demonstrated it in presentations until Art Fry attended one. Fry sang in his church choir, and was frustrated by the bookmarks he used, which didn't stay in place. He realized that Silver's material was perfect for this sort of temporary adhesion. He presented it to his supervisors and, while they were sceptical, they realized that they were using the sticky papers much more than their flagship Scotch tape. So, for the next five years, Silver and Fry were set to work on perfecting the machines to make the notes. In 1978, ten years after the invention, they were introduced as Press n' Peel pads, and after two years of market testing they were rebranded as Post-it notes and put on sale. One year after the official launch, the packs brought in more than $2 million in sales. Today, they generate more than $1 billion a year. **DG**

⊙ NAVIGATOR

👁 FOCAL POINTS

1 STICKINESS
The tackiness is achieved, not by using a weak adhesive as one might suppose, but by embedding tiny plastic balls in the adhesive. The degree of stickiness of the notes depends on the number and size of the balls. The balls prevent the bond from becoming permanent.

2 COLOR
The Post-it note has an iconic, classic form: square and yellow. In fact, it was only yellow because the lab next door had scrap yellow paper available for testing. This recalls Steve Jobs' original idea of defining the iMac by its colors, rather than its function. Now many other colors and shapes are sold.

🕐 DESIGNERS' PROFILE

1931–53
Arthur "Art" Fry was born in Minnesota and was a tinkerer from a young age. He moved to the University of Minnesota, and was recruited as an undergraduate for 3M in 1953.

1941–66
Spencer Silver was born in Texas in 1941. He majored in chemistry at Arizona State University and completed a doctorate in organic chemistry from the University of Colorado in 1966.

1966–96
Spencer Silver filed twenty-two patents during his career at 3M. The adhesive he and Fry invented for Post-it notes was adapted for other products, such as medical bandages and interior decorating kits, but he never received any royalties. He retired from 3M in 1996 in order to concentrate on his paintings. Art Fry also retired in the early 1990s. Both have been inducted into the US National Inventors Hall of Fame.

▲ The Sticky Note Exhibition was one feature of the Work Zone of the Millennium Dome in London. The exhibition, which was open to visitors throughout the year 2000, underlined how ubiquitous and convenient the Post-it note had become in business life.

SCOTCH "MAGIC" TAPE

Among 3M's other well-known adhesive products is the pressure-sensitive cellulose tape known as Scotch tape. Although the concept was originally developed in 1845, Dr Richard Drew (1899–1980) designed 3M's product in the 1930s. The name "Scotch" was derived from a pejorative association of the nation with "stinginess" at the time, because of the product's weak adhesion.

GRAPHIC SIGNPOSTS

1 Lou Dorfsman worked on his haute relief wall graphic at the CBS headquarters, New York, in 1965.

2 Derek Birdsall oversaw many iconic covers for influential women's magazine *Nova*, including this one from 1967.

3 Massimo Vignelli's New York subway map was introduced in 1972.

Italian-born Massimo Vignelli (1931–2014), who moved to New York in the 1960s, was a prolific designer in the European modernist tradition, and he is best known for his graphic design. From his American Airlines corporate identity (1967), which remained unchanged for fifty years, to his modular subway signage for the New York Transit Authority (1966–70) and the city's subway map (see image 3), Vignelli's work has reached millions. "I was always seeking to affect the lives of millions of people—not through politics or entertainment but through design," he said. A huge fan of Helvetica (see p.276), Vignelli was dedicated to clarity and concision: "I like design to be semantically correct, syntactically consistent, and pragmatically understandable." Not everyone approved of the results. The subway diagram, which he co-designed with Bob Noorda (1927–2010) in 1972, was particularly controversial. Executed in Helvetica (which would later be adopted across the New York subway in 1989), the map followed the principles of the London underground map (1933; see p.202) designed by Harry Beck (1903–74) and represented the network in a graphic, systematic way, rather than attempting to reproduce the geographical reality. "The most beautiful spaghetti work I've ever done," said Vignelli. However, unlike sprawling London, New York is laid out in a rigorous grid pattern and the divergence of Vignelli's diagram from the truth on the ground proved too much for many New Yorkers. As soon as the map was introduced,

KEY EVENTS

1962	1962	1963	1963	1965	1966
The *Sunday Times* magazine is published for the first time. It is the first UK color supplement.	Gino Valle (1923–2003) co-designs mechanical indicator boards. They are widely adopted in airports and railway stations, and become an industry standard.	Jock Kinneir is commissioned to design a signage system for UK roads and invites Margaret Calvert to assist him.	Richard Guyatt organizes an exhibition titled "GraphicsRCA: Fifteen Year's Work of the School of Graphic Design" at the RCA.	Valle designs the Cifra 3 travel clock for Italian display company Solari di Urbine (see p.348).	Massimo Vignelli designs the subway sign system for the New York Transit Authority. It is based on a modular system of panels.

complaints flooded in from those incensed at its "inaccuracies," such as the representation of Central Park, shown much smaller and the wrong shape. In 1979, the map was withdrawn in favor of a new design based on geography.

Few complaints greeted the British motorway signage (see p.346) designed by Jock Kinneir (1917–94) and Margaret Calvert (b.1936) in a ten-year development program that began in the late 1950s. Unlike Vignelli, who flew the flag for Helvetica at every opportunity, Kinneir and Calvert surmised that the British public might find the Swiss sans serif font a little austere. The font they designed for the signage—Transport—was clear, legible, and shared similar antecedents to Helvetica, but it was more rounded and friendlier. A landmark of public service design, the signage has guided drivers from Land's End to John o' Groats, and it is now such an entrenched part of the country's visual identity that it is difficult to imagine what says "Britain" more.

Maps and signage set graphic designers the task of making navigation easier, more comprehensible, and safer for the traveler. "Navigation" in another sense can also be a requirement of texts, in which legibility is seen as a form of location. A classic example is the work of UK typographer Matthew Carter (b.1937) for US telecommunications giant Bell Telephone. In 1974 he designed a new typeface—Bell Centennial—to replace Bell Gothic, in which the company had previously printed its telephone directories. The challenge was to come up with a font that could be printed at high speed on cheap paper and retain its legibility. Carter's solution was to incorporate notches, or "ink traps," into the corners of the letters to allow for the spread of ink. The new typeface retained its clarity even when condensed. The result was fewer two-line address entries, fewer columns overall, and a considerable saving in paper.

US type designer W. A. Dwiggins (1880–1956) first used the term "graphic design" in the 1920s, and it was reintroduced by Richard Guyatt (1914–2007), who set up the school of graphic design at the Royal College of Art (RCA) in London in 1948. A proponent of a new cross-disciplinary approach, Guyatt mounted the first exhibition of graphic design at the RCA in 1963. Alumni included many who would go on to be prominent in the field, such as Alan Fletcher (1931–2006). Derek Birdsall (b.1934), who later taught at the school during the 1980s, was a colleague of Fletcher. Highly influential, his career encompasses the design of Penguin book covers, Pirelli calendars, and art direction for the seminal British magazine *Nova* (see image 2), as well as his redesign of the *Book of Common Worship* (2000), for which he chose Gill Sans.

Graphics also has its playful side. An iconic work of the 1960s is the "wall of words" (see image 1) designed by Lou Dorfsman (1918–2008), director of design at Columbia Broadcasting System, for the cafeteria of the New York headquarters designed by Eero Saarinen (1910–61). "Gastrotypographicalassemblage," as Dorfsman called it, was 35 feet (10.5 m) long, 8 feet (2.5 m) tall, and featured 1,450 letters, hand-milled from solid pine. It spelled out food-related words. **EW**

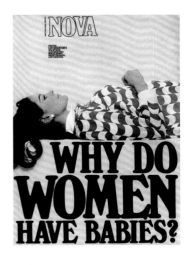

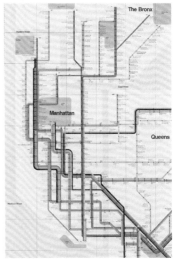

1966	1967	1971	1972	1972	1974
Lou Dorfsman's "wall of words" is completed and installed in the CBS cafeteria.	Vignelli designs the corporate identity for American Airlines. It remains in use for fifty years.	The Rolling Stones commission John Pasche (b.1945), a student at the RCA's school of design, to come up with their lips and tongue logo.	Vignelli designs the subway diagram for the New York Transit Authority. It arouses immediate controversy.	Pentagram, a leading British design studio, is founded by Alan Fletcher, Kenneth Grange, Theo Crosby, Bob Gill, and Mervyn Kurlansky.	Typographer Matthew Carter creates the Bell Centennial typeface for Bell Telephone in the United States.

Motorway Signage 1963

JOCK KINNEIR 1917–94   MARGARET CALVERT b.1936

👁 FOCAL POINTS

1 TYPEFACE
The typeface is a version of Akzidenz Grotesk. It was later named Transport. A sans serif font, it is more rounded than European modernist lettering. Upper and lower case letters were used, as this was deemed more legible than capitals only.

2 REFLECTIVE MATERIAL
The white elements on the motorway signs were made of a special reflective material that increased its visibility at night when caught in a car's headlights. The blue background was non-reflective, thus heightening the contrast.

3 COLOR
Sky blue, the background color of the motorway signs, is recessive in daylight; in other words, it does not jump out like "advancing" shades of red and orange. At night, the blue reads black, an equally effective foil for white lettering and numerals.

4 SPACING AND PROPORTION
Once the typeface had been designed, specific attention was paid to kerning (the spacing between certain combinations of letters). The size of the lettering relative to the sign was also scaled proportionately.

Jock Kinneir and Margaret Calvert's design has influenced road signage around the world.

T he signage created by Jock Kinneir and Margaret Calvert in the early 1960s for the United Kingdom's road network was part of an ambitious program of government-sponsored information design, conducted between 1957 and 1967. It was a model of coherence and legibility, and it transformed the way drivers navigated their way around the nation's roads. Instantly recognizable from Land's End to John o' Groats, and largely taken for granted, the signage effectively serves to brand the United Kingdom. The program was designed to coincide with the expansion of the road network and the construction of new motorways, which began in the late 1950s. The first section of the first motorway—the M1—ran from Watford to Rugby and it opened in 1959. At that time, existing road signs were chaotic and inconsistent and there were valid concerns that they would prove confusing and dangerous to motorists driving at speed (there was no speed limit in the 1950s).

The government committee set up to review the issue appointed Kinneir in 1963; he was a graphic designer who had previously designed the signage at Gatwick, London's newest airport. Kinneir, in turn, asked Calvert, a former student of his at Chelsea School of Art, to assist. It was an immense and complicated project. The immediate priority was to devise a system for the new motorways; later the pair was commissioned to come up with an equivalent for all other roads. From the outset, the motorway signs were conceived as maps of upcoming junctions. The main aim was to reduce information to the essence, and extensive testing was carried out to ensure readability at speed. For the lettering, Kinneir and Calvert came up with a new typeface, a sans serif font that was later named Transport. Great attention was paid to weight, spacing, and kerning, as well as to layout, scale, and proportion. **EW**

SYMBOLS AND PICTOGRAMS

For the road sign program, the committee specified the use of symbols rather than words. Kinneir and Calvert adopted the codes laid down by the Geneva Protocol of 1949: triangles for warning signs, circles for commands, and rectangles for information. While many of the symbols were abstract—no entry, no right turn, for example—the red triangle warning signs featured pictograms. Most of these were drawn by Calvert, who imbued them with character and personality. The triangle alerting drivers to beware of farm animals, for example, featured a pictogram of Patience, a cow on her cousin's farm. The leaping deer pictogram has been singled out as especially pleasing. Calvert has said that the "children crossing" sign (right) was the hardest to realize, but also the most satisfying. The previous sign had shown a boy in a school cap leading a little girl. Calvert's version, more egalitarian in keeping with the times, featured a girl leading a little boy. The girl was based on a photograph of herself as a child.

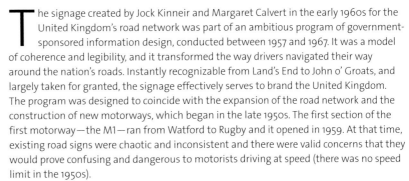

Cifra 3 1965
GINO VALLE 1923–2003

Plastic
3⅞ x 7 x 3¾ in.
10 x 18 x 9.5 cm

 **NAVIGATOR**

First and foremost a prolific architect, responsible for many significant buildings in Italy and around the world, Gino Valle was also an industrial designer who held firmly to the belief that products should reflect the user's needs. Notably, he collaborated with Italian manufacturer Zanussi on the identity of its washing machines and refrigerators. The Cifra 3 clock, which Valle designed in 1965 for display company Solari di Urbine, became a bestseller soon after its launch in 1966. No longer in production, but highly sought after, it is included in the collections of New York City's Museum of Modern Art and London's Science Museum. The clock makes use of a mechanism similar to those in split-flap indicator boards, which Solari also manufactured. Its crisp graphics and minimal form have made it a classic of post-war Italian design. The housing of the clock is made of plastic, the shape entirely determined by the rotating mechanism within the cylinder. As the roller blades move, individual plastic tiles or "cards" audibly flap into position.

Much of Valle's architectural work was carried out in and around his hometown of Udine, near Venice, where his father, Provino Valle, also had an architectural practice and where his son carries on the family tradition. The town features a church designed by Provino in commemoration of World War I and a monument to the Resistance designed by Valle himself, who was taken prisoner by the Germans in World War II and interned in Mauthausen camp following his activities with the Italian Resistance. **EW**

👁 FOCAL POINTS

1 CLEAR FRONT

The curved face of the clock is clear, revealing the movement of the parts. There are two rolls of numerals: 48 plastic flaps for the hours and 120 for the minutes. Flip clocks only work in one direction; in other words, they only flap downward, aided by gravity. A knob is used to wind the clock forward.

2 TYPEFACE

The typeface is Helvetica, chosen for its modernity. The numbers that show the hours are in bold face so that the clock can be read more easily from a distance. Instead of the familiar ticking sound of a clock, time is marked by an appealing flipping sound as each minute passes.

3 CYLINDRICAL FORM

The clock's cylindrical form entirely reflects the flipping mechanism of the roller blades that it contains; there is nothing superfluous about Valle's design and no ornamentation. The clock's simple futuristic shape is accentuated by the use of plastic for the casing.

🕐 DESIGNER PROFILE

1923–63

Born in Udine, Italy, Gino Valle studied architecture at the University of Venice and continued his studies at Harvard University in Massachusetts. During the 1950s he designed a number of buildings, mostly near Udine. In the late 1950s he began his fruitful associations with Zanussi and Solari. He won the Compasso d'Oro in 1956 and again in 1962.

1964–2003

International recognition included a one-man show at the Royal College of Art in London in 1964. Although Valle refused to work in commercial real estate development, he remained a prolific architect, employed in the United States, Germany, and France as well as in Italy. He also taught at universities in Europe and South Africa and at Harvard.

SOLARI BOARDS

The mechanism behind split-flap indicator boards (right), ubiquitous in railway stations and airports around the world until the advent of digital displays, was the brainchild of Solari's founder, self-taught engineer Remigio Solari. Valle worked on the design of the boards with inventor John Myer. Clearly visible from any angle and requiring little power, so-called Solari boards rapidly became an industry standard. They made the same noise as the Cifra 3 clock, and for many people the sound of changing arrivals and destinations is evocative of an earlier age of travel.

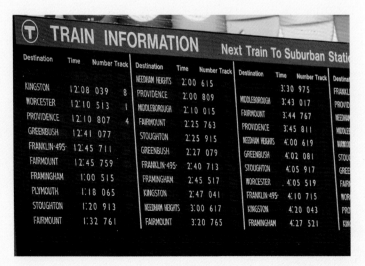

PLASTIC FANTASTIC

F or designers in the post-war period, the sculptural properties of plastic offered the opportunity to create an object that was made in one piece, or "monobloc." It was both an esthetic and a commercial aim, with the potential to bring design to a wider audience via a simplified manufacturing process. Initially, technical limitations meant that this vision could not be realized. The Tulip chair (1956; see p.294) by Eero Saarinen (1910–61) was designed originally to be manufactured as a single form. Instead, the molded fiberglass seat shell had to be mounted on a separate cast aluminum base. However, the all-white finish and flowing lines of the design create the illusion of material unity. Despite the efforts of many designers, the first one-piece plastic chair was not put into production until 1967, although its concept dated back to the beginning of the decade. This was the Panton chair (1960; see p.352) by Danish designer Verner Panton (1926–98), which takes the radical form of a cantilever. Although it has become a design icon, it was notoriously difficult to manufacture and has had a checkered production history.

KEY EVENTS

1960	1961	1963	1964	1965	1966
Verner Panton designs the first one-piece, molded plastic chair (see p.352). It takes the radical form of a glossy cantilever with a flared base.	The elegant Selene chair, designed by Vico Magistretti, is the first injection-molded chair in glass-reinforced plastic.	Robin Day designs the Polyprop chair, a molded plastic seat supported by tubular steel legs. The chair goes on to sell millions worldwide.	Yrjö Kukkapuro (b.1933) designs the Karuselli chair. With a fiberglass base and shell and upholstered in leather, this classic Finnish chair swivels and rocks.	Joe Colombo (1930–71) begins his design for the Universale monobloc chair. It is manufactured from 1968 by Kartell.	Swiss designer Hans Theo Baumann (b.1924) introduces a range of cutlery for children.

British designer Robin Day (1915–2010) took a different approach for his Polyprop chair (see image 2), which consists of a molded plastic shell supported by bent tubular steel legs. This design has the distinction of being the most commercially successful plastic chair ever made, selling in millions in twenty-three countries. It was the first to use injection-molded polypropylene, which had been invented almost a decade earlier in 1954. Stackable and available in a wide range of colors, the Polyprop is a familiar sight in public settings, from doctors' surgeries to school halls the world over.

By the mid to late 1960s, plastic had entered the arena of fashion and Pop Art. Notable designs that reflected this trend included the inflatable Blow chair (1967; see p.372), by the Milan-based studio of Jonathan de Pas (1932–91), Donato d'Urbino (b.1935), and Paolo Lomazzi (b.1936), and the Bubble chair (1968; see image 1)—a clear plastic shell suspended on a chain from the ceiling—by Eero Aarnio (b.1932). In the late 1960s plastic acquired a certain chic, thanks not only to technical improvements in the material itself, but also, more significantly, to the efforts of Italian designers to raise its status. Vico Magistretti (1920–2006) specialized in furniture and lamps, including the Chimera floor lamp (1969; see p.356), and produced pioneering examples in plastic. His sculptural Selene chair (1968) is comfortable, affordable, and stackable; the monobloc design is made from compression-molded fiberglass and has been reissued by the Heller company. Another Italian design classic is the Valentine typewriter (1969; see p.334). Designed for Olivetti by Ettore Sottsass (1917–2007), its casing is made from a bold red plastic that was chosen for its own merits, rather than its ability to mimic another "superior" material.

Plastic, of course, is not a single material but a family whose characteristics vary widely, the very feature that has made it so indispensable in the modern world. One of the ways in which Italian designers gave their plastic creations additional cachet was by opting for materials such as ABS (acrylonitrile butadiene styrene), which offered glossy surfaces that were visually appealing and tactile. ABS features widely in the designs marketed by Italian firm Kartell, which produced numerous desirable plastic products during this period.

While Italian designers sought to impart plastic with a new status—an esthetic of its own—its cheapness and versatility saw it adopted in products, both seen and unseen, including household appliances, cars, flooring, and electrical and plumbing goods; there was scarcely a product on the market that did not include a plastic element. During the early 1970s, conflict in the Middle East and the resulting oil crisis provided a wake-up call for a society that had become increasingly dependent on oil and the synthetic products of the petrochemical industry. Plastic was no longer cheap and the disposability of the Pop Art movement no longer looked like a sensible response to a world of limited resources. Plastic did not go away, but the days when designers saw the material as offering a "brave new world" of possibilities were over. **EW**

1 Eero Aarnio's Bubble chair (1968) consists of a blown hemisphere of acrylic containing cushions. It is suspended from the ceiling by a chain and steel ring, because the designer did not favor a transparent pedestal support.

2 The Polyprop chair (1963) by Robin Day has been manufactured in several different versions, including upholstered, with holes for drainage for use in the garden, and in children's sizes.

1967	1968	1968	1969	1969	1973
Anna Castelli Ferrieri (1918–2006) designs the modular Componibili units (see p.354). They are made of ABS plastic.	Eero Aarnio designs the Bubble chair. It appeals to exhibitionists who like to be exposed to public view.	Sergio Mazza (b.1931) designs the Toga—a stacking chair made from one continuous piece of fiberglass. It is produced by Mazza's company Artemide.	Ettore Sottsass designs the Valentine typewriter (see p.334) for Olivetti. The red plastic casing shows a positive commitment to plastic as a material.	Magistretti exploits plastic's flexibility and translucency to dramatic effect with his furled Chimera floor lamp (see p.356).	Following tensions in the Middle East, OPEC launches an oil embargo. The resulting oil crisis sees plastic prices rise dramatically.

Panton Chair 1960
VERNER PANTON 1926–98

✶ NAVIGATOR

Polyurethane foam
32¾ x 24 x 19¾ in.
83 x 61 x 50 cm

The work of Verner Panton represents a departure from what is typically conceived as Scandinavian modern design. Instead of using natural materials and traditional organic forms, he relished both space-age esthetics and brash synthetics, which led to a reputation among his Danish contemporaries as an *enfant terrible*. "The main purpose of my work," he said, "is to provoke people into using their imagination."

With its continuous back, seat, and base, the Panton chair represented the fulfilment of a dream shared by many post-war designers: to achieve a one-piece chair design in plastic. Although many previous plastic chairs looked as if they were monobloc, closer inspection would reveal the inevitable seams and joints that designers tried so hard to conceal. Bold, colorful, and sexy, the Panton chair won immediate acclaim when it was first exhibited at the Cologne Furniture Fair in 1968, and it has since become a design icon for a new generation. Its cantilevered form was groundbreaking, and its luscious curves and high glossy finish are clear references to automotive design. The design was not put into production until seven years after it was conceived: Panton's imagination was always a little ahead of what could be achieved technically. **EW**

👁 FOCAL POINTS

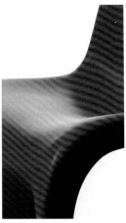

1 CONTOURED BODY SHELL
Panton's aim was to design a comfortable, all-purpose, affordable plastic chair. Although the seat and backrest of the chair are contoured carefully to fit the human frame, comfort is not the sole issue. Even when the chair is unoccupied, its curves and indentations give it a strong, almost animated presence. Viewed in profile, the cantilevered form is perfectly balanced. The chair was designed to be stackable and therefore versatile.

2 BRIGHT COLOR
The designer used bright color to arouse and stimulate. "Most people spend their lives living in dreary gray-beige conformity, mortally afraid of using colors," he wrote. Plastic could deliver color extremely well and this chair boldly announces the synthetic nature of the material.

3 LIPPED EDGE
The lipped edge that runs all the way around the flowing form of the Panton chair serves the practical function of giving the chair additional strength and rigidity. These qualities were of prime importance at the early stage of the development of plastics technology, when the chair was initially produced. At the same time, this lipped edge contributes to the fluid, almost sensuous lines of the chair's design. It was inspired by a stack of buckets.

4 FLARED BASE
The long sweep of the flared base resembles a tail fin or car bumper. Contemporary references to popular art and culture are a feature of Panton's work, and this design rapidly became an icon of the Pop art movement. More recently in 1995, it appeared on the cover of *Vogue* magazine.

🕐 DESIGNER PROFILE

1926–55
Verner Panton graduated in architecture from the Royal Danish Academy of Fine Arts in 1951. He spent two years working in the architectural office of Arne Jacobsen (1902–71), where he assisted in the design of the Ant chair (1952). Panton then set up his own practice in Copenhagen.

1956–60
The futuristic Cone chair (1958) and all-red interior, both designed for the Komigen inn on the island of Funen, caused a sensation, as did Panton's redesign of the Astoria restaurant in Trondheim, with its bright colors and Op Art influences.

1961–69
Panton designed lamps, furniture. and textiles for companies such as Fritz Hansen and Louis Poulsen. By the time the Panton chair was put into production in 1967, the designer had settled in Switzerland.

1970–98
Panton's psychedelic landscape installation, Visiona II, at the Cologne Furniture Fair in 1970, was hugely influential in its use of synthetic materials and space-age esthetics. His later work was an exploration of pure geometric forms.

PRODUCTION PROBLEMS

Once Verner Panton (above) had designed his unique chair, it proved notoriously difficult to produce and it took him three years to find a manufacturer. In collaboration with Vitra, Panton's chair was finally introduced to the public in 1967. Plastics technology had advanced significantly since the war, but it was nowhere near as sophisticated as it is today. Following technological developments, the Panton chair was made in greater numbers, but in 1979 Vitra withdrew it from production because the available plastics were not strong enough to support a sitter's weight without cracking. The chair was subsequently relaunched in 1990 in both polypropylene and polyurethane hard foam.

Componibili Modules 1967

ANNA CASTELLI FERRIERI 1918–2006

This display of Componibili modules combines round- and square-profile units. The door sizes vary, too, and castors have been fitted to some modules.

⬖ **NAVIGATOR**

Anna Castelli Ferrieri and her husband Giulio Castelli (1920–2006) founded the Milanese manufacturer Kartell in 1949, and it quickly became known for its innovative designs in plastic. Ferrieri had trained as an architect, and from the mid-1960s she designed many of the company's products.

Her Componibili modules, a set of storage units, were hugely successful and are still in production today. Used singly or in tiers, Componibili provide adaptable, functional storage for any area of the home. They are available in various sizes and in square or round formats, although the round shape is more common. Readily stacked by means of a vertical overlap, the units require only one lid per tower and may be fitted with castors. The distinctive sliding doors are operated by means of a simple finger hole.

The flexible functionality of the design depends heavily on the use of plastic, in this case acrylonitrile butadiene styrene (ABS), a type of thermoplastic. ABS is strong, shiny, and resistant; its most familiar application is in Lego, the children's building system.

In the late 1960s, plastic was mostly considered a low-status material, but Ferrieri helped to transform that reputation by giving her high-quality designs a strong and modern visual identity. She was aided in this by other inspired Italian designers, such as Gino Columbini, Vico Magistretti, Marco Zanuso, and Joe Colombo. Her Componibili are displayed at the Museum of Modern Art in New York City and at the George Pompidou Centre in Paris. In 1972, the New York City department store Bloomingdale's used the units to create an entire New York skyline in a memorable shop window display. **PS**

FOCAL POINTS

1 GLOSSY MATERIAL

The Componibili are made from ABS, a tough, high-quality, glossy plastic that Italian designers in the 1960s used extensively to give everyday objects a luxurious appearance. The ultra-modern material also gave the units a contemporary, space-age look in a domestic setting.

2 POP COLORS

In line with the neo-modern Pop aesthetic of the 1960s, the Componibili units were originally available in white, black, and red; other colors are now available. The finger hole used for opening the doors had an additional visual function as a striking black spot on the white and red versions.

3 FUNCTIONALITY

The Componibili units combined visual and functional simplicity. Each of the individual "stories" had an overlapping door that, when opened, traveled around the inner side of the module. The sliding doors meant that the units remained totally functional in restricted spaces.

▲ Ferrieri designed these striking Polo stools for Kartell in the 1970s. Made from metal and plastic, they were also available in other combinations of white, black, and red components.

DESIGNER PROFILE

1918–48

Anna Castelli Ferrieri was born in Milan in 1918. She studied architecture at Milan Polytechnic, and worked alongside the architect and designer Franco Albini (1905–77) for a period of time. She married Giulio Castelli in 1943, and edited the monthly magazine *Casabella* from 1946 to 1947.

1949–63

In 1949 the Castellis founded Kartell, a company that specialized in making objects from high-quality plastic. At first Kartell focused on manufacturing automobile accessories, but it shifted to objects for the domestic environment in 1963.

1964–75

Ferrieri personally began to design objects for Kartell in 1965. Commercially, her two most successful designs were the 4822/44 stool and the Componibili modular units.

1976–2006

Ferrieri became Kartell's art director in 1976. The combination of Giulio Castelli's background as a chemical engineer and her training as an architect proved to be highly successful.

KARTELL

Kartell earned a reputation not only for design but also fot experimentation in plastics technology. From the late 1950s onward, the company worked with leading architects and designers of the day, including in recent years Philippe Starck (b.1949) and Antonio Citterio (b.1950), designer of the Battista folding extension table (1991; above). Giulio Castelli's son, Claudio Luti (b.1946), intensified Kartell's collaboration with designers, and the company made revolutionary use of polycarbonate to create transparent furniture items.

Chimera Floor Lamp 1969

VICO MAGISTRETTI 1920–2006

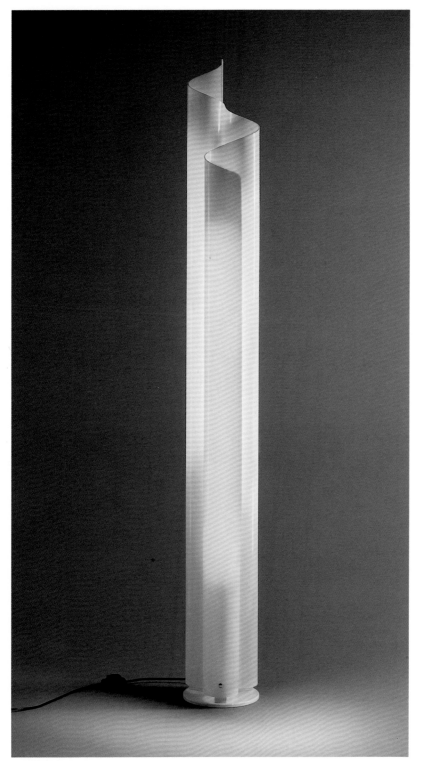

1 SCULPTURAL FORM
The Chimera was conceived as a piece of sculpture that emitted light and was intended to be equally intriguing whether or not it was switched on. Its curved, wavy form was made possible by the literally plastic qualities of the material from which it was fabricated.

2 TRANSLUCENT MATERIAL
The lamp was made of methacrylate, which is also known as acrylic and by a number of trade names, including Plexiglas. The lamp's curved surfaces were achieved by heating the material and bending it while it was still hot. The lamp's base was made of lacquered steel.

The Chimera floor lamp was one of the most expressive lighting designs created by Italian furniture designer and architect Vico Magistretti for the Artemide company. His other designs, including the Dalu and Eclisse, were more rational and overtly functional. For a brief time, Magistretti moved away from his strict, neo-modern approach to design and aligned himself with the more metaphorical, Pop-oriented designs of radical groups such as Archigram and Superstudio, which were adding figurative elements to otherwise functional products and introducing elements of kitsch and irony. The Chimera is a rare example of Magistretti playing with imagery, and allowing his design to operate simultaneously on the levels of function and expression.

The Chimera is named after the fire-breathing monster of Greek mythology that is part lion, part goat, part snake. While Magistretti's design is no such hybrid, its furled top resembles a flickering flame, especially when the lamp is illuminated. A powerful, evocative object, the Chimera lamp brings an emotional quality to the space it inhabits. A key element of the design is the soft, diffused quality of ambient light that is emitted, and the lamp is intended to enhance the space it illuminates by accentuating its volume. Thus, the owner can adjust the three separate light sources set within the vertical body to vary the intensity of the light emitted, according to the time of day. The lamp's shell is made from translucent opal methacrylate, which has visual warmth when illuminated; the material contributes to the muted effect. **PS**

◈ NAVIGATOR

Illuminated or not, the elegant, undulating Chimera serves as a sculptural spatial object.

◷ COMPANY PROFILE

1960–71
Artemide was founded by Ernesto Gismondi (b.1931) and Sergio Mazza (b.1931) in 1960 at Pregnana Milanese, near Milan. It focused on lighting products created by well-known designers. Its first lamp, Alfa, had been designed by Mazza in 1959.

1972–85
In 1972 Artemide launched one of its most successful lamps, Tizio, designed by Richard Sapper (b.1932). It took the international reputation of the company to a new level. The flexible task light appeared in interiors across the globe.

1986–THE PRESENT
In 1986 Artemide had another huge success with Tolomeo, designed by Michele de Lucchi (b.1951) and Giancarlo Fassina (b.1935). Since then, Artemide has been awarded many prizes, including the Compasso d'Oro in 1995 and the European Design Prize in 1997.

◄ In 1966 Magistretti produced these preliminary sketches for lamps that eventually would be taken into production by the Artemide company, first as the Chimera (1969), and then as the Mezzachimera (1970).

SPACE AGE

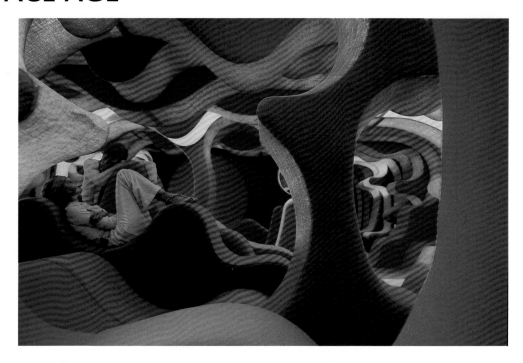

Interest in space exploration gripped the public imagination throughout the 1960s, culminating in the Apollo moon landing in 1969, hence the term "space age" as a description of the decade. Although it specifically alludes to space exploration, space age is an evocative term that conjures up a gamut of other technological advances, from computing to plastics to aeronautics, as well as the visual culture and iconography of space travel as manifested in fashion, design, and film. One of the most tangible spin-offs from the National Aeronautics and Space Administration's (NASA) space programme was Mylar, a synthetic foil developed for spacesuits to protect astronauts from radiation. It was later adopted by the US wallpaper industry as a decorative silvered finish.

For furniture designers, the space age was a philosophical construct as well as a practical aspiration. It was about breaking the mold and pushing boundaries. Harnessing new materials and technology, space-age designers explored radical concepts that challenged prevailing esthetics and conventions, demonstrating creative ingenuity and technological awareness. Danish-born Verner Panton (1926–98) and Finnish-born Eero Aarnio (b.1932) epitomized the rebellious aspect of space-age design. Turning their backs on Scandinavian traditions, they embraced manmade materials such as plastics and explored a

KEY EVENTS

1957–58	1961	1962	1963	1963	1964–65
The Soviet Union launches two unmanned satellites, Sputniks 1 and 2, in 1957; the United States launches its Explorer 1 satellite in 1958.	Russian cosmonaut Yuri Gagarin (1934–68) becomes the first man in space, orbiting Earth in a Vostok spacecraft on 12 April.	Telstar, the first communication satellite, is launched, enabling news and images to be transmitted around the globe.	Three giant golf ball-shaped radomes are erected as part of a Ballistic Missile Early Warning System at RAF Fylingdales in North Yorkshire, England.	Eero Aarnio designs the Ball chair (see p.360), a large fiberglass sphere supported on a pedestal.	US Mariner 4 space probe sends back close-up images of Mars in 1964; Russian cosmonaut Aleksey Leonov (b.1934) takes a space walk in 1965.

self-consciously futuristic vocabulary of geometric shapes and artificial colors. Panton's work became increasingly daring and adventurous over the course of the decade, culminating in his legendary Visiona II installation at the Cologne Furniture Fair in 1970 (see image 1).

French designers, such as Pierre Paulin (1927–2009) and Olivier Mourgue (b.1939), also embraced space-age design. Paulin's Ribbon chair (1966) and Tongue chair (1967) for the Dutch firm Artifort looked like something from outer space, although their fluid, twisting upholstered forms were fabricated from tubular steel, padded with synthetic foam. Mourgue's quirky biomorphic Djinn chair and sofa (see image 2) were also ahead of their time.

Italian designers were at the forefront of technological developments in furniture and lighting during the 1960s, particularly in the field of plastics. Esthetically and conceptually, they were also extremely advanced. One of the most influential figures of the decade was Joe Colombo (1930–71), who relished the opportunity of creating installations—or "environments," as they were known—as well as individual furniture designs. His Tube chair (1969) for Flexform consisted of a group of padded cylinders that could be linked together in various configurations. When not in use, the rolls could be stored inside each other like Russian dolls, a highly original concept.

Pattern designers were also prompted to develop new space-age imagery by recent breakthroughs in science and technology. Eddie Squires (1940–95) and his colleague Sue Palmer (b.1947) created an extraordinary collection to celebrate the Apollo moon landing, featuring images of rockets and astronauts. What united all these designers from diverse disciplines was their enthusiasm for the space age, and their desire to take design into another realm. **LJ**

1 Verner Panton's space-age environment was created from interlocking Pantower sculptural foam-covered seats for Bayer at the Cologne Furniture Fair in 1970 to promote synthetic home furnishings.

2 Olivier Mourgue's Djinn rubber and foam sofa of 1965 looked so futuristic that it was chosen to furnish the space station in the science-fiction film *2001: A Space Odyssey* (1968).

1967	1968	1968	1969	1969	1970
US architect Buckminster Fuller (1895–1983) creates a huge spherical geodesic dome for the US Pavilion at the Montreal Expo.	Finnish architect Matti Suuronen (1933–2013) designs the Futuro House, an ovoid fiberglass pod on steel legs resembling a space capsule.	Stanley Kubrick's (1928–99) film *2001: A Space Odyssey* features Olivier Mourgue's Djinn chairs and Arne Jacobsen's (1902–71) AJ cutlery (1957).	Neil Armstrong (1930–2012) and Buzz Aldrin (b.1930) become the first men to walk on the moon on 21 July.	The Anglo-French supersonic aircraft Concorde (see p.362) takes its maiden flight in March and breaks the sound barrier in October.	Verner Panton creates his striking space-age Visiona II installation at the Cologne Furniture Fair for German chemical company Bayer.

Ball Chair 1963
EERO AARNIO b.1932

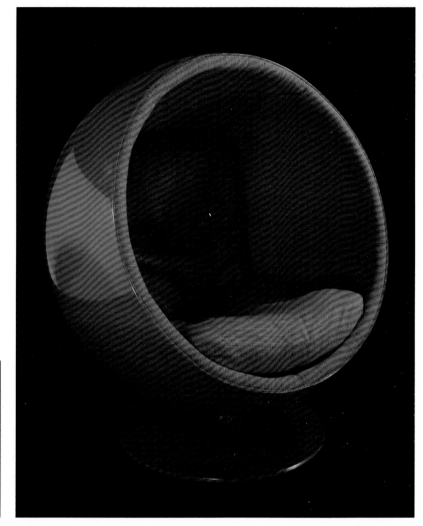

⊕ NAVIGATOR

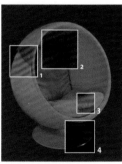

The Ball chair is made from fibreglass and upholstered in fabrics such as cashmere or leather.

Eero Aarnio was at the forefront of a new generation of iconoclastic young designers who transformed the design world during the 1960s. He broke away from the restrained esthetics and natural materials associated with Finnish design and started experimenting with plastics, particularly fiberglass-reinforced polyester resin. Aarnio was part of the liberated Pop generation who believed that design should look to the future and express the ideas and interests of young people. Capturing the zeitgeist of the Swinging Sixties, the Ball chair became an icon and was featured in the cult television series *The Prisoner* (1967–68) and the film *The Italian Job* (1969). The Ball chair reflects the idealism of the space age, the idea of exploring new frontiers. Echoing the shape of an astronaut's helmet, it was boldly futuristic, like something from a science-fiction film. Circular motifs had already been widely adopted by textile and wallpaper designers and cylindrical forms were increasingly prevalent in modern buildings. Spheres marked a natural progression. Plastics, the materials of the future, were the solution, as they could be molded into exciting forms hitherto unimagined in the history of furniture. The Ball chair was a beacon of space-age modernity in concept, color, and shape. **LJ**

👁 FOCAL POINTS

1 SHELL
The spherical shell is molded from fiberglass-reinforced polyester resin. The most remarkable feature of this chair is its spherical form, sliced open to create a seat. The Ball chair embraced a new vocabulary of circular forms, expressing the futuristic aspirations of the Space Age.

2 INTERIOR
The sphere provides the opportunity to create a self-contained environment. Padded with foam and upholstered with fabric, the interior enables the sitter to curl up inside as if in the womb. Optional extras, such as speakers, reinforce the idea of retreating from the world.

3 COLOUR
Space-age design was characterized by a high-intensity palette. Tomato red and zingy orange were popular, expressing the energy of Pop design. Black and white featured prominently, reflecting the influence of Op Art. The Ball chair appeared in all four colors.

4 PEDESTAL
The Ball chair eschews conventional legs in favor of a circular pedestal base. Low and wide to provide balance and prevent the chair from toppling over, the base is made of aluminum sprayed with an enamel finish to match the color of the seat, so that the two elements harmonize visually.

🕐 DESIGNER PROFILE

1932–59
Eero Aarnio was born in Helsinki, Finland. After studying at the School of Applied Arts in Helsinki from 1954 to 1957, he began practicing as a furniture designer.

1960–69
From 1960 to 1962, Aarnio worked as a designer for the Finnish furniture company Asko Oy, continuing his relationship with the firm after establishing his own design practice in 1962. Moving away from Scandinavian traditions, he began experimenting with plastics. Some of his most iconic designs were created over the next few years, including the Ball chair, the Bubble chair (1965), and the Pastilli chair (1968).

1970–PRESENT
In addition to furniture, product design, and interior design, Aarnio pursued other interests in photography and graphic design, for example. From 1978 to 1982 he ran a design studio in Germany. Since then his design office has been based at Veikkola in Finland. Always forward-looking, Aarnio embraced computer-aided design in the 1980s and remains active as a designer in the 21st century.

SPHERICAL DESIGNS

Redolent of the 1960s, there is something arresting about spherical designs, be it a chair, a building, or a lamp. Spherical buildings were pioneered by Buckminster Fuller in his geodesic domes, such as the US Pavilion at the Montreal Expo in 1967. In domestic products, spheres were successfully exploited by Hugh Spencer and John Magyar in their globe-shaped record-player speakers for the Clairtone Sound Corporation in Canada (c. 1963), and by Arthur Bracegirdle in his plastic television console for the US firm Keracolor (c. 1969). Verner Panton was one of the first designers to adopt circular and spherical forms, initially in his Moon lamp for Louis Poulsen (1960). His Flower Pot pendant lamps (1968), juxtaposing spherical and hemispherical forms, were produced in similar colors to Aarnio's Ball chair.

Concorde 1967

VARIOUS

Although Concorde was a technical marvel, it proved inefficient and expensive compared to other planes. Its last commercial flight took place on 24 October 2003.

✦ NAVIGATOR

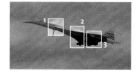

Along with the landing of Apollo 11 on the moon in 1969, the aeronautical event of the decade was the maiden flight of Concorde, the world's first supersonic passenger aircraft, on 2 March 1969. Conceived by the British Aircraft Corporation (BAC) in 1961, Concorde was brought to fruition by an Anglo-French team after BAC joined forces with the French company Sud-Aviation (part of Aérospatiale). Originally known in the United Kingdom as "Concord" (meaning agreement), the French spelling was adopted after the first prototype—Concorde 001—was unveiled in Toulouse on 11 December 1967.

The Olympus 593 turbojet engine used to power Concorde was developed by Rolls-Royce's Engine Division at Bristol. Known as twinspool, it had two separate compressors, each driven by its own turbine, so it was effectively two engines in one. Fuel was injected into a combustion chamber containing hot compressed air, then ignited. Hot gases ejected through the rear jet pipe drove the turbine and provided forward thrust.

Following Concorde's maiden flight, testing continued until 1 October 1969, when it became truly supersonic and broke the speed of sound, cruising at 1,350 miles per hour (2,180 km/h). Concorde made its first transatlantic crossing in September 1971, but it was five years before the aircraft entered service and began scheduled flights. **LJ**

1 WINGS

Concorde had large, slender, triangular wings extending over half the length of the fuselage. To facilitate both subsonic and supersonic flying, the wings were ingeniously shaped, both widthwise in terms of camber and taper, and lengthwise in terms of droop and twist.

2 BODY

The main structural material was a copper-based aluminum alloy, with some components being milled from solid lumps of metal. Chosen for its lightness, strength, and flexibility, the metal was rigorously tested before being approved, including its ability to withstand "creep," which is the deformation caused by interaction between mechanical loadings and high temperatures.

3 FUSELAGE

Concorde had an unusually long, slender fuselage measuring 204 feet (62 m). The reason for its strikingly elegant body shape was to make the plane as streamlined and aerodynamic as possible in order to reduce drag. Only this way could it break the speed of sound.

◀ Although Concorde's droop snoot was visually striking, the reason behind it was technical rather than esthetic. Dipping the nose and lowering the visor ensured that the pilot had much better visibility during take-off and landing. Once the plane had reached sufficient altitude, the nose was straightened, making it more streamlined so the plane could fly faster, while protecting the flight deck from the extreme heat and pressure caused by flying at supersonic speed.

POP

1 The figures on the collage for the cover of *Sgt. Pepper's Lonely Hearts Club Band* suggest the zeitgeist of Pop in the 1960s.

2 Mary Quant cosmetics, such as this lipstick and nail varnish (*c.* 1966), are easily recognizable by the daisy logo.

3 Peter Murdoch's disposable Chair Thing was created from a single piece of die-cut, folded card.

The emergence of built-in obsolescence during the 1950s, combined with the concept of disposability and the growth of youth culture and its associated spending power, influenced a radical new approach to design, based on values linked to ephemerality, that rejected the old idea of "form follows function" (see p.168). Rather than the top-down approach of the early modernists, Pop brought people power into play.

The earliest manifestation of Pop was in fine art. The collage *Just What Is It That Makes Today's Homes So Different, So Appealing* (1956) by UK artist Richard Hamilton (1922–2011) is generally considered to represent the birth of a movement that derived its subject matter from consumer culture. On both sides of the Atlantic, artists such as Patrick Caulfield (1936–2005), Roy Lichtenstein (1923–97), and Andy Warhol (1928–87) drew on imagery from cartoons, advertising, food packaging. and television news to make works that both celebrated popular taste and commented on it ironically.

Unsurprisingly, given such antecedents, the Pop ethos first spread to the highly reactive media of fashion and graphic design, before reaching the

KEY EVENTS

1959	1963	1964	1965	1965	1966
The Austin Mini car (see p.366) is launched. It becomes a British icon in the 1960s and a symbol of Swinging London.	Mary Quant, known for her design of the miniskirt, wins the first ever Dress of the Year award.	Finnish textile designer Maija Isola (1927–2001) designs the iconic Unikko (poppy) print pattern (see p.368), presaging the flower-power era.	Peter Murdoch designs a child's chair made of paper. It is the first paper chair designed for mass production and sells in large numbers.	The Lytegem Lamp (see p.370) by Michael Lax is brought into production. Its sphere and cube design epitomizes the "fun'" side of Pop.	An exhibition of works by Aubrey Beardsley (1872–98) is held at London's Victoria and Albert Museum. It helps shape Pop poster design.

disciplines of furniture design and architecture, whose long lead times naturally make influences slower to appear. It was also overwhelmingly linked to young people and to the lifestyle accessories of the new throwaway culture—such as clothing, records, and posters—that they increasingly desired as a means of distinguishing themselves from their parents' generation. In parallel was the explosive growth of pop music.

For a time in the early 1960s, coinciding with the arrival of the Beatles and the Rolling Stones on the music scene, Swinging London was the epicenter of pop culture. In fashion UK designer Mary Quant (b.1934) led the way, with miniskirts, knee socks, and pinafores, showcased by leggy, doe-eyed models such as Twiggy (b.1949), expressing their child-like inspiration. Quant leveraged her brand, launching a line of cosmetics in 1966 that was an instant success, and its packaging's simple shapes reflected those of her clothes designs (see image 2). The clothes, which were cheap enough to appeal to a younger generation, were sold through the new retail environment of the boutique, emblazoned with bold color inside and out, where customers could shop to the sound of loud music. The rapid turnover of designs brought a frenzy to the fashion scene. Many of the boutiques were located in Carnaby Street, where the entrepreneur John Stephen (1934–2004) owned several such outlets. Tommy Roberts's (1942–2012) Mr Freedom store on the King's Road in Chelsea offered highly desirable items to young Londoners, and attracted clients that included Twiggy and Mick Jagger (b.1943). Fashion photography was transformed in those years, with working-class newcomers, such as David Bailey (b.1938) and Terence Donovan (1936–96), making a big impact.

In the world of graphic design, record covers served as blank canvases for the cultural mood. Robert Freeman's (b.1936) photographs of the Beatles appeared on one of their album covers, while Pop artist Peter Blake (b.1932) worked with his then wife Jann Haworth (b.1942) on the sleeve cover of the *Sgt. Pepper's Lonely Hearts Club Band* album of 1967 (see image 1). Posters to adorn the bedroom walls of young people also received the Pop treatment.

While Pop fashion and graphic design were, by their nature, ephemeral (there was even a fad for dresses made out of paper), furniture began to show a similar influence. In the UK, Peter Murdoch (b.1940) designed his polka-dot paper chair in 1968 (see image 3) and Roger Dean (b.1944) produced his Sea Urchin foam chair (1968) for Hille, which is cited as the forerunner of the bean bag. In France the work of Pierre Paulin (1927–2009), with its free-flowing forms, was directly influenced by the Pop revolution, while in Italy the anti-designers, Superstudio, Archizoom, Gruppo NNNN, and others, inspired by the radical work of architect and designer Ettore Sottsass (1917–2007), embraced the anti-form, anti-chic, and, ultimately, anti-design Pop ethos. Their creations, such as Archizoom's Dream beds (1967) envisaged a world in which fantasy and reality were united, and there were no physical boundaries. **PS**

1967	1967	1967	1967	1968	1969
The Beatles release *Sgt. Pepper's Lonely Hearts Club Band*. The album's innovative Pop artwork features cardboard cut-outs of famous people with the band.	Ettore Sottsass's show of Pop-influenced totem ceramics, "Miljö för en ny planet" (Landscape for a new planet), is held in Stockholm.	The British pavilion at the Expo held in Montreal pays homage to Pop design, and features mannequins wearing clothes designed by Quant.	Italian manufacturing company Zanotta launches the inflatable Blow chair (see p.372). It is one of the first pieces of furniture made from PVC.	The Milan Triennale of 1968 was closed prematurely because of student protests. Many of the anti-designers contributed to it.	Tommy Roberts opens the Mr Freedom boutique in London, selling brightly colored Pop fashions with bold graphics by young designers.

Austin Mini Cooper S 1963

ALEC ISSIGONIS 1906–88

👁 FOCAL POINTS

1 ROOF
While the standard Mini was available in one overall color, the Cooper S has a roof-panel color that contrasts with the rest of the shell. The two-tone body panels and interior trim make the Cooper S styling distinctive. Its grille and badge are also different.

2 INTERIOR
As well as higher engine capacity, there are a number of different design details between the Mini and Mini Cooper S. The seat covers were made of vinyl in two colors with brocade in the middle, and three different styles of sun visor were available.

3 WHEEL
The standard Mini and the Cooper S were made on the same assembly lines. The wheels of the Mini are 10 inches (25.5 cm) in diameter, but the Cooper S has perforations to make them appear racier. The Cooper S also came with radial ply tires.

4 WINDOW
The Mini is small because Issigonis designed it with a transverse engine and front-wheel drive layout, so 80 per cent of the floor plan is available for passengers and luggage. The windows are as large as they could be to give passengers a sense of space.

The standard Austin/Morris Mini, designed by Alec Issigonis, was launched in 1959. It was intended as a people's car, a small, cheap model that would put Britain on wheels. It was meant to compete with its European equivalents—Germany's VW Beetle (see p.210), France's Citroen 2CV, and Italy's Fiat's 600 and 500 among them. Although Issigonis had already entered that field working on the Morris Minor of 1948, until the arrival of the Mini, Britain lagged behind other countries in the small car market.

The Austin Mini was quickly a great success. Its innovative design with its compact dimensions revolutionized the small-car market. Initially, the Mini was not conceived as a high-power competition car and only had an engine capacity of 848 cc. But the owner of the Cooper Car Company, John Cooper (1923–2000), the creator of Formula One and rally cars, saw the potential in the Mini and worked with Issigonis to create the Mini Cooper with a racing tuned 997 cc engine, twin carburettors, and and front disc brakes. It was launched in 1961, and the more powerful Mini Cooper S, with a 1,071 cc engine and larger disc brakes, followed two years later. They proved successful as rally cars and won the Monte Carlo Rally in 1964, 1965, and 1967. The car nearly won the 1966 race, but was disqualified after the finish because its headlights contravened the rules. Approximately 14,000 Cooper S models were built between 1962 and 1967. The Cooper models represent only 2.5 percent of all the Minis ever made. The Mini had a production run of 5.3 million units and became the bestselling British car in history. **PS**

◈ NAVIGATOR

The boxy shape of the Mini became a familiar sight on the fashionable streets of London during the 1960s.

◷ DESIGNER PROFILE

1906–48

Born in Smyrna (then a Greek port, now Izmir, Turkey), Alec Issigonis moved to England where he studied engineering at Battersea Polytechnic. In 1936 he took a job at Morris Motors and was involved in the design of the Morris Minor (1948).

1949–88

Issigonis left Morris Motors to work for Alvis, where he helped Alex Moulton (1920–2012) create his revolutionary bicycle. He then returned to British Motors (the merged Morris and Austin), where he worked on the Mini. He also worked with Italian studio Pininfarina on British Motors' Austin 1100 (1963).

SWINGING LONDON

Although the Mini was designed as a people's car for families, it soon took on a different image as a symbol of Swinging London. It became the preferred car of a number of celebrities, both female and male. Magazines and newspapers showed it whizzing round London's streets and models, such as Twiggy, were photographed getting out of Minis in their miniskirts. The Beatles also drove Minis, as did many actors, including Steve McQueen (1930–80), Dudley Moore (1935–2002), and Peter Sellers (1925–80). The Mini even became a film star itself and models, including the Cooper S, appear in the 1969 film *The Italian Job* (above) as the getaway cars in a gold heist.

▲ The small size and light weight of the Cooper and Cooper S gave them a competitive edge as rally cars. They were used by top drivers, including James Hunt (1947–93) and Jackie Stewart (b.1939).

Unikko (Poppy) Textile 1964

MAIJA ISOLA 1927–2001

The large scale of the repeated
motif expresses confidence
and energy.

 NAVIGATOR

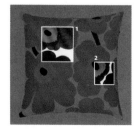

One of the most recognizable and enduring prints designed by Maija Isola for
Finnish textile company Marimekko, Unikko (or "poppy") was designed during
the heyday of Pop. With the design's second wave of popularity coinciding with
the revival of interest in decorative pattern in the early 2000s, it has become something
of a Marimekko trademark. The fame of the print is such that it has been featured as
livery on Finnair jets, in a blue, green, and gray colorway.

Isola designed more than 500 patterns for Marimekko during her thirty-eight-year
association with them. Throughout her life she took inspiration from many different
sources, ranging from nature to folk art. She was provoked to create this pattern when
Armi Ratia, one of Marimekko's founders, publicly declared that the company did not
produce floral prints, presumably as an implied criticism of the kind of demure patterns
that were common in furnishing and dress materials at the time. Unikko was Isola's
response. It married two elements of her previous work: inspiration directly taken from
nature and a strong graphic approach. **EW**

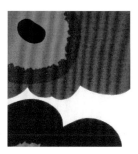

1 COLOR

Well-judged clashing shades of pink and poppy red are offset by a crisp, white background with accents of black. The bold colors are youthful and enthusiastic, and capture the irreverent mood of Pop. Other equally strong colorways—notably blue and yellow—have been introduced over the years.

2 GRAPHIC EDGE

Like many Finnish designers, Isola was profoundly influenced by nature. Expressed in a crisp, graphic style, with flat patterning, her motifs are punchy and memorable. Exuberance comes from the exploding forms of the poppies and the asymmetry of the pattern.

⊙ DESIGNER PROFILE

1927–51

Born in Riihimäki, Finland, Maija Isola studied at the Central School of Industrial Arts in Helsinki and graduated in 1949. Her first textile designs, screen-printed cotton fabrics, were created for Printex, a Helsinki-based textile company that was founded in the same year. In 1951 Marimekko was set up by Viljo Ratia and his wife, Armi, to promote Printex fabrics within its collections of furnishing fabrics and dress materials. Isola began an association with the company that would last nearly forty years.

1952–2001

During her years as principal textile designer for Marimekko, Isola created more than 500 prints. Some of the most memorable include Kivet (1956), Putkinotko (1957), Lokki (1961), Ananas (1962), Melooni (1963), Unikko (1964), Kaivo (1964), Tuuli (1971), and Primavera (1974). Isola's daughter, Kristina, joined Marimekko in 1964 at the age of eighteen and worked alongside her mother. During Kristina's childhood, Isola traveled widely in search of artistic inspiration, leaving her daughter to be raised by her grandmother. During the latter part of her life, Isola left behind the world of textiles and devoted herself to painting.

ADAPTABLE DESIGNS

Few pattern designs have been as successful as Unikko across so many different applications. Bed linen, wall panels, wellington boots, cosmetic bags, and shower curtains are just some of the products to feature the well-known print. In recent years, Irish designer Orla Kiely (b.1963) has created similarly iconic and adaptable patterns, including her stylized "stem" motif (above). This simple graphic print has found its way onto phone cases, audio equipment, and even London's double-decker buses.

▲ The striking Kaivo pattern (far right), with its large-scale repeat, was designed by Isola for Marimekko in the same year as Unikko. Tribal art was an inspiration for the bold, wavy pattern with its graphic contours and strong color contrasts. Kaivo has been reissued in new colorways devised by Isola's daughter Kristina.

Lytegem Lamp 1965

MICHAEL LAX 1929–99

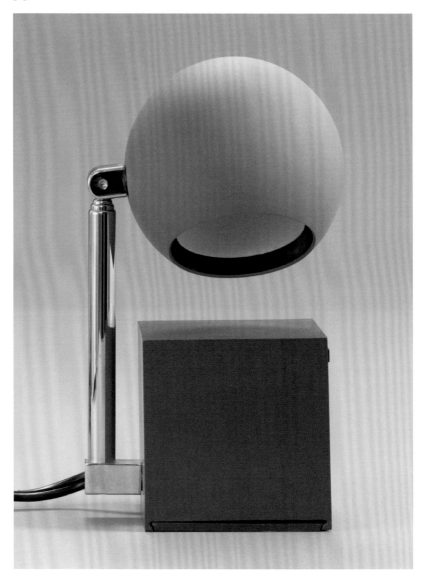

Plastic, zinc and aluminum
5 x 3 x 3½ in.
38 x 7.5 x 9 cm

👁 FOCAL POINTS

1 NECK
The strongest feature of the reading light is the functionality and flexibility made possible by its telescoping neck, which swivels 360 degrees. Its offers two levels of light intensity, which can be achieved by the flick of a switch on the cube base. The base is weighted for stability.

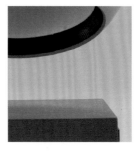

2 SPHERE AND CUBE
The lamp consists of a sphere resting on a cube. As such, it epitomizes the Bauhaus approach to design and recalls interwar modernism. Lax's use of metal and that of the three basic colors—black, white, and red—reinforced his commitment to the modernist design esthetic.

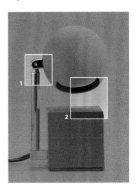

Designed in 1964 and manufactured by Lightolier in the following year, Michael Lax's telescoping reading light is an icon of 1960s design. It epitomizes the period's neo-modernism, Pop sensibility, and focus on lifestyle. The cube base houses a transformer and the ball reflector extends on a telescopic arm. While the design performs its function, enabling its user to read with the aid of an intense, localized light, made more accessible by its telescoping neck, its simple geometric forms add a strong sculptural presence to its environment. Flexibility is built into the design: it can be used as a table task lamp or it can be wall mounted and used as a sconce.

A highly acclaimed and successful industrial designer, Lax's primary interest, however, was sculpture, a discipline to which he dedicated his later life. His background in ceramics gave him an instinctive feel for materials and handcrafting. Lax came out of the Scandinavian tradition. Having spent time in Finland, he saw how that country's designers combined craft sensibilities with the esthetic of Pop. Throughout his designing career he remained committed to adding sculptural form to everyday utensils. In addition to his enameled ironware cookware designs for Copco, he created glassware and tableware for Mikasa and Rosenthal, a bath for American Cyanamid, and containers for Tupperware. He also worked in exhibition and graphic design, and created a series of wooden equipment for children's playgrounds. The Lytegem light is in the permanent collection of the Museum of Modern Art in New York City. **PS**

① DESIGNER PROFILE

1929–55
Born in New York, Lax trained in ceramics, graduating in 1947 from the New York School of Music and Art in New York City and in 1951 from Alfred University in Alfred, New York. In 1954 Lax won a Fulbright Fellowship to Finland, where he learned about modern Scandinavian design.

1956–99
Lax worked on dinnerware for Russel Wright (1904–76). In 1960 Lax began working for Copco. This was followed by work for Lightolier. In 1977 he won the Rome Prize and went to Italy, returning there in 1984 to work on sculpture.

COPCO TEA KETTLE

Lax worked for Copco from 1960, creating a line of cast-iron and porcelain enamel cookware. Cast-iron cookware had been very traditional in its design. His enamel-coated tea kettle (1962; above) features a bent teakwood handle, and became a design icon. The cast-iron pieces were manufactured in Denmark. Redolent of Scandinavian examples, it introduced a new esthetic to the United States. Copco later offered the kettle in a range of bright colors—red, blue, and yellow—which was innovative at the time. Lax continued to contribute designs to Copco throughout the 1980s.

▲ The telescoping neck on the Lytegem Lamp allows the height to be adjusted from 6½ inches (16.5 cm) to 15 inches (38 cm). There is also a humorous element, because the light has the appearance of a visitor from outer space.

Blow Chair 1967
VARIOUS

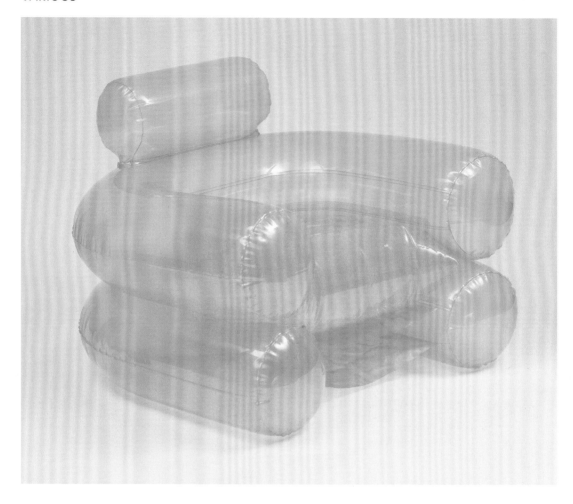

PVC plastic
33 x 47⅛ x 40¼ in.
84 x 119.5 x 102 cm

 NAVIGATOR

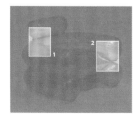

Designed by the Italian studio De Pas, D'Urbino, Lomazzi for the Italian company Zanotta, the Blow chair was the first mass-produced inflatable chair. It is an example of a form of seating that transformed the nature of furniture from static, conservative, status-ridden objects to flexible, lifestyle-oriented artefacts that worked around people's lives. Its lightness, transparency, compactness, and portability suited the ideals of the Pop generation. Given that the chair was inflatable, it was seen as an ephemeral object and appealed to young people who did not want to be tied down by material possessions. It was also as usable outdoors as indoors, even in a swimming pool.

The Blow chair is radical from a technological perspective, being one of the first furniture items to be made of polyvinyl chloride (PVC). It was the first piece of furniture designed by the group of architect-designers—Jonathan de Pas (1932–91), Donato D'Urbino (b.1935), Paolo Lomazzi (b.1939), and Carla Scolari—and they based it on an inflatable raft. It is made from individual sheets of PVC joined together using high-frequency welding—a process in which high-frequency waves are passed through the plastic. The heat under pressure seals the cells of the material together.

Zanotta showed that there was an international market for Pop furniture design that was affordable and in stark contrast to contemporary high-style Italian design. The Blow chair helped give Zanotta an international reputation. **PS**

👁 FOCAL POINTS

1 SEAMS
A great deal of research went into the high-frequency welding process to join the seams of the PVC skin. The novel techniques involved were inspired by the space race. The result is a strong plastic chair that can withstand being inflated so that it feels solid and can support the weight of a sitter. The chair came with an air pump to inflate it.

2 TRANSPARENCY
The Blow chair was originally available in blue, yellow, and red, as well as clear PVC. But all the chairs produced were transparent. This was a deliberate strategy on the part of its designers to show that they were rejecting the hard, solid forms of design modernism. The chair embodies the playful spirit of freedom and fun at the time.

▲ Designed by Piero Gatti (b.1940), Cesare Paolini (1937–83), and Franco Teodoro (1939–2005) for Zanotta, the Sacco (1968) is a fabric cover filled with polystyrene beads. Unlike modernist furniture icons, the beanbag's form is determined by how a sitter wants to sit.

INFLATABLE FURNITURE

The mid to late 1960s saw a wide range of inflatable and disposable furniture designs created in a number of different countries. Denmark's Verner Panton (1926–98) started before the others, creating an inflatable stool in the 1950s, which was launched on the market in 1960. He went on to create a number of other similar pieces. In Britain, architect Arthur Quarmby (b.1934) designed an inflatable pouffe in 1965 for Pakamac Special Products. The clear PVC inflatable seat cushion was octagonal in shape, with a central column that was not inflated to help maintain the cushion shape and indicate the seat. In France, Vietnamese-born Quasar Khanh (b.1934) invented a car, the Quasar-Unipower or Cube (right), manufactured from 1967 to 1968. The boxlike car had plastic inflatable seats, a glass roof, and sliding glass doors. Khanh also produced his Aerospace line of inflatable furniture in a Parisian toy factory between 1968 and 1972, effectively making them by hand.

THE MODERN CONSUMER

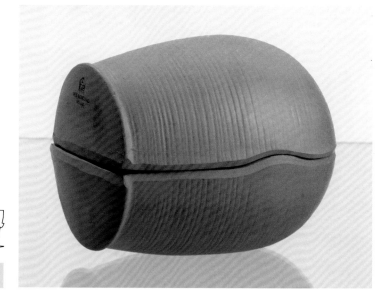

1 Habitat launched the terracotta chicken brick in 1968. It was sold with a recipe card and acts like a traditional clay oven.

2 Ikea's Poem chair from 1977 has a layered bentwood frame, and aimed to be comfortable, durable, and attractive.

By the mid 1960s a new group of middle-class consumers had emerged in Britain, Europe, and the United States. With greater levels of disposable income than previous generations, and essentially forward looking in outlook, they aspired to a lifestyle that placed modern design at its center. Expressed in the kind of clothes they wore, the furnishings they chose for their homes, and even the food they ate, that concept of a good life was bound up with social status. These new consumers were not inclined to acquire their possessions piecemeal over years; neither were they entirely confident of their tastes. By and large, although up to date and relatively wealthy, they had not traveled much abroad. All these factors combined to create a market for preselected or directional ranges of goods sold in a single outlet, along with more exotic products from far-flung locations.

A handful of far-sighted retailers understood the new market and could anticipate its tastes. They also put design at the heart of their retailing strategies, and used their own educated eyes to select the goods they put in their shops. In England, that approach was exemplified by Terence Conran's (b.1931) groundbreaking Habitat stores. From a background in textile and furniture design, and restaurant ownership, Conran opened his first Habitat in Chelsea, near to the heart of Swinging London, in 1964 (see p.378). His stock brought together traditional items—a revived Chesterfield sofa, bentwood chairs, and brightly colored enamel mugs—with contemporary design from

KEY EVENTS

1962	1963	1964	1964	1966	1969
Terence Conran imports the Carimate chair (1960; see p.376) by Italian architect Vico Magistretti (1920–2006) into Britain.	The first Ikea store outside Sweden opens in Oslo, Norway. It is the first of many overseas stores.	Conran opens the first Habitat store in London, with a stock of 2,000 practical furnishing items and a fresh approach to retailing.	Habitat sells continental quilts, also known as "duvets," reportedly after Conran used one in Sweden. They transform British bedding.	A second London-based Habitat store opens near to the influential furniture store Heal's.	Conran launches a mail-order catalog, Habitat Creative Living by Post, delivering nationwide to people who cannot visit its London stores.

Italy and Scandinavia, as well as vernacular objects—such as rugs and baskets—from India and elsewhere. The eclectic look he created was of the moment. Products were displayed in domestic settings—or piled high like goods on the French market stalls he so admired—and customers could either equip their entire homes or leave with a Habitat wooden spoon. Both routes allowed them to buy into the lifestyle that Conran was cleverly offering them.

Not only was the overall look of the store innovative, Conran was the first to bring a number of items into the British home, such as the chicken brick (see image 1), the garlic press, the Japanese paper lantern, and the duvet. His far-sighted approach to homemaking enabled him to see the mass potential of these and other objects. Habitat expanded its number of stores both in London and the provinces and, by the 1970s, it had helped design become a household word. Habitat also introduced a successful catalog, flat-pack furniture that could be assembled at home, and a complete House Pack that was delivered in a crate.

Like Conran, the founder of the Swedish furniture company Ikea, Ingvar Kamprad (b.1926), understood the concept of lifestyle. Kamprad provided Swedish consumers with flat-pack furniture from 1956, anticipating the need for cheap, modern furniture for post-war homes. He also introduced a catalog and a showroom before Conran, in 1951 and 1953 respectively. Kamprad opened the first Ikea store in Sweden in 1958. From the 1960s, he began to create simple and cheap furniture ranges, including the Poem—later Poäng—chair (1977; see image 2) by Japanese designer Noboru Nakamura.

The 1980s saw the huge expansion of Ikea in countries such as Italy, France, the United Kingdom, and the United States. The formula was the same in all the stores. Above all, Ikea communicated its Swedish origins by using blue and yellow in its branding. Kamprad realized that Sweden was linked internationally with the concept of good modern design, and he played heavily upon that well-established reputation while making it available to a wider audience than ever before.

On entering an out-of-town Ikea store, which looked much the same in every country, customers were first introduced to a number of complete room settings that allowed them to enter imaginatively into the modern lifestyle. They could then purchase the goods they had already seen integrated into interior settings. All Ikea's goods were in the modern style, and Kamprad used a wide range of young Swedish designers to create his products for him.

By the mid 1980s, largely due to the efforts of Conran and Kamprad, the modern lifestyle had been heavily democratized and good modern design had entered the lives of millions of people in the industrialized world. **PS**

1973	1973	1974	1976	1977	1981
The first Ikea store outside Scandinavia opens in Zurich, Switzerland.	Habitat's first international store opens in Paris, France. The store is the first of many international locations.	Conran publishes *The House Book*, which becomes an important guide for young people furnishing and decorating their first homes.	Ingvar Kamprad publishes *The Testament of a Furniture Dealer*, his manifesto outlining the Ikea furniture retail concept.	Habitat introduces its House Pack containing everything needed for a three-bedroom house, from sofas to beds, which is delivered to customers in a crate.	The brainchild of Conran and forerunner of the Design Museum, the Boilerhouse exhibition space opens at London's Victoria and Albert Museum.

Carimate Chair 1960

VICO MAGISTRETTI 1920–2006

Lacquered beech wood and
paper-rope seat
29 x 23 x 19 in.
74 x 58 x 47 cm

✦ NAVIGATOR

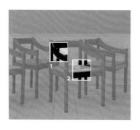

Modern Italian design has its roots in the reconstruction period after World War II, when political and economic aid enabled Italian industry to develop and recover. Italian architect Vico Magistretti worked in Milan at that time, in the climate of reconstruction that characterized post-war Italy. His emphasis was on creating new mass housing and furnishings, creating a number of simple stacking and folding items that could fit easily into the apartments being constructed around Milan.

By the late 1950s, Italy had been transformed into a modernized, industrialized country and its designers began to reflect that. In 1959 Magistretti, a keen golfer, designed a chair for the lounge of the Golf Club Carimate in Lombardy. In 1962 Italian furniture company Cassina took on production of the chair. The chair quickly became a success and could be found in many Italian restaurants throughout the 1960s.

By the early 1960s, thanks to publicity surrounding the Milan Triennales, the British design community became aware of the progressive objects being created in Italy. In 1962 Terence Conran imported the Carimate chair to Britain. Initially, it was only available by mail order, but when the original Habitat store opened in Chelsea, London, in 1964, it was visible on the shop floor. It suited Habitat's mix of modern and vernacular perfectly, and was easily assimilated into the Conran esthetic. **PS**

◉ FOCAL POINTS

1 COLOR

The most shocking feature of the Carimate was its color. Instead of leaving the wood a natural color, Magistretti stained it bright red, a color one would have expected to see in a plastic chair. In doing so, he aligned his design with the bright colors of the Pop environment.

2 SEAT

Magistretti uses traditional materials in his chair that evoke a rural simplicity in a stylish modern design with smooth lines that suggests urban sophistication. The seat is made out of high-resistance woven paper-rope. The smooth supports and legs are made from beech wood.

◷ DESIGNER PROFILE

1920–46

Vico Magistretti was born in Milan into a family of architects. In 1939 he began to study architecture at the Politecnico di Milano university. In 1943 he moved to Lausanne, Switzerland, and continued his studies there. In 1945 he returned to Milan, graduated, and went to work in his father's firm. He showed pieces of furniture at the "Riunione Italiana per le Mostre di Arredamento" (Italian Assembly for Furniture Exhibitions) show the following year as part of the Milan Triennale.

1947–59

Magistretti played a key role in the reconstruction years in Italy, creating architecture and furniture items. He exhibited extensively, winning awards at the 1951 and 1954 triennales.

1960–69

Magistretti focused on architecture during this period, although he also produced iconic furniture items and lighting designs for Cassina, Artemide, and Oluce.

1970–2006

From the late 1970s, Magistretti taught at the Royal College of Art in London. Among the key designs he created are the Maralunga sofa (1973) and the Sindbad sofa (1981).

▲ The most notable feature of the Carimate chair is its blend of vernacular influences and striking modernity. The combination is also seen in the Superleggera chair (1955; see p.171) by Italian architect and designer Giò Ponti (1891–1979) for Cassina—it is based on the Italian Chiavari chair created in 1807.

SELENE STACKING CHAIR

While the Carimate chair had vernacular origins, Magistretti's Selene chair (1968; above), produced by Artemide, belonged firmly to the 20th century. Made of compression-molded fiberglass, it was one of the first all-plastic, stackable chairs to be produced. Its glossy surface gave it an ultramodern look. It was not manufactured in one piece and the legs need to be fixed on after production. Magistretti's innovative S-shape cross-section design of the leg helps the sheet material's stability. The result is a sculptural chair that, because of its material, was cheap and quick to manufacture, making it accessible to a wide audience.

Habitat Interior 1964

TERENCE CONRAN b.1931

With products stacked high, the first Habitat shop acted as a retail space and warehouse.

✪ NAVIGATOR

Terence Conran's first store on the Fulham Road in Chelsea, London, created a model that he was to replicate many times over subsequent years. It exemplified an entire new way of life that was modern, informal, and inviting.

In early 1960s Britain, most furniture stores and departments were highly conservative places, reflecting the caution of the buyers that ran them. Customers frequently had to wait for a long time for their orders to be filled. One of the reasons why Conran decided to launch Habitat was his frustration at being unable to sell his own furniture via these staid outlets or, once he had, to see them properly displayed and marketed.

Habitat could not have been more different. There was an appealing immediacy about what it offered, with many items being available to take away on the day of purchase or flat-packed for self-assembly.

The staff in the first Habitat store wore uniforms designed by Mary Quant (b.1934) and had Sassoon-style haircuts. Jazz music played in the background to create a relaxed setting in which customers could browse at ease. Even the logo was striking. "The success of the Habitat logo," said Conran, "came from having a good name to start with and putting it together with the lower-case type style that was right for its time." The total effect was one of exuberant eclecticism unified by a single controlling eye. **PS**

⊚ FOCAL POINTS

1 ECLECTIC MIX
Industrial-style shelves were piled high with modern and vernacular products mimicking the look of continental market stalls. The most striking feature of the store was the eclectic mix of objects—old chairs, Mediterranean terracotta casseroles, pots, and modern designs—that filled it.

2 SETTING
Visually, the first Habitat interior had a breezy Mediterranean feel, evocative of the cookery writing of Elizabeth David (1913–92), whom Conran much admired. Many of the larger items of furniture were arranged in room settings, and fresh flowers adorned the tables.

3 BRICK AND WOOD
Above all else, the choice of materials that determined the fabric of the 1964 Habitat interior emphasized the role of texture. Ceramic tiles, exposed bricks, and painted wood showed a commitment to natural materials—the honesty of materials that Conran admired.

⏱ DESIGNER PROFILE

1931–52
Terence Conran was born in Kingston upon Thames, England. He studied textile design at London's Central School of Arts and Crafts and then set up his own furniture-making business.

1953–63
Conran visited France for the first time. On his return, he opened his first restaurant, the Soup Kitchen, in London. In 1956 he founded the Conran Design Group. By 1962 he had opened a furniture-making factory at Thetford in Norfolk.

1964–PRESENT
He opened the first Habitat store. In 1968 the Design Group merged with Ryman. In 1973 The Conran Shop opened in London, selling upmarket products. In 1992 Sweden's Ikano Group bought Habitat. Conran continues to develop restaurants and to work with London's Design Museum.

▲ (Left to right) Habitat buyer Zimmi Sasson, Terence Conran's then-wife Caroline, and Terence pictured shortly after the original Habitat shop opened in May 1964.

THE DESIGN MUSEUM

One of Conran's greatest contributions to the world of design is the Design Museum in London, which he both conceived and funded. Using the Boilerhouse Project at London's Victoria and Albert Museum as a template through the 1980s, in 1989 the Design Museum opened in Shad Thames (right). Conran's commitment to the idea of modern design for everybody was expressed through its exhibitions and programs that focused on explaining what design, and the design profession, meant for a lay audience. The museum spawned other examples around the globe, providing a model of how design can be presented in a museum context. The success and expansion of the Design Museum over nearly three decades led to its relocation in 2016 to a larger site in Kensington, London.

COUNTERCULTURE

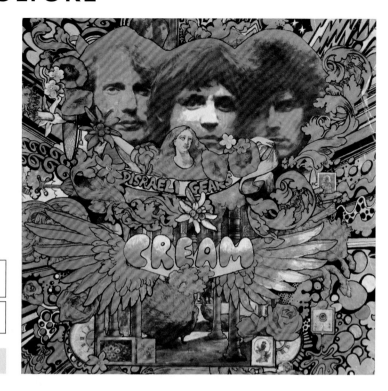

1 Martin Sharp's cover design for Cream's album *Disraeli Gears* (1967) shows a psychedelic pattern over a photograph of band members.

2 Gerald Holtom's logo for CND was adopted as the Ban the Bomb symbol by British anti-nuclear campaigners, such as this group protesting in London in 1959.

3 After Che Guevara's death, Jim Fitzpatrick sent copies of his poster depicting the revolutionary to left-wing political activist groups in Europe.

Early in the 1960s, a cultural phenomenon developed against the establishment, predominantly among young people, and starting in the economically buoyant United States. From there, it spread to Britain and throughout much of the Western world. It was a period when various sociopolitical events triggered social tensions regarding gender equality, civil liberties, women's rights, and the Vietnam War (1955–75).

New manifestations of Bohemianism emerged in the hippy culture. Hippies felt alienated from middle-class society, which they saw as dominated by materialism and repression, and they developed their own lifestyle and dress. They promoted openness and tolerance, and sought spiritual guidance from sources outside the Judeo-Christian tradition, particularly in Buddhism and other Eastern religions. Astrology was popular, sexual liberation abounded, and the recreational use of hallucinogenic drugs, particularly marijuana and LSD, was justified as a way of expanding consciousness. Folk and rock music were an integral part of the counterculture, with singers such as Bob Dylan (b.1941) and Joan Baez (b.1941) and groups such as The Beatles, Grateful Dead, Jefferson

KEY EVENTS

1963	1963	1964	1965	1966	1967
In June, photographs of Vietnamese Buddhist monk Thich Quang Duc (1897–1963) self-immolating in protest circulate	US President John F. Kennedy (1917–1963) is assassinated in November. This leads to diminished trust in government.	In December, US folk singer Joan Baez leads six hundred people in a demonstration against the Vietnam War in San Francisco.	US Quaker Norman Morrison (1933–65) self-immolates in front of the Pentagon to protest the United States' involvement in the Vietnam War.	US graphic designer Milton Glaser (b.1929) creates a poster to use as an insert for *Bob Dylan's Greatest Hits* (1967) album (see p.382).	In January the Human Be-In takes place at Golden Gate Park, San Francisco, initiating the hippy Summer of Love.

Airplane and The Rolling Stones also identifying with the movement. Public gatherings, including music festivals and protests, were an important aspect. Across Britain, in opposition to nuclear weaponry, Ban the Bomb protests occurred, and in 1958 British designer Gerald Holtom (1914–85) created a logo for the British Campaign for Nuclear Disarmament (CND) that became the internationally recognized symbol for peace (see image 2).

Contemporary visual arts represented the revolutionary political, social, and spiritual beliefs. Graphic design in particular, especially posters and music album covers, used psychedelia to represent prevalent feelings. The word "psychedelic" is a combination of the Greek words *psyche* and *delos*, meaning "mind (or soul) manifesting." To this end, colors were juxtaposed to create vibrating images and typography was contorted. Influences derived from Pop Art and Op Art, and from the sinuous forms of Art Nouveau (see p.92). Several graphic designers came to prominence, creating unprecedented styles that were imitated for decades. Hapshash and the Coloured Coat was a British graphic design and musical partnership between Michael English (1941–2009) and Nigel Waymouth (b.1941). From the early 1960s, they produced psychedelic posters advertising underground happenings in London clubs and at music concerts. Their styles reflected elements of Alphonse Mucha (1860–1939) and Aubrey Beardsley (1872–98), among others. Their new screen-printing technique enabled them to gradate from one color to another on a single separation, and they often used expensive metallic inks, which was unusual in advertising posters. They helped initiate the commercial sale of posters as art.

Martin Sharp (1942–2013) was an Australian artist, cartoonist, songwriter, and film-maker who became known as Australia's foremost Pop artist. He created psychedelic, abundantly filled, vibrantly colored posters and album covers for Dylan, Donovan (b.1946), Cream (see image 1), and other prominent musicians, and much of his early work was featured in the Australian satirical counterculture magazine *Oz*, which he co-founded in 1963, and the British version that launched in 1967.

In 1966 US designer Wes Wilson (b.1937) created a groundbreaking poster with red, flamelike lettering on a green background advertising a rock concert at the Fillmore Auditorium in San Francisco. Inspired by the work of Viennese Secessionist Alfred Roller (1864–1935), Wilson created a flowing lettering style, which filled all available space and that was emulated in psychedelic posters.

In 1968 just after the Argentine-born revolutionary Che Guevara (1928–67) died, Irish artist Jim Fitzpatrick (b.1943) created a two-tone portrait of him, a personal protest regarding the manner of his death. Based on a photograph by Cuban photographer Alberto Korda (1928–2001), the image became a controversial icon of the era (see image 3), representing anti-imperialism and leftist radicalism. Over the years it has become an international symbol of resistance to oppression. **SH**

1967	1968	1968	1969	1969	1975
In October Argentine Cuban revolutionary and Communist Che Guevara is executed by the Bolivian army. He is regarded as a martyred hero by leftists.	The rock musical *Hair*, featuring peace-loving, long-haired hippies, opens on Broadway in the United States and then in London's West End.	US writer Stewart Brand (b.1938) launches the *Whole Earth Catalog* counterculture magazine.	In July, US road movie *Easy Rider* is released. It explores the counterculture lifestyle, and the rise and fall of the hippy movement.	In August Woodstock, a three-day open-air music festival, is held in Bethel, New York, and attracts an estimated total of 400,000 visitors.	The capital of South Vietnam is captured in the Fall of Saigon in April, marking the end of the Vietnam War.

Bob Dylan Poster 1966

MILTON GLASER b.1929

Prolific US graphic designer Milton Glaser has created hundreds of posters and several seminal images, including this psychedelic Bob Dylan poster of 1966 and the "I ♥ NY" logo of 1977. He also co-founded Push Pin Studios in 1954 with fellow graphic designers Edward Sorel (b.1929), Reynold Ruffins (b.1930), and Seymour Chwast (b.1931), and in 1968, *New York Magazine* with journalist Clay Felker (1925–2008).

The Dylan project occurred early in Glaser's career when John Berg (1932–2015), then art director at Columbia Records, asked him to create a poster to be folded and packaged into *Bob Dylan's Greatest Hits* LP released in 1967. "This was probably my third or fourth poster," Glaser recalls. More than six million copies were distributed, making it one of the most widely circulated posters of all time.

Glaser's transformation of Dylan's curly hair into a tangled rainbow was inspired by other sources, as he has said: "I was interested in Art Nouveau at the time. That was an influence for the colors and shapes in the picture." For the single word, Dylan, at the bottom right corner of the poster, he used his blocky typeface, Baby Teeth, for the first time, which he designed in 1964 when inspired by the reduced letter forms he saw on a hand-painted sign in Mexico City. After the launch of this poster, the font appeared in many places and became synonymous with the era. **SH**

✦ NAVIGATOR

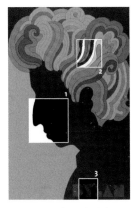

Milton Glaser's psychedelic poster of folk-rock star Bob Dylan captures the spirit of the flower-power era.

👁 FOCAL POINTS

1 SILHOUETTE

The idea for the silhouetted profile with kaleidoscopic hair evolved from Glaser's admiration of *Self-Portrait in Profile* (1957) by French artist Marcel Duchamp (1887–1968). Glaser recalled first seeing it: "I was astonished at the amount of energy and power... from a simple black silhouette."

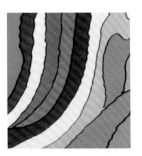

2 HAIR

While Glaser admired modernism, he reacted against its strict authoritarianism and austerity. In accordance with modernist ideals, the poster shows a certain amount of restraint, but the curving, colorful hair against the black profile contradicts the less-is-more philosophy.

3 LETTERING

Baby Teeth is one of Glaser's earliest and most successful typefaces. As well as being inspired by a Mexican sign that he saw, it derives from a Futurist typeface used in advertising and propaganda in Fascist Italy during the 1920s and 1930s that was intended to represent speed and modernity.

🕐 DESIGNER PROFILE

1929–53

Milton Glaser was born in the Bronx, New York. He attended the High School of Music and Art and the Cooper Union art school, both in New York City. With a scholarship, he studied under Italian painter Giorgio Morandi (1890–1964) at the Accademia di Belle Arti in Bologna, Italy.

1954–PRESENT

Glaser co-founded Push Pin Studios, which had a profound effect on graphic design. In 1968 he launched *New York Magazine*. In 1974 he established his studio, Milton Glaser, taking on a variety of design disciplines. In 1983 he co-founded the publication design firm WBMG, which has been responsible for the design for more than fifty periodicals.

▲ Studying under Morandi, painter of *Still Life* (1949; above), transformed Glaser's attitudes toward design. He learned to draw inspiration from movements that developed before modernism.

BACK TO THE PAST

By the late 1960s and early 1970s, modernism began to be challenged by a growing popular interest in styles and design movements from the past, particularly in Britain. A sequence of stylistic revivals—initially focusing on Art Nouveau (see p.92) and Art Deco (see p.156)—had the effect of opening a huge dressing-up box. On the domestic front, the focus shifted from modernizing (and often destroying) old housing stock to preserving and restoring original period features. Stripped pine replaced chromed steel and fiberglass; futuristic sci-fi designs were rejected in favor of quaint finds in flea markets or antique emporia. Embracing traditional furniture types alongside the modern, designer Terence Conran (b.1931) revived the Chesterfield sofa, and artist Peter Blake (b.1932) took inspiration from 19th-century folk art and vernacular culture, such as fairground carousels and old letterforms. To begin with, this was largely a British phenomenon, but soon other European countries, along with the United States, followed suit (see image 1).

Mass media—notably costume dramas on television and in film—helped to foster the nostalgic, romanticizing mood. The television adaptation of *The Forsyte Saga* by John Galsworthy, set in the early decades of the 20th century and screened by the BBC in 1967, was an enormous popular hit, with 19 million watching the final episode the following year. In the cinema, *Bonnie*

KEY EVENTS

1964	1966	c. 1966	1967	1968	1968
Barbara Hulanicki sets up Biba as a mail-order company. Within two years she has moved into "retro" clothing and opened Biba in Kensington.	John Jesse moves from his market stall in Portobello Road market to a shop in Kensington, where he sells Victoriana and Arts and Crafts items.	John McConnell (b.1939) designs his first Biba logo. This one is Celtic and Art Nouveau in inspiration and reflects the retro mood of the mid-1960s.	The film *Bonnie and Clyde*, starring Warren Beatty and Faye Dunaway, is released. Its costumes of the 1930s confirm a fashion trend.	Bevis Hillier publishes *Art Deco of the 20s and 30s*, a book that helps to fuel a craze for the style and make it fashionable, especially in London.	A Bauhaus exhibition held at London's Royal Academy shows that even modernism is being viewed through a nostalgic lens.

and Clyde (1967), *Women in Love* (1969), and *The Boy Friend* (1971) had a similar effect, while *The Go-Between* (1971) and *Barry Lyndon* (1975) were notable for their meticulous attention to period detail. The Aubrey Beardsley exhibition at the Victoria and Albert Museum (1966) in London helped to spread the new enthusiasm for Victoriana, while a spate of publications—including *Art Deco* (1968; see image 2) by Bevis Hillier (b.1940)—were also hugely influential.

Several British entrepreneurs were quick to respond to the mood. The dealer John Jesse was among the first to see the potential of Victorian, Arts and Crafts (see p.74), and Art Deco collectibles when he opened a shop in Kensington, in the heart of fashionable London, after running a stall in Portobello Road market. Barbara Hulanicki (b.1936), founder of Biba (see image 3), reimagined the old Derry and Toms department building top to bottom as an Art Deco extravaganza.

During the immediate post-war period, urban renewal had seen many slum or bomb-damaged streets replaced by both high-rise and low-rise council housing of chiefly modernist character. At the same time, a great many historic houses, too expensive to maintain after the war, were destroyed. Now the pendulum was swinging in the opposite direction, and conservation became a preoccupation. Properties dating from Georgian, Victorian, and Edwardian times were increasingly sought after by young middle-class homeowners who took pains to restore their original architectural detailing. Period-style fabrics, wallpapers, and paints, of varying degrees of authenticity, were produced by firms such as Colefax and Fowler, Laura Ashley (see p.388), and Farrow and Ball (which originally manufactured paint for the National Trust). By the 1970s and 1980s the idea of the "English Country House style," promulgated by numerous glossy magazines, had crossed the Atlantic. At the upper end of the market, Georgian style supplanted Victoriana as an aspirational look, complete with faux marbled paint finishes and windows festooned with ruched shades.

As Britain's manufacturing infrastructure went into decline, a heritage industry sprang up to fill the vacuum it had formerly occupied in the national identity. From the refurbishment of grand stately homes, initiated in the 1950s by John Fowler and the National Trust, to the recreation of industrial centers for the tourist gaze, Britain reconstructed selected aspects of its past. The Jorvik Viking Centre in York, the Ironbridge Gorge Museum, and the refurbishment of Liverpool's Albert Dock were notable examples, as were neo-classical designs, such as a scheme for Richmond-upon-Thames by Quinlan Terry (b.1937).

The desire to integrate the present into the past did not prove a short-lived phenomenon. Rather it became part of a dominant approach toward design from the 1970s up to the present. While over the years the fads and styles changed—Victorian pine gave way to mid-century modern teak, for example— the stylistic purity of modernism and its faith in the future was replaced by a new eclecticism that found solace in history. Nothing spoke more clearly of that past than the designed objects it had spawned. **PS**

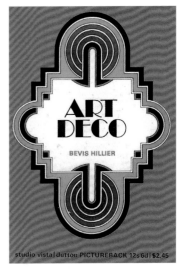

studio vista|dutton PICTUREBACK 12s 6d|$2.45

BIBA

22 CONDUIT STREET LONDON W1

1969	1971	1972	1974	1974	1984
John McConnell produces another logo for Biba, this time one that is inspired by the Art Deco style of the 1930s.	*The Boy Friend*, directed by Ken Russell, is released. Its huge success is partly due to its costumes and sets, which reflect the glamor of Art Deco.	Gillian Naylor (1931–2014) publishes a book on the Arts and Crafts design movement, sparking renewed interest in it.	Sarah Collier and Susan Campbell design their Cottage Garden print (see p.386) for Liberty, a firm commonly associated with historical revivalism.	The Victoria & Albert Museum in London stages an exhibition called "The Destruction of the Country House'," stimulating an upsurge of popular interest.	The Jorvik Viking Centre is opened in York, heralding the spate of British heritage-inspired projects initiated in the 1980s and 1990s.

Cottage Garden Textile 1974

COLLIER CAMPBELL

This screen-printed cotton furnishing fabric has a dense floral print.

NAVIGATOR

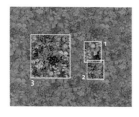

In 1961 Susan Collier (1938–2011), a self-taught painter and designer, took her portfolio to Liberty of London, which bought six of her designs on the spot and commissioned more. It was the beginning of what would be a long and fruitful association, during which time Collier and her sister, Sarah Campbell (b.1946), brought great energy and freshness to textile design, in the process transforming Liberty into a major wholesaler of printed fabric. Characteristic of the sisters' methodology was a painterly approach to pattern making and an insistence that this quality be closely reproduced in the finished print. Early acclaim came when Yves Saint Laurent (1936–2008) commissioned the sisters to create exclusive patterns for his first ready-to-wear collection in 1971. The same year, Collier was appointed Liberty's design and color consultant, a post she held until 1977; soon after, she and her sister launched Collier Campbell. From the outset, the designs were produced for a variety of different fabrics, including lawn, wool, silk, linen union, and cotton, and for applications that ranged from dresses, scarves, and accessories to furnishings. This both reflected and helped to foster a growing closeness between fashion and home furnishing, a trend that would increase over the decades that followed. Cottage Garden, designed in 1974 and manufactured by Liberty in 1977, has the nostalgic mood of a period when both fashion and interior design mined the past for decorative and design influences. A classic of English style, it recalls 19th-century motifs, yet avoids pastiche. Collier was influenced by nature, especially butterflies, birds, and garden flowers. She also had a great eye for color, a trait fostered by her mother, actress Patience Collier. **EW**

◉ FOCAL POINTS

1 PAINTERLY DESIGN
All of Collier Campbell's designs began as painted artworks. The designers insisted that a loose, fluid quality be retained in the printing of the fabrics, so that brush marks, for example, remained visible. Collier has cited artist Henri Matisse as a major influence.

2 COLOUR SENSE
Cottage Garden, like other Collier Campbell designs from this period such as Bauhaus (1972), Tambourine (1976), and Kasak (1973), shows a deliberate attempt to move away from traditional Liberty colorways in favor of palettes that are more expressive and suggestive of mood.

3 "CHEAT THE REPEAT"
Collier's motto was "cheat the repeat." Hand painting allowed Collier Campbell to avoid the mechanistic patterning of conventional textile design and to achieve a livelier sense of rhythm. "I was politically motivated to produce beautiful cloth for the mass market," remarked Collier.

◷ DESIGNERS' PROFILE

1938–60
Born in Manchester, Susan Collier displayed a love of color and nature from an early age. A self-taught painter, she initially worked for freelance designer Pat Albeck (b.1930), and sold early sketches to scarf companies such as Richard Allen and Jacqmar.

1961–74
In 1961 Liberty bought six of Collier's designs. She was retained by the company from 1968 and appointed design and color consultant in 1971, the same year that Yves Saint Laurent commissioned her designs for his first ready-to-wear collection. Sarah Campbell, Collier's younger sister, assisted her from an early age and later while studying design at Chelsea College of Art. After Campbell sold her graduation design to Liberty in the late 1960s, she began producing patterns for the company, too, and was retained as a designer in the early 1970s.

1975–2010
Campbell left Liberty in 1975 to design under her own name for French dress fabric company Soieries Nouveautés. Two years later, Collier also left the company and the two sisters formed Collier Campbell. For the next thirty years, Collier Campbell produced a large number of painterly designs for a wide range of clients, including Jaeger, Habitat, Marks and Spencer, Rodier, Fischbacher, Martex, and P. Kaufmann. They won the Prince Philip Designers Prize in 1984. In 1988 they were commissioned by Terence Conran to design the carpeting for Gatwick Airport's North Terminal.

2011–PRESENT
Collier died of cancer in 2011 at the age of seventy-two. Campbell continues to design under her own name, producing both commercial work and bespoke projects in a range of different materials.

CÔTE D'AZUR TEXTILE

One of Collier Campbell's best-known and loved designs is Côte d'Azur, a summery, Matisse-like pattern shot through with Mediterranean color and light. Designed for luxury Swiss textile brand Christian Fischbacher, the cotton furnishing fabric is part of the "Six Views" collection, for which the designers won the Prince Philip Designers Prize in 1984, the first women to receive this accolade. This version of Côte d'Azur (right) dates from the early 1980s, when the studio achieved some of its greatest successes and its patterns appeared everywhere: on the catwalk, on Marks and Spencer's best-selling duvet cover, on the carpets at Gatwick Airport's North Terminal, and on scarves, drapes, and pillow covers. Other patterns that were particularly successful during this period include Bauhaus and Tambourine. Collier Campbell was always keen to bring its designs to a wider audience and at one point launched its own clothing catalog business, selling direct to customers.

Cottage Sprig Wallpaper 1981

LAURA ASHLEY 1925–85

Cottage Sprig, a Victorian pattern in origin, was cleverly updated by the Laura Ashley firm to appeal to consumers nostalgic for that era.

The Welsh fashion designer and businesswoman Laura Ashley succeeded in developing a nostalgic domestic esthetic that contrasted strongly with the dominant, futuristic, masculine esthetic of Pop. Discovering soft floral motifs in Victorian pattern books, she applied them to both clothing and interior decoration. In a bedroom, for example, she might use the same pattern for a wallpaper, for a bed covering, and as a fabric for upholstering chairs. She preferred patterns with repeated small motifs that created a restful environment and contributed to the look of a particular lifestyle.

One of her most popular patterns, Cottage Sprig, was launched in 1981. It is believed to have been discovered in a Victorian children's book, entitled *Cox and Box*, by textile designer Brian Jones, who worked for Ashley for many years. By redrafting and recoloring it, Jones ensured that it was appropriate for the 1980s. It was applied across a range of domestic products, from wallpaper to wall tiles and china, and quickly became a design that defined the early 1980s. It was hugely evocative of a Victorian world, not that of the urban middle classes but of the more modest rural milieu that Ashley had known in her childhood. Pine dressers and bentwood chairs were displayed to complement the look. Cottage Sprig was fresh, pretty, feminine, and based on the natural world.

The Laura Ashley firm also published books providing advice to young people wanting to decorate and furnish their homes in the simple, country style that Ashley advocated. *The Laura Ashley Book of Home Decorating* (1984), to which she contributed a foreword, was the most successful and it helped spread her style far and wide. **PS**

 NAVIGATOR

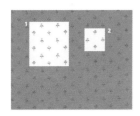

◉ FOCAL POINTS

1 REPETITIVE PATTERN
Ashley realized that repetitive patterns using small motifs lent themselves to many applications in the home and were soothing in their effect. Cottage Sprig may have enjoyed particular success because the floral motif is also anthropomorphic, perhaps suggesting children waving.

2 NATURAL INSPIRATION
Most of Ashley's patterns had their origins in the world of nature, and, like the Victorian pattern makers before her, she was hugely inspired by flowers, plants, and birds. Natural images are unthreatening, and she used harmonious blends of pastel colors to increase consumer enjoyment of them.

◀ A magazine advertisement of the 1980s illustrates how Laura Ashley fabrics, wallpaper, china, and other artefacts may be combined harmoniously to suggest a comfortable lifestyle governed by good taste.

THE LAURA ASHLEY COMPANY

Laura Ashley (seated, right, c. 1980) produced her first dress in 1966 and opened the first store with her name on it in South Kensington, London. two years later. Two more shops opened in 1970, in Shrewsbury and Bath. By the end of the 1970s the company had expanded massively, and there were over seventy shops across the world. The company expanded into home furnishings in the 1980s, but Laura Ashley died in 1985 and the company was undoubtedly most successful when it was linked to the creative individual whose vision had inspired it. Her husband and co-founder Sir Bernard retired as chairman in 1993, becoming honorary president until 1998. After further financial decline of the company in the 1990s, the Laura Ashley Design Service was launched in 1999. Today, production is centered on a single site in Powys, where paint, wallpaper, and drapes are made. The firm now operates just over two hundred stores across the United Kingdom, and it launched a new girls-wear line in 2011.

THE APPLIANCE OF SCIENCE

1 The third-generation Toyota Corolla was billed as the "ultimate family car" when it was introduced in April 1974.

2 Philips's tape players became bestsellers because of the rise in popularity of pre-recorded music cassettes.

3 The TRS-80 microcomputer was an appealing alternative to the build-your-own hobbyist machines available in 1977.

Discussions about design often focus on what is visible. But good design is sometimes a question of what is not seen: the appliance of science that goes on behind the scenes. Here, the input of engineers and technicians is critical. The Beolit 400 portable radio (1970; see p.392) is a case in point. Designed by Jacob Jensen (1926–2015), the sleek, minimal casing proclaimed an exclusive product aimed at the top end of the transistor market. However, the radio was also distinguished by its impressive sound quality. The Danish consumer-electronics company Bang & Olufsen, which manufactured the Beolit range, had long been devoted to what it termed "honest music reproduction," which had been a particular interest of co-founder Peter Bang (1900–57) when the firm was first launched in 1925. Jensen's role as product designer was to express this quality in the physical object that enclosed the unseen audio device.

The 1970s was a period on the cusp of technological change. Microprocessors were first mass produced in 1971. Six years later, one of the earliest mass-produced home computers was launched in the United States: the TRS-80 (see image 3). Made by Tandy, the computer was sold through the company's Radio Shack stores for less than $600. The digital age was just around the corner, yet home computing was dismissed in some quarters as a passing fad. Not so the pre-recorded music cassette, a format that grew increasingly popular, either for

KEY EVENTS

1963	1970	1970	1971	1972	1973
Philips launches the battery-operated EL 3300. It captures the imagination of the amateur recorder and even some broadcasting concerns.	The Sharp QT-8B Micro Compet handheld calculator is introduced. It is the first mass-produced calculator to be battery powered.	Bang & Olufsen launches the Beolit 400 portable radio with casing designed by Jacob Jensen.	Microprocessors are mass produced for the first time. The first general microprocessor is the Intel 4004.	German industrial designer Richard Sapper (1932–2015) creates the Tizio desk light (see p.394).	Arab members of OPEC place an embargo on the United States and other countries supporting Israel in the Yom Kippur War.

use in car stereos or in compact cassette recorders such as the Philips EL 3302 (1967; see image 2), which became a bestseller worldwide. The first pocket calculators date from the 1970s. Microwave ovens decreased in size and price and sales began to take off by the end of the decade.

In the motor industry, there was an enormous shift after the oil crisis of 1973. Suddenly compact, lightweight fuel-efficient models looked preferable to the large, heavy "gas-guzzlers" produced by Ford and General Motors. In 1974 the Volkswagen Golf (see p.396) small family hatchback was launched. It brought Giorgetto Giugiaro's (b.1938) cool styling to the mainstream and its angular, "folded paper" esthetic influenced car design during the 1970s. The same year, the latest model of the Toyota Corolla (see image 1) offered new safety and comfort features, while maintaining the low running costs that were to prove so important; it became the bestselling car worldwide.

During this period, Japanese car manufacturers began to dominate, eventually overtaking the United States by 1980. Rigorous quality control and the increased use of computers and robotics increased precision in Japanese car manufacturing, and hence the reliability of their products. Fuel injection, which became more commonplace during the 1970s, also helped smooth the path; it was more fuel efficient, during a newly energy-conscious time, was better at cold starts, and did without the need for a mechanical choke. By contrast, carburettors required frequent tuning and were prone to flooding. Improved rust proofing, which was introduced a little later, enhanced longevity. Increasingly, consumers expected cars to be safe, even if it took legislation to bring manufacturers to heel. The first seat-belt design dates from the 19th century, but the legal requirement for seat belts to be fitted in cars was first enacted in Australia in 1970. Airbags, similarly, have a relatively long design history. Ford and General Motors introduced them into certain models in the 1970s, partly because few drivers used seat belts.

Innovation had an impact on household appliances, too. In 1978 German company Miele became the first appliance manufacturer to produce washing machines, dryers, and dishwashers controlled by microprocessors. Miele's marketing slogan "Always better," encapsulates a design approach whereby goods are engineered to outperform their competitors, to last longer, and to take intelligent advantage of the latest developments in technology. Companies such as Miele have built their brands and their profits by ensuring their products do not break down and require frequent replacement. Naturally, such premium goods command premium prices. For the consumer who is willing and able to make the investment up front, the benefits are peace of mind and, often, status. For the producer, the goal is to establish brand loyalty based on reputation. The 1970s was a time when high-end, robust consumer goods began to become aspirational. The trend intensified for the rest of the 20th century and is still evident in the 21st century. **EW**

1974	1974	1974	1975	1977	1978
In January, world oil prices are four times higher than they were before the oil crisis began in October 1973.	The Toyota Corolla's export figures increase to more than 300,000 units annually. It becomes the bestselling car worldwide.	Volkswagen debuts the Golf. It becomes one of the top ten bestselling cars of all time.	Steven Sasson (b.1950) at Eastman Kodak creates the first working prototype of a digital camera.	Tandy/Radio Shack launches the TRS-80 Micro Computer System. It sells nearly twice as many units as originally projected.	Miele becomes the first appliance manufacturer to produce washing machines, dryers, and dishwashers controlled by microprocessors.

Beolit 400 Portable Radio 1970

JACOB JENSEN 1926–2015

Aluminum and plastic
8 ⅝ x 14 x 2 ⅜ in.
22 x 36 x 6 cm

The name "Beolit" refers to Bang & Olufsen's range of portable radios (as BeoVision refers to their televisions, and so on down through the product lines), with "BeO" being a latinized version of "B&O." The Beolit 400 and 600 portable radios were designed by Jacob Jensen for Bang & Olufsen, and were manufactured between 1970 and 1975. Visually, there was not much difference between the two models, but the 600 included AM, was mains as well as battery powered, and had a more refined tuning pointer. The 600, in particular, was an enormous success, with 600 a day being made for a period at the B&O factory in Struer.

Jensen was consultant head of design at B&O for over two decades from 1965, creating many of the superlative objects that defined the B&O esthetic and helped to cement the brand's reputation for outstanding quality. He designed many of their radios, some in a colorful Mondrian-like style, often experimenting with materials and finishes, such as teak and Nextel, but his design signature was perhaps most clearly expressed by the Beolit 400 and 600.

The radios' design is so cool and minimal that their function is not immediately apparent. An aluminum frame holds two textured plastic trays that can be unclipped to change the batteries. The station indicator, a metal ball dragged by a magnet down a groove in the aluminum profile, is protected by a glass cover. The radio can be turned to lie on its side, balancing on its handle, when required. Jensen's design is confident and intelligent, neither pretentious nor keen to please: the epitome of the sleek 1970s. **JW**

✪ NAVIGATOR

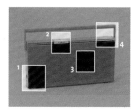

◉ FOCAL POINTS

1 RECTILINEAR SHAPE
Thin, flat, and elongated, the Beolit 400 has an anonymous presence and does not immediately proclaim its function. Lacking the usual profusion of prominent knobs and other controls, its sleek, modern lines and minimal detailing were to establish it as a design icon very quickly.

3 TEXTURED PANELS
The plastic side panels have textured outer surfaces, which contribute to the radio's overall impression of high quality. Jensen defined perfectionism in design as "the ability to rework, almost infinitely, over and over," saying also, "That 'over and over' is for me the cruellest torture."

2 STATION INDICATOR
Under a transparent panel, the station indicator consists of a metal ball recessed in the aluminum frame; the ball is moved by a magnet on the control slider. This feature, designed to prevent sand from getting into the casing, was altered slightly in the 600 model.

4 ALUMINUM FRAME
Two plastic panels or sides, which can be removed to change the batteries, form a "sandwich" with the central frame of aluminum. The aluminum handle extending from the frame can be folded down to support the radio and lift it off the ground when played on its side.

◷ DESIGNER PROFILE

1926–53
Born in 1926 in Copenhagen, Jacob Jensen was admitted in 1948 into the School of Applied Arts, where his teachers included Hans J. Wegner and Jørn Utzon. Graduating in 1952, he got a job at the first Danish industrial design studio, Bernadotte & Bjørn, where he designed the melamine mixing bowl called Margarethe that is still in production today.

1954–80
In 1956 Jensen visited industrial designer Raymond Loewy in New York, and went on to work with Richard Latham, Bob Tyler, and George Jensen, who had worked for Loewy and were now practicing as LTJ in Chicago. Jacob Jensen became a partner in LTJ in 1960, and director of LTJ Europe from 1975. Meanwhile, he founded the Jacob Jensen Design studio in Copenhagen in 1958. His signature style of slim objects in black and chrome, from doorbells to smoke alarms, wristwatches to toasters, won him many prizes. He was also influential as Assistant Professor in Industrial Design at Chicago University from 1959 to 1961. Jensen began his long association with Bang & Olufsen in 1965, eventually creating more than 230 products for them. In 1975 the Museum of Decorative Art Copenhagen devoted an exhibition to Jensen's work, and in 1978 an exhibition at the Museum of Modern Art in New York City entitled "Design For Sound" showed twenty-eight of his audio products for B&O. Jensen would work with Bell Express, F&H Scandinavia, and many other companies in addition to Bang & Olufsen.

1981–2015
In 1990 he handed his LTJ Europe company directorship to his son, Timothy Jacob Jensen, who expanded into Shanghai and Bangkok. Jacob Jensen died in 2015, aged eighty-nine.

JENSEN'S WEISZ WATCHES

Jensen claimed his style was inspired by the landscape around him, in particular the way the land meets the sea and the sky on his fjord in northern Jutland. It inspired the large collection of watches he made in collaboration with S. Weisz Uurwerken BV outside Amsterdam. For example, his Chronograph 605 (above) has pared-down, simple lines, is minimalist in design, and draws on geometrically pure forms. Functionality and high-quality materials are key, and all Jensen's watch designs take account of the fact that a watch acts as a piece of jewelry as well as a timepiece.

Tizio Desk Light 1972

RICHARD SAPPER 1932—2015

ABS plastic, aluminum,
metal alloy
30 x 30 in.
76 x 76 cm

⚙ NAVIGATOR

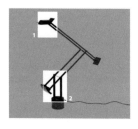

Designed by Richard Sapper for Artemide, Tizio instantly rewrote the rules for desk light design. Along with the Tolomeo task light (1987) by Michele de Lucchi (b.1951), which it inspired, Tizio is one of Artemide's greatest successes. The Italian word *tizio* is used to denote a man for whom one has no name—"that fellow"—and it specifies a certain masculine character that was integral to Sapper's design. Ernesto Gismondi (b.1931), founder of Artemide, remarked that one of Tizio's outstanding qualities is that it looks extremely handsome (in the masculine) no matter how it is positioned.

The first balanced-arm task light was the Anglepoise (1932—35; see p.172), designed by British engineer George Carwardine (1887—1947), and the use of springs enabled the adjustable folding arm to counteract the force of gravity. Sapper took the articulated arm idea to a new level of luxurious, minimalist sophistication. He left no wires visible, which increases the sleekness of the lamp's lines, and there are no springs, only counterweights. In the 1990s some improvements were made to the aluminum head: a glass cover and a thin wire handle were added, the latter so that the head could be tilted comfortably even when it had become hot to the touch. Tizio is available in black, white, and metallic gray, and in a variety of sizes, but the original and best known is the Tizio 50 in black. A more recent LED-powered version includes a dimmer. **JW**

1 INNOVATION
Sapper's construction of Tizio was highly innovative: it is powered using a 12-volt transformer in the swivel base, and the electricity runs through the two parallel arms of the frame so that there are no visible cables. Tizio was also the first light fixture to use a halogen lamp, which had previously been used mainly in the car industry.

2 FLEXIBILITY AND BALANCE
Tizio is a muscular, floating-arm lamp that swivels in four directions. It is all about kinetic movement and balance, and can be adjusted using only one hand. Two square counterweights complete Tizio's striking appearance, as if a nodding donkey pump has been transformed into a fine and elegant tabletop sculpture.

🕐 DESIGNER PROFILE

1932–69
Richard Sapper was born in Munich. He gained a business degree from the University of Munich. Sapper's first job was in the styling department of Daimler-Benz in Stuttgart. In 1958 he moved to Milan, where he opened his own practice.

1970–2015
In the 1970s Sapper was a design consultant for Fiat and Pirelli. From 1980 he became chief industrial design consultant for IBM, creating the design for the ThinkPad 700C laptop computer in 1992 (see p.434). He also designed ships and cars, electronics, furniture, and kitchen appliances. His clients included Alessi, Artemide, Kartell, and Knoll.

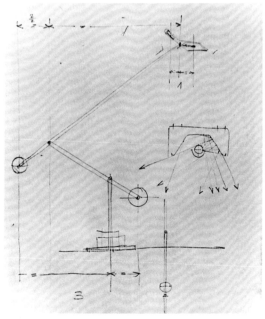

▲ Maneuvrability was vital to the design of the Tizio, as Sapper's design sketches reveal. Sapper claimed that he designed the Tizio because he could not find a work lamp that suited his needs.

THE HALLEY SERIES

Sapper returned to lighting design in 2005 with the Halley series (above) of warm white LED task lights for Lucesco. Unparalleled for movement and maneuvrability, the design uses counterbalances rather than springs or tension knobs to produce perfect balance through its movements. Each joint has full vertical and horizontal motion, creating fluid movement. The lightweight head has an integral fan to cool the LEDs. The name refers to Halley's Comet, the only comet visible to the naked eye that might appear twice in a human lifetime. Sapper may have been hoping that Tizio's meteoric success may be repeated twice in his lifetime with Halley, his second task light. Sadly, Lucesco closed in the wake of the 2008 financial crisis and the Halley is no longer manufactured.

Volkswagen Golf Mk1 1974

GIORGETTO GIUGIARO b.1938

👁 FOCAL POINTS

1 BUMPERS AND LED DISPLAYS
Several amendments were made to Mk1 in 1980. These included larger rear lamp clusters more in line with Giugiaro's original concepts, a new dashboard with updated instrument display and LED warning lights, molded black plastic bumpers and, for US versions, rectangular headlights.

2 WINDOWS
One of the exhilarating design aspects of the Golf Mk1 was the amount of sky that could be seen through the windshield, side windows, and the rear window of the hatchback. The glasshouse feel offered the liberating experience of an open mind and the freedom of the open road.

3 COMFORT AND HANDLING
The interior had quality materials and finishes that added all-important style and comfort. The Golf was firmly sprung and damped with McPherson strut front suspension and torsion beam rear suspension. It held the road well and was sharp without being uncomfortable.

4 "FOLDED PAPER" STYLE
From the early 1970s, Giugiaro introduced the angular "folded paper" design concept, which became highly influential in 1970s car design. The angularity gave the Volkswagon Golf a cool, assertive edge, disguising the economy drive that had become a necessity.

G iorgetto Guigiaro's Golf Mk1 was a small family car with three doors and a hatchback, and it was intended as a front-wheel drive, front engine, water-cooled replacement to the Volkswagen Beetle (1941): a neat and efficient family car. "Italy was a poor country after the Second World War, so we designers had to work with the few things that we had at our disposal," noted Giugiaro. "Minimal use of materials, avoidance of superfluous repetition: simple designs born out of necessity." However, the designer created much more than a make-do-and-mend vehicle. The Golf was an instant success, and by October 1976 one million cars had rolled off the production line.

The car was a deeply European concept: small and unpretentious, it was ideal for parking in awkward urban spaces. However, the key to its success was an Italian sense that putting family first was not in any way second best. Here was a small vehicle with a powerful sense of confidence: a true family car that was stylish and speedy. It neither needed to be a playboy racer nor a power-hungry saloon to prove its worth. In addition, the after-hours project for a "Sport Golf" grew into the Golf GTI, which was released in the late 1970s and started the boom in hot hatches that continues to this day. Volkswagen's in-house team adapted Giugiaro's design into the longer, wider Golf Mk2, which arrived in 1983. It sold 6.3 million units before the 1991 launch of Mk3. Of all his designs, the Golf gave Giugiaro the most satisfaction, but he is not sentimental. "Beauty comes down to mathematics," he said. "When designing a car, you don't start from emotions." **JW**

Styled by Giorgetto Giugiaro, the Volkswagen Gold Mk1 is a compact hatchback with front-wheel drive.

⏱ DESIGNER PROFILE

1938–66
Giorgetto Giugiaro was born in Garessio, Piedmont, Italy. He moved to Turin to study art and technical design. Dante Giacosa (1905–96), Fiat's technical director, saw his car sketches and hired him to work at Fiat in 1955. In 1959 Giugiaro became head of design for Bertone. He left in 1965 to join Ghia.

1967–95
Giugiaro set up his own company, Ital Styling, freelancing for different companies. A year later he co-founded Italdesign, offering engineering and styling services for the motor industry. The company has styled Alfa Romeos, BMWs, Ferraris, Lamborghinis, Lotuses, and Maseratis. Giugiaro has also designed camera bodies for Nikon, telephones, guns, a pasta shape and watches. In 1995 he was awarded a Golden Steering-Wheel for lifetime achievement and another for his Fiat Punto design.

1996–PRESENT
In 2010 Volkswagen bought 90 per cent of his company. In 2015 Giugiaro resigned.

▲ Launched in 1980, when manufacturers were packing cars with technological gadgets and power-hungry luxuries, the basic, cheap, and practical Fiat Panda (above) was a breath of fresh air. It won Giugiaro an Italian Compasso d'Oro industrial design award in 1981.

CORPORATE IDENTITIES

PanAm　Bali

© PanAm Japan

P roducts have long had distinct visual identities, but the idea of producers also having them was not developed until after World War II. On a sinister note, it was the Nazi Party's preoccupation with appearances that first alerted the world to the potential of a unified corporate identity. In business, possessing a corporate identity became particularly valuable at times of takeovers and mergers. Companies needed to communicate by means of visual sign language, which in turn was reflected by the public's increasing ability to interpret the messages conveyed. A clear corporate identity became crucial when there was no physical product on sale. As Colin Forbes (b.1928) of the design firm Pentagram wrote, "It challenges the designer to create a memorable identity for companies whose distinctive features have been blurred by universal technology or regulation." Such companies include airlines or banks, which offer services, not products. In this world, "A single office and a letterhead may be the only manifestation of a highly sophisticated service, and the first impressions can be the most important."

KEY EVENTS

1961	1962	1964	1965	1971	1971
The World Wildlife Fund creates its logo, a graphic representation of a giant panda, spotlighting its work in the conservation of threatened species.	Graphic design consultancy Fletcher Forbes Gill is founded in London; it is later renamed Pentagram.	Chermayeff and Geismar redesign the Mobil logo, in blue with a red "o'." The company's Pegasus winged horse logo is retained for some uses.	Michael Wolff and Wally Olins found Wolff Olins in London, becoming leading international corporate identity consultants.	Portland State University student Carolyn Davidson (b.1943) creates the tick-like "Swoosh" trademark of the newly named Nike, Inc.	Raymond Loewy (1893–1986) subtly redesigns the scallop shell logo of the Shell oil company to the form used today.

The most familiar element of any corporate identity is usually its logo or trademark, which on the surface is purely a graphic product. The company identity usually consists of one or two words, which must be configured in a way that is clear but also distinctive and memorable, conveying through its visual style the values of the company concerned. As Ivan Chermayeff (b.1932) and Tom Geismar (b.1931) of the New York-based branding and graphic design firm Chermayeff & Geismar wrote, "Trademark design challenges us to use all the magic and intelligence at our command, all our skill, knowledge, vision, and ability in the creation of a single, clear, direct image that will embody the character and aspirations of the organizations that come to us in search of identity."

The contributions of graphic design to corporate identity extend much further than creating a logo; they extend to letter headings, vehicle liveries, corporate gifts such as calendars, and many aspects of the corporation's advertising. The Mobil oil company became a client of Chermayeff and Geismar in the 1970s, following an introduction by architect and industrial designer Eliot Noyes. After creating the Mobil logo in a custom-designed sans-serif font—presented in blue with the "o" as a pure circle—they designed posters for the wide variety of arts sponsorship then undertaken by the company. The posters drew on a variety of techniques, including simple hand drawing, collage, and simplified geometric renderings of buildings. All were intrinsically intriguing and yet unrelated to the core business; similarly, their posters for PanAm in 1973 (see image 1) "built the brand" in a subtle and indirect manner.

Corporate identity goes beyond simply possessing a "house style" when it claims to transform not only the public perception of an organization but also its internal cohesion. In such cases, the idea behind the brand and the need to protect it acquire additional urgency, informing the corporation's entire outlook on the world. Like many other former state agencies, the UK National Grid, the infrastructure provider for electricity generators, was privatized in 1990. As John McConnell (b.1939), also of Pentagram, wrote of his work for them (see image 2), "the shared attitudes, values and priorities of a company are often called its corporate culture. Corporate design has first to identify this culture and then give it visual expression." The potential of this activity for misleading the public has been identified, and McConnell stressed that designers must check a corporation's aspiration against its reality, warning that "some companies and their accomplice designers go so far as to believe that corporate design will actually produce unwarranted, if desired, perceptions of an organization." Thus, companies are encouraged to use their design consultant as a "critical friend" who, like a therapist, penetrates to the soul of a company, builds up its strengths, and treats any sickness. Design firms working to shape and improve how the world perceives a corporate client may be retained for the purpose for decades. **AP**

1 Two of a series of advertisements created by Chermayeff & Geismar for PanAm in 1973 highlight in a brilliantly simple way the airline's diversity of destinations while simultaneously showing people why they might want to go to them.

2 The bold logo designed for the UK National Grid by John McConnell and Justus Oehler of Pentagram in 1989.

1971	1972	1977	1977	1987	1997
Starbucks found their corporate identity on a logo based on a 16th-century Norse woodcut of a twin-tailed mermaid, known as the Siren.	IBM's logo (see p.400) is rethought by Paul Rand (1914–96), who uses horizontal stripes to suggest "speed and dynamism."	Commissioned by New York State in 1976, Milton Glaser (b.1929) produces the "I♥NY" logo, with black type and the heart in red.	Rob Janoff designs the Apple logo *pro bono* for Steve Jobs, who adds rainbow colors to show that Macintosh computers have color displays.	Javier Mariscal (b.1950) devises the charming figure of CoBi (see p.402) for the Barcelona Olympic Games of 1992.	Ex-Prime Minister Margaret Thatcher criticizes new British Airways tail fin designs by Newell and Sorrell: "We fly the British flag, not these awful things."

IBM Logo 1972

PAUL RAND 1914–96

The basic design of the IBM logo has remained constant since 1972, and it is one of the most recognized in the world.

NAVIGATOR

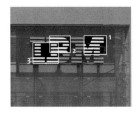

International Business Machines originated in 1911, becoming a multifaceted information-handling and machine-production business before 1939. After World War II, with the potential for rapid development of mainframe computers, its old-fashioned and confused image was threatened by the design-conscious Olivetti of Italy, which inspired the new second-generation president, Thomas Watson Jr (1914–93), to seek professional help.

In 1956 Watson hired the architect Eliot Noyes (1910–77) as consultant director of design. Noyes had worked with Walter Gropius (1883–1969) and Marcel Breuer (1902–81), and also with Charles Eames (1907–78) on the exhibition "Organic Design in Home Furnishings" at the Museum of Modern Art in New York City in 1940. Noyes selected Paul Rand as graphic designer for IBM, who revised the existing logo to become the familiar chunky three letters, which he modified with horizontal stripes in 1967.

For Rand, this was a new experience, and he realized the need to create a corporate manual to explain the changes to the employees of the vast organization, working with the help of Marion Swannie and building up a reliable team of graphic designers within the company. This focus on the company name was not a diversion, for as Noyes said at the time, "because IBM's products are too complex to be understood by the average buyer, the buyer must rely on IBM's name." With product packaging in bright colors, with a mixture of stripes and patterns of repeating letters, Rand brought a touch of glamor that had rarely been seen in the world of office equipment. **AP**

👁 FOCAL POINTS

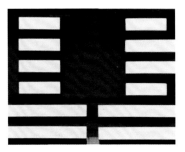

1 SERIF

The previous logo consisted of the letters IBM set in outline Beton Bold. Rand's version of 1956 replaced it with City Medium, bolder letterforms, and more conspicuous serifs. Lettering styles of this type, first popular in the 1820s, are known as "slab-serif Egyptians." They were revived in the 1930s as display faces with a retro feel, and were thought to be compatible with modernist sans serif types.

2 STRAIGHT LINES

Rand simplified the letterforms so that they consisted of straight lines and segments of circles, making them easier to redraw without making mistakes. The thin parallel lines reminded Rand of the security stripes on a banknote or check, and helped add authority and link the letters together to form a harmonious whole, but an IBM employee said they reminded him of a striped prison uniform.

3 STRIPES

"Paul felt that people shouldn't be hit over the head with this logo," explained IBM designer Swannie, who became Rand's second wife. He played with the logo in different ways, turning it into multicolored outlines on black, and adding the stripes to the logo in stages, with thirteen stripes in 1967 and a simpler eight stripes, shown here, in 1972. Rand felt the stacked stripes suggest speed and dynamism

🕐 DESIGNER PROFILE

1914–39

Born Peretz Rosenbaum in Brooklyn, New York, Rand grew up in a poor Orthodox Jewish family that ran a grocery store. He studied art at night classes and was inspired by finding graphics magazines in bookshops and in the New York Public Library. Typographer Ervine Metzl (1899–1963) helped Rand (who had changed his name to avoid anti-Semitic prejudice) to get good graphic commissions and develop an imaginative and fresh style; he became art director for *Esquire* magazine.

1941–96

Rand joined the William H. Weintraub advertising agency, introducing a new, often almost wordless, style based on abstract and Surrealist art. In 1947 Rand published *Thoughts on Design*, discussing the use of symbols in advertising, the use of collage, and other techniques. He created classic covers for art books published by Wittenborn. Among his other activities, Rand illustrated children's books.

THE LOGO

Short for "logotype," a combination of letters cast in one piece in the days of metal printing, the logo has become a feature of modern life. Historically, logos and brand names occurred almost by accident, but that age of innocence is past. The logos of business corporations and other more transitory affairs, such as each Olympic Games, are designed after consultation and testing. Multiple meaning is needed, although if they become too clever, they may not work. Some are pictorial, some are composed only of letters, and some are in between. Often a new typeface is designed, or an existing one is modified, on the basis that the style of lettering will speak volumes about the message.

▲ Rand redesigned the IBM company logo in 1956 (above) under Noyes's direction. It marked the first step toward an integrated corporate design program at the computer company.

CoBi Mascot 1987
JAVIER MARISCAL b.1950

As the lasting visual image of the Barcelona Olympic Games in 1992, Josep M. Trias's official identity for the event—a figure conveyed in mid-leap in just three brushstrokes—has long been eclipsed by a small cartoon sheepdog created by designer and illustrator Javier Mariscal. First conceived in 1987, CoBi was named after the Organizing Committee for the Barcelona Olympic Games (COOB'92), and is widely regarded as the most successful mascot ever created for an Olympics. Mariscal was asked to produce a design that was not traditional, and in referencing Spanish art and culture he did just that, realizing a vision of what a mascot could achieve commercially for both the organization and the host city. CoBi was a decidedly avant-garde creation, yet the mascot's cute comic-book appearance belied its significance as a cultural export. By the time the Games opened he was ubiquitous, appearing in sponsorship tie-ups with Danone and Coca-Cola, on posters, toys, and licensed souvenirs, even in a twenty-six-episode cartoon called *The CoBi Troupe*. He appeared in hundreds of different guises: as a representative of each of the Olympic sports, as a spectator or tourist, and in many supporting and service roles. Trias's figure was a masterly example of graphic brevity, but CoBi was its messy opposite: full of life and charm, and perfect for the reinvented city. **MS**

⚽ NAVIGATOR

A Barcelona '92 poster features both CoBi in a dominant position and, almost hidden, the official logo of the Games.

👁 FOCAL POINTS

1 HAND-DRAWN STYLE
CoBi's angular face and flattened perspective were inspired by the Cubist style pioneered by Picasso. The black outlines that define the flat, unmodeled color elements and the lack of shading also recall the graphic style of comic books. Other detailing is left to the viewer's imagination.

2 COLOR PALETTE
Mariscal avoided primary colors to distance his CoBi figure from other cartoon figures used commercially. The color palette he used tends toward pastel shades. The figure and its background have a freshness that tied in with the intention of showing Barcelona in a new light.

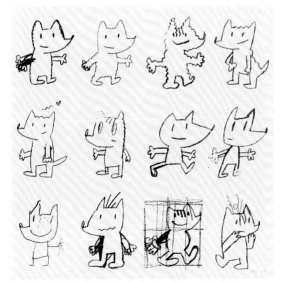

FOLLOWING PICASSO

In his treatment of the CoBi mascot's physical appearance, Mariscal was influenced by details of a series of forty-four paintings that Pablo Picasso (1881–1973) executed in 1957. Picasso had reinterpreted the famous portrait *Las Meninas* (1656) by Diego Velásquez (1599–1660), reimagining it in his Cubist style (below).

▲ In this series of preliminary sketches of the CoBi mascot, Mariscal was exploring its basic form and applications. It was only later that it was given the uniform of a COOB'92 official.

OBJECTS OF DESIRE

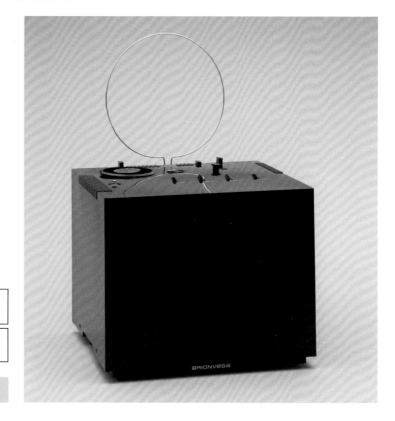

1

2

3

1 The Black 201 television set (1969), designed by Marco Zanuso, exemplified the esthetic that an object's appearance primarily should be an expression of its technological function.

2 Weighing 30 lb (13.6 kg), the Sony CRF-320 radio (1976) in stylish black and chrome offered more controls than any radio enthusiast would reasonably expect.

3 A US magazine advertisement of the 1970s helps to establish the idea that a pair of Calvin Klein jeans is a must-have object of desire, and tacitly that the owner is equally desirable.

By the 1970s, attacks by author Vance Packard, among others, on the colossal waste resulting from conspicuous consumption were forcing a re-evaluation of the role of design in the market place. Post-war strategies to drive sales—such as built-in obsolescence—now seemed crude and simplistic, and the public was increasingly suspicious of advertisers' claims and more experienced in decoding their messages. Yet, as design allied itself ever more closely with retail culture, the problem remained: how to persuade people to buy new goods when their needs were broadly taken care of?

One answer was to address "wants" rather than "needs." A version of this approach has long been the *raison d'être* of the fashion industry, where wanting the "new" motivates people to refresh their wardrobe each season. In product design, novelty might be similarly be expressed in the superficial allure of styling, an approach that was successful in the 1930s and 1940s with streamlining, or it might rest in improved technical specification and functionality, making

KEY EVENTS

1969	1972	1973	1974	1975	1977
Marco Zanuso designs his Black 201 television set for Brionvega. It has the appearance of an all-black box when the screen is not lit up.	Richard Sapper designs the all-black Tizio light for Artemide. It becomes a neo-modernist icon, found in every "well-designed" interior.	With Florian Seiffert (b.1943) and Robert Oberheim (b.1938), Dieter Rams creates the minimal Sixtant 8008 electric shaver with a grip feature.	Sony launches its CF 1480 all-black portable radio. With its circular dial, it is reminiscent of a radar monitor and has a strongly masculine appeal.	With Dietrich Lubs (b.1938), Dieter Rams creates the AB 20/20 tb, a squared-off version of the "phase 3" traveling clock.	Sony launches its portable TV set, nicknamed "Citation" -after a type of jet. Its appearance is inspired by the spare look of jet cockpit monitors.

previous models seem outdated, whether or not they still performed their jobs. A third way, and one that now came to the fore, was to surround design with the aura of high culture. Elevating the value and status of design necessarily raised conspicuously designed products to objects of desire, a phenomenon that *Cult Objects* (1985), a book by Deyan Sudjic (b.1952), was to explore.

In the late 1970s, many such cult objects shared a "matt-black esthetic" that first emerged in the 1960s and 1970s in the styling of Italian goods. The Black 201 television set (1969; see image 1) that Marco Zanuso (1916–2001) had designed for Brionvega, for example, had set the tone, as had the Tizio light (see p.394) for Artemide, also realized in black, designed by Richard Sapper (b.1932). The use of that single color denoted a thoughtful restraint that became the marker of "good design" for many people. It was widely used, especially in the arena of high-technology products, which were increasingly sold on the basis of their sleek appearance and not solely on their functionality.

In Germany, Braun's minimal artefacts had also achieved cult status by the 1970s, with the work of Dieter Rams (b.1932) receiving worldwide acclaim for its rigor. His traveling clocks, calculators (see p.406), electric shavers, and watches appealed, above all, to the design-conscious male consumer. The Japanese company, Sony, embraced the same esthetic in its hi-tech products. In the early 1970s, many radios (see image 2), television sets, hi-fi equipment, and cameras had black-and-chrome bodies conforming to the masculine formula for "good design" that Germany had already perfected. But other colors crept back, as in their Walkman TPS-L2 stereo cassette player (1978; see p.408).

The matt-black esthetic denoted not only seriousness; generally speaking, it also promised a high degree of quality. A corollary of the elevation of design into the realm of high culture was the rapid emergence of the "designer label," a badge of distinction in some cases, in others a hollow tag justifying a premium price point. This trend first emerged in the fashion industry, notably in the highly competitive (and lucrative) market for jeans. Names such as Calvin Klein (see image 3), Gloria Vanderbilt, Giorgio Armani, Gianni Versace, and Donna Karan, among others, were used to inject individualism into otherwise bland, mass-produced goods. The same licensing strategy, pioneered by Pierre Cardin, saw designers' names applied to bed linen, homewares, and elsewhere.

Calvin Klein Jeans

By the 1980s and 1990s, the aura that had been attached to many "objects of desire" in the previous decade was transferred to their creators, who increasingly defined themselves as artists. The spectrum of so-called "designer" goods gradually broadened until it was even possible to talk of "designer water'." This mass-manufactured, brand-name designer culture was quick to invade the high street. Even countries such as China produced vast numbers of copies of branded luxury goods, and within that context the word "designer" took on a whole new significance. As a consequence, the "designer" concept became ever more firmly entrenched in the world of commerce and retail. **PS**

1979–84	1980	1981	1982	1984	1985
James Dyson (b.1947) develops 127 different prototype vacuum cleaners. His first commercial model, the "G-Force," is marketed in Japan in 1983.	The Japanese brand Muji is launched as part of the Seiyo chain of supermarkets. Its vision is to reject foreign luxury in favor of minimalist goods.	With Caroline Thorman, Ron Arad (b.1951) founds his design and production studio, One Off. The studio/store is based in London.	A Sony exhibition is held at the Boilerhouse in London's Victoria & Albert Museum, curated by Stephen Bayley (b.1951).	A year after Phillipe Starck (b.1949) refurbishes President Mitterrand's private apartments, he designs the Café Costes in Paris, his first public interior.	Deyan Sudjic publishes his book, *Cult Objects*, in which he looks back at how Western culture imbued certain objects with special status and desirability.

Braun ET22 1976

DIETER RAMS b.1932   DIETRICH LUBS b.1938

The ET22 calculator, which Dieter Rams designed with Dietrich Lubs for Braun, was the first of a series of such objects that the company released through the 1980s, culminating in the ET66, launched in 1987. Because of the ET22's early date, it lacks some of the technological sophistication of the later model. However, esthetically and functionally, it is distinctive, appealing, and defined the design direction that followed.

The ET22 was characterized by its minimal appearance and its simple user-friendly interface with its functions arranged in a logical sequence. Its black body, multicolored buttons, and clear lettering invited touch and did not distract from the task in hand. The rounded lower corners invited the user to slip it into a breast pocket. However, unlike the later model, it depended on sliding switches, and its LED display was improved upon later.

As design director for Braun, Rams set the *modus operandi* for his team and established the company's design philosophy, which was both to make technology accessible and to create timeless products that outlasted the vagaries of fashion. He went further than that, however, seeing his objects as being pleasurable to use, both because of their direct relationship with the human body and because of their restrained, pleasing appearance. He has described design as replacing the old-fashioned butler inasmuch as, when it is well executed, it makes life easier for everyone. Taking ideas from the Bauhaus (see p.126), another of his aims is "to make things that recede into the background." **PS**

Metal and plastic
5¾ x 3⅛ x 1 in.
14.5 x 8 x 2.5 cm

FOCAL POINTS

1 COLOR
The ET22 interacts with its users through the visual impact of the small number of colors used. The black body provides the background for a number of brown buttons and a single yellow one designated for the Equals function. The numerals and symbols in white stand out against the dark background.

2 BUTTONS
Rams treats the ET22 as a small, sculptural object. The minimum amount of buttons are arranged in an orderly manner, employing a dark, minimalist color palette. The circular and rectangular buttons are convex in shape, which provides the user with a smooth physical experience.

DIETER RAMS AND APPLE

Both Steve Jobs (1955–2011), the late founder of Apple, and Jonathan Ive (b.1967), its chief designer, have acknowledged the work of Rams as a source of inspiration in the creation of iconic products such as the iPod (2001) and iPhone (2007). The Calculator application on the first iPhone made a clear reference to Braun's ET66 with its rounded buttons and characteristic choice of colors. In this homage, Ive was co-opting the appearance of a familiar and well-loved icon in the creation of what would become another. Similarly, Braun's T3 radio (1958; right), also designed by Rams, has an obvious echo in iPod, which shares the same central control dial. Such influences, however, are more than skin deep. Rams' design philosophy is rooted in a coherent approach, equally evidenced by the best Apple products.

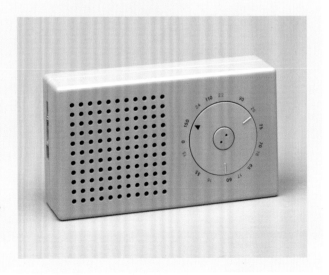

Walkman TPS-L2 Stereo Cassette Player 1978

SONY CORPORATION

👁 FOCAL POINTS

1 ESTHETICS

The first Walkman had a blue and silver case. A few years later, it was available in silver, blue, black, or red. In 1988 Sony launched the iconic "yellow monster" Sports Walkman. However, ultimately the appeal of the Walkman was less about appearance and more about the miniaturization of technology.

2 FUNCTIONALITY

The functionality of the Walkman was minimal. The user simply had to turn the machine on and off and fast-forward the cassette. Sony was familiar with these control mechanisms from its work on tape recorders from the 1940s onward. It merely had to further reduce their size.

A lthough Sony did not invent the associated technology, the Japanese company was the first to exploit the market for magnetic cassettes. As experts in well-designed miniaturized electronics—the firm produced its first tape recorder in 1955—it was ready in the late 1970s to take advantage of the shift from vinyl records to cassette tapes, the medium that increasingly enabled people to listen to music while on the move. The Walkman—a compact, high-quality music player—was initiated by Sony's co-founder Masaru Ibuka (1908–97), who was a frequent traveler. The prototype was made in 1978 and the finished product, which had been widely tested with users, was first introduced in 1979 in Japan, where it was a great success. This achievement was repeated when the music player finally arrived on the international market. The Walkman was a very simple object. In essence, it consisted of a container for the cassette and a pair of lightweight earphones. Its launch coincided with the crazes for aerobics and jogging, and the product was widely used in sporting contexts. However, in the 1990s the Walkman was overtaken by personal CD players. Sony was quick to work with the new format. **PS**

 **NAVIGATOR**

Metal alloy case
6 x 3 ½ x 1 ⅜ in.
15 x 9 x 3.5 cm

🕐 COMPANY PROFILE

1946–62

Masaru Ibuka and Akio Morita established Sony in 1946 as Tokyo Tsushin Kogyo. In 1949 it created the first prototype for a magnetic tape recorder, which was launched a year later. The company changed its name to Sony Corporation in 1958. Sony launched the world's first direct-view portable television—the TV8-301—in 1960, followed by the world's smallest and lightest all-transistor television—the TV5-303—in 1962.

1963–PRESENT

Bestselling products have included the Trinitron color television, introduced in 1968, and the Walkman launched in Japan a decade later. Sony continued to develop new products, among them a portable CD player (later called the Discman) in 1983 and a camcorder. In 1993 Sony Computer Entertainment Inc. was established, and in the 21st century, Sony entered the mobile phone market in a joint venture with Ericsson.

MARKETING THE WALKMAN

A great deal of effort was put into marketing the Sony Walkman. The idea behind the campaign was to introduce the idea of "Japaneseness" to the rest of the world. This was seen as being synonymous with high technology and miniaturized products, items that were both smart and small. As the Walkman was a new product with a new functionality, and its appearance was fairly utilitarian, people had to be persuaded to buy it. This was done through extensive launch, poster, and advertising campaigns. The Walkman's key advantage over other music-listening products was the fact that it could be carried around. This transformed the way we could listen to music: instead of being a private activity, carried out indoors, it became a public activity. Consequently, the first marketing campaign involved demonstrations of people using Walkmans while engaged in sports and physical activity. A poster campaign was also developed (right). A particularly memorable example showed a young scantily clad Western woman listening to a Walkman while being watched by an older Japanese man in traditional dress; another depicted young people roller skating while using their Walkmans. The emphasis was firmly on the idea of youth and fun and the sense of freedom that comes from being able to listen to music on the go.

PUNK

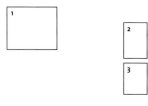

1 Singer Joey Ramone on stage during a performance by the Ramones in 1977. The backdrop has an Arturo Vego adaptation of the presidential seal.

2 Model and actress Jordan (b.1955) outside Malcolm McLaren and Vivienne Westwood's shop, Sex, in London in 1976.

3 A poster for a concert by Californian punk group the Dead Kennedys promotes a band member for mayor of San Francisco.

Punk music exploded onto the scene in New York City and London in the mid-1970s. The graphic style that accompanied the music and fashions was forcefully influential and remains in widespread use. The Ramones first played at the club CBGB in New York City in August 1974, and after the furious opening two-minute song it was clear that the hippy era was over.

Mexican-born graphic designer Arturo Vega (1947–2013) created the logo and graphics for the Ramones. Subversive, anti-establishment, and anti-consumerist, his parody of the US Presidential Seal was intended as a hardcore assault. Vega's adaptation of the seal (see image 1) replaced the motto "E Pluribus Unum" ("out of many, one") with "Hey ho let's go" after the opening lyrics of the band's first single "Blitzkrieg Bop" (1976).

British impresario Malcolm McLaren (1946–2010) and his girlfriend British fashion designer Vivienne Westwood (b.1941) were in New York a few months later, and recognized the future in what the Ramones were doing. Returning to London, McLaren formed a band that became the Sex Pistols. A few months previously, in spring 1974, McLaren and Westwood had rebranded Too Fast To Live Too Young To Die, their boutique in London, with a new name: Sex (see image 2). It sold bondage and fetish gear that—along with safety-pinned ears and noses, Mohican hairstyles dyed in peacock shades, and torn and ripped clothing—became the insignia of the genuine punk.

KEY EVENTS

1973	1974	1974	1974	1975	1976
The oil crisis begins. It leads to a global stock-market crash that causes a recession in most of the Western world.	US band Television's singer Richard Hell (b.1949) is one of the first to spike his hair and wear torn clothing fastened with safety pins.	The Ramones form. The band cements the elements of Punk music and attitude, and its members adopt the same stage surname.	Malcolm McLaren and Vivienne Westwood refurbish their shop in Chelsea in London and rename it "Sex."	The Sex Pistols perform for the first time at St Martin's College of Art in London, followed by performances at other art schools.	The Sex Pistols inspire a rash of new bands in London: The Clash, The Slits, Siouxsie and the Banshees, X-Ray Spex, and The Damned.

British artist Jamie Reid (b.1952) designed graphics for the Sex Pistols. A member of McLaren's Glitterbest management team, based in offices in London, Reid designed the posters, T-shirts, fliers, and album covers for the Sex Pistols in the manner of ransom notes. It was a perfect visual mode for titles such as *Never Mind the Bollocks, Here's the Sex Pistols* (1977; see p.412).

Posters and fliers that announced punk concerts flew in like messengers of havoc. Deliberately amateurish, like the music they were advertising, they disseminated shock, using recycled paper scraps, assemblage, and collage like that for a concert headlined by the Dead Kennedys (1979; see image 3). Mixing crude stenciling with sloppy Dadaist montages, they tore up the typesetters' traditional grid and replaced it with chaotically disordered text. The ripped-up record sleeves and posters that expressed something so vital to the disaffected youth of the time owed much to German artist Kurt Schwitters (1887–1948) and the Dada movement. Many punk musicians and managers had been to art school, along with their graphic designers, and knew the revolutionary graphics of Russian Constructivism. A larger-than-life theatricality formalized the personae of punk groups and musicians in both the United States and the United Kingdom, and aliases were adopted to project a new identity. Johnny Rotten (b.1956), The Slits, X-Ray Spex, The Clash, Poly Styrene (1957–2011), The Damned, and Black Flag are some of the characteristically consonant-rich names that were so well served by punk's graphic designers.

Women became much more prominent than previously was the norm in British subculture groups, often appearing in transgressive fetish gear. The visual elements of sadomasochism and of Neo-Nazism were laced with a threatening, reactionary machismo, and images of violent sexualities.

In punk magazines and printed materials, aggression was expressed with off-center, oversized lettering, and pixellated photography cropped at savage angles. Multiple planes and fonts were smashed together with primitive force. Above all, punk visuals always presented an anarchic eyeful.

Posturing—adopting the style without understanding the substance of punk values—was considered even worse than joining the establishment. Authenticity was vital and so a do-it-yourself esthetic born of necessity was also a visual expression of legitimacy.

The earliest punk magazines or punkzines of the 1970s were inspired by science fiction as well as rock fanzines, and later titles of the 1980s, 1990s, and after the millennium continue punk graphic traditions. *Punk* magazine was formed in New York in 1976 and other titles such as *Sniffin' Glue* formed in London in 1976, *Flipside* and *Slash* in Los Angeles in 1977, and *Maximumrocknroll* in San Francisco in 1982 became seminal.

Punk graphic style remains expressive in the 21st century, and is gaining in strength and use, spreading to high-street fashion logos, new typefaces, and advertising as a stylistic shorthand for authentic youth culture. **JW**

1976	1976	1976	1977	1977	1977
The Sex Pistols embark on the 'Anarchy Tour' in Britain, supported by The Clash and The Damned. Fearing violence, many venues cancel tour dates.	Singer Joey Ramone (1951–2001) appears on the front cover of *Punk* magazine, drawn by founding editor John Holmstrom (b.1954).	McLaren recruits art school friend Jamie Reid to work on the Sex Pistols management team and create artwork.	Sid Vicious (1957–79) joins the Sex Pistols and the band also signs to US record label A&M Records.	The Sex Pistols' single "God Save the Queen" is released in May. Reid designs the cover showing Queen Elizabeth II with type across her face.	The album *Never Mind the Bollocks, Here's the Sex Pistols* is released in October with a sleeve designed by Reid.

Never Mind The Bollocks, Here's The Sex Pistols 1977

JAMIE REID b.1947

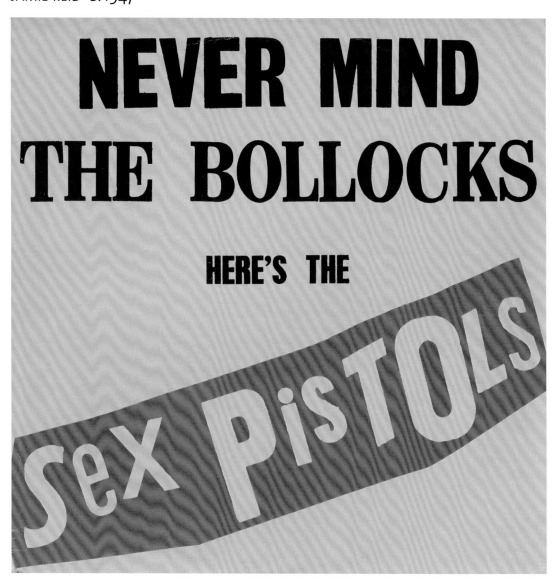

👁 FOCAL POINTS

1 PINK AND YELLOW
Reid's Situationist influences ran through his designs, and for *Never Mind the Bollocks* he subverted the language of consumerist slogans to invigorate the punk message. The pink-and-yellow colorway came from his graphic reworking of a banal marketing standard: the Day-Glo sticker.

2 LETTERING
The ransom-note typography reflects Reid's interest in cheap collage techniques. On this sleeve, as with that for the single "Anarchy in the UK" (1976), the words "Sex Pistols" are displayed using ten separate and differently sized letters, effectively establishing a countercultural logo.

W hen it was released in 1977, *Never Mind the Bollocks, Here's the Sex Pistols* grabbed the attention of punk fans, the media, and the law courts. It brought the sound and image of punk into one cohesive form that was recognizable to a much broader audience. Just as the music was radically different to what had gone before, so was designer Jamie Reid's artwork, which packaged it.

Invited to work with the band in 1975 by their manager Malcolm McLaren, Reid had previous experience with the Situationist movement through his own publisher, the Suburban Press, and this influenced the direction he would take in his designs. While his artwork for the Sex Pistols' first two singles had incorporated handwriting, the Union Jack, safety pins, and a torn portrait of the queen, his album sleeve relied solely on typography and bright colors. Emerging from a pink strip placed over an acid yellow background, the band's name was rendered in a series of clashing typefaces cut out in a ransom-note style from newspapers. Most of the words were displayed in a heavy butcher-block type, but "the bollocks" was rendered in a serif font. As a typographic cover, the lettering remains the most distinctive and influential part of the design, and it is widely credited to performer and Sex Pistols fan Helen Wellington-Lloyd (b.1954), who had previously used cut-out letters for punk flyers.

Making a collage with visual elements garnered from his Situationist esthetic, Reid used this subversive type style throughout the Sex Pistols' discography. It was blunt, loud and angry, and perfectly suited to the cause. **MS**

The use of the phrase "never mind the bollocks" on the cover led to an obscenity case in Britain where its etymology was defended in court.

DESIGNER PROFILE

1947–75
Jamie Reid was born in Croydon in south London and attended Wimbledon Art College and Croydon Art School in the early 1960s. In 1966 he designed the cover of *Heatwave*, a publication allied to the Situationist International group, and four years later he co-founded a neo-Situationist printing press, the Suburban Press.

1976–85
From 1976 to 1980 Reid worked with the Sex Pistols, creating sleeve artwork and publicity materials for the band's singles and albums, and he was also involved in the production of graphic art for *The Great Rock 'n' Roll Swindle* (1980) feature film. He continued to work on music projects for a range of acts, including Bow Wow Wow, Rhys Mwyn and Anhrefn, Afro-Celt Sound System, and Half Man Half Biscuit. He also held numerous international exhibitions of his work.

1986–PRESENT
From 1986 to 1990 Reid worked at Assorted Images graphics studio in London and in 1989 he began to work at Strongroom recording studio in London. He also produced cover artworks for artists including Boy George (b.1961). In 2008 his art was placed in the permanent collection at Tate Britain. In 2011 he staged "Peace Is Tough," which exhibited work from his archive and the 365 paintings that make up his "Aspects of the Eightfold Year" project about birth, life, and death. Social campaigning and spirituality remain a significant part of his life and art.

PUNK TYPOGRAPHY

Punk typography covers a variety of techniques that have several shared qualities: a rough, unschooled appearance, the use of found materials, and a do-it-yourself attitude. Ransom-note lettering was often accompanied by handwritten type that similarly conveyed a challenge to the uniformity of properly set and printed type. Punk fanzine *Sniffin' Glue* (above) featured a masthead scrawled in founder Mark Perry's handwriting, while countless flyers, posters, and record artwork incorporated the handmade mark of their creator. In the United States, another technique came to be added into the countercultural mix: Labelmaker. A handheld printing machine, Dymo's product enabled users to punch out individual letters onto an adhesive plastic strip, forming words or phrasing of their own making. It was printing type on-demand in effect—and subverted an existing technology, so was well suited to the punk ethos.

5 | Contradiction and Complexity 1980–95

POSTMODERNISM

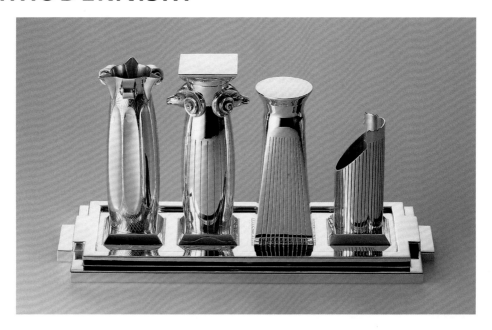

1 Charles Jencks's five-piece silver Tea and Coffee Piazza (1983) for Alessi features a coffee pot with ionic-type volutes.

2 Robert Venturi's Queen Anne side chair (1984) overtly references history to create an object of fantasy.

3 Michele de Lucchi's chair for Memphis Group, First (1983), consists of a circular steel tube that supports a backrest.

I n the early 1960s the Pop movement heralded a shift in values away from the tenets of modernism. From then on, design became increasingly driven by consumerism. After the 1970s, design and designers became more aligned with marketing, the mass media, and brand creation. Postmodernism grew out of this break with modernist tradition. It operated as a high cultural movement that critiqued the past and as an ironic response to popular culture that fed on it. By the 1970s, the production-oriented concept of design was replaced by an emphasis on consumption. Within the popular manifestation of postmodern design the media played an important role, giving consumers, who were increasingly intrigued by the past, access to a range of lifestyles.

Through the 1980s and 1990s the culture of consumption, with design at its center, affected everyday life, from shopping to tourism, and embraced leisure activities, from visiting heritage sites, museums, and theme parks to buying branded fashion items. As town centers emulated theme parks, and shopping malls were transformed into fantasy environments, it became difficult to separate real from designed experiences.

Efforts were also made by manufacturers and designers to create a high cultural design movement that responded to popular culture and contained within it a critique of the past. The Memphis Group experiment of the early 1980s, led by veteran Italian designer Ettore Sottsass (1917–2007), was

KEY EVENTS

1977	1979–84	1979	1980	1980	1981
Charles Jencks publishes *The Language of Post-Modern Architecture*, the first book to reference the concept in its title.	Robert Venturi makes a set of nine chairs for Knoll International, all of which are inspired by the past and can be described as postmodern.	Italian design group Studio Alchimia launches a collection of objects entitled "Bauhaus 1" which critiques the values of modernist design.	Ettore Sottsass, Michele de Lucchi, Matteo Thun (b. 1952), and others meet in Milan and form the Memphis Group to design furniture.	Austrian architect Hans Hollein (1934–2014) creates a controversial postmodern facade for his unit at the Venice Biennale.	Memphis holds a show in Milan to coincide with the prestigious annual "Salone del Mobile" (Furniture Fair). It causes an uproar.

important in that context. It began as a gallery-based phenomenon, but was quickly transformed from an avant-garde activity into a stylistic alternative to modernism in the marketplace. The power of postmodernity, which prioritized the importance of material goods in the context of consumption, imbued Memphis products like Sottsass's Carlton room divider (1981; see p.418) with added value, although it was made of cheap plastic laminates rather than fine woods. While Memphis remained an elite manifestation—the Memphis designers produced an annual show of handmade pieces from 1981 onward—the endless mass-market reproduction of Memphis-style patterns become part of the popular culture upon which the group was commenting. However, objects like First (see image 3), by Memphis co-founder Michele de Lucchi (b.1951), were intended for a broad public and the chair became a bestseller.

As part of a strategy to move its image forward and become linked in its customers' minds with a cultural program, the Italian company Alessi, which had been producing metal tableware and kitchenware since the early 20th century, invited well-known international, postmodern architects and designers—including the Italian Aldo Rossi (1931–97) and Americans Michael Graves (1934–2015), Robert Venturi (b.1925), and Charles Jencks (b.1939)—to create a limited-edition series of Tea and Coffee Piazzas. The resulting designs were intended only for exhibition purposes and included Jencks's notoriously impractical tea and coffee set in column shapes with rams' heads as handles (see image 1). Yet the collection had the knock-on effect of suggesting that the other goods that Alessi presented in its specialist retail outlets had something in common with museum objects.

Graves and German designer Richard Sapper (b.1932) created kettles for Alessi (see p.420) that took the concept of postmodern design to a new level of meaning. The designs communicated a complex sociocultural message to a wide community of consumers without necessarily having to perform their primary utilitarian function. Their purchasers knew that they had been created by well-known designers, and were manufactured by a design-conscious company that only sold its goods through selected retail outlets.

The same strategy was employed by US companies, which sought to invest their products with added value in a similar way. Knoll International launched a furniture collection created by Venturi, including his Queen Anne side chair (see image 2) of molded plywood with a laminated finish. The collection included a variety of major historical furniture styles: Chippendale (see p.26), Empire, Hepplewhite, Sheraton, Biedermeier, Gothic Revival, Art Nouveau (see p.92), and Art Deco (see p.156). SwidPowell Design also worked with designers from the Memphis stable, and Formica used similar names to work on its Colorcore series of objects. By the end of the 1980s, the concept of postmodern design had become synonymous with a highly self-conscious use of decoration and stylistic quotation. **PS**

1982	1982	1983	1983	1985	1987
The Portland Building in Oregon opens. Designed by Michael Graves, the postmodern structure has a cartoon-like quality.	SwidPowell Design releases houseware by postmodern designers and architects such as Richard Meier (b.1934).	Richard Sapper designs a kettle for Alessi that quickly becomes a postmodern icon. It features a coxcomb motif and a melodic brass whistle.	Alessi introduces its Tea and Coffee Piazzas, designed by postmodern designers. They are distributed to museums around the world.	Sottsass announces he is leaving the Memphis collective. He concentrates his energies on his architectural practice, Sottsass Associati.	The last Memphis show is held in Milan. The demise of the influential group signals the end of the postmodern design movement.

Carlton Room Divider 1981

ETTORE SOTTSASS 1917–2007

Wood, plastic laminate
76¾ x 74¾ x 15¾ in.
195 x 190 x 40 cm

Among the objects displayed at the first Memphis show in Milan was Italian designer Ettore Sottsass's Carlton room divider, or shelving system. It quickly became one of the iconic objects of that seminal exhibition. Sottsass had gathered a group of young colleagues around him, among them Michele de Lucchi, George Sowden (b.1942), Martine Bedin (b.1957), and Nathalie du Pasquier (b.1957), and he also invited a number of international collaborators to join them to create a set of objects that would directly critique design modernism. The unorthodox shapes, bright colors, patterned surfaces, and the plastic laminate that they used for their objects—Carlton among them—combined to make a strong visual attack on conventional esthetic values in design. The objects were only intended to be prototypes, but they were widely photographed and reproduced in the international design press.

In spite of their outrageous esthetic, Memphis designs are simple, functional household furnishings, such as shelving systems, sofas, lights, and ceramic artefacts. As such they do not stray completely from conventional design applications. Nor do they ignore the question of function. Rather they reprioritize the role of design, emphasizing meaning over utility, and seeing designed objects as carriers of cultural significance. Sottsass understood the paradoxes that were inherent in postmodernism and used the Memphis experiment to bring them to the attention of the design community. **PS**

✪ NAVIGATOR

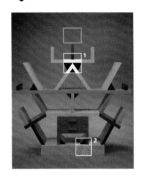

◉ FOCAL POINTS

1 SHELF

As is the case for many of the Memphis objects, Carlton is hand made from a processed wood base covered with colored plastic laminate produced by Italian company Abet Laminati. The latter is used to emphasize surface and because it is a material without any high cultural associations.

2 BASE

For Carlton's base, Sottsass used the decorative Bacterio pattern in black and white that he developed for Studio Alchimia in 1978. It resembles bacteria observed through a microscope. The shelving unit's playful, bright colors are matched carefully to create a visual symmetry.

OCEANIC LIGHT

The diagonal composition and bold colors of de Lucchi's Oceanic table light (1981) is typical of early Memphis designs. More than many other Memphis designs, it is a strong visual metaphor, resembling a sea serpent. At the same time it is a fully functioning table lamp. Each of its three striped pillars represents a functional element: the light source, the switch, and the power connection. The object cleverly combines its overt functionality with the Memphis commitment to expressive form, bright color, and emphasis on surface and object symbolism. Made from enameled steel, the lamp was manufactured by Artemide.

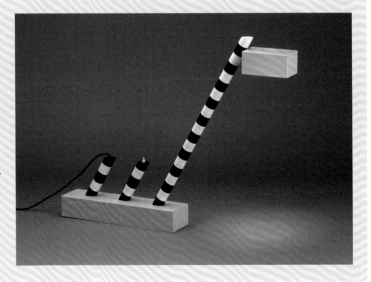

Alessi Whistling Bird Tea Kettle 1985

MICHAEL GRAVES 1934–2015

Stainless steel, polyamide
Height 8⅞ in./22.5 cm
Width 9½ in./24 cm
Diameter 8⅝ in./22 cm

✦ NAVIGATOR

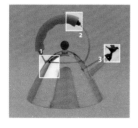

The 9093 kettle that US architect Michael Graves designed for Italian brand Alessi was launched in 1985. It came at a time when he was creating buildings in the postmodern idiom that depended on the use of color and traditional references. Graves's link with Alessi came through his work on the company's Tea and Coffee Piazza brainstorming project. Alessi asked him to design a kettle that would develop and popularize, through mass manufacture, some of the ideas he had initiated there. The kettle became a design icon.

The kettle demonstrates many of Graves's postmodern ideas in action. It has a cartoon look to it, especially with its Disneyesque spherical knob on the lid and the other two at either end of the rubber handle. Graves worked on Disney theme parks and he was fascinated with the idea of bringing mass and high culture together in one design. There is also a Pop feel to the object with its bird whistle, which sings when the water boils.

In 2015 Alessi celebrated the success of the kettle by launching a version, Tea Rex, which has a dragon, rather than a bird, at the end of its spout. Graves designed it just before his death, choosing a dragon because it symbolizes strength and good luck in Chinese folklore. His 9093 kettle remains one of Alessi's most successful products. **PS**

👁 FOCAL POINTS

1 BODY
The kettle's stainless-steel mirror-polished body and conical shape suggest 1930s Art Deco objects that feature a similar finish and hard geometrical profile. This helps create a sense of nostalgia— the kettle is not electric but is used on a hob, recalling old-fashioned country kitchens.

2 HANDLE
The 9093 kettle was Graves's first mass-produced design. He used blue and terra-cotta red colors for the grooved rubber grip covering the arc-shaped handle and the small whistle. He selected them for their symbolism— blue evokes the sky and coolness, and red the earth and heat.

3 WHISTLE
The plastic bird-shaped whistle positioned at end of the kettle's spout adds the element of sound to what is a strong visual design and suggests whistling kettles on a range. There is a playfulness to Graves's design, particularly in his choice of the whistle, which is reminiscent of a child's toy.

🕐 DESIGNER PROFILE

1934–61
Born in Indianapolis, Indiana, Michael Graves trained in architecture at the University of Cincinnati in Ohio. He then studied at Harvard University's Graduate School of Design.

1962–79
Graves began teaching at Princeton University. In the 1970s he was a member of the New York Five group of architects known as the "Whites" because of their white modernist buildings.

1980–2015
Graves' work began to include color, figuration, and traditional elements, and had more in common with postmodernism. He designed the Portland Building (1982) and the Humana Building (1985) in Louisville, Kentucky. In 2003 Graves became paralyzed from an infection of the spinal cord and he devoted the rest of his life to design for disability.

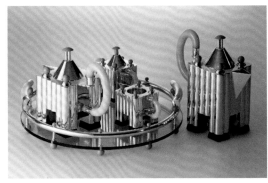

▲ Graves's silver Tea and Coffee Piazza set for Alessi treats the key components of a classic service—teapot, coffee pot, sugar bowl, tray, and milk jug—as if they are architectural elements.

ALESSI 9091 KETTLE

German industrial designer Richard Sapper created Alessi's first designer kettle, the multisensory 9091, in 1982. Unlike Graves, Sapper is more a late modernist than a postmodern designer, and he is best known for the Tizio desk lamp (1972) he created for Artemide. Nevertheless, Sapper indulged in a little light-heartedness on the Alessi kettle project. This is demonstrated by the kettle's coxcomb motif handle, and its two-tone brass whistle, which produces a short and pleasant melody when steam exits. The whistle contains two pipes that Sapper created with the aid of a German craftsman who made tuning pipes for musical instruments. The pipes are pitched at two notes to create a harmony when the water in the kettle boils.

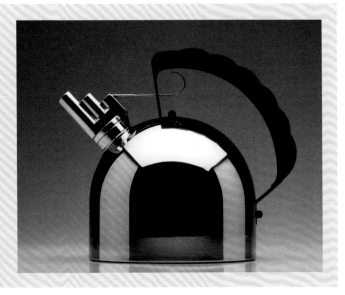

INDUSTRIAL CHIC

1 The Haçienda club in Manchester, England, had an urban theme, with striped columns and bollards mapped out the dance floor.

2 The armrests on Jasper Morrison's Thinking Man's chair are fitted with flat drinks holders.

3 Tom Dixon's S-chair is made from welded steel. The rush upholstery was done by a British basket-making firm.

Design underwent some rather unexpected twists and turns during the 1980s. Although some designers continued to pursue modernist ideals, the 1970s also witnessed the Crafts Revival. During the early 1980s, the picture was complicated by the rise of postmodernism and the vogue for Industrial Chic. Both were triggered by dissatisfaction with the blandness of mainstream design, although the solutions they proposed were entirely different. Whereas the Memphis group delighted in self-consciously artificial, hyper-decorative, pattern-laden objects, Industrial Chic started out as an anti-design movement promoting budget-conscious, down-to-earth, do-it-yourself furniture and furnishings made from industrial materials.

The origins of Industrial Chic can be traced to the fashion for High Tech during the late 1970s. High Tech design was closely linked to High Tech architecture, a revitalized modernist idiom pioneered by architects such as Richard Rogers (b.1933) and Renzo Piano (b.1937) at the Pompidou Centre in Paris (1977) and Norman Foster (b.1935) in the Sainsbury Centre at the University of East Anglia (1978) in England. Inspired by such factory-style public buildings with their externalized steel structures, High Tech designers advocated the use of heavy-duty industrial materials, such as wire mesh and heavy-duty rubber flooring. They also suggested that low-key utilitarian products from trade catalogs, such as steel lockers, could be used in domestic settings.

KEY EVENTS

1978	1981	1982	1983	1985	1985
The influential book *High Tech: The Industrial Style and Source Book for the Home* by Joan Kron and Suzanne Slesin is published.	Ron Arad establishes a shop and design studio in London called One Off, selling his Rover chair and Kee Klamp furniture.	Ben Kelly designs The Haçienda club in Manchester, England, for Factory Records. It reinvigorates the nightclub genre.	One-time Funkapolitan bass guitarist and hip-hop club owner Tom Dixon starts welding sculptural furniture and lighting from scrap metal.	Dixon sets up Creative Salvage with Mark Brazier-Jones (b.1956) and Nick Jones (b.1963); they show their scrap-metal pieces in a vacant shop in London.	Sheridan Coakley establishes a furniture company, SCP, and teams up with Jasper Morrison and Matthew Hilton.

Industrial decline and urban dereliction also played a part in fostering Industrial Chic. Disused buildings such as factories and warehouses were colonized by artists, architects, and designers and turned into loft apartments and studios. In Manchester, England, architect Ben Kelly (b.1949) designed The Haçienda club (1982), incorporating industrial features such as bollards, cat's-eyes, and diagonal-striped warning markings. Because conventional furnishings looked out of place in these large, bare spaces with their brick walls, cast-iron pillars, steel girders, and concrete floors, designers had to come up with ways of domesticating these non-domestic interiors. By using low-cost, mass-produced materials and off-the-peg components, and adopting simple construction techniques and rough-and-ready fabrication methods, designers were able to create innovative furniture with minimal capital outlay.

In Britain, Industrial Chic was championed by a new generation of iconoclastic young designers in London, providing a channel for raw energy and creative spontaneity during the bleak early 1980s. Recession and unemployment forced them to become more resourceful and entrepreneurial, to make the most of limited resources, and maximize their ingenuity and skills. Israeli-born architect Ron Arad (b.1951), who shocked the design world with his Rover Chair (1981; see p.424) made from an abandoned car seat mounted on scaffolding, was one of the leading lights. Another key protagonist was Tom Dixon (b.1959), co-founder of an inventive trio called Creative Salvage, who constructed composite furniture from railings, pipes, and other scrap metal, exhibited in pop-up displays in vacant stores.

Although there was an element of crossover from High Tech, the British reincarnation of Industrial Chic was less about simply reappropriating existing products and more about exploiting industrial materials as a vehicle for new ideas. Matthew Hilton (b.1957) and Jasper Morrison (b.1959), although later associated with more restrained minimalist design, both dabbled with Industrial Chic early in their careers. Morrison created his skeletal Thinking Man's chair (1986; see image 2) from flat bar and tubular steel, while Hilton's Antelope table (1987; see p.452) for Sheridan Coakley Products (SCP) is a theatrical hybrid sculpture juxtaposing sand-cast aluminum legs with medium density fiberboard (MDF), stained and polished to resemble wood.

In the hands of maverick designers such as Dixon, Industrial Chic was imaginative, playful, and energetic. Dixon's designs were eye catching and provocative. Openly disrespectful of modernist conventions such as functionalism, he co-opted a steering wheel as the base for his iconic S-chair (1987; see image 3). In spite of the small scale of their initial enterprises, Dixon and Arad rose to prominence. Within a few years, they were both being courted by leading European firms such as Vitra and Cappellini, and hailed as the saviors of British design. What had started out as a radical anti-establishment movement was promoted by lifestyle magazines as Industrial Chic. **LJ**

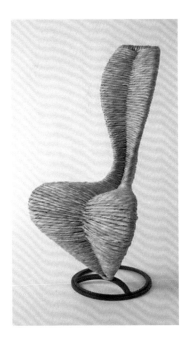

1986	1986	1986	1987	1987	1989
French-born André Dubreuil (b.1951) teams up with Dixon and starts producing welded steel furniture, such as his Spine chair (see p.450).	Swiss company Vitra produces Arad's Well Tempered chair, made from die-cut sheets of stainless steel.	Morrison designs the Thinking Man's chair, made from tubular and flat bar steel, later manufactured by Cappellini from 1988.	Dixon's S-chair is put into production by the Italian firm Cappellini, mounted on a steering-wheel pedestal with a rush-woven seat.	SCP produces Matthew Hilton's Antelope table, combining cast-aluminum antelope legs with a circular stained and polished MDF top.	Ron Arad Associates becomes the new vehicle for Arad's architecture and design practice and the workshop for his One Off furniture.

Rover Chair 1981

RON ARAD b.1951

Tubular steel, leather, and cast-iron Kee Klamp joints
31½ x 24 x 36 in.
80 x 61 x 91.5 cm

⚙ NAVIGATOR

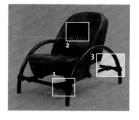

Ron Arad has had a remarkable career since establishing One Off, his combined workshop, studio, and store in 1981. The son of a sculptor, he originally had ambitions to become an artist but shifted his focus to architecture after moving to London from his native Israel in 1973. Arad got drawn into the design world inadvertently after the success of his Rover chair. The idea for this design was triggered by a chance visit to a scrapyard, where he saw a disembodied seat from a Rover V8 car. Although the vehicle itself had reached the end of its useful life, the leather-covered seat was still in good condition. Realizing that the seat would make a comfortable easy chair, Arad came up with the idea of mounting it on a tubular steel frame bolted together with scaffolding clamps, a low-tech, low-cost solution born out of necessity rather than ideology, due to lack of resources and skills. Although the raw industrial esthetic appealed to Arad, his decision to use off-the-peg building materials was largely for cost and simplicity.

Having developed a satisfying no-nonsense solution to a practical construction problem, Arad went on to design a whole range of furniture utilizing scaffolding poles fixed together with cast-iron Kee Klamp joints. In addition to storage systems, shelving, and desks, he designed the Round Rail bed (1981), with arched bed ends and a wire mesh platform supporting the mattress. Arad's work later took a different direction and became increasingly sculptural after he began fabricating chairs from welded sheet steel. **LJ**

FOCAL POINTS

1 KEE KLAMP JOINTS
Arad used cast-iron Kee Klamp scaffolding joints to attach the different sections of the frame together. Employed by builders, these off-the-peg industrial components were cheap and readily available. Because of their intended application, they were strong, reliable, and simple to use. Arad used the Kee Klamp system for a range of low-cost furniture, including beds.

2 ROVER CAR SEAT
The leather-covered seat was an authentic piece of salvage from a classic British car, the Rover V8. Because the seats were reclaimed, each one was unique and carried the evidence of its use. The concept of the ready-made was pioneered by artist Marcel Duchamp (1887–1968) as early as 1913. Arad raised the status of the seat by mounting it on a frame.

3 TUBULAR STEEL FRAME
The chair's frame is made from heavy-duty wide-gauge. tubular steel scaffolding poles, fixed together by Kee Klamp joints. The structure consists of four straight lengths supporting the seat, and two arched sections forming the armrests and legs. Tubular steel had been used in furniture since the 1920s, but it had not been exploited in such an overtly industrial way.

DESIGNER PROFILE

1951–79
Ron Arad was born in Tel Aviv. He studied at Bezalel Academy of Arts and Design in Jerusalem from 1971 to 1973, then moved to London. From 1974 to 1979, he studied at the Architectural Association in London.

1980–88
In 1981 Arad and his partner Caroline Thorman established One Off, a store, design studio, and workshop producing furniture using industrial and recycled materials. His work became increasingly sculptural in the mid 1980s after he began using welded steel.

1989–PRESENT
In 1989 he established Ron Arad Associates, the base for his architecture and design practice. He has designed furniture for leading Italian firms. From 1994 to 1997 he was professor of Product Design at the University of Technology in Vienna. From 1997 to 2009 he was professor of Furniture Design (later Design Products) at the Royal College of Art in London.

STEEL CHAIRS

Tubular steel has been used for chair frames since the 1920s. Up to the 1980s, however, steel had rarely been used for chair seats. Arad's welded sheet steel chairs, known as the "Volumes" series, created from 1988 onward, were doubly innovative. Not only did the metal provide the structure as well as the cladding, Arad left dints and scorch marks on the surface so that the chairs looked unfinished. His Well Tempered chair (right) for Vitra, designed two years earlier, was based on different principles. Made from sheets of tempered stainless steel, folded to create the seat and armrests, the metal is held in place by wing nuts and bolts to prevent it springing flat. Along with the color and sheen of the metal, this fixing method accentuates the design's industrial esthetic.

STYLE BIBLES

1 French lifestyle magazines became extremely popular, including those published by existing women's magazines, *Elle* and *Marie Claire*.

2 Launched in 1990, *Martha Stewart Living* was selling 1.2 million copies per issue by 1995.

The deregulation of the financial markets in the 1980s had the immediate and intended effect of heightening competition between banks and other lending institutions. For the consumer, the direct result was that it became easier than ever before to obtain a mortgage or to take out a personal loan, and many people did. Property values soared, particularly in formerly moribund inner city areas where "gentrification" saw working-class neighbourhoods transformed by middle-class incomers. In a reversal of the demographic trend of the immediate post-war years, in which new suburbs were settled by those escaping cities and rural areas, young professionals aspired to live right in the heart of things. Fueling and reflecting this trend was a boom in lifestyle publishing, highly illustrated books and glossy magazines targeting new homeowners (see image 1). Loftily aspirational for the most part, such titles injected the fashion cycle into the realms of interior design, decoration, gardening, and cookery. "Real Homes" features, supplemented with advice on "How to Get the Look," were as much about satisfying a voyeuristic desire to peep through the keyhole as they were about selling paint, sofas, or faucets.

KEY EVENTS

1980	1981	1984	1985	1986	1988
The Face (see p.428) is published in the United Kingdom. It is a monthly music magazine covering street style, politics, and fashion.	*World of Interiors* magazine is founded by Kevin Kelly; the title is bought by Condé Nast in 1983.	Habitat launches the rustic Country collection and a year later introduces the City Living collection to cater for modern urban dwelling.	*French Style* by Suzanne Slesin and Stafford Cliff is published. It is the first in the bestselling *Style* series.	*The Englishman's Room* by Alvilde Lees-Milne (1909–94) and photographer Derry Moore is published.	UK fabric designer Tricia Guild publishes *Design and Detail: A Practical Guide to Styling a House*. The book's photography is by David Montgomery.

In 1974 Terence Conran (b.1931) published his first *House Book*, which arose directly out of the popular Habitat catalogs. These featured Habitat staff and Conran family members and sold a way of life, delivered in a simple do-it-yourself kit form. The *House Book* began as an in-house training manual for the shop staff, but grew to be one of the bestselling style bibles of all time. At the heart of its appeal was choice, within arbitrated limits. Readers could acquaint themselves with different types of bed linen and door handles, for example, safe in the knowledge that these items had already received the stamp of approval from one of the United Kingdom's leading retailers.

In the United States, the doyenne of lifestyle publishing was Martha Stewart (b.1941). *Martha Stewart Living* (see image 2), first published by Time Inc. in the United States in 1990, wrapped up homemakers' concerns—familiar since the days of Mrs Beeton—into one all-encompassing brand. Stewart guided readers through all elements of cookery, design, decor, and entertainment, presenting these traditional skills as serious areas of interest for forward-thinking professional women. Domestic style took on an exotic, international dimension, too. In 1985 Suzanne Slesin and Stafford Cliff published *French Style*, the first in a popular series of style books that went on to include Greece, the Caribbean, Japan, and other destinations, sanctioning the import of vernacular traditions of decoration into home territory.

Hand in hand with the success of lifestyle publishing went the increased prominence of the style makers. Editors Ilse Crawford (b.1962) at *Elle Decoration*, Min Hogg (b.1938) at *World of Interiors*, and Paige Rense (b.1929) at *Architectural Digest* became powerful taste makers, alongside photographers including Derry Moore (b.1937) and David Montgomery (b.1937). Stylists such as Olivia Gregory, Faye Toogood (b.1977), and Sue Skeen emerged from behind the scenes; the word "genius" was used to describe them with surprising frequency. Skeen's white-on-white interiors were particularly influential. After extensive careers at magazines, these stylists were employed to prop catalogs for leading design firms, and their input had a phenomenal impact on sales.

The rise of the style bible culminated in *Wallpaper**, launched by Tyler Brûlé (b.1968) in 1996. Breaking the mold of the conventional "shelter" magazine, Brûlé and his team did not shoot real interiors. Instead, they composed aspirational sets from scratch and filled them with Gucci-clad models. *Wallpaper** was the interiors magazine for the generation weaned on Bret Easton Ellis and MTV, and was the first to champion a late 1970s style. Described as an exercise in optimism, it was also unashamed about blurring the lines between editorial and advertising, a boundary about which previous publications had been coy.

The establishment of the World Wide Web in 1991 served as a harbinger of change, and with the advent of high-speed wireless networking, large numbers of photographs could be downloaded with increasing ease. It was not long before readers were lusting after beautiful interiors online. **JW**

1989	1990	1993	1994	1996	2004
Elle Decoration, a sister publication of the French fashion magazine *Elle*, launches its first issue in the United States.	Time Inc. launches the magazine *Martha Stewart Living*; by 1994 it is appearing monthly.	The half-hour weekly show *Martha Stewart Living* debuts on US television.	The first web-based diary—Justin's Links from the Underground—is created by US journalist Justin Hall (b.1974).	Canadian journalist Tyler Brûlé launches style and fashion magazine *Wallpaper**.	Maxwell and Oliver Ryan launch the online decor site Apartment Therapy; by 2010 it reaches five million readers a month.

The Face Magazine 1980

NICK LOGAN b.1947   NEVILLE BRODY b.1957

Issue number 26 of *The Face*,
released in June 1982.

L aunched in London in May 1980, *The Face* was a monthly independent music magazine. Providing a totally new slant on modern music, it is often credited with defining a whole generation. Here, for the first time, music was seen in the context of politics, street style, fashion, and culture, and pages were heavily photo-led in the manner of a glossy fashion magazine. Although it was decidedly a music magazine, it was one that invited the world into the secrets of street style.

Publisher Nick Logan was a talented journalist from east London who had previously created the teen magazine *Smash Hits* (1978–2006) and had been an editor at the *New Musical Express* in the 1970s. "What *The Face* does is combine racy copy with a lot of photography—people do underestimate the power of good pictures," said Logan when the magazine was launched. When the staff could not get good pictures, they printed big lettering over the top of bad ones, or cropped them at odd angles. "It was a big laboratory. . . . Great courage is what set this magazine apart," said designer Neville Brody. From 1981 to 1986, Brody's work at *The Face* made him the best-known graphic designer of his generation. His style drew on the work of Russian Suprematist El Lissitzky (1890–1941), and also of Jan Tschichold (1902–74), the Bauhaus (see p.126), and the De Stijl movement (see p.114). The resulting radical page layouts and inventive typefaces were at the very heart of the magazine's appeal. Furthermore, Brody and the stylists and writers who created *The Face* refused to limit their scope. They wanted to create ambiguity and a flexible dialog, and they aimed to be as creative as possible. The ferocity of this passion burned through every page of the magazine, but Brody considers it a failure: "The failure was that people copied it. . . . It became a copycat culture." In 2011 *The Face* was added to the permanent collection of the Design Museum in London. **JW**

FOCAL POINTS

1 ENERGY AND VERVE
On each cover, Brody's simple, diagonally divided black-and-red (sometimes blue-and-red) square behind the title seemed to open the door to an offbeat, asymmetrical energy. Inside, blocks of text might be placed horizontally or vertically on the page. Brody later said that *The Face* was not about design elements, but about communication as an organic thing that evolves with society.

2 TYPE
Brody contorted letterforms, mutating type for headlines and story leads but leaving the main body text in more legible lettering. His first custom typeface came with Issue 50 and in the subsequent five or six issues, new typefaces such as Industria appeared with dizzying speed. It created a new graphic vocabulary that was imitated by advertising, retail, and publishing giants.

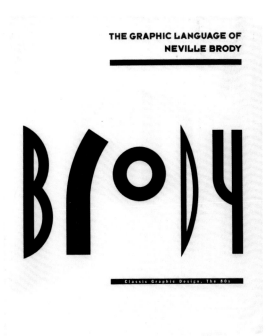

THE GRAPHIC LANGUAGE OF
NEVILLE BRODY

▲ The first volume of *The Graphic Language of Neville Brody* was published in 1988, and immediately became the world's best-selling graphic design book. It was published alongside a retrospective of the designer's work at the Victoria and Albert Museum in London, which attracted more than 40,000 visitors and went on to tour Europe and Japan.

THE VIRTUAL DESKTOP

E arly computers were the size of rooms or buildings, but their interfaces are not often given much thought. Users interacted with them by turning dials or inserting punched cards to run programs. Ticker tapes showed the outputs in strings of numbers and letters, while punched cards had holes precisely encoding data. The first true displays were redesigns of the cathode-ray tube television, giving the computer per-pixel control over the screen. For these, a new kind of language needed to be invented that made sense in the context of what users already knew. Following the typewriter, information was displayed on a screen, with a keyboard allowing users to enter and delete data—what is known as a "command-line interface."

The first concept of what a graphical user interface (GUI) could be came from Vannevar Bush (1890–1974), the head of the US Office of Scientific Research and Development for military purposes during World War II. He posited a memex computer, storing all a person's documents, images, and memories linked by hypertext, accessed through a graphical interface. Douglas Engelbart (1925–2013), a US computer pioneer at the Augmentation Research

KEY EVENTS

1981	1983	1984	1985	1985	1988
The Xerox Star 8010 is released, with a WYSIWYG GUI and an icon-based file system. Despite being based on the Alto workstation, it is a commercial failure.	Former members of the Xerox Parc team aid in the development of the Apple Lisa.	The Apple Macintosh 128K is launched and becomes the first commercially successful GUI-based personal computer.	Commodore launches the Amiga with the Workbench GUI, with multitasking, advanced animation hardware, and four-channel eight-bit sound.	Steve Jobs leaves Apple and founds a new company, NeXT. Some members of the original Apple Macintosh design team follow him to NeXT.	Jobs launches the NeXT Computer workstation with the GUI NeXTSTEP operating system.

Center at the Stanford Research Institute in California, took this concept and ran with it. His team created the oN-Line System (NLS) collaboration system in the 1960s, inventing the mouse, computer monitor, and screen windows as they did.

Sadly, Engelbart's team was dissolved and the technology was sold on. Many of his team members went to work at the nearby Xerox Parc, where they continued the work they had started and in 1973 built the Xerox Alto personal computer. The WYSIWYG (what you see is what you get) GUI this computer used added key elements, such as icons and menus, to allow users to move, copy, and delete items as if they were doing it by hand. In 1981 the Xerox Star 8010 (see image 1) was released, with a WYSIWYG GUI and an icon-based file system. Despite being based on the Alto, it was a commercial failure.

When Steve Jobs (1955–2011) and the design team at his personal computer company, Apple Computer, visited Parc, they recruited several Xerox Parc employees and bought access to the Alto with Apple stock options. Their GUI designs for the Apple Lisa personal computer and the subsequent Macintosh (see p.432) built on the Alto's technology, while introducing skeuomorphism to further reinforce the desktop metaphor.

The early Microsoft Windows operating system (1985) encouraged its users to explore the hard drive through a file manager and programs through a program manager. Microsoft chief executive officer Bill Gates (b.1955) wanted to license the Mac OS for Windows, but was rejected by Apple. Although the first version of Windows licensed certain Apple GUI elements, such as icons and windows, later versions continued to use them, arguing they were derived from earlier Xerox designs. In 1988 Apple sued Microsoft but lost. Gates wrote to Jobs: "Hey, Steve, just because you broke into Xerox's house before I did and took the TV doesn't mean I can't go in later and take the stereo."

Microsoft seized the advantage with Windows 95 (see image 2), which introduced the Start menu and taskbar, putting all running programs in one place, which has better multi-application support and a more modern look. It soon became the most popular operating system, thanks to it being bundled with cheap IBM PCs.

After leaving Apple in 1985, Jobs founded a new company, NeXT, which launched a high-end computer system, aimed at institutions such as universities. The NeXT Computer launched in 1988 was powerful with an elegant and advanced GUI, featuring 3D icons, a dock for frequently used applications, and submenus that could be torn off as individual windows and repositioned on the screen for easy access.

By 1994, the Mac OS was still in use, but looking outdated. An internal effort to replace it, Copland, was stymied due to internal politics, and Apple's prospects looked increasingly hopeless. Yet when Jobs returned to Apple in 1996, he brought with him the NeXTSTEP operating system, which became the basis of a new Apple operating system—OS X—that helped to revive the company's fortunes. **DG**

1 The Xerox Star 8010 was the first commercial system to use a GUI employing a desktop metaphor with icons and folders.

2 Microsoft's Windows 95 had a taskbar running along the foot of the screen. Documents and applications could be launched via the Start menu.

1990	1990	1992	1992	1995	1996
The world's first World Wide Web server runs on a NeXT Computer at CERN, the European centre for particle physics near Geneva, Switzerland.	Microsoft launches Windows 3.0 (see p.432), which proves a strong rival to the GUIs of the Apple Macintosh and Commodore Amiga.	Microsoft releases Windows 3.1. It incorporates Truetype font support, providing scalable fonts to Windows applications.	IBM launches the ThinkPad 700C notebook computer, created by US industrial designer Richard Sapper (b.1932; see p.434).	Microsoft releases Windows 95. It soon becomes the most popular operating system for personal computers.	After its efforts to upgrade the Mac OS fail, Apple announces it will buy NeXT and that Jobs will return to Apple.

Microsoft Windows 3.0 Operating System 1990

MICROSOFT CORPORATION

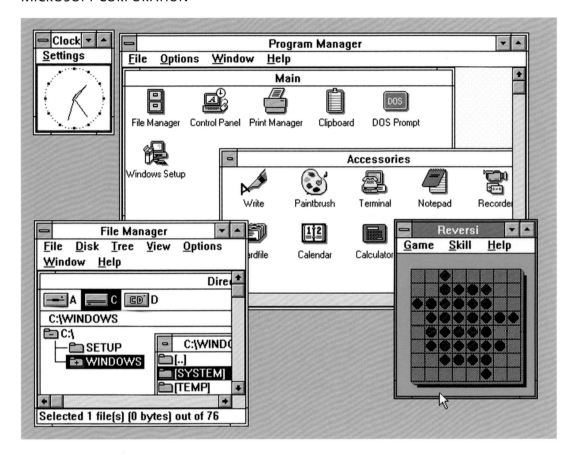

Windows 3.0 was the first truly successful Windows product for Microsoft. It featured a redesigned interface and improvements in speed, and (in 1991) extensive multimedia support. By the arrival of Windows 3.1 (1992), ten million copies had been sold.

NAVIGATOR

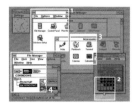

Before Windows, Microsoft relied on its MS-DOS operating system (1981) to manage the computer hardware for the user, and run software such as word processing programs. MS-DOS was far from intuitive and required specialist knowledge, however, so Microsoft began work on a new operating system called Interface Manager; this was renamed Windows by the time it shipped in 1985. Based on MS-DOS, Windows was distinguished by its original graphical user interface (GUI), which included drop-down menus, scrolling windows, and mouse support. At just $99, it was also cheap.

Microsoft's Windows and Apple's Mac OS look similar because they both owe a lot to Douglas Engelbart (see p.430). Englebart's team created the first graphical user interfaces for its oN-Line System. Many team members went on to create the Xerox Parc Alto personal computer (1973), which was the first machine to use the desktop metaphor and a GUI. Much of Apple's Lisa and Macintosh UI was drawn from this, and Microsoft licenced certain aspects of the Windows 1.0 interview from Apple.

Windows could run multiple programs simultaneously, and came with a variety of useful bundled software, including Paint, Write, Calendar, a clock, a card filer, a calculator, Notepad, and a game called Reversi. Windows 2.0 (1987) also introduced two core software packages, Excel and Word, but its slow speed meant that it did not sell well at all. Since Windows 3.0 (1990), however, the OS has gone from strength to strength. StatCounter's April 2016 survey estimates that around 85 percent of computers are running a variety of Windows (less than 10 percent run Mac OS X), although many are built on the Windows NT system (1992) rather than the original Windows code base. **DG**

◉ FOCAL POINTS

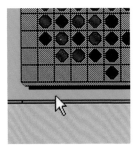

1 WINDOWS

Originally invented by Douglas Engelbart's team, windows are user interface containers of other elements, normally files or software. Microsoft's windows were introduced with Windows 1.0, but were not allowed to overlap until Windows version 2.0, for fear of legal action.

2 CURSOR

Following the practice of Apple and Xerox, Microsoft's GUI was mouse-operated. The mechanical device allowed users to map hand movements to screen movements and interact with icons and menus using buttons—a revolutionary step for users accustomed to typing in commands.

3 ICONS

The Xerox and Apple PCs used icons, and Microsoft followed. Icons are shortcuts to software applications and files, and their imagery allows users to see what objects are on their desktop, and where they are. Icons enabled users with no knowledge of code to access software for the first time.

4 MULTIMEDIA

Windows 3.0 with Multimedia Extensions (1991) was the first operating system to come bundled with a CD-ROM drive and a sound card, allowing users to experience accurate sound and video for the first time. The drives were slow and the sound was poor, but the advance seemed revolutionary.

◷ DESIGNER PROFILE

1955–74

Microsoft cofounder Bill Gates was born in 1955 to a wealthy family in Seattle. At thirteen he wrote his first computer program—a game—on a terminal at his school. Within a year, he and three friends were employed by a nearby computer corporation to hunt out bugs; by fifteen they were writing software. He enrolled at Harvard in 1973 but dropped out in 1974 to start his own business.

1975–84

Gates and his friend Paul Allen formed Microsoft, to develop programming languages. In 1980, IBM approached them to create an operating system for their new personal computer. Rather than develop their own operating system, Microsoft bought an OS clone, selling it to IBM as MS-DOS. Soon, IBM hired them to develop another OS, called OS/2.

1985–2001

In 1985, Microsoft launched its own OS, Windows, which became dominant from 1990. In 1995, Gates shifted the company's focus to the new Internet with Windows 95. In 2001, the company released its first games console, the Xbox.

2002–PRESENT

In the early 21st century, Gates gradually stepped away from Microsoft, resigning his last official role (as chairman) in 2014. He now focuses on the charitable foundation he runs with his wife, Melinda; it has assets valued at more than £23.56 billion ($34.6 billion). In 2015, his net worth was estimated at £54 billion ($79.2 billion).

VIRTUAL REALITY

The next steps in GUIs are being taken by very different products: Facebook's Oculus Rift (above), Microsoft's HoloLens, and HTC's Vive (all 2016). Virtual reality and augmented reality human-computer interfaces have entirely different rule systems and interaction points to those of the typical GUI—notably, they have 3D interfaces. This means that their virtual interfaces need new interaction devices, ranging from the depth-and-motion recognition of Microsoft's Kinect (2010) to the strange, banglelike controllers of Oculus Touch (2016)—but all of this is in its infancy.

ThinkPad 700C 1992

RICHARD SAPPER 1932 – 2015

The ThinkPad 700C came with a 25 MHz 486SLC processor, up to 8 MB of RAM, and a 120 MB hard drive. It weighed 7 pounds 10 ounces (3.5 kg).

 NAVIGATOR

When the ThinkPad 700C was released, it was like nothing else. The sharp, black look was meant to evoke the mystery of the bento or cigar box. Opening it up revealed the bento's surprises—a mysterious red nubbin among the concave keys and a large, bright color monitor. Where other laptops were gray or beige with small monochrome screens, the 700C's color 10 ⅜-inch (264-mm), 640 x 480 video graphics array (VGA), thin-film-transistor (TFT) display was the big selling point, because it was unheard of in a laptop and had been custom developed by IBM—hence the high retail price.

It was an engineering challenge for the independent designer Richard Sapper, IBM's lead notebook designer Kazuhiko Yamazaki, and the IBM design team based in Yokohama, Japan, to collaborate on the project from different parts of the globe. Their success was facilitated by a Sony digital communications system that transmitted high-resolution images over phone lines, and was established in several IBM design centers globally.

The ThinkPad series quickly garnered more than 300 awards for quality and design, and went on to have over 200 different models, selling more than 100 million notebook computers over the years. Chinese firm Lenovo acquired the brand in 2005, yet many of the original ThinkPad design team still work on the series, including Sapper. **DG**

👁 FOCAL POINTS

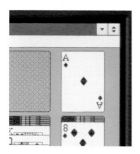

1 RED RUBBER

Between the G and H keys sits the TrackPoint, a small, rough red nubbin designed to replace a touchpad, touchball, or a mouse. It is more sensitive than a mouse with worse acceleration, but experienced users can use it just as well. The red rubber coloring serves to identify it in low light.

2 CASING

The dark finish adds a sense of mystery, tying in with the cigar-box shape, the rank of glowing light-emitting diodes at the panel's rear, and the featureless matt finish, which gives so little away. It also helps supply contrast and user focus to the high-end TFT screen, to aid the hardware perform its function.

3 SCREEN

Although Sapper's design was key in launching the ThinkPad, equally important was its power and functionality. It had a large 10 ⅜-inch (264-mm) TFT screen, unheard of in a portable computer. It also had a concave-keyed keyboard that was easy to type on and a removable hard drive.

▲ The ThinkPad has become an icon of the computing industry. In what is a rapidly changing environment, the ThinkPad is a classic technology brand. Its design has evolved to accommodate innovations while retaining the esthetic of a simple black box.

TS 502 RADIO

Sapper created the TS 502 radio with Italian designer Marco Zanuso (1916–2001) for Italian electronics company Brionvega in 1963. When closed, it is a nondescript rounded box. "We wanted to make objects for the home that do not show they are technology products unless you use them," said Sapper. The radio won multiple prizes, and is in the permanent collection at the Museum of Modern Art in New York City. Sapper and Zanuso went on to design a series of radios and televisions. An updated 1977 version—the TS 505—is still on sale.

PROBLEM SOLVING

1 Compact discs and compact disc players were introduced in Japan in 1982 before being rolled out worldwide in 1983.

2 The Aeron chair (1992) was designed "as a metaphor of human form" and there are no straight lines in the design.

3 The high-tech Carna wheelchair (1989) was named after Carna, the Roman goddess of health and vitality.

Creative problem solving has been the task of designers throughout history, but in the late 20th century it became more involved and more complicated as new technologies emerged at an unprecedented rate. In addition, rapidly increasing populations experienced greater needs and underdeveloped countries faced complex requirements. Frequently, innovative creative solutions resulted in the production of iconic items that made a considerable impact on their target markets for at least a decade. These were often a blend of design, invention, and engineering, such as the pocket-sized Sony Walkman (see p.408), created by Nobutoshi Kihara (1926–2011) in 1979, the compact disc, designed by the Philips/Sony design team in 1982 (see image 1), and the Swatch watch, first produced by Nicolas G. Hayek (1928–2010) in 1983.

In *Design for the Real World* (1970), designer Victor Papanek (1927–98) wrote about the social responsibility of design. This principle became an underlying theme of that decade and beyond, with an increasing consideration of ergonomics in design practice, as concerted efforts were made to create more efficient, safer, and user-friendly products. Designers investigated ways in which the human form functioned and, accordingly, created objects that were convenient and comfortable for users. For example, in 1979 Hans Christian Mengshoel (b.1946) produced the Balans kneeling chair. For office use, the chair addressed the physical problems that were arising as people were sitting at their desks for increasing lengths of time. In the 1990s, Donald Chadwick (b.1936) and William Stumpf (1936–2006) excelled in the field of ergonomic

KEY EVENTS

1980	1981	1983	1984	1985	1986
The Rubik's Cube, invented by Ernő Rubik (b.1944), is named "toy of the year" and sales peak over the next three years.	The nonconformist Memphis design group holds its first exhibition in Milan.	Philippe Starck (b.1949) designs the private apartments of French President, François Mitterrand.	Jean-Louis Dumas (1938–2010) creates the Hermès Birkin bag for actress Jane Birkin after the contents of her basket spill out on an aeroplane.	Michael Graves (1934–2015) designs his Art Deco-inspired postmodernist Whistling Bird kettle (see p.420) for Alessi.	IBM develops the laptop computer for commercial distribution, and Fujifilm develops the disposable camera for commercial use.

design. Manufactured from recycled aluminum and polyester, the groundbreaking biomorphic Aeron chair (see image 2) that they created for Herman Miller was the result of extensive research, trials, and consultation. During the 1980s and 1990s, the computer age was not only creating the need for new office seating, desk, and lighting designs, but also it enabled product and graphic designers to utilize sophisticated programs to carry out aspects of their work that had traditionally been drawn or made by hand. CAD/CAM (computer assisted design/computer-assisted manufacturing) provided imaginative new possibilities in planning and production.

Papanek's reasoning also inspired a greater awareness that design should address issues relating to the environment and ecological concerns. Soon after *Design for the Real World* was published, architect and designer Misha Black (1910–77) began discussing the role of the designer as being a force for social good, not simply to design products for commercial gain. Overall, there emerged a growing sense that design could be a powerful influence on social improvement. During the 1980s, designers began to focus more on green issues, such as designing products using materials that could be recycled, and consumers became increasingly sensitive to environmental issues.

Additionally, Japanese designers created a vast range of affordable products, each aiming to appeal to at least three of the five human senses. Designers everywhere needed to confront all these design issues if they were to be successful. Resulting solutions included household gadgets, such as those manufactured by OXO, founded in 1989 by industrial engineer Sam Farber (1924–2013). Developed for Farber's wife, who had arthritis in her hands and found using kitchen utensils difficult and often painful, OXO's Good Grips range of utensils focused on handle design and quality components (see p.440). The handles were made of Santoprene (a soft and flexible polypropylene plastic/rubber), they did not slip, and they were at once practical, ergonomic, and comfortable to use. In Japan industrial designer Kazuo Kawasaki (b.1949) also pursued personal problem-solving projects after both his legs were paralysed in a car accident in 1977. He designed the lightweight titanium and aluminum Carna wheelchair (see image 3), which had additional components that could be added to the frame according to personal needs.

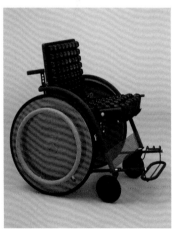

Other problem-solving designs of the period included the Double Plus calculator, designed by Donald Booty Jr. (b.1956) for Zelco Industries in 1986. It was ergonomically shaped for ease of handling, and featured a large plus key so that the addition function—the most commonly used key—could be accessed speedily. Also developed for ease of use were various models of the lightweight foldable Maclaren baby buggy, originally created in 1965 by aeronautical engineer Owen Finlay Maclaren (1907–78). These included the Sovereign (1984), which became the bestselling pushchair in the United States, and the Duette (1991), a double buggy that would fit through a standard doorway. **SH**

1988	1989	1990	1991	1993	1994
After filing for his first patent in 1979, Andrew Ritchie (b.1947) commences full-time production of his folding Brompton bike (see p.438).	The Design Museum moves to the south bank of the River Thames in London. Its transformation is led by Terence Conran (b.1931).	Industrial designer Ross Lovegrove (b.1958) opens his own practice, Studio X, in London.	Trevor Baylis (b.1937) creates the wind-up radio, powered by human muscle power rather than batteries or electricity.	James Dyson (b.1947) launches his dual cyclone vacuum cleaner—the DC01— (see p.442) on the UK market.	The rise of personal computers creates a need for new typefaces. Matthew Carter (b.1937) designs Verdana, which works well in low resolution.

Brompton Folding Bike 1988

ANDREW RITCHIE b.1947

Brompton bikes are custom built to suit the needs of the rider from a range of more than 16 million combinations of colors and components.

NAVIGATOR

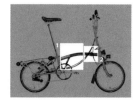

Seen by many as the classic folding bicycle, the Brompton has been a huge success since full-time production started in 1988. Designed by Andrew Ritchie, it was inspired by the aluminum Bickerton folding bike (1971). Ritchie believed that a different metal and a different folding system would make the design more efficient, and that lightweight folding bikes would be more desirable to commuters and urban cyclists if they could conveniently fold and store them on trains or in cars. In 1975, after persuading ten friends to each invest a relatively small amount of money, he spent a year creating a prototype folding bicycle in his London apartment. As his home overlooked the Brompton Oratory, he named his bike the Brompton. The first prototype was crude but Ritchie persevered and made two more, finally creating a steel bike with small wheels, downward-pointing handlebars, and hinges that folded the wheels inwardly, thus enclosing the oily chain and the chain wheel. The convenient and compact folding mechanism aroused some interest among several manufacturers, but ultimately they all declined to produce it, believing that no market existed for such a bicycle.

Ritchie filed a patent and began producing the Brompton himself. Initially, he made and sold thirty. Over the next few years, he produced and sold many more. Convenient, light, and strong, the bike can be folded and unfolded in approximately ten to twenty seconds. In 1986 he received private funding from the founder of Naim Audio, Julian Vereker, who had bought two Bromptons in 1982. An additional sum was raised from friends, relatives, and other Brompton owners, and in 1987 Ritchie set up a fully equipped factory. As demand surpassed the factory's capacity, he expanded in 1994 and again in 1998. Brompton soon became the largest bicycle manufacturer in the United Kingdom. **SH**

👁 FOCAL POINTS

1 "HUMPBACK" FRAME
Early models of the bike featured what was known as a "humpback" frame. This was because the tools that were available at the time were not sophisticated enough to create a more gentle bend. Later models benefited from an improved tool that produced a more elegant curve.

2 HINGE
Little has changed in the structure of the bike; it has the same hinged frame and small wheel size that Ritchie designed originally. The bike has two big wing-nut type fixings to secure the two hinges; the rear triangle and wheel simply swing underneath the frame.

🕐 DESIGNER PROFILE

1947–75
Andrew Ritchie graduated in engineering from the University of Cambridge, England, in 1968 and subsequently worked as a computer programmer for Elliott Automation, which later became part of Marconi. In the mid 1970s, his father introduced him to a man who was trying to raise money for the Bickerton bike, the first genuinely folding bicycle. Ritchie decided he could improve on the Bickerton's design.

1976–85
Although the bicycle trade in the United Kingdom was in decline, Ritchie worked on his prototype for a year. After unsuccessfully trying to license the design with the popular bicycle manufacturer Raleigh, he persuaded thirty people to place an order for a bike and pay £250 in advance. He then made fifty bikes and sold all of them within eighteen months.

1986–PRESENT
With funding from a variety of sources, Ritchie opened a factory under a railway arch in Brentford, and production began in 1988. The business was profitable from the start, and Brompton now exports to forty-four countries around the world.

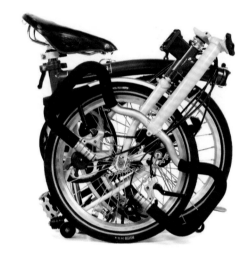

▲ The Brompton has a hinge at the front, so the handlebars tuck down, and one at the back that doubles as a suspension point. Small castor wheels allow the folded bike to be towed along.

PERFECTIONISM

Ritchie is a perfectionist and until 1987 he made all his folding bikes himself, with only one additional helper. Despite the huge demand today, the components of the Brompton bicycle are mainly made on site and each bike is hand brazed by skilled craftsmen at the London factory (right). They make sure that each bicycle is tough, unique, and fit for purpose. Every brazer is trained by Brompton for a period of eighteen months and has a personal signature that they stamp on the parts of the bike that they work on. Today, Brompton makes almost 50,000 bikes a year.

Good Grips Hand Tools 1990

DAVIN STOWELL b.1953

Santoprene, ABS plastic, and stainless steel
(Left to right) Measuring spoons, jar opener, pizza wheel, can opener, sink strainer, garlic press, swivel peeler, ice cream scoop, tongs

Largely self educated as a designer, Davin Stowell founded Smart Design in New York in 1980; the company has since become widely known for its innovative thinking in relation to combining the physical and digital with a strong ethical and public service commitment. In 1989 Stowell was approached by Sam Farber, an industrial designer and owner of a family kitchenware business. Farber's wife Betsey suffered from arthritis and had difficulty grasping many everyday kitchen tools, a vegetable peeler in particular. Farber had more or less retired, but his wife's predicament prompted him to seek a solution in collaboration with Smart Design. Dan Formosa (b.1953) was one of the designers at Smart who worked on the project and recalled, "First thought was, let's go larger—a handle that has some direction and some friction. . . . We go out to hardware stores, sports shops, wherever, to get ideas, borrow ideas, get some inspiration." The answer came in the form of an ergonomic, oversized, black rubber handle—similar to those used on a bicycle—with an extra flexible finger grip positioned close to the super-sharp blade. It was not only easy to use, but also visually appealing. Two versions of the vegetable peeler were made: one serrated, the other with a swivel blade.

Similar adaptations were made throughout an entire range of kitchen utensils, especially in relation to items such as the can opener, where conventional designs were difficult to operate. There was also a strand of proactive thinking: the egg separating cup was designed to have hollows for the white and the yolk, and the sink strainer—normally a messy item that was awkward to clean—was reworked in a flexible plastic version, based on a plunger, which throws off the collected bits when it is flipped. The products in the Good Grips range were more expensive than standard kitchen utensils, but they were immediately popular on the market. This prompted Farber and his son, John, to set up a new division in the family business to manufacture the utensils; they called it OXO, apparently because the name reads the same in any direction. By 1992 the OXO Good Grips range was so successful that the Farbers sold the company to General Housewares, and, after another change of ownership, Good Grips remains a current brand. **AP**

 NAVIGATOR

FOCAL POINTS

1 MECHANISM

The catch on the simple spring holds the jaws closed around the can as pressure is applied. It is released with a touch of the thumb. The sharp cutting wheel engages against the underwheel with cogs to increase the mechanical effectiveness. According to tests, the openers work equally well for left-handers. All Good Grips products are produced only in black.

2 ERGONOMICS

The turning handle is made from solid plastic with a non-slip surface, as are the grip handles. A hinged insert, with a small magnet attached below, picks up the lid when the can is opened. The opener is therefore safe and easy to use, and allows the user to see through the hole what is going on. The Good Grips can opener won the Arthritis Foundation Design Award in 1992.

KITCHEN CLASSICS

The arrival of the named designer in the kitchen is a post-1945 phenomenon. It led to kitchenware crossing the barriers between art, craft, and product design and entering the field of "design classics." The cast-iron casserole of 1959 (above) by Finnish designer Timo Sarpaneva (1926–2006), with its dual function detachable teak handle, is a prime example. It can be used in the oven, on the hob and at the table.

Dyson Dual Cyclone™ DC01 1993

JAMES DYSON b.1947

FOCAL POINTS

1 ATTACHMENTS
One of Dyson's innovations for the DC01 was his design for storing attachments on the machine itself. Although not a unique idea, this was unusual. The attachments—colored gray to match the machine— clipped easily onto the body, which enhanced the cleaner's convenience and accessibility.

2 YELLOW
After his pink G-Force, Dyson made the DC01 in striking gray and yellow ABS plastic. The body of the machine is gray and the moving parts are bright yellow. More controversial is the transparent area where the dust collects; in traditional vacuum cleaners, this would have been hidden in a bag.

In 1976 British engineer and inventor James Dyson noticed that his vacuum cleaner was losing suction. He opened it up and saw that the machine drew in air through the sides of the porous dust bag and that the bag soon clogged up, which led to poor suction. At around the same time, he visited a sawmill where he witnessed a system of expelling waste. The mill used a cyclone, which spun air around a large cone to remove the sawdust by centrifugal force. Dyson concluded that if he added a cyclone mechanism to a vacuum cleaner, there would be no need for a bag and therefore no loss of suction would occur. He made a prototype by removing the bag from his own vacuum cleaner and replacing it with a cardboard cyclone. It worked.

Dyson's revolutionary bagless vacuum cleaner—the G-Force—first went on sale in Japan, as he struggled to find a licensee for it in the United Kingdom and the United States. Manufacturers saw the product as a threat because disposable bags made them huge profits. However, in 1991, the G-Force won the International Design Fair prize in Japan, and Dyson used the prize money to create a dual cyclone vacuum cleaner. This was the DA001, but it was replaced the following year by the DC01—an improved version of his original cyclone cleaner. Market research had shown that a transparent dust container would be unpopular, but Dyson and his team made one anyway. As soon as it was launched in the United Kingdom in 1993, the DC01 drew positive attention. The efficiency of the suction, the machine's unusual grey and yellow appearance, and the transparent dust container that instantly showed users when it needed emptying were all appreciated. Within eighteen months, it had become the country's bestselling vacuum cleaner. **SH**

ABS, polycarbonate, and polypropylene plastic

⏲ DESIGNER PROFILE

1947–73
James Dyson was born in Norfolk, England, and attended the Byam Shaw School of Art in London. He then studied furniture and interior design at the Royal College of Art, but changed to engineering from 1966 to 1970.

1974–84
In 1974 Dyson created the Ballbarrow, a modified version of a wheelbarrow that used a ball instead of a wheel. The design was featured on the BBC and won the Building Design Innovation Award. Next, he designed the Trolleyball—a trolley with ball wheels that launched boats—and then the Wheelboat, which could travel on both land and water. In 1978 he came up with the idea of a bagless vacuum cleaner and took five years developing it. He produced the G-Force in 1983 and spent two years trying to find someone to license it.

1985–95
Dyson took his G-Force to Japan where he began working with a company that imported Filofax. In 1993 he established the Dyson company and research center, where he created many more versions of the vacuum cleaner before launching the DC01. That same year, he launched the dual cyclone DC02, which became the second bestseller in the United Kingdom.

1996–PRESENT
In 1996 Dyson launched the DC02 Absolute, with special air filters and a bacteria-killing screen, and from then onward he continued to produce new revolutionary versions of his vacuum cleaners each year. He began selling them in the United States from 2002. In 2005 he introduced the Dyson DC15, replacing the conventional wheels with ball wheels like those of his Ballbarrow.

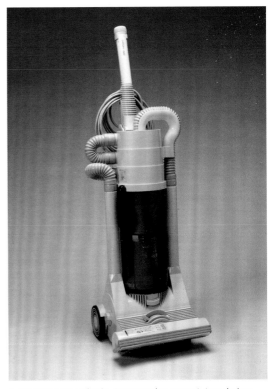

▲ Between 1979 and 1984, Dyson made 5,127 prototype designs. Although his pink G-Force cleaner of 1985 functioned well, the bagless design caused controversy and brought him little success. However, he refused to give up and followed his instincts.

MINIMALISM

1 At his London residence (1997–99), John Pawson designed the kitchen counter to appear as though it was passing uninterrupted through the glass wall into the garden.

2 Muji's stackable polypropylene (PP) storage drawers are compact and space saving, thus providing an excellent solution to many storage issues.

3 The Snow chest of drawers (1994) is part of a multifunctional range designed by Thomas Sandell.

After the overblown excesses of postmodernism and the succession of period-style revivals that had been such a feature of interior design in the 1970s and 1980s—the popular vogue for Georgian, Victorian, and Edwardian makeovers—the 1990s saw a return to the basic principles of modernism. Classical pastiche was out and in came a new appreciation for the radical design movements of the early 20th century. Minimalism was a style like any other, but the difference was not that there was very little in the dressing-up box but that the dressing-up box had been discarded altogether.

The oft-quoted "less is more" phrase coined by Ludwig Mies van der Rohe (1886–1969)—rephrased by Dieter Rams (b.1932) as "less but better" and by R. Buckminster Fuller (1895–1983) as "do more with less"—had long inspired a persistent strand of design thinking: one that prioritized function and eschewed superficial ornament in favor of the honest expression of materials. Minimalism went a step further, resulting in highly refined designs—in architecture, interiors, fashion, and furniture—that played with abstract notions of space, light, and immateriality.

It is perhaps no coincidence that the trend for minimalism in design, particularly in the design of interiors, should emerge at a time of economic recession, on the back of belt-tightening and falling markets. Superficially, a virtually empty interior could be seen as an austere rejection of consumerism and a reflection of a more sober global mood. Similarly, "no-brand" goods and clothing, such as those produced by Japanese retailer Muji (see image 2),

KEY EVENTS

1986	1990	1991	1991	1992	1993
Japanese designer Shiro Kuramata designs "How High the Moon," a minimal chair made of steel mesh (see p.446).	Philippe Starck (b.1949) brings minimalist design to kitchenware with the Juicy Salif (see p.466) created for Alessi.	The World Wide Web and public access to the Internet are launched.	Japanese "no-brand" retailer Muji opens its first international store in London.	Black Wednesday sees a run on the pound, the forced exit of sterling from the European Exchange Rate Mechanism, and the beginning of recession.	Jil Sander's flagship store opens in Paris, designed by minimalist architect Michael Gabellini.

advertised the fact that they needed no advertising at a time when the "added value" of branding seemed suspect and not worth paying for. Yet, paradoxically, minimalism—done well—was expensive. In many Western countries, property was becoming a significant area of investment, and despite periods of negative equity, relatively high house prices meant that space was increasingly at a premium. Minimalism celebrated pure space—and plenty of it.

There was not a great deal for the eye to rest upon in minimalist interiors, so surfaces and finishes had to be near perfect, particularly when conventional architectural features were removed or suppressed. A case in point is "shadow-gapping"—a common feature of the most sophisticated minimalist spaces. Shadow-gapped walls have no skirting boards, and the plane of the plastering finishes slightly above the floor on an inset metal fillet. This "look-no-hands" type of detailing is notoriously difficult and costly to achieve. Consequently, what these near-empty spaces contained in the way of furniture and fittings had to be worthy of scrutiny. Companies manufacturing licensed reproductions of great icons of modern design, such as the LC4 chaise longue (1928; see p.140) by Le Corbusier (1887–1965) and Mies's Barcelona chair (1929), saw sales increase as these pieces were selected to be displayed like art objects in domestic interiors that more closely resembled contemporary art galleries than homes. At the more affordable end of the spectrum, minimalism also had an influence. The Snow chest of drawers (see image 3), for example, designed by Thomas Sandell (b.1959) and Jonas Bohlin (b.1953) and manufactured by Swedish company Asplund, demonstrates esthetic restraint, combined with the human quality strongly associated with Scandinavian modern design. Part of a range of storage furniture, there is nothing that overtly says "bedroom" about the piece: it has the unassuming functional emphasis that makes it adaptable to a number of different uses and contexts.

The most influential figure in minimalism, then and now, is British architectural designer John Pawson (b.1949). His serene, pure interiors (see image 1), along with his later range of household wares, owe a great deal to a formative period in his design education, when he spent time in Japan and met architect and designer Shiro Kuramata (1934–91). The ancient Zen concept of "thinglessness" is evident in Pawson's seamless spaces, in which walls are pure white planes, floors are expanses of wood or limestone, and all the accoutrements of daily life are concealed in cupboards behind floor-to-ceiling, flush-paneled doors. The power of this contemplative approach has seen Pawson execute commissions for a diverse range of clients, from the Calvin Klein Collections Store in Manhattan (1993–95) to the Abbey of Our Lady of Nový Dvůr in Bohemia, Czech Republic (1999–2004). Other seminal interiors of the 1990s were the retail environments created by US architect Michael Gabellini (b.1958) for clients such as Nicole Farhi, Salvatore Ferragamo, and Bergdorf Goodman, as well as the Guggenheim and Cooper Hewitt museums. **EW**

1994	1995	1995	1997	1998	2000
Thomas Sandell and Jonas Bohlin design the Snow chest of drawers, a pared-down example of updated Scandinavian modern design.	Retail giant IKEA launches its PS range, featuring designs by named designers, including Sandell.	The Calvin Klein Collections Store opens in New York City, designed by John Pawson.	Pawson begins work on Pawson House, his minimalist family residence in Notting Hill, London.	The Glo-ball lighting range by Jasper Morrison (b.1959) reduces light fittings to the bare essentials.	The LEM bar stool by Shin (b.1965) and Tomoko Azumi (b.1966) is named product of the year at the International Interior Design Awards.

"How High the Moon" Chair 1986

SHIRO KURAMATA 1934–91

👁 FOCAL POINTS

1 ARCHETYPAL FORM
Japan does not have a tradition of seat furniture, and this design expresses an archetypal Western form, with the armrests, back, and seat of an armchair. The way that the mesh is contoured in well-defined plump curves suggests upholstered comfort.

2 NO INTERNAL FRAME
Unlike conventional pieces of seat furniture, this chair is manufactured with no supporting internal framework. The steel mesh material both expresses the form and comprises its structure, a unity that gives power and coherence to the design as a whole.

3 TRANSPARENCY
Kuramata plays with notions of transparency. A transparent object both occupies space and is absent from it. It also has an apparent weightlessness that makes it appear to float. What better accompaniment to a minimal interior than a chair that is barely there?

4 WIRE MESH
The chair is constructed out of nickel-plated steel mesh. In addition to transparency, the material gives the form a shimmering quality, which reinforces its sense of immateriality. Kuramata often employed materials that have an industrial esthetic.

At first glance, the work of Shiro Kuramata appears to distil a particularly Japanese esthetic in its refined minimalism. However, there are other more poetic preoccupations expressed in his designs, which help to explain why one of the designer's most fruitful creative associations was with postmodernist Ettore Sottsass (1917–2007), who asked him to work with his Milan-based design and architecture group Memphis in the late 1980s. Part of a generation that put Japan on the international design map, Kuramata was also noted for his experimental minimalist interiors, notably a number of sushi restaurants in Tokyo and the boutiques he created for Issey Miyake.

Throughout his career, Kuramata was fascinated by lightness and transparency: "I am attracted to transparent materials because transparency does not belong to any special place but it exists and is everywhere, nevertheless." Acrylic, glass, aluminum, and steel mesh, which crop up frequently in his work, carry the meaning of his designs as much as they express their forms. "How High the Moon," constructed entirely of nickel-plated steel mesh, has no supporting framework, which adds to its dematerialized quality, as does the reflective sheen of the metal. Like all of Kuramata's designs, its meticulous craftsmanship owes a great deal to Japanese traditions of making, which do not distinguish between "art" and "craft." Central to the design are a number of tensions: between its apparent ephemerality and its generous accommodating curves; and between the suggestion of solidity and a material that is full of light and air. The chair does not so much invite you to sit in it as question whether or not you could. **EW**

✦ NAVIGATOR

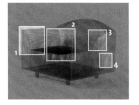

Perforated zinc and steel mesh, nickel plated
29½ x 37½ x 32 in.
75 x 95.5 x 81.5 cm

⏱ DESIGNER PROFILE

1934–65

Shiro Kuramata was born in Tokyo. After training in traditional woodworking techniques at high school, he worked in a furniture factory. He then studied interior design at the Kuwasawa Design School in Tokyo, where he was introduced to the concepts and practice of Western interior design. He went on to work as a designer of floor and window displays for a Tokyo department store before opening his own design office in 1965.

1966–81

Kuramata became interested in industrial techniques and transparent materials. Notable designs from this period include a light made of acrylic, a glass table and chair, and a tall chest of drawers with a serpentine curve. He received the Japan Cultural Design Award in 1981.

1982–89

During the 1980s the designer collaborated with Ettore Sottsass and his design group Memphis. Notable designs in addition to "How High the Moon" include the concrete Kyoto table (1983), Miss Blanche chair (1988), and a transparent flower vase (1989). He also created boutique and restaurant interiors, few of which have survived.

1990–91

Kuramata was awarded the Ordre des Arts et des Lettres by the French government. He designed the Laputa free-standing glass washbasin in 1991 and died at the age of fifty-six in the same year.

▲ One of the most beautiful of Kuramata's designs is this acrylic chair (1988), named after Blanche DuBois from *A Streetcar Named Desire* (1947). Creating the chair was a complex process. The acrylic had to harden yet remain clear; the flowers had to preserve their color without bleeding into the acrylic.

FORM FOLLOWS FUN

1 The Wink chair (1980), by Toshiyuki Kita for Cassina, has colored covers on each part that can be switched and washed easily, adding to the whimsy and fun.

2 In the design of the Duplex stool (1980), Javier Mariscal (b.1950) repeats the strategy "First surprise, then fascinate, then convince."

3 The witty Lucellino table light (1992) by Ingo Mauer has handcrafted goose-feather wings.

The US and European recessions of the early 1990s were over swiftly, and money flooded back into the system from North Sea oil, booming tech industries, and a cacophony of buoyant stock and property trades. The Western world began to look more prosperous and more fun, and there was a lot of new real estate in which to play. In order to express this new prosperity, playfulness, color,and superfluous decoration began to reappear.

Ettore Sottsass (1917–2007) and the design group Memphis had already, in the early 1980s, cut a jubilant path away from the monochrome rigors of modernism. In addition, industrial designers were growing in stature to become owners of their own brands. Consumers began to be interested in the designers' characters, and their jokes. For example, the Duplex stool (see image 2) by Estudio Mariscal seems to spin on its multicolored legs like a tipsy dancer lost in pleasure. Similarly cheerful is the Wink chair (see image 1) by Toshiyuki Kita (b.1942). It has ears like Mickey Mouse and presents a friendly versatility in bold blocks of color—just for the fun of it. In Munich, masterful designers such as Ingo Maurer (b.1932) allowed the witty side of their nature free rein (see p.454). His Birds series was launched in 1992 with the Lucellino table light (see image 3), a halogen bulb with wings, and the Birds, Birds, Birds chandelier, in which twenty-four bulbs fly skyward from a central point. There is no functional need for goose-feather wings on these lights, and that is the point: they provide an emotional narrative that references freedom and an irrepressible dash of wit.

KEY EVENTS

1986	1987	1992	1993	1996	2002
André Dubreuil (b.1951) creates the metal-framed Spine chair (see p.450). The curves of the steel rods recall Rococo ornamentation.	Matthew Hilton (b.1957) designs the three-legged Antelope table (see p.452) as a private commission.	Ingo Maurer launches the Birds series. It grows to include Birds, Birds, Birds, Seven off the Wall, Birdie's Nest, and Birdie's Busch.	Ron Arad (b.1951) designs the Bookworm bookshelf in sprung steel (later PVC). It arranges books on a sinuous. gravity-defying curve.	The Jack light by Tom Dixon (b.1959) is a light, a stacking seat, and a sculptural object all in one.	The Campana Brothers design the limited edition Banquete chair. It is made from stuffed animals: alligators, pandas, sharks, for example.

Italian designer Achille Castiglioni (1918–2002) and his brother Pier Giacomo (1913–68) had, since the 1960s, always included elements of whimsy in their designs. They thought that the industrial design world lacked focus on the important little pleasures of life. The Snoopy table lamp they created in 1967 for Flos, for example, provided the opportunity to smile as well as being a serviceable down light, while their Taraxacum pendant lamp (1960) also for Flos, designed to resemble a dandelion flower, embodies a "superfluous" narrative relating to time and the blowing of childhood dandelion clocks. Taraxacum directly influenced Marcel Wanders (b.1963) and the design of his Zeppelin light (2007) for Flos, which likewise is a decorative, narrative piece. Wanders was also influenced by Castiglioni and the Memphis group, and since his early collaboration at Droog design collective he has been central in defining the "form follows fun" esthetic. "Superficiality and spectacularity are genuine qualities, whether we like it or not," he said. Similarly, the Campana Brothers (Humberto, b.1953, and Fernando, b.1961) in Brazil have developed their postmodernist vision in a jokey manner, using stuffed animal motifs on seating and spirals of colorful strips in their iconic Sushi chairs (2002).

Leisure space became a major area for fun design, too, such as at the fashionable Sketch restaurant in London. Here, the pursuit of pleasure informs every design decision, and a programme of artist-conceived interiors rolls out biannually. The dining room created by artist Martin Creed (b.1968) in 2012 was a riot of disparate pattern, color, and form, in which every piece was a surprise and an entertainment. It was swept away in 2014 to make way for the sugar-almond pink dining room by India Mahdavi (b.1962), with its playful velvet upholstery, drawings by David Shrigley (b.1968) on the walls, and Missoni-style patterned tiles on the floor. The excess of old Hollywood is referenced in the sea of retro pink, gently clashing with copper bar and table lamps, offset by the gleam of steel lamps atop the plump banquettes.

However, it is in the lighting market that playfulness has been most central to design. Elaborating on Maurer's avian theme, Volière by Mathieu Challières is a family of lights, retailed by Conran from 2006, made to resemble copper birdcages inhabited by a colorful flock of feathered friends. Their function is to divert and charm. Animals are a recurring reference in many "fun" pieces, including fish in the porcelain Shoal installations (2007) by Scabetti and dragonflies in Fauna by Michele de Lucchi (b.1951). For his own label, Produzione Privata, the latter designer also created an homage to Florence's renaissance dome in his Brunellesca pendant (2015), for the sheer joy of it. The bottom is edged with an LED strip as if in afterthought. Custom design is part of this high-on-the-hog wave of design, in which luxury, extravagance, and exclusivity can play major roles. Where modernism championed mass production to provide functional and affordable design for all, these hedonistic designs tend to be more inspired by limited editions available at escalating prices. **JW**

2009	2007	2012	2014	2015	2015
The Fauna Dragonfly pendant lamp, from the Nature series by Michele de Lucchi, features a delicate cut-out metal dragonfly.	The Zeppelin light by Marcel Wanders for Flos uses the same technology as Achille Castiglione's Taraxacum pendant lamp from 1960.	Martin Creed creates the new dining room for Sketch restaurant in London. Every object is mismatched and introduces an element of surprise.	India Mahdavi's interior for London's Sketch restaurant references Hollywood glamor and voluptuous excess.	Commissioned by the Council for Culture and Art, Anagrama design firm creates arched bookshelves for the Conarte Library in Monterrey, Mexico.	Anagrama creates a giant maze in the Kindo children's clothing store near Monterrey.

Spine Chair 1986

ANDRÉ DUBREUIL b.1951

👁 FOCAL POINTS

1 MATERIAL QUALITY
The seat of the Spine chair is formed of flat metal struts bent inward, and the front feet rest on small steel plates. The chair frame is made of hand-bent steel rods, round in section, welded together. It is demonstrably the product of a workshop rather than manufactured in a factory.

2 STYLISTIC QUOTATION
The curves of the chair echo the flowing lines of Baroque and Rococo furniture. However, the chair is not a replica: the historical quotation is at the service of an original artistic sensibility. Although the chair is not a one-off design, it is a statement piece for those interested in style.

The work of André Dubreuil, who prefers to be referred to as an artisan rather than a designer, has often taken as a point of departure the Baroque and Rococo designs of the 17th and 18th centuries, a period during which France became the pre-eminent producer of luxury goods and the arbiter of high fashion throughout Europe. At the same time, the curlicues of welded metal of the Spine chair are also indelibly of the mid 1980s, when postmodernism provided a context for the pluralistic quotation of style and detail.

Dubreuil was taught to weld by Tom Dixon (b.1959), the maverick self-taught British designer whose early work consisted chiefly of furniture created from welded salvage. Dubreuil's own background included a period when he worked as an antique dealer, which may account for his abiding interest in historical styles. Light, airy, and curvaceous, the Spine is a chair to be viewed and appreciated for its beauty, rather than one to be sat in for long periods. The continuous flowing lines of the back and seat have a calligraphic quality: the chair looks as much drawn as constructed. Unlike metal-framed modernist furniture, the design is a celebration of curves executed in round steel rods. Although some models have been manufactured with a black painted finish, an unpainted waxed finish was the designer's original intention. Unusually for Dubreuil, the Spine chair was created as one of a series and it is still made today. **EW**

Waxed steel
33¾ x 27¾ x 36½ in.
86 x 70.5 x 93 cm

DESIGNER PROFILE

1951–87

Born in Lyon, France, Dubreuil was interested in art from an early age. In 1967 he moved to London to study at the Inchbald School of Design. His early pieces, which he hand made in his apartment using a minimum of equipment, included chandeliers, sconces, and candlesticks.

1988–PRESENT

In 1988 he set up a workshop in London, trading as André Dubreuil Decorative Arts. He worked with steel, copper, and iron, but also created pieces incorporating ceramics and glass. In 1996 Dubreuil took over his parents' estate, an 18th-century chateau in the Dordogne, and embarked on its restoration. In 2010 he returned to France and now runs his workshop from the estate. Clients have included Chanel and Louis Vuitton.

PARIS CHAIR

Made of waxed steel sheet, the three-legged Paris chair (1988; above) is imbued with great personality. Its decoration, created using an acetylene torch, resembles animal print, thereby adding further vitality and animation to the piece. An avowed opponent of machine manufacture, Dubreuil dislikes replicating his work. The designs that he is prepared to reproduce are all hand made and no two are exactly alike.

▲ Unlike modernist metal furniture, in which every effort was made to conceal the marks of making, here they are left exposed by the wax finish applied to the steel.

Antelope Table 1987

MATTHEW HILTON b.1957

Aluminum, sycamore, and MDF
Height 28 in./71 cm
Diameter 33 in./84 cm

✦ NAVIGATOR

There is a long tradition of zoomorphism in furniture design, dating back to the ancient civilizations of Egypt, Greece, and Rome. At a time when deities typically took parahuman forms—hybrids of men and beasts—it was common to find representations of animal feet or heads on thrones and other seats of power. In the 18th century, Neoclassical furniture borrowed from these antecedents and often featured claw feet. This convention has survived to this day in the form of the claw feet that support cast-iron bathtubs. Matthew Hilton's Antelope table, a theatrical, sculptural design, makes such hybridization more overt. The table originated as a one-off design for a private client, who had seen a candlestick that Hilton had designed and commissioned him to produce an item of furniture that summoned up a similar mood. For the design, Hilton combined traditions of craftsmanship and handmaking with techniques of mass manufacture. Like the contrast of materials used, this gives the design an interesting tension and dynamism. The Antelope table dates from the early part of the designer's career, soon after he began his creative association with progressive furniture company SCP. **EW**

◉ FOCAL POINTS

1 ZOOMORPHIC FORM
Two of the legs of this tripod table have the attenuated form of antelope legs, animating the design with great movement and energy, as if it was about to leap across the room. Side tables are typically restrained items of furniture, but the theatrical, sculptural quality of this design demands attention.

2 CONTRASTING MATERIALS
Part of the drama of this piece arises out of the bold contrast of the materials used. The antelope legs are made of sand-cast aluminum; the other supporting leg is sycamore. The top is made of medium density fiberboard (MDF), stained and polished to resemble wood.

⏱ DESIGNER PROFILE

1957–99
Born in Hastings, England, Matthew Hilton graduated with a degree in furniture design. He designed products for Paul Smith and Joseph Pour La Maison before joining product design company Capa. He set up his own design studio in 1984, and began collaborating with UK retailer and manufacturer SCP. In 1986 SCP launched Hilton's Bow shelving at Milan, his first design to be put into production, and went on to produce and market many of his designs for chairs, sofas, and tables.

2000–PRESENT
A retrospective of Hilton's work was held at London's Geffrye Museum in 2000. The same year he became head of furniture design at Habitat. In 2005 he was named Royal Designer for Industry, for his services to furniture design. In 2007 he launched a new business, Matthew Hilton Limited, formed on the basis of a licensing deal with Portuguese company De La Espada.

▲ The Balzac chair (1991) is SCP's bestselling chair to date. With a beech frame, oak legs, and leather upholstery, it is a contemporary reworking of the traditional club chair. Its deep rounded form arose out of Hilton's observations of the way people like to sit.

HYBRID NO. 1

A playful, energetic quality similar to that of Hilton can be seen in the work of young Turkish designer Merve Kahraman (b.1987), who has spent time in the design practices of Tom Dixon and Tord Boontje (b.1968). Her Hybrid no. 1 (above), a chair in which antlers grow out of the back rail, and Hybrid no. 2, a chair with rabbit ears, transform their sitters into hybrids themselves. Both pieces are hand made. Hybrid no. 1 has a textured paint finish on the antlers and a special pattern carved into the upholstery that recalls deer hide. The bunny of Hybrid no. 2 is more feminine, with cream leather upholstery and a cream painted finish.

Porca Miseria! 1994

INGO MAURER b.1932

👁 FOCAL POINTS

1 CUTLERY IN MOTION

In addition to the porcelain elements, Porca Miseria! contains cutlery—longer, thinner shapes glinting in the light, extending the appearance of movement. The spectrum of color, as the light filters through layers of porcelain, ranges from white to cream and from buff to blue and the darkest shades of gray.

2 EXPLOSION OF LIGHT

When viewed at a distance, the translucency of the porcelain material creates an optical effect: the eye sees it simply as an explosion of light coming out of the shadows. In this sense, it is the purest pendant light that has ever been, as there does not appear to be any form to it.

The term *porca miseria* is an Italian profanity and one of the many characteristically humorous names used by the great German designer Ingo Maurer for his lights. Originally Maurer called this pendant "Zabriskie Point," inspired by the dramatic explosion in the last scene of the film of the same name, directed by Michelangelo Antonioni in 1970. However, a group of Italians came to view the pendant at a private launch in 1994 and muttered *"porca miseria"* (holy cow, or similar) in amazement. Liking the sound of it, Maurer changed the name immediately.

This light is an emotional piece, expressing a moment of frustration or possibly a nexus of anger in the most magical and beautiful way. A number of cool, white porcelain dishes are broken with a hammer, or simply dropped at random on the floor, and reassembled as if spinning out from a single light source in a violent centrifugal whirlwind. The quality of the porcelain adds a breathtaking, translucent glow to the light and a halo to the violence of the explosion. Suspended on two steel cables, the Porca Miseria! is less a source of ambient light and more a sculpture that glows. Emotion, backed by technological sophistication, is at the heart of all Maurer's design. This light belongs in the genre of beautiful broken things—or shattered things—and could be said to be the ultimate expression of the Japanese principle of *wabi-sabi* in light. **JW**

◆ NAVIGATOR

This is a limited-edition piece. It takes four people five days to make one pendant, and only ten can be made in a year.

◷ DESIGNER PROFILE

1932–99

As a teenager Ingo Maurer was apprenticed as a typesetter, then studied graphic design in Munich. In 1963 he founded Design M to manufacture lamps of his own design and in 1966 released Bulb, which was instantly recognized as a masterpiece. Other well-known designs include One From The Heart (1989) and the winged light bulb Lucellino (1992).

2000–PRESENT

In 2002 the Vitra Design Museum toured "Ingo Maurer: Light—Reaching for the Moon" across Europe and Japan. Another exhibition was staged at the Cooper Hewitt National Design Museum in New York City in 2007. Maurer was honoured with the Compasso d'Oro lifetime achievement award in 2011 and is widely admired for mentoring new talent.

▲ The explosion at the end of *Zabriskie Point* is a slow-motion ballet of destruction, set to music by Pink Floyd. Ironically, Maurer's destructive explosion looks like the dawn of creation.

LED WALLPAPER

One of the first designers of lights to embrace LED technology, Maurer has been exploring the unique esthetic effects of LEDs and printed circuit boards since the mid 1990s. In 2011, with characteristic experimental flair, he took light away from fixtures and into the walls with his illuminated LED wallpaper (right). Manufactured in a choice of white or green matt non-woven wallpaper, the conducting paths are printed double sided as a closed circuit. Distributed over them are white, red, and blue LEDs. The red and blue diodes form optical cuboids, and the white lights are spread irregularly around them. At full strength they reach a total of 60 watts. Maurer and his team worked with the manufacturers at Architects Paper for three years to develop the product, which won the Interior Innovation Award at Euroluce in 2012.

DECONSTRUCTED TYPOGRAPHY

The standard block of text is so neutral in appearance, so even tempered, so sterile in its machine-like perfection, that it can seem as if the words have come out of nowhere. The design of writing has evolved to suggest an unnaturally calm, measured voice, as though there were an all-knowing, God-like presence behind the words, rather than a fallible human being.

French philosopher Jacques Derrida (1930–2004) suggested deconstructing writing, to uncover its underlying structures and reveal how it affects the way people read, write, and think. The first design discipline to take to these ideas was architecture. But, as writing is the first concern of deconstruction, the natural field for applying its principles is typography—as Derrida explored in his experimental book *Glas* (1974). How typographers went about this varied.

US graphic designer Katherine McCoy (b.1945) and her students at Cranbrook Academy of Art in Michigan took the most academic approach, drawing upon philosophy and art theory to produce work that blew apart typographic convention. Their compositions—typically posters such as "Typography As Discourse" (1989; see p.458) by Allen Hori (b.1960)—were often dense, chaotic, off-grid affairs, with multiple layers of hierarchy and an unusual interplay between text and image that sought to challenge the basic left-to-right linearity of typography and to make the reader aware of the process of reading. Cranbrook graduate Edward Fella (b.1938) rejected the prevalent slick, corporate esthetic of the time and chose to create work that embraced subjectivity and irregularity, like his posters for the Detroit Focus Gallery, produced between 1987 and 1990 (see image 2). Likewise, fellow graduate Jeffery Keedy (b.1957) employed ambiguity and randomness in designs, such as those for the *Fast Forward* catalog (1993; see image 1) of students' work at the California Institute of Arts.

Such ideas reflected a mood of dissatisfaction with the bland, characterless, humorless seriousness of modernism, which meant that the design world was receptive to new ideas and approaches. There was a sense that modernism's near-religious devotion to purity of geometry, material, and process neglected other, more subtle aspects, such as the need for human character and expression. The austere, minimalist esthetic of modernism, and its claim of exclusivity over functionalist rigor—of transcending the fads and foibles of passing styles—was unraveling and revealing itself to be just another style.

In typography, the resulting postmodern turn toward playfulness, expression, and anything-goes experimentation recalled earlier 20th-century typographic innovators, such as the Dadaists, Futurists, and Concrete Poets. In designing *Emigre* magazine, Dutch-born Rudy VanderLans (b.1955) and Czech-born Zuzana Licko (b.1960) had license to break all the rules, bringing mismatched typefaces at multiple sizes and alignments together in a single spread. Licko rejected centuries-old arguments regarding type legibility in *Emigre*, claiming simply that "you read best what you read most." Freed from traditional constraints, Licko created typefaces with new forms derived from the low-resolution computer environment. Similarly, US typographer Barry Deck (b.1962) sought to create type that reflects the imperfect language of the real world with his typeface Template Gothic (1990; see p.460).

The availability of the desktop computer was a key development, as it made the manipulation of typography possible for any designer, and in radical and creative ways previously impossible. Maverick magazine designers, such as Neville Brody (b.1957) at *The Face*, and David Carson (b.1954) at *Ray Gun* (see p.462), used the computer in tandem with traditional media to create a rich, creative process, and their work influenced a generation of designers.

In recent years there has been a notable retreat to the clean page design associated with modernism. In some ways deconstructed typography is a victim of its success, becoming the latest, fashionable style until it has its time and becomes passé. However, it is forgivable for businesses and organizations to wish to communicate a single, authoritative, neutral voice. One suspects that the calm, measured voice from nowhere is here to stay. **TH**

1 Jeffery Keedy's book spread from *Fast Forward* (1993), designed with Shelley Stepp, uses digital technology to morph typefaces, sometimes beyond recognition.

2 Edward Fella creates a highly unusual typographic composition in this *Nu-Bodies* (1987) poster for Detroit Focus Gallery.

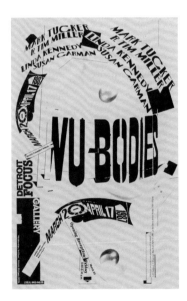

1988	1989	1990	1991	1991	1992
The Museum of Modern Art in New York City holds an influential exhibition, "Deconstructivist Architecture."	Allen Hori's "Typography as Discourse" poster is an example of how poststructuralist theory is influencing graphic design.	US designer Philip B. Meggs (1942–2002) publishes the how-to guide, "De-constructing Typography," in *Step-by-Step Graphics* magazine.	Katherine and Michael McCoy (b.1944) produce the book *Cranbrook Design: The New Discourse*, documenting the school's work in the 1980s.	US rock group Nirvana releases the album *Nevermind*, bringing the grunge esthetic to a global audience.	The music magazine *Ray Gun* is published, under the experimental art direction of David Carson.

Typography As Discourse 1989
ALLEN HORI b.1960

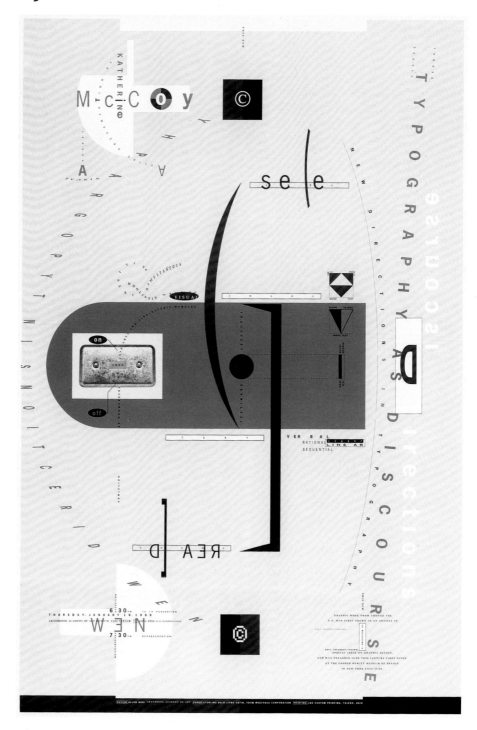

The poster takes as its subject a lecture on typography
given by Katherine McCoy, the co-chair of the design
department at Cranbrook Academy of Art.

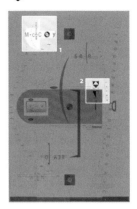

O nce described as "the most dangerous design school in the world," nowhere were the ideas of deconstructed typography explored with more serious intent than at Cranbrook Academy of Art in Michigan. Led by Katherine McCoy, a former industrial designer, students at Cranbrook were encouraged to draw on a wide range of academic texts to reconsider typographic conventions from first principles.

Allen Hori's poster, by discarding traditional page grids and text hierarchy, aims to represent the content — "typography as discourse" — through the form. Unlike a regular student essay, there is no single way to read this piece. Words travel in multiple directions, are reversed in grand, sweeping curves, and are set in small, delicate, miniature compositions. The typography could be said to resemble a conversation, with stronger and weaker voices, main points and sub-points, quick interjections, stumbled rephrasings, and moments of clarity.

Although one critic publicly labeled the school's output as ugly — perhaps unfairly for what is, after all, student work — Hori's poster has an elegance, a compositional balance, and an almost musical playfulness, that has come to make it an iconic piece representing this time of extraordinary creativity and intellectual boldness at Cranbrook. **TH**

👁 FOCAL POINTS

1 LAYERS

The hierarchy between text elements is organized in a novel manner through a complex series of fluid, overlapping layers. Top-level information is placed on the highest layer, with the reader able to explore areas of particular interest further.

2 GRAPHICS

Influenced by French post-structuralist theory, a key concept at Cranbrook was inviting the reader into a critical play with the piece, where meaning was not just the responsibility of the author, but constructed through the reader's encounter with a work.

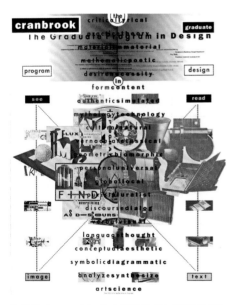

▲ McCoy's own poster from 1989 for the design course at Cranbrook, displaying many of the compositional themes that run through students' work.

MIT VISIBLE LANGUAGE WORKSHOP

In 1973 Muriel Cooper (1925–94), a renowned book designer, co-founded the MIT Visible Language Workshop in order to explore how the computer created new possibilities for typographic design. Cooper and her students developed what they called "information landscapes," where text occupied a virtual three-dimensional space on screen. Like at Cranbrook, the intention was to create a dynamic relationship between the reader and the text.

INTRRR ODUCT ION

Layouts from Issue 19 of *Emigre* magazine in 1991 featuring Template Gothic.

Futura (see p.146), Helvetica (see p.276), Univers, and other modernist typefaces aimed at perfection—to reduce letter shapes to their most essential, primary forms. In so doing it was claimed they became effectively invisible, presenting the content they carried with crystal-clear sharpness, unmuddied by what were viewed as the unnecessary quirks and ornaments of traditional serif typefaces.

Barry Deck's typeface Template Gothic tries something different. It offers a direct challenge to the tenets of high modernism by expressing and embracing the ambiguity and messiness that is human communication. Deck sought to create type that was not perfect, that better reflected the imperfect language of the real world. He was attracted to the raw imperfection of an old sign he found in his local laundrette that had been hand drawn from crude lettering templates. In Template Gothic, he sought to replicate its naive charm as a digital typeface, as well as the degradation that comes from repeated photomechanical reproduction. He embraced the subtle effects that a typeface can have on the way a text is read, creating typefaces with their own, subjective tone of voice. He pushed this idea of expressiveness in typography to its limit, even seeking to imbue typefaces with specific individual characteristics, such as angst, deviation, and perversion.

Template Gothic subsequently became an emblematic typeface of the grunge esthetic, and later entered the canon of design respectability upon being acquired by New York City's Museum of Modern Art for its 2011 Architecture and Design Collection. As Canadian philosopher Marshall McLuhan (1911–80) stated with such memorable brevity: "the medium is the message." Whether a crudely painted store sign or a professionally designed modernist typeface, form, as well as content, carries meaning. **TH**

◆ NAVIGATOR

Template Gothic 1990
BARRY DECK b.1962

stance.
peface de
DECK
RRY
published

II C

711

Emigre m
e Graphics
045-

idence to:

1 LETTERFORMS

A range of unusual features distinguish Template Gothic from most professional typefaces, giving it a naive, untutored feel. Unbalanced forms, inconsistent letter shapes, oddly tapering strokes, cut-off serifs, and an overall quirkiness set it apart from its modernist rivals.

2 MIXED TERMINALS

The endings of letters show wide inconsistency, varying from thick lines to thin lines, sometimes tapering off, and ending in either a rounded shape or an unusual cut-away triangular serif. This is matched by unusual variations in stroke thickness that could horrify many type designers.

3 LINE THICKNESS

Alongside the naive charm of hand-drawn lettering, Deck wanted to celebrate how repeated photomechanical reproduction creates interesting visual effects. Line thicknesses appear overly expanded or contracted, losing their definition, and are cut away at seemingly arbitrary angles.

▲ Template Gothic was released by Emigre Fonts in 1991 and gained popularity after being featured throughout Issue 19 of *Emigre* magazine, both in the layouts and on the cover.

JONATHAN BARNBROOK AND BASTARD

British type designer Jonathan Barnbrook (b.1966), like Deck, displays a lack of reverence for the traditions of typography, often creating typefaces that conjoin radically different historical styles into surprising new forms. With Bastard (right), released in 1990, Barnbrook aimed to bring Bastarda, a medieval script, into the computer age. He created a modular kit of parts that gives the typeface a slightly crude feel, with some astonishingly bold, starkly geometric curves on the upper case, but a lower case that retains the strokes of the Gothic scribe with a nib pen.

Ray Gun 1992 – 2000
DAVID CARSON b.1954

Issue 1 of *Ray Gun* appeared in November 1992, and featured US singer Henry Rollins (b.1961) on the cover.

⚙ **NAVIGATOR**

David Carson is as close as typographic design comes to its own rock star. With hundreds of awards to his name, international press coverage, filled lecture halls, and a bestselling debut book, his influence over a generation of designers is incalculable. A professional-level surfer, Carson learned his craft designing surfing and skateboarding magazines, and it was perhaps this surfer's attitude that he brought to design, helping to create the loose, carefree grunge esthetic of the early 1990s. His natural eye, plus his lack of formal training, gave him a freedom and willingness to experiment.

In 1992 Carson helped found the music magazine *Ray Gun* and, as its art director with no oversight, gave himself free rein to reinvent magazine design inside out, sometimes even in a literal sense: for one issue the magazine started in the middle and worked outward in both directions. His playful, energetic, and inventive designs never sat in the background, but always demanded attention and asked more of the reader.

Carson took roughly the opposite, non-academic approach to page design that the students at Cranbrook Academy of Art followed, yet ended up challenging its conventions in a markedly similar way. By following his intuition, expressing himself, and simply having fun, Carson gave voice and character to typography in a way few have matched. **TH**

1 MIXED TYPEFACES
Radically different typefaces are mixed freely in a way that recalls the punk esthetic of a previous generation, yet this time with more control. Stroke thicknesses are kept uniform, with a fluid but definable baseline, allowing room for creativity in the typeface choices and letter spacing.

2 LOGO
An otherwise bland, ordinary sans serif is transformed in Carson's hands into a lively, dynamic composition by a few simple interventions. Conjoined letters, a mix of upper and lower cases, a sole serif added to each letter, and an offset alignment all add up to create a logo with great character.

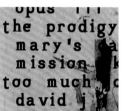

3 INDENTS
Seemingly arbitrary indents are added to badly spaced type, creating an esthetic with attitude. Overlaid onto a dark image, the words become hard to read in places, challenging the sanctity of legibility in typography and asking the reader to work harder in engaging with the cover.

🕐 DESIGNER PROFILE

1954–79
David Carson was born in Corpus Christi, Texas. He graduated with a degree in sociology from San Diego State University. He became a professional surfer, reputedly reaching a ranking high of ninth in the world.

1980–87
Carson attended a two-week graphics course at the University of Arizona. He taught at a high school in San Diego, California, from 1982 to 1987. After attending short graphic design courses in Oregon and Switzerland, he found work designing skateboarding and snowboarding magazines.

1988–91
His design talents were spotted by *Beach Culture*, a quarterly surfing magazine. He art directed six issues and gained attention in the design press for his innovative style, winning him more than 150 design awards. He moved on to *Surfer* magazine for two years.

1992–99
Carson founded *Ray Gun* magazine with publisher Marvin Scott Jarrett, and began to gain recognition beyond the world of graphic design, being featured in *The New York Times* and *Newsweek*. In 1995 he left *Ray Gun* to found his own studio, David Carson Design in New York, and his rebellious, counterculture esthetic proved a hit with corporate clients such as Nike, Levi's, and Pepsi. He published *The End of Print* (1995), which is reported to have sold more than 200,000 copies, an unprecedented amount for a graphic design book.

2000–PRESENT
Carson moved to Charleston, South Carolina. In 2011 he published *The Book of Probes*, an experimental rendition of the writings of media theorist Marshall McLuhan. He has a studio in New York, where he continues to work as a freelance creative director for major clients.

◀ Carson was once so uninspired by an interview with the musician Bryan Ferry (b.1945) that he set the entire piece (left) in Zapf Dingbats, a typeface consisting solely of graphic symbols, in *Ray Gun* Issue 21 in November 1994. Perhaps the ultimate rebellious act of deconstructed typography, the article could, in theory, be translated back into English by converting the piece letter by letter into a regular typeface.

SUPERSTAR DESIGNERS

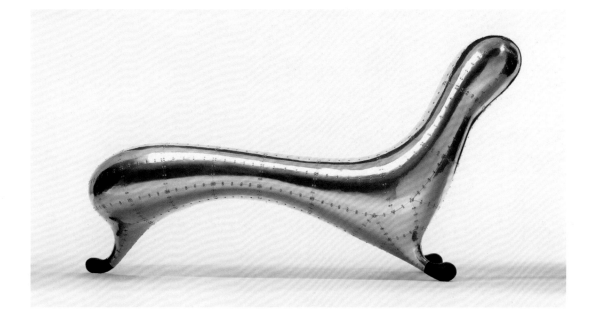

During the 1990s, a number of flamboyant media-savvy designers became superstars, brands in their own right, and none more so than French designer and *enfant terrible* Philippe Starck. (b.1949). Designers had been household names before—Raymond Loewy (1893–1986), who had a genius for self promotion, was a notable early example—but in this period their reach and celebrity became truly international. This development was fostered by a growing design awareness among the public at large, fed by coffee table books, magazine articles, exhibitions. and faster Internet connections.

On the world stage, the decade was marked by intense change as the legacies of the post-war era fell away and a new order emerged. Germany reunited, the Soviet Union disbanded, Japan went into recession, and the United States under President Clinton enjoyed one of the longest periods of sustained growth on record. European cities became truly multicultural hubs to rival New York City. A fascination with metals and materials that gleamed, last prominent in Art Deco style (see p.156) and to some extent Pop (see p.364), came to the fore as accents in an otherwise neutral palette. Clear acrylic and silver, mirrored glass and polished steel became key phrases in the syntax of showman designers, and consumers adopted the universally accepted esthetics of a few chosen taste makers, among them Starck, Terence Conran (b.1931), Ron Arad (b.1951), Karim Rashid (b.1960), Christian Liaigre (b.1943),

1990	1992	1993	1993	1993	1994
Philippe Starck designs the Juicy Salif for Alessi, made from cast and polished aluminum.	Free Trade Agreements in the EU reduce trade barriers such as import quotas and tariffs.	The home-furnishings firm Holly Hunt signs a licensing agreement to manufacture and distribute Christian Liaigre designs in the United States.	Terence Conran reopens Quaglino's restaurant in London (see p.468).	Marc Newson designs the aluminum and lacquer Orgone chair. Its fluid form recalls the designer's Lockheed Lounge chaise longue (1988).	Ron Arad completes his design of the public spaces for the Opera House in Tel Aviv. The concrete foyer features a wall made from bronze rods.

Tom Dixon (b.1959), and Marc Newson (b.1963). Consumers associated these superstar designers with individualism, enlisting them to create focal pieces for homes and public spaces, spiced with plenty of theatricality (see images 1 and 2). The concept of the "design icon" as a type of universal currency also grew during this time. Buying an Alessi kettle (see p.420), for example, was a means of tapping into an elite sphere.

US entrepreneur Ian Schrager (b.1946) introduced the concept of "lobby socializing" in his designer hotels—from the Royalton in New York to the Delano in Miami—in which Starck's design was the principal draw. Increasingly, these spaces became themed, theatrical environments where the superstar designer reigned. Starck said he intended many of his designs to "liberate the user from the humdrum reality of everyday life." As public taste for design grew, flamboyance became a useful tool for designers who needed to present themselves in ever more memorable ways in a competitive market. A pink suit, unusual eyeglasses, or a felt cloche hat, for example, might become a useful mnemonic, adding power to a message and distinguishing a designer from the crowd. Showmanship implies great artistry, but showy designs did not always bear scrutiny in the cold light of day, particularly when scant attention was paid to function. Occasionally, they did not work well at all, overturning the principle that had long been a benchmark of what constitutes "good design." One example is Starck's Juicy Salif lemon squeezer (1990; see p.466), which performs rather better as a sculptural object than as a squeezer. **JW**

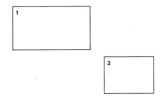

1 The Lockheed Lounge (1988) by Marc Newson was made by hammering numerous aluminum panels onto a fiberglass mold.

2 Karim Rashid created the Aura table (1990) by hand painting sheets of glass. These could be arranged on the metal legs in a number of configurations.

1994	1995	1995	1995	1998	1998
Tom Dixon's stacking plastic Jack light is mass produced by Eurolounge, bringing him to the forefront of industrial design.	Karim Rashid designs the Arp bar stool. Its wavy seat becomes a trademark of the designer.	Nobu restaurant opens in New York City, designed by British designer David Collins (1955–2013).	The Soho House private members club is founded in London, specifically for people from the creative industries.	Designed by Liaigre, the Mercer hotel opens in New York. His striking wenge wood furniture in the lobby makes him a household name.	The brightly colored iMac is launched. Apple took advice from a candy-wrapper company when deciding on the colors.

Juicy Salif Lemon Squeezer 1990

PHILIPPE STARCK b.1949

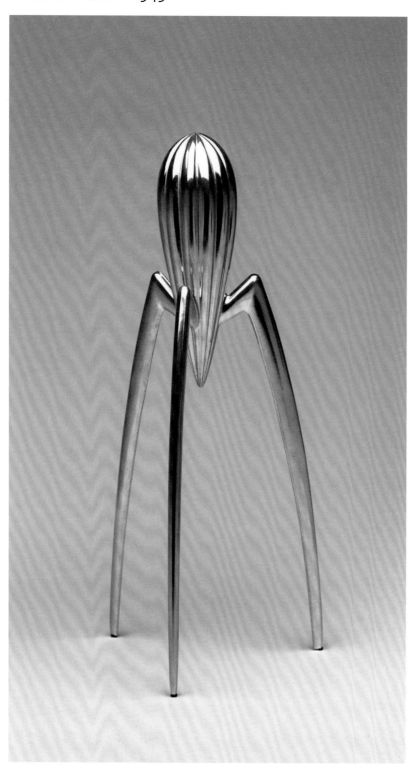

FOCAL POINTS

1 METAL HEAD

In theory, the lemon juice is meant to flow down the fluted runnels in the metal head toward a point at the bottom and into a glass below. But in practice, the juice simply pours everywhere. "It's the most controversial squeezer in the century," said a delighted Alberto Alessi, director of Alessi.

2 MATERIAL

The squeezer is made of mirror-polished aluminum casting. Alessi has also produced gold-plated versions of Juicy Salif, emphasizing its sculptural presence. They were never intended for use, because the citric acid in the lemon juice would damage and discolor the metal.

Rarely has a simple kitchen utensil been so controversial. Designed by Philippe Starck in 1990, it has been celebrated as a supreme example of form over function, and is ranked among the greats of contemporary design. However, for many, the Juicy Salif appears to have been designed as a practical joke. It is equally well known for its striking beauty and the fact that it is not fit for purpose. Its critics say that the juice, far from angling down into a receptacle placed below, sprays at random across kitchen surfaces. Furthermore, unlike almost every other lemon squeezer available on the market, the Juicy Salif will not fit into a kitchen drawer. Rather than be hidden from sight, it insists on being treated more like an ornament, sculpture, or feature of a kitchen environment. For his part, Starck remains unperturbed. "It is not meant to squeeze lemons," he said, but "to start conversations."

The birth of the idea for the Juicy Salif is amusing and characteristic of its designer. Starck was having lunch in a restaurant on the Amalfi coast, pondering a commission from Alessi, who wanted him to design a tray. Lacking lemon for his dish of calamari, he was suddenly struck by an idea and began scribbling on a paper napkin. Twenty-five years later, the napkin is a prize exhibit in the Alessi Museum. Alberto Alessi remembers: "I received a napkin from Starck; on it, among some incomprehensible marks—tomato sauce, in all likelihood—there were some sketches. Sketches of squid. They started on the left and as they worked their way over to the right, they took on the unmistakable shape of what was to become the Juicy Salif lemon squeezer." **JW**

◈ NAVIGATOR

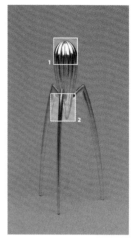

Mirror-polished aluminum casting
5½ x 4½ x 12 in.
14 x 11.5 x 30.5 cm

◷ DESIGNER PROFILE

1949–89

Born in Paris, Philippe Starck was apprenticed to Pierre Cardin in 1969. During the 1970s he designed the interiors of two iconic Paris nightclubs and moved on to larger hospitality spaces with Ian Schrager in the 1980s and 1990s.

1990–PRESENT

Prolific, controversial, and highly visible, Starck's designs include office furniture for Vitra and luggage for Samsonite. His Louis Ghost chair for Kartell (2002) was a bestseller and his Gun lamps for Flos (2005) caused a stir. In 2014 he launched a collection of low-energy prefab houses with Riko.

▲ The Theme Building at Los Angeles International Airport (1961) was designed by Pereira & Luckman Architects. Its two massive arches and UFO-style design have made it an iconic landmark.

DURAVIT

The Starck 1 toilet, bathtub, and washbasin series is based on the traditional bucket, tub, and washbowl—timeless, historic forms that Starck has reinterpreted with impeccable contemporary elegance. Launched in 1994, the archetypal shapes, translated into ceramic and acrylic and crafted by hand, were such a success that he went on to design the Duravit Design Center in Hornberg, Germany (2005; above). Cut into the facade and visible for miles across the Black Forest area, a giant toilet spans three floors. Again, Starck's sense of humor prevails, along with an attitude that hygiene and humankind's daily ablutions are to be celebrated rather than hidden. Studies in London real estate markets proved that the installation of a Starck 1 bathroom could increase the value of a property by 3 per cent.

Quaglino's Ashtray 1993
TERENCE CONRAN b.1931

Hand-cast aluminum
Diameter 3½ in./9 cm

✦ NAVIGATOR

Terence Conran reopened London's old Quaglino's restaurant on Valentine's Day 1993. It was a huge, expensive, exhilarating gamble. Glassed-in dining rooms overlooked a main floor surrounded with angled mirrors, and the grand, sweeping staircase gave diners the chance to make an entrance like stars in a Busby Berkeley film. Conran used the strong calligraphic image of the letter "Q" everywhere: on uniform buttons, menus, glasses, wine lists, bar coasters, matches, all promotional literature and, of course, the coveted ashtray. An etched glass screen behind the central banquette was decorated with the letter "Q," as was the metal balustrade on the magnificent staircase. The letter reflects the restaurant logo, which was originally designed by James Pyott.

Conceived at a time when smoking was still very much permitted indoors, the ashtray seemed to endorse the pleasures of sophisticated smoking—often between courses. Black versions were created for use as cruets; identical in form, they were powder coated in polyester. Frequently, the alloy metal-walled ashtrays were snaffled by diners and borne home as trophies of memorable nights out. In 2003 Quaglino's held an amnesty during which 1,500 ashtrays were returned. **JW**

◉ FOCAL POINTS

1 MATERIAL

Quaglino's ashtray is made of hand-cast aluminum, which was gravity fed, using resin sand. It was originally made in Hastings, England, by the Harling Foundry, but production moved to India when the foundry could no longer cope with the quantities. Twelve were made in bronze and there was a special 10th anniversary edition.

2 OLDSTYLE FONT

The ashtray is made in the shape of a "Q" in an Oldstyle font, a type with a bookish appeal. These oldest of fonts were originally created with a quill: every curve has a transition from thick to thin, and all letters tend to have a diagonal stress. A waved diagonal crosses the confines of the "O" to complete the "Q."

◀ Tucked away in the heart of Mayfair in London, Quaglino's was conceived in the spirit of a great Parisian brasserie in Montparnasse. It was not a traditional British eatery, where hushed diners politely pretended not to notice one another, but a thrillingly public, theatrical space where cigarette girls prowled and everyone present participated in the performance.

BUTLER'S WHARF

Design showmanship is a natural expression of ambition on a grand scale. Few ambitions have been grander than Conran's revitalization of a neglected area on the South Bank of the Thames in London. In 1983, when Conran and Partners purchased twenty-three redundant warehouses immediately adjacent to Tower Bridge, the present-day landmarks of the Oxo Tower, the Globe, Borough Market, and Tate Modern were still in the future. The project was an enormous gamble. Gradually, the former industrial site was transformed into Butler's Wharf, a vibrant mix of retail outlets, restaurants, and residential apartments, along with a cultural centre. People began flooding to the area to live, shop, and eat, as well as to visit exhibitions at the former banana warehouse that in 1989 became the Design Museum. "We changed the South Bank," Conran said. "Tate Modern would never have put itself into Bankside if it hadn't seen the success of Butler's Wharf and our little Design Museum."

FOUND OBJECTS AND READY-MADES

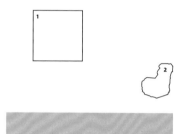

1 The original Tide chandelier (2005) by Stuart Haygarth is constructed from objects found washed up on a beach in Kent, UK. The different-shaped, translucent objects are arranged in a perfect sphere to reflect the shape of the moon, which controls the tides that wash up the plastic debris.

2 The Rag chair (1991) by Tejo Remy is constructed from layers of discarded rags bound together. Each chair is unique, and the owner can contribute their own rags to be incorporated into the design.

Like many developments in design, the use of found objects—or creative recycling—has its origins in the art world. French surrealist Marcel Duchamp (1887–1968) introduced ready-made elements into fine art in 1913 with the *Bicycle Wheel* stool, followed by *Bottlerack* (1914) and the infamous *Fountain* (1917). Duchamp saw "ready-mades" as an antidote to the purely visual "retinal" art that prevailed at the time. A few decades later, Pablo Picasso (1881–1973) said of his bicycle seat and handlebar assemblage piece *Bull's Head* (1942), "If you were only to see the bull's head and not the bicycle seat and handlebars that form it, the sculpture would lose some of its impact." Traces of a previous identity become a vital feature of the new object and provide opportunities for complex meaning, from witty puns to sharp social comment.

Creative recycling soon found its way into furniture design. Initially, it was a means of expressing paradox, irony, and surprise, but by the 1990s environmental concerns about waste and the consumption of finite resources had been added to the equation. From the 1950s onward in Milan, the Castiglioni brothers—Achille (1918–2002) and Pier Giacomo (1913–68)—were the most notable early designers to embrace the narrative opportunities provided by found objects. Two of their decorative lights manufactured by Flos—the Arco (1962) and Toio (1962)—are classic ready-made designs. "I see around me a professional disease of taking everything too seriously," said Achille. "One of my secrets is to joke all the time." The Castiglione brothers did not mention Duchamp by name, but they adapted his principles for their purpose. In 1957, they created the Sella stool from a bicycle seat and the Mezzadro stool made from a tractor seat. Mezzadro stools were updated continually as new tractor models were introduced to the market. Italian architect Gae Aulenti (1927–2012) also echoed Duchamp's bicycle theme when she designed the Tavolo con ruote (Table with wheels) for FontanaArte in 1980. She followed with the iconic Tour table in 1993, in which four pivoting bicycle wheels with chrome forks support a thick glass tabletop.

In the 1990s, the creative recycling field grew to incorporate designers such as Tejo Remy (b.1960) and Marcel Wanders (b.1963) at Droog in the Netherlands. Wanders, in particular, has been quoted as drawing inspiration from Achille Castiglioni. The tone of design that uses found objects became increasingly thoughtful, concerned with the environment, social responsibility, and waste, as seen in Remy's Rag chair (see image 2) and the Tide chandelier (see image 1) by British designer Stuart Haygarth (b.1966). In the latter example, the material is multicolored plastic detritus collected from the beach. The littoral shore had become a spoiled and littered space, and Haygarth transformed it into an elegant orb with a singular presence.

Since the millennium, found-object design has been instrumental in the idea of furniture being perceived as sculpture or design/art, and consequently realizing escalating prices at international auction. Designed by Raffaele Celentano (b.1962) for German firm Ingo Maurer, the Campari light (2002) falls on the light-hearted side of ready-mades and rapidly became a runaway success for bars and restaurants across the capitals of the world. By contrast, the Kebab lamp (2003) by London-based Committee is sold by Established and Sons in limited editions of eight per year. It is an "anti-design" piece—made by skewering a miscellany of spent found objects made of porcelain or plastic—that raises questions about mass production, consumption, and retail. Created for the Smithsonian in Washington, D.C., the TransPlastic chair (2007) by Brazilian brothers Humberto (b.1953) and Fernando Campana (b.1961) is a conceptual piece in which colored plastic chairs, lights, and trash are embedded within wicker, as if encouraging an all-powerful nature to engulf a material whose dominion is over. More recently, Piet Hein Eek (b.1967) in Eindhoven in the Netherlands designed the Scrapwood series of furniture and wallpaper (2013), finding an almost nostalgic beauty in material from the trash heap and a return to the soft warmth of wood. **JW**

1998	1999	2002	2003	2003	2011
The sculpture *My Bed* (1998) by British artist Tracey Emin (b.1963) reignites the debate surrounding ready-mades and art.	Stuart Haygarth's Millennium chandelier is made from spent black party poppers collected on the streets of London the morning of the millennium.	The Campari light by Raffaele Celentano for Ingo Maurer lends a Warholian (Pop Art) red glow to bars and restaurants.	The Campana Brothers create the Favela chair, a love song to the ingenuity of Brazil's shanty town dwellers.	The Kebab lamp by Committee is a skewer of found porcelain and plastic objects, later described as a "car boot [yard] sale in a lamp."	The Marie Coquine chandelier by Philippe Starck (b.1949) for Baccarat is designed around a white umbrella with a curved wooden handle.

85 Lamps Chandelier 1992

RODY GRAUMANS b.1968

Light bulbs, cords, and sockets
39⅜ x 39⅜ in.
100 x 100 cm

 NAVIGATOR

Designed in 1992 by product and interior designer Rody Graumans, the 85 Lamps chandelier was released as part of Droog's first collection at the Milan Furniture Fair in 1993. It was an instant success. The materials used are a minimalist's idea of what might be needed to construct a chandelier: wires, connectors, and light bulbs. The bare essentials are transformed into a voluminous feature light, both resplendent and luxurious, by the use of scale and repetition—two key features that are more readily associated with contemporary art than domestic fittings and fixtures.

The 85 Lamps chandelier is made like a bunch of flowers held upside down: the cords gathered nearest the ceiling swoop down and flare out to 85 light bulbs, or lamps, jostling for space below. One detail that contributes much to the success of the piece as an object is the ball of wire connectors at the top. Graumans could have set his connectors into a different shape, such as a flat ceiling rose, or arranged them in a drooping formation. The opposite of pretentious, the chandelier is humorously indifferent to the formalities of luxury, which a chandelier has traditionally defined. Yet the 85 Lamps chandelier manages to create a new definition of luxury for contemporary sensibilities. It is as if someone made a genuinely luxurious ball gown from one hundred plain white T-shirts. **JW**

◉ FOCAL POINTS

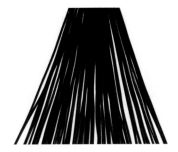

1 HOMAGE TO THE BULB
Graumans' chandelier design refers back to one of the earliest masterpieces of contemporary lighting: Ingo Maurer's Bulb of 1966. In homage to the incandescent bulb, Maurer treated his subject with a reverence usually reserved for grander material. Graumans applied the same principle to his chandelier for the luxurious and design-savvy interiors of the early 1990s.

2 BLACK CASINGS
Despite the ready availability of colored and braided flex for lighting, and a general movement in Dutch design for friendly colors, the 85 Lamps has always remained studiously monochrome. The casings for the lamps and the wire have only ever been available in black, and this creates a powerful chiaroscuro contrast to the halo of golden light below when the piece is lit.

3 CONNECTORS
The one element of 85 Lamps that shows the hand of the designer, almost despite himself, is the cluster of wire connectors at the top. The size of the ball of connectors is perfectly judged to create a balance in the chandelier as a whole, completing a harmonious visual integrity. It is a purely esthetic judgement that owes nothing to concept or theory.

◷ COMPANY PROFILE

1968–1992
Rody Graumans was born in the Netherlands. He was educated at Hogeschool voor de Kunsten in Utrecht and later at Gerrit Rietveld Academie in Amsterdam. By the age of twenty-five he had created a design classic: the 85 Lamps Chandelier.

1993–99
Renny Ramakers (b.1948) and Gijs Bakker (b.1942) founded Droog in Amsterdam in 1993. It was established as an anti-modernist, no-nonsense design collective, in which the theories of the Bauhaus were overturned for something more anarchic, narrative, and even sometimes baroque. Among the founding principles of the studio was a sober simplicity, coupled with a dry sense of humor or, some might say, a particularly Dutch form of wit. Graumans' design offered a witty new form of unashamed opulence for the design-loving classes. In the early 1990s the Droog collective strove to provide usable products that were readily available at relatively accessible prices. The firm launched the careers of a generation of Dutch designers, including Hella Jongerius (b.1963), Richard Hutten (b.1967), and Jurgen Bey (b.1965).

2000–PRESENT
In addition to its flagship site in Amsterdam (Hotel Droog) and a showroom in Tokyo, Droog premises were opened in Manhattan in 2009 and in Hong Kong in 2014. Graumans' 85 Lamps continues to be sold in Droog stores and also by multiple online design retailers, but the designer has been singularly silent and does not give interviews. One of the reasons for this may be the wild commercial success of his piece, which may be cheap to assemble but costs a significant sum to buy. He continues to live and work as a product designer in Gouda, in the western Netherlands, but his name is not associated with any further Droog products.

LED VERSION

In 2012 the 85 Lamps chandelier was reissued with dimmable LED lamps. The new version (above) offers an 83 per cent saving on energy consumption, compared to the original incandescent version, and because the LED bulbs are supposed to last much longer, it also saves time on bulb replacement. In this way, 85 Lamps became an ecological form of luxury, a knowing adaptation that entirely chimes with Graumans' original idea for the piece.

6 | The Digital Age
1995–present

THE ONLINE REVOLUTION

L ittle has had a greater impact on modern society than the arrival of the Internet. A design in itself, if an intangible one, it has in turn created new design disciplines, from the design of websites to video games. Established design spheres, such as typography, have also been transformed by the requirements of online communication.

Growing out of analog communication systems and nuclear-hardened military networks, the Internet is an unusual example of international collaboration done right, mixing math, hardware, and open access in a unique fashion. Yet, for modern consumers, it is an ubiquitous background tap, dripping information into their ears and eyes, that they barely notice.

Underlying every online interaction are some of the most brutal, large-scale structures around. The Internet runs on millions of racked servers (see image 1) of crude utilitarian appearance buried in old mines, in freezing bunkers, and in high-security compounds in city centers. Leviathan tubes of pure glass lie under the seas alongside the disconnected copper cables of their predecessor technology, the telegraph. Battalions of satellites orbiting the planet let every computer know where it is. Striding cell phone towers dot the landscape. And US technology company Google is building more and more billion-dollar server farms the size of small towns across the world.

KEY EVENTS

1995	1996	1996	1998	1999	2001
Shopping websites Amazon and eBay launch, although it takes several years before consumers are comfortable sharing bank details online.	The Hotmail web-based email service is launched. US technology company Microsoft buys it a year later, and localizes it for markets worldwide.	Microsoft introduces the web-friendly font Verdana (see p.478) to coincide with the launch of its Internet Explorer 3.0 web browser.	Google launches as a search engine. It goes on to pioneer targeted advertising with Google AdWords and expand into all forms of online software.	Napster launches, allowing peer-to-peer file sharing. Users can share audio files on the Internet. It is shut down for copyright infringement in 2001.	Microsoft releases the Xbox (see p.480) games console; the next year it launches Xbox Live, which allows gamers to play together online.

By contrast, each device that accesses it is a miracle of miniaturization. Each one is smaller than a single transistor valve from the first computers, but is a million-fold more powerful. Functionality dreamed of at the turn of the century is a standard part of many devices—global-positioning systems, speakers, always-on cell data connections, multiple cameras with facial recognition, biometric tracking, gyroscopes, and direct bank-payment links.

To the user, that is all invisible. A tap on an iPhone screen creates visual and tactile feedback much like tapping a sheet of paper—but that is generated by screens comprised of millions of high-density switches and actuators, with the subsequent action created by the processing power and features of the device interacting with software running on distant servers.

Transferring data between two locations using wires is not a new idea—the electrical telegraph was doing so the mid 19th century. But these connections were typically direct, meaning each node could only ever talk to one other at a time. This was also true of the first local area networks (LANs) and wide area networks (WANs), meaning that users could be frustrated if they needed to switch information sources. In 1969, the US Department of Defense's Advanced Research Projects Agency Network (ARPANET) was the first network to implement packet switching, allowing computers to connect to multiple machines at the same time.

The user-friendly Internet did not arrive until 1989. Tim Berners-Lee (b.1955), a researcher at the European Organization for Nuclear Research (CERN) in Switzerland, created the structure of what was called the "World Wide Web" and became known as the "Internet." The design motive was to enable users reading a document to be able to click the references or hyperlinks and see them immediately, whether they were graphics, speech, or video. To ensure that the references were always available, Berners-Lee built a web server using a NeXT computer, and wrote the first web browser. He then built the first web pages to describe the project itself, which were simple text documents. To enable users to always find the right document, Berners-Lee developed: a system of globally unique identifiers, called Uniform Resource Locators (URLs); a programming language to publish and read documents called the Hypertext Markup Language (HTML); and the Hypertext Transfer Protocol (HTTP) to enable web browsers to communicate with servers. These are still the basis of nearly all Internet traffic.

The Internet started to realize its potential in the 2000s, and it was only with the advent of mobile-cellular technology that it became nearly universally accessible. The rapidly accelerating capacity and data-access speeds of storage, married with higher speed Internet connections and the increased accessibility of user-generated sites such as Facebook (2004; see image 2), meant that more users had the capacity to access it. Over time, Berners-Lee's invention has revolutionized almost every field of the global economy. **DG**

1 Racks of computer servers located around the world form the lifeblood of the Internet and make communications possible with web browsers.

2 The Facebook website built its business around people's relationships and encouraged social networking online.

2003	2005	2009	2009	2011	2015
MySpace leads the social-media revolution. It becomes the largest social networking site until it is surpassed by Facebook in 2008.	The YouTube video-sharing website launches. It allows users to watch videos or upload their own creations for free.	Swedish programmer Markus "Notch" Persson (b.1979) starts to develop the Minecraft video game (see p.482), updating players via his website.	The anonymized digital currency Bitcoin is released. At its peak in 2013, one bitcoin is worth $1,242—up from less than a cent at launch.	The Silk Road website launches and trades illegal goods on the dark web—a sector of the web not indexed by search engines. It is shut down in 2013.	According to the International Telecommunication Union, approximately 43 per cent of the world's population uses the Internet.

Verdana 1996

MATTHEW CARTER b.1937

The Verdana font was created to address the challenges of on-screen display.

F or the launch of the web browser Internet Explorer 3.0 in 1996, Microsoft needed new fonts that were web friendly. Previous computer-specific fonts were more functional than attractive, because of the low resolutions of the user interfaces on screens, and did not scale up well. Earlier print fonts were adapted from type and did not scale down well. But the two fonts Georgia and Verdana, designed by English typographer Matthew Carter for Microsoft, were created with screen reading in mind.

Verdana in particular has been long regarded as among the most legible fonts around, ideal for online interaction. It is mostly a sans serif font, because of the problems that interlaced, low-resolution screens had with the fine detail on horizontal serifs, but several of the more linear letters have retained them. Despite the lack of serifs, Carter has kept much of their calligraphic beauty while ensuring legibility. The font has hand-hinting done by US type engineer Tom Rickner (b.1966), to ensure it has the sharpest appearance at any size. It also has a large x-height (the size of the lower-case letters), large counters, and wide spacing to make it clearer on computer displays.

From 1996, Verdana has been bundled with every version of the Windows operating system, as well as Microsoft Office and Internet Explorer, and has been on Mac OS since 2011. Carter has expressed surprise at the ubiquity of Georgia and Verdana—he had expected that many more web-specific fonts would have emerged to displace them. Instead, the fonts have often spread beyond the web to print because of the desire for consistent corporate branding. **DG**

 NAVIGATOR

FOCAL POINTS

1 COUNTERS
To improve the legibility of the font, Carter increased the sizes of any small aspects of the lettering. So the x-height was increased, giving his capitals less impact. He also increased the size of the counters—the empty areas that are enclosed by a letterform—for the same reasons.

2 SANS SERIF
Older computer monitors were low resolution and used cathode-ray tubes to generate the image, so fine details, such as swashes and serifs, would fade away at smaller sizes, losing consistency. Carter removed serifs where possible, but left them on certain letters like lower-case j and upper-case i.

DESIGNER PROFILE

1937–57
Matthew Carter was born in London. He interned at the Enschedé printing company in Haarlem, Holland, where he learned the art of punch cutting—making metal type by hand.

1958–79
After leaving Enschedé, Carter worked as a freelancer in London, where he designed the logo for the satirical magazine *Private Eye* in 1962, which is still in use. In 1965 he joined Linotype in New York, where he stayed for fifteen years. There he designed the Bell Centennial (1978) typeface for AT&T.

1980–1990
In 1980 Carter was appointed typographical adviser to Her Majesty's Stationery Office, remaining in the post for four years. In 1981 he co-founded the Bitstream digital type foundry, which was eventually bought by Monotype.

1991–PRESENT
In 1991 Carter co-founded the Carter and Cone type foundry, where he produced Verdana, Georgia, and Tahoma. Carter has also designed type for *Time*, *The Washington Post*, *Wired*, and *Newsweek*. In 2015 he completed a redesign of *The New York Times Magazine* logo. He continues to design fonts.

♣ SOPHIA CC
AABCDEE FF
GHIIJKK
LMMNOPQRR
STTUVWXX
YZ & ÆŒ
1234567890
CEFGHLRTTZ

▲ Since forming Carter and Cone, Carter has focused on more personal font projects, such as Sophia (1993; above). The design of this titling face was taken from the hybrid alphabets that flourished at the end of the Byzantine Empire. It is a mingling of Greek letterforms, Roman classical capitals, and sharp uncials.

IKEA CATALOG FONT

Because of its initial design for web use, Verdana has sometimes met with opprobrium when used in print. In 2009, Ikea decided to homogenize its branding and changed the font it had used in its print products to match its online presence. So the Swedish furniture manufacturer replaced the specially commissioned variation of Futura (see p.146), Ikea Sans Futura, that it had used for fifty years with Verdana (above). Such was the outrage among experts that an online petition asking Ikea to "get rid of Verdana" was started.

Microsoft Xbox 2001

VARIOUS

The Xbox came with an Intel Pentium III processor running at 733 MHz, 64 MB of RAM and 10 GB of hard-disk storage.

The Microsoft Xbox games console is a black and green rugged plastic box embossed with the shape of a giant X. The look was designed by Teague, and the interior was designed by four people, including technical director Seamus Blackley (b.1967). Inside this shell is essentially a hacked-apart laptop computer running the DirectX 8 graphics engine from the Windows operating system on a cut-back version of Windows 2000. This hardware was chosen so that game developers familiar with Windows-based personal computers, or PCs, could transition to developing for the console. Because PC components were cheaper, it could also afford to be more powerful, with a processor and memory twice the speed of the Sony PlayStation 2, its contemporaneous competitor. Uniquely, it had a hard drive, allowing it to store large amounts of content — music and saved games — locally rather than on separate memory cards.

What was notable, however, was the inclusion of an Ethernet network port on the rear of the device. In 2002, a year after the Xbox was released, Microsoft launched Xbox Live, which allowed fee-paying subscribers to download content and connect with other players via a broadband connection. Although earlier consoles had online functionality, the Xbox was the first to integrate it and support it so thoroughly. This meant that, like the players on PCs, Xbox users could play together, and 150,000 players became subscribers in the first week. By 2004 Xbox Live had 1 million subscribers, and by 2009 the number had grown to 20 million. Microsoft got what it wanted — a foothold in the living room. **DG**

 NAVIGATOR

FOCAL POINTS

1 CONTROLLER
The original game controller launched with the Xbox was large and heavy, and alienated the younger demographic Microsoft hoped to win over. Instead, the Japanese edition Controller S was introduced, with smaller grips that fit small hands better and roomy thumb sticks.

2 DISC TRAY
The Xbox was digital-media friendly. Users could also rip music from standard audio CDs to the hard drive, then play them from there while gaming. Some games also allowed players to access audio data. It was also capable of playing DVDs, although users needed a DVD Movie Playback Kit.

3 CONTROLLER PORT
Xbox had multiplayer options. Consoles feature four controller ports, system link cables allowed for up to four consoles to be linked together for sixteen players in the same game, and Xbox Live allowed more users to connect via the Internet. Xbox made it easy to play video games online.

XBOX 360

Two designs serving the same function could not be more dissimilar. The Xbox's successor, the Xbox 360 is off-white, gray, and silver, with a purity of line that echoes ceramics rather than electronics. It was designed in 2005 by an international team led by hardware designer Jonathan Hayes (b.1968), and was design rather than function led. Hayes says the form was inspired by a sculpture, *Bird in Space* (1923), created by Romanian artist Constantin Brancusi (1876–1957): "It traces a bird's flight. It captures the essence of upward thrust."

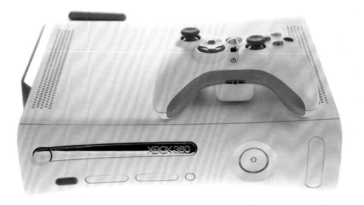

Minecraft 2009

MARKUS PERSSON b. 1979

Minecraft is a 3D open-world game with no specific goals for a player to accomplish.

It is unusual for a video game to merit attention from people other than hardcore players. But Minecraft is a very unusual game, which is creative, co-operative, and child friendly. The game is devoid of purpose—it does not even have a tutorial—but it is full of purposeful actions. Minecraft is procedurally generated from a random number seed, meaning no two players should experience the same unless they share their code. This both saves on hand-coding layouts and creates an infinite number of possible layouts for players to explore. Minecraft players initially have to work out what they can do in the world, experimenting with hitting creatures and plants, before exploring the keyboard. When they find the Crafting menu, then the real game begins. When night falls and monsters emerge, the game changes again, from one form of survivalism to another.

Many of the design elements of the game are inherited from Swedish programmer Markus "Notch" Persson's other favorite games. Persson, again unusually, developed Minecraft entirely in public from 2009, updating his website daily with information and talking to players until the full version was released in 2011. This served to market the game, and it soon drew attention. Minecraft sold 20,000 copies after a year and 1 million copies within two years. More than 70 million copies have been sold. **DG**

NAVIGATOR

1 HAND-DRAWN FIGURES

The blocky humans are an example of coder art—Persson made them rather than employing a game artist. They were originally designed for another project, Zombie Town. Their limited body structure saves on animation time and processing power.

2 PICKAXE TOOL

Tools, such as the pickaxe, can be unlocked through combining basic resources harvested from the world, and the tools allow players to explore more of the world, with greater safety and speed, on the surface, on the sea, and under the ground.

🕐 DESIGNER PROFILE

1979–2003

Markus Persson was born in Stockholm, Sweden. He began programming at the age of seven, producing his first game, a text-based adventure, a year later.

2004–09

Persson worked at Midasplayer, later King.com, which went on to make Candy Crush Saga. In 2009 he moved to Jalbum, a photo-sharing service, and started work on Minecraft.

2010–PRESENT

Minecraft sold enough copies a day for Persson to go full time and he co-founded developer Mojang. In 2014 Microsoft bought Mojang for $2.5 billion. Persson left the company.

◀ Introduced in 2010, The Nether is a hell-like dimension inside Minecraft. It can only be accessed by acquiring the toughest material in the game, obsidian, and shaping it into a portal big enough to step through, then setting it alight. Although The Nether sounds daunting, players go there for the rare materials, and because it acts as a shortcut between areas of the Overworld.

TECHNOLOGY ON THE MOVE

2

3

1 From the Motorola DynaTAC (far left) to the iPhone (far right), cell phones have diminished in size while growing hugely in capability.

2 The BlackBerry enjoyed popularity with business users, many of whom liked its miniature QWERTY keyboard.

3 The Motorola Razr became the world's bestselling clamshell phone.

I n the early 1990s, cell phone technology was the domain of science fiction writers, as it had been since the novelist Robert Heinlein first wrote about cell phones in *Space Cadet* (1948). Even in 2000 Iain M. Banks was still writing in his far-future *Culture* series about "terminals," or small, voice-controlled multifunction devices that allowed users to video call and access data remotely. It is a sign of how quickly cell phone technology has advanced that, by 2005, Banks' work already seemed woefully outdated.

The early cell phone designers faced a formidable array of challenges, including battery accommodation, keyboard and user interface design, the keyboard lock, water-vulnerable ports, robustness, and screen legibility. Then there were the infrastructure challenges. Early cell phones used radio or satellite technology, with users having to hunt down their connections, and coverage was often patchy. Masts were soon evident across the landscape, and they were a design challenge in themselves. Now city dwellers have become used to seeing a crown of white plastic prongs surmounting any building sufficiently high to improve coverage. Elsewhere, masts are disguised as trees and cacti, placed in church towers, or hidden behind billboards.

The first cell phone systems were designed for the German railway networks at the end of World War I. Yet these were only mobile in the same

KEY EVENTS

1998	1999	2001	2003	2007	2008
Nokia produces the first phone with interchangeable fascias, the 5110 (see p.488). They started the trend for cells to be customizable.	The first device to carry the BlackBerry name, the BlackBerry 850, is launched. It is an email pager and the first device to integrate email fully.	NTT DoCoMo launches the first 3G network, allowing users to access video and download apps.	The Nokia 1100 and 1110, despite being low-end feature phones, sell over 250 million units each, becoming the world's bestselling cells.	Apple releases the very first iPhones. Consumers rush to buy the 4 GB ($499) and even more alluring 8 GB ($599) versions.	Google unveils the first Linux-based Android-powered cell phone, the HTC Dream.

way that the later truck and car-based systems were; there was no way that a single person could carry them, and few people could afford them.

In contrast, the Motorola company's Walkie-Talkies and Handie-Talkies of the 1940s were portable, albeit with difficulty. However, these were half-duplex systems, meaning that only one person could talk at a time, and only on a local radio network. Motorola kept going, however, and created their first prototype cell phone in 1973—the DynaTAC (see image 1). Motorola's lead designer used it to ring the head of Bell Laboratories, their arch-competitor, presumably parodying the fact that Alexander Graham Bell made the first landline phone call. The phone's form remained a strictly utilitarian "brick" shape of angular plastic, no great advance from the military phones and Handie-Talkies of the past. Yet the DynaTAC phone was revolutionary in its "cell" mast system; this enabled phones to move between the masts without losing signal. Further, the masts did not interfere with each other, which massively increased the number of calls that could be made simultaneously.

Until 1998, cell phones, particularly the giant "brick" car phones familiar from movies like *Wall Street* (1987), were mostly still the preserve of business people. But everything changed with the launch in that year of Nokia's line of consumer phones, including the 5110 (see p.488) and their interchangeable faceplates. Soon, with many cell companies competing for business, the prices of handsets were driven down. Low-cost text messaging, first introduced in 1992, soon gained immense popularity.

Innovations were rapid, but fragmented. Camera phones arrived in 2000 with Sharp's Japan-only J-SH04, with a 0.1 MP sensor. In 2001 3G arrived, though it was prohibitively expensive in most countries. RIM's launch of the BlackBerry (see image 2) in 2003 won business support because of its always-on email service and its encrypted private messaging services. The iconic Motorola Razr (see image 3) signaled the last hurrah of the feature phone in 2004, and the Nokia N95 of 2007 heralded the smartphone revolution.

However, the most significant generator of smartphones was not to be Finland, home of Nokia, but Silicon Valley in northern California. From the beginning of the 21st century onward, companies based in that small area had begun to create designs that would go on to govern many aspects of everyday life. Silicon Valley, the birthplace of the microprocessor, was also the home of Apple and Google, corporations that sold the notion that with the aid of their products and services we would all be better off: smarter, healthier, better informed, more efficient, more social, and more entertained.

The pursuit of perfection has always characterized Apple products and, in particular, the design approach of the company's chief design officer Jonathan Ive (b.1967), who led the team that created the iPhone. Launched in 2007, and quickly followed by the iPhone 3G in 2008, the iPhone established itself as the control panel of its users' lives, blurring even further the boundary between the

2008	2010	2011	2013	2014	2015
Nokia sells more camera phones than Kodak sells film-based cameras, at the same time becoming the biggest manufacturer of any kind of camera.	Apple kick-starts a new handheld computing platform, the tablet, which combines a large screen and touchscreen interface.	The first cells with MasterCard PayPass and/or Visa payWave certification appear, using an embedded secure element and/or SIM card for payments.	The Pebble Smartwatch is launched. It connects via Bluetooth with a smartphone to display data on the wrist.	Although Flappy Bird is the most popular free game downloaded from the App Store, its creator withdraws it because of its addictive nature.	The Apple Watch is unveiled by Tim Cook. It is Apple's first wearable device, designed to liberate the user from their smartphone.

4 Steve Jobs launched the iPad on January 27, 2010: "iPad creates and defines an entirely new category of devices that will connect users with their apps and content in a much more intimate, intuitive, and fun way than ever before."

5 The Punkt MP 01 is a simple cell phone used only for texts and phone calls. Turning its back on the smartphone revolution, the Swiss Punkt company is happy to call its product a "dumbphone" and market it to a new kind of customer.

real and the digital. However, the idea was not new. The first PDA, or personal digital assistant, was the Psion Organiser (1984), which included a diary, address book, and calculator, and Apple had also tried a touchscreen-driven, handheld digital assistant with the Newton in 1993. Palm was established as the leading PDA, and Nokia and BlackBerry had evolved the same concept with their smartphones. Yet, in 2007, the iPhone—thinner, lighter, faster, more intuitive—really shook up the field.

With the exception of Apple, no other company had looked quite so holistically at this complex product, which had to bristle with different technologies—wireless connectivity, microphone, camera, touchscreen—yet remain small and light, and tough enough to survive heavy usage. It had to be computationally powerful and still run for at least a day on a battery charge. Furthermore, it had to be a pleasure to hold, easy to use, and manufactured on an enormous scale to Apple's high level of quality. The result was a balance of physical and digital design, made in the vast factories of Shenzhen, China.

Created by Ive and his team of designers, the iPhone's glass and aluminum industrial design was a model of material quality. Its software, designed by a team led by Scott Forstall (b.1969), was a model of ease of use. The first iPhone eschewed physical keyboards in favor of a capacitive touchscreen. From this screen sprang a user interface based on natural sweeps and gestures, served by software that subtly taught users how it functioned through tactile-looking buttons and responsive swooshing animations.

With the arrival of smartphone companies like Apple, HTC, and Google, there was a global divergence. The Nokia 1100 and 1110 sold over 500,000 units, mainly in the developing world, where these simple phones began to be used for micropayments. Meanwhile, the developed world raced ahead with increasingly complex smartphone technology. The arrival of the iPhone spurred Google to change the core design of its own smartphone software, Android. Soon GPS systems for tracking location, biometric systems for tracking health, always-on data, virtual reality headsets, and tiny peripherals were on offer.

Cell technology was not exclusively restricted to phones, of course – users of laptops, tablets, and e-readers, such as Amazon's Kindle (2004; see p.490), could also communicate or access information on the move. In a short space of time, such devices had a wide-ranging impact on the structure of traditional media industries, such as publishing and print journalism.

Apple went on to market the iPhone's software, later known as iOS, as keenly as its hardware, updating it simultaneously with each year's new model. However, it was when the App Store opened in 2009 that the iPhone truly came alive. Any developer was able to create software, from games such as Candy Crush Saga (2012) and Flappy Bird (2013) to apps such as Uber (2010; see p.492) and Tweetbot (2011). Apple maintained a firm hand overall, however, barring any app that did not comply with its sometimes controversial rules over content and competing commercial services. Earlier, in 2001, the company had opened its first bricks-and-mortar stores, followed by its flagship outlet in SoHo, New York City, in 2002. Apple Stores, which rapidly proliferated worldwide, challenged established notions of retailing, with their Genius Bars, their enthusiastic young sales personnel, and their distinctive minimal design, all of which carried through the image of the brand every bit as effectively as Apple's high-quality white accessories and packaging.

In 2010 Apple chief executive Steve Jobs (1955–2011) revealed the iPad (see image 4) using the words "revolutionary" and "magical," standard language for communicating Silicon Valley's innovation. The next major leap in the pursuit of perfection was made in 2015 with launch of the Apple Watch, which marked a further incursion of digital devices into personal realms. By the mid 2010s, the physical limits of silicon were starting to be reached. Amid claims that Silicon Valley's boom was a bubble about to burst, concerns began to be voiced, both about the environmental cost of such high-volume production and about the impact that constant connectivity was having on real-life relationships and social exchanges. With the ownership of a smartphone no longer conveying the prestige it once had, other means of signaling status began to appear on the market. The cell MP 01 (2015; see image 5), designed by Jasper Morrison (b.1959) for Swiss brand Punkt, is focused on making calls and sending texts only; it is aimed at the executive who is too busy on important matters to receive calls or be disturbed in any way. **DG/AW**

Nokia 5110 1998

FRANK NUOVO b.1961

FOCAL POINTS

1 CASING

Nokia aimed to make the cell phone a piece of technology that could be personalized. The Nokia 5110 cover could be removed easily by pressing the locking catch at the top, for example with a coin. The phone came with a real-time clock, and an alarm could be set to go off at a specified time.

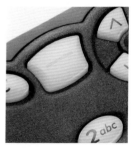

2 BUTTONS

The Nokia 5110 is sturdily constructed with large, translucent buttons that make the keypad easy to navigate. The Navi Key below the display, combined with the graphical menu system, made it easy for users to send Short Message Service (SMS) texts of up to 160 characters in length.

N okia was among the first manufacturers to design a cell phone casing. It was the Nokia 101 1G and 1011 2G (the first mass-produced GSM, or Global System for Mobile Communications) models of 1992 in which the Finnish firm demonstrated its ability to encase the modern technology in a modernist shell where form followed function. Leading the project was Frank Nuovo from the design consultancy Designworks, and he went on to become Nokia's chief of design.

The 101 was the first phone Nuovo worked on. He ensured that the key layout was well spaced and placed for ease of use, with key size and color to reflect their importance and function. The microphone and earpiece were put at a comfortable distance, and there was a large screen. The business-oriented 6110 (1998) and the consumer-oriented 5110 were built on this, acting as a design midpoint between the 101 and the mass-produced icon that was the 3310 (2000). The 6110 was smaller and lighter than any other Nokia phone, and the iridescent skin gave a flair that belied its businesslike design. An infrared port allowed it to communicate with a PC. But it was the removable cases on the 5110 that really made the design a style icon. Each could be popped off and replaced with an expensive Nokia design or, quickly, a range of aftermarket ones.

Nokia's star has waned in recent years: the company never pursued a consistent strategy and was left in the shade by the closed Android and iOS operating systems, leaving an array of obsolete products in its wake. In 2014 Nokia sold its cell phone business to Microsoft, which continued producing its phones under the Lumia name. **DG**

Injection-molded ABS and polycarbonate
5⅛ x 1⅞ x 1¼ in.
13.2 x 4.75 x 3.1 cm

⏱ DESIGNER PROFILE

1961–94

In 1986 Frank Nuovo graduated in industrial design from the Art Center College of Design in Pasadena, California. He went to Designworks, where he designed a range of products, from consumer electronics to automotive products. He worked with Nokia from 1989 as consultant design director.

1995–PRESENT

Nuovo joined Nokia as chief of design. He established an internal design group, which worked on core designs. Nuovo helped launch Nokia's luxury brand, Vertu, in 1997 and in 2006 he moved to work on it full time. When Nokia sold Vertu in 2012, Nuovo left to concentrate on Design Studio Nuovo, which designs consumer electronics for major corporations.

▲ The Nokia 5110 gave consumers the choice to have a phone that was not black or gray, thanks to its colorful Xpress-on covers. They helped the cell phone become a fashion accessory.

SCIENCE FICTION

Cell phone design has been influenced by science fiction. Nokia's sliding **8110** (1996; right) was used extensively in *The Matrix* (1999–2003) trilogy (spring-loaded, to pop open when needed), and Samsung's clamshell-designed **SGH-T100** (2002) bears the influence of *Star Trek: First Contact* (1996). The Official Star Trek Communicator (2016) acts as a Bluetooth hands-free device for any cell phone.

Amazon Kindle 2007

LAB126 est. 2004   AMAZON est. 1994

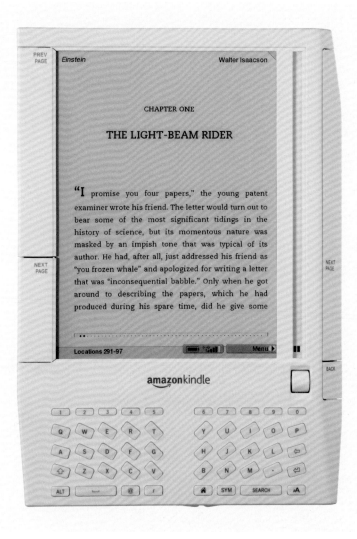

The first-generation Kindle weighed 10 ounces (289 g) and could store 200 e-books.

 NAVIGATOR

The Kindle was designed by a group—Lab126—set up in 2004 by Jeff Bezos (b.1964), founder of Amazon. The team's brief was to create a product that would reflect what the company would be doing in twenty years' time. After initial experiments with MP3 players and set-top boxes, Bezos directed them to focus on what he loved: reading. Bezos was closely involved with the team, though his demands for simplicity but also an ever-expanding feature set seemed contradictory. Lab126's solution was the Kindle—an e-reader with extremely low-power demands, a simple screen that worked in any light conditions, storage for e-books, and a 3G connection that made book downloads simple.

Since that launch in 2007, Amazon has released a new design at least yearly, each year bringing more diversification in the number of models available. No other e-reader has matched the Kindle's speed of evolution. The entire device is now smaller and slimmer, while the screens have stayed the same size but are clearer and brighter, looking more and more like a freshly cut page of paper. In 2010 Amazon was able to announce that, through its activities, e-book sales had surpassed paperback sales for the first time. **DG**

👁 FOCAL POINTS

1 TEXT
Lab126 wanted an e-reader requiring only low power, and MIT Media Lab's E Ink technology was the answer. It consists of an unlit screen that resembles a printed page. When the power cuts out, the current image is retained. Power is needed only when the user turns to the next page.

2 BATTERY LIFE
The E Ink technology and the fast flash memory were chosen in the service of battery life. The original Kindle had a battery life of around four days (in use with 3G on). When not in use, the Kindle uses no power at all, although it will still display a single image for an indefinite period of time.

3 INTERNET ACCESS
Amazon made a deal with Qualcomm and AT&T to have free unlimited 3G access for users to browse the Amazon store and download books. The Whispernet feature stores a user's progress across devices, removing the need for slow, unreliable synchronizing of data with a desktop computer.

▲ Amazon launched a tablet version of its e-reader, the Kindle Fire (above), in 2011, followed by the HD version in 2012 and the HDX in 2013. The device features a color display, as well as access to the Amazon Appstore, streamable movies, and television shows.

KINDLING AMAZON

Designing the Kindle was one task; building it and selling it turned out to be a much larger one, taking more than three years. The initial E Ink displays turned out to be poorly built, and would degrade rapidly after just one month—thankfully, this was fixed ahead of launch (right). Meanwhile, the bespoke wireless chip for Whispernet had been co-designed by the US semiconductor company Qualcomm, which was also going to be its supplier. But Qualcomm was prevented from selling any of its equipment while it was being sued by a competitor, Broadcom. Despite these issues, the Kindle was a success at launch, because it addressed many of the standard problems of contemporary e-readers. Even so, Amazon heavily underestimated how many Kindles would be sold, causing a shortage at launch.

Uber 2010

GARRETT CAMP b.1978   TRAVIS KALANICK b.1976

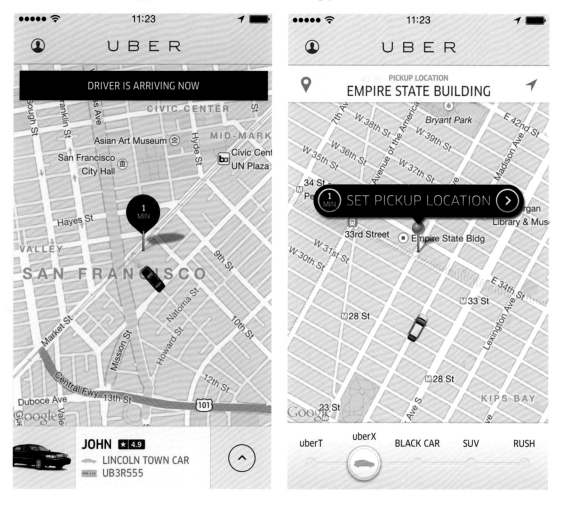

Uber runs a driver and passenger review system to ensure quality of service. A star rating appears beside the driver's name.

 NAVIGATOR

Apps are where smartphone hardware and network connectivity come together through design, where subtle ideas can make the difference between success and failure. And occasionally success is so great that whole industries are transformed. Indeed, few changes have been as sweeping as those brought about by Uber in the taxi business. It is a model of how smartphones and apps—so utterly alluring in their convenience—have become pervasive, and how design enabled them.

Simplicity is key to Uber's success, because the short sequence of taps required to book a taxi addresses a swathe of problems with the traditional way that the process works: from the uncertainty of when a car will arrive and how long it will take, to knowing what the fare will be and finding enough change to pay for it. Behind the easy interface of Uber is an incredibly complex network infrastructure that keeps constant tabs on the fleet of Uber cars, in which the drivers run their own app—UberPartner—which reports their position and status. Uber's "surge pricing" system increases fares in areas that are busy. This feature was designed to attract more drivers to the particular area that is experiencing high demand. In order to keep prices low, Uber does not employ any drivers or own any cars. Each driver is self employed and therefore remains in thrall to competition for fares and to Uber's review system. **AW**

FOCAL POINTS

JOHN ★ 4.9
LINCOLN TOWN CAI
UB3R555

1 SIMPLICITY
Central to Uber is its simplicity. It relies on GPS, so on opening the app, it shows a map of your location. Once you hit the "Set pickup location" button and state your destination, your taxi will be on its way. The app keeps you updated as to how long the taxi will be and it takes your payment at the end.

2 MAP VIEW
On Uber's map view, you can see cars steadily patrolling nearby streets in real time, a point of reassurance that your ride is mere minutes away. Some researchers claimed that these visualizations were not representative of reality, but Uber was quick to refute this point.

3 USER-FRIENDLY FEATURES
The Uber app has many user-friendly features, including being able to easily split the fare with other passengers who have an Uber account. The app also gives information about the car and its driver, including a star rating that is calculated by Uber's review system.

DESIGNER PROFILE

1976–2000
Travis Kalanick was born in Los Angeles and studied computer engineering at University of California, Los Angeles. In 1998 he dropped out to co-found Scour and to build a search engine and peer-to-peer file-sharing service. However, a copyright infringement lawsuit drove the firm into bankruptcy in 2000.

2001–07
In 2001 Kalanick co-founded another peer-to-peer file-sharing service called Red Swoosh, which enabled users to transfer large media files. Akamai Technology acquired the firm for $19 million in 2007.

2008–09
Kalanick founded Uber as UberCab with fellow entrepreneur Garrett Camp and became the company's chief executive. Although he was feeling burned out by the pressure of running his previous ventures, he was talked into taking the project forward by Camp, who championed the cell app idea.

2010–PRESENT
In 2010 the Uber service was launched in San Francisco. It expanded into a new city every month throughout 2011, and in December 2011 it was introduced in Paris, its first non-US location. The app was designed to predict where demand would be high and where passengers were likely to go. It also optimized where drivers patrolled and which drivers were alerted to new requests. A test made by its data scientists in 2014 concluded that during quiet times drivers should simply park rather than patrol, thereby reducing fuel consumption and reducing emissions. In 2014 Kalanick featured at position 290 in the Forbes top 400 richest Americans list, with an estimated worth of $6 billion.

DRIVERLESS CARS

In 2015 Kalanick stated that he saw his company's future in self-driven cars, thereby introducing another step along a road of disruptions to the taxi industry. He claimed that driverless cars, such as the one designed by Google (right), could help to reduce congestion in cities and to ensure greater road safety, a marker of how Uber should "embrace the future." Kalanick's concerns were less focused on Uber's network of drivers, which numbered 160,000 by the end of 2014. He explained, "The reason Uber could be expensive is because you're not just paying for the car—you're paying for the other dude in the car."

DEVELOPMENTS IN PLASTIC

Despite growing environmental concerns, in the 21st century plastic is still everywhere. It is in homes, workplaces, cars, in the packaging of the products, and in many products themselves. One of the reasons for such ubiquity is that it is cheap. Even more persuasive is the fact that plastic is incredibly versatile: it can perform almost any function conceivable. Depending on the precise formula or type of plastic, it can be soft and malleable, rigid and robust, and it can be woven, colored, opaque, translucent, or transparent. It can also be recycled, which is less of an advantage, ecologically speaking, than it might first appear, because recycled plastic takes energy to produce and there can be a significant deterioration of quality.

If plastic is so common in daily life that it is taken it for granted, its presence in landfill and the world's oceans is rapidly becoming a problem of global proportions. Low-cost plastic products are routinely discarded without further thought, and the cheapest and most thoughtlessly discarded are plastic bags, which are polluting the world's seas in their millions. While the so-called "Great Pacific Garbage Patch" has not been reliably measured (estimates range anywhere between the size of Texas to twice the size of the United States), it is an undoubted threat to marine life. Plastic does not biodegrade; it photo-degrades and over time disintegrates along with the toxic chemicals used in its production, finding its way into the food chain.

KEY EVENTS

1996	1997	2000	2002	2002	2002
French designer Philippe Starck follows up his polypropylene Lord Yo chair with the Dr No chair. Both chairs revive a contemporary plastic esthetic.	Parties to the Kyoto Protocol agree the broad outlines of targets for reducing greenhouse gas emissions.	Jasper Morrison designs his groundbreaking Air chair, a minimal one-piece design produced by gas injection.	Starck's Louis Ghost chair is issued. Made of injection-molded polycarbonate, it brings wit and glamor to plastic products.	British designer Michael Young designs the colorful Yogi Family of outdoor furniture.	Bangladesh becomes the first country in the world to ban plastic bags, after they were discovered to have choked local drainage systems during floods.

Despite the scale of the problem plastic poses for sustainable development, designers still want to work with the material because it allows them to experiment with form and achieve desired functionality. It also has the potential to bring products to a mass audience at a low cost.

An added attraction is that recent developments in plastics technology mean that it is possible for designers not simply to design in plastic, but to design the plastic itself. When German designer Konstantin Grcic (b.1965) was working on the prototype of his Myto chair (2007; see p.494), he discovered that it was possible to fine-tune his design by altering the composition of the plastic (Ultradur, produced by the German company BASF), thus changing the chemistry, not the geometry. Computer simulation made this possible. Designing on computer also made possible Grcic's earlier Miura bar stool (2005), a monoblock design with complex free-form surfaces.

One way of reducing the impact of plastic is to use less of it. A groundbreaking design that demonstrates this approach is Air chair (2000; see p.492) by British designer Jasper Morrison (b.1959). Unlike the Myto, which was manufactured using conventional injection molding, the Air chair was produced by gas injection, which is more expensive. Gas injection pushes the plastic to the very edge of the mold. This creates a hollow and permits changes of section from thick to thin. Where a chair needs to be stronger—the legs—the sections can be thicker; where it bears less weight—in the back—the section can be thin. Made of polypropylene, like British designer Robin Day's (1915–2010) original Polyprop chair (1963) with metal legs, the stackable Air chair differs in that it is made from just one piece of plastic.

The designer who is perhaps most responsible for the return of plastic to something approaching the glamorous status it enjoyed before the oil crisis of 1973 is Philippe Starck (b.1949). Executed in polypropylene, his early plastic chair designs Lord Yo (1994) and Dr No (1996) were variations on traditional forms produced with such wit and flair that the image of plastic was instantly elevated. But it was his Louis Ghost chair (2002; see image 2) that brought true desirability to plastic furniture. Made of injection-molded polycarbonate, the design reduces the Baroque form of a classic Louis XV chair of the 18th century to a barely there, shadowy presence redolent with irony. Most effective in its pure transparent version that does not interrupt the view, creating an impression of space, it is also available in different colors, along with black. Despite a relatively high price tag, the chair has been a bestseller for US furniture and lighting company Kartell, selling 1.5 million pieces in the first ten years of its production.

More overtly whimsical, if not comic, is the brightly colored Yogi Family (2002; see image 1) of outdoor furniture created by British designer Michael Young (b.1966) for Italian firm Magis. Low to the ground, curved, and cartoon-like in form, this is furniture that does not take itself too seriously. **EW**

1 Designer Michael Young uses plastic to create fun, vibrant pieces, such as his Yogi Family of outdoor furniture.

2 The Louis Ghost armchair is made from a single injection-molded polycarbonate, which is a recyclable plastic.

2005	2007	2012	2014	2014	2015
Konstantin Grcic designs the Miura bar stool, a complex multisurface form modeled with the aid of a computer.	Grcic designs the Myto chair, a one-piece cantilevered form showcasing German chemical company BASF's product, Ultradur.	Starck's Louis Ghost chair has sold 1.5 million pieces since its launch, making it a bestseller for manufacturer Kartell.	The European Parliament passes a directive to reduce the use of plastic bags by 80 per cent by 2019.	The state of California passes a law banning single-use plastic bags.	England falls in line with the rest of the United Kingdom and introduces a 5p charge for single-use plastic carrier bags in large stores.

Air chair 2000

JASPER MORRISON b.1959

Polypropylene with glass fiber
30½ x 20⅛ x 19¼ in.
77.5 x 51 x 49 cm

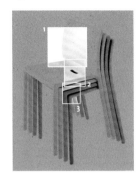
The Air chair is a strikingly simple chair, molded in one piece from gas-injected polypropylene and glass fibre, designed by Jasper Morrison and manufactured by Magis in Italy. The design was one of the first uses of gas-injected polypropylene, and the technology allowed for lower retail prices than expected for designer furniture.

Morrison was inspired to create the Air chair when Eugenio Perazza (b.1940), owner of Magis, showed him a smooth length of tube made by gas injection, a process then in its infancy. Morrison's idea for the design began from the legs up. He imagined a perfect wooden chair, then sought to make it lighter, more durable, more robust, and stackable.

Earlier injection-molding processes involved packing a mold cavity with plastic material, but stresses were introduced, surfaces were uneven, and the mold sometimes warped. By using the inert gas medium, pressure was distributed smoothly and evenly through the mold, requiring less pressure, minimizing warping, and strengthening the end product. There was vastly improved surface definition, too. Less material was needed because of the hollow core, saving as much as 30 per cent on production costs. The hot plastic solidified faster, resulting in faster productivity.

Morrison's simple design, the smooth plastic material, and the revolutionary production have resulted in a contemporary design icon. Over time Morrison has developed the product range to include folding chairs, an armchair, and tables. **JW**

👁 FOCAL POINTS

1 CHAIR BACK
The curve of the chair back supports the spine and small of the back, and elegantly extends further down and out through the back legs. While straight lines define the width of the chair, the depth curves in this subtle arabesque, and has Asian and Scandinavian echoes running through it.

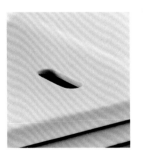

2 SEAT
The seat and back support have identical and generous widths, and are set flush and square with the width of the legs. Despite the basic nature of the material and lack of decorative or soft upholstered elements, the ample width creates a feeling of generosity and comfort.

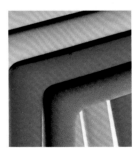

3 COLOR
Originally, the Air chair was made in eight colors, and consumers were encouraged to buy an assortment. The colors are fresh and upbeat—as if to prove that a functional object need not lack character. The range has been extended to include white, to enhance the chair's minimalism.

GLO-BALL FAMILY

Morrison's goal for the first Glo-Ball light, designed for Italian firm Flos in 1998 and released a year later, was to achieve maximum diffusion of ambient light with no glare, using simple, functional construction. His inspiration was the full moon on a clear night. The diffusers are hand blown into a natural, flattened sphere from externally acid-etched, flashed opaline glass. Inside is a transparent, injection-molded polycarbonate diffuser support. Over time, Glo-Ball has grown into a family, comprising at least three sizes in each typology: suspension, ceiling, floor, wall, and table lights (above). They provide a clean, soft, white light and look at their best, like planets, when clustered.

Myto Chair 2007
KONSTANTIN GRCIC b.1965

Polybutylene terephthalate (PBT)
32¼ x 21⅝ x 20⅛ in.
82 x 55 x 51 cm

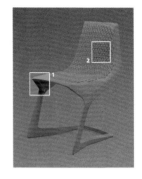

Myto is a chair made from a single piece of plastic, using the minimum amount of polybutylene terephthalate (PBT) and manufactured in Italy by Plank. It is designed to be light, strong, comfortable, stackable, compact, and striking. It is also cantilevered, which to the design community was a statement of astonishing ambition when it was unveiled at the K 2007 plastics fair in Düsseldorf, Germany.

A cantilever chair has no back legs to support its structure, and is known to be the most challenging form to realize. The best-known examples are legendary and include some of the most famous designs of the 20th century, such as MR10 (1927) by Ludwig Mies van der Rohe (1886–1969), B32 (1928) by Marcel Breuer (1902–81), and the Panton chair (1960; see p.352).

In 2006 German chemical manufacturer BASF commissioned Konstantin Grcic to design a product using its Ultradur High Speed plastic, a fast-flowing PBT. It was the material's characteristics that led him to develop a cantilevered chair, conceived as a monoblock plastic-injection molding. Unbowed by the weight of history, Grcic wanted his chair to be light and supple, with a perforated seat and back. Myto took only one year to develop. Grcic believes that chairs should not only be utilitarian—they should also have a personality. He conceived Myto's perforations to look like animal skin, and the chair as a whole to have a reptilian quality with a precise outline and round, but tense, surfaces. "Sometimes animals assume that position when they're ready to pounce," he said. **JW**

👁 FOCAL POINTS

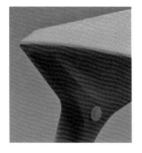

1 ANGULAR FORM
Myto combines an industrial style with boldly experimental, artistic elements. Some say the chair looks like a man on his knees, others that its angular forms suggest an Eastern European esthetic. The strong and stable frame is the mainstay into which the seat and the backrest fit.

2 PERFORATIONS
The material's flowability, coupled with its strength, excited Grcic because it allowed "an elegant transition from thick to thin cross sections." The form of the chair is based on a solid supporting frame, which dissolves into net-like perforations in a symmetrical structure.

CLERICI BENCH

The Clerici seating range, designed by Grcic for Italian furniture manufacturer Mattiazzi, was launched at the Salone del Mobile furniture fair in Milan in 2015. The range comprises a classical wooden bench and lower, upholstered versions made from solid oak or stained ash. Assembled from flat wooden planes stained to show the natural grain, the red bench (right) is particularly striking. The bench's silhouette, with its framed negative spaces, is reminiscent of paintings by Piet Mondrian (1872–1944) and the De Stijl style (see p.114).

SHOCK TACTICS

1 The stainless-steel Fruit Bowl (2000) by Gijs Bakker is designed in the shape of a droplet of water.

2 Tejo Remy's chest of drawers (1991) is made from found drawers bound together with a jute strap.

3 The chair backs of the Tree trunk bench (1999) by Jurgen Bey are cast in bronze.

E mergent artists and designers invariably question the esthetics and ethos of their predecessors. It is all part of the ongoing cycle of youthful rebellion: one generation's cutting edge is the next generation's old hat. Shock tactics are often adopted as a way of gaining instant notoriety, as with punk during the 1970s (see p.410) and the Young British Artists (Damien Hirst, Tracy Emin, et al.) during the 1990s. Paralleling the rise of the YBAs was a radical Dutch design collective called Droog. Established in 1993 by jeweler Gijs Bakker (b.1942), who specialized in the avant-garde (see image 1), and cultural commentator Renny Ramakers (b.1948), Droog championed the work of up and coming designers, such as Hella Jongerius (b.1963) and Jurgen Bey (b.1965), who challenged the fundamental assumptions and orthodoxies prevalent in mainstream design. The 1980s had been a time of rampant materialism and the triumph of style over substance. Rejecting the superficiality and intellectual paucity of this approach, Droog turned design on its head, emphasizing the significance of ideas and creative exploration—rather than styling and end products—and giving birth to conceptual design, the sister of conceptual art.

Although beauty is in the eye of the beholder, it was generally accepted until recently that one of the main purposes of design was to make the world

KEY EVENTS

1997	1997	1997	1998	1998	1999
The Design Academy Eindhoven moves to a new building called De Witte Dame (The White Lady).	El Ultimo Grito is co-founded by Roberto Feo (b.1964) and Rosario Hurtado (b.1966) in London, producing witty conceptual designs.	Designersblock is launched as a satellite exhibition at 100% Design in London, providing a showcase for experimental work by emergent designers.	At the Milan Furniture Fair, Salone Satellite is created as a platform for young designers.	Ron Arad becomes head of the newly created design products department at the Royal College of Art in London.	Trend forecaster Li Edelkoort is elected chairwoman of Design Academy Eindhoven, an influential tenure that lasts ten years.

a more beautiful place. Droog rejected this notion and provided a platform for designers with an alternative agenda who felt compelled to create objects that, by conventional standards, were crude, unsophisticated, or unfinished. Bey's Tree trunk bench (see image 3), a huge log with a row of chair backs inserted along the top, epitomized the rawness of this philosophy. Jongerius's Soft Urn (1993) was another classic Droog creation. Made from silicon rubber, the walls of the vessel are pliable and no attempt was made to disguise the mottled brown coloring of the material or to remove the joint lines created by the mold. Yet, although it was visually low key, this was a statement piece, all the more arresting for its naked simplicity. Summing up the Droog ethos, Ramakers noted: "A sparing use of resources, the frequent recycling of materials, products and typologies, a deliberate lack of style, and the makeshift nature of some designs—all this registered as a critique of the prevailing overconsumption and the equating of design with style and technical perfection."

For the extrovert Marcel Wanders (b.1963), Droog provided a vital jumping-off point and a means of gaining exposure. His gravity-defying Knotted chair—made from knotted cord with a carbon core impregnated with epoxy resin—was initially launched under the auspices of Droog in 1996 and later put into production by Italian style leaders Capellini in 2005. In addition to shaping the course of design directly through its startling collection of products— for example, the much-copied chest of drawers (see image 2) by Tejo Remy (b.1960) and 85 Lamps (1993; see p.472) by Rody Graumans (b.1968)—Droog has had a secondary impact on design by influencing the work of mainstream practitioners such as Philippe Starck (b.1949). Starck's Attila stool-table (1999), an absurdly kitsch creation featuring a large plastic gnome, would probably never have seen the light of day without Droog. Shock tactics have become the stock in trade for many other internationally successful designers, from Front in Sweden to the Campana Brothers (Humberto, b.1953, and Fernando, b.1961) in Brazil. Front's debut project, Design by Animals (2003), included a wooden table routed with wiggly lines replicating patterns bored by insects and a roll of wallpaper gnawed by rats.

The Netherlands continues to provide fertile territory for Droog, with the Design Academy Eindhoven acting as a hothouse and breeding ground. Conceptual design has also been firmly rooted at the Royal College of Art since the mid 1990s, fueled by the enlightened Ron Arad (b.1951) during his tenure as professor of design products from 1998 to 2009. In the United Kingdom, shock tactics are often mediated by wit and humor, as in the playfully subversive designs of Gitta Gschwendtner (b.1972) and Carl Clerkin (b.1973). Gschwendtner's macabre Strangled Lights (1998)—ceramic lampshades strangled by their own cable— were featured in an exhibition called "The Uncanny Room" in 2002, along with Clerkin's Long Crawly Thing, a bench resembling a centipede with a long, padded seat and numerous cabriole legs. **LJ**

2001	2001	2002	2004	2005	2009
Dutch designer Marcel Wanders co-founds the controversial Moooi brand in the Netherlands and acts as art director.	Wanders creates the Airborne Snotty vase (see p.502), using shock tactics to grab people's attention.	"The Uncanny Room" exhibition in London features works by ceramicist Richard Slee (b.1946) and glassmaker Emma Woffenden (b.1962).	The "Beauty and the Beast: New Swedish Design" exhibition at the Crafts Council in London highlights the work of radical Swedish designers.	Philippe Starck designs his provocative "Guns" collection for Italian lighting brand Flos. It includes a Kalashnikov AK-47 table light (see p.504).	Tord Boontje (b.1968) replaces Ron Arad as head of design products at the Royal College of Art, continuing until 2013.

Airborne Snotty Vase: Influenza 2001

MARCEL WANDERS b. 1963

Polyamide
6 x 6 x 6 in./15 x 15 x 15 cm

Dutch designer Marcel Wanders has spent his whole career delighting and upsetting people in equal measure. Although he started off as a radical outsider, he has become successful commercially, heading up a large and prolific design studio that attracts leading clients from all over the world. Wanders deliberately flouts conventions, and thrives on notoriety. While his admirers applaud the audacity of his over-the-top designs, his detractors are shocked by his apparent self-indulgence and his blatant disregard for good taste.

Wanders has been at the hub of creative developments in the Netherlands since the mid 1990s. Playful, mischievous, and uninhibited, Wanders delights in pure, unfettered experimentation. There is an almost puerile, adolescent quality to some of his designs, a disconcerting mix of naivety and sophistication. His Airborne Snotty vases, with their repellent mucus-inspired forms, were conjured up by means of rapid prototyping. Their bizarre forms were created by enlarging images of tiny particles from a 3D scan of a human sneeze. As if this were not extraordinary enough, the five designs in the series were each named after different diseases of the nasal cavity: influenza, sinusitis, coryza (runny nose), pollinosis (hay fever), and ozaena (fetid discharge). As well as pushing the technology of 3D printing to its limits, Wanders has pushed the boundaries of good taste far beyond most people's comfort zone. **LJ**

⬡ NAVIGATOR

👁 FOCAL POINTS

1 CURVES
The fluid, irregular form was created by using a 3D scanner to record the scattered mucus particles emitted during a human sneeze. Scanners are associated with precision engineering or medical procedures, but Wanders co-opted them to create this experimental vessel design.

2 HOLLOW
Once the scan of the sneeze had been transferred to a computer, five particles were chosen from the 3D digital image. Each particle was enlarged and used as the basis for a vase. The vessel was created by manipulating the image to make a hollow for holding a flower stalk.

3 PLASTIC
This vase was built from polyamide plastic using a digitally controlled process known as "rapid prototyping." This technique, sometimes referred to as "3D printing," was developed as a means of producing accurate one-off prototypes, but in this case the model was the end product.

🕐 DESIGNER PROFILE

1963–88
Marcel Wanders was born in Boxtel in the Netherlands. He graduated in 1988 from the Hogeschool voor de Kunsten (ArtEZ Institute of the Arts) in Arnhem, having been expelled from the Design Academy Eindhoven.

1989–PRESENT
Wanders was initially associated with the radical Dutch design group Droog, but rose to fame after establishing his own design studio, Wanders Wonders, in Amsterdam in 1995. In 2001 he co-founded the design brand Moooi.

▲ The Knotted chair (1996) established Wanders's reputation. To make it rigid, the cord is soaked in epoxy resin. Once hardened, it becomes sufficiently strong to withstand a person's weight.

Kalashnikov AK47 Table Light   2005

PHILIPPE STARCK   b.1949

C reated for the Italian lighting brand Flos, Philippe Starck's table lamp in the form of a Kalashnikov AK-47 semi-automatic assault rifle is a member of his "Guns" collection, along with a bedside model, whose base is a replica of a Beretta pistol, and an M16 rifle floor lamp. The desire to shock may not have been one of his avowed aims—he claimed that the collection was "nothing but a sign of the times"—but the gold-plated imagery was to prove no less provocative than its astronomic price tags.

In his musings on the collection, entitled *To Life, To Death*, Starck noted that: "Designed, manufactured, sold, dreamed, purchased, and used, weapons are our new icons . . . We get the symbols we deserve." As a comment on geo-politics, terrorism, and the arms trade, the designs were controversial and inevitably gave rise to allegations of bad taste. Yet they highlight deeper paradoxes, intrinsic in the relationship between designers and industry, or rather designers appropriating the critical freedoms of artists while producing commercial work intended for sale. As Deyan Sudjic (b.1952), leading design critic and director of London's Design Museum, wrote in *The Language of Things* (2009), "For a designer to make a critical object is to bite the hand that feeds him." If a Kalashnikov table lamp is an irony, he goes on, it is one that "is likely to escape the attention of the Chechen warlords or Colombian godfathers who would find it a congenial accessory for their living rooms." **EW**

⬡ NAVIGATOR

Gold-plated, die-cast aluminum
36½ x 20 in.
92.4 x 50.8 cm

👁 FOCAL POINTS

1 BLACK SHADE
The AK-47's barrel pokes into a black shade, which Starck described as a symbol of death; the crosses that decorate the shade's interior are "to remind us of our dead ones." A less expensive version of the lamp was also made available, with a chromed silver finish and a white shade.

2 GOLDEN BODY
The lamp body, a replica of a Kalashnikov AK-47 assault rifle, is made of die-cast aluminum, coated with injection-molded polymer, and finished in 18-carat gold plating. Starck explained that the expensive gold plating was intended to represent "the collusion between money and war."

MIXED MESSAGES

"I am a designer and design is my only weapon, so I use it to speak about what is important," Starck has said. Superficially, lamps in the form of gold-plated weaponry might be seen to glorify war, violence, and bloodshed, or even to constitute a kind of macho "bling," but both Starck and the Flos company have been at pains to distance themselves from such simple interpretations. For its part, Flos has stated that 20 per cent of sales from the collection are to be donated to Frères des Hommes, a charity dedicated to eliminating global poverty.

Starck himself has been rather more ambiguous. He has said that he would donate a portion of the sales from the table lamp to Médicins sans frontières, the international medical humanitarian organization. The remainder would go as a commission to Mikhail Kalashnikov (1919–2013), the Soviet designer of a gun that has sold over 100 million copies worldwide (some to the East German People's Police, right) and who never received any royalties for it.

NEW BRITISH DECOR

U ntil the turn of the 19th century, pattern was accepted as an integral feature of domestic interiors, be it Jacquard-woven silk damask hangings or block-printed Arts and Crafts wallpapers. With the advent of modernism, pattern became more contentious. A split opened up between the minimalists, who denounced ornament as crime, and the maximalists, who relished color and pattern. This battle has continued to the present.

During the 1990s it was the minimalists who held sway. Wallpaper had become deeply unfashionable and furnishing fabrics lost their pizzazz. Magnolia walls were the order of the day. Decoration was a dirty word. The resurgence of pattern around the millennium was a reaction against this vacuum, reflecting a hunger for greater visual stimulation. By the start of the 21st century, attitudes were changing.

Key players in this volte face were Glasgow-based design partnership Timorous Beasties, who had pluckily kept the pattern flame alive during the 1990s with their imaginative, witty, screen-printed fabrics, such as Glasgow Toile (2004; see p.510). The duo later expanded into wallpaper, acting as a catalyst for its subsequent revival. The miraculous renaissance of wallpaper was one of the design sensations of the 2000s. The freedom with which young

KEY EVENTS

1990	1997	1997	1999	1999	2000
Textile designers Paul Simmons (b.1967) and Alistair McCauley (b.1967) establish a partnership, Timorous Beasties, in Glasgow, Scotland.	Dominic Crinson (b.1963) develops a technique for digitally printing tiles, launching his first collection the following year.	Designer Tracy Kendall (b.1957) launches the Graphic collection of large-scale floor-to-ceiling hand screen-printed wallpapers.	James Bullen produces his Trompe L'Oeil Illusionary Prints collection after graduating from the Royal College of Art (RCA) in London.	RCA textile graduate Deborah Bowness establishes a studio designing wallpaper friezes.	Dutch designer Hella Jongerius starts to incorporate embroidery into her designs, including a large porcelain vase, Giant Prince.

designers embraced this alien medium gave it a contemporary relevance and opened up new markets. Panoramic wallpapers with floor-to-ceiling patterns had been one of the curiosities of the wallpaper industry during the 19th century. This archaic idea was revived by Deborah Bowness (b.1974), who recognized the potential of frieze wallpapers to transform interiors. Instead of exterior vistas, Bowness created self-referential interior landscapes featuring photographs of everyday objects, such as clothes on hooks (see image 1).

Computer-aided design opened up new opportunities for experimentation, and digital printing plays a significant role in production. Digital technology has transformed the look of contemporary design, triggering a revolution in the esthetics of surface pattern, not just in textiles and wallpapers but in other fields such as laminates and tiles. Pattern designer James Bullen (b.1968) has harnessed the creative potential of computer technology. His Trompe L'Oeil Illusionary Prints, launched in 1999, included arresting designs such as Padded Cell (1999; see image 2). Created by scanning details from close-up photographs, then stretching the images and altering their tonal balance, Bullen's virtual textures have a strange, eerie beauty. As well as being digitally printed on fabrics, such as silk velvet, they were also applied to plastic laminates and mats.

Pattern is deep rooted in the British psyche. So when Dutch-born designer Tord Boontje (b.1968) designed his Garland light (see p.508) with its cascading leaves and flowers, it was no surprise that it was greeted with enthusiasm, becoming a bestseller for British store Habitat in 2002. The vogue for ornament spread over the next few years as designers—from Front design group in Sweden to Hella Jongerius (b.1963) in Holland—embraced decoration, relishing the chance of engage with a design idiom that had been taboo. **LJ**

1 Deborah Bowness's Frocks wallpapers (2000) are like *trompe l'oeil* works of art. The colors are mixed by hand and applied by silk-screen printing.

2 James Bullen's *trompe l'oeil* Illusionary prints were originally developed for fabrics, but he later applied the designs to a range of wall art.

2002	2004	2004	2005	2005	2007
Tord Boontje's Garland light is put into production by Habitat and becomes a bestseller.	Boontje creates an installation *Happy Ever After* at the Milan Furniture Fair featuring his laser-cut textiles.	Timorous Beasties launches the Glasgow Toile printed fabric, a subversive reinterpretation of traditional toile de Jouy textiles.	Timorous Beasties is nominated for Designer of the Year at the Design Museum in London.	Jongerius designs the Jonsberg group of ceramic vases for Ikea's PS range, featuring printed, impressed, and pierced patterns.	Timorous Beasties co-curates the "Peacock Among the Ruins" exhibition at Dundee Contemporary Art in Scotland, and opens a showroom in London.

Garland Light 2002

TORD BOONTJE b.1968

W hen Dutch-born Tord Boontje launched his festooned Garland light for Habitat and his glittering Blossom chandelier for Swarovski in 2002, he unleashed a tidal wave of decorative design. The Garland light was the centerpiece of the designer's Wednesday collection, a group of designs that incorporated fairy-tale images of leaves, flowers, and animals. Other pieces included a wooden table with a punched stainless steel top, decorated using a CNC (computer numerically controlled) machine, and glass bowls embellished on the underside with pinprick patterns resembling embroidery. These designs were particularly striking because Boontje's previous work was radically different in character: plain, austere, and utilitarian, with no hint of decoration. His Rough and Ready furniture (1998), constructed from scrap wood and old blankets, was about the hardness of living in the city. With the Garland light, Boontje consciously abandoned austerity in favor of lavish over-the-top decoration. Unashamedly romantic, the design was inspired by the birth of his daughter and reflected the designer's growing interest in the history of pattern making and ornament. Technologically innovative and esthetically groundbreaking, it was made from thin photo-etched metal with a gold, copper, or silver finish. Marking the triumphant return of decoration after a period when minimalism was the norm, the Garland light heralded an exciting phase in Boontje's career and a new era in design. **LJ**

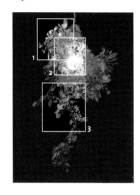

Etched metal
63 in./160 cm

FOCAL POINTS

1 SHADOW EFFECTS
Because of the fineness and delicacy of the photo-etched pattern, the "lampshade" resembles lace. It acts as a decorative filter, casting pretty shadows on the ceiling and walls. This creates a unique ambiance that is totally different in character to conventional lights.

2 PHOTO-ETCHED METAL
Cut from an extremely thin sheet of metal, the intricate pattern was produced by photo etching, a low-cost process commonly associated with the manufacture of medical filters and computer components. The soft metal was bent into shape around the light bulb.

3 FLORAL PATTERN
The most striking feature of this light is the extravagant floral decoration. A dense cluster of tiny leaves and flowers envelops the light bulb, cascading and climbing and entwining the flex. The floral garland shields the bulb directly, as if a real plant were growing over the lamp.

BOONTJE AND SWAROVSKI

Boontje was one of several leading designers invited by Swarovski to reinvent the chandelier as part of its Crystal Palace project at the Milan Furniture Fair in 2002. His Blossom chandelier (above), conjuring up a blossom-laden branch, was an extraordinary creation, its steel frame encrusted with Swarovski cut-glass crystals illuminated by programmed flashing LED lights. The sheer decorative exuberance of this piece— its twinkling, fairy-tale quality—combined with its rampant floral imagery and the luxurious decadence of the materials prompted a flurry of media attention.

Glasgow Toile 2004

PAUL SIMMONS b.1967   ALISTAIR MCAULEY b.1967

Glasgow Toile is hand printed on linen, and available in red and blue versions.

◆ NAVIGATOR

Founded in 1990 by Paul Simmons and Alistair McAuley, Timorous Beasties injected a breath of fresh air into British textiles and wallpapers at a time when commercial pattern design had become predictable and tame. Although Timorous Beasties initially supplied patterns to established firms, they found the constraints of mainstream design too restrictive, so they began producing their own work independently.

Rampant eclecticism and playful subversion are the hallmarks of Timorous Beasties' designs. Drawing inspiration from diverse sources, ranging from television and the internet to historical sample books, they juxtapose apparently incongruous and incompatible elements to create thought-provoking and visually stimulating hybrid designs. One of their most effective ploys has been to interweave historical and contemporary elements, as in Glasgow Toile, which co-opts the composition and colouring of 18th-century toile de Jouy fabrics to explore 21st-century social problems in a post-industrial landscape. The design is deliberately misleading. At first glance, it appears to be a conventional toile. Only on closer inspection is the true nature of the subject matter revealed. The mismatch between the initial perception and the sudden shock of recognition heightens the impact of the design. **LJ**

👁 FOCAL POINTS

1 CHURCH
The design incorporates Glasgow landmarks such as the Free Church in Maryhill, designed by Charles Rennie Mackintosh (1868–1928), and the Necropolis graveyard with its mausoleums. Several modern buildings are also represented, including three high-rise towers.

2 TREE
While adopting the style of historical toile de Jouy fabrics, Timorous Beasties has given the genre a 21st-century twist by replacing idyllic rural scenes with gritty snapshots of urban life. Including a tramp swigging from a can of lager, a youth urinating against a tree, and a junkie shooting up on a park bench.

🕓 DESIGNERS' PROFILE

1967–89
Paul Simmons and Alistair McAuley were both born in 1967. They met at Glasgow School of Art in 1984, where they specialized in printed textiles, graduating in 1988. Simmons then did a Master of Arts at the Royal College of Art in London, while McAuley worked briefly in a fashion and textile studio and then did a postgraduate course in Glasgow.

1990–2003
The duo established Timorous Beasties in 1990, initially producing screen-printed textiles in short runs to commission. Wallpapers were added soon afterward, triggering a revival in this hitherto unfashionable medium.

2004–PRESENT
Timorous Beasties opened a shop in Glasgow and launched their Glasgow Toile at Designersblock in London. In 2005 they were nominated for Designer of the Year at the Design Museum. In 2007 they opened a showroom in London and co-curated an exhibition examining the history of the use of the natural world in interior design, "Peacock Among the Ruins," at Dundee Contemporary Art. Their latest projects include bespoke artworks for the Hilton Metropole hotel in Brighton, England in 2015.

▲ Toile de Jouy textiles were produced in Britain and France from the mid 18th century. They featured idealized scenes, such as swains and shepherdesses in a rural landscape.

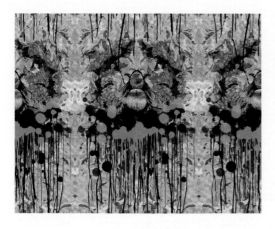

WALLPAPER AS A WEAPON

When Timorous Beasties started out in the early 1990s, wallpaper was unfashionable and not an obvious vehicle for artistic experimentation. Largely as a result of their creative energy, wallpaper has been revitalized and is widely used in interiors again. Timorous Beasties exploit its visual potential to the full, not just as a design statement but as a decorative weapon that can grab people's attention. Their designs start life as drawings, hence their vigor and immediacy. They are then manipulated on a computer to create vivid, multilayered compositions, and printed using a mixture of matt and glossy pigments in startling color combinations, sometimes with metallic highlights. At their most extreme, their wallpapers are high voltage works of art, as in Bloody Empire, featuring bee motifs spattered with drips of paint.

HANDS-ON DESIGN

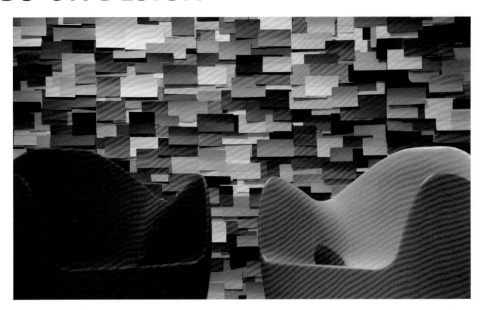

1 Another Color (2013) is part of Tracy Kendall's bespoke collection. The colored papers are stitched onto a wallpaper backing.

2 The Eight-Fifty lamp (1999) by Claire Norcross has attracted much critical acclaim. The plastic cable ties can be dyed as required.

3 Max Lamb's Anodized chair (2015) is made from three aluminum plates bolted together. It is available in smooth and rough versions.

In addition to the revival of decorative pattern, one of the more surprising developments in contemporary design since the millennium has been the renewed appreciation of craft. These two trends are not unrelated, as both ornament and handcraft had been sidelined during the 1990s. Furthermore, the mainstream design world had been somewhat suspicious of craft ever since the revival of the 1970s, when craftspeople made a decisive break with industrial design. Even after craft workers updated their image during the 1980s and were known as designer-makers, "pure" craft was still held at arm's length by technology-driven industrial designers, and it received little coverage in the design press. These divisions were reinforced by the education system, which tended to channel students in one direction or another, rather than encouraging cross-fertilization. It is no coincidence that the change in attitude toward craft began to take root following the introduction of a more free-thinking approach to design education in leading institutions such as the Royal College of Art in London and the Design Academy Eindhoven in the Netherlands.

Since the millennium, craft has taken on a new lease on life, not only as a creative medium in its own right, but also specifically in relation to design and manufacturing, where it is now recognized that a hands-on approach can be a valuable part of the process. Handmade objects, such as the subtle porcelain vases of Edmund de Waal (b.1964) and the raw-edged furniture (see image 3) of Max Lamb (b.1980), are now seen as tokens of authenticity in an

KEY EVENTS

1996	1997	1998	2001	2002	2002
Dutch designer Hella Jongerius (b.1963) exhibits at the "Self-Manufacturing Designers" exhibition at Stedelijk Museum in Amsterdam.	Humberto and Fernando Campana exhibit at the Milan Furniture Fair for the first time and team up with Edra the following year.	Dutch designer Jurgen Bey (b.1965) establishes his own design practice in Rotterdam, having previously been a partner in Konings + Bey since 1990.	The "Industry of One" exhibition at the Crafts Council Gallery in London focuses on the emergence of designer-makers since the 1980s.	Phaidon publishes *Spoon*, an overview of contemporary international product design, including the work of craft-based practitioners.	Maarten Baas creates his first collection of Smoke furniture as part of his degree show at the Design Academy Eindhoven in the Netherlands.

age of ever-increasing automation and digitization. As an increasing number of our everyday experiences are mediated through computers and digital devices, the reassuring tangibility and stimulating physicality of craft offer a welcome relief to the remoteness of the virtual world. The remarkable sculptural designs (see p.516) of Humberto (b.1953) and Fernando Campana (b.1961), the intriguing hybrid furniture (see p.518) by Martino Gamper (b.1971), and the extraordinary mastery of materials demonstrated by Thomas Heatherwick (b.1970) provide a compelling case for the legitimacy and vitality of craft in the 21st century.

There are several other factors that have nurtured a more hands-on approach to design. Whereas in the past, skilled trades such as cabinetmaking and glassmaking were taken for granted in Europe, the wholesale shift of production to the Far East, particularly China, has resulted in considerable loss of skills and expertise in countries such as the United Kingdom. Companies like Ercol, which produces high-quality, well-crafted furniture using a combination of skilled handwork and machines, are now a rarity, so there is a renewed appreciation of their products and skills. Although electrical goods benefit from standardization, in other areas of domestic design, such as furnishings, the one-size-fits-all approach leads to blandness. This is why hand weavers such as Eleanor Pritchard (b.1971) and Margo Selby, who apply their craft skills to machine-woven fabrics, have proved so successful, creating textiles enriched by color, texture, and pattern. Similarly, in the field of wallpapers, independent designer-makers, such as Tracy Kendall (b.1957), have whetted people's appetites for visually stimulating bespoke works of art printed or, in the case of her textural 3D designs such as Another Color (see image 1), stitched by hand.

Lighting is another field in which designer-makers, such as Claire Norcross and Sharon Marston (b.1970), have transformed the medium by developing products in which hands-on construction or decoration is an integral feature of the design. Norcross's Eight-Fifty Lamp (see image 2), a giant pom-pom created using plastic cable ties, was later manufactured as a pendant lamp by Habitat, where the designer was head of lighting for several years. While there, she recognized the potential of the Garland light (2002; see p.508) by Tord Boontje (b.1968) for Habitat, which successfully translated the craft esthetic of cut-paper silhouettes into digitally designed, industrially made products.

In addition to enlivening the mass market, the reappraisal of craft has had a significant impact on avant-garde design. In the Netherlands—birthplace of the Droog collective—hands-on design has been championed. The first generation of Droog designers consciously exploited the imperfection of handmaking as a way of distinguishing their work from the slickness of commercial design. Their approach has influenced younger designers, for example Maarten Baas (b.1978), who has embraced the principle of craft production as a means of preserving the dynamic spontaneity of his work. Although Baas's designs (see p.514) are not craft in the traditional sense, they are emphatically hands on. **LJ**

2002	2007	2009	2009	2011	2012
The Crafts Council Gallery mounts an exhibition called "Home Made Holland: How Craft and Design Mix."	The 100 Chairs in 100 Days installation by Martino Gamper in London is subsequently exhibited all over the world.	Edmund de Waal completes his commission *Signs and Wonders* for the Victoria and Albert Museum in London.	Tord Boontje succeeds Ron Arad (b.1951) as head of design products at the Royal College of Art in London.	The Victoria and Albert Museum in London mounts an exhibition titled "Power of Making;" it features one hundred handcrafted contemporary objects.	Thomas Heatherwick creates a spectacular cauldron for the Olympic Games in London.

Smoke Series 2002–04

MAARTEN BAAS b.1978

Burned solid wood, finished with epoxy resin,
and fire-retardant foam leather upholstery
41¼ x 28¼ x 28¼ in./105 x 72 x 72 cm

Although the work of Maarten Baas is strongly conceptual, it is also concerned with the physical processes of making and unmaking. The designer's commitment to hands-on design is indicated by his decision to establish a workshop on a farm in the south of the Netherlands, where most of his furniture is produced. Ironically, the pieces of furniture for which he is best known, the Smoke series, were created by burning and partially destroying existing objects. This perversity is fundamental to Baas's ethos.

The idea of re-appropriation is not new, and can be traced back to Marcel Duchamp a century ago. Baas's "authorship" of the Smoke series lies in the process of transforming "found" objects and preserving their remains. The result has several potential readings: as a mischievous reflection on the fickleness of fashion, as a critique of society's wastefulness, or as a comment on the bourgeois propensity for nostalgia, for example. Challenging conventions on several fronts, the Smoke series is anarchic and open ended. It is up to us what we make of these curious pieces. **LJ**

FOCAL POINTS

1 PRESERVING RELICS
The charred remains of the chair, sections of which were destroyed altogether, have been carefully preserved by coating them in epoxy resin. As well as hardening the fragile structure and flaking surface of the wood, the epoxy acts as a preservative and prevents further decay.

2 GOTHIC TRADITION
Viewed objectively, the Smoke chair can be appreciated on a purely esthetic level as a manifestation of the centuries-old Gothic tradition. This interpretation is reinforced by the self-consciously macabre, black leather, deep-buttoned upholstery of the Baroque-style chair.

DESIGNER PROFILE

1978–2004
Maarten Baas was born in the Netherlands and studied at the Design Academy Eindhoven before going to the Politecnico di Milano in Italy. In 2000 he returned to the Design Academy Eindhoven and created the Smoke series in 2002 for his graduation show. In 2004 three Smoke pieces were produced by Moooi.

2005–PRESENT
Baas teamed up with Bas den Herder in 2005 to establish Studio Baas & den Herder. His Clay furniture was shown at the Milan Furniture Fair in 2011. The workshop began to produce and distribute pieces by other designers under the name Den Herder Production House in 2012.

BAROQUE DINING

By burning furniture, such as the Baroque chair (above) reproduced by Dutch label Moooi, as part of the "making" process, Baas deliberately set out to outrage people, thereby gaining instant notoriety and establishing his reputation as an agent provocateur. He filmed his conflagrations to draw attention to the extreme nature of his techniques and to prove that this was no mere visual trickery; the stunt is part of the design.

Favela Chair 2003

HUMBERTO CAMPANA b.1953　FERNANDO CAMPANA b.1961

👁 FOCAL POINTS

1 FRAMELESS STRUCTURE
Unlike a conventional chair, the Favela has no internal frame. It is constructed entirely from strips of untreated wood, nailed together by hand to create a load-bearing structure. The prototype was assembled from recycled waste materials, but the production version is made from pine or teak.

2 ORDER OUT OF CHAOS
Although this design appears to be chaotic, the components were meticulously assembled to create a structurally sound chair. The timber strips are all different shapes and sizes, which makes each chair unique. The random pattern of the wood is a key element in the chair's esthetic appeal.

The arresting sculptural furniture designed by Humberto and Fernando Campana has attracted considerable acclaim since it was first exhibited at the Milan Furniture Fair in 1997. The Favela chair, one of their most iconic pieces, was originally conceived in 1991 and has been produced by Italian firm Edra since 2003. Inspired by the wooden shacks in the slums (*favelas*) of São Paolo, Brazil, it pays homage to the resourcefulness and creativity of the residents of these shanty towns, who exploit any available scrap materials to build and furnish their homes. Melding virtuoso handling of materials with dazzling sculptural flair, the Favela chair embodies all the hallmarks of the Campana Brothers' unashamedly hands-on approach to design.

The complexity of the designs and the unconventional materials and fabrication techniques make their furniture very labor intensive to produce. Each design requires a high level of manual dexterity. Although recycled materials provide the starting point for many of their designs, the Campana Brothers have harnessed all manner of raw materials and products, from steel wire to coconut matting and mounds of soft toys. As the designers explain, "First comes the material, then the form, and finally we elaborate the function of the product by studying its ergonomics, limitations and capabilities." **LJ**

 NAVIGATOR

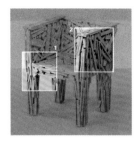

Pine or teak
29 x 26¼ x 24½ in.
74 x 67 x 62 cm

⏱ DESIGNER PROFILE

1953–84

Humberto and Fernando Campana were both born in São Paolo, Brazil. After graduating from the University of São Paolo in 1977, Humberto initially practiced as a lawyer before pursuing his passion for sculpture. Fernando joined him after studying architecture at the Art College of São Paolo from 1979 to 1984.

1985–97

Having started to make experimental furniture, such as the Vermelha chair, the Campana Brothers exhibited at commercial galleries in São Paolo and New York City during the 1990s, but their big breakthrough came when they participated in the Milan Furniture Fair in 1997.

1998–2004

In 1998 Italian firm Edra began producing the Campana Brothers' designs, and in the same year they became the first Brazilian designers to have their work exhibited at the Museum of Modern Art in New York City. In 2004 a major retrospective was held at the Design Museum in London.

2005–PRESENT

Collaborating with diverse firms, including Swarovski, Louis Vuitton, Camper, Alessi, and Venini, Estudio Campana continues to create groundbreaking designs. Its first hotel interior was completed in Athens, Greece, in 2011, and elements of the design clearly recall the Favela chair.

RESOURCEFUL USE OF MATERIALS

In times of hardship, people are obliged to make do and mend by using leftover scraps or by recycling components from defunct products. The resulting creations not only serve a practical purpose, but also provide an outlet for creativity, as in the case of rag rugs and quilts. Resourcefulness in the face of adversity is a constant source of inspiration for the Campana Brothers, and although the designers themselves are not obliged to be self reliant, the ingenuity they have witnessed in the *favelas* of São Paolo has prompted them to devise new applications for commonplace materials such as corrugated cardboard, bubble wrap, and hosepipe. Their Vermelha chair (1993; right) was inspired by a large bunch of rope that they bought from a street stall. The resulting chair, which is "upholstered" with brightly colored hand-knotted rope, is not about recycling as such but re-appropriating existing materials and giving them new life and purpose by harnessing their sculptural potential.

100 Chairs in 100 Days   2005–07

MARTINO GAMPER b.1971

Like his mentor Ron Arad, Martino Gamper has a free-thinking approach to design, but his work is difficult to categorize because he ignores traditional boundaries and bridges multiple disciplines spanning art, craft, and design. "I'm a designer in that my work is functional and I care about the usability of my product," he reflects, "but an artist in that I like to think about what my work means in its particular context. And I create like a craftsman, using traditional tools to make things out of other things."

Furniture often provides the starting point for Gamper's projects, which are often self-initiated. In 100 Chairs in 100 Days, his most ambitious project to date, he salvaged parts from a large collection of vintage furniture and used these components to create one hundred new hybrid chairs. Each piece incorporates recycled parts from two or three separate chairs, and a chair back, for example, might be repositioned to serve as a seat or legs. Avoiding the temptation to match like with like, Gamper deliberately paired up apparently incompatible materials, such as plastic and plywood, and juxtaposed components from different eras or in contrasting styles. As a trained cabinetmaker, Gamper already had the requisite skills to attach the components together, but his aim was creative spontaneity rather technical perfection. Witty and imaginative, 100 Chairs in 100 Days reaffirms the value of manual dexterity and mental agility in the digital age. **LJ**

❖ NAVIGATOR

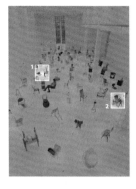

The installation on display in 2009 at the Triennale Design Museum in Milan, Italy.

👁 FOCAL POINTS

1 RECYCLED COMPONENTS
Gamper chose to cut up and disassemble a collection of old chairs to create a pool of components. Working quickly and spontaneously, he re-appropriated parts from various sources to create original pieces that display a curious mélange of physical characteristics.

2 DESIGN HYBRIDS
The mutant chairs are playful and quirky, but have slightly sinister connotations. They are deliberately ungainly and ugly by conventional standards. Whereas in plant hybrids, diverse physical characteristics are blended, in these pieces each incongruous element remains separate.

⏱ DESIGNER PROFILE

1971–2000
Born in Italy, Martino Gamper served an apprenticeship as a cabinetmaker. He studied sculpture at the Academy of Fine Arts in Vienna, but later switched to product design. In 1997 he moved to London, where he completed an MA in design products at the Royal College of Art in 2000.

2001–08
After establishing his studio, Gamper engaged in a variety of design activities. 100 Chairs in 100 Days received the Furniture Award at the Brit Insurance Designs of the Year in 2008.

2009–PRESENT
Gamper has created several designs for the furniture industry, including the Vigna chair for Magis and the Sessel chair for Established & Sons, both in 2010. The following year he won the Moroso Award for Contemporary Art. Recent projects include Post Forma at the British Art Show (2015).

◀ Gamper's L'Arco della Pace (2009) was one of the items featured in the "design is a state of mind" exhibition at London's Serpentine Gallery in 2014. Curated by the designer, the show was centered around "interesting things collected by interesting people on interesting shelves."

DESIGN WITH A CONSCIENCE

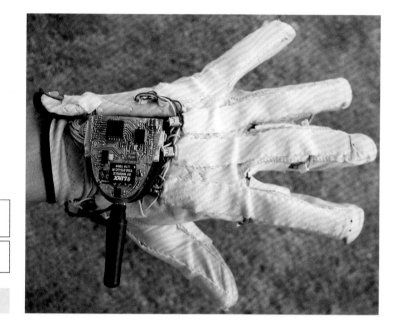

1 The award-winning Braille glove allows sign language users to communicate easily with people who are not trained in sign language.

2 The lightweight LifeStraw is only 12 inches (31 cm) long and 1⅛ inches (3 cm) in diameter.

3 The Ecosan toilets are made in South Africa and shipped as components for local assembly.

The idea of design with a conscience might share many of the same aims as sustainable design (see p.524), but the definition described here is different: design conceived proactively for people who do not constitute an economic market in the usual sense. This includes making products more cheaply for a broader market, as in the case of One Laptop per Child (see p.522), or seeking solutions to problems not previously recognized because of the lack of articulate demand. Designers in this field have empathized with a particular problem and realized how an effective solution could be found. This was the message put across by Austrian-born Victor Papanek (1923–98), who wrote in the preface to the second edition of *Design for the Real World* in 1985, "We are all citizens of one global village and we have an obligation to those in need."

Papanek's ideas developed alongside socialist economist E.F. Schumacher's insight concerning the need for "intermediate technology" to ensure that modernization in the post-war world would not involve the implant of over-sophisticated devices, which might break down and be abandoned, where a simpler alternative would do the job equally well. This type of thinking informed the design of the Freeplay wind-up radio (1995), created by Trevor Baylis (b.1937) in response to the need to disseminate healthcare information to remote areas in Africa, where there was no electricity supply and where batteries were unaffordable.

KEY EVENTS

1996	1998	1999	2002	2003	2004
At the BBC Design Awards, Trevor Baylis wins the prize for best product and best design for his Freeplay radio.	*Ecological Sanitation* is published by Stockholm Environment Institute. It stimulates the spread of expertise in safe human waste recycling.	Vestergaard Frandsen introduces the PermaNet, a long-lasting insecticidal bed net that helps to protect sleepers against malaria.	Eighteen-year-old Ryan Patterson invents the Braille glove for transferring hand movements into words on screen.	The Full Belly Project is founded in Wilmington, North Carolina, to produce labor-saving devices.	Wangari Maathai becomes the first environmentalist and the first African woman to win the Nobel Peace Prize.

Design with a conscience is not necessarily about products. It is possible to skip the fossil fuel and heavy infrastructure stage and move straight to renewables and local networks, replacing biomass cooking fuel, for example, with solar power. Not only is the labor of wood gathering avoided, but also smoke pollution and long-term deforestation. Kenya, where founder of the Green Belt Movement and Nobel Peace Prize winner Wangari Maathai faced official persecution for her pro-democracy activities, is now the world leader in the installation of small-scale solar power systems and harnessing geothermal energy.

Water supply and sanitation make a crucial difference to life chances. There are several relatively low-cost techniques for directing water to villages and for drilling wells that can be carried out locally. Furthermore, instead of an expensive and potentially polluting water-carried sewage system, as used in developed countries, a dry composting toilet such as the Ecosan (see image 3) offers a more reliable system. It has the potential for extracting useful chemical products, while avoiding the water table contamination problem of conventional pit toilets. Water contamination often occurs in the wake of natural disasters, adding the risk of disease to what are already challenging conditions for both survivors and rescuers. LifeStraw (see image 2), produced by Swiss company Vestergaard Frandsen, is a compact, portable plastic filter. Tiny purifying pores within the cartridge remove bacteria and parasites as water is sucked through the tube. One LifeStraw can purify 220 gallons (1,000 l) of water. The award-winning design has been used in many disaster-hit areas, such as Haiti after the earthquake and Pakistan after the floods, both in 2010. Larger versions that can be deployed long term are also distributed for family use, and a consumer version has been developed for hikers and trekkers.

Developed countries need fresh design approaches, too. The Design School Kolding in Denmark reformed itself in the early 21st century to turn students into investigators who could redefine a problem. In one real-life project, they were asked to design a robot that could take blood samples from anxious hospital patients. They realized that if the robot resembled a human in any way, the patient's fear of the procedure would remain. Consequently, they came up with a simple dolphin-shaped armrest that performs the process out of sight of the patient and thus reduces stress.

A major, if rather different, aspect of design with a conscience is concerned with the frailties of the human body, whether lifelong or induced by age or accident. Nominated by *Time* magazine as one of the best inventions of 2002, the Braille glove (see image 1) by Ryan Patterson (b.1983) translates sign language into text. Patterson was still in high school when he had the idea for the device, which was inspired by an occasion when he spotted a deaf woman having difficulties ordering food at a takeaway. The glove senses hand movements, which are transmitted wirelessly to a small monitor, where they appear as words. **AP**

2005	2006	2008	2013	2013	2014
The non-profit organization One Laptop per Child (OLPC) is established to create low-cost, robust laptops for distribution in developing countries.	The Design School Koning joins the Robocluster project to create a robot that can take samples of blood from patients.	Italian firm Italcementi Group develops TX Active, a self-cleaning cement that breaks down the airborne pollutants found in cities.	The Full Belly Project launches Soap for Hope, an initiative set up to reuse the soap that is discarded from hotels and other establishments.	The WAM (Wearable Assistive Materials) research project is launched. It aims to create a wearable exoskeleton to support walking.	The drinkable book project is established with the aim of creating pages of silver-impregnated water-purifying paper.

One Laptop per Child (OLPC) XO Laptop 2006

YVES BÉHAR b.1967

Metals and plastic
9½ x 9 x 1¼ in.
24.2 x 22.8 x 3.2 cm

I n 2005 the interdisciplinary digital advocate Nicholas Negroponte spoke at the World Summit on Information Technology in Tunis, demonstrating a $100 laptop produced for the non-profit organization One Laptop per Child (OLPC), set up by him and former colleagues from the MIT Media Lab. The aim was to extend Internet use in developing countries by means of a new, simplified, low-cost model that would be sufficiently robust to withstand accidents. Swiss designer Yves Béhar signed on with OLPC that year, and those requirements were the basis of his design for the XO laptop for OLPC. Bright green was used to reduce misappropriation of the child-intended OLPC XO on the black market.

Designing the OLPC XO required rethinking all the components and attempting to adapt them to the needs and capacities of their child users. Passive cooling was used in place of a fan, and drives and ports were reduced to USB only. A hand-cranked generator was included in the early models, but a simple solar panel is now used to recharge the exceptionally long-lived battery. The shockproof casing includes its own carrying handle. The screen relies on low-energy LED rather than the conventional cold cathode fluorescent lamp. The software is either Windows or an open-source alternative, as was the original intention. Wikipedia offered static copies of its articles as part of the preloaded software. But despite these strengths, some pupils stopped using the OLPC XO after a while, and questions arose whether the laptop was well enough tuned to the needs of its users, and whether OLPC supplied enough training in the XO's use. **AP**

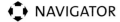

⊙ NAVIGATOR

👁 FOCAL POINTS

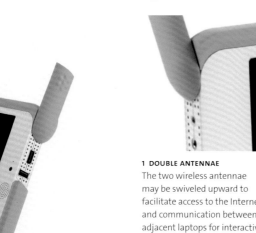

1 DOUBLE ANTENNAE
The two wireless antennae may be swiveled upward to facilitate access to the Internet and communication between adjacent laptops for interactive learning. In their closed position, they double as locking devices, sealing the USB and other ports from dust.

2 KEYBOARD
The electronic works (consisting of flash memory rather than a hard drive) are located behind the screen rather than beneath the keyboard. With no sophisticated wiring or circuit boards, the keyboard is less vulnerable to damage.

3 ADJUSTABLE SCREEN
The screen rotates through 180 degrees and may be laid flat for greater convenience as a reading device. Many children in developing countries are schooled outdoors in bright sunlight, so the designer had to ensure that that screen was readable in those conditions.

🕐 DESIGNER PROFILE

1967–99
Yves Béhar was born in Switzerland and studied there and in California, where he worked in Silicon Valley before setting up the design company Fuseproject in 1999.

2000–PRESENT
He is involved in many aspects of idealistic design, including membership of the Founders Circle of the Cradle to Cradle Products Innovation Institute and chief creative officer of the wearable technology company Jawbone. In 2008, he redesigned the NYC Condom logo, packaging, and vending machines for a program to reduce HIV/AIDS and teen pregnancy in the city. His designs for low-cost customized child spectacles for the international campaign "See Better to Learn Better" have been piloted in Mexico and San Francisco. In 2011, the Condé Nast Innovation and Design Awards recognized him as Designer of the Year.

◄ In recent years, the OLPC organization has faced criticism that XO use has had little impact on test scores. Its response is that the XO has proved a powerful tool of "self-empowered learning."

SUSTAINABILITY

1 Puma's Clever Little Bag shoe packaging can be reused by the consumer and is fully recyclable at the end of its life.

2 With the Replenish Refill System, a reusable bottle is attached directly to a concentrate refill pod.

3 The Nest Learning Thermostat learns about a user's domestic heating needs to program itself and save energy.

The term "sustainable development" was popularized in *Our Common Future* (or the Brundtland report) published by the World Commission on Environment and Development in 1987. It defined sustainable development as that "which meets the needs of the present without compromising the ability of future generations to meet their own needs." Yet sustainability existed before it was given a name. Traditional societies have devised low-tech ways of storing water, conserving heat inside buildings with insulation (the principle of the igloo), and developing natural cooling by designing shapes that will create updraft, all guided by experience rather than scientific theory. However, folk wisdom only goes so far, and many opportunities for harnessing natural processes were overlooked.

Units of measurement, such as ecological and carbon footprints, explain the problems of unsustainable lifestyles in relation to the carrying capacity of a local area, a city or the world. The Brundtland report linked the words "sustainable" and "development," but many dispute the possibility that development, in the conventional form of economic growth, can ever be sustainable. Instead of measuring success by gross domestic product, the Happy Planet Index correlates survey data country by country, based on the experience of well-being, life expectancy, and reduction of ecological footprint. This metric implies that the consumption-based goals of Western society are unsustainable, thus suggesting a different role for design in a sustainable future, with a broader overview of its potentially harmful effects.

KEY EVENTS

1995	1997	1998	2000	2002	2005
The Centre for Sustainable Design is established in Farnham, Surrey, England, at what became the University for the Creative Arts.	The Kyoto Protocol international treaty to fight global warming by reducing greenhouse gas emissions is adopted.	Construction starts on the Vauban sustainable district in Freiburg, Germany. It becomes one of the most celebrated model sustainable districts.	Building begins on the Beddington Zero Energy Development (BedZED) in south London, designed by British architect Bill Dunster (b.1960).	Michael Braungart and William McDonough publish *Cradle to Cradle: Remaking the Way We Make Things*, advocating upcycling.	US sportswear maker Nike launches the Nike Considered sustainable line of shoes with the Considered boot made from hemp.

Some argue that sustainability can be achieved largely through technical fixes, allowing the fundamental assumption of economic and population growth to continue as it has since the Industrial Revolution. If this were to be reversed in the form of a steady-state economy and a stable population, which is a common commitment among sustainability campaigners, many kinds of imaginative thinking would be needed to make the transition, all of which might be defined in a wider sense as design—not necessarily of products, but of processes and ways of sharing resources to provide something beyond personal gratification in use and waste after use.

While much of the design world has continued to be largely unconcerned about sustainability, there are signs in some quarters of an increased environmental awareness. The retro trend among fashion-oriented consumers brings benefits of sustainability by reverting to older forms of manufacture and materials. Cradle to cradle design, as advocated by US architect and designer William McDonough (b.1951) and German chemist Michael Braungart (b.1958), builds a second life use into products without waste or degradation. Japanese design studio Nendo's Cabbage chair (2008; see p.528) is an example of how the waste material created during the manufacture of pleated fabric has found new purpose by being upcycled as a furniture item. Banning built-in obsolescence by making products easy to repair is another proposal.

Disposable packaging creates huge environmental problems, particularly in the world's oceans. Swiss designer Yves Béhar's (b.1967) packaging for shoe manufacturer Puma, the Clever Little Bag (2010; see image 1), addresses the wastage created by cardboard boxes and plastic bags. It replaces the traditional shoe box and plastic shopping bag with a cardboard frame wrapped in a non-woven polyester bag, which can be repurposed for creative reuse and is recyclable. The Replenish Refill System (2014), dreamed up by US entrepreneur Jason Foster, is designed for common household cleaning products, most of which contain 90 per cent water and only 10 per cent actual ingredients. Foster turned the problem on its head—his reusable bottle (see image 2) attaches to refill pods and the user simply mixes with water from their own tap.

Sustainable energy involves the use of renewable energy and energy efficiency. The Solar Tree street lamp (2007; see p.526) by Welsh designer Ross Lovegrove (b.1958) is an instance of street furniture that employs renewable energy but also promotes the issue of sustainability through its role as a piece of public art. The connectivity of things can also help to cut energy use. Many domestic white goods give consumers information about their power consumption rating. In this context, smart metering has a role to play. The Nest Learning Thermostat (2011; see image 3), invented by US home-automation company Nest Labs, learns a user's heating requirements and programs itself accordingly. It can also be remotely controlled by an app on a smartphone, tablet, or laptop, so there is no need to heat an empty home. **AP**

2006	2010	2012	2012	2015	2016
An Inconvenient Truth—a documentary based on former US Vice President Al Gore's (b.1948) lectures on global warming—is released.	One of the driving forces behind the iPod (2001) and iPhone (2007), US designer Tony Fadell (b.1969) leaves Apple to co-found Nest Labs.	The book *The Shape of Green: Esthetics, Ecology, and Design* by US architect Lance Hosey argues that sustainable design needs to be beautiful.	The Cradle to Cradle Products Innovation Institute is created to bring about a large-scale transformation in the way things are made.	The United Nations Framework Convention on Climate Change's Paris Agreement marks a historic turning point for the reduction of global warming.	Steve Howard, chief sustainability officer at Swedish furniture retailer Ikea, says consumption of home furnishings is at its peak.

Solar Tree Street Lamp 2007

ROSS LOVEGROVE b.1958

For some years, it has been common to see small solar panels powering items of street furniture. The Solar Tree street lamp was created in 2007 by Welsh designer Ross Lovegrove with technical input from Sharp Solar, a subsidiary of Japanese electronics maker Sharp Electronics, and manufactured by Italian firm Artemide for the Museum für Angewandte Kunst (Museum of Applied Arts) in Vienna. The street lamp was not the first of its kind to be made, but it represents an advance on the esthetic quality of its predecessors.

The Solar Tree's low-energy LEDs are powered by solar energy, harvested from the upper faces of the flower-shaped heads. The energy is stored in batteries so that even in winter the street lamp will run off grid for three overcast days. In sunny weather, it can feed into the grid. The lamp is regulated automatically to switch on and off, and to dim, in relation to ambient light levels.

In 2012 a Solar Tree was exhibited in London as part of the Clerkenwell Design Week festival. Lovegrove spoke of how for some people, it is enough for street furniture to be in the background and unobtrusive. But Lovegrove wanted to bring the imaginative quality of domestic lighting into the public realm, asking: "Where's the poetry in the way these lights look or the way that street furniture looks. . . where's the forgiveness and the softness and the beauty of these objects?" **AP**

◈ NAVIGATOR

The Solar Tree's steel poles are painted with outdoor epoxy paint in a light green color shading into white.

👁 FOCAL POINTS

1 PHOTOVOLTAIC CELLS
Lovegrove argues in favor of making sustainable design look attractive to avoid the tendency to marginalize it. The Solar Tree street lamp evokes biological forms, like buds on branches. The upper faces of the heads at the end of each pole contain photovoltaic cells to collect solar energy.

2 CURVED POLES
The Solar Tree street lamp uses color and forms suggestive of the Art Nouveau (see p.92) movement of the 19th century, a period when much original thinking about the expressive potential of electric lighting took place. The Solar Tree's cluster of curved poles are like the stalks of a plant.

3 BENCH
The concrete and steel circular bench around the base of the Solar Tree makes it a social meeting place in an urban environment. The poles and heads also provide shade, just like the leaf canopy and branches of a tree. The poles reach a maximum height of 18 feet (5.5 m) above street level.

OFF GRID

The most obvious argument in favor of going off grid is economic, because global energy prices are rising, but the argument for the low environmental impact of small-scale renewable energy sources is equally strong. As climate change brings more extreme weather, the prospect of surviving a minor emergency is attractive. According to British environmentalist Rob Hopkins (b.1968), a co-founder of the Transition Network charity, resilience is a key concept for the future. This involves developing local resources, and being adept in a range of skills, such as how to grow food, repair items, maintain energy systems, and look after livestock.

Cabbage Chair 2008

NENDO f. 2002

👁 FOCAL POINTS

1 LAYERS

The chair's shaggy appearance is achieved by peeling back layers of material. The chair is made by taking a roll of pleated, unwoven fabric that has been cut layer by layer from the top to mid-height along its radius. Miyake coined the name "Cabbage chair," referring to the chair's layered structure.

2 SEAT

The height of the seat is determined by the position of the ring of tape that holds the roll of fabric in place. The layers created form a stable structure, which is suitable for someone to sit on comfortably without any extra support. The pleats add elasticity and a springy resilience to the chair.

The Cabbage chair was made by Japanese design studio Nendo in 2008 for the "XXIst Century Man" exhibition in Tokyo, curated by Japanese fashion designer Issey Miyake (b.1938). Miyake asked Nendo to make furniture from the pleated paper that is a by-product of the process of putting pleats into fabric, as used extensively by Miyake and which is normally discarded. The pleated paper sheets are rolled into a drum and secured with tape before being thrown away. The first idea was to combine this product with other materials, but instead, as Nendo co-founder Oki Sato (b.1977) explained, "we just started peeling the sheets back from the drum, like corn husks. We didn't really design it—we found it. We had a roll and we started peeling."

The transformation of the lengths of paper into a chair was achieved by taking a roll of pleated paper, binding it with a belt of tape a little above half way up, and then cutting into the upper section to that the outer "leaves" peel away. Using the paper version as a prototype, Nendo went on to make full-scale versions of the chair in unwoven fabric. The chair has been produced in a variety of colors, with tonal variations of each color—white, blue, lime green, orange, and cherry red. Nendo's original intention was that it could be shipped simply as a roll of material and left to the purchaser to assemble, thus reducing distribution costs. **AP**

Unwoven fabric
25¼ x 29½ x 29½ in.
64 x 75 x 75 cm

◄ Nendo created the Patchwork-glass collection for British glass manufacturer Lasvit in 2013. It combines the fine cut-glass techniques particular to Bohemian glass with a old production method for sheet glass, in which glass blown in a cylinder is cut away, opened up, and flattened. Nendo reheated items decorated with traditional cut-glass patterns, then sliced them open and reattached them to each other to create one large object. The process was similar to piecing together fragments of cloth to create a patchwork quilt.

EMOTIONALLY DURABLE

The concept of "emotionally durable design" was outlined by British academic Jonathan Chapman (b.1974) in his book of the same name in 2005. It has entered the discussion of sustainable design, asserting the need for products to satisfy consumers in ways that mean that they do not go out of fashion: they are cherished and retained rather than thrown away. This may lead to designs with a retro look and feel—as with the traditional-style products sold by German retailer Manufactum, such as the cardboard suitcase (right)—a witty reinvention of what is standard, or where the inherent visual and tactile qualities combine with a freshness of appearance.

MODERN RETRO

Taken together, the words "modern retro" are a blatant contradiction, since the essence of "modern" is to foreswear the past. Nevertheless, the modern period has seen several waves of historical revival. Most people react against the style of their parents, who in turn at one time reacted against the style of theirs. It is therefore not unusual for people to rebel by going back to granny's wardrobe and grandfather's technology.

Although considered by some to be trivial in their motivation and effect, such revivals are important in terms of museology, collecting, and popular taste. In 1960 an exhibition of Art Nouveau at the Museum of Modern Art in New York City sparked a revival of this particular Proto-modernist style that was understood by writer Susan Sontag as an expression of camp: affectionate irony that was sceptical of the present. This pattern has persisted in later revivals. As the 1960s ushered in the period of cultural pluralism and relativism known as Postmodernism, in which the single, rigid connection between style and sociopolitical morality that underpinned modernism was abandoned, the broader history of the recent past gained in significance. In the 1970s and

KEY EVENTS

1997	1998	1999	1999	2004	2007
The Italian Smeg company launches its FAB range of retro-style refrigerators in five colors. Other types of appliance are later added to the range.	Volkswagen launch the New Beetle after presenting the world with its "Concept One" show car, a redesign of their classic Beetle lineage, in 1994.	The BBC launch digital audio broadcasting (DAB). Roberts Radios introduce their retro-styled R60 Revival DAB in the early 2000s (see p.534).	"Hipster" or "fauxhemian" style comes to mean knowing about exclusive things before anyone else.	The Vitra Home Collection relaunches "modern classic" chairs drawn from ranges from the 1930s to the 1960s.	A new interpretation is launched of the iconic Fiat 500 (see p.532). The car joins a trend of redesigned, updated classics that began with the VW Beetle.

1980s, revival of Art Deco followed that of Art Nouveau, after which came mid-century modern, a style that remains dominant after emerging in the 1990s and gaining the name 'retro' at that time.

The revivals follow a recognizable pattern, initiated by style leaders who set the trend in the antiques trade, scholarship and museums, and then in reproductions and popular media. The conservation of buildings forms part of the cycle, especially as obsolescence is perceived to occur ever sooner after construction. In the 1970s, preservation of historic districts began to be justified not only on antiquarian grounds but also as a stimulus for urban regeneration and tourism; the Art Deco hotels of Miami Beach in Florida are a case in point.

Retro taste is good for business. It was symptomatic of a wider trend that in 1964 the Italian furniture manufacturer Cassina acquired rights to reproduce designs by Le Corbusier, which had been forgotten by all but a few specialists, although he was still alive at the time. This led to the concept of the 'modern classic' in furniture. Inspired by films such as *Bonnie and Clyde* (1967), light floral prints and long dresses were made popular by Laura Ashley in reaction against the Mary Quant look, and men's trousers became impossibly wide. Graphics for album sleeves accelerated the trend, such as *A Collection of Beatles' Oldies* (1966), designed by David Christian, and *Sgt. Peppers Lonely Hearts Club Band* (1967), by Peter Blake and Jann Haworth. In the eclectic carnival of revival that followed in the 1970s, elements from different styles were freely mixed together, as were examples of high art (in reproduction, often as posters) and the low arts of advertising and product packaging, which the Pop Art movement had elevated in status.

In *Retro — The Culture of Revival* (2006), Elizabeth Guffey identifies modern retro as 'a kind of subversion in which the artistic and cultural vanguard began looking backwards in order to go forwards'. The final irony was achieved, perhaps around the turn of the millennium, when the word 'retro' on its own was used to denote what had previously been called 'modern'. During a cycle now lasting over fifty years, it has become clear that retro is not a brief aberration in the path of progress, but an intrinsic part of a new way of seeing and understanding the world. It is made ever more compelling on one side by the increase in accessible imagery online, and on the other by the desire to resist the virtualization of so many experiences by celebrating real time and tactile events, such as eating cupcakes while reading a hardback book, or riding a chunky retro town bike (see image 1) through the preserved or reconstructed streets of a city, wearing leather shoes and woollen clothing. It may also be a form of ecological protest, in which the rapid turnover of consumerism is replaced by a focus on objects that, offering more than mere technical efficiency, provide 'emotional durability'. The retro styling of the Smeg fridge-freezer range (see image 2), for example, places it squarely in that category. **AP**

1 A retro-styled bicycle from the Skeppshult company in Sweden. The basket and chainguard mark it as a Liberty print special limited edition.

2 A FAB fridge-freezer from the Italian maker Smeg. The firm introduced the colourful, retro-styled FAB range in 1997 with a simple refrigerator model.

2008	2011	2012	2013	2015	2015
The publisher Penguin issues its first ten Clothbound Classics (see p.536), reasserting the printed book as a beautiful, lasting object in its own right.	While keeping the feel of its original watch, Cartier issues the Cartier Ronde Solo, a slightly redesigned version of its classic Cartier Ronde.	The Dr. Martens shoe brand reports that 2011–12 was its bestselling season of all time, partly because of a revival of the fashions of the 1990s.	Braun reissues its iconic ET66 calculator, which was designed collaboratively by Dietrich Lubs and Dieter Rams and first released in 1987.	Converse redesigns its well-known canvas basketball shoe—the Chuck Taylor All Star—to appeal to a wider range of non sports-playing fans.	The Ray-Ban company announces its New Wayfarer Classic model; the redesign includes a smaller frame and slightly softer eye shape.

Fiat 500 2007

ROBERTO GIOLITO b.1962

The new Fiat 500 offered enhanced space, comfort, and performance when compared to the original 500, but it was its retro styling that most appealed to buyers.

 NAVIGATOR

In 1957 Italy's prime car manufacturer, Fiat, created the original 500 (Cinquecento or "Topolino" after Mickey Mouse), designed by Dante Giacosa (1905–96). As its smallest four-seater passenger car with a rear engine, it predated the Austin Mini by two years. It was to become a national icon, but production ceased in 1975. Fifty years later, Fiat revived the model with new rounded bodywork that evoked the original in a deliberately nostalgic manner, designed by Roberto Giolito (b.1962) and Frank Stephenson (b.1959).

The original 500 was cramped inside but the new version was much more capacious, while still looking small and nippy like the original. The differences between the old and new 500s were highlighted in a special edition of 2014, devised by the furniture designer Ron Arad (b.1951), in which the outline of the original 500 was superimposed in white on the bodywork of the new black car. Attention was given to reducing the thickness of the internal finishes to gain more space. The dashboard in front of the passenger seat retracts when required, and the front seat may then be pushed forward to increase back seat leg room. (This cannot be done with the driver's seat, and the Fiat Trepiùno, launched in 2004, acknowledged the problem in a humorous way—the name means "three plus one more.")

Safety was never a great concern of the original 500, nor would its old-style macho Italian drivers have wanted it. In Italy exhaustive testing and the presence of airbags made the new model a very different proposition, but a "naked" version was made available at a lower price for sale in countries with less stringent safety standards. **AP**

👁 FOCAL POINTS

1 CHROME DETAILING
The reuse of chrome to highlight features such as the door handles, window trim, bumpers, and mirrors links the car with its predecessor. However, the decorative chrome accent terminating the side molding at the rear is a new feature; the original 500 had no such molding.

2 WINDOWS
The designers of the new 500 wanted to achieve a sense of transparency combined with protection for the occupants. The large glazed area is set above a relatively high "belt line," while the high wheel arches and driver position take advantage of SUV (sport utility vehicle) design.

3 HEADLIGHTS
The round headlights help to give the car the creaturelike quality that contributed to the 500's original appeal in the 1950s. Similarly, the edge of the bonnet runs between the headlights and continues with an upward curve at each end, which gives the car a smiling appearance.

🕐 DESIGNER PROFILE

1962–89
Roberto Giolito joined Fiat in 1989 as a designer qualified in the use of computers; he had a parallel career as a jazz bassist.

1990–PRESENT
Car design is a team activity. Giolito worked on Fiat's Zic electric car with aluminum frame (1994) and the Ecobasic (2000), a diesel city car entirely made from recyclable materials.

His Multipla family car, with an exceptionally compact body but spacious interior, was produced between 1998 and 2010. Like the new 500, the Multipla was originally a well-loved vehicle from Fiat's back catalog. After his early success with the new 500, Giolito has remained at Fiat. In the motor trade he is reputed to be "the most important designer you have never heard of."

ICONS REVISITED

Other famous small cars of the mid 20th century have been reinvented to strengthen brand identity and present technical innovation in a friendly and familiar form. They include the Volkswagen Beetle, the British Mini-Minor, and the BMW Mini Hatch. The Beetle (Typ 1) was launched in 1938 and continued in production until 2003, but already in 1994 the company had introduced the "Concept One," nostalgically modeled on the Beetle. This was followed by the "New Beetle" (1998; right), with bodywork resembling its predecessor but a front rather than rear engine.

Roberts RD60 Revival DAB Radio 2008

ROBERTS RADIOS est. 1932

The RD60 Revival: 1950s in styling but fronting technology of the twenty-first century.

◆ NAVIGATOR

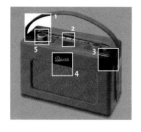

The Roberts Radio company was founded in 1932 by Harry Roberts (1910–59), and its products, solidly built and sometimes featuring reassuringly old-fashioned wooden panels, were a familiar sight in British homes, both before and after World War II. The RD60 Revival DAB (digital audio broadcasting) radio, which works both on mains and batteries, is based on the Roberts R66 of 1956. That model had been developed into the R200, which in the late 1980s was included in the background of a nostalgic TV advertisement for Martini; the radio was widely noticed and sparked a surge in demand.

By the early 1990s, however, cheaper foreign products, a break in family continuity of ownership, and new technology were threatening the viability of the company. It was acquired by the private Glen Dimplex Group in 1994, and since then it has redefined its visual identity while updating technically. As a company history of 2012 puts it, "the trend for nostalgia, despite living in an increasingly digital era, appears to remain unabated both in the UK and across the globe." The first "Revival" radios had appeared in 1993, and the new technology of DAB radio, launched in the 1999, was given a "Revival" housing. **AP**

1 CARRYING HANDLE

Where radio is now commonly heard via a miniature device and earphones, the RD60 Revival DAB savors the humor of the original design of 1956 with its prominent carrying handle, inspired by Harry Roberts' wife's handbag. Once again, radio is a shared listening experience.

2 PUSH-BUTTON CONTROLS

Roberts gave new roles to conventional push-button controls, such as switching between the radio's FM and DAB capabilities. In 1999, Roberts ran tests with the BBC prior to its introduction of digital audio broadcasting, and so was ready to launch its first DAB models in 2000.

3 CASING COLORS

Color has played a vital role in transforming the fortunes of the Roberts brand. The first RD60 Revival DAB was red, but the design became available in fourteen colors, mostly pastels. Limited editions have included a Revival in the livery of Cath Kidston's popular "Kempton Rose" pattern.

4 GOLD PLATING

Roberts radios are an excellent example of how retro styling can command a premium in today's market, even in the field of electronics. The tactile, hand-finished case and the gold plating of the logo and other metal parts complement electronic components with a reputation for quality.

5 RETRO CONTROL KNOB

In an era of technology being commonly operated by way of a touchscreen, many consumers enjoy the tactile experience of twiddling a smooth knob to find their preferred station. However, the Revival DAB offers the best of both worlds with automatic tuning and station presets.

▲ Viewed from the top, the Roberts RFM3 radio features all the knobs and push buttons of the original Revival and its DAB version, but clearly lacks the Revival's self-consciously retro styling.

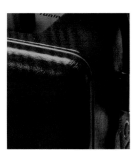

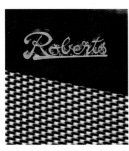

ROBERTS RADIO COMPANY

Harry Roberts (1910–59) founded the company in 1932, supplying the brand name and the commercial brains; his partner, the engineer Leslie Bidmead, oversaw the internal workings and probably also had a considerable input into the casings. Many of their radios had wooden panels, which contributed to the resonance of their tone. In 1956 the R66 model was launched, eventually to be developed into the R200 (above, in a special edition). In 1994 Roberts Radio was acquired by the Glen Dimplex Group. The previous year had seen the launch of the Roberts Revival model, which traded on the vogue for nostalgia. The Revival DAB followed the launch of Roberts' first DAB models in 2000.

Penguin Clothbound Classics 2008

CORALIE BICKFORD-SMITH b.1974

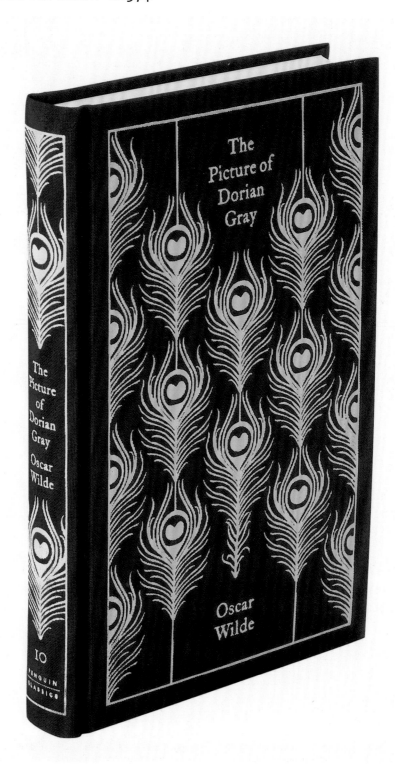

◈ NAVIGATOR

Cloth, board, and paper
5¼ x 8 x 1 in.
13.6 x 20.3 x 2.8 cm

Penguin Clothbound Classics first appeared as a series of ten books in 2008 and, since then, a further forty-four hardback editions have been published. Across the collection the approach by designer Coralie Bickford-Smith was to connect the disparate titles by means of beautiful, illustrative patterning and sumptuous, physical design. The books invoke the heritage of Victorian bookbinding while appealing to the eye of the modern reader. Each fabric-covered, B-format edition was treated as a tactile artefact as much as a classic text. The materials used referenced 19th-century book production methods, and the conceit was that these were editions to be cherished.

For each title, Bickford-Smith hinted at the book's contents by illustrating symbolic elements from the narrative. By using visual motifs that fitted easily into a grid, she ensured that the series would still tie together coherently. Fine details were difficult to achieve with pigment foil, so Bickford-Smith chose illustrations that would reproduce well: the horse-chestnut leaf on the cover of *Jane Eyre* symbolizes a pivotal moment in the story; the cover of *Dracula* features the garlic flowers that the heroine hangs around her neck to ward off the bloodthirsty protagonist.

As print publishing continued to be threatened by the effects of readers moving towards tablets and ebooks, the Clothbound Classics series was a conscious attempt to evoke a sense of both timelessness and quality. Bickford-Smith's solution was to treat each book very much as an object, celebrating its physical presence in the world. **AP**

◉ FOCAL POINTS

1 COLOR AND MOTIF
For the cloth binding of each title, Bickford-Smith looked for a color that would express an element of the subject matter. Her black-and-white treatment of Oscar Wilde's *The Picture of Dorian Gray*, for example, refers to the illustrations of Aubrey Beardsley (1872–98), one of Wilde's contemporaries. Her peacock feather motif, which extends to the book's spine, alludes to the dual personality and vanity of the Dorian Gray character.

2 CASLON TYPEFACE
Bickford Smith chose to use the typeface Caslon for the main cover typography across the entire collection. Designed by William Caslon in 1722, the serif face worked well with the pigment foil, giving the feel of a hand-blocked impression when used on the cloth covers. The elegant construction of the typeface also complemented Bickford-Smith's visual motifs. The use of a single typeface helped to establish visual coherence across the series.

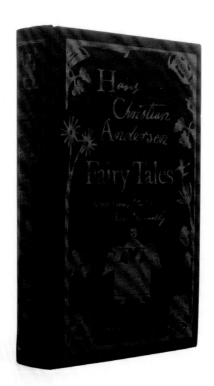

▲ One of the first covers Bickford-Smith designed for Penguin was for the 200th-anniversary edition of Hans Christian Andersen's *Fairy Tales* (2005). Foregoing a paper wrap-around jacket, its design was to inform the look of the forthcoming Clothbound Classics.

THE PUBLIC REALM

The term "public realm" refers to a physical reality, to the places owned in common on behalf of the people and to a conceptual space for freedom of information and discussion. Both have been seen as important to a good society. Architects, industrial designers, transport designers, traffic engineers, landscape architects, and artists have become watchful of infringements on physical spaces, whether by neglect or clutter, or by privatization in the form of shopping malls or gated housing. Technology crudely retrofitted to urban spaces in the form of signage, tramlines, wires, and pedestrian barriers is apt to take over unless controlled. Growth in car ownership in the 20th century only made it worse, and this visual anarchy provoked a reaction in favor of tidying up.

The pedestrianization of the city center began in the 1960s and has proved to bring social and commercial benefits. In the 1970s the discipline of space syntax developed to help urban planners simulate the social effect of their designs by collecting data about pedestrian movement, for example, revealing the correlation between pedestrian pathways and retail footfall. The radical concept of shared space pioneered by Dutch road-traffic engineer Hans Monderman (1945–2008) also proved influential. Shared space is a subtler alternative to pedestrianization in which street safety is increased by removing barriers and kerbs to rely on the intelligence of drivers. This is used effectively

KEY EVENTS

c. 1995	1995	1996	2001	2002	2004–08
The US Project for Public Spaces introduces its collaborative Placemaking process to shape the public realm to maximize shared value.	The book *Great Streets* by US urban designer Allan B. Jacobs (b.1928) examines the physical characteristics of the world's best streets.	English space-syntax theory pioneer Bill Hillier (b.1937) publishes *Space is the Machine* on how people relate to space in built environments.	*Blue Carpet* by Thomas Heatherwick uses innovative tiling to define a public space in Newcastle-upon-Tyne, England.	The first Paris Plage transforms an underutilized road along the banks of the Seine in Paris into man-made beach for the summer.	Hans Monderman leads the European Shared Space project to develop new policies and methods for the design of public spaces with streets.

on London's Exhibition Road 2011; see image 2), which adopts a less delineated route for through traffic, encouraging motorists to drive more cautiously, adhere to the speed limit, and have greater consideration for pedestrians. The design of transport systems—from vehicles to stops, signage and information—makes a vital contribution to empowering citizens and reducing car use, too. The redesign of the iconic Routemaster bus (2012; see p.542) by British designer Thomas Heatherwick (b.1970) aims to encourage people to use public transport by giving users the freedom to get on and off at will easily.

While changing streetscapes by decluttering is a component of public-realm design, there is a need for good street furniture, which has been addressed by many manufacturers working with designers. Strength and simplicity are key to success, reducing the need for repair or maintenance, and sometimes performing a dual function, as when seating patterns guide pedestrian flow, or seating forms part of raised planting beds or water features.

Public art is often included in outdoor improvement schemes, with dramatic interventions, such as *Cloud Gate* (2004; see image 1) by Anish Kapoor (b.1954) in Millennium Park, Chicago, that help to define the identity of a place and make it uniquely memorable. In some instances, an improvement to a conventional element can become an artwork, as with the structural installation *Dash Fence* (2007; see p.540) by Marc Newson (b.1963) in Miami, Florida.

Insofar as design in the public realm encourages inner-city living and walking and cycling rather than driving, it can be shown to make a positive contribution to limiting carbon emissions, reducing crime, and improving air quality. Better open spaces also lead to a stronger feeling of community. **AP**

1 Made from stainless steel, the surface of Anish Kapoor's *Cloud Gate* sculpture in Chicago reflects its surroundings.

2 The streetscape developed for Exhibition Road in London, where several museums are located, has a kerb-free single surface, using visual and tactile lines to distinguish pedestrian "comfort zones."

2007	2007	2007	2009	2011	2016
For the first time, the world's urban dwellers outnumber the rural population, with more than half of humanity living in towns and cities.	The *Public Space, Public Life* report analyses public life and space in Sydney, providing a blueprint on how to make the city center people friendly.	The British Department for Transport publishes *Manual for Streets* with guidance for practitioners involved in designing streets.	The first phase of the High Line linear park in New York City is completed. It is built on an elevated section of disused railway.	The Governing Council of the United Nations Human Settlement Programme adopts the first-ever public-space resolution on international policy.	Habitat III, the third UN conference to be held on Human Settlements, looks at sustainable urban development in the upcoming decade.

Dash Fence 2007
MARC NEWSON b.1963

The Dash fence structural installation in Miami is 100 feet (30.5 m) in length.

The Dash fence was created after Australian-born designer Marc Newson won Design Miami's Designer of the Year Award in 2006. Each winner is asked to create a permanent, site-specific installation that will enhance the Miami Design District. Newson designed a fence for the Design and Architecture High School (Dash).

Miami is a city in Florida suffused with water and light, and Newson's design plays on this. The Dash fence was inspired by the ripples on the ocean. The fence's appearance shifts based on point of view: it is possible to see through the fence when the viewer is close, but from a distance the fence appears opaque and forms an effective screen. The fence appears to undulate as the viewer walks by.

The fence was difficult to produce, owing to the number of components and the need to find a manufacturer capable of producing it. Newson said, "The end result works very well as a fence with sculptural qualities. Standing in front of it, one can see through it like blinds, but from the sides it gives a striped ripply effect."

The fence is an unusual piece of public art and design by Newson. The commission acknowledges the potential for environmental improvements that take a conventional element, such as a security fence, that is usually produced to a low standard, and transform them into something attractive that, in this case, also helps to advertise the mission of the institution that it serves to protect. **AP**

✦ NAVIGATOR

1 RIPPLE EFFECT
The optical effect of rippling is enhanced by the protrusion of the horizontal stays that form a pattern along the length of the fence. It is also enhanced by subtle variations of light and shade across the surface.

2 RAILING
The Dash fence consists of a thin metal frame of 400 vertical fins of varying depths. They are positioned to create a series of changing patterns with an undulating effect like the ripples of the ocean.

3 HORIZONTAL BAR
The horizontal bars show through like ridges in the sand at low tide, catching the light. The transparency close up allows a view into and out from the Dash courtyard, giving a sense of what lies beyond.

◀ Newson designed the Qantas First Class lounge in the Sydney international terminal in 2007. Sculptural oak dividers separate the space into bays that are aerodynamically shaped, like a section of an airplane wing.

LIMITED EDITIONS

Newson's work straddles the worlds of design for production and a more rarefied market of one-off pieces and limited editions, in which the boundary between product design and fine art blurs. The exclusive edition world allows for a high level of perfection in the making process. As Newson explained in relation to his show "Transport" (2010) in New York City premiering the Aquariva (right) leisure speedboat, "Twenty-two boats doesn't sound like a lot, but for a luxury company like Riva, it represents a substantial proportion of their production, and in the context of Gagosian Gallery where it was shown, it seemed logical. This product is entirely hand made, so there was no real economy of scale in making more."

Routemaster 2012

THOMAS HEATHERWICK b.1970

The Routemaster uses diesel-electric hybrid technology. A battery pack powers the electric motor that drives the wheels.

◆ NAVIGATOR

The Associated Equipment Company Routemaster (1954–68) designed by London Transport was the classic double-decker London bus, with its open rear platform and a functionalist esthetic. However, most of the original Routemasters were withdrawn from normal passenger service in 2005 because of safety problems, poor disabled access, and the need for a second operator to check tickets and passes. A new Routemaster was proposed and coachbuilder Wrightbus won the production contract with its proposal for a bus with a chassis 10 feet (3 m) longer than its predecessor—to accommodate two staircases—and a hybrid electric-diesel engine. Thomas Heatherwick's design practice, Heatherwick Studio, was commissioned to do the design.

Among the requirements were a secure driver's cabin, a low floor, and a rear platform that could be closed during one-man operation. Heatherwick Studio adopted the curved corners in order to disguise the extra bulk, and provided the distinctive motif of the continuous areas of glass winding up each of the stairs—that are consequently lighter than in previous models—and which extends to form the bands of windows on the upper level on each side. The bus has bench-type seats like the original Routemaster. **AP**

1 WINDOWS

Two levels of windows wrap around the bus like ribbons and light the two staircases. The large front window is angled toward the pavement to enhance visibility, allowing the driver to see any small children standing beside the bus.

2 DOORS

The bus has two doors, in addition to a door enclosing the open platform, because speed of loading and unloading passengers is critical. The central door is ramped to enable access for wheelchair users and children's buggies.

3 REAR PLATFORM

The hop-on, hop-off rear open platform was a feature of the original Routemaster. It gave passengers freedom and the bus character. The new Routemaster incorporates an open platform, but it is enclosed outside peak hours.

◄ The skills that workers at London Transport gained in working with aluminum by building bomber aircraft during World War II were used after the war to develop a lightweight double-decker bus. They built the Routemaster RM1 for London, and the first Routemaster entered service at Crystal Palace in February 1956.

OLYMPIC CAULDRON

London is a popular tourist destination and the red double-decker bus is one of its icons. The new Routemaster was designed to refresh the bus's image. It was introduced in 2012, the same year in which Heatherwick Studio's Olympic Cauldron (right) appeared at the opening ceremony of the London Summer Olympics. Each participating country carried part of the cauldron's structure into the stadium, in the form of petal-shaped objects of polished copper. The components were laid out to form a pattern like a flower, each was lit, and the construction rose up into a compact mass—a process reversed in the closing ceremony. Heatherwick Studio demonstrated its ability to span a range of public-realm designs with memorable results.

3D PRINTING

1 These 3D-printed Molecule shoes (2014) were designed by Francis Bitonti and manufactured using Adobe software.

2 The Materialized Sketch chair (2006) by Front was built up in layers of ABS-like resin and strengthened with ceramic filler.

3 Designed by Janne Kyttanen, the Lily. MGX lamp won the Red Dot Design award in 2005.

The advent of plastics had freed designers from material limitations and expanded the range of forms they could make; the arrival of 3D printing liberated them still further. Objects with intricate internal structures that would be impossible to mold or mill could pop into existence at the touch of a button, fully formed, having been manipulated on a computer screen. It was a process of fabrication that was wrested from the factory floor and established on the desktop. Consequently, 3D printing was soon lauded as a revolution in manufacturing and design. Indeed, the ability to produce unique objects quickly caused change across a broad spectrum. It was not only employed in advanced medical procedures and in the studios of artisan designers, but it also raised big questions about copyright and the control of easily reproduced forms, including firearms. In addition, 3D printing offered the potential to reshape the existing production and distribution industry to be more environmentally friendly.

The term "3D printing" is used to describe the general method of production in which a three-dimensional object is built up, layer by layer (see image 1). Also known as additive manufacturing, it comprises many different processes that use many different materials. For example, stereolithography (SLA) utilizes computer-directed ultraviolet light to harden a liquid

KEY EVENTS

2000	2005	2006	2007	2009	2010
Dutch designer Janne Kyttanen's graduation project leads to the founding of Freedom of Creation, a design company based on 3D printing.	British engineer Adrian Bowyer (b.1952) begins the RepRap project to create an open-sourced 3D-printing machine that can reproduce its own parts.	Sjors Bergmans and Marc van der Zande create Head Over Heels, the world's first wearable 3D-printed shoe.	Shapeways is launched in New York City. It allows users to submit their own 3D models and have them printed.	US firm MakerBot launches its first 3D printer, Cupcake CNC. Demand is so high that the company asks owners to print parts to build more.	Materialise creates an accurate full-size replica of Tutankhamun's mummy for a National Geographic exhibit.

photopolymer, whereas selective laser sintering (SLS) employs lasers to fuse metal or thermoplastic in powder form. Fused deposition modeling (FDM) sets down layers of hot plastic, metal, or clay, which harden as they cool. Each process has a particular application—some produce fine detail; others create stronger objects—but they all conjure form from formlessness.

The pioneering method of 3D printing was stereolithography, invented by Chuck Hull (b.1939) in 1983 as a way of efficiently creating small parts for prototype product designs. The first thing he made was a black eye-wash cup. In 1986 he founded 3D Systems—the first company to be based on 3D printing technology—and initially his new production method was used in big industry as an accessory to traditional fabrication, quickly prototyping parts for medical equipment, cars, and aeroplanes, for example. Prior to the advent of 3D printing, every new plastic or metal part had needed a cast or mold, which was expensive and time consuming to produce. However, 3D printing creates bespoke objects effortlessly, and all that is required to realize the design is a 3D CAD (computer-aided design) drawing. The process has wide applications, too. For example, medical researchers soon discovered that it can be used to create highly complex objects, such as implants and prosthetics that exactly fit patients' bodies (see p.550).

The possibilities of 3D printing also appealed to furniture and product designers, as well as architects. Some designers particularly enjoy the material qualities of 3D-printed objects. For example, Janne Kyttanen (b.1974) explored the textured, diaphanous, and often brittle nature of SLS with products such as Lily (see image 3), Lotus, and Twister (2002), lighting designs produced in collaboration with 3D-printing specialist Materialise. Others, such as the Swedish design group Front, launched the Sketch furniture project (see image 2), which used computer software to translate the designers' movements, as they "drew" furniture in the air, into data that could be printed out in physical forms.

The mass media latched onto the transformative nature of 3D printing, reporting on remarkable medical advances on the one hand and expressing concerns over projects such as the Liberator (2013), a printed gun, on the other. However, the furore over the latter overlooked the fact that the gun barely worked—its material tending to shatter—and the excitement over the possible scales of production was dampened by the fact that printing and curing typically took hours, and objects usually required milling and polishing, too. Furthermore, the promise of democratizing production was countered by the sheer level of knowledge required for successful prints. Fortunately, 3D-printing technology is constantly improving, from print speeds to the more efficient employment of high-quality materials, such as glass and metal. It is still very much in its infancy, and its impact has yet to be charted and understood fully. In a world in which the digital and the physical are increasingly becoming intertwined, the potential of 3D printing is still being written. **AW**

2011	2012	2012	2013	2013	2015
Online 3D printing service i.materialise offers gold and silver as material options.	Michael Eden (b.1955) creates the PrtInd vase (see p.546). It has a soft touch coating to give it a tactile feel.	A Dutch hospital fits the first 3D-printed replacement jaw, made from titanium powder fused by laser, to an eighty-three-year-old patient.	Olaf Diegel (b.1964). adds the Steampunk guitar (see p.548) to the range of 3D-printed guitars offered by his company, ODD.	Cody Wilson, founder of Defense Distributed, releases models for a 3D-printed gun called the Liberator.	Foster and Partners unveils a proposal for robots to 3D print habitable structures on Mars using the Regolith Additive Construction process.

PrtInd Vase 2012

MICHAEL EDEN b.1955

Nylon with soft-touch
mineral coating
Height 11¾ in./30 cm
Diameter 9½ in./24 cm

⟨⟩ NAVIGATOR

Michael Eden's work often explores the relationship between a 3D-printed object and its historic source. The PrtInd vase is a reproduction of the Portland vase (see p.33), a Roman cameo glass vessel that was made between AD 5 and 25. It has been estimated that the original version took its creator at least two years to produce, steadily cutting away a top layer of white glass to reveal a lower layer of violet-blue glass. This ancient vase has been copied many times, including by Josiah Wedgwood (1730–95), who produced a meticulous reproduction in ceramics in 1790 after four years of trials. Eden's copy is consciously less meticulous, because it is based on visual information that he found via search engines. He was inspired by a Google project in which users could explore a museum through their browser. It allowed them to look at objects in detail, but Eden was interested in the fact that they were viewing the pieces only on a screen. The PrtInd vase is faceted, thus revealing the polygons that comprise computer attempts to represent ellipsoids in 3D, and the decorations are simplified and sometimes missing because Eden could not see them in his reference material. **AW**

1 NYLON
The vase was printed in nylon by Selective Laser Sintering, a process that slowly creates 3D forms from thousands of layers of melted and fused powder. It was coated first with a compatible primer and then with a colored mineral coating, and finally a soft-touch material to give a tactile feel.

2 DECORATION
Eden took an image of the original vase's back and front into Photoshop and extrapolated what the rest of the vase had looked like. He reduced the colors to black and white and used his CAD application to extrude the image as a raised 3D form on the surface of the vase.

🕐 DESIGNER PROFILE

1955–80
Michael Eden studied industrial design at Leeds Polytechnic. While there he was introduced to working with clay, which he enjoyed for the speed with which it allowed him to realize his ideas. However, he left the course before graduating and went on to join his wife's business making slipware.

1981–2007
Eden worked as a professional potter and specialized in functional slipware. He was attracted to making things with computers, but the exacting nature of programming did not match his love of the plastic properties of clay until he discovered 3D printing.

2008–PRESENT
In 2008 Eden completed an MPhil research project at the Royal College of Art in London, exploring how digital technology could be combined with his experience as a potter and ceramicist. It culminated in his first 3D-printed work, the Wedgwoodn't tureen (2008). Eden is represented by ceramics gallery Adrian Sassoon. He had a solo show at the Holbourne Museum in Bath, England, in 2015–16.

▲ Eden manually modeled the faceted form of the vase in his CAD application, Rhino, copying the 2D outline of the original from a Google search image and revolving it to produce a fully 3D form.

3D-PRINTED WEDGWOOD

In order to create the 3D-printed Wedgwoodn't tureen (above), Eden had to formulate new processes for every aspect. These included learning new software to create its form and understanding the tolerances and quirks of 3D printing itself. He wanted to recreate an object that would hold significance for being reproduced through 3D printing, so he chose a piece by Wedgwood because of the latter's recognizability and role in the Industrial Revolution. Although Eden's tureen shares the shape of the original, which was part of the Wedgwood creamware catalog of 1817, it could only have been produced through 3D printing. Eden took a 2D image and used his CAD software to produce a 3D tureen shape. For the finished surface treatment, he chose bright colors to move as far away as he could from a traditional ceramics palette, thereby revealing the contrast between the possibilities that Wedgwood enjoyed and what can be achieved today.

Steampunk 3D-Printed Guitar 2013

OLAF DIEGEL b.1964

3D-printed Duraform (nylon) PA outer body, maple inner core,
airbrushed paint, and clear satin lacquer
Weight 7 lb/3.2 kg

The free-form nature of 3D printing has the capacity to question the customary presentation of familiar objects. Although Olaf Diegel's guitars retain the well-known shapes of Telecasters and Les Pauls, their bodies shrug away their traditional structures. For example, a Les Paul's top and back panels are solid maple, but Diegel's equivalent—the Atom—is a chassis of curved framework that evokes the patterns of oil on water. And a Telecaster's body is solid wood, but that of Diegel's Steampunk guitar is filled with moving gears and a piston. The latter is printed in nylon as a single unit, emerging with all the gears and the piston in place and in working order.

One of the assumptions made about 3D-printed guitars is that they do not sound as good as the "real thing." Diegel says that there is almost no difference, and that the sound of a guitar is more defined by its strings and pickups than by its body. In fact, the Steampunk features many traditional components in addition to its 3D-printed body. It has a Warmoth Pro Telecaster maple neck, chrome Gotoh locking tuners, and a chrome Schaller 475 bridge; Diegel's philosophy is to use 3D printing where it has the advantage. **AW**

◉ FOCAL POINTS

1 AIRBRUSHED FINISH
Diegel paints most of his guitars himself, but the finish on the Steampunk is airbrushed by hand by Ron van Dam, an airbrush specialist based in New Zealand. The guitar is printed over a period of eleven hours by 3D Systems' Cubify bureau service on an sPro 230 machine.

2 INTERNAL GEARS
The main challenge of the Steampunk was to ensure there was enough clearance between the gears so that they could be printed *in situ* and rotate freely when complete. 3D printing is not highly precise, so many tests were needed to reach a balance of print tolerance and tightness.

◷ DESIGNER PROFILE

1964–92
Born in New Zealand, Olaf Diegel studied electronics at the University of Natal in Durban, South Africa, before taking a variety of jobs around the world, including teaching English in Japan.

1993–2001
Having moved back to New Zealand, Diegel was employed at a lighting company, where he began to model products in 3D software. In the mid 1990s, he heard about 3D printing and recognized its potential in manufacturing prototype parts. No machines were available in New Zealand so he had his first component, a handle, made in Australia.

2002—PRESENT
In 2002 Diegel was appointed an associate professor at Massey University's Institute of Technology and Engineering in New Zealand. He made his first 3D-printed guitar, the Spider, in 2011. It was as big a form as he could fit in the 3D-printing machine that he had at the time. He subsequently blogged about its construction and people started requesting to buy copies. This prompted Diegel to establish his own company—ODD—to manufacture 3D printed guitars. In 2014 he became professor of product development at Lund University in Sweden, but he continues to run ODD.

3D-PRINTED VIOLIN

One of the best-known 3D-printed musical instruments is the 3Dvarius (2015; above), a violin that does not follow many standard elements of violin construction, as it is electric and a completely different shape. Its maker, Laurent Bernadac, claims that its form is modeled to work with the way sound propagates through its structure, and that it is far more durable than a standard violin.

3D-Printed Vertebra 2014

LIU ZHONGJUN b.1958

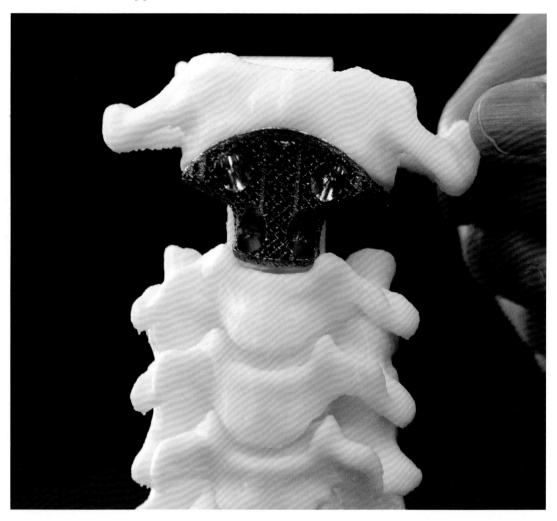

Titanium implants are used because they are biocompatible and rarely rejected.

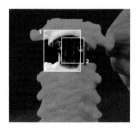

The possibilities offered by 3D printing have proved a natural fit for medicine. In August 2014, Liu Zhongjun and his team at Peking University Third Hospital in China pioneered the use of 3D printing to replace the second vertebra in the neck of a twelve-year-old boy with a 3D-printed titanium one. The boy, called Minghao, needed the five-hour operation to remove a malignant tumor from his spine, windpipe, and internal and external carotid arteries. The second vertebra, otherwise known as the axis, is a critical one because the head pivots on it. Usually, it is replaced by a standard hollow titanium tube and the patient's head is held in place with a frame and pins during a healing process that takes at least three months. However, by using a 3D-printed vertebra that was not only a precise fit but also stronger, Minghao's recovery was more efficient, as natural bone grew into the new vertebra's honeycomb structure. He was also expected to recover a great deal of his original movement. At Cornell University in New York, researchers have worked on a different form of 3D-printed spinal implant to replace damaged discs. Normally, disc disease is treated by fusing vertebrae together, which reduces movement. Their method prints stem cells into structures that are inserted into the damaged area. The structures dissolve over time as new spinal cells grow. **AW**

⊙ FOCAL POINTS

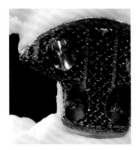

1 COMPLEX SHAPE

The 3D-printing process and titanium material that formed the replacement vertebra had been regularly used for surgery before. The difference was the complexity of shape that 3D printing could bring to this implant, which allowed it to fit better and required less infrastructure to hold it in place.

2 HONEYCOMB STRUCTURE

The intricate composition of the 3D-printed vertebra would be very difficult to cast using traditional methods while maintaining structural strength. The honeycomb structure allows bone to grow throughout it to strengthen and naturally bond the replacement with the rest of the patient's body.

⊕ DESIGNER PROFILE

1958–2008

Liu Zhongjun graduated from Beijing Medical College (now known as Peking University Medical and Health Science Center) in 1987. He joined Peking University Third Hospital's Department of Orthopedic Surgery, where he became chairman of his department and the chair of the university's Research Center of Spinal Surgery. While there, he was awarded millions of Chinese yen in research grants for his work in the field of spinal surgery, particularly for studies into spinal tumors. He also oversaw his team performing some 2,500 procedures a year.

2009–PRESENT

Liu and his team worked on using titanium 3D-printed implants for several years. They launched the program and developed the first model in 2009, began testing the method on sheep in 2010, and started clinical trials on humans in 2012. After Liu and his team had utilized implants on more than fifty volunteer patients with great success, the Chinese health authority was prompted to begin approving them for wider use, ready for Minghao's orthopedic spine surgery in 2014.

▲ A 3D printed-model, of a child's heart for example, provides surgeons with considerably more information than an MRI or CT scan, thus enabling them to diagnose problems more easily.

3D BIOPRINTING

Artificially growing biological tissue is a notoriously difficult process, particularly because of the challenge of keeping nutrients flowing consistently to all cells. However, in 2014 a research team at Harvard University in Massachusetts, led by materials scientist Jennifer Lewis, used a 3D printer to print a protein matrix and living cells in a similar pattern to the way in which they are found in a living body, including a vascular system that delivered nutrients (right). The process, which Lewis refers to as "3D bioprinting," is a long way from printing full organs, but it is a key step in that direction.

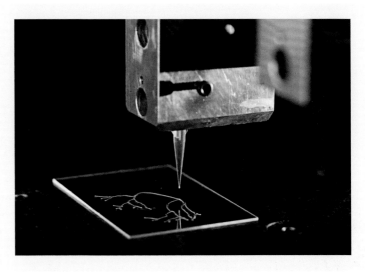

GLOSSARY

ABS
Acrylonitrile butadiene styrene: a very durable type of oil-based plastic.

Abstract Expressionism
A US movement in abstract art, dating from the 1940s and 1950s, pioneered by Jackson Pollock and Mark Rothko, which placed the emphasis on spontaneous mark making.

aerodynamics
The study of how air passes over solid moving bodies. See *streamlining*.

Aestheticism
A late 19th-century British design movement that promoted "art for art's sake."

Art Deco
A pervasive decorative style that flourished between the 1920s and 1940s, characterized by stepped profiles, smooth curves, opulent materials, and the vibrant colors of the Ballets Russes.

art glass
Sculptural, decorative glass produced in limited editions by named designers, rather than designs for mass manufacture.

Art Nouveau
An international movement in art and design characterized by sinuous, organic shapes and natural forms.

Arts and Crafts
A mid-to-late 19th-century movement in design and architecture, spearheaded by William Morris, which looked back to a preindustrial craft tradition when artifacts were made individually by hand.

Bakelite
The first fully synthetic material, invented by Leo Baekeland in 1907, and available only in brown and black. Bakelite was made of phenol and formaldehyde.

Baroque
An exaggerated operatic architectural style of the 17th and early 18th centuries.

Bauhaus
One of the most seminal design schools of all time, the Bauhaus (1919–33) fomented modernist ideals across a wide range of disciplines.

bentwood
A technique pioneered by Michael Thonet in which lengths of wood, often beech, were bent into curved shapes by the use of metal clamps and heating by steam.

brand
The overarching identity of a product or manufacturer as expressed in visual messaging, such as a logo, packaging and advertising, and in its perceived values in the marketplace.

cabriole leg
A chair leg that curves outward where it attaches to the seat and inward where it reaches the floor.

cantilever chair
A chair whose seat and frame are supported by a single base rather than four legs.

classicism
A style of architecture and design originally developed during the Renaissance, which harked back to the "orders" of ancient Greece and Rome. Classicism was revived during the 18th century

and became the dominant influence on taste.

collage
Artwork or design composed by piecing together fragments from a variety of other sources, often including "found" materials.

collotype
An early photographic process used for printing in high volumes.

Constructivism
A post-Revolution Russian movement that insisted that art, design, and architecture should act primarily as agents of social change.

corbel
A supporting structure projecting from a wall or similar surface.

corporate identity
The visual means—through signage, logos, printed communication, and the like—by which a company presents itself both to its customers and employees.

counter
In typography, the enclosed area of a letter or character.

Craftsman style
The late 19th-century US variant of the Arts and Crafts movement, typified by the work of Gustav Stickley.

Cubism
An art movement of the early 20th century that brought different views of the same subject together in the same picture plane. Picasso and Braque were its most influential proponents.

daguerreotype
An early photographic

process, invented by Louis Daguerre in the early 19th century, which enabled an image to be captured on a silvered copper plate.

De Stijl
An early 20th-century Dutch movement in art, design, and architecture that prioritized abstract geometric forms and primary colors.

diffuser
In lighting design, a shade or any other screen that spreads or softens the effect of a light source.

dynamic obsolescence
A term coined by GM's influential car designer Harley J. Earl to describe a marketing strategy whereby customers were persuaded to buy new models on the basis of updated styling alone.

ergonomics
The study of the interaction between the human form and capabilities and objects or systems.

Expressionism
A German art movement of the early 20th century that focused on conveying subjective emotion or mood.

faience
Tin-glazed earthenware pottery, originating in Italy.

Fauvism
An early modernist art movement, typified by the use of strong nonrepresentational color, often to communicate the emotional state of the artist.

fiberglass or GRP
Plastic that has been reinforced for extra strength with glass fibers.

font
Narrowly defined as a set of type in one specific face and size; generally used more loosely as a synonym for the word "typeface."

Futurism
An early Italian art movement that celebrated modern technologies and products such as the automobile and the airplane.

gas injection molding
A technique of molding plastic that involves the injection of gas into the mold, thus creating hollows and permitting changes of section to be made.

Googie architecture
A form of modern architecture influenced by automobile culture, jet aircraft, and the Space Age.

Gothic
An architectural style dating from the medieval period and subsequently revived in the mid-to-late 19th century. Common features include the pointed arch, flying buttress, and ribbed vault.

grid
A geometric layout used by graphic designers to order the placement of type and illustrations on a page

Hi Tech
A short-lived design and architectural style characterized by the reuse or repurposing of industrial and commercial spaces and fixtures and fittings.

hot metal
A method of typesetting in which molten metal is shaped into "slugs" of characters that are inked.

injection molding
A technique for mass-manufacturing products and parts by injecting molten plastic into a mold.

International Typographic Style
A rigorous, pure, and minimal graphics style that emerged in postwar Switzerland. The typeface Helvetica is a famous example.

Jacquard loom
A mechanical loom dating from the beginning of the 19th century that uses perforated cards to create complex patterns.

Japonisme
A decorative style of the late 19th century, heavily influenced by imported Japanese prints and artifacts.

jasperware
A fine, matt porcelain or stoneware first devised by Josiah Wedgwood in the late 18th century. The most famous type, still made today, is Wedgwood Blue.

Kitsch
A form of taste that knowingly embraces the camp, lowbrow, or mass-produced.

ladderback
A traditional type of chair with a back featuring evenly spaced horizontal bars.

logo
A graphic symbol or name consistently rendered in the same style to represent a product or company.

lowercase/uppercase
Lowercase or miniscule letters are uncapitalized; uppercase are capitalized.

matt-black esthetic
High-end technology products, such as hi-fi equipment and calculators, were often produced in matt-black casings or finishes during the 1970s to emphasize their seriousness and sophistication.

Minimalism
A rigorous offshoot of modernism, heavily influenced by traditional Japanese notions of "thinglessness," which was especially influential during the late 20th century.

modernism
The dominant design style of the early 20th century, modernism rejected ornament in favor of a stripped-back machine esthetic that prioritized function and pure form.

modular
A furniture or furnishing system comprising multiple identical components, such as modular shelving or seating.

monobloc
A design produced all in one piece or as a single casting.

monocoque
A design where the skin is structural—such as an aircraft's stressed fuselage or a ship's hull.

Neoclassicism
See *classicism*.

nylon
A family of synthetic materials, first produced in 1935, with a range of applications, including fabrics.

offset lithography
A method of volume printing, dating from the late 19th century, where an image is transferred from a metal plate to rollers and then onto paper or other media.

Palladianism
A form of classicism or Neoclassicism inspired by the work of the Italian architect Andrea Palladio.

Perspex
Like Plexiglas, a trade name for a lightweight, shatterproof thermoplastic, used as an alternative to glass.

photosetting
A form of typesetting in which a photographic process is used to set type on photographic paper.

planned obsolescence
The practice, common in the 1950s and 1960s, of designing domestic goods (particularly appliances) so that they had a short period of usefulness and would need frequent replacement.

Plexiglas
See *Perspex*.

plywood
Laminated sheets of thin wood (often softwood), glued together and often faced with a veneer of a more expensive or attractive hardwood. Plywood may be formed into curves under steam pressure.

point
The smallest unit in typography. In digital type, there are seventy-two points to an inch.

polycarbonate
A type of strong thermoplastic that has many varied uses in design and engineering.

polypropylene
A versatile thermoplastic used in packaging, textiles, mechanical parts, and furniture.

polythene
The most common plastic, with a widespread use in packaging.

Pop
An early 1960s art, fashion, and design movement that took inspiration from popular youth culture, consumerism, and ephemerality.

Postmodernism
A late 20th-century movement in design and architecture that turned its back on the purism of modernism and embraced stylistic quotation.

production line
A development in mass production, pioneered by Henry Ford, that placed products for assembly on a moving belt to speed manufacture.

Productivism
A Soviet graphic design movement that saw graphics as the means to bring art into the life of the masses.

Punk
Punk rock's raw untutored sound had its graphic counterpart in DIY collages and anarchic graphics.

quality control
A US manufacturing discipline, whereby all aspects of production are rigorously monitored to meet quality standards. It was widely adopted by Japanese companies after 1945.

Rationalism
A postwar version of modernism, popular in Germany and Switzerland, and to some extent Italy, in which products reflected a problem-solving approach.

ready-made
A work of art or design composed by collaging together found objects to make an entirely new creation.

repeat
In textiles, the design element, figurative or abstract, that is repeated across fabric to create a pattern.

La Ricostruzione
The Italian term for the country's postwar economic reconstruction, which was heavily design led.

Rococo
A French decorative style, dating from the 18th century, that is lighter, more elegant, and more playful than Baroque.

Royal Warrant
In the United Kingdom a Royal Warrant is awarded to producers and manufacturers that supply the Royal Household. It is therefore seen as a badge of quality.

Scandinavian Modern
Postwar design from Denmark, Sweden, Finland, and Norway characterized by clean contemporary lines, natural forms, bright color, and a distinctly human appeal.

screen printing
A printing technique that involves transferring a photographic image or graphic design from a mesh screen onto paper, fabric, and the like.

serif/sans serif
A serif is the hook that completes the main stroke of a letter. Sans serif typefaces lack hooks and flourishes of this kind.

splat
A supporting element of a chair, either horizontal on the chair back, or vertical, between the seat and the arm.

streamlining
Smooth, teardrop-shaped contours that were applied to a wide range of products in the 1930s, echoing aerodynamic principles.

styling
In product design, focusing on external appearance rather than function or specification.

Suprematism
A Russian art movement of the early 20th century that exalted pure abstract or geometric forms over representational imagery.

task light
An often repositionable light whose prime function is to provide targeted illumination for working or reading. The Anglepoise, with its moveable arm, is a famous example.

trademark
A sign or symbol, often protected by law, that identifies a particular product or producer.

tubular steel
Hollow steel tubing, originally used in bicycle manufacture, was widely adopted by early modernist furniture designers to create minimal frameworks for seating and tables.

typeface
A type design, generally encompassing an alphabet, numbers, punctuation marks, and other special characters.

unjustified/justified
Unjustified text does not have a fixed line length; justified text has fixed margins, either to the right or the left or both.

user interface
The means by which a computer user interacts with the computer system, generally via software.

veneer
In cabinet making, a thin layer of decorative wood applied over a baser wood that comprises the main frame or structure of an item of furniture.

virtual reality
A computer-generated version of three-dimensional reality, with which users can interact.

Vorticism
A short-lived British art and literary movement, dating from World War I, that rejected traditional subjects in favor of abstract evocations of the machine age.

***washi* paper**
Strong, high-quality Japanese paper derived from the bark of shrubs and trees, most commonly the mulberry.

x-height
The height of the notional letter "x" in a typeface.

zoomorphism
The use of references from the animal kingdom in design, especially of furniture—chair legs in the form of antelope legs, or ball and claw feet, for example.

CONTRIBUTORS

Dan Griliopoulos (DG)
is an award-winning journalist who has also written books and video games since 2002. As a freelance writer he has contributed to hundreds of publications, ranging from *The Sunday Times* to *Wired* and *The Guardian,* but he prefers to write for specialist publications such as *PC Gamer* and *Edge.* Despite being color blind he is also a painter and photographer. Griliopoulos won an MA in Politics, Philosophy, and Economics from the University of Oxford. He lives in London's East End with his partner and daughter.

Susie Hodge (SH)
is an art historian (MA FRSA), author and artist who has had more than a hundred books published, mostly on the history of art and design, practical art, and history. She also writes magazine articles and web resources for museums and galleries, and provides workshops and lectures for schools, universities, museums, galleries, businesses, festivals, societies, and groups around the world. A regular contributor to radio and television news programs and documentaries, she began her career as an advertising copywriter, beginning at Saatchi & Saatchi and moving to J. Walter Thompson. She has also held teaching posts in a number of schools and colleges.

Lesley Jackson (LJ)
is an independent writer, curator, and design historian specializing in 20th-century design. An authority on the 1950s and 1960s, she has written extensively on textiles, furniture, and glass. Her books include *The New Look: Design in the Fifties* (1991); *"Contemporary": Architecture and Interiors of the 1950s* (1994); *The Sixties: Decade of Design Revolution* (1998); *Robin and Lucienne Day: Pioneers of Contemporary Design* (2001); *20th-Century Pattern Design* (2001); *Alastair Morton and Edinburgh Weavers* (2012); *Ercol: Furniture in the Making* (2013); and *Modern British Furniture: Design Since 1945* (2013).

Alan Powers (AP)
has written widely on 20th-century art, architecture, and design. His recent books include *100 Years of Architecture* (2016) and *Edward Ardizzone* (2016). He teaches, lectures widely, curates exhibitions, and leads study tours for ACE Cultural Tours. For many years he has been involved with the Twentieth Century Society and he is coeditor of its journal, *Twentieth Century Architecture.*

Mark Sinclair (MS)
is deputy editor of *Creative Review* magazine in London. He has written books on narrative illustration, including *Pictures and Words: New Comic Art and Narrative Illustration* (2005), and on identity and logo design, including *TM: The Untold Stories Behind 29 Classic Logos* (2014). He has contributed essays to three titles for Unit Editions, including *Supergraphics* (2010) and *Type Only* (2013). His writing has also appeared in *Print* magazine, and the *Independent* and *The Guardian.*

Penny Sparke (PS)
is a professor of Design History and the director of the Modern Interiors Research Centre at Kingston University, London. She studied French Literature at the University of Sussex from 1967 to 1971 and, in 1975, was awarded a PhD in the History of Design. She has taught at Brighton Polytechnic and the Royal College of Art, London, and has worked at Kingston University since 1999. Among her many publications are *An Introduction to Design and Culture: 1900 to the Present* (1986); *Design in Italy: 1860 to the Present* (1989); *As Long as It's Pink: The Sexual Politics of Taste* (1995); *Elsie de Wolfe: The Birth of Modern Interior Decoration* (2005); and *The Modern Interior* (2008). Sparke is currently working on a book about plants and flowers in interiors.

Elizabeth Wilhide (EW)
is the author of many books on design and interiors, including *William Morris: Decor and Design*

(1991); *The Mackintosh Style* (1995); *Sir Edwin Lutyens: Designing in the English Tradition* (2000); *Surface and Finish* (2007); and *Scandinavian Home: A Comprehensive Guide to Mid Century Modern Scandinavian Designers* (2016). As co-author she has contributed to many of Terence Conran's books, including *The Essential House Book* (1994); *Conran on Design* (1996); *Plain Simple Useful* (2014); and *Conran on Color* (2015). She wrote titles for the Design Museum's "How to Design a…" series, including *Light, Chair, Typeface,* and *House* (all 2010). She is also the author of two novels, *Ashenden* (2013) and *If I Could Tell You* (2016).

Jenny Wilhide (JW)
has written on design, art, and lifestyle subjects for the *Evening Standard, The Spectator,* the US *Robb Report,* the *Telegraph Magazine, Homes & Gardens, Country & Town House,* and *Formula Life* magazine. She wrote a monthly column with Tamasin Day-Lewis in the UK *Reader's Digest* under editor Sarah Sands, and a regular shopping page in the programs of the Royal Opera House, Covent Garden. She was senior contributing editor to *Europe's Elite 1000* (2001 edition). She also has had a career as an actress, playing leading roles for the United Kingdom's National Theatre, as well as UK and US television dramas and movies.

Alex Wiltshire (AW)
is a writer on technology and video games. He was one of the founding editorial team of the design magazine *Icon,* and edited the leading video game magazine *Edge.* He has written technology and game design columns for the publications *Dezeen* and *Rock, Paper, Shotgun* respectively. He also wrote the bestselling *Minecraft: Blockopedia* (2014), edited *Britsoft: An Oral History* (2015), and has contributed to *Guinness World Records Gamer's Edition.* He has also helped to curate a major exhibition about video games for the Victoria & Albert Museum, London.

INDEX

Page numbers in **bold** refer to illustrations.

PICTURE CREDITS

(Key: top = t; bottom = b; left = l; right = r; centre = c; top left = tl; top right = tr; centre left = cl; centre right = cr; bottom left = bl; bottom right = br)

18 Mary Evans Picture Library **19t** Mary Evans Picture Library **19b** © 2016. Image copyright The Metropolitan Museum of Art / Art Resource / Scala, Florence **20** Getty Images **21r** Getty Images **22** Bridgeman Images **23c** TopFoto **23b** Wikipedia **24-25** © Victoria and Albert Museum, London. **26-27** Courtesy of Peter Harrington **28** Image copyright The Metropolitan Museum of Art / Art Resource / Scala, Florence **29** Image copyright The Metropolitan Museum of Art / Art Resource / Scala, Florence **30** Alamy **31** Wikipedia **32** © Victoria and Albert Museum, London. **33b** © The Trustees of the British Museum **34-35** © Victoria and Albert Museum, London. **36** Bridgeman Images **37** Getty Images **38-39** © 2016. The British Library Board / Scala, Florence **40** Division of Home and Community Life, National Museum of America History, Smithsonian Institute. **41** Bridgeman Images **42** Vitra Design Museum **43t** Getty Images **43b** AKG Images **44** © 2016. Digital image, The Museum of Modern Art, New York / Scala, Florence **45** Bridgeman Images **46** Getty Images **47t** Getty Images **47b** Wikipedia **48** Alamy p49b TopFotp **50, 51bl** Courtesy of Victorinox AG **51br** Alamy **52** Alamy **53** © Victoria and Albert Museum, London. **54** © Victoria and Albert Museum, London. **55c** Bridgeman Images **55b** Alamy **56** Bridgeman Images **57t** Carl Dahlstedt / Living Inside, Owner of the house, Emma Vom Bromsen www.emmavonbromssen.se **57b** Corbis **58-59** Getty Images **60-61** Getty Images **63bl** AKG Images **63br** Getty Images **64** Science & Society Picture Library **65l** SPL **65r** Wikipedia **66** Superstock **67bl** getty Images **67br** Advertising Archives **68** Alamy **69t** TopFoto **69b** Christie's Images, London / Scala, Florence **70** Advertising Archives **71b** Getty Images **72-73t** Campbell Soup Company **73b** Mary Evans Picture Library **74** © Victoria and Albert Museum, London. **75t/b** Bridgeman Images **76** Bridgeman Images **77b** Digital Image Museum Associates / LACMA / Art Resource NY / Scala, Florence **78** Bridgeman Imagesw**79b** Mary Evans Picture Library **80** Bridgeman Images **81br** © Victoria and Albert Museum, London. **82** © Victoria and Albert Museum, London. **83t/b** Bridgeman Images **84** © Victoria and Albert Museum, London. **85t** Bridgeman Images **85b** © 2016. Image copyright The Metropolitan Museum of Art / Art Resource / Scala, Florence **86** Alamy **87** © 2016. Digital Image Museum Associates / LACMA / Art Resource NY / Scala, Florence **88** Getty Images **89t** © Victoria and Albert Museum, London. **89b** Alamy **90** Mary Evans Picture Library **91** Getty Images **92-93** AKG Images **94t/b** © Victoria and Albert Museum, London. **95** 4Corners Images / Pietro Canali **96-97** Alamy **98** The Macklowe Gallery **99** Courtesy Sotheby's New York, Collection of Sandra van den Broek. **100** Getty Images **101t** Getty Images **101b** Alamy **102** Bridgeman Images **103t** © MAK, MAK – Austrian Museum of Applied Arts / Contemporary Art **103b** © Auktionshaus im Kinsky GmbH. **104** Ellen McDermott © Smithsonian Institution.© 2016. Cooper-Hewitt, Smithsonian Design Museum / Art Resource, NY / Scala, Florence **105b** TopFoto **106** © 2016. Digital image, The Museum of Modern Art, New York / Scala, Florence **107** AKG Images **110** Getty Images **111t/b** Getty Images **112** AKG Images **113bl** Alamy **113br** Magic Car Pics **114** © DeAgostini Picture Library / Scala, Florence **115** © Victoria and Albert Museum, London. **116, 117t** Images courtesy of Pallucco **117b** Getty images **118** Museum of Applied Arts and Sciences **119t** Museum of Applied Arts and Sciences **119b** © AEG **120** © 2016. Photo Scala, Florence, © Rodchenko & Stepanova Archive, DACS, RAO, 2016. **121t** © The Wyndham Lewis Memorial Trust / Bridgeman Images **121b** Digital image, The Museum of Modern Art, New York / Scala, Florence **122** © Christie's Images / Bridgeman Images **123** © 2016. Digital image, The Museum of Modern Art, New York / Scala, Florence **124** Photo: Brigitte Borrmann© 2016. Photo Scala, Florence / bpk, Bildagentur fuer Kunst, Kultur und Geschichte, Berlin, © DACS 2016. **125bl** Photo: Brigitte Borrmann© 2016. Photo Scala, Florence / bpk, Bildagentur fuer Kunst, Kultur und Geschichte, Berlin, © DACS 2016. **125br** © 2016. Digital image, The Museum of Modern Art, New York / Scala, Florence, © DACS 2016. **126** Alamy **127t** AKG Images **127b** Getty Images **128b** Getty Images **128t** © 2016. Digital image, The Museum of Modern Art, New York / Scala, Florence, © The Josef and Anni Albers Foundation / Artists Rights Society (ARS), New York and DACS, London 2016 **129** © Victoria and Albert Museum, London. **130** © 2016. Digital image, The Museum of Modern Art, New York / Scala, Florence, © DACS 2016. **131b** © 2016. Digital image, The Museum of Modern Art, New York / Scala, Florence, © DACS 2016. **132** © 2016. Neue Galerie New York / Art Resource / Scala, Florence, © DACS 2016. **133bl** © 2016. Digital image, The Museum of Modern Art, New York / Scala, Florence **133br** © 2016. Digital image, The Museum of Modern Art, New York / Scala, Florence, © DACS 2016. **134** Bridgeman Images **135t** © Villa Tugendhat, David Zidlicky, © DACS 2016. **135b** Stockholms Auktionsverk **136** Bridgeman Images **137bl** Alamy **137br** © 2016. Digital image, The Museum of Modern Art, New York / Scala, Florence **138** © 2016. Digital image, The Museum of Modern Art, New York / Scala, Florence **139b** Getty Images **139t** Bonaparte chair by Eileen Gray, images supplied by Aram Designs Limited, holder of the worldwide licence for Eileen Gray Designs **140** © 2016. Digital image, The Museum of Modern Art, New York / Scala, Florence, © ADAGP, Paris and DACS, London 2016 / © FLC / ADAGP, Paris and DACS, London 2016. **141** © ADAGP, Paris and DACS, London 2016 / © FLC / ADAGP, Paris and DACS, London 2016. **142** AKG Images **143** Bridgeman Images **144** PA Photos, with permission by Chanel **145bl** Image courtesy of Chanel **145br** Alamy, with permission by Chanel **146** © DACS 2016 **147b** Wikipedia **148** Barcelona® Table, 1929 designed by Ludwig Mies van der Rohe and manufactured by Knoll, Inc. Image courtesy of Knoll, Inc., © DACS 2016. **149c** Alamy, © DACS 2016. **149b** Digital image, The Museum of Modern Art, New York / Scala, Florence **150** © 2016. Image copyright The Metropolitan Museum of Art / Art Resource / Scala, Florence **151** © Victoria and Albert Museum, London. **152** © Victoria and Albert Museum, London. **153** © 2016. Digital image, The Museum of Modern Art, New York / Scala, Florence **154** Blue Marine rug and E1027 side table by Eileen Gray, images supplied by Aram Designs Limited, holder of the worldwide licence for Eileen Gray Designs **155** © Christie's Images / Bridgeman Images **156** Bridgeman Images **157t** Bridgeman Images **157b** Getty Images **158** © 2016. Christie's Images, London / Scala, Florence **159** Bridgeman Images **160** Bridgeman Images **161** Alamy **162** © Victoria and Albert Museum, London. **163b** Collection Het Nieuwe Instituut, archive(code): OUDJ, inv.nr.: ph1705, Copyright Pictoright **163t** Getty Images **164** Getty Images **165** © Victoria and Albert Museum, London. **166** Alamy **167t** Image Courtesy of The Advertising Archives **167b** Cooper-Hewitt, Smithsonian Design, Museum / Art Resource, NY / Scala, Florence, 2297 **168** Alamy **169** Photo credits: Dorotheum Vienna, auction catalogue 4 November 2015 **170** Image courtesy of FontanaArte Spa **171** © 2016. DeAgostini Picture Library / Scala, Florence **172** Original patent application, 1935. This one relates to ex UK. **173b** Anglepoise® Type 1228™, 2008. Image copyright Anglepoise **174** © 2016. Digital image, The Museum of Modern Art, New York / Scala, Florence **175** Modernity Stockholm **176** © 2016. Digital image, The Museum of Modern Art, New York / Scala, Florence **177bl** © 2016. Digital image, The Museum of Modern Art, New York / Scala, Florence **177br** © Victoria and Albert Museum, London. **178** © Victoria and Albert Museum, London. **179t/b** Isokon Plus **180** Alamy **181** Getty Images **182** © Kameraprojekt Graz 2015 / Wikimedia Commons / CC-BY-SA-4.0 **183bl, br** Getty Images **184, 185c** Greg Milneck **185b** Getty Images **186** © 2016. Digital image, The Museum of Modern Art, New York / Scala, Florence **187c** © 2016. Digital image, The Museum of Modern Art, New York / Scala, Florence **187b** Getty Images **188** Getty Images **189t** Getty Images **189b** Rex / Shutterstock

190 © Victoria and Albert Museum, London. 191 Getty Images 192 Getty Images 193t Mary Evans Picture Library 193b Wikipedia 194 Getty Images 195 Getty Images 196 © Victoria and Albert Museum, London. 197 Getty Images 198 Cooper-Hewitt, Smithsonian Design Museum/Art Resource, NY/Scala, Florence "199bl © 2016. Digital image, The Museum of Modern Art, New York/Scala, Florence" 199br Getty Images 200 Alamy 201t TBC 201b © 2016. Digital image, The Museum of Modern Art, New York/Scala, Florence 202 © TfL from the London Transport Museum collection 203bl © Victoria and Albert Museum, London. 203br Getty Images 204 © 2016. Digital image, The Museum of Modern Art, New York/Scala, Florence 205r Getty Images 206, 207t Getty Images 207b www.mad4wheels.com 208 © 2016. Digital image, The Museum of Modern Art, New York/Scala, Florence 209b AKG Images 210 Rex/Shutterstock 211br Image Courtesy of The Advertising Archives 211bl The Picture Desk 212 © 2016. DeAgostini Picture Library/Scala, Florence 213b © 2016. DeAgostini Picture Library/Scala, Florence 213t Science & Society Picture Library 214 Getty Images 215 Getty Images 216, 219 © IWM 217 Getty Images 218 Mary Evans Picture Library 220 © Victoria and Albert Museum, London. 221c AP/Press Association Images 221b © Victoria and Albert Museum, London. 244 © Victoria and Albert Museum, London. 255 AKG Images, © DACS 2016 266 © 2016. Cooper-Hewitt, Smithsonian Design Museum/Art Resource, NY/Scala, Florence 227 AKG Images 228 Image courtesy of PP Møbler 229c Getty Images 229b Image courtesy of CARL HANSEN & SØN A/S 230 © Republic of Fritz Hansen 2016 231t © Christie's Images/Bridgeman Images 231b © Republic of Fritz Hansen 2016 232 © 2016. Digital image, The Museum of Modern Art, New York/Scala, Florence 233t/b Louis Poulsen A/S 234 © Stig Lindberg/DACS 2016. 235b Image courtesy of Phillip, www.phillips.com, © DACS 2016 235t © Victoria and Albert Museum, London. 236 © Victoria and Albert Museum, London. 237t © Victoria and Albert Museum, London. 237b © Victoria and Albert Museum, London. 238 AKG Images, © DACS 2016 239t Photo Rauno Träskelin, © DACS 2016 239b Tapio Wirkkala Rut Bryk Foundation, photographer Hans Hansen., © DACS 2016 240 Bukowski Auctions, © Stig Lindberg/DACS 2016. 241t SVENSK FORM 241b AKG Images, © DACS 2016 242 STRING FURNITURE AB 243bl STRING FURNITURE AB 243br Fritz von der Schulenburg/The Interior Archive 244 © 2016. Digital image, The Museum of Modern Art, New York/Scala, Florence 245l Rex/Shutterstock 245r Getty Images 246 © 2016. Digital image, The Museum of Modern Art, New York/Scala, Florence 247 © 2016. Digital image, The Museum of Modern Art, New York/Scala, Florence 248 © 2016. Digital image, The Museum of Modern Art, New York/Scala, Florence 249t Getty Images 249b Rex/Shutterstock 250 Alamy 251l © Christie's Images/Bridgeman Images 251r © 2016. Digital image, The Museum of Modern Art, New York/Scala, Florence 252 Rex/Shutterstock 253 Rex/Shutterstock 254 © Christie's Images/Bridgeman Images 255 © Victoria and Albert Museum, London 256 Vitra 257t © Vitra Design Museum 257b Getty Images, © Calder Foundation, New York/DACS London 258 TBC, © Stig Lindberg/DACS 2016. 259b Bukowskis Auctions, © Stig Lindberg/DACS 2016 259t Rydboholms Textil AB, Scandinavian Design Online AB, © Stig Lindberg/DACS 2016. 260 Corbis 261t © Victoria and Albert Museum, London. 261b Getty Images 262 Alamy 263 © Victoria and Albert Museum, London. 264 © Victoria and Albert Museum, London. 265l © 2016. Digital image, The Museum of Modern Art, New York/Scala, Florence , © DACS 2016 265r © Victoria and Albert Museum, London. 266 Digital image, The Museum of Modern Art, New York/Scala, Florence 267t Image Courtesy of The Advertising Archives 267b Digital image, The Museum of Modern Art, New York/Scala, Florence 268 Corbis 269b AKG Images 270 © 2016. Digital image, The Museum of Modern Art, New York/Scala, Florence 271 TopFoto, © DACS 2016. 272 © 2016. Digital image, The Museum of Modern Art, New York/Scala, Florence 273t Corbis 273b © BRAUN P&G 274l © 2016. Digital image, The Museum of Modern Art, New York/Scala, Florence 274r © 2016. Digital image, The Museum of Modern Art, New York/Scala, Florence 275 © 2016. Cooper-Hewitt, Smithsonian Design Museum/Art Resource, NY/Scala, Florence 276 FontShop 277 Courtesy of American Airlines 278 Bridgeman Images 279 © Victoria and Albert Museum, London. 280 AKG Images, © The Isamu Noguchi Foundation and Garden Museum/ARS, New York and DACS, London 2016. 281 © The Isamu Noguchi Foundation and Garden Museum/ARS, New York and DACS, London 2016. 282 Getty Images 283 Flaminio Bertoni 284 © 2016. Digital image, The Museum of Modern Art, New York/Scala, Florence 285 © 2016. Digital image, The Museum of Modern Art, New York/Scala, Florence 286b © Christie's Images/Bridgeman Images 286t Bridgeman Images 287 Bridgeman Images, © The Isamu Noguchi Foundation and Garden Museum/ARS, New York and DACS, London 2016. 288 VITRA 289 © 2016. Christie's Images, London/Scala, Florence 290 © Bonhams, London, UK/Bridgeman Images 291b Bridgeman 292 AKG Images, © ARS, NY and DACS, London 2016, Courtesy of Knoll, Inc 293 © 2016. Image copyright The Metropolitan Museum of Art/Art Resource/Scala, Florence 294 © 2016. Digital Image Museum Associates/LACMA/Art Resource NY/Scala, Florence, Courtesy of Knoll, Inc 295 Getty Images 296 © Victoria and Albert Museum, London. 297t Image Courtesy of The Advertising Archives 297b © 2016. Digital image, The Museum of Modern Art, New York/Scala, Florence 298 © 2016. Digital image, The Museum of Modern Art, New York/Scala, Florence 299l © 2016. Digital image, The Museum of Modern Art, New York/Scala, Florence 299r Superstock 300 Alamy 301 Image Courtesy of The Advertising Archives 302 Getty Images 303 Image Courtesy of The Advertising Archives 304 Alamy 305t Getty Images 305b London Records catalogue no. LL997 306 Rex/Shutterstock 307 Rex/Shutterstock 308 Getty Images 309t Image Courtesy of The Advertising Archives 309b © Victoria and Albert Museum, London. 310 © 2016. Digital image, The Museum of Modern Art, New York/Scala, Florence 311l Bridgeman Images 312r Gibbs Smith Cover Archive 313 Getty Images 314 Getty Images 315t Image Courtesy of The Advertising Archives 315b Gale Family Library, Minnesota Historical Society 316 General Motors Media Archive 317 Rex/Shutterstock 318 Alamy 319t Getty Image 319b Alamy 320 Alamy 321 Alamy 322 Getty Images 323 Favcars.com 324 Alamy 325r Alamy 325l © 2016. Christie's Images, London/Scala, Florence 328 Alamy 329t Corbis 329b Image Courtesy of The Advertising Archives "330 © 2016. Digital image, The Museum of Modern Art, New York/Scala, Florence" 331 Getty Images 332 Reproduced by permission of Penguin Books Ltd 333 © The Economist Newspaper Limited 2016. All rights reserved 334 © 2016. Digital image, The Museum of Modern Art, New York/Scala, Florence, © ADAGP, Paris and DACS, London 2016. 335bl © 2016. Digital image, The Museum of Modern Art, New York/Scala, Florence, © ADAGP, Paris and DACS, London 2016. 335br Image Courtesy of The Advertising Archives 336 Getty Images 337 Image Courtesy of The Advertising Archives 338 With permission by McDonald's 339 With permission by McDonald's 340 www.nycoffeecup.com 341t Getty Images 341b Bridgeman Images 342 © 2016. Digital image, The Museum of Modern Art, New York/Scala, Florence 343l Corbis 343r Image Courtesy of The Advertising Archives 344 Getty Images 345t Image Courtesy of The Advertising Archives 345b © 2016. Digital image, The Museum of Modern Art, New York/Scala, Florence 346 Alamy 347 Getty Images 348 © 2016. Digital image, The Museum of Modern Art, New York/Scala, Florence 349 Getty Images 350 ADELTA, eero-aarnio.com 351 © Victoria and Albert Museum, London. 352 VITRA 353 Verner Panton Design 354 Dwell Media 355 AKG Images 356 Fondazione studio museo Vico Magistretti 357 Fondazione studio museo Vico Magistretti 358 Verner Panton Design 359 Bridgeman Images 360 Ball Chair, design Eero Aarnio, ADELTA. 361 Getty Images 362 Alamy 363 Corbis 364 Alamy 365t Getty Images 365b © Victoria and Albert Museum, London. 366 Rex/Shutterstock 367l Getty Image 367r Rex/Shutterstock 368 Image courtesy of Marimekko 369l/r Alamy 370 Alamy 371bl © 2016. Digital image, The Museum of Modern Art, New York/Scala, Florence 372 Copyright Zanotta Spa - Italy - check against images 373t © 2016. Digital image, The Museum of Modern Art, New York/Scala, Florence. Copyright Zanotta Spa 373b Getty Images 374 Habitat 375 Alamy 376 Image courtesy of ©1stdibs, Inc. 2016 377l © Victoria and Albert Museum, London. 378 Habitat 379t Habitat 379b Alamy 380 Alamy 381t Getty Images

381b Rex / Shutterstock **382** Getty Images **383** Getty Images **384** Getty Images **385b** Image Courtesy of The Advertising Archives **386** © Victoria and Albert Museum, London. **387** © Victoria and Albert Museum, London. **388** Laura Ashley **389t** Image Courtesy of The Advertising Archives **389b** Getty Images **390** © Toyota Motor Sales, U.S.A., Inc. **391t** Alamy **391b** Alamy **392** © 2016. Digital image, The Museum of Modern Art, New York / Scala, Florence **393** The credit for both pictures is Jacob Jensen Design A/S. **394** Courtesy of Richard Sapper Design, Photographs by Serge Libiszewski **395bl** Courtesy of Richard Sapper Design **395br** Artemide SpA, Photo Miro Zagnoli. **396** Italdesign, © Volkswagen AG **397** Rex / Shutterstock **398l** © 2016. Digital image, The Museum of Modern Art, New York / Scala, Florence **398r** © 2016. Digital image, The Museum of Modern Art, New York / Scala, Florence **399** Pentagram / John McConnell **400** Alamy, © Copyright IBM Corporation 1994, 2016. **401bl** © Copyright IBM Corporation 1994, 2016. **401br** Corbis **402** Estudio Mariscal **403bl** Estudio Mariscal **403br** Akg Images, © Succession Picasso / DACS, London 2016. **404** © 2016. Digital image, The Museum of Modern Art, New York / Scala, Florence **405t** Alamy **405b** Image Courtesy of The Advertising Archives **406** Copyright BRAUN P&G **407** © 2016. Digital image, The Museum of Modern Art, New York / Scala, Florence, Copyright BRAUN P&G **408** © Victoria and Albert Museum, London. **409** Image Courtesy of The Advertising Archives **410** Getty Images **411** Rex / Shutterstock **412** © 2016. Digital image, The Museum of Modern Art, New York / Scala, Florence **413** Getty Images **416** Tea & Coffee Piazza tea and coffee service in 925 / 1000 silver by Charles Jencks for Alessi **417t** © 2016. Digital image, The Museum of Modern Art, New York / Scala, Florence **417b** © 2016. Museum of Fine Arts, Boston. All rights reserved / Scala, Florence **418** © 2016. Image copyright The Metropolitan Museum of Art / Art Resource / Scala, Florence, © ADAGP, Paris and DACS, London 2016. **419** © 2016. Image copyright The Metropolitan Museum of Art / Art Resource / Scala, Florence, © ADAGP, Paris and DACS, London 2016. **420** 9093 kettle in 18 / 10 stainless steel mirror polished with handle and small bird-shaped whistle in PA, light blue by Michael Graves for Alessi **421t** Tea & Coffee Piazza tea and coffee service in 925 / 1000 silver by Michael Graves for Alessi **421b** TopFoto, 9091 kettle in 18 / 10 stainless steel mirror polished and melodic whistle in brass and handle in PA, black by Richard Sapper for Alessi **422** The Haçienda designed by Ben Kelly RDI **423t** AKG Images **423b** © Victoria and Albert Museum, London. **424** © 2016. Digital image, The Museum of Modern Art, New York / Scala, Florence **425** Bridgeman Images **426** Getty Images **427** © Copyright 2016, Martha Stewart Living Omnimedia, Inc. All rights reserved. **428** Alamy **429** Brody Associates **430** DigiBarn Computer Museum **431** Getty Images **432** © 2016 Microsoft **433** © 2016 Oculus VR, LLC **434** Courtesy of Richard Sapper Archive, Photo by Aldo Ballo **435t** Lenovo UK & Ireland **435b** © 2016. Digital image, The Museum of Modern Art, New York / Scala, Florence **436** Rex / Shutterstock **437t** Bridgeman Images **437b** © 2016. Digital image, The Museum of Modern Art, New York / Scala, Florence **438** Brompton Bicycle Ltd **439t** Brompton Bicycle Ltd **439b** Corbis **440** Smart Design. **441** Marjatta Sarpaneva **442** Alamy **443** Getty Images **444** Alamy **445t** Images courtesy of Muji **445b** ASPLUND, Photographer Louise Bilgert **446** © Victoria and Albert Museum, London. **447** © 2016. Digital image, The Museum of Modern Art, New York / Scala, Florence **448** PHOTO : Mario CARRIERI, Museum of Modern Art, New York, Centre Georges Pompidou, Paris, Vitra Design Museum, Weil Rhein, Germany, Museum fur Kunst und Gewerbe, Hamburg **449** (c) Ingo Maurer GmbH, Munich. **450** © Victoria and Albert Museum, London. **451** © Victoria and Albert Museum, London. **452** © Victoria and Albert Museum, London. **453bl** Alamy **453br** Photo Tamer Yilmaz. **454** (c) Ingo Maurer GmbH, Munich. **455b** (c) Ingo Maurer GmbH, Munich. **455c** Alamy **456** Art Director, Mr Keedy, designer, Shelley Stepp **457** Digital image, The Museum of Modern Art, New York / Scala, Florence **458** ALLEN HORI, DESIGNER **459bl** Katherine McCoy © 1989 **459br** MIT Media Lab **460** ©barnbrook / virusfonts **461** Emigre #19, 1991, Design by Rudy VanderLans, Template Gothic typeface by Barry Deck **461b** ©barnbrook / virusfonts **462** With permission by David Carson **463** With permission by David Carson **464** © Christie's Images / Bridgeman Images **465** Bridgeman Images **466** © 2016. Digital image, The Museum of Modern Art, New York / Scala, Florence, Juicy Salif citrus-squeezer in aluminium casting mirror polished by Philippe Starck for Alessi **467bl** TopFoto **467br** Alamy **468** Quaglino's ashtray by Conran and Partners **469t** Alamy **469b** Alamy **470** Images courtesy of Droog, www.droog.com **471** Images courtesy of Droog, www.droog.com **472** Images courtesy of Droog, www.droog.com **473** Images courtesy of Droog, www.droog.com **476** Rex / Shutterstock **477** Alamy, Facebook © 2016 **478** Getty Images **479bl** Carter & Cone Type Inc. **479br** IKEA **480** © 2016 Microsoft **481** Alamy **482** © 2016 Microsoft **483** © 2016 Microsoft **484b** Alamy **485t** Getty Images **486** Rex / Shutterstock **487** Alamy **488** Alamy **489** Rex / Shutterstock **490** Amazon **491t** Alamy **491b** Getty Images **492** © 2016 Uber Technologies Inc. **493** Rex / Shutterstock **494** Michael Young Ltd. **495** AKG Images **496** Jasper Morrison Ltd, Photo Credit: Walter Gumiero **497** Rex / Shutterstock **498** © 2016. Digital image, The Museum of Modern Art, New York / Scala, Florence **499** Photo by by Gerhard Kellerman **500** © 2016. Photo The Philadelphia Museum of Art / Art Resource / Scala, Florence] **501t** Bridgeman Images **501b** Alamy **502** by Marcel Wanders, www.marcelwanders.com **504** © 2015 Oliva Iluminación. Todos Los Derechos Reservados. **505** Getty Images **506** WALLPAPER frocks by deborah bowness, Photo by Clare Richardson **507** Created by James Bullen. **508** Studio Tord Boontje **509** Bridgeman Images **510** Glasgow Toile by Timorous Beasties **511b** Glasgow Toile by Timorous Beasties **511t** Corbis **512** Tracy Kendall Wallpaper **513b** Photo by Erika Wall **513t** Claire Norcross © 2016. All Rights Reserved. **514** Maarten Baas, www.maartenbaas.com, Photo: Frank Tielemans **515** Maarten Baas, www.maartenbaas.com, Photo: Bas Princen **516** Sotheby's **517** © 2016. Digital image, The Museum of Modern Art, New York / Scala, Florence **518** Courtesy of Martino Gamper **519** Corbis **520** Photoshot **521t** Alamy **521b** Image supplied by Ecosan South Africa - www.ecosan.co.za **522** Courtesy of fuseproject **523** Courtesy of fuseproject **524** Getty Images **525t** Getty Images **525b** Getty Images **526** Alamy **527** Alamy **528** Courtesy of nendo inc **529** Getty Images **529b** Manufactum Ltd. **530** Alamy **531** Rex / Shutterstock **532** Rex / Shutterstock **533** Alamy **534** © Roberts Radio **535t** Alamy **535b** Getty Images **536** Reproduced by permission of Penguin Books Ltd. **537** Reproduced by permission of Penguin Books Ltd. **538** Alamy **539** AKG Images **540** © 2016 Marc Newson Ltd **541c** Getty Images **541b** © 2016 Marc Newson Ltd **542** Alamy **543c** Getty Images **543b** Alamy **544** Corbis **545t** © Victoria and Albert Museum, London. **545b** Janne Kyttanen © Materialise **546** Image courtesy of Adrian Sassoon, London **547l** Image courtesy of Adrian Sassoon, London **547r** Image courtesy of Adrian Sassoon, London **548** Olaf Diegel, ODD Guitars **549** Thomas Tetu - lesimagesdetom.fr **550** Reuters **551** Corbis **551** Lori K. Sanders / Lewis Lab, Wyss Institute at Harvard University